v. Beseler-Jacobs

LAW DICTIONARY

v. Beseler-Jacobs

LAW DICTIONARY

Fachwörterbuch
der anglo-amerikanischen Rechtssprache

DEUTSCH — ENGLISCH

3., völlig neu bearbeitete Auflage
von Barbara Jacobs

1971
WALTER DE GRUYTER · BERLIN · NEW YORK

v. Beseler-Jacobs

LAW DICTIONARY

technical dictionary
of the Anglo-American legal terminology

GERMAN — ENGLISH

3., completely new and revised edition
by Barbara Jacobs

1971

WALTER DE GRUYTER · BERLIN · NEW YORK

Die 1. Auflage erschien im Jahre 1929,
die 2. Auflage erschien im Jahre 1947
unter dem Titel
Dora v. Beseler
Taschenwörterbuch
der Rechts- und Geschäftssprache

The first edition was published in 1929,
the second edition was published in 1947
with the title
Dora v. Beseler
Taschenwörterbuch
der Rechts- und Geschäftssprache

ISBN 3 11 002187 0

Satz und Druck: Max Schönherr, 1 Berlin 65

INHALT — CONTENTS

VORWORT

Das vorliegende Wörterbuch stellt eine grundlegende Neubearbeitung des letztmals 1947 erschienenen „Taschenwörterbuch der Rechts- und Geschäftssprache" dar.

Die zunehmende Verflechtung der Rechtsbeziehungen zwischen der Bundesrepublik und den englischsprechenden Ländern machte seine Neuauflage zu einem dringenden Erfordernis. Neben den umfangreichen vorhandenen Rechtslexika soll es mit seinem handlichen und trotzdem umfassenden Volumen eine echte Lücke auf diesem Gebiet ausfüllen. Um dieser Aufgabe gerecht zu werden, beschränkt sich das „Law Dictionary" ausschließlich auf die Fachterminologie des Rechtsbereiches, unter selbstverständlicher Berücksichtigung sich überschneidender Disziplinen.

Die individuelle Rechtsentwicklung in Deutschland und den angelsächsischen Staaten hat zu kaum überbrückbaren unterschiedlichen Konzeptionen geführt. Daher war es die Hauptaufgabe der Verfasserin, für nicht korrespondierende Rechtsbegriffe und Institutionen möglichst äquivalente Termini zu erbringen.

Trotz des Taschenbuchformates bietet dieses Lexikon eine Vielheit von Synonymen, auf die die Verfasserin in Anbetracht des reichen Wortschatzes der englischen Sprache nicht verzichten konnte. Diese Tatsache ermöglicht es wiederum seinem Benutzer, das ihm zutreffend erscheinende Wort selbst auszuwählen.

Somit will das als rein juristisches Fachlexikon erstellte „Law Dictionary" sowohl dem Praktiker als auch dem Wissenschaftler bei seiner Arbeit zur Verfügung stehen.

Mannheim, August 1971

Barbara Jacobs

Diplom-Übersetzerin

PREFACE

The present dictionary constitutes a fundamentally new edition of the „Taschenwörterbuch der Rechts- und Geschäftssprache“ published in 1947.

The increasing entanglement of law relations between the Federal Republic of Germany and the English-speaking countries made this new edition an urgent necessity. Besides the already existing voluminous law dictionaries, in its handy and nevertheless comprehensive form, it is intended to fill an actual gap in this field. In order to meet these requirements the "Law Dictionary" has exclusively been limited to the legal terminology taking into account all overlapping disciplines.

The individual legal development in Germany and the Anglo-American states led to nearly unbridgeable differences of legal conceptions. Therefore, it has been the author's main task to present equivalent terms for those noncorresponding legal concepts and institutions.

Though edited as a pocketbook this dictionary offers a multitude of synonyms which could not be neglected in view of the rich vocabulary of the English language. This fact, on the other hand, allows the user to select himself the expression which he thinks to be adequate.

The author hopes that this law dictionary will be able to render helpful assistance to all lawyers in practice and theory.

Mannheim, August 1971

Barbara Jacobs
Graduated Translator

A

abänderlich alterable, amendable, changeable, commutable, modifiable, revisable, variable
Abänderlichkeit alterability
abändern alter, amend, change, commute, correct, improve, modify, rectify, revise, vary
Abänderung alteration, amendment, change, commutation, correction, improvement, modification, rectification, revision, variation
Abänderungsantrag amendment
abänderungsfähig s. abänderlich
Abänderungs
—plan plan of alteration, modified plan, scheme of improvement
—vorschlag proposal of amendment, (proposed) amendment
Abandon abandonment, relinquishment, dereliction
Abandon
—erklärung declaration (notice) of abandonment
—frist limitation of abandonment, period allowed for declaration of abandonment
—klausel abandonment clause
abandonieren abandon, relinquish
Abandonierung abandonment, relinquishment
abarbeiten work off
Abart modification, subspecies, variation, variety
Abbau axe, cut, decontrol, demolition, discharge, dismissal, exhaustion, exploitation, gradual abolition, mining, reduction, relaxation, removal, retrenchment, withdrawal, working
abbauen abolish, axe, cut, decontrol, demolish, discharge, dismantle, dismiss, exhaust, exploit, lift, reduce, remove, retrench, withdraw, work
Abbau
—entschädigung leaving indemnity, terminal (severance) pay
abbaufähig exploitable, workable
Abbau
—konzession mining concession
—lizenz mining licence
—recht mining right, right of exploitation
—verlust mining loss
abberufen call back (home), recall, relieve, remove, suspend
Abberufung recall, removal, suspension
—sschreiben letters of recall
abbestellen cancel, countermand, discontinue, withdraw
Abbestellung cancellation, countermand, discontinuance, withdrawal
abbezahlen clear (pay) off, discharge, pay in (by) instalments, repay
Abbezahlung clearing (paying) off, discharge, part payment, payment by (in) instalments (on account), repayment
Abbild copy, diagram, duplicate, graph, image, representation, reproduction
Abbildung copy, illustration, picture, representation
Abbitte apology, deprecation, excuse, recantation
Abbitte
— leisten (abbitten) apologize (for), excuse, recant
abbrechen break off (down, up), call off, cease, cut, demolish, discontinue, dismantle, drop, interrupt, sever, stop
Abbruch breach, breakdown, breaking down (off), cession,

damage, derogation, discontinuance, dismantling, interruption, prejudice, rupture, severance
— **erleiden** be impaired
— **tun** be detrimental (prejudicial) to, damage, derogate, detract from, impair, injure, interfere with, prejudice
abbüßen atone for, expiate
—, **Strafe** serve a sentence, sit in, undergo judgement
Abbüßung atonement, expiation
abdanken abdicate, discharge, dismiss, resign, retire
Abdankung abdication, discharge, dismissal, resignation, retirement
—**surkunde** deed (document, instrument) of abdication
abdienen complete, fulfil, serve, work off
Abdruck copy, impress, impression, imprint, mark, print, reprint, reproduction, seal, stamp
Finger- finger-print
abdrucken impress, print, reprint
abdrücken discharge, fire (off)
Abdrucksrecht copyright, printing licence (se)
aberkennen abjudicate, deny, deprive of, disallow, dispossess
Aberkennung abjudication, degradation, denial, deprivation, disallowance, dispossession, forfeiture, loss
— **der bürgerlichen Ehrenrechte** civil degradation, deprivation (loss) of civil rights
— **der Staatsangehörigkeit** denaturalization, expatriation
abfällig adverse, critical, depreciatory, derogatory, detractive, disapproving, disparaging, unfavo(u)rable
Abfangen interception
abfangen catch, intercept, snatch
abfassen compose, draft, draw up, formulate, frame, make out, prepare, set up, word, write
Abfassung composition, drafting, drawing up, formulation, framing, preparation, setting up, tenor, wording, writing
abfertigen attend to, clear, deal with, dismiss, dispatch, expedite, forward, handle, process, put off (with), send off, serve
Abfertigung attendance, clearance, dealing with, despatch, dispatch(ing), expedition, forwarding, handling, process, rebuff, refusal
Abfertigungs
—**gebühren** clearance payment, forwarding charges (fees), handling fees
—**schein** bill of clearance, clearing certificate, customs certificate (declaration, permit), dispatch (forwarding) note, permit
—**vorschriften** dispatch (forwarding) instructions (regulations)
abfinden buy out, compound with, compensate, content, indemnify (for), pay off, satisfy, settle
sich — mit be reconciled with, come to terms with, compound (settle) with, make a compromise with, put up with, reconcile oneself with, resign oneself to, tolerate
—, **sich mit den Tatsachen** face facts
Abfindung agreement, allowance, buying out, compensation, composition, compounding, indemnification, indemnity, paying off, portion, satisfaction, settlement, severance pay
Abfindungs
—**betrag (-geld, -summe)** compensation, composition, indemnity
—**vertrag** deed of composition, settlement (agreement)
—**zahlung** composition payment
Abfluß drain, efflux, outflow
abfordern charge, claim, demand, request (from)
abführen discharge, pay (off, over), remand, remove, transfer
Abführung payment, removal

Abgabe assessment, customs, delivery, duty, excise, fee, impost, imposition, levy, rate, royalty, sale, surrender, tax, toll, tribute
Stimmen- vote
Abgaben dues
abgabenfrei duty-free, royalty-free, tax-exempt (-free)
Abgaben
—freiheit exemption from taxation (duty), immunity
—ordnung revenue regulations, taxe code
—pflicht liability to pay taxes (duties), tax liability, taxability
abgaben
—pflichtig dutiable, liable to duty (tax, taxation), taxable
Abgabenwesen fiscal system, system of taxation (imposts and taxes), taxation
abgeben cast, cede, deliver, depute (to), dispense with, dispose of, draw, express, give (up), hand over, make, pass, pronounce, renounce, sell, surrender, turn over
abgekürzt abbreviated, abridged, summary
abgelaufen expired, mature, (over)due
abgelten compensate, discharge, meet, pay (off), remunerate, satisfy
Abgeltung compensation, composition, discharge, settlement
abgemacht agreed, arranged, settled, stipulated, understood
Abgeordneter delegate, deputy, representative
Abgesandter ambassador, delegate, emissary, messenger
abgesondert preferential, separate, special
abgrenzen define, delimit, demarcate, limit, mark off, restrict
Abgrenzung definition, delimitation, demarcation, limitation, restriction
abhalten celebrate, deliver, give, hold, keep, observe
— von deter (from), detain, hinder, hold (keep) off, prevent (from), restrain (from)
Abhaltung celebration, detention, hindrance, holding, observance
abhandeln debate on, discuss, negotiate, settle, treat (of)
Abhandlung discussion, essay, paper, treatise
—, wissenschaftliche dissertation
abhängig ancillary, conditioned (by), contingent (on), controlled, dependent on), depending, subject to, supervised
—, gegenseitig interdependent
Abhängiger dependant, dependent
Abhängigkeit dependence (cy)
—, gegenseitige interdependence
Abhängigkeitsverhältnis condition (state) of dependence, dependent relation, subordinate position
abhelfen adjust, correct, ease, meet, rectify, redress, relieve, remedy, remove, satisfy, supply
Abhilfe correction, redress, relief, remedy
abhören intercept, listen to illicitly, overhear, tap
Abkomme (Abkömmling) descendant, offspring
Abkommen agreement, arrangement, charter, contract, convention, covenant, deed, pact, settlement, stipulation, treaty
Abkunft birth, descent, extraction, lineage, origin, parentage
abkürzen abbreviate, abridge, condense, curtail, reduce, shorten
Abkürzung abbreviation, abridgement, condensation, curtailment, reduction, shortening
Ablage file(s), filing, records
—ort filing cabinet, place of records (deposit)
Ablauf completion, end, ending, expiration, expiry, extinguishment, lapse, maturity, termination
ablaufen become due (payable), end, expire, fall due, fall in,

come to an end (close), lapse, mature, **run out, terminate**
Ablauf
—frist term (of expiration), time of limitation, time limit
—termin date of expiration (maturity), deadline, expiration (termination) date, term
Ableben death, decease, demise
ableben decease, die
ablegen file, give (up), make, pass, render, take
—, Eid swear, take an oath
—, Zeugnis bear witness, give evidence, testify
ablehnen challenge, decline, deny, disagree, disclaim, dismiss, negative, object to, overrule, refuse, reject, repudiate, rule out, throw down (out), turn down, vote down (out)
Ablehnung challenge, condemnation, denial, disagreement, disapprobation, disapproval, dismissal, exclusion, nonacceptance, objection, refusal, rejection, repudiation
ableisten complete, fulfil, perform, serve, take
Ableistung fulfilment, performance, serving
ableiten deduce (from), derive (from), distract (from), divert, draw off, trace (from)
Ableitung derivation, distraction, diversion
ablenken avert (from), distract (from), divert (from), draw off, ward off
Ablenkung averting, distraction, diversion
—smanöver diversion
ableugnen abnegate, contest, deny, disavow, disown, traverse
Ableugnung abnegation, dementi, denial, disavowal, disclaimer, traverse
abliefern deliver, hand over
Ablieferung delivery
ablösbar commutable, redeemable
—, nicht irredeemable
ablösen alternate with, commute, compound, discharge, exchange (for), liquidate, pay off, redeem, relieve, repay, replace, settle, substitute (for), supersede, withdraw
Ablösung commutation, discharge, liquidation, redemption, relay, relief, repayment, settlement, supercession, withdrawal
Ablösungs
—anleihe redemption loan
—bestimmungen redemption provisions
—recht right of redemption
abmachen agree (upon), arrange, conclude, covenant, make, make an agreement (arrangement), settle, stipulate, transact, wind up
Abmachung agreement, arrangement, contract, convention, covenant, settlement, stipulation, transaction
abmelden,
polizeilich give notice of departure to the police
Abmeldebescheinigung,
polizeiliche leaving permit
Abmeldung,
polizeilich (formal) notice of departure
Abnahme, acceptance, decline, decrease, diminution, dwindling, falling off, loss, purchase, reduction, shrinkage, taking delivery, taking over
—bedingungen terms of acceptance
abnehmen accept, administer, buy, decline, decrease, deprive of, diminish, dwindle, fall off, handle, lessen, purchase, relieve of, take delivery, take over, tender
Abnehmer buyer, client, consumer, customer, purchaser, taker, vendee
abnorm abnormal, anomalous, exceptional, exorbitant, irregular, unnatural, unusual
Abnormalität abnorm(al)ity
abordnen delegate, depute, deputize

Abordnung delegation, deputation
Abraten dissuasion
abraten advise (warn) against, dissuade from
abrechnen account, allow, deduct, discount, liquidate, balance (clear, settle, square) accounts (with), settle (square) with, subtract
Abrechnung account, allowance, clearing, deduction, discount, liquidation, settlement, statement of account
Abrede agreement, arrangement, denial, stipulation, understanding
in — stellen challenge, deny, disavow, disclaim, dispute
—treffen agree, make an agreement (arrangement)
Abruf recall
—, auf at (on) call
abrufen call back (in), recall
abrüsten disarm
Abrüstung disarmament
Absage cancellation, countermand, decline, denial, negative reply, rebuff, recall, refusal
absagen call off, cancel, countermand, decline, deny, recall, refuse, withdraw
Absatz break, circulation, distribution, market, marketing, outlet, paragraph, pause, sale, selling, stop, subsection, subparagraph
Absatz
—bedingungen market(ing) conditions, terms of sale
—beschränkungen marketing (sales) restrictions
absatzfähig marketable, saleable
Absatz
—fähigkeit marketability, saleability
—gebiet market, marketing area, outlet
abschaffen abolish, abrogate, annul, discharge, discontinue, dismiss, dispose of, do away with, invalidate, redress, remove, repeal, rescind
Abschaffung abolition, abolishment, abrogation, annulment, discontinuance, discharge, dismissal, redress, removal, repeal, rescission
abschätzbar appraisable, assessable, estimable, rat(e)able, valuable
—, nicht inestimable
abschätzen appraise, assess, estimate, evaluate, rate, value
Abschätzer appraiser, assessor, valuer
Abschätzung appraisal, appraisement, assessment, estimate, estimation, valuation
abschieben deport
Abschiebung deportation
Abschied departure, discharge, dismissal, leave, resignation, separation
— geben discharge, dismiss
seinen —
nehmen resign, retire, hand in (send in, tender) one's resignation
Abschiedsgesuch resignation
sein — einreichen tender one's resignation
abschießen discharge, fire (off)
Abschlag abatement, allowance, decline, deduction, diminution, discount, fall, instalment, part payment, rebate, reduction, refusal
—szahlung instalment, part payment, payment on account
abschlagen abate, decline, fall off, refuse, reject, turn down
abschlägig (in the) negative
—e Antwort
(—er Bescheid) denial, negative reply, rebuff, refusal
abschließen agree, arrive at, balance, close, complete, conclude, contract, effect, execute, lock (up), make, settle, shut up, sign, strike, terminate, transact, wind up
abschließend concluding, conclusive, definitive, final
Abschluß balance, balancing, business, close, closing, completion, conclusion, ending,

settlement, signing, termination, transaction, winding up
Abschluß
—termin closing date, settling day
—zahlung final payment
—zeugnis terminal report
Abschnitt chapter, counterfoil, coupon, cut, paragraph, part, period, portion, section, sector, segment, term
abschnittsweise in (by) sections, in portions (stages)
abschrecken deter, discourage, frighten, intimidate
abschreckend deterrent, exemplary
Abschreckung deterrence, discouragement, intimidation
—smittel deterrent, determent
abschreiben cancel, copy, countermand, deduct, depreciate, engross, plagiarize, transcribe, write off (out)
Abschreibung cancellation, depreciation
Abschrift copy, duplicate, transcript, transcription
abschwächen diminish, extenuate, lessen, mitigate, reduce, weaken
Abschwächung decline, decrease, extenuation, weakening
abschweifen deviate, digress (from), diverge (form)
abschwören abjure, deny (recant, renounce) by oath, forswear, swear off
Abschwörung abjuration, denial by oath
absehbar conceivable, foreseeable, imaginable, measurable, reasonable, recognizable, visible, within sight
in —er Zeit within reasonable time
absehen conceive, foresee, perceive
— auf aim (drive) at, have in view
— von abandon, abstain from, disregard, dispense with, drop, leave out of account (consideration)
Absender consignor, forwarder, return address, sender
absetzbar marketable, removable, salable
Absetzbarkeit removability, salability
absetzen deduct, depose, dethrone, discharge, dismiss, dispose of, distribute, market, remove, sell
Absetzung deduction, deposition, dethronement, discharge, dismissal, removal, suspension
Absicht aim, design, end, intent, intention, mind, object, plan, purpose, will
absichtlich deliberate, intended, intentional, on purpose, wilful
absichern cover, guard, secure
absitzen, Strafe serve one's sentence, sit in
absolut absolute
absondern detach (from), divide, isolate, seclude (from), segregate, separate, set apart (aside), sever
Absonderung abstraction, detachment, isolation, seclusion, segregation, separation
abspalten separate
Abspaltung separation
abspenstig alienated, disloyal, unfaithful
— machen alienate (estrange) from, entice away
absperren bar, barricade, block, bolt, confine, isolate, lock, obstruct, separate, shut up, stop
Absperrung barricade, blocking, isolation, obstruction, separation, stoppage
Absprache agreement, appointment, arrangement, stipulation, understanding
absprechen abjudicate, agree, deny, disallow, dispute, refuse, stipulate
Absprechung abjudication, denial, disputation
abstammen be derived (descended) from, derive from, descend from
Abstammung birth, derivation, descent, extraction, origin

Abstand distance, interval
—nahme desistance, discontinuance
— nehmen von abstain from, desist from, discontinue, dispense with, refrain from, renounce
Abstandsgeld (-summe) compensation, forfeit (option) money, indemnification, indemnity
abstatten give, make, render
abstellen abate, abolish, correct, rectify, redress, remedy
Abstellung abolition, redress
abstempeln mark, stamp
abstimmen adjust, balance, ballot, compare, control, coordinate, divide, harmonize, poll, reconcile, vote
Abstimmung adjustment, balancing, ballot, control, coordination, division, harmonizing, poll, reconciliation, vote, voting
Volks- plebiscite, popular vote, referendum
abstrakt (in the) abstract
Abstraktion abstraction
abstreiten argue down, contest, contradict, deny, dispute, gainsay
Abstrich curtailment, cut, deduction
—e economies
—e machen economize, make cuts
abstufen grade, graduate
Abstufung graduation
abteilen divide, separate
Abteilung branch, department, detachment, division, group, section, separation
—schef departmental chief
(—sleiter) (head, manager), head of a department
abtragen clear (off), discharge, liquidate, pay off, redeem
abträglich adverse, detrimental, harmful, injurious, prejudicial, unfavo(u)rable
Abtragung liquidation, payment. redemption
abtreiben commit (procure, produce) abortion
Abtreibung abortion, foeticide
—smittel abortifacient
abtrennen detach, separate, sever
Abtrennung separation, severance
abtretbar assignable, conveyable, transferable
Abtretbarkeit assignability, transferability
abtreten assign, cede, convey, relinquish, resign, retire, surrender, transfer
Abtreter assigner, ceder, transferrer, transferor
Abtretung assignment, cession, conveyance, relinquishment, surrender, transfer
Abtretungs
—erklärung declaration of assignment
—recht right of assignment
—urkunde deed of assignment (cession), deed (instrument) of conveyance, transfer deed
—vertrag contract of assignment (cession, conveyance, transfer)
abtrünnig disloyal, faithless, unfaithful
Abtrünniger deserter, renegade
aburteilen abjudicate, condemn, decide, sentence, bring to trial, try
Aburteilung abjudication, condemnation, sentence, trial
abvermieten sublet, underlet
abwägen consider, weigh
abwälzen devolve on, remove, shift off
abwandern migrate
Abwanderung migration
abwechseln alternate (with), change, rotate, vary
abwechselnd alternate, alternating, by turns, in rotation (turn), changeable
Abwechslung alternation, change, rotation, turn, variation
Abwehr defence, protection, resistance
Abwehr
—aktion defensive (precautionary) action
—krieg defensive war(fare)
—maßnahme defensive (precautionary) measure

—streik defensive strike
—waffe defensive weapon
abweichen depart, deviate, differ, diverge, vary
abweichend deviating, different, discrepant, dissentient, divergent, at variance (with), varying
Abweichung departure, deviation, difference, discrepancy, divergence, variation
—sklausel deviation clause
abweisen decline, dismiss, dishono(u)r, nonsuit, reject, refuse, repel, repulse, turn down
Abweisung denial, disclaimer, dismissal, nonacceptance, nonsuit, rebuff, refusal, rejection, repulse
—sbescheid nonsuit
(—surteil)
abwendbar avertible, avoidable, preventable
abwenden avert, avoid, prevent, protect (against, from), save from, ward off
Abwendung averting, avoidance, prevention
abwerfen bear, drop, yield, return
abwerten depreciate, devalorize, devaluate, devalue
Abwertung depreciation, devalorization, devaluation
—sklausel devaluation clause
abwesend absent
Abwesender absentee
Abwesenheit absence, contumacy, nonappearance, nonattendance, nonexistence
—, dauernde absenteeism
Abwesenheits
—erklärung declaration of absence
—liste absentees' list
—pfleger curator absentis, trustee in absentia
—urteil judgement in default, sentence in absence
—verfahren proceedings in contumacy
—vermutung presumption of absence
abwickeln adjust, arrange, carry through, complete, effect, execute, liquidate, manage, settle, transact, wind up
Abwickler liquidator
Abwicklung adjustment, arrangement, dealing (with), development, disposal (of), liquidation, management, settlement, transaction, winding up
Abwicklungs
—behörde liquidation department
—verfahren liquidation (winding up) procedure
abzahlen clear off, discharge, pay off, pay by (in) instalments
Abzahlung discharge, instalment, liquidation, part payment, payment (in full), payment on account, payment by instalments, paying off, settlement
Abzahlungs
—kauf hire (instalment) purchase
—kredit instalment credit
—system hire-purchase system, instalment plan (system)
—verkauf hire (instalment) sale
—vertrag hire-purchase contract (agreement), instalment contract
Abzeichen badge, decoration, distinguishing badge (mark), insignia, mark, sign
abziehbar deductible
abziehen abate, deduct, discount, subtract, withdraw
Abzug abatement, allowance, deduction, discount, reduction, subtraction
abzugsfähig deductible
Acht ban, excommunication, ostracism, outlawry, proscription
achtbar hono(u)rable, reputable, respectable
Achtbarkeit hono(u)rability, respectability
achten abide, esteem, hono(u)r, observe, respect
ächten ban, boycott, ostracize, outlaw, proscribe

Achtung attention, esteem, estimation, regard, reputation, respect
Ächtung ban, ostracism, outlawry, proscription
Administration administration
administrativ administrative
Administrator administrator, agent, steward, trustee
administrieren administer, manage
adoptieren adopt
Adoptierter adoptee
Adoption adoption
Adoptions
—beschluß adoption order
—vertrag deed (contract) of adoption
Adoptiv
—eltern adoptive parents
—mutter adoptive mother
—sohn adoptive son
—tochter adoptive daughter
—vater adoptive father
Adressant addresser, consignor, drawer, sender, writer
Adressat addressee, consignee, drawee, payee
Adresse address, direction
—nänderung change of address
adressieren address, consign, direct
—, falsch misdirect
Advokat advocate, attorney (at law), barrister (at law), counsel, counsellor (at law), lawyer, solicitor
Advokaten
—gebühr lawyer's fee
—stand (Advokatur) attorneyship, bar, barristership, legal profession, solicitorship
Affäre affair, business, case, job, matter
Agenda agenda, order of the day
Agent agent, broker, emissary, representative, solicitor
Agenten
—gebühr (-kommission) commission
—geschäft agency business
Agentur agency, agent's office, branch (office), office, representation
—vertrag agency agreement (contract)
Aggression aggression
aggressiv aggressive
Agitation agitation, propaganda, public excitement
Agitator agitator, fomenter, propagandist
agitatorisch agitating, agitatorial, propagandistic
agitieren agitate
Ahn ancestor, forbear, forefather
ahnden avenge, discipline, punish, revenge
Ahndung disciplining, punishment, retribution, revenge
Akademie academy, college, university
Akademiker academician, graduate, university man
akademisch academic(al)
akkreditieren accredit, open a credit
Akkreditiv credentials, letter of credit
Akt act, action, deed, expression, performance
Akte act, deed, document, file, record
Akten deeds, documents, files, folders, records, register, rolls
Akten
—bündel file
—einsicht (-nahme) inspection of documents (the file, the files, the records)
aktenkundig on the record
— machen place on record
— sein be on record
aktenmäßig documentary, on the record
Akten
—notiz memo(randum), note
—stück deed, document
—vermerk file mark, memorandum, note
—zeichen file number, reference mark (number)
Aktie share, stock
Stamm- common share (stock), ordinary (original) share
Vorzugs- preference (preferential, preferred, priority) share, preferred stock

Aktien
—abschnitt coupon, dividend warrant
—ausgabe issue of shares (stock), share issue
—bank incorporated bank, joint-stock bank
—besitz holdings, shareholding, stockholding
—besitzer shareholder, stockholder
—börse stock exchange
—gesellschaft incorporated company, joint-stock company (corporation), public limited company
—gesetz Companies Act (GB), company (corporation) act (law)
—händler (-makler) share broker, stock broker, stock jobber
—inhaber shareholder, stockholder
—kapital capital stock, joint stock, share (stock) capital
—kurs share (stock) price
—recht company (corporation) law
—schiebung stock jobbing
—zertifikat (-schein) share (stock) certificate (warrant)
Aktion action, operation, process
—, gemeinsame joint action
Aktionär shareholder, stockholder
—srechte stockholder's rights
—sversammlung general meeting, meeting of shareholders (stockholders)
Aktions
—ausschuß executive committee
—bereich range of action
—freiheit freedom of action
—kommission council of action
aktiv active, effective, favo(u)rable
— legitimiert empowered (entitled) to sue
Aktiva assets
Aktiv
—bestand assets, actual (effective) strength
—geschäft active business
—legitimation ability (capacity, power, right, title) to sue
—masse (-vermögen) assets
Aktivität activity
Aktualität topical interest, topicality
aktuell current, immediate, topical
Akzept acceptance
akzeptabel acceptable
Akzeptant acceptant, drawee
Akzeptation acceptance
akzeptfähig bankable, negotiable
Akzeptfrist limitation (period, term) of acceptance
akzeptieren accept, hono(u)r
—, nicht dishono(u)r
Akzise excise (duty), indirect tax
Alarm alarm
—, blinder false alarm
alarmbereit in constant readiness, on the alert
Alarm
—bereitschaft alert
— —, in s. alarmbereitschaft
—ruf (-signal, -zeichen) alarm
alarmieren alarm
alarmierend alarming, alerting
alias alias, before, otherwise
Alibi alibi
sein — beweisen (erbringen) establish (prove) one's alibi, set up an alibi
alimentär alimentary
Alimentation alimony
—sklage bastardy procedure
Alimente alimony
Alimenten
—forderung claim for maintenance
—klage action for alimony, action (suit) for maintenance
alimentenpflichtig liable to pay alimony
Alimenten
—prozeß bastardy procedure
—urteil bastardy order
alimentieren pay alimony, support
Alkohol alcohol, liquor, spirits
alkoholfrei non-alcoholic
Alkohol
—gegner prohibitionist

—gehalt alcoholic strength (percentage)
Alkoholiker alcoholic, alcoholist, habitual drinker
alkoholisch alcoholic
Alkoholismus alcoholism
Alkohol
—monopol liquor state monopoly, monopoly of (in) brandy
—probe alcohol(ic) test
—schmuggel bootlegging, liquor smuggling
—schmuggler bootlegger, liquor smuggler, rumrunner
—verbot prohibition
—vergiftung alcoholism
allein alone, exclusive, single, sole, solitary
Allein
—berechtigung exclusive (sole) right
—besitz exclusive (sole) possession
—eigentum exclusive (sole) ownership (porperty)
—eigentümer exclusive (sole) holder (owner, proprietor)
—erbe sole heir
—handel monopoly
—händler monopolist, sole agent
—herrscher absolute ruler, autocrat, monarch
—hersteller monopolist, sole manufacturer (maker, producer)
—inhaber sole owner
alleinig exclusive, sole
alleinstehend alone, single, solitary, unmarried
Allein
—verkauf (— -srecht) exclusive (sole) right to sell (of sale), (sales) monopoly
—vertreter exclusive (sole) agent, sole representative
—vertretung exclusive (sole) agency, sole representation
—vertrieb exclusive (sole) agency (distribution)
allgemein common, general, public, overall, universal
— anerkannt generally accepted
— bekannt sein be a matter of common knowledge, be public property, be widely known
— gebräuchlich general, universal
allgemeingültig generally accepted
allgemeinverständlich intelligible to all, popular
Allgemein
—begriff general idea (concept)
—gültigkeit universality
—gut common knowledge, public property
—heit general(ity), public, universality
—wissen general knowledge
—wohl common weal
Allianz alliance, league
alliieren ally, enter into an alliance
Alliierter ally
alljährlich annual, every year, yearly
allmählich by degrees, gradual, little by little, successively, step by step
alltäglich daily, every day
Almosen alms
—empfänger almspeople
Altbesitz old holding (possession)
alteingesessen old-established
Altenteil annuity
Alter age, seniority
Alters
—folge (order of) seniority
—fürsorge old age relief
—grenze age limit, limit of age
—rente old age pension
—versicherung old age insurance
—vorrecht (right of) seniority
—zulage seniority allowance, superannuation (allowance)
alternativ alternative
Alternative alternative, choice, option
Alternativvorschlag alternative proposal
Ältestenrat council of elders (aldermen), alderman
Amnestie act of grace, amnesty, general pardon
—erlaß amnesty decree
—gesetz amnesty law

amnestieren amnesty, pardon
Amortisation amortization, redemption, repayment
amortisierbar amortizable, redeemable, repayable
amortisieren redeem, repay
Amt agency, board, bureau, charge, function, office, position, post
Amt, im in official position
Amt, um -s wegen officially, ex officio, by virtue of office, upon own motion
amtieren act as, be in charge, hold office, officiate
amtierend acting, officiating
amtlich official, functional
Amts
—alter length of service, seniority
—anmaßung (unjustified) assumption of office (public authority)
—antritt accession to office, entering into office
—arzt health (medical) officer
—befugnis (official) authority, competence, competency
—bereich (-bezirk) competence, jurisdiction
—bescheid direction
—bezeichnung official title
—blatt official gazette
—dauer term of office
—diener usher, marshal
—eid oath of office
—einführung inauguration
—enthebung dismissal (removal, suspension) from office
—gebühren official charges (duties, fees)
—geheimnis official secret
—gericht inferior (county, police, local) court, magistrate('s court), Assizes (GB), Judge of the Peace (GB), Petty Sessions (GB)
—gewalt competence, competency, official authority (power)
—handlung official act (function)
—mißbrauch abuse of (official) power, malversation
—niederlegung resignation from office
—periode term (period) of office
—richter county (district) judge, magistrate
—schreiber bailiff, clerk
—siegel official seal
—sitz official residence
—sprache official language
—stunden official hours
—träger functionary, holder of office, office holder (bearer)
—übernahme accession to (entrance into) office
—unterschlagung embezzlement in office (official position), malversation, misappropriation of public funds
—vergehen malfeasance in office
—vorgänger predecessor in office
—vormund public (statutory) guardian
—vorsteher official in charge
—walter (-leiter) functionary
—zeit tenure of office, term (of office)
analog analogous
Analogie analogy
Analyse analysis
analysieren analyse
Anarchie anarchy
Anarchist anarchist
anarchistisch anarchist
anbahnen initiate, prepare
anbelangen concern, regard, relate to
anberaumen appoint, fix, schedule
Anbetracht,
in — von in consideration of, considering, in view of
anbieten offer, present, quote, tender
andernfalls else, in the contrary case, on the other hand, otherwise
ändern alter, change, correct, modify, rectify, reverse, vary
Änderung alteration, change, correction, modification, rectification, reversion, variation
anderweitig otherwise
andeuten announce, foreshadow, indicate, suggest

Andeutung announcement, hint, indication, suggestion
andeutungsweise allusively, by way of suggestion, in outlines
androhen menace, threaten, warn
Androhung menace, threat, warning
unter — von under the threat of
aneignen acquire, appropriate, contract, usurp
Aneignung acquisition, adoption, annexation, appropriation, conversion
aneinandergrenzend adjacent, adjoining
Anerbieten offer, proposal, proposition
anerkannt accepted, acknowledged, admitted, certified, established, proved, recognized
—, allgemein generally accepted (approved)
—ermaßen admittedly
anerkennen accept, acknowledge, admit, recognize
Anerkenntnis acceptance, acknowledgement, admission
—urteil consent judgement (decree), judgement by admission (consent), judgement (decree) by confession
Anerkennung acknowledgement, admission, authentication, legitimation, recognition
Anerkennungs
—gebühr recognition fee
—schreiben letter of acknowledgement
—urkunde deed of acknowledgement (recognition)
Anfall accrual, devolution
anfallen accrue, devolve upon, fall due
Anfallsrecht revisionary interest, right to succeed
Anfang beginning, commencement, origin, outset, start
Anfangs
—kapital initial (opening) capital
—kurs opening price (rate) (quotation)
—schwierigkeiten initial difficulties
—stadium initial stages
—tag (termin) initial date
anfechtbar avoidable, contestable, defeasible, disputable, impugnable, rescindable, voidable
Anfechtbarkeit nullity, voidability, voidableness
anfechten appeal, avoid, challenge, contest, defeat, dispute, impeach, impugn, make void, oppose, trouble
Anfechtung appeal, avoidance, contestation, impeachment, impugnment, nullification
Anfechtungs
—erklärung declaration of (a)voidance
—klage action for avoidance (annulment, nullification), action to set aside
—kläger plaintiff in a nullity action (suit)
—prozeß annulment proceedings
—recht right of avoidance
anfordern call for, claim, demand, request
Anforderung call, claim, demand, request
—, auf on demand (request)
Anfrage application, inquiry, question
anfragen apply, inquire, interpellate, question
anfügen (ad)join, affix, annex, append, attach, enclose
anführen allege, cite, plead, quote, state
Anführer chief, commander, leader, ringleader
Anführung adduction, allegation, citation, quotation, specification, statement
—szeichen quotation marks
Angabe declaration, description, information, specification, statement
—, falsche misrepresentation
Angaben data, details, particulars, statements
—, wissentlich falsche knowingly false statements
angeben allege, declare, specify, state

angeblich alleged, pretended, ostensible
angeboren inborn, inherent, innate
Angebot bid, offer, quotation, tender
angebracht advisable, appropriate, convenient, seasonable, suitable
angehen concern, regard
angeklagt accused of, charged with, committed for, tried on
Angeklagter accused, culprit, defendant, delinquent, prisoner
Angelegenheit affair, business, case, concern, matter
angemessen adequate, appropriate, proper, reasonable, suitable
Angemessenheit adequacy, adequateness, appropriateness, reasonableness
angeschuldigt accused of, charged with
Angeschuldigter accused, defendant
angesehen distinguished, esteemed, notable, reputable
angestammt
—es Recht ancestral (hereditary) right, birthright
Angestellten
—versicherung employees' social insurance
Angestellter clerk, employee, functionary, member of staff, official
angewandt applied
angewiesen depend(ent) on
Angewiesener drawee
angleichen adjust, assimilate, coordinate, equalize
Angleichung adaption, adjustment, assimilation
angliedern adjoin, affiliate, annex
Angliederung adjoinment, affiliaton, annexation, incorporation
angreifbar attackable, contestable, disputable, vulnerable
angreifen approach, attack, handle, tackle, touch
Angreifer aggressor, attacker, invader
angrenzen adjoin, be adjacent (adjoining) to, border on, verge on
angrenzend adjacent, adjoining, contiguous, neighbo(u)ring
Angriff aggression, assault, attack
in — nehmen cope with, embark (up)on, tackle, take in hand
anhaften adhere, attach, be inherent in
Anhaltspunkt basis, clue, criterion, lead, reference point
Anhang annex, appendage, appendix, enclosure, schedule, supplement
anhängig pending
— machen bring in an action against
Anhängigkeit pendency
anhäufen accumulate, accrue, amass, pile up
Anhäufung accumulation, aggregation, increase
anheften affix, attach
anheimfallen devolve upon
anhören hear
Anhörung hearing
Ankauf purchase
ankaufen buy, purchase
anklagbar impeachable, indictable, triable
Anklage accusation, charge, impeachment, indictment, prosecution
— erheben enter (prefer) a charge
Anklage
—bank dock
—behörde prosecution
—beschluß indictment
—schrift (bill of) indictment, charge sheet
—verfahren procedures of indictment, prosecution
—verlesung arraignment
anklagen accuse of, arraign for, bring an action against, charge with, indict of
Ankläger accuser, informer, plaintiff
Ankläger, öffentlicher public prosecutor
ankündigen announce, give notice, notify

Ankündigung announcement, notice, notification, proclamation
—sschreiben letter of advice
Anlage appendix, enclosure, exhibit, investment
—papier investment part (stock)
—vermögen fixed assets, invested capital, investments
Anlaß cause, ground, motive, occasion, reason
anläßlich on the occasion of
anlegen affix, attach, invest
Anleihe advance, credit, loan,
—vertrag loan contract
Anleihe advance, credit, loan
Anliegen adjacency, desire, matter, request
anliegen be adjacent to, border on
anliegend adjacent, adjoining, attached, enclosed, neighbo(u)ring
Anlieger abutter, neighbo(u)r
—recht neighbour right
anmaßen arrogate, assume, usurp
anmaßend arrogant, overbearing, presumptuous, pretentious, usurping
Anmaßung arrogance, arrogation, assumption, pretension, usurpation
Anmelde
—formular registration (application) form
—frist period (limitation, term) of registration (application, notification)
—gebühr filing (registration) fee
—pflicht compulsory registration, obligation to notify
anmeldepflichtig notifiable
Anmelde
—stelle registration (filing) office (agency)
—termin application (registration) date
anmelden announce, notify, register
Anmeldung announcement, application, booking, declaration, registration, report
Anmerkung annotation, comment, (foot)note
Annahme acceptance, adoption, assumption, passage, passing, presumption, reception, supposition
—bedingungen conditions (terms) of acceptance
—frist term (period) (limitation) of acceptance
—protest protest for non-acceptance
—vertrag contract of adoption
—verweigerung non-acceptance, refusal to accept
—verzug default of acceptance
—zwang obligation to accept, duty of acceptance
Annalen annals, records
annehmbar acceptable, admissible
Annehmbarkeit acceptability
annehmen accept, adopt, assume, pass
annektieren annex
Annektierung annexation
(Annexion)
Annuität annuity
annullieren annul, cancel, declare null and void, make void, nullify, set aside
Annullierung annulment, cancellation, nullification
anonym anonymous
Anonymität anonymity
anordnen arrange, direct, dispose, group, instruct, order
Anordnung arrangement, direction, directive, disposition, grouping, instruction, order, regulation
anpassen accommodate, adapt, adjust
Anpassung accommodation, adaption, adjustment
anpassungsfähig adaptable, flexible, versatile
Anpassungs
—fähigkeit adaptability
—zeitraum period of adaption
anraten advise, recommend
anrechnen allow, charge, credit, debit, deduct, put to account, set off
Anrechnung charge, debiting, deduction
Anrecht claim, right, title
Anrede address

anregen animate, incite, propose, suggest
Anregung proposition, suggestion
anrichten cause
anrüchig disreputable
Anrüchigkeit disrepute
anrufen appeal, call, invoke
Anrufung appeal, invocation
ansammeln accumulate, accrue, amass, collect
Ansammlung accumulation, accrual, aggregation, collection, concentration, heap, massing
ansässig domiciled, domiciliated, resident, residing
anschaffen acquire, buy, purchase
Anschaffung acquisition, purchase
Anschaffungs
—kosten cost (actual) price
—preis purchase price
—wert original (cost) (acquisition) value
Anschauung conception, idea, notion, opinion, perception, point of view, viewpoint
Anschein appearance, look, probability
Anschlag attempt, conspiracy, plot
—brett bulletin (notice) board
anschlagen, öffentlich placard
anschließen adopt, affiliate, annex, incorporate, join
anschließend adjacent, ensuing, following, next, subsequent
Anschluß affiliation, annexation, connection, joining
—berufung cross-appeal
— — einlegen cross-appeal
—revision cross-appeal
Anschreiben cover note, covering letter
Anschrift address
—sänderung change of address
anschuldigen accuse, charge, incriminate
Anschuldigung accusation, charge, incrimination
—, falsche false denouncement
Ansehen esteem, reputation, standing
ansehen consider, look at, regard, view
ansehnlich considerable, important
ansetzen appoint, assign, fix, schedule
Ansicht opinion, (point of) view, viewpoint
—, zur on approval, for inspection
—ssache matter of opinion
Ansinnen unfair demand, unreasonable request
anspielen allude to, hint at, insinuate
Anspielung allusion, hint, insinuation
Ansprache address, speech
ansprechen address, speak
Anspruch claim, demand, pretension, right, title
— erheben raise (put forward) a claim
— geltend machen enforce a claim
Anspruchs
—abtretung assignment (transfer) of a claim
anspruchs
—berechtigt entitled to claim
—los unpretending, unpretentious
Anspruchs
—verjährung limitation of claims, prescription
anspruchsvoll demanding, pretentious
Anstalt establishment, institute, institution
Anstand behavio(u)r, complaint, objection
—sgefühl sense of decency
anstandslos promptly, readily, unhesitatingly, without difficulties (objections)
Anstands
—regeln rules of etiquette, social conventions
anstandswidrig improper, indecent, unseemly
anständig decent, fair, proper, respectable
Anständigkeit decency, fairness, propriety, respectability

ansteckend contagious, infectious
Ansteckung contagion, infection
anstehen be (come) up for, defer, delay
anstellen appoint, draw, employ, engage, make
Anstellung appointment, employment, engagement, position
—, feste definite appointment, permanent position (post)
Anstellungs
—bedingungen conditions (terms) of employment
—vertrag employment contract
anstiften abet, cause, incite, initiate, instigate, provoke
Anstifter abettor, instigator
Anstiftung abetment, incitement, initiation, instigation
Anstoß erregen cause (give) offence to
— nehmen disapprove, take offence at (exception to)
anstößig indecent, objectionable, offensive, scandalous, shocking
anstreben aim at, aspire to, endeavo(u)r, strive for
anstrengen endeavo(u)r, make an effort, strive
Anstrengung attempt, effort, endeavo(u)r, exertion, exhaustion, strain
Ansturm assault, attack, onslaught, run
Ansuchen application, petition, request, solicitation
ansuchen apply for, ask, petition for, request, solicit
Anteil allotment, contingent, contribution, interest, part, portion, quota, share
anteilig proportional, proportionate, pro rata, sharing
anteilsberechtigt participating, entitled to a share
Anteilschein share, share certificate
Anteilseigner shareholder
(-sinhaber)
anteilsmäßig proportionate, in proportion, pro rata
Antrag application, motion, offer, petition, plea, proposal, proposition, request
— stellen plead, put a motion
antragen offer, propose, tender
Antrags
—formular application form
—frist period (limitation) of application
—gegner opponent, respondent
Antragsteller appellant, applicant, claimant, person applying, petitioner, proposer
antreten accept, begin, enter, furnish, offer, start, take up
Antrieb drive, impetus, impulse, initiative, motive
Antritt accession, commencement, entrance, entry, start
Antritts
—rede inaugural address (speech)
—vorlesung inaugural lecture
antun harm, hurt, injure
Antwort answer, reply, response
antworten answer, reply, respond
Antwort
—schein reply coupon
—schreiben letter of reply
—schrift answer, replique
—telegramm reply telegram
anvertrauen confide, entrust, give (put) in charge
anvertraut entrusted, in trust
anverwandt related
Anverwandter, nächster next of kin
anwachsen accrue, augment, increase
Anwalt advocate, attorney (-at-law), barrister, counsel(lor), lawyer, legal adviser, solicitor
Anwalts
—beruf legal profession
—büro chambers, law office
Anwaltschaft bar
Anwalts
—gebühren (-honorar) legal fees
—kammer bar association (council), Chamber of Lawyers
—kanzlei chambers, law office
—kosten lawyer's charges (fees)
—praxis legal practice
Anwärter aspirant, candidate, expectant, revisioner
Anwartschaft claim (to), expectancy, prospect (of)

—srecht claim
anweisen allot, assign, direct, instruct, order, transfer
Anweisung allocation, assignment, direction, directive, instruction, order, regulation, remittance, transfer
Anweisungs
—empfänger payee
—gebühr transfer fee (charge)
anwendbar applicable, practicable, relevant
Anwendbarkeit applicability, practicability
anwenden apply, employ, use, utilize
Anwendung application, employment, use, utilization
Anwendungs
—bereich (-gebiet) field of application, scope
—möglichkeit applicability, use
Anwesen land property, real estate
anwesend present
Anwesenheit attendance, presence
—sliste attendance list
anzahlen make (pay) a deposit, pay on account (down)
Anzahlung advance (down) payment, first instalment, deposit, payment on account, part payment
— leisten (machen) pay on account, pay a deposit (on)
Anzeichen indication, mark, sign, signal, symptom
Anzeige advice, advertisement, announcement, charge, declaration, denouncement, information, notice, notification, report
— erstatten denounce, inform against, lay (prefer) an information against
anzeigen announce, charge, declare, denounce, inform, notify, report (to the police)
Anzeigepflicht duty (obligation) to notify
anzeigepflichtig notifiable, reportable
anzetteln devise, hatch, lay, plot
Anziehung attraction
—skraft attraction
anzüglich offensive, personal, suggestive
anzweifeln dispute, doubt, question
Apanage apanage, life annuity
Appell appeal
Appellant appellant
appellieren appeal
Approbation approbation, licenc(s)e
—surkunde practising certificate
approbieren admit
approbiert licensed, qualified
Äquivalent equivalent
äquivalent equivalent
Arbeit effort, employment, job, labo(u)r, occupation, pains, task, trouble, work
arbeiten labo(u)r, operate, run, work
Arbeiter hand, labo(u)rer, worker, workman
—, (un)gelernter (un)skilled worker
Arbeiter
—abordnung workers' delegation
—ausschuß workers' committee
—aussperrung lockout
—ausstand strike
—bewegung labo(u)r movement
—familie worker's (working class) family
—frage labo(u)r question
—führer labo(u)r leader, boss
—fürsorge industrial welfare, workers' relief
—genossenschaft workers' co-operative society
—gesetzgebung labo(u)r legislation
—gewerkschaft trade (labo(u)r) union
—klasse working class
—mangel labo(u)r shortage
—organisation labo(u)r organization
—partei labo(u)r party
—rat works (workers', shop) council
—regierung labo(u)r government
—schaft labo(u)rers, working class, workmen, workers

—schutz labo(u)r protection
—schutzgesetzgebung factory laws, social legislation
—unfallgesetz workmen's compensation act
—verband (-vereinigung) workers' union (association)
—versicherung industrial insurance, workmen's compensation
—versicherungsgesetz s. -unfallgesetz
—vertretung labo(u)r representation
—wohlfahrt workmen's assistance
Arbeitgeber employer, management, master
—anteil employers' contribution (share)
—organisation (-verband) employers' (trade) association (federation)
—schaft employers, management
Arbeitnehmer employee, worker
—anteil employee's contribution (share)
—verband (-vereinigung) employees' association, workers' (trade, labo(u)r) union
—schaft employees
Arbeits
—abkommen labo(u)r contract, wage agreement
—amt labo(u)r office (exchange)
—ausschuß study group, working committee
—bedingungen terms of employment
—bereich range of work, sphere (field) of activity (operation)
—bescheinigung certificate of employment, labo(u)r permit
—bummelei absenteeism
—einkommen earned income
—entgelt remuneration
—erlaubnis labo(u)r permit
arbeitsfähig able to (capable of) work, able-bodied
Arbeits
—fähigkeit capacity to (fitness for) work
—frieden industrial peace
—gebiet field of activity
—gefängnis workhouse
—gemeinschaft collaboration, study group, team, union
—genehmigung labo(u)r (working) permit
—gericht labo(u)r (industrial) court
—gesetz labo(u)r law
—gesetzgebung labo(u)r legislation
—gruppe working group (team)
—haus workhouse
—konflikt labo(u)r (industrial, trade) dispute (conflict)
—lohn pay, wage
arbeitslos idle, out of work, unemployed
Arbeitsloser unemployed, workless
Arbeitslosen
—fürsorge (-unterstützung) dole, unemployment benefit (assistance, relief)
—versicherung unemployment insurance
Arbeitslosigkeit unemployment
Arbeits
—ministerium Ministry of Labour (GB), Department of Labor (USA)
—niederlegung strike, walkout
—ordnung working regulations
—papier working papers (permit)
—recht industrial law, labo(u)r legislation (law)
arbeitsscheu work-shy
Arbeits
—schutz industrial safety
—schutzgesetz industrial safety law
—sitzung working meeting (session)
—streitigkeiten labo(u)r dispute
—tag workday, working day
—teilung division of labo(u)r
arbeitsunfähig disabled, incapacitated
Arbeits-
—unfähigkeit disability, disablement, incapacity for work, invalidity
—unfall working (industrial) accident
—verfassung labo(u)r charter

—vergütung pay, remuneration
—verhältnis employment, job, post
—verhältnisse working conditions
—vertrag employment (labo(u)r, work) contract
—verweigerung refusal to work
arbeitswillig ready to work
Arbeits
—zeit hours of work, working time (hours) (period)
—zeitabkommen agreement of working hours, contract for guaranteed employment
Arbitrage arbitrage
—klausel arbitrage clause
arbitrieren arbitrage
Archiv archives, records, record office
Archivar archivist, keeper of (public) records, recorder, registrar
Ärgernis annoyance, indecency, mischief, nuisance, scandal, vexation
—, öffentliches public scandal
— erregen excite a scandal
Arglist fraud, malice
arglistig cunning, fraudulent, malicious
—e Täuschung wilful deceit, fraud
Argument argument, point
argumentieren argue about, reason with
Armen
—fürsorge poor relief (assistance)
—pfleger relieving officer, poormaster
—recht poor law, legal aid
—unterstützung s. -fürsorge
Arrest, arrest, confinement, detention, seizure
Arrestant detained, prisoner
Arrest
—befehl distraint order, arrest report, warrant of arrest, writ of attachment
—strafe detention, sentence of confinement
arrestieren apprehend, arrest, take into custody
Art class, fashion, manner, method, mode, kind, sort, species, style, type
arteigen characteristic
Artikel article, clause, paragraph, section
Assessor assessor(y), assistant judge, junior barrister
Assisengericht court of assizes
Assistent aid, assistant, clerk
Assoziation association, partnership
assoziieren associate, enter into partnership
assoziiert associated, cooperant
Asyl asylum, refuge, sanctuary, shelter
—recht right of sanctuary (asylum)
Aszendent ascendant
Attaché attaché
Attentat attempted assassination, criminal attempt (attack), outrage, perpetration
Attentäter assailant, perpetrator
Attest attestation, certification, certificate
attestieren attestate, certify
aufbewahren deposit, have (keep) in custody, file, keep, preserve
Aufbewahrung custody, preservation, (safe) keeping, safe custody
Aufbewahrungs
—frist retention period
—ort depository, place of deposit (keeping), repository
—schein deposit receipt
aufbieten call up, summon
Aufbietung summons
aufbürden burden, charge, impute
aufdecken detect, disclose, discover, reveal, unveil
Aufdeckung detection, disclosure, discovery, exposition, exposure
Aufdruck impression, imprint
aufdrucken (im)print
aufdrücken affix, press, put, set
aufeinanderfolgend consecutive, successive

Aufenthalt abode, domicile, residence, sojourn, stay, whereabouts
Aufenthalts
—bestätigung residence certificate
—bewilligung (-erlaubnis, -genehmigung) staying (residence) permit
—dauer duration of stay, time of residence
—kontrolle supervision (control) of residence (aliens)
—ort domicile, place of sojourn (abode), residence
—verbot local banishment
—verlängerung prolongation of residence (stay)
auferlegen impose, inflict
Auferlegung impositon, infliction
auffassen comprehend, conceive, grasp, understand
Auffassung comprehension, conception, interpretation
—svermögen intelligence, intellectual grasp, perceptive faculty
auffindbar discoverable, traceable
auffinden discover, find (out), locate, trace
Auffindung discovery, finding
auffliegen blow up, clear out, fail
auffordern ask, call, invite, request, summon, urge
Aufforderung call, demand, invitation, order, request, summons
aufführen enumerate, list, (re)present, specify, state
Aufführung enumeration, listing, performance, (re)presentation, specification, statement
—srecht acting rights, right of performance
Aufgabe abandonment, assignment, advice, business, concern, direction, discontinuance, dispatch, duty, function, instruction, job, office, quotation, relinquishment, renunciation, resignation, retirement, surrender, task, work
Aufgaben
—bereich competence, scope of duties (functions)
—gebiet field of activity
aufgeben abandon, discontinue, dispatch, drop, forgo, give up, leave, post, quit, relinquish, renounce, resign, retire, set aside, surrender, waive
Aufgebot public summons (notice, citation), banns (of marriage), proclamation, publication of banns
— bestellen publish the banns
Aufgebots
—termin date fixed by public summons
—verfahren public citation, procedure (proceedings) by public summons, public summons
Aufgeld agio, extra(-)charge, premium, surcharge
aufgliedern analyse, break down, departmentalize, itemize, specify, subdivide
Aufgliederung analysis, breakdown, classification, departmentalization, itemization, specification
aufgreifen, pick up, take up
aufhalten delay, detain, halt, live, reside, retard, stay, stop
aufhebbar voidable
aufheben abolish, abrogate, annul, break off, cancel, discontinue, dissolve, put aside, quash, repeal, rescind, reverse, revoke, set aside, suspend, terminate, withdraw
Aufhebung abolition, abrogation, annulment, cancellation, discontinuance, dissolution, putting aside, quashing, repeal, rescission, reversal, reversion, revocation, setting aside, suspension, termination, withdrawal
Aufhebungs
—antrag application (motion) for setting aside (cancellation)
—bestimmung (-klausel) cancellation clause

—klage action for rescission
aufhetzen incite, instigate
Aufhetzung agitation, incitement, instigation
aufklären clear up, elucidate
Aufklärung clearing up, elucidation, explanation, instruction
aufkommen assume, be answerable (responsible, liable) for, compensate, guarantee
aufkündbar subject to notice, terminable
aufkündigen call in, cancel, denounce, foreclose, give notice, revoke
Aufkündigung notice, recalling, revocation, termination
Auflage charge, direction, edition, imposition, injunction, instruction, order
— machen raise a to-do
auflassen cede, convey, transfer
Auflassung cession, conveyance, transfer
Auflauf accrual, assembly, riot
auflegen edit, issue, publish
auflehnen, sich lean up against, oppose, rebel, revolt
Auflehnung mutiny, opposition, rebellion, resistance, revolt
auflösbar dissolvable, soluble, solvable
auflösen annul, break up, cancel, disband, disentangle, disintegrate, dismiss, dissolve, liquidate, rescind, resolve, unravel, wind up
Auflösung annulment, breaking up, cancellation, disbandment, disentanglement, disintegration, dismissal, dissolution, liquidation, rescission, resolution, unravelling, winding up
Aufmerksamkeit alertness, attention, courtesy, vigilance
Aufnahme absorption, acceptance, admission, admittance, beginning, drawing up, entering, entrance, establishment, incorporation, initiation, insertion, integration, introduction, reception, starting, taking up
—bedingungen terms of admission
aufnahmefähig admissible, capacious
Aufnahme
—fähigkeit capacity
—gebühr admission (initiation, entrance) fee
—gesuch application for admission
—prüfung entrance examination
aufnehmen admit, draw up, embody, hear, include, incorporate, initiate, insert, integrate introduce, list, raise, start, take up
Aufpreis additional price, premium, surcharge
aufreizen incite, instigate, provoke
aufreizend inflammatory, provocative
Aufreizung incitement, instigation, provocation
Aufruf appeal, call(ing in), proclamation, summons
aufrufen appeal, call (in), proclaim, summon
Aufruhr insurrection, mutiny, sedition, rebellion, revolt, riot, uproar
Aufrührer agitator, fomenter, instigator, insurgent, mutineer, rebel
aufrührerisch inflammatory, insurgent, mutinous, seditious, rebellious
aufschieben adjourn, defer, delay, postpone, put off, suspend
aufschiebend dilatory
Aufschiebung adjournment, postponement, suspension
Aufschlag additional (extra) charge, premium, rise, surtax
Aufschluß explanation, information
aufschlußreich informative, instructive
Aufschrift address, direction, heading, inscription, legend, title
Aufschub adjournment, deferment, delay, postponement, reprieve, respite, stay, suspension

Aufsehen sensation, stir
— **erregen** cause (create) sensation
aufsehenerregend sensational, startling
Aufseher attendant, foreman, guardian, inspector, supervisor
Aufsicht control, inspection, supervision, surveillance
— **führen** control, superintend, supervise
aufsichtführend controlling, superintendent, superintending
Aufsichts
—**amt** control office (board)
—**beamter** control officer, inspector, superintendent, supervisor
—**befugnis** right of control
—**behörde (-instanz, -organ)** supervising (controlling) authority
—**führender** s. -beamter
—**personal** superintending (supervising) staff
—**rat** supervisory board
—**ratsmitglied** member of the supervisory board
—**ratssitzung** meeting of the supervisory board
—**vorsitzender** chairman of the supervisory board
—**recht** right of control
Aufstand insurrection, mutiny, rebellion, revolt, sedition, (up)rising
aufständisch rebellious, seditious
Aufständischer insurgent, rebel
aufstellen appoint, formulate, lay down, make (out, up), nominate, present, set up
Aufstellung drawing up, list, making up, nomination, preparation, schedule, statement
—, **genaue** specification
aufteilen allot, apportion, dismember, distribute, divide (up), parcel
Aufteilung allocation, allotment, dismemberment, distribution, division, parcelling, partition
Auftrag charge, duty, direction, instruction, mandate, (com)mission, order
—, **ohne** uncommissioned, without authority
—, **ohne offiziellen** without official status
auftragen charge, commission, instruct, order
Auftraggeber client, customer, employer, mandator, orderer, principal
Auftragnehmer assignee, consignee, contractor, supplier
Auftrags
—**annahme** acceptance of order
—**bestätigung** confirmation of order
—**formular** order form (blank, sheet)
auftragsgemäß as ordered, due to order
Auftrags
—**vertrag** agency contract
auftreten act (behave) as, appear (before, in), take the floor
Auftreten appearance, behavio(u)r, occurrence
Aufwand expenditure, expense
—**sentschädigung** expense allowance
aufwenden spend
Aufwendungen advances, expenditure, expenses, outlays
— **machen** incur advances
aufwerfen bring up, raise, set forth
aufwiegeln foment, incite, instigate, stir up
Aufwiegelung agitation, fomentation, incitement, instigation, sedition, stirring up
Aufwiegler agitator, fomenter, instigator
aufwieglerisch agitating, inflammatory, seditious
aufzählen enlist, enumerate, itemize, specify
Aufzählung enlistment, enumeration, itemization, specification
augenfällig conspicuous, evident, obvious
Augenschein appearance, evidence, examination, inspection
in — nehmen examine, inspect
augenscheinlich apparent, evident, obvious

Augenzeuge eyewitness
—nbericht eyewitness report
Auktion (sale by open) auction, (public) sale
Auktionator autioneer
Auktions
—bedingungen auction terms
—gebühren auction fees
—lokal (-saal) auction (sale) room
—termin auction day
ausarbeiten compose, draw up, elaborate, prepare, work out
Ausarbeitung composition, drawing up, elaboration, preparation, working out
ausbedingen reserve
Ausbedingung reservation
ausbeuten exploit, sweat, utilize, work, take advantage of, turn to account
Ausbeuter exploiter, sweater
Ausbeutung exploitation, sweating, utilization, working
—srecht right of exploitation
ausbezahlen buy out, pay (off, out)
ausbilden cultivate, develop, educate, instruct, school, train
Ausbildung development, education, instruction, schooling, training
—szeit training period (time)
Ausbleiben absense, default (of appearance), nonappearance, nonattendance
ausbleiben fail to appear, stay (remain) away
ausbrechen break out, break jail (gaol)
Ausbrecher jail (gaol) breaker
Ausbruch breaking out, escape, jailbreak, outbreak, outburst
ausbürgern denaturalize, deprive of citizenship, expatriate
Ausbürgerung denaturalization, deprivation of citizenship, expatriation
ausdehnen enlarge, extend
Ausdehnung enlargement, expansion, extension, extent
Ausdehnungs
—bedürfnis expansionism
—politik expansionist policy
Ausdruck expression, manifestation, phrase, term
ausdrücken express, utter
ausdrücklich explicit, express(ed), intentional, on purpose
auseinandergehend different, differing, divergent
auseinandersetzen argue, arrange, come to terms, compound, explain, make clear, point out
Auseinandersetzung argument, arrangement, conflict, discussion, dispute, explanation, liquidation, settlement
auserwählen choose, elect, select
Ausfall breakdown, deficiency, deficit, failure, loss
—bürgschaft deficit (deficiency) guarantee, indemnity bond
ausfallen be cancelled (omitted), fall out
ausfertigen draw up, execute, exemplify, issue, make out
Ausfertigung copy, execution, issue
Ausflucht excuse, pretext, subterfuge
Ausflüchte machen make up excuses, resort to (use) subterfuge
ausfragen cross-examine, inquire, interrogate, question
Ausfuhr export, exportation
—abgabe export duty
—artikel export article (item)
—beschränkungen export restrictions
—bestimmungen export regulations
—bewilligung (-erlaubnis) export licence (permit)
—handel export trade
—kontingent export quota
—kontrolle export control
—sperre export ban (embargo)
—steuer export duty
—überschuß export surplus
—verbot export embargo
—zoll export duty
ausführbar achievable, practicable, workable
Ausführbarkeit feasibility, practicability

ausführen carry out (through), commit, declare, effect, execute, explain, perform, perpetrate, realize, state
ausführen, näher give particulars (details), specify
ausführend executive
ausführlich ample, detailed, in detail, explicit
Ausführung application, carrying out, declaration, design, execution, explanation, fulfilment, implementation, performance, perpetration, realization, statement
Ausführungs
—bestimmungen implementing (executive) regulations
—verordnung carrying-out ordinance, executive order
ausfüllen fill (in, out), complete
Ausgabe distribution, edition, expense, expenditure, issue, issuing
—bedingungen terms of issue
—kurs rate of issue
Ausgang close, conclusion, day off, end(ing), event, issue, leave, outcome, result, termination
Ausgangs
—beschränkung curfew
—punkt starting-point, point of departure
ausgeben circulate, distribute, edit, issue, spend
Ausgeber editor, issuer
ausgebildet educated, schooled, trained
—, voll fully qualified
ausgedehnt extended, extensive, vast, wide-spread
ausgehen derive from, emanate from, originate from, proceed from, start from
Ausgehverbot confinement, curfew
ausgemacht agreed (upon), established, settled, stipulated
ausgenommen except, excluded, excluding, safe, with the exception of
Ausgleich arrangement, balance, balancing, compensation, compromise, equalization, offset, reconciliation, settlement
ausgleichen adjust, arrange, balance, compensate, compromise, offset, reconcile, settle
ausgleichend
—e Gerechtigkeit retributive justice
Ausgleichs
—forderung equalization claim
—verfahren clearing procedure
—zahlung discharge, equalization payment, severance pay, settlement
Ausgleichung accommodation, adjustment, arrangement, balancing, compensation, equalization, settlement
aushändigen deliver, hand over
Aushändigung delivery, handing over, surrender
Aushang bulletin, notice, placard, poster
aushängen post
auskaufen buy out
Auskunft information, inquiry, report
Auskunftei information bureau (office), inquiry office (agency)
Auslagen disbursement, expenses, outlays
—erstattung reimbursements
Ausland foreign country (countries)
fürs — bestimmt outward(-) bound
—, im abroad
—, vom from abroad
Ausländer alien, foreigner
ausländisch (from) abroad, alien, external, foreign
Auslands
—abteilung foreign department
—anlagen foreign investments, investments abroad
—anleihe foreign loan
—aufenthalt stay abroad
—bank foreign (overseas) bank
—beteiligung foreign investment
—gelder foreign capital
—geschäft foreign business (transaction)
—gläubiger foreign creditor

—guthaben foreign credit balances (holdings)
—kapital foreign capital
—handel foreign trade (commerce)
—kredit foreign credit
—paß foreign passport, passport for travels abroad
—schuld foreign debt
—vermögen foreign (external) assets (holdings), property abroad
—währung foreign currency (money, exchange)
—wechsel foreign bill of exchange
auslassen cancel, leave out, let out, omit
Auslassung deletion, omission, remark, utterance
auslaufen end, expire, run out, terminate
auslegen construe, disburse, display, exhibit, explain, expose, expound, interpret, lay out (open)
—, falsch misconstrue, misinterpret
Auslegung exegesis, exhibition, explanation, interpretation
—, falsche misconstruction, misinterpretation
Auslegungs
—bestimmungen (-vorschriften) interpretation clause
—frage matter of construction (interpretation)
—regel (-vorschrift) rule of interpretation
ausleihen hire (out), lend (out), loan
Ausleiher lender
Ausleihungen borrowings, lendings
Auslese assorting, choice, digest, selection
ausliefern deliver (up), extradite, hand over, surrender
Auslieferung delivery, extradition, surrender
Auslieferungs
—antrag request to extradite (for extradition)
—bedingungen terms of extradition (delivery)
—verbot prohibition of delivery
—verfahren extradition proceedings (procedure)
—vertrag delivery contract, extradition treaty (agreement)
Auslobung public reward, offer (promise) of reward
auslöschen cancel, delete, extinguish, obliterate
Auslöschung cancellation, deletion, extinction, obliteration
auslosen draw (by lots)
Auslosung drawing (of lots, by lot)
auslösen arouse, call forth, produce, ransom, redeem
Auslösung redemption
ausmachen agree, arrange, fix, locate, make out, settle, stipulate
Ausmaß degree, dimensions, extent, measurement, proportions, range, scale, scope
Ausnahme exception, exemption
—bestimmungen exceptional provisions, saving clause
—erlaubnis exception permit
—fall exceptional case
—gesetz emergency law
—gesetzgebung emergency legislation
—stellung exceptional (special, privileged) position
—zustand (state of) emergency
— — verhängen declare (establish, proclaim) martial law
ausnehmen except, exempt
ausnutzen benefit by, exploit, make profit of (by), profit by, take advantage of
Ausnutzung employment, exploitation, utilization
ausplündern pillage, plunder, rob, sack
Ausrede excuse, pretext, subterfuge
—, faule lame (poor, thin) excuse
Ausreise departure, exit
—erlaubnis (-genehmigung) exit permit
—visum exit visa
ausreißen desert, leave, run away
ausrotten eradicate, exterminate, extirpate, stamp out

Ausrottung eradication, extermination, extirpation, genocide, uprooting
Aussage declaration, pleadings, statement, testimony
—, schriftliche deposition
aussagen declare, depose, plead, state, testify
Aussageverweigerung refusal of testimony
ausscheiden eliminate, exclude, renounce, retire, rule out, separate, withdraw
Ausscheiden removal, resignation, retirement, withdrawal
Ausscheidung elimination, removal, separation
ausschlagen decline, disclaim, refuse, reject, renounce
ausschlaggebend casting, decisive, determining
ausschließen disbar, disqualify, except, exclude, expel, preclude, ostracize, suspend
ausschließlich exclusive, sole
Ausschließung disbarment, disqualification, elimination, exclusion, expulsion, suspension
—sverfahren foreclosure proceedings
Ausschluß disbarment, disqualification, exclusion, exemption, expulsion, foreclosure
unter — der Öffentlichkeit in camera, in private
Ausschlußurteil judgement of exclusion
Ausschreibung announcement
Ausschreitung excess, riot, transgression, outrage
Ausschuß board, commission, committee, panel
ausschütten declare, distribute, pay
Ausschüttung declaration, distribution, payment
Außen
—dienst field (foreign) service
—handel foreign trade
—handelsbilanz balance of payments
—minister Foreign Minister, Foreign Secretary (GB), Secretary of State (USA)
—ministerium Foreign Ministry, Foreign Office (GB), State Department (USA)
—politik foreign policy
—stelle (field) agency, branch office
—wirtschaft foreign trade
außer
—dienstlich private, unofficial
—ehelich extra(-)marital, illegitimate
—etatmäßig extra-budgetary, supernumerary
—gerichtlich extra-judicial, private, out of court
Außerkraftsetzung abrogation, legal renouncement, repeal
äußern comment, declare, express, give, present, utter
außerordentlich eminent, exceptional, extraordinary, extreme, outstanding, singular, uncommon, unusual
außerplanmäßig additional, extraordinary, supernumerary, unscheduled
äußerst extreme, final, latest, outermost, supreme, utmost
außerstande inapt, incapable, not in a position, unable
Äußerung comment, declaration, expression, observation, remark, statement, utterance
Aussetzen cessation, failure, intermittence, interruption, stoppage, suspension
aussetzen allow, announce, bequeath, expose, interrupt, put out, set out, stay, suspend
Aussetzung bequest, exposure, interruption, stay, suspension
—santrag motion to stay proceedings
aussöhnen reconcile
Aussöhnung reconciliation
aussondern select, separate
Aussonderung selection, separation
—srecht right of separation (severance), right to preferential settlement
aussperren lock out, shut out
Aussperrung lockout
Aussprache debate, discussion, exchange of views

aussprechen declare, deliver, express, pass, pronounce
Ausspruch dictum, observation, remark, statement, utterance
Ausstand strike, walkout
ausständig outstanding, striking, on strike
Ausständiger striker
ausstatten endow, equip, staff
Ausstattung dowry, endowment, equipment, outfit
ausstehend open, outstanding, overdue, owing, receivable
ausstellen draw (up), execute, give, make (out), issue
Aussteller drawer, executor, issuer, signer
Ausstellung drawing, execution, issue, making out
Ausstellungs
—datum (-tag) date (day) of issue
—jahr year of issue
—ort place of issue, issuing place
Aussteuer dowry, endowment, outfit
aussteuern endow, give a dowry
ausstoßen banish, eject, excommunicate, expel
Ausstoßung banishment, ejection, excommunication, expulsion
ausstreichen cancel, cross out, delete, expunge, strike out
Ausstreichung cancellation, crossing out, deletion, striking out
Austausch barter, exchange, interchange
austauschbar exchangeable, interchangeable
Austauschbarkeit exchangeability, interchangeability
austauschen barter, exchange, interchange
austreten leave, retire, secede, withdraw
Austritt retirement, secession, withdrawal
—serklärung notice of withdrawal, resignation
ausüben carry on, commit, conduct, exercise, exert, perform, perpetrate, practise
ausübend executive, practising
—e Gewalt executive power
Ausübung carrying on, execution, exercise, exertion, performance, perpetration, practice
Auswahl choice, selection
—recht option, right of choice
auswählen choose, select
Auswanderer emigrant
Auswanderung (e)migration
auswandern (e)migrate
Auswanderungs
—amt (-behörde) board of emigration
—beamter emigration officer
—büro (-agentur) emigration office (agency)
auswärtig external, foreign
Auswärtiges Amt Foreign Office (GB), State Department (USA), Foreign Ministry
auswärts away from home, nonresident, out-of-town, outdoors, outside, outward
auswechselbar exchangeable, interchangeable, replaceable
auswechseln exchange, interchange, replace
Auswechslung exchange, interchange, replacement
Ausweg alternative, exit, outlet, way out
ausweichen avoid, elude, evade, sidestep
ausweichend evasive, non-committal
Ausweichklausel escape clause
Ausweis certificate, evidence, identity card, permit, proof, return, statement, voucher
ausweisen banish, deport, eject, establish (prove) one's identity, evict, exile, expel
Ausweiskarte card (certificate) of identity (identification), identity card, pass, permit
ausweislich according to, as evidenced by, as shown in
Ausweispapiere identity papers (documents)
Ausweisung banishment, deportation, eviction, exile, expulsion, proof of identity

Ausweisungs
—befehl (-beschluß) deportation warrant (order), expulsion order
—recht right to expel
—verfahren expulsion proceedings
auswerten analyse, evaluate, exploit, interpret, utilize
Auswertung analysis, evaluation, exploitation, interpretation, utilization
—sverfahren evaluation method
auszahlen buy out, disburse, pay (off, out)
auszählen count (out)
Auszählung count (out), counting
Auszahlung buying out, disbursement, paying off, payment
Auszahlungs
—anordnung (-anweisung) disbursing order, order to pay
—datum (-termin) date of payment
—liste payroll
Auszug abridgement, abstract, excerpt, extract, statement, summary
auszugsweise abbreviated, in abstracts
authentifizieren authenticate, certify, legalize, verify
authentifiziert authentic(al), authenticated, verified
Authentifizierung authentication, legalization, proof of authenticity
authentisch authentic(al), authenticated, genuine
Authentität authentity, genuineness
Autor author, writer
Autorisation authorization, permission
autorisieren authorize, empower
Autorität authority, expert
Autorschaft authorship
Aval guarantee, surety(ship), warranty
avalieren guarantee
Avis (letter of) advice, information, notification
avisieren advise, inform, notify, give advice

B

Bagatelle bagatelle, trifle, trifling matter
Bagatellgericht court of summary procedure (jurisdiction)
—sbarkeit (Bagatelljustiz) summary jurisdiction
bagatellisieren belittle, make light of, minimize, play down, underrate, understate
Bagatell
—sache petty case (cause), summary offenc(s)e
—schaden petty case of damage
Bande band, clan, clique, crew, crowd, gang, ring
Banden
—diebstahl gang robbery
—führer gangleader, ringleader
Bandit bandit, ganster, outlaw
Banditentum (-wesen) banditry
Bank bank, banker, banking house (firm, institute), bench, dock
Bank
—abteilung banking department
—agent bank agent (broker)
—angestellter (-beamter) bank official (clerk)
—gesetz banking law, bank act
—gesetzgebung bank legislation
Bankier banker, financier
Bank
—note bank note, (bank) bill
—raub bank robbery

—recht bank(ing) law
—wechsel bank bill
Bankrott bankruptcy, failure, insolvency
bankrott bankrupt, insolvent
Bankrotterklärung declaration of bankruptcy
Bankrotteur bankrupt
Bann ban, banishment, domination, excommunication, influence, interdict, jurisdiction, outlawry, power, precinct, proscription, sway
bannen ban, banish, boycott, cast out, excommunicate, exile, exorcize, obviate, ostracize, outlaw, proscribe
Bann
—meile outskirts, precinct, suburbs
—recht prerogative (privilege, right) to ban
—ware contraband (goods)
bar (in) cash
Bar
—abfindung cash settlement
—bestand cash in hand
—geld cash
—vermögen cash (assets)
—wert cash value
—zahlung cash payment
— —, gegen against (for) cash
beabsichtigen aim, consider, contemplate, intend, mean, propose
beabsichtigt deliberate, intended, intentional, wilful
beachten consider, (bear in) mind, notice, observe, pay attention to, take care, take into account, take notice of
beachtenswert noteworthy, remarkable
beachtlich considerable, marked, noticeable, remarkable
Beachtung attention, consideration, notice, observance, regard
Beamten
—herrschaft bureaucracy
—laufbahn official career
—tum bureaucracy, officialdom
Beamter civil servant, clerk, executive, functionary, officer, official
beanspruchen call for, claim, demand, pretend, require
Beanspruchung claim, demand, pretension
beanstanden challenge, contest, demur to, object, oppose, protest, refuse, reject, take exception to
Beanstandung complaint, objection, protest(ation), reclamation
beantragen apply for, demand, make a motion, file a petition, move, petition, plead, propose, request
beantworten answer, reply, respond
Beantwortung answer, reply, response
bearbeiten act upon, consider, deal with, handle, have in hand, prepare, process, treat, work (at, out)
Bearbeitung consideration, dealing with, handling, preparation, processing, treatment, working
beaufsichtigen control, inspect, look after, superintend, supervise, watch over
Beaufsichtigung control inspection, superintendence, supervision, surveillance
beauftragen authorize, charge, commission, direct, empower, entrust, instruct, order, retain
beauftragt appointed, authorized, charged, commissioned, directed, empowered, instructed, ordered
Beauftragter agent, attorney, commissioner, delegate, deputy, mandata(o)ry, nominee, proxy, representative
Bedachter beneficiary, legatee, recipient
Bedenken concern, consideration, deliberation, doubt, hesitation, objection, reflection, scruple
— haben hesitate
bedenken, consider, deliberate, doubt, hesitate, object, reflect, waver

bedenkenlos unscrupulous, without hesitation
Bedenkfrist (-zeit) time for consideration (reflection)
bedenklich critical, diffident, doubtful, dubious, objectionable
bedeuten imply, mean, represent, signify
bedeutend considerable, distinguished, important, remarkable
bedeutsam considerable, significant, suggestive
—, rechtlich legally relevant, relevant in law
Bedeutung importance, meaning, significance
bedeutungslos insignificant, irrelevant, meaningless, unimportant
Bedeutungslosigkeit harmlessness, insignificance, irrelevance, unimportance
bedeutungsvoll important, significant, weighty
Bedeutungswandel change of meaning
bedienen, sich avail of, make use of
bedingen postulate, presuppose, stipulate
bedingt conditional, contingent, limited, qualified
Bedingtheit conditionality, limitation, relativity
Bedingung clause, condition, provision, proviso, qualification, requirement, stipulation, term
Bedingungsklausel proviso
bedingungslos reserveless, unconditional, unqualified
bedrängen dun, press, urge
Bedrängnis affliction, distress
bedrohen endanger, menace, threaten
bedrohlich menacing, ominous, threatening
Bedrohung assault, menace, threat
bedürfen necessitate, need, require, want
bedürftig destitute, indigent, necessitous, needy, poor
Bedürftigkeit destitution, distress, indigence, neediness, poverty
beeiden (beeidigen) affidavit, confirm by oath, evidence by oath, give sworn evidence, swear to, take an oath upon
beeidigt sworn, under oath
Beeidigung confirmation by oath
beeinflussen affect, influence, inspire, prejudice
Beeinflussung influence
—, ungebührliche undue influence
beeinträchtigen affect, encroach upon, impair, infringe, injure, prejudice
Beeinträchtigung encroachment, impairment, infringement, injury, prejudice
beenden (beendigen) put an end to, terminate
Beendigung completion, conclusion, end(ing), termination
beerben be heir of, inherit, succeed to
Beerbung succession
befähigen enable, qualify
befähigt able, capable, fit for, gifted, qualified, talented
Befähigung aptitude, capacity, competence, efficiency, gift, qualification, skill, talent
—szeugnis certificate of qualification, proof of ability (qualification)
befangen bias(s)ed, partial, prepossessed, prejudiced, shy, timid
unbefangen free of prejudice, unprejudiced
als — ablehnen challenge
Befangenheit bias, partiality, prejudice, prepossession, shyness
Befehl command, decree, direction, instruction, order, warrant
befehlen bid, command, decree, direct, instruct, order, tell
befinden consider, deem, find, regard, think
befolgen abide by, adhere to, comply with, follow, meet, obey, observe, take

Befolgung adherence, compliance with, observance
befragen ask, consult, examine, inquire, interrogate, interview, query, question
Befragung consultation, examination, interrogation, interview, query, questioning
befreien clear off, discharge, dispense from, exempt from, exonerate, liberate, release, relieve, set free
befreit exempt from, free(d) from
Befreiung discharge, exemption, exoneration, liberation, release
Befreiungs
—klausel exemption clause
—schein exemption certificate
—vorschrift exemption provision
befriedigen appease, content, meet, pay off, satisfy
befriedigend satisfactory, satisfying
Befriedigung appeasement, gratification, paying off, payment, satisfaction, settlement
befristen put a deadline, fix a period for, set a time limit on
befristet limited, for a fixed period, temporary, on time
—er Anspruch deferred claim
Befugnis authority, authorization, competence, competency, jurisdiction, power, privilege, right
—überschreitung excess of power
befugt authorized, having authority (power), competent, empowered, entitled, privileged
Befund data, evidence, facts, findings, opinion, outcome, report, result
befürworten advocate, back, endorse, favo(u)r, plead for, recommend, second, sponsor, support
Befürworter advocate, backer, sponsor, supporter
Befürwortung endorsement, plea, recommendation, support
begaunern cheat, swindle, victimize
begeben dispose of, endorse, issue, proceed to, negotiate, sell
—, sich eines Rechtes waive (desist from, forgo, give up, yield, renounce) a right
Begebenheit (Begebnis) affair, event, happening, incident, occurrence
Begebung issue, negotiation, sale, waiver
begehen commit, make, perpetrate
Begehr demand, desire, request
Begehren demand, petition, request
begehren apply, claim, covet, demand, desire, petition, request, require, seek, solicit
Begehung commisson, committal, perpetration
Beginn beginning, commencement, outset, start
beginnen begin, commence, start
beglaubigen accredit, attest, authenticate, certify, confirm, legalize, notarize, verify
beglaubigt accredited, attested, certified, legalized
—e Abschrift certified (legalized) copy
—, notariell notarized
Beglaubigung accreditation, attestation, authentication, certification, legalization, verification
Beglaubigungs
—gebühr legalization fee
—schreiben letter of credence, credentials
—vermerk attestation clause
—zeuge attesting witness
begleichen balance, pay (off, up), settle
Begleichung payment, settlement
zur — von in settlement of
Begleit
—brief (-schreiben) accompanying (covering) letter, letter of advice
—umstände accessory (attendant, concomitant) circumstances, res gestae
—wort word of explanation

begnadigen amnesty, pardon, reprieve
Begnadigung amnesty, clemency, pardon, reprieve
Begnadigungs
—gesuch petition for mercy (pardon, clemency)
—recht power (right) of pardon (mercy)
begrenzen confine, limit, mark off, restrict
Begrenzung limit(ation)
Begriff conception, idea, notion, term
—sbestimmung definition
begründen argue, constitute, create, establish, found, justify, prove, give reasons for, set up, substantiate
begründet justifiable, justified, reasonable, substantiated, well-founded
—e Rechte vested rights
—er Verdacht reasonable suspicion
—er Zweifel reasonable doubt
Begründung argumentation, (statement of) arguments, establishment, (explanatory) proof, foundation, founding, initiation, motivation, reasons, substantiation
Berufungs- (Rechtsmittel) reasons (grounds) for an appeal
Urteils- grounds of judgement
mit dem —, daß on the grounds that
zur — in support of
Begründungs
—frist period (limitation) of giving reasons
begünstigen abet, aid and abet, assist, back, connive in, countenance, encourage, favo(u)r, foster, patronize, promote, support
Begünstiger abettor, accessory, accomplice
Begünstigter beneficiary, devisee, legatee
Begünstigung abetment, aiding and abetting, assistance, help, tenance, furtherance, patronage, preference, preferential treatment, promotion, protection, support
Begünstigungs
—klausel preferential (benefit) clause
—tarif preferential tariff
begutachten appraise, examine, give (express) an opinion
Begutachter appraiser, expert, referee
Begutachtung appraisement, examination, (expert) opinion, expertise
behaftet affected with, afflicted with, involved in, subject to
behalten hold, maintain, keep, retain
behandeln attend, deal with, handle, manage, treat
Behandlung dealing with, handling, processing, treatment
Beharren insistence, insisting, maintenance, persistence, persistency
beharren adhere to, insist on, keep to, maintain, persevere persist in, stand to, stick to
beharrlich constant, persistent, persevering, perseverant, steadfast, steady, unwavering, unyielding
Beharrlichkeit constancy, insistence, persistence, perseverance, steadfastness
behaupten affirm, allege, assert, claim, contend, defend, hold, insist, keep, maintain, plead, remain steady, stand one's ground, state
Behauptung affirmation, allegation, assertion, assurance, conjecture, contention, declaration, maintenance, statement
beheben adjust, clear away, do away with, eliminate, make good, meet, obviate, overcome, rectify, redress, relieve, remedy, remove, resolve
Behebung adjustment, elimination, obviation, redress, relief, removal
beheimatet domiciled, resident
behelligen annoy, bother, importune, molest, trouble

Behelligung bother(ation), molestation, trouble
beherbergen accommodate, give shelter to, house, lodge, shelter
beherrschen command, control, dominate, govern, master, reign, rule, sway
beherrschend dominating
Beherrscher master, ruler, sovereign
Beherrschung command, control, domination, mastery, ruling, supremacy, sway
behilflich helpful, serviceable
behindern hamper, handicap, hinder, impede, obstruct, restrain
Behinderung hindrance, impediment, obstruction
Behörde administration, agency, (public) authority, board, department, magistracy, office
behördlich authoritative, government(al), official
beibehalten abide by, adhere to, keep (on, to up), maintain, retain, stick to
Beibehaltung adherence to, keeping, maintenance, retention
beibringen adduce, administer, allege, bring, cause, furnish, inflict, obtain, procure, produce, provide, submit, supply, teach
Beibringung production
beiderseitig bilateral, common, mutual, reciprocal
beiderseits mutually, on both sides, on either side, reciprocally
beifolgend adjoined, annexed, attached, enclosed, subjoined
beifügen add, adjoin, affix, annex, append, attach, attribute, enclose
Beifügung addition, attribute, enclosure
Beihilfe abetment, aid, aiding and abetting, assistance, help, collaboration, subsidy, subvention
— leisten aid and abet, assist
Beilage addition, annex, appendix, enclosure, exhibit, supplement
beiläufig casual, incidental, occasional, secondary
beilegen add, adjoin, adjust, annex, arrange, assume, compromise, enclose, join, settle
Beilegung addition, accommodation, adjustment, arrangement, assumption, attribution, composition, enclosure, imputation, settlement
beiliegend adjoined, enclosed
beimessen ascribe to, attach, attribute, give credit to
Beimessung attribution
Beiname by-name, nickname, sobriquet, surname
beiordnen (ad)join, appoint, assign, coordinate
Beiordnung adjunction, assignment, coordination
beipflichten agree with (to), approve of, assent to, concur with
Beipflichtung agreement, approbation, assent, concurrence
Beirat advisor, advisory committee (board, council, panel), counsel
Beischlaf cohabitation, coition, sexual intercourse
Beisein assistance, presence
im — von in the presence of
beiseite schaffen abstract, appropriate, do away with, purloin, remove, take away
Beiseiteschaffung abstraction, killing, removal, stealing
Beisitz assessorship
beisitzen assess, associate, sit in (on), be a member of
Beisitzer assessor, associate judge, juror, juryman, member
Beispiel demonstration, example, instance, model, precedence
beispielsweise by way of (as an) example, for instance
Beistand advisor, advocate, aid, assistance, counsel, help, lawyer, legal adviser, support
Beistands
—abkommen (-pakt) (-vertrag) treaty (pact) of mutual assistance
—verpflichtung assistance obligation

beistehen aid, assist, give (lend) (render) assistance, help, plead for, stand by, support
Beisteuer aid, contribution, subsidy, subvention
beisteuern contribute to(wards), help, subsidize, subvention
beistimmen agree with, approve, assent, concur with, consent to
Beistimmung agreement, approval, assent, consent
Beitrag contribution, portion, premium, quota, share, subscription
beitragen conduce to, be conducive, contribute, help, promote
Beitragsanteil quota, share, subscription fee
beitragsfrei free (of contribution), non-contributory
Beitragspflicht contribution liability
beitragspflichtig liable (subject) to contribution, contributory
Beitragspflichtiger contributory
Beitragszahlung contribution, subscription
beitreibbar collectible, enforceable, recoverable
—, nicht irrevocable, unrecoverable
—, gerichtlich nicht unenforceable
beitreiben collect, enforce, exact, recover
Beitreibung collection, exaction, recovery
—skosten collection charges
beitreten accede, agree, approve, assent, concur with, enter, join
Beitritt accession, joining
Beitritts
—abkommen (-vertrag, -urkunde) deed of consent (accession)
—bedingungen conditions (terms) of membership
—erklärung declaration of accession, enrolment
—gesuch application for membership
—pflicht compulsory membership **(-zwang)**
beiwohnen assist at, attend, cohabit, participate, be present at, witness
Beiwohnung attendance, cohabitation, presence
bejahen accept, affirm, answer in the affirmative, assent, aver, consent
bejahrt advanced in years, aged, elderly
Bejahung acceptance, affirmation, affirmative answer
bekämpfen assail, attack, combat, fight against, oppose, prevent against, resist, struggle
Bekämpfung combat, fighting, prevention, struggle
bekannt acquainted, familiar, (well-)known, noted, notorious
—ermaßen (-lich) notoriously, as is well known, as you know
Bekanntgabe (Bekanntmachung) advertisement, announcement, communication, disclosure, notice, notification, proclamation, promulgation, publication
bekannt geben (— machen) advertize, announce, disclose, make known, give notice, notify, make public (known), publish, proclaim, promulgate, report
Bekanntmachung advertisement, announcement, bulletin, communiqué, disclosure, poster, promulgation, public notice, publication
Bekanntschaft acquaintance (ship), friends, familiarity, knowledge
bekennen acknowledge, admit, avow, confess, own
—, schuldig plead guilty
Bekenntnis admission, avowal, confession, creed, denomination
beklagen bemoan, bewail, complain, deplore, lament, pity
Beklagter appellee, contestee, defendant, respondent
bekleiden fill, hold, occupy
bekräftigen affirm, aver, confirm, corroborate, endorse, ratify, sanction, substantiate

—, eidlich affirm upon (by) one's oath
Bekräftigung affirmation, confirmation, corroboration, endorsement, sanction, substantiation
—, eidliche affirmation on (upon) oath
zur — von in confirmation of
bekunden declare, demonstrate, depose, manifest, reveal, show, state, testify
Bekundung declaration, demonstration, deposition, evidence, manifestation, testimony
Belang case, concern, consequence, importance, issue, matter, moment, relevance
—, ohne of no account, immaterial, irrelevant
—, von material, of importance (interest), important
Belange affairs, concerns, interests, matters
belangen concern, go to law with, indict, proceed against, prosecute, sue, take legal action against
belanglos immaterial, inconsequential, insignificant, irrelevant, negligeable, petty, unimportant
belangreich considerable, important, of importance, momentous, relevant
Belangung (legal) action, prosecution, suit
belassen leave, maintain, retain
belasten burden, charge, debit, discriminate, encumber, incriminate
belastend discriminating, incriminating, incriminatory
—es Material incriminating (incriminatory) evidence (documents)
—e Umstände incriminating circumstances
belästigen annoy, bother, inconvenience, molest, pester, trouble
Belästigung annoyance, bother, importunity, inconvenience, molestation, nuisance, trouble
Belastung burden, charge, encumbrance, incrimination, strain
Belastungs
—material incriminatory evidence (documents)
—zeuge witness for the prosecution (crown)
Haupt- principal witness for the prosecution
Beleg authority, document, (piece of) evidence, proof, receipt, record, voucher
belegbar verifiable
belegen authenticate, document, evidence, prove, support by, verify
—, mit einer Strafe impose (inflict) a penalty on, impugn
belehren advise, caution, inform, instruct
Belehrung advice, caution, information, instruction
beleidigen affront, assault, hurt, dishonour, injure, insult, outrage, offend (against), give offence to, wrong
beleidigend abusive, injurious, insulting, offending, offensive
Beleidiger insulter, offender
Beleidigter injured (offended) person (party)
Beleidigung abuse, affront, injury, insult, offence
—, gröbliche gross insult
—, tätliche assault and battery
—, verleumderische libel and slander
Beleidigungsklage (-sprozeß) action (suit) for libel (slander)
Belieben choice, convenience, discretion, option, pleasure, will
beliebig arbitrary, discretionary, optional
belohnen recompense, remunerate, reward
Belohnung award, premium, prize, recompense, remuneration, reward
bemächtigen get hold of, take possession of, seize, usurp
bemängeln blame, censure, complain of, criticize, find fault with

Bemängelung censure, complaint, criticism, remark
bemerken note, notice, observe, perceive
bemerkenswert notable, noteworthy, remarkable
Bemerkung comment, note, observation, remark, statement
bemessen adjust, assess, determine, estimate, measure by, proportion
Bemessung assessment, determination, proportioning, proportionment, rating
Bemessungs
—grundlage assessment basis
—zeitraum assessment period
bemühen endeavo(u)r, exert, strive, trouble
Bemühung effort, endeavo(u)r, exertion, pains, trouble
benachbart adjacent, adjoining, contiguous, neighbo(u)ring
benachrichtigen advise, announce, give notice, inform, notify
Benachrichtiger informant
Benachrichtigung advice, announcement, information, notice, notification
—sschreiben letter of advice
benachteiligen discriminate against, handicap, injure, prejudice, wrong
benachteiligend detrimental, injurious, prejudicial
Benachteiligter injured party (person)
Benachteiligung detriment, disadvantage, discrimination, handicap, injury, prejudice
Benannter nominee
Benehmen behavio(u)r, conduct, demeanour
Benehmen, ungehöriges improper (undue) conduct
benennen appoint, call, (de)nominate, designate, name, propose, term
Benennung appointment, (de)nomination, designation, naming, nomenclature
—srecht right of nomination
benötigen need, require, want
benutzen (benützen) employ, profit by, (make) use (of), utilize
Benutzer (Benützer) user, utilizer
Benutzung (Benützung) employment, use, utilization
—, mißbräuchliche abuse, misuse
Benutzungs
—gebühr utilization charge (fee)
—recht right to (of) use
—zwang compulsory use
beobachten comply with, follow, keep, notice, obey, observe, respect, shadow, study, watch
Beobachter observer
Beobachtung observance, observation
beordern command, commission, direct, order, summon
beraten advise, confer, consult, counsel, debate, deliberate on, discuss
beratend advisory, consultative, consulting, deliberative
Berater adviser, consultant, counsel, counsel(l)or
Rechts- legal adviser
beratschlagen deliberate on, debate, discuss
Beratschlagung deliberation, conference, consultation
Beratung advice, conference, consideration, consultation, counsel, deliberation, guidance
berauben bereave, deprive of, dispossess, divest of, expropriate, plunder, rob, strip of
Beraubung bereavement, deprivation, plunder, plunderage, robbery, spoliation
berechenbar calculable, computable
berechnen account, calculate, charge, compute, count, determine, estimate, evaluate, quote, reckon, value
berechnend calculating, diplomatic, politic
Berechnung calculation, charge, computation, determination, estimate, evaluation, policy, quotation, valuation
berechtigen authorize, constitute, empower, entitle, justify, license, qualify, warrant

berechtigt authorized, competent, entitled, justified, lawful, legitimate, rightful
Berechtigter entitled person (party)
Anspruchs- claimant
Nutzungs- beneficiary, usufructuary
Stimm— (Wahl-) elector, voter
Zahlungs— payee
Berechtigung authorization, competence, eligibility, justification, licence, power, qualification, right, title, warrant
—sschein certificate, scrip, warrant
Bereich area, compass, domain, field, orbit, province, range, reach, scope, sphere, sweep
bereichern enlarge, enrich
Bereicherung addition, enlargement, enrichment
—, ungerechtfertigte unjustified enrichment
bereinigen clear (up), remove, settle, square, validate
Bereinigung adjustment, correction, settlement, validation
Bereitschaft preparedness, readiness, willingness
bereitstellen arrange for, make available, furnish, provide, supply
Bereitstellung provision, supply
bereuen regret, repend (of)
Bereuung repentance
bergen salvage, shelter
Bergung salvage, wrecking
—skosten salvage charges
Bericht account, advice, bulletin, communiqué, information, minutes, report, return, statement
Jahres— annual report
— erstatten give (render) an account of, give (make) a report of, report on
berichten advise, give (render) an account, inform, report
Berichterstatter commentator, correspondent, informant, referee, reporter
Berichterstattung report, statement
berichtigen adjust, balance, correct, pay, rectify, remedy, settle
Berichtigung adjustment, correction, payment, rectification, settlement
Berichtsjahr year under review
Berichtszeitraum reporting period
berüchtigt ill-reputed, infamous, notorious
berücksichtigen allow for, consider, take into consideration (account), bear in mind, pay regard to, make allowance for
—, nicht disregard
Berücksichtigung consideration
unter — von allowing for, with regard to, in the light of, in consideration of
Beruf business, calling, career, duty, function, job, line, mission, occupation, office, profession, province, trade, vocation
—, freier free-lance (liberal) profession
berufen appoint, call, convene, convoke, designate (to), nominate
sich — auf adduce, appeal to, plead, quote, refer to
berufen authorized, able, competent, qualified
beruflich by profession (trade), occupational, professional, vocational
Berufs
—ausübung exercise of a profession
—eignung qualification
—geheimnis professional secret, secrecy
—genossenschaft professional association
—verband (-vereinigung) trade association, professional union
—verbrecher habitual (professional) criminal
—vertretung professional representation
—zweig branch line, professional field
Berufung (notice of) appeal, appointment, call, convocation,

nomination, reference, vocation
— **abweisen** dismiss an appeal
— **einlegen** (give notice of) appeal, lodge (prefer) an appeal
— **stattgeben** allow an appeal
Berufungs
—**antrag** petition of appeal
—**ausschuß** appeal committee, review board
—**beklagter** appellee, respondent
berufungsfähig appealable
—, **nicht** nonappealable
Berufungs
—**frist** limitation of appeal
—**gericht** appellate court (tribunal), court of appeal
— —**sbarkeit** appellate jurisdiction
—**instanz** appellate instance
—**klage** appeal
—**kläger** appellant, appealing party
—**recht** right of appeal
—**richter** judge of appeal, appellate judge
—**schrift** petition (instrument) of appeal
—**urteil** appellate judgement, judgement of appeal
—**verfahren** appellate proceedings, procedure of appeal
—**verhandlung** hearing of appeal
beruhen auf be based (founded) on, depend on, be due to
berühren affect, concern, handle, mention, touch (upon)
beschädigen damage, disable, injure, mutilate
Beschädigter injured party (person)
Beschädigung average, damage, injury, mutilation
beschaffen furnish, procure, provide, secure, supply
Beschaffenheit character, condition, constitution, design, disposition, nature, property, quality, state, structure
Beschaffung acquisition, attainment, procurement, production, provision, supply
beschäftigen employ, engage, give work (employment), occupy
sich — mit be concerned with, deal with, engage in, occupy oneself with, work at (on)
Beschäftigung activity, business, employment, engagement, job, occupation, pursuit, work
—**snachweis** certificate of employment
beschatten shadow
Beschattung secret control, shadowing
Bescheid advice, answer, decision, decree, direction, information, instruction, notice, order, ruling
Amts— official notice
bescheinigen acknowledge, attest, authenticate, certify, verify, vouch for
Bescheinigung acknowledgement, attestation, certificate, certification, receipt, voucher
beschenken bestow (up)on, make a donation, present
Beschenkter donee
Beschenkung bestowal, donation
beschimpfen abuse, affront, call names, insult, revile
Beschimpfung abuse, affront, injury, insult, outrage, vituperation
Beschlag attachment, seizure
mit — belegen arrest, attach, confiscate, distrain, embargo, engage, impound, occupy, seize, sequester, sequestrate
Beschlagnahme (-nahmung) arrest, attachment, confiscation, distrain, distress, embargo, garnishment, impoundment, requisition, seizure, sequestration
Beschlagnahme
—**recht** right of seizure (confiscation)
—**verfügung** charging order, warrant of arrest
beschlagnahmen attach, confiscate, distrain, distress, embargo, impound, requisition, seize sequester, sequestrate
beschlagnahmt confiscated, seized, sequestrated

beschließen close, conclude, decide, determine, end, finish, resolve, rule, settle, terminate, wind up, vote
Beschluß close, conclusion, decision, decree, determination, end, order, resolution, resolve, termination, vote
beschlußfähig sein form a quorum
Beschlußfähigkeit competence, quorum
Beschluß
—fassung resolution, resolve
—unfähigkeit absence (lack) of a quorum
beschneiden curtail, cut (down), reduce, retrench, shorten
Beschneidung curtailment, cut, reduction, retrenchment
beschönigen excuse, extenuate
Beschönigung excuse, extenuation
beschränken confine, cut, limit, narrow, restrain, restrict
beschränkend limiting, restrictive
beschränkt conditional, confined, limited, narrow, restricted
Beschränkung confinement, limit (ation), restraint, restriction
beschreiben characterize, describe, give a description of, specify
Beschreibung description, specification
beschuldigen accuse of, arraign, charge with, impute, incriminate, inculpate
Beschuldiger accuser
Beschuldigter accused, culprit, defendant, suspect
Beschuldigung accusation, charge, imputation, incrimination, inculpation
beschützen defend (from), guard, patronize, protect, screen, shelter, shield
Beschützer defender, patron, protector
Beschützung protection
Beschwerde appeal, complaint, declaration of dissent, grievance, protest, remonstrance
Beschwerde
— abweisen dismiss a complaint
— einlegen lodge (make) a complaint (protest), protest (against)
— führen appeal to, complain of, make complaints about
— stattgeben allow a complaint
Beschwerde
—führer appellant, complainant
—recht right of complaint
—schrift bill (memorandum) of complaint, remonstrance
—verfahren procedure of complaint
beschweren, sich appeal to, complain about (of), lodge (make) a complaint, make complaints about
beschwichtigen appease, calm, pacify, quiet, soothe
Beschwichtigung appeasement, pacification
beschwindeln bamboozle, cheat, deceive, swindle, trick
beschwören confirm by oath, swear to, take an oath upon
Beschwörung confirmation by oath, swearing
beseitigen abolish, dispose of, do away with, eliminate, get rid off, liquidate, overcome, redress, remedy, remove, set aside, settle
Beseitigung abolition, accommodation, disposal, elimination, liquidation, redress, removal, settlement
besetzen fill (up), occupy, staff, take (possession of)
Besetzung appointment, filling, occupation
besichtigen examine, inspect, survey, view, visit
Besichtigung examination, inspection, visit(ation)
besiegeln seal, put a seal on
Besitz estate, possession, property
Grund- holding, tenure
Privat- private ownership
Besitz
— ergreifen take possession (hold) of

—anspruch claim to possession, title
—aufgabe dereliction
besitzen hold, occupy, possess
Besitzentsetzung (-entziehung) dispossession, expropriation
Besitzer holder, occupant, owner, possessor, proprietor, tenant
Besitz
—ergreifung occupancy, occupation, seizin, seizure, taking possession, usurpation
—interesse possessory interest
—klage possessory action
—recht legal possession, ownership, possessory right (title), right of occupation (possession)
—stand possessory title, ownership, seizin
—störung trespass
—titel title (deed)
—tum (legal) estate, possession, property, tenure
Besitzung (real) estate, possession, property
Besitz
—übertragung conveyance of title, transfer of possession (property)
—urkunde title deed (document)
—wechsel change of title (ownership)
Besonderheit characteristic, individuality, particularity, peculiarity, speciality
besorgen attend to, arrange for, deal with, handle, manage, perform, prepare, procure, provide, supply
besprechen agree upon, arrange, discuss, talk over
—, sich confer, consult, deliberate (on)
Besprechung conference, conversation, deliberation, discussion, talks
—sraum conference room
bessern (a)meliorate, amend, better, improve, reform
Besserung (a)melioration, amendment, betterment, improvement, reform
—sanstalt house of correction, corrective institution, reformatory
besserungsfähig improvable
Besserungsmittel corrective (means)
bestallen appoint, install, invest with
Bestallung appointment, installation, investiture, investment
—surkunde certificate, commission, diploma, (letters-)patent, deed of appointment
Bestand amount, consistence(cy), continuance, durability, duration, endurance, existence, number, permanence, stability, standing, stock, store, supply
Rechts— legal validity
beständig constant, continual, continuous, firm, lasting, permanent, perpetual, persistent, stable, steadfast
Beständigkeit constancy, continuance, durability, permanence, (cy), perpetuity, perseverance, stability, steadiness, steadfastness
Bestandsaufnahme (-sverzeichnis) inventory
Bestandteil component, constituent, element, ingredient, part
bestätigen acknowledge, affirm, approve, certify, confirm, corroborate, endorse, probate, ratify, sanction, substantiate, support, uphold
—, amtlich authenticate, authorize
bestätigend, affirmative, approving, confirmative, confirming, confirmatory, corroborative
Bestätigung acknowledgement, attestation, certification, confirmation, corroboration, endorsement, ratification, sanction, substantiation, verification
Bestätigungs
—schreiben letter of confirmation, credentials
—urteil confirmatory judgement
—vermerk authentication, notice of confirmation

bestechen bribe, buy, corrupt, suborn, tamper with
Bestecher briber, corrupter, suborner
bestechlich bribable, corrupt, corruptible, venal
unbestechlich incorruptible
Bestechlichkeit corruptness, corruptibility, venality
Bestechung bribery, corruption, subornation
Bestechungs
—geld bribe, hush-money
—unwesen bribery and corruption
—versuch attempt at (of) bribery, attempted bribery
Bestehen composition, continuance, existence, insistence, passing, persistence, presence, subsistence
bestehen be composed of, consist of, continue, endure, exist, last, overcome, pass, persist, stand, subsist
— auf insist on, persist in
—, nicht fail
bestehlen rob, steal
bestellen appoint, attend to, book, brief, call, cite, commission, constitute, deliver, direct, instruct, nominate, order, reserve, summon
Besteller buyer, customer, deliverer, orderer, purchaser, subscriber
Bestellformular order form
Bestellter appointee
Bestellung appointment, booking, commission, delivery, nomination, order
besteuerbar assessable, chargeable, rat(e)able, taxable
Besteuerbarkeit taxability
besteuern assess, excise, rate, tax, levy (impose) a tax on
Besteuerung taxability, taxation
besteuerungsfähig assessable, rat(e)able, taxable
Besteuerungs
—freigrenze tax immunity limit, exemption
—grenze limit of taxation (assessment)
—satz rate of assessment, tax rate
—system tax(ation) system
—vorschriften tax(ation) prescriptions
bestimmbar appreciable, ascertainable, definable, determinable
bestimmen appoint, appropriate, ascertain, assign, decide, decree, define, design, designate, destine, determine, direct, fix, induce, intend, lay down, order, prescribe, rule
bestimmend decisive, determinant, determinative, determining
Bestimmung appointment, ascertainment, assessment, decision, decree, definition, designation, destination, determination, disposition, fixation, fixing, regulation, vocation
—, vertragliche article, clause, provision, stipulation, term
Bestimmungs
—ort place (lieu) of destination
bestrafen castigate, chastise, penalize, punish, sentence
—, mit Gefängnis gaol, imprison, jail
—, mit Geld fine
—, mit Tod sentence to death
Bestrafung castigation, chastisement, penalization, penalty, prosecution, punishment
Bestreben (Bestrebung) aspiration, attempt, effort, endeavo(u)ur
bestreitbar challengeable, contestable, disputable
un— incontestable, indisputable, unquestionable
bestreiten argue against, call in question, challenge, contest, deny, dispute, doubt, meet, supply, traverse
Bestreitung argument, contestation, payment, supply
Besuch attendance, call, visit (ation)
besuchen attend, call, visit
—, häufig frequent
Besucher attender, caller, frequenter, guest, visitor

Besuchs-
—raum parlo(u)r
—zeit visiting hours
betätigen manifest, operate, practise, realize
—, sich participate in, take an active part in, work
Betätigung activity, manifestation, occupation, participation, practice, work
—sfeld field of action, sphere of activity
beteiligen, jmd. (make a) partner, give a share (an interest) in
—, sich — an cooperate, contribute, engage in, join in, participate, take part in
beteiligt sein an be interested in, be involved in, have (take) an interest (a share) in
Beteiligter concerned, participant, partner, party (concerned, interested), person involved
Beteiligung attendance, complicity, contribution, cooperation, holding, interest, investment, participation, partnership, share
Beteiligungs
—gesellschaft affiliate, affiliated (holding) company, subsidiary
—klausel participation clause
beteuern affirm, assert, asseverate, assure, protest, swear
Beteuerung affirmation, assertion, assurance, asseveration, declaration, protestation
betonen accentuate, emphasize, insist on, point out, stress
Betracht
außer — lassen leave out of account
in — kommen come into question
nicht in — kommen be out of question
in — ziehen allow for, make allowance for, consider, take into account (consideration)
betrachten consider, contemplate, inspect, regard, watch
beträchtlich considerable, essential, important, substantial
Betrachtung consideration, contemplation, inspection, reflection, study
Betrag aggregate, amount, sum
Betragen behavio(u)r, conduct, demeanour
betragen amount to, behave, conduct
—, sich schlecht misbehave, misconduct
betrauen appoint, entrust (charge) with
Betrauter fiduciary, trustee
Betreff concern, reference, regard, respect, subject
betreffen affect, concern, refer to, relate to, touch
betreffend concerned, concerning, under consideration, in the matter of, in question, in re, regarding, respective
Betreiben management, practice, prosecution, pursuit
betreiben carry on, conduct, follow, manage, practise, prosecute, pursue, run, work
betreuen assist, attend, care for, take care of, handle, look after, nurse
Betreuung care
Betrieb activity, business, enterprise, establishment, factory, firm, management, operation, plant, undertaking, working, works
Betriebs-
—anlage plant
—einstellung shutdown
—kapital (-vermögen) business (floating, trading, working) capital
—kosten (-unkosten) operating (working) cost (expenses)
—leitung management
—obmann shop (works) steward
—ordnung factory (works) regulations
—rat factory (shop, works) committee (council), firm's council
—stillegung (-störung) shutdown
—unfall industrial (working) accident
— —versicherung industrial accident insurance

—vereinbarung factory agreement
—vermögen trading capital
—vorschriften operating instructions, plant (shop, working) regulations
betroffen affected, afflicted, concerned
Betrug cheat(ing), deceit, deception, fraud, imposition, impostor, swidler
betrügen bamboozle, cheat, deceive, defraud, double-cross, dupe, humbug, swindler
Betrüger cheat, counterfeit(er), deceiver, defrauder, fraud, impostor, swindle
Betrügerei cheating, deceit, fraudulence, imposition, imposture, trickery
betrügerisch deceitful, fraudulent, swindling
in —er Absicht fraudulently, with intend to defraud
betrunken drunk(en), inebriate(d), intoxicated
Betrunkener drunken man (person), drunkard, inebriate
Betrunkenheit (state of) drunkenness, intoxication
Bettelei beggary, begging, mendicity, mendicancy
betteln beg (for), cadge
Bettler beggar, mendicant
beurkunden acknowledge, attest, authenticate, certify, depose, document, legalize, prove, record, register, verify
—, notariell notarize
—, durch einen Zeugen witness
Beurkundung attestation, authentication, certification, legalization, notarization, registration, verification
—svermerk attestation clause
beurlauben give (grant) leave, suspend
Beurlaubung leave, suspension
beurteilen criticize, estimate, judge, pass (award, pronounce) judgement (up)on, rate, review
—, falsch misjudge
—, richtig seize up
Beurteiler critic, judge
Beurteilung judgement, opinion, rating, review
—, falsche misjudgement
—, kritische criticism
—, milde leniency
Beute booty, loot, plunder, prey, prize, spoil
Beuterecht right of seizure, prize law
Bevölkerung inhabitants, people, population
bevollmächtigen accredit, authorize, commission, empower, give (invest with) power (of attorney)
bevollmächtigt authorized, empowered, commissioned, plenipotentiary
Bevollmächtigter (authorized) agent, assignee, authorized person, attorney (in fact), delegate, deputy, envoy, mandatary, mandatory, plenipotentiary, proxy, representative, trustee
Bevollmächtigung authorization, power of attorney
—, durch by proxy
bevor before, prior to
—, nicht not until
bevormunden hold in tutelage, regiment, tutor
Bevormundung regimentation, tutelage
bevorrechtigen prefer, privilege
bevorrechtigt preferential, preferred, privileged
Bevorrechtigung preference, prerogative, priority, privilege
bevorzugen favo(u)r, prefer, privilege
bevorzugt favo(u)red, preferential, preferred, privileged
Bevorzugung favo(u)ritism, preference, preferment
bewachen guard, watch (over)
Bewachung custody, guard
—, unter under custody (the guard of)
unter — halten keep in custody
bewaffnen arm, armour, equip with arms
bewaffnet armed
—er Widerstand armed resistance
unbewaffnet unarmed

bewältigen accomplish, conquer, cope with, manage, master, overcome
bewahren guard, keep, preserve, protect, save (from)
bewähren prove, verify
—, **sich** stand the test, prove a success (useful)
—, **sich nicht** be (prove) a failure, be of no use
Bewahrer custodian, guardian, keeper, preserver
bewahrheiten prove (come) true, verify
bewährt approved, proved, reliable, successful, tested, tried, trusty
Bewahrung keeping, preservation, protection
Bewährung confirmation, probation, proof, verification
—, **auf** on probation
— **gewähren** place on probation
— **erhalten** be placed on probation
—**sfrist** (limitation, period of) probation
— — **gewähren** grant probation
bewegen induce, instigate, move, persuade
Beweggrund ground, incentive, inducement, instigation, motive, reason, stimulus
beweglich flexible, movable
—**es Eigentum** movable (personal) property (estates), movables
Bewegung motion, movement, tendency, trend
—**sfreiheit** freedom of action (movement)
Beweis argument, demonstration, (piece of) evidence, exhibit, proof, substantiation, witness
— **antreten** produce (prove) (offer) evidence
— **erbringen (führen)** furnish (produce) evidence (proof)
— **erheben** hear evidence
— **würdigen** estimate evidence
— **des ersten Anscheins** prima facie evidence
Beweisaufnahme hearing of evidence (witnesses)
beweisbar demonstrable, evidenceable, provable
Beweisbeschluß order of evidence
beweisen argue, demonstrate, evidence, give (furnish) evidence, prove, substantiate
Beweis-
—**führung** argumentation, demonstration, reasoning
—**grund** argument
—**kraft** conclusiveness, conclusive (probatory) force
beweiskräftig conclusive, convincing, demonstrative, probative
Beweis
—**last (—pflicht)** burden (onus) of evidence (proof)
—**material** evidence material
—**mittel** evidence, proof
—**recht** law of evidence
—**regeln** rules of evidence
—**sicherung** preservation of evidence
—**stück (—urkunde)** exhibit, piece of evidence, proof, voucher
—**termin** date for evidence
—**verfahren** rules of evidence
—**würdigung** estimation of evidence
bewerben apply for, bid, run for, solicit, tender
Bewerber applicant, aspirant, candidate, competitor
Bewerbung application, solicitation, candidature
—**sgesuch (-sschreiben)** (letter of) application
bewerten appraise, appreciate, assess, estimate, judge, price, rate, value
Bewertung appraisal, assessment, estimate, estimation, judgement, rating, valuation
bewilligen allocate, allot, allow, appropriate, concede, grant, license
Bewilligung allocation, allotment, allowance, appropriation, authorization, concession, grant, permission, permit, licenc(s)e
bewirken bring about, cause, effect, lead to, occasion, pro-

duce, provoke, give rise to, result in
bewirtschaften administer, carry on, conduct, manage, ration, run, work
Bewirtschaftung administration, control, management, rationing, running, working
bewohnbar (in)habitable
bewohnen inhabit, live in, occupy, reside in
Bewohner citizen, inhabitant, inmate, lodger, occupant, resident, roomer, tenant
bewußt aware, conscious, deliberate, intentional, knowing
Bewußtsein consciousness
bezahlen compensate, discharge, honour, pay, remunerate, settle
Bezahler payer
Bezahlung consideration, compensation, discharge, payment, remuneration, settlement
bezeichnen brand, characterize, denominate, denote, designate, express, indicate, label, mark, name, nominate, qualify, signify, specify, ticket
bezeichnend characteristic, expressive, significant, typical
Bezeichnung characterization, denomination, denotation, designation, expression, indication, label, mark, name, nomination, term
bezeugen attest, certify, testify, warrant, (bear) witness
Bezeugung attestation, certification, testimony
bezichtigen accuse of, charge with, incriminate
Bezichtigung accusation, charge, incrimination
beziehen buy, draw, get, move into, obtain, occupy, procure, receive, subscribe, take (up)
sich — auf refer to, relate to
Bezieher buyer, customer, drawer, subscriber
Beziehung association, connection, connexion, reference, regard, relation, relationship, respect
Beziehungen affiliations, contacts, relations
beziehungsweise respectively
Bezirk area, borough, circuit, compass, county, district, division, domain, province, region, ward
Bezirks-
—amt district board
—ausschuß (-rat) county (district) council
—gefängnis county gaol
—gericht district (county) court
—notariat district notary
—richter district judge (magistrate)
—vorsteher district (county) commissioner
bezirksweise districtial, by districts
Bezogener acceptor, drawee, payee
Bezug procurement, purchase, reference, regard, respect, subscription, supply
Bezüge drawings, emoluments, income, pay, receipts, remuneration, salary
bezüglich concerning, in regard (respect) of, referring to, regarding, relating to, in the matter of
Bezugnahme reference
unter — auf with reference to, referring to
Bezugs-
—anweisung delivery order
—bedingungen terms of delivery
—marke supply coupon
—recht claim, option, priority of right, privilege, preference right, right, subscription privilege
—schein delivery order, supply permit
bieten (make a) bid, give, offer, present
Bieter bidder
Bigamie bigamy
Bigamist bigamist
Bilanz balance (sheet), outcome, result
bilanzieren (strike the) balance
Bilanz
—veröffentlichung publication of the balance sheet

—verschleierung cooking of a balance sheet
—ziehung striking of the balance, balancing
bilateral bilateral
bilden constitute, create, educate, establish, form, make up, organize, set up
Bildung constitution, creation, education, establishment, formation, knowledge, organization
billig equitable, fair, just, moderate, reasonable, right
billigen agree to, approve of, authorize, consent, pass, sanction
Billigkeit equity, equitableness, fairness, justice, justness, reasonableness
Billigkeits-
—anspruch equitable claim, claim of equity
—gericht Court of Equity (GB)
—gerichtsbarkeit equitable jurisdiction
—gründen, aus on the grounds of equity, for reasons of fairness
—recht equity, law of equity
—rechte equitable interests
Billigung agreement, approbation, approval, assent, authorization, consent, sanction
bindend binding, mandatory, obligatory, valid
Bindung bond, commitment, engagement, liability, obligation
Bitte petition, request, solicitation, supplication
bitten ask, petition, request, solicit, supplicate (for)
Bitt-
—gesuch (—schrift) petition
—steller petitioner, supplicant
blanko (in) blank
Blanko
—akzept acceptance in blank, blank acceptance
—unterschrift blank signature, signature in blank
—vollmacht blank power of attorney, blanket authority, unlimited powers (authority)
—wechsel blank bill
bleiben abide by, continue, insist (on), keep, persist (in), remain, stay, stick to
bleibend enduring, lasting, permanent
Blockade blockade
— brechen run a blockade
Blockade
— brecher blockade runner
— bruch blockade run(ning)
blockieren block, blockade, obstruct
Blockierung blockade, obstruction
bloßstellen compromise
Bloßstellung compromise, exposure
Bluff bluff, strike
bluffen bluff
Bluffer bluffer
Blut
—gruppe blood group
—probe blood test
—schande incest
—schänder incestuous person
blutschänderisch incestuous
blutsverwandt consanguine, consanguineous, related by blood
Blutsverwandter blood relation
—, nächster next of kin
Blutsverwandtschaft blood relationship, consanguinity, kinship
Bluttat murder
Boden, Grund und ground(s), land, land(ed) property, premises, real estate, territory
Bonus bonus, gratification, premium
Börse stock exchange
börsenfähig marketable, negotiable
Börsen-
—fähigkeit negotiability
—gesetz stock exchange law
—kurs exchange rate, market price (rate)
—makler exchange (stock) broker
—notierung (market) quotation
—ordnung exchange regulations
—papiere shares, securities, stocks
—preis market price (rate)
—recht stock exchange law
—schwankungen market fluctuations

—spekulant stock jobber
—spekulation stock jobbing
—zettel stock exchange list, list of (market) quotations
—zulassung admission to the stock exchange
bösartig bad, evil-minded, malicious, malignant, virulent, wicked
Bösartigkeit badness, malignancy, malignity, virulence(cy)
böswillig malevolent
—e Absicht wilful malice
in —er Absicht with malice aforethought (prepense)
Böswilligkeit malevolence
Bote commissioner, courier, emissory, messenger, runner
Amts— usher
Botengang commission, errand
Botschaft communication, embassy, errand, message, mission, news
Botschafter ambassador
Boykott boycott
— verhängen put under a boycott
boykottieren boycott
Boykottierung boycotting
Branche
branch, business, line, trade
Brand brand, fire, trademark
in — setzen set on fire, set fire to
brandmarken brand, denounce, denunciate, stigmatize
Brandmarkung denouncement, stigmatization
Brandschaden fire damage
brandstiften commit arson, raise fire, set fire to
Brand-
—stifter arsonist, incendiary, fire raiser
—stiftung arson, incendiarism, fire raising
—versicherung fire insurance
Brauch convention, custom, habit, practice, routine, tradition, usage, use
brauchbar able, efficient, practicable, serviceable, useful, usable, utilizable, workable
Brauchbarkeit practicability, serviceableness, usability, usefulness

Braut betrothed, bride, fiancée
—ausstattung (—aussteuer) bridal outfit, trousseau
Bräutigam betrothed, bridegroom, fiancé
Brautstand betrothal, time of engagement
brechen break, infringe, run, transgress, violate
—, Ehe commit adultery
Brief charter, deed, document, instrument, letter, note
Brief-
—geheimnis secrecy of letters
—grundschuld unregistered land charge
—hypothek unregistered mortgage
brieflich by letter (mail)
Brief-
—schulden unregistered debts
—siegel letter seal
—telegramm letter telegram
—verkehr (-wechsel) correspondence, exchange of letters
—zensur postal censorship
bringen bring, yield
—, an sich acquire, appropriate
—, mit sich involve
—, zum Abschluß bring to a conclusion
Bringer bearer, bringer, carrier
Bringschuld debt payable to the creditor (at creditor's domicile)
Broschüre booklet, brochure, folder, pamphlet
Bruch breach, break(age), infraction, infringement, rupture, violation
—stück fragment
—teil fraction
Brückengeld (bridge) toll
brutal brutal, cruel, inhuman
—er Mensch brute
— behandeln brutalize
Brutalität brutality
brutto gross
Buch book, ledger, register, volume
— führen keep a record (an account) of
buchen account, book, enter into the books, list, make an entry of, record, register, write down

Buch-
—führer (—halter) accountant, bookkeeper, recorder
—führung (—haltung) accounting, bookkeeping
—gläubiger book creditor
—grundschuld registered land charge (lien)
—hypothek registered mortgage
—prüfer auditor
—prüfung audit
— —sbericht auditor's report
—schuldner book debtor
Buchung booking, entry, registration
—sbeleg (—sunterlage) voucher
Buchwert book value
Budget budget, estimates
Bummelstreik go-slow strike
Bund alliance, association, confederacy, confederation, federation, league, union
Bundes-
—angelegenheit federal matter
—anstalt federal institution (corporation)
—anzeiger federal gazette
—arbeitsgericht federal supreme labour (industrial) court
—bank federal bank
—beamter federal officer
—behörden federal authorities
—bezirk federal district
—finanzhof federal supreme finance court
—gebiet federal territory
—genosse ally, confederate
—gericht federal court
—gerichtsbarkeit federal jurisdiction
—gerichtsentscheidung federal decision
—gerichtshof federal supreme court
—gesetz federal law
—gesetzgebung federal legislation
—hauptstadt federal capital
—haushalt federal budget
—kanzler federal chancellor
—mächte confederate powers, confederates
—minister federal minister
—ministerium federal ministry
—mitglied member of a federation
—parlament federal parliament (diet)
—präsident president of a federation
—rat federal council
— —sbeschluß federal decree
—regierung federal government
—republik federal republic
—sozialgericht federal supreme social (welfare) court
—staat federal state
—steuer federal tax
—tag (—versammlung) federal diet (parliament)
—verfassung federal constitution
— —sgericht federal constitutional court
—verordnung federal order (ordinance)
—verwaltung federal administration
— —sgericht federal supreme administration (administrative) court
—versammlung federal meeting
Bündnis agreement, alliance, confederacy, confederation, league, pact
—vertrag treaty of alliance
Bündnis- und Freundschaftsvertrag treaty of alliance and friendship
Bürge bail, guarantee, guarantor, security, sponsor, surety, voucher, warrantor
bürgen answer for, (be, go) bail (for), guarantee, stand surety, vouch for, warrant
Bürger citizen, civilian, commoner, freeman, townsman
—krieg civil war
—kunde civics
bürgerlich civic, civil, middle-class
—e Ehrenrechte civil rights
—es Gesetzbuch (BGB) civil code
—es Recht civil law
—er Tod civil death
Bürgermeister burgomaster, maire, mayor
—amt town hall
Bürger-
—pflicht civic duty

—recht civic right, citizenship, freedom of a city
—schaft citizens
—tum citizens, citizenship
—versammlung town meeting (assembly)
—wehr civic (national) guard, militia
Bürgschaft bail, bond, collateral, guarantee, guaranty, security, surety, warranty
— leisten s. bürgen
bürgschaftsfähig bailable
Bürgschaftsleistung bailment, guarantee, guaranty, security, surety(ship)
Büro agency, bureau, office
—angestellter clerk, (office) employee
Bürokrat bureaucrat
Bürokratie bureaucracy, officialdom, officialism
bürokratisch bureaucratic
Büropersonal office personnel (employees), clerical staff
Büroschluß closing time
Bürostunden (—zeit) office hours
Buße atonement, expiation, fee, fine, forfeit, payment, penalty
— auferlegen fine
büßen atone (for), be fined, expiate, pay for, pay the penalty, suffer for

C

Charakter capacity, character (istic), characteristic (distinctive), feature, disposition, nature, type
charakterfest of firm (strong) character, resolute, staunch
Charakterfestigkeit (—stärke) firmness (strength) of character, resolution, staunchness
charakterisieren characterize
Charakterisierung (Charakteristik) characterization
charakteristisch characteristic, distinctive, typical
Charakterkunde characterology
charakterlos characterless
Charakterlosigkeit lack (want) of character (principle)
Charaktermerkmal (—zug) characteristic (feature)
charakterschwach weak
Charakterschwäche weakness of character
Charta (Charter) charter, deed, grant
Charterpartie (-vertrag) charter party, freight contract
Charterer charterer
chartern charter
Charterung chartering
Chef boss, chief, employer, head, manager, principal, senior (partner)
Chiffre cipher, code
—schlüssel cipher key
—telegramm cipher (code) telegram
Chiffreur cipherer
chiffrieren cipher, code
Clique band, gang, set
Code code
—telegramm code telegram
Coupon s. Kupon
Courtage brokerage, commission, courtage

D

Dachgesellschaft holding (parent) company
Dachorganisation control unit, controlling body, top (parent) organization
darbieten offer, present
Darbietung (re)presentation
darlegen disclose, expose, lay open, put forward, represent, reveal, set forth, state
—, eingehend detail, particularize, specify
Darlegung explanation, exposé, exposition, representation, statement
Darleh(e)n advance, credit, loan
Darlehns-
—bank loan bank
—geber creditor, lender
—kapital loan capital
—nehmer (—schuldner) borrower, debtor
—schulden loans, loan debts
—urkunde bond, loan certificate
—vertrag loan contract
—zins loan interest
darleihen lend (out), loan
darstellen constitute, describe, mean, represent, show, signify
—, falsch misrepresent
darstellend descriptive, representative
Darstellung description, presentation, recital, representation, statement
—, falsche misrepresentation
dartun demonstrate, evidence, prove, set forth, show
Dasein existence
Daseinsberechtigung right of existence
Daten datas, details, facts, particulars
datieren date (from)
datiert dated
undatiert undated
Datowechsel dated bill
Datum date
Dauer continuance, duration, length, life, period, permanence, permanency, term, (length of) time
—auftrag standing order
dauerhaft durable, lasting, stable
Dauerhaftigkeit durability, lastingness, solidity, stability
dauern continue, endure, last, take
dauernd continuous, lasting, permanent
davonkommen escape, get away (off)
davonlaufen run away
davonschleichen steal away
dazugehören belong to, form part of
dazukommen come along
Dazwischentreten interference, intervention
dazwischentreten (-kommen) intercede, interfere, intervene
dazwischenwerfen interject, interpose
Debatte debate, discussion
debattieren debate, discuss
Debet debit
Debet-
—anzeige (—note) debit note
—saldo debit balance
debitieren charge, debit
Debitor debtor
dechiffrieren decipher, decode
Deckadresse cover address
decken conceal, cover, excuse, hide, justify, meet, protect, reimburse, screen, secure, shield
sich — mit be in accordance with, be identical with, coincide with, conform to, correspond with
Deckname cover name, pseudonym
Deckung consideration, cover, coverage, guarantee, meeting, payment, protection, reimbursement, screening, security, shielding
Deckungs-
—betrag cover, margin
—klausel covering clause

—note covering note
—spanne margin
Dedikation dedication
dedizieren dedicate
de facto de facto, in fact
defamierend defamatory
Defamierung dafamation
Defekt damage, defect, deficiency, fault, imperfection
defekt damage, defective, faulty, incomplete
defensiv defensive
Defensivbündnis defensive alliance
Defensive defensive
Defensivpakt defensive pact
definierbar definable
definieren define
Definition definition
— geben give a definition of
definitiv definite, definitive, final
Defizit deficit, deficiency, shortage
Deflation deflation
deflationistisch deflationary
Deflationspolitik deflationary policy
Defloration defloration
Deflorations-
—anspruch defloration title
—klage action (suit) for defloration
deflorieren deflower
Defraudant defrauder
Defraudation deceit, embezzlement, fraud
defraudieren deceive, defraud, embezzle
dehnbar elastic, extensible, flexible, vague, wide
Dehnbarkeit ambiguity, extensibility, flexibility, vagueness
Dekade decade, ten-day period
dekadent decadent, degenerate
Dekadenz decadence, degeneracy
Dekan dean
Dekanat deanery, deanship
Deklamation declamation, recitation
deklamatorisch declamatory
deklamieren declaim, recite
Deklarant declarant
Deklaration declaration, entry, return
deklarieren declare, enter, register
Dekret decree, order
— erlassen issue (pass) a decree
dekretieren decree, order
Delation delation
delatorisch criminative
Delegation delegacy, delegation
delegieren delegate
Delegierter delegate, representative
Delikt delict, misdemeanour, offenc(s)e, tort, tortious (punishable, unlawful, wrongful) act
Delikts-
—fähigkeit (—haftung) criminal responsibility, tortious liability
—handlung tortious (illicit) (criminal) act, crime
—klage action in tort
Delinquent accused, criminal, defendant, delinquent, offender (of the law)
Delkredere del credere, guarantee (ty)
Demagoge demagogue
Demagogie demagogy
demagogisch demagogic
Demarkation demarcation
—slinie demarcation line
Dementi contradiction, dementi, denial
dementieren contradict, deny
dementsprechend (demgemäß) (demnach) accordingly, consequently, corresponding to, correspondingly
demgegenüber (dementgegen) as against
Demission demission, resignation
— einreichen submit (hand in) one's resignation
demissionieren resign (office)
demobilisieren demobilize, disarm
Demobilisierung demobilization, disarmament
Demokrat democrat
Demokratie democracy
demokratisch democratic
demokratisieren democratize
Demokratisierung democratization
Demokratismus democratism

demolieren demolish, destroy
Demolierung demolition, destruction
Demonstrant demonstrator
Demonstration demonstration
— veranstalten make a demonstration
demonstrativ demonstrative
demonstrieren demonstrate, show, take part in a demonstration
Demontage dismantling, dismounting
demontieren dismantle, dismount, pull down
Demoralisation demoralization
demoralisieren demoralize
Demoskopie population research, opinion poll
demoskopisch
—e Untersuchung public opinion research
Demut humbleness, humility, meekness
demütig humble, meek, submissive
demütigen humble, humiliate, mortify
Demütigung humiliation, mortification
Denk(ungs)art mentality, mindedness, way of thinking
denkbar conceivable, imaginable, possible, thinkable
denken believe, conceive, consider, imagine, reflect, suppose, think
denkend rational, reasoning, thinking
denkfähig intelligent, rational
Denk-
—fähigkeit intelligence
—fehler false reasoning, fallacy
—freiheit freedom of thought
—gewohnheit habit of thought
—prozeß process of reasoning (thought)
—schrift exposé, memoir, memorandum, memorial
—vermögen intelligence, intellectual power
denkwürdig memorable, noteworthy, remarkable
Denk-
—würdigkeit memorability
—zettel lesson, reminder

Denunziant denouncer, denunciator, informer
Denunziation denunciation, information
denunzieren denounce, denunciate, inform against
Depesche cable, despatch, dispatch, telegram, wire
depeschieren cable, telegraph, wire
Deponent bailor, deponent, depositor
deponieren bail, deposit
Deponierung deposition
Deportation deportation, transportation
deportieren deport, transport
Deportierter deportee
Depositar (Depositär) bailee, depositary, trustee
Depot custodianship, deposit(ory), depot, storehouse, warehouse
Deputat allowance (in kind), emolument
Deputation delegation, deputation
deputieren delegate, depute
Deputierter delegate, deputy
Derogation derogation
Deserteur deserter
desertieren desert
Desertion desertion
Designation designation
—srecht right of appointment (designation)
designieren designate
Desintegration disintegration
desintegrieren disintegrate
desinteressiert disinterested
despektierlich disrespectful, contemptuous
Despot despot, tyrant
Despotie (Despotismus) despotism
despotisch despotic
destruktiv destructive
Deszendent descendant
Deszendenz descent
Detail detail, retail
ins — gehen go into detail(s) (particulars)
im — verkaufen sell (by) retail, retail
Details details, particulars
— angeben give details (particulars), particularize

Detail
—geschäft retail business (shop, trade)
—handel retail trade
—händler retail dealer, retailer
detaillieren detail, itemize, particularize, specify
detailliert detailed, in detail
Detaillierung itemization, particularization
Detektei detective agency
Detektiv detective, investigator
—büro detective agency (office)
deuten construe, explain, interpret
—, falsch misconstrue, misinterpret
deutlich clear, conspicuous, distinct, obvious, plain, precise, spectacular
Deutlichkeit conspicuousness, clearness, distinctness, plainness
Deutung construction, explanation, interpretation
—, falsche misconstruction, misinterpretation
eine andere — zulassen admit (be open to) another interpretation
Devise device, motto
Devisen foreign currency (exchange)
Devisen-
—abkommen foreign exchange agreement
—ausgleichsfonds foreign exchange equalization fund
—beschränkungen exchange restrictions
—bestände foreign exchange holdings (funds)
—bestimmungen (—vorschriften) foreign exchange regulations
—bewirtschaftung foreign exchange control
— —sstelle exchange control board
—bilanz foreign exchange balance
—gesetz foreign exchange law
— —gebung foreign exchange legislation
—kontingent foreign exchange quota
—kontrolle foreign exchange control
—kurs exchange rate
—markt foreign exchange market
—notierung foreign exchange quotation
—reserve foreign exchange reserve
—schieber currency profiteer
—schiebung currency manipulation
—schmuggel currency smuggling
—sperre exchange embargo
—stelle foreign exchange department (office)
—vergehen currency offence
—zuteilung allotment of foreign exchange
Devolution devolution
Dezentralisation decentralization, departmentalization
dezentralisieren decentralize, departmentalize
Dezernat department, section
Dezernent departmental chief (head, expert)
Diakon deacon
Diäten allowances, emoluments
dichthalten keep silence
Dieb burglar, pilferer, plagiarist, plagiary, thief
Taschen— pickpocket
Diebes-
—bande gang of thieves
—gut stolen goods
Diebstahl burglary, larceny, pilfery, theft
Taschen— pocket-picking
—, einfacher petty (simple) larceny
—, geistiger plagiarism
—, schwerer aggravated (grand) larceny
Diebstahls
—klausel theft clause
—versicherung insurance against burglary and theft
dienen serve (as, for)
Diener attendant, servant, subordinate
dienlich expedient, helpful, serviceable, subservient, useful
— sein be helpful, be of service, subserve

Dienlichkeit helpfulness, serviceableness, subservience (cy), usefulness
Dienst attendance, duty, employ (ment), function, office, service, turn
—, außer off-duty, retired, ex service
—, im on duty, in service
—abzeichen badge (insignia) of office (rank)
—alter seniority, length of service, time in grade
—antritt entrance upon (into) service (office)
—anweisung service instruction
—barkeit bondage, easement, servitude, subjection
—bereich competence (cy), province, area of responsibility
—bezüge (—einkommen) official income, salary
—eid official oath, oath of office
— — ablegen (leisten) be sworn in
—enthebung discharge, dismissal, removal, suspension
—entlassung dismissal (from office) (from service)
dienstfrei exempt from service, off duty
Dienst-
—gebrauch official use
— —, für den for official purposes (use)
—geheimnis official secret, secrecy
—grad official rank
diensthabend in charge, on duty
Dienst
—handlung official function
—herr employer, master, principal
—jahr year of service
—leistung service (rendered)
Dienstleistungs-
—betrieb public service company
—gewerbe service trade
—vertrag service contract
—zeugnis testimonial
dienstlich official, functional
Dienst
—ordnung service regulations
—pflicht official duty
— — vernachlässigen neglect one's duties
—rang official rank
—raum office
—sache official matter (business)
—siegel official seal
—stempel official stamp
—stelle agency, department, office
—strafe disciplinary punishment
—strafverfahren disciplinary proceedings
—stunden office hours
—telegramm service (official) telegram
diensttuend in charge, on duty
Dienst-
—vergehen breach of duty, official misdemeanure, disciplinary offence
—verhältnis employment, service
— —se terms of employment
dienstverpflichten conscript, direct to work
Dienst
—verpflichtung conscription, direction to work
—vermerk service notice, office memorandum
—verschwiegenheit official secrecy
—vertrag contract of employment, service (labo[u]r) contract
—vorschrift service instruction (regulation)
—waffe service pistol
—weg official channels
— —, auf dem through official channels
—wohnung official residence
—zeit service period, office hours
—zeugnis testimonial
—zwang compulsory service
Diffamation (Diffamierung) defamation
diffamieren defame
Differenz balance, difference, disagreement, dispute, dissension, residual
differenzieren differentiate
Differenzierung differentiation
differieren differ
diffizil delicate, difficult
Diktat dictate, dictation

Diktator dictator
diktatorisch dictatorial
Diktatur dictatorship
diktieren dictate
dilatorisch dilatory
Ding affair, cause, matter, object, thing
dingbar hir(e)able
dingen bribe, engage, hire
dingfest machen apprehend, arrest, put in prison, seize
dinglich ad rem, real
Diplom certificate, charter, diploma
Diplomat diplomat(ist)
Diplomatie diplomacy
diplomatisch diplomatic
diplomiert certificated, diplomaed
direkt direct, first-hand, immediate
Direktion administeration, direction, directorate, board (body) of directors (managers), management
Direktive direction, instruction, rule
Direktor director, governor, manager, president
Direktorat directorship, directory
direktorial directorial
Direktorium directorate, directory, board (body) of directors (managers), management
diskreditieren discredit, bring discredit on
Diskrepanz discrepancy, disparity, divergence (cy)
diskret dicreet, judicious, tactful
Diskretion discretion, discreetness
—, bewahren maintain (exercise) discretion
diskriminieren discriminate (against)
diskriminierend discriminatory
Diskriminierung discrimination
Diskurs conversation, discourse, talk
Diskussion argument, debate, discussion
zur — stehend under discussion
Diskussions-
—basis basis for discussion
—freiheit free discussion
—teilnehmer debater, panel member
—veranstaltung forum, panel (discussion) meeting
diskutable discussible
diskutieren argue, debate, discuss, dispute
Dispens dispensation, exemption
— erteilen grant dispensation
dispensieren dispense from, excuse from, exempt from
Dispensierung dispensation
disponieren dispose, make arrangements, plan ahead
Disposition arrangement, disposal, disposition, order, planning ahead
—srecht right of disposal
Disput dispute
Disqualifikation (Disqualifizierung) disqualification, ineligibility
Dissertation dissertation, thesis, treatise
Distrikt area, district, quarter, region, section
Disziplin discipline
Disziplinar-
—ausschuß disciplinary committee
—behörde disciplinary authority
—bestimmungen disciplinary regulations
—fall disciplinary matter
—gerichtsbarkeit disciplinary jurisdiction
—gewalt disciplinary power
—hof disciplinary court
disziplinarisch disciplinary
— vorgehen take disciplinary action
Disziplinar
—maßnahme disciplinary action
—strafe disciplinary punishment (penalty)
—verfahren disciplinary action (proceedings)
—vergehen disciplinary offence
disziplinieren discipline
Divergenz divergence (cy)
divergieren diverge
Dividende dividend
Dividenden-

—ausschüttung declaration (distribution) (payment) of dividend
—erklärung declaration of dividend
—schein dividend coupon (warrant)
Doktrin doctrine
doktrinär doctrinaire
Dokument deed, document, evidence, (legal) instrument, paper, proof, record
dokumentarisch documentary
Dokumenten-
—sammlung collection of documents, file
—veröffentlichung publication of documents
—wechsel documentary (acceptance) bill
dokumentieren demonstrate, document, prove (support) by documents (documentary evidence), reveal, show
Dokumentierung documentation, documentary evidence (proof)
Dolch dagger, poniard
Domäne (crown, state) domain, demesne, estate, province, realm, sphere
dominieren dominate, domineer, predominate, prevail, rule (over)
dominierend dominating, prevailing
Domizil domicile, residence
Domiziliant domiciliant, payee
domizilieren domicile
Domizilierung domiciliation
Domizilwechsel domiciled bill
Doppel copy, duplicate
Doppelehe bigamy
doppelsinnig ambiguous, equivocal
Doppelsinnigkeit ambiguity, equivocation
doppelt double, in duplicate, twice, twofold
Dosis dose
Über- overdose
Dotalrecht (—system) dotal system
Dotation dotation, endowment
dotieren allocate, appropriate, dotate, endow
Dotierung allocation, appropriation, dotation, endowment
Dozent instructor, lecturer, professor, reader
dozieren lecture (on), profess (in)
Drang desire (for), pressure, rush, stress, urge, urgency
drängen dun, force, press for, push, urge
drastisch drastic
dreifach threefold, triple, in triplicate
dreimonatlich quarterly
Dreiviertelmehrheit three-fourths majority, three-quarters vote
dringen auf demand, insist on, persist in, press for, urge
dringend exigent, imminent, imperative, instant, pressing, strong, urgent
—es Bedürfnis (Erfordernis) exigence (cy)
dringlich instant, pressing, urgent
Dringlichkeit emergency, instancy, pressure, priority, urgency
Dringlichkeits-
—antrag application (motion) of urgency
—beschluß urgency resolution
—erklärung declaration of urgency
—fall case of emergency (urgency)
—liste priority list
—maßnahme urgency measure
—stufe degree of urgency, priority
— —, höchste top priority
Drittausfertigung triplicate
Drittel third (part)
Dritter third party (person)
Drittschuldner garnishee
Droge drug
Drohbrief threatening letter
drohen bluster at, fulminate against, menace, threaten
drohend imminent, impending, menacing, threatening
Drohung menace, threat
—, leere bluff, bluster
—, schwere fulmination
Druck compulsion, duress(e), force, impression, pressure, print(ing), strain

—, **unter** under compulsion (duress, pressure)
— **ausüben** exercise (exert a) pressure on
unter — setzen put pressure on, pressurize
unter — stehen be under pressure
Druck
—**erlaubnis** imprimatur, printing licenc(s)e
—**mittel anwenden** exercise pressure
—**sache** printed matter
dubios doubtful, dubious
Dubiosen doubtful debts
Duell duel
Duellant dueller, duellist
duellieren duel, fight a duel
duldbar endurable, sufferable, tolerable
Duldbarkeit endurability, tolerableness
dulden accept, acquiesce in, allow, bear, countenance, endure, permit, put up with, suffer, sustain, tolerate
duldsam indulgent, patient, tolerant
Duldsamkeit indulgence, tolerance, toleration
Duldung admission, permission, sufferance, tolerance, toleration
Duplikat copy, counterpart, duplicate, replica
Duplizität duplicity
durch-
—**arbeiten** work through (over)
—**beraten** discuss
—**blicken lassen** hint (at), indicate, insinuate, suggest, give to understand
—**brechen** break (through), infringe, run
—**brennen** abscond, bolt, make off
—**bringen** bring (get) through, carry, pass
— —, **Antrag** carry a motion
— —, **Geld** dissipate, squander
— —, **Gesetz** pass a bill
—**denken** meditate on, think over
—**dringen** get through, penetrate
Durchdringung penetration
durchdrücken press (force, push) through
Durcheinander confusion, disorder, turbulence
durcheinander in disorder (confusion)
— **bringen** put into disorder, confuse, upset
— **kommen** get into disorder
durchfahren go (pass) through
Durchfahrt passage
Durchfahrts-
—**recht** right of passage (way, transit)
—**zoll** transit duty
Durchfall failure
durch-
—**fallen** fail
—**fechten** fight out (through)
Durchfuhr passage, transit
—**bescheinigung** transit certificate
—**bewilligung (—erlaubnis)** transit permit
—**handel** transit trade
—**land** transit country
—**recht** right of passage (transit) (way)
—**verbot** transit embargo
—**zoll** transit duty
durchführbar feasible, practicable, workable
Durchführbarkeit feasibility, practicability, workability
durchführen accomplish, carry out (through), complete, conduct, enforce, execute, fulfil, perform, pursue, realize
Durchführung accomplishment, completion, enforcement, execution, performance, pursuit, realization
Durchführungs-
—**bestimmungen** executive (implementing) regulations, rules of application
—**verordnung** carrying-out ordinance, executive order
Durchgang passage, transit
—, **freier** free transit
Durchgangs-
—**abgabe** transit duty

—gebühr transit charge
—güter transit goods
—land transit country
—recht right of way
—schein transit bill (pass)
—verkehr transit traffic
—visum transit visa
durchgehen be carried, examine, go through, pass, be passed, revise
durchgreifen, hart resort to (take) drastic measures
durchgreifend drastic, radical, strong, trenchant, uncompromising
durchhalten endure, hold out, stay
Durchhaltevermögen endurance, holding out, stay
durchkommen get (come) (pass) through, pass
—, nicht fail, be defeated
durchkreuzen cross, frustrate, traverse
Durchkreuzung crossing, frustration, prevention
durchlassen let pass, let through, pass
durchlesen read through (over), peruse
durchleuchten clear up, examine into
durchmachen endure, experience, go (pass) through, suffer, undergo
Durchreise passage, transit
—, auf der on one's way through
Durchreise
—erlaubnis transit permit (certificate)
—visum transit visa
durchschauen see through (into)
Durchschlag (—schrift) copy, duplicate
Durchschnitt average, level, mean standard
—, im on an average
— berechnen average
durchschnittlich average, common, mean, medium, normal, ordinary
durchsehen examine, peruse, review, revise
durchsetzbar enforceable
durchsetzen carry (through), effect, enforce, penetrate, push
—, sich assert oneself, prevail, make (fight, push, win) one's way
Durchsetzung assertion, enforcement, penetration
Durchsicht examination, inspection, perusal, revision
durch-
—sickern leak out, transpire
—sprechen discuss, talk over
—stöbern ransack (for)
—streichen cross (strike) out, cancel
—suchen search
Durchsucher searcher
Durchsuchung search
Durchsuchungs-
—befehl search warrant
—recht right of search
durchtrieben artful, crafty, cunning, sly, tricky
durchweg always, throughout, without distinction (exception)
dürftig inadequate, indigent, insufficient, needy, poor, slim
Dürftigkeit inadequacy, indigence, insufficiency, neediness, poorness
Dynast dynast
Dynastie dynasty
dynastisch dynastic(al)

E

ebenbürtig equal, worthy
— sein be of equal birth (rank), be the equal of, be on a par with
nicht — sein not to be the equal of, not to be equal in rank, not to be of equal rank
Ebenbürtigkeit equality (of birth)

Ebene level, standard
—, **auf höchster** on top level
echt authentic, genuine, lawful, legitimate, natural, pure, real, true
Echtheit authenticity, genuineness, legitimacy, purity, reality, trueness
— **bestreiten** dispute validity
— **feststellen** authenticate
Echtheits-
—**beweis** proof of authenticity
—**zeugnis** certificate of authenticity
Edikt decree, edict
— **erlassen** issue an edict
Effekt effect, result
Effekten (goods and) chattels, movables, papers, securities, shares, stocks
Effekten-
—**börse** stock exchange
—**handel (—verkehr)** stock broking, stock jobbing
—**händler (—makler)** stock broker, stock jobber
—**markt** stock market
effektiv actual, effective, efficient, real, virtual
Effektivbestand actual balance, real stock
Effektivwert actual (real) (true) value
effektuieren carry out, effect, execute
Effektuierung execution
Ehe marriage, matrimony, wedlock
—, **aus erster** of one's first marriage
—, **anfechtbare** contestable (voidable) marriage
—, **nichtige** void marriage
—, **wilde** cohabitation, concubinage
—, **in wilder — leben** cohabit with
—, **zerrüttete** ruined (destroyed) marriage
— **anfechten** contest the validity of a marriage
— **auflösen** cancel a marriage
— **brechen** commit adultery
— **eingehen (—schließen)** celebrate (conclude) a marriage, marry
— **scheiden** divorce
— **trennen** separate (dissolve) a marriage
Ehe-
—**anfechtung** action (petition) for nullification of marriage
—**aufgebot** marriage banns
—**brecher** adulterer
—**brecherin** adultress
ehebrecherisch adulterous
Ehe-
—**bruch** adultery
— — **begehen** commit adultery
—**frau** wife
—**fähigkeit** nubility
—**gelöbnis** promise of marriage
—**gesetz** marriage law (act)
—**hindernis** impediment of marriage
—**kontrakt** marriage contract (settlement)
—**leute** husband and wife
ehelich conjugal, legitimate, matrimonial, true, in wedlock
für — erklären legitimate, legitim(at)ize
ehelichen marry
Ehelichkeit legitimacy
Ehelichkeits-
—**erklärung** declaration of legitimacy, legitimation
—**vermutung** presumption of legitimacy
ehelos single, unmarried
Ehelosigkeit celibacy, single life
ehemalig alias, ex, former, previous
Ehe-
—**mann** husband
—**mündigkeit** marriageable age, nubility
—**nichtigkeit** nullity of marriage
Ehenichtigkeits-
—**erklärung** nullification of marriage
—**klage** action (petition) for the nullification of marriage
Ehe-
—**paar** (married) couple
—**recht** marriage law
—**sache** marriage matter
—**scheidung** divorce

Ehescheidungs-
—gericht divorce court
—grund cause of (ground for) divorce
—klage petition for divorce
—prozeß (—verfahren) divorce proceedings (suit)
—recht divorce law
—urteil decree of divorce
— —, provisorisches decree nisi
— —, endgültiges decree absolute
Ehe-
—schließung (contraction of) marriage
—stand married state, matrimony, wedlock
—streitigkeit matrimonial (conjugal) dispute
—tauglichkeit fitness (qualification) for marriage
— —szeugnis certificate of marriage qualification
—trennung separation of marriage
—versprechen promise of marriage
—vertrag marriage contract (settlement)
—zerrüttung wrecking of marriage
Ehrabschneider calumniator, slanderer
Ehrabschneiderei defamation, slander
Ehrauffassung (sense of) hono(u)r
ehrbar decent, honest, hono(u)rable, reputable, respectable
Ehrbarkeit decency, honesty, integrity, reputability, respectability
Ehre credit, dignity, distinction, hono(u)r, pride, reputation
— abschneiden defame
ehren hono(u)r, respect
Ehrenamt honorary function
ehrenamtlich honorary, unpaid
Ehrenbezei(u)gung hono(u)r, respect, salute, tribute
Ehrenbürger (einer Stadt) honorary citizen (freeman) [of a city]
—recht honorary citizenship (freedom) [of a city]
Ehren
—gast guest of hono(u)r
—geleit suite, retinue
—gericht (— —shof) court of hono(u)r
ehrenhaft hono(u)rable, honorary, honest, respectable, upright, worthy
Ehrenhaftigkeit honesty, integrity, uprightness
ehrenhalber honorary, for hono(u)r's sake, honoris causa
Ehrenmann man of hono(u)r
—mitglied honorary member
— —schaft honorary membership
—pflicht duty of hono(u)r, honorary obligation
—platz place (seat) of hono(u)r, pride of place
—posten honorary post
—präsident honorary president
—recht law of hono(u)r
—rechte, bürgerliche civil rights
— — aberkennen deprive of civil rights
—, Aberkennung der deprivation (loss) of civil rights, civil degradation
—rettung vindication of hono(u)r, rehabilitation, whitewash(ing)
ehrenrührig calumnious, defamatory, disgraceful, dishono(u)rable, slanderous
Ehren
—sache matter of hono(u)r
—schuld debt of hono(u)r
—schuß salute
—strafe degrading (dishono[u]ring) punishment
—titel honorary title
—urkunde certificate of hono(u)r
—wache guard of hono(u)r
ehrenvoll creditable, hono(u)rable, respectable
Ehrenvorsitz honorary chairmanship (presidency)
Ehrenvorsitzender honorary chairman (president)
ehrenwert creditable, hono(u)rable, respectable
Ehrenwort parole, word of hono(u)r
— brechen break one's parole
— geben give one's word of hono(u)r, pledge one's hono(u)r

Ehren
—zahlung payment for hono(u)r
—zeichen badge of hono(u)r, decoration, mark of distinction, medal
ehrerbietig respectful
Ehrerbietung duty, reference, regard, respect, respectfulness
Ehrgefühl sense of hono(u)r
Ehrgeiz ambition
ehrgeizig ambitious
ehrlich faithful, honest, respectable, reliable, straight, upright
Ehrlichkeit fairness, honesty, straightness, uprightness
ehrlos disgraceful, dishono(u)rable, infamous
Ehrlosigkeit disgracefulness, dishonesty, infamy
ehrsam honest, hono(u)rable, respectable
Ehrsamkeit honesty, respectability
Ehrung compliment, distinction, hono(u)r tribute
Ehrverletzung defamation, insult, slander
Ehrverlust civil degradation, deprivation (loss) of civil rights
Eid oath
—, falscher false oath
—, wissentlich falscher perjury
falschen — leisten commit perjury, perjure (forswear) oneself
— ablegen (—leisten) swear (an oath), take an oath upon
— abnehmen administer an oath
— brechen break (violate) an oath
—, auf (up)on oath
—, unter under oath
unter — aussagen testify on oath
unter — bestätigen confirm by oath
unter — stehen be under oath
unter — vernehmen hear (cross-examine) under oath
— es Statt, an in lieu of oath
an — — erklären (an — — versichern) declare (affirm) in the form of affidavit, affirm in lieu of oath
Eid
—brecher perjurer
—bruch perjury, violation of oath
eidbrüchig guilty of perjury
Eides-
—ablegung (—leistung) taking of an oath
—abnahme administration of oath
—entbindung release from oath
—formel form of oath
eidesstattlich in lieu of oath
—e Erklärung (—e Versicherung) affidavit
— versichern affirm in lieu of oath
Eides
—verletzung violation of an oath
—verweigerung refusal to take an oath
Eidgenosse confederate
—nschaft confederation, league
eidgenössisch confederate, federal
eidlich by (on, under, upon) oath, sworn
—e Aussage (—e Erklärung) sworn statement, affidavit, deposition
—e Zeugenaussage sworn testimony
— aussagen swear, declare upon oath
— vernehmen hear (cross-examine) under oath
Eifersucht envy, grudge, jealousy
eifersüchtig envious, jealous
eigen characteristic, curious, individual, inherent, odd, own, particular, peculiar, private, proper, queer, separate, special, strange
Eigenart character, characteristic (features), quality
eigenartig curious, odd, original, peculiar, queer, special, strange
Eigenartigkeit curiousness, peculiarity, strangeness
eigenartigerweise curiously (strangely) enough, strange to say

Eigenbesitz freehold, private property, proprietary possession
Eigenbesitzer private owner, proprietary possessor
Eigengesetzlichkeit autonomy, inherent laws
eigenhändig personal, with one's own hand
Eigenheit particularity, peculiarity
Eigen
—kapital capital stock
eigenmächtig arbitrary, autocratic, independent, unauthorized
— handeln act on one's own authority (responsibility)
—mächtigkeit arbitrary action, arbitrariness
—name proper (family) name
—nutz self-interest, selfishness
eigennützig self-interested, selfish
Eigennützigkeit self-interestedness, selfishness
eigens (e)specially, expressly, particulary, on purpose
Eigenschaft attribute, capacity, characteristic, feature, nature, peculiarity, position, property, quality, status
in seiner — als in one's capacity as
eigenstaatlich autonomous, national, sovereign
Eigenstaatlichkeit autonomy, sovereignty
eigentlich actual, essential, intrinsic, precise, proper, real, true, virtual
Eigentum estate, ownership, possession, property, proprietorship
Grund— land property, real estate
—, bewegliches personal (movable) property (estate), chattels, movables, personalty
—, geistiges literary property
—, unbewegliches real property (estate), immovables
Eigentümer holder, owner, proprietor, proprietary
Grund(stücks)— land owner

Eigentums-
—anspruch property right, title
—beschränkung restriction of property
—delikt property offenc(s)e
—entsetzung expropriation
—erwerb acquisition of property
—klage claim of ownership
—nachweis proof of title
—recht ownership, (right of) property, proprietary (right), proprietorship, title
—schutz protection of property
—steuer property tax
—störung trespass (on property)
—titel title, deed of property
—übergabe (—übertragung) conveyance (transfer) of title (property)
—vergehen property offenc(s)e
—vorbehalt reservation (retention) of ownership (title) (property)
Eigentümerin proprietress
Eigenwechsel promissory note
Eigenwert intrinsic value
eignen, sich be adequate, fit, suit, be suitable
Eigner owner, proprietor
Eignung appropriateness, aptitude, fitness, qualification, suitability
—sprüfung aptitude test
einbegreifen comprise, include
einbegriffen including, included
— sein in be included in
einbehalten detain, keep back, retain, withhold
Einbehaltung detention, retention, withholding
einberufen call (up), convene, convoke, summon
Einberufung convening, convocation, summoning, summons
einbeziehen comprehend, cover, include, incorporate
Einbeziehung inclusion, incorporation
Einblick glimpse, insight
einbrechen break in(to), burgle, commit burglary, invade
Einbrecher burglar, housebreaker, picklock
—bande gang of burglars
einbringen bring (pay) in, con-

tribute, enter, introduce, invest, move, put, yield, return
Einbringung contribution, introduction
Einbruch breaking in, burglary, housebreaking, incursion, inroad, invasion, irruption, trespass
—sdiebstahl burglary, housebreaking
einbruchsicher burglar-(theft-) proof, thief-resisting
Einbruchsversicherung burglary (theft) insurance, insurance against burglary and theft
einbürgern naturalize
wieder— repatriate
—, sich become customary
Einbürgerung naturalization
Wieder— repatriation
Einbürgerungs-
—antrag (-gesuch) application for naturalization
—urkunde certificate (document) of naturalization
Einbuße damage, forfeiture, loss
— erleiden suffer a loss
einbüßen forfeit, lose
eindeutig clear, plain, unambiguous, unequivocal
Eindringen forcible (unlawful) entry, infiltration, influx, intrusion, invasion, irruption, penetration
eindringen break in(to), enter by force, infiltrate, invade, penetrate
eindringlich insistent, pressing, urgent
Eindringlichkeit emphasis, force, insistence, urgency
—, mit aller with all insistence
Eindringling intruder
Eindruck impress(ion), imprint
Einehe monogamy
einengen confine, constrict, limit, narrow, restrict
Einengung confinement, constriction, limitation, restriction
einerseits — andererseits on the one hand, and on the other hand
einfach common, ordinary, plain, simple, single
Einfachheit plainness, simplicity
der — halber for the sake of simplicity
Einfall collapse, idea, incursion, inroad, inspiration, invasion, irruption, raid
einfallen break in, collapse, invade
Einfalt innocence, simplicity
einfältig innocent, simple
einfinden, sich appear (in, before), arrive, turn up
einflechten insert, interpose, introduce, put in, weave into
Einfluß authority, hold, influence, sway
— ausüben exercise an influence (on)
Einflußbereich (—gebiet, —sphäre) sphere of influence
einflußreich influential
einfordern call in (for), collect, demand
Einforderung call for, calling in, collection
einfügen insert, interpose, put in
—, sich adapt oneself, conform, fit in(to)
Einfügung adaptation, insertion, interpolation
Einfuhr import, importation
Einfuhr
—abgabe import duty
—agent import agent
—artikel import article (item)
—beschränkungen import restrictions
—bestimmungen import regulations
—erklärung import declaration (entry)
—erlaubnis (—bewilligung) import licenc(s)e (permit)
— —schein import certificate
—handel import trade
—händler importer
—kontingent import quota
—monopol import monopoly
—sperre import embargo (ban)
—steuer import duty
—überschuß import surplus
—verbot import embargo
—zoll import duty, customs
einführen establish, import, inaugurate, initiate, install, in-

stitute, instruct, introduce, present, recommend, set up, start
Einführung establishment, importation, inauguration, initiation, installation, institution, instruction, introduction
—sschreiben letter of introduction
Eingabe application, memorial, petition, statement
— machen submit (make) an application, file a petition, address a memorial to, memorialize (for)
Eingang arrival, entrance, entry, receipt
Eingänge incomings, receipts, takings
eingangs at the beginning (outset)
Eingangs
—anzeige notice of receipt
—bestätigung acknowledgement of receipt
—datum date of receipt
—zoll entrance duty
eingeben administer, hand (send) in, inspire, present, propose, recommend, submit, suggest
eingeboren aboriginal, native
Eingeborener native
Eingebung inspiration, suggestion
Eingehen acceptance, accession, agreement, cessation, compliance, consent, contraction, death, decay, decline, discontinuance, extinction, reaction (to)
eingehen arrive, assume, come in, conclude, contract, embark upon, enter, go in, incur, make, be plausible, undertake
cease to exist, die (off), discontinue, become extinct, be extinguished, perish
eingehen auf accede to, accept, agree to, comply with, consent to, descend to, enter (go) into, inquire into, yield to, react to, refer to, respond to
eingehend careful, detailed, in detail, exhaustive, incoming, thorough
— wiedergeben particularize
eingemeinden communalize, incorporate, municipalize
Eingemeindung communalization, incorporation, municipalization
eingestandenermaßen admittedly, avowedly
Eingeständnis admission, avowal, confession
eingestehen admit, avow, confess
eingetragen incorporated, registered
eingliedern classify, enrol (in), incorporate, integrate
Eingliederung classification, enrolment, incorporation, integration
Eingreifen encroachment, engagement, interference, intervention
eingreifen encroach, engage in, impinge upon, infringe upon, interfere, intervene, invade, meddle in, step in
Eingriff encroachment, impingement, inroad, interference, intervention, invasion, operation, usurpation
einen verbotenen — vornehmen perform an illegal operation
eingruppieren classify, group
Eingruppierung classification, grouping
Einhalt gebieten stop, bring to a stop, put a stop to
einhalten abide by, adhere to, comply with, fulfil, keep (to), meet, obey, observe, stick to, stop
—, Zeit be punctual
—, Frist observe the appointed time
Einhaltung adherence, compliance, fulfilment, meeting, observance
Nicht— non-compliance, nonobservance
einheimisch domestic, domiciled, home, inland, native, resident
Einheimischer inhabitant, native, resident
Einheit entity, standard, uniformity, unit, unity

einheitlich coherent, consistent, homogeneous, standardized, undivided, uniform, unitary
Einheitlichkeit cohesion, conformity, consistency, homogeneity, uniformity, unity
Einheits
—bestrebungen unitary tendencies
—bewegung unitary movement
—staat unitary state
—wert standard (basic) value
einholen apply for, ask for, call for (in), collect, gather, obtain, procure, recoup, recover, search, seek
Einholung collection, obtaining, procuring, recoupment, recovery
einig united
— sein agree, be in agreement (conformity), be agreed (on)
nicht — sein disagree, be in disagreement
— werden come to terms (an agreement) with
einigen unify, unite
—, sich agree, come to terms (an agreement) (an understanding) with, settle with
—, sich gütlich come to a friendly (amicable) settlement (agreement)
Einigkeit agreement, concord, harmony, unanimity, union, unity
Einigung agreement, arrangement, settlement, understanding, unification, union
— erzielen arrive at (come to) an agreement, reach a settlement
Einigungs
—bestrebungen efforts to reach an agreement
—versuch attempt at conciliation
einkassieren cash, collect, encash
Einkassierung cashing, collection, encashment
einklagbar actionable, claimable, enforceable, suable
einklagen sue for, take legal proceedings for, prosecute
Einklang accord, harmony, unison
in — mit in accordance (conformity) with
in — bringen bring in accordance with, coordinate, harmonize, reconcile
in — stehen be in harmony (keeping) with, be compatible with
nicht in — stehen mit be incompatible with
Einkommen earnings, emoluments, income, revenue
Jahres— annual income, annuity
— aus Arbeit earned income
— aus Vermögen unearned income
einkommen come in, be paid in
— um apply for, ask for, make an application (petition) for, petition for
Einkommens-
—besteuerung taxation of income
—erklärung income return (statement)
—steuer income tax
—steuererklärung income tax return
— — abgeben make (file) an income tax return
—steuerveranlagung income tax assessment
—überprüfung means test
einkreisen encircle, isolate
Einkreisung encirclement, isolation
Einkünfte earnings, emoluments, income, receipts, revenue, takings
einladen convoke, invite, summon
Einladung invitation
auf — von at the invitation (request) of
Einlage contribution, deposit, enclosure, investment
Einlaß admission, admittance, entrance
— gewähren grant admission
sich — verschaffen force an entrance into
Einlaßgebühr admission (entrance) fee
einlassen admit (into), let in(to)
sich — join issue

sich — auf accede to, agree to, comply with, consent to, yield to
sich nicht — auf refuse (to)
sich — in embark (up)on, engage in, enter in, venture on
sich — mit associate with, have intercourse (intimacy) with
Einlassung appearance, defenc(s)e
einlegen deposit, enclose, enter, lodge, make, put in, pay into
—, Anschlußberufung cross-appeal
—, Berufung appeal, lodge (prefer) an appeal against
—, Beschwerde lodge a complaint against
—, Protest (Verwahrung) enter (lodge) (make) a protest against
—, Revision appeal to
—, Veto veto, put a (one's) veto on
einleiten begin, initiate, institute, introduce, open, preface, prelude, start
—, Prozeß bring an action against, take proceedings against
—, Untersuchung institute an inquiry
—, Verhandlungen enter into (open) negotiations
—, Verfahren initiate (institute) (start) legal proceedings against, prosecute (for)
einleitend introductory, opening, prefatory, preliminary
Einleitung beginning, initiation, institution, introduction, opening, preamble, preface, preliminary, prelude, prologue, starting
einlenken give in, relent, yield
einleuchten be clear (evident, obvious, plausible)
einleuchtend clear, evident, obvious, plausible
einliefern deliver, deposit, hand in, submit
—, ins Gefängnis imprison, put into jail
Einlieferung deposit, delivery, handing in
—, ins Gefängnis imprisonment
einliegend enclosed
einlösbar redeemable
einlösen discharge, fulfil, keep, meet, pay, redeem, take up
—, Scheck cash (pass) a cheque
einen Scheck nicht — reject a cheque
—, Wechsel hono(u)r (protect) a bill
einen Wechsel nicht — dishono(u)r a bill
Einlösung discharge, keeping, payment, redemption, repayment, withdrawal
— eines Schecks cashing (passing) of a cheque
— eines Wechsels hono(u)ring (protection) of a bill
Einlösungstermin date of redemption (maturity)
einmalig non-recurring, single
einmischen, sich interfere, intervene, (inter)meddle in, mingle
Einmischung interference, intervention, (inter)meddling
Nicht— non-interference, non-intervention
einmütig harmonious, of one mind, solid, unanimous
Einmütigkeit agreement, concord, harmony, solidarity, unanimity, unity
Einnahme capture, collection, occupation
Einnahmen earnings, proceeds, receipts, returns, revenue, takings
Einnahmequelle source of income (revenue)
einnehmen capture, collect, conquer, earn, hold, occupy, receive, take (in, up), take possession of
einordnen arrange, classify, dispose, file, incorporate, integrate, range
—, sich join
Einordnung arrangement, classification, filing, incorporation
einräumen accord, admit, allow, (con)cede, give, grant, open, own, permit, resign, yield
Einräumung admission, allowance, concession, grant(ing), opening

einrechnen include in
Einrechnung inclusion
Einrede defenc(s)e, demurrer, exception, objection, plea, protest(ation), remonstrance
— erheben demur, enter a plea
einreden persuade
einreichen bring in, deliver, file, give, hand in, lodge, prefer, present, put in, send in, submit, tender
Einreichung entering, filing, handing in, lodging, presentation, sending in, submission, tendering
einreihen class (with), classify, enrol, enter (in), file, incorporate, subsume
—, sich join
Einreihung filing, subsumption
Einreise entry (into)
Einreise-
—erlaubnis (—bewilligung, —genehmigung) entry permit
—visum entry visa
einreisen enter
einrichten arrange for, constitute, dispose, establish, equip, found, furnish, institute, introduce, organize, set up, start
sich — auf prepare for
Einrichtung arrangement, disposition, equipment, establishment, foundation, furniture, installation, institution, introduction, organization, regulation
Einrichtungen accommodations, facilities
—, soziale social (welfare) institutions (organizations)
einsammeln collect, gather
Einsammler collector, gatherer
Einsammlung collection, gathering
Einsatz action, activity, application, appointment, assignment, employment, engagement, risk, share, use, venture
—, im in action
einschalten incorporate in, insert, intercalate, interpolate, interpose, put in
—, sich get into, interfere, interpose, intervene, join
Einschaltung insertion, intercalation, interference, interpolation, interposition, intervention, participation
einschätzen appraise, assess, estimate, rate, value
Einschätzung appraisal, appraisement, assessment, estimation, rating, valuation
einschicken send in, remit
einschieben insert, intercalate, interpolate, put in
Einschiebung insertion, intercalation, interpolation
einschlägig applicable, apposite, competent, pertinent, relevant, respective
einschleichen creep (slip) (steal) in(to)
einschließen comprise, enclose, include
einschließlich (unter Einschluß von) comprising, included, including, inclusive
einschmuggeln smuggle in
einschneidend decisive, drastic, trenchant
einschränken confine, curtail, cut down, hamper, limit, modify, qualify, reduce, restrain, restrict, retrench
—, sich economize, retrench, curtail one's expenses
einschränkend limitative,restrictive
Einschränkung confinement, curtailment, economizing, limitation, modification, qualification, reduction, reserve, restriction, retrenchment
— machen make a reserve
mit —en restrictively, with certain qualifications
ohne —en unconditionally, unreservedly, without reserve
Einschreibebrief registered letter
per — by registered letter
einschreiben enlist, enrol, enter in(to), inscribe in, matriculate, record, register
Einschreibung enlistment, enrolment, entry, matriculation, registration

Einschreiten interference, intervention, stepping in, (taking of legal) proceedings against
einschreiten interfere, intervene, step in
— **gegen** proceed against, take measures against
—, **gerichtlich** proceed against, prosecute, take action against, take legal steps (proceedings) against
einschüchtern intimidate, exert undue influence
Einschüchterung intimidation, undue influence
—**sversuch** attempt at intimidation
einschwören swear in
einsehen appreciate, apprehend, examine, grasp, inspect, look into, realize, understand
einseitig biassed, one-sided, partial, prejudiced, unilateral
Einseitigkeit one-sidedness, partiality
einsenden contribute, remit, send in, transmit
Einsender contributor, remitter, sender, transmitter
Einsendung contribution, remittance, sending in, transmittal
gegen — von on receipt of
einsetzen apply, appoint, assign, bring into action, constitute, designate, employ, engage, establish, found, insert, install, institute, nominate, put in, set up, use, utilize
—, **sich** go for, identify with, push, sponsor, stand up for
—, **Leben** risk (venture) one's life
Einsetzung appointment, designation, establishment, insertion, installation, institution, nomination, setting up
Einsicht discernment, examination, inspection, perusal, understanding
— **nehmen** examine (into), inspect, look into, peruse
einsichtig (einsichtsvoll) discerning, judicious, reasonable, sensible
Einsichtnahme inspection, perusal
einsparen economize, reduce, retrench, save
Einsparung cut, economizing, restriction, retrenchment, saving
Einspruch appeal, caveat, contestation, demurrer, exemption, objection, opposition, plea, protest, protestation, remonstrance, veto
— **einlegen** enter a caveat, file an objection, enter (lodge) a protest against, protest, veto
— **erheben** demur, exempt against, raise objection, make a plea against, protest (remonstrate) against
Einspruchs-
—**frist** limitation of protest (veto)
—**recht** right of protest, veto
—**schrift** appeal
—**verfahren** opposition proceedings
einstecken accept, pocket, put up with, swallow
einstehen für answer for, be answerable for, be (go) bail for, guarantee, give security for, be (stand) surety for, vouch for, warrant
einstellen break off, cease, close (down), discontinue, dismiss, drop, employ, engage, give up, nolle-pros, shut down, quash, stay, stop, suspend
—, **sich** appear, arise, attend, come up, ensue
sich — auf adjust (adapt) one's mind to, provide for, respond to
Einstellung attitude, cessation, discontinuance, employment, engagement, nolleprosequi, shutdown, stop, stoppage
—, **vorläufige** stay, suspension
Einstellungs-
—**bedingungen** terms of employment
—**beschluß** order to stay proceedings
einstimmig unanimous
Einstimmigkeit accord, agreement, unanimity

einstufen assess, categorize, class, classify, grade, graduate, group, rate
Einstufung assessment, categorization, classification, grading, graduation, rating
einstweilen in the interim, (in the) meantime, (in the) meanwhile, for the present, for the time being
einstweilig interim, interlocutory, provisional, temporary
—e Anordnung provisional arrangement, temporary order
—e Verfügung interim injunction, interlocutory order, temporary decree
eintauschen barter, exchange, trade in
einteilen arrange, class, classify, dispose, distribute, divide into, grade, graduate, group
Einteilung arrangement, classification, disposition, distribution, division, graduation, grouping, schedule
Eintrag entry, item, record, register, registration
eintragen book, bring in, enrol, enter (into), incorporate, inscribe, insert, list, record, register, yield
einträglich gainful, lucrative, paying, profitable, remunerative, worthwile, yielding
—, wenig (nicht) gainless, profitless, unremunerative
Einträglichkeit lucrativeness, profitableness
Eintragung booking, enrolment, entry, inscription, insertion, recording, registration, registry
—, falsche misentry
Eintragungs-
—bescheinigung (—schein, —urkunde) registration certificate
—bewilligung authorization for registration
—vermerk note of entry
—zwang compulsory registration
Eintreffen appearance, arrival, realization
eintreffen appear, arrive, be realized, come to pass, come true, happen, turn up
eintreibbar collectible, enforceable, exigible, recoverable
eintreiben call in, collect, enforce, exact, recover
Eintreibung collection, enforcement, exaction, recovery
—skosten collection charges
eintreten arise, come about, ensue, enter (into), eventuate, happen, join, occur, step in, take place
— für advocate, answer for, champion, intercede for, plead a cause, support, stand for, take up the cause of
Eintritt access(ion), admission, admittance, beginning, entrance, entry, incidence, ingress
einverleiben annex, embody, include in(to), incorporate
Einverleibung annexation, inclusion, incorporation
Einvernehmen agreement, concord, harmony, understanding
im — mit in accordance (agreement) (harmony) with
in bestem — on excellent terms
in bestem — stehen be on the best terms
gegenseitiges — mutual understanding
geheimes — secret understanding
gutes — good understanding
in gutem — on friendly terms
gütliches — friendly understanding
in vollem — in complete agreement
sich ins — setzen mit communicate with, come to an understanding with, consult with
einverstanden sein mit accept, acquiesce in, agree, approve, be agreed on, consent
sich — erklären mit agree (consent) to, associate with, concur with (in)
Einverständnis acquiescence, agreement, approval, assent, consent, fiat, harmony, understanding

im — mit in accordance (agreement) (conformity) with
—, gegenseitiges mutual consent
—, geheimes collusion, connivance
in geheimem — mit in collusion with
—, stillschweigendes tacit understanding
— erzielen come to an understanding
— geben give approval to
Einverständniserklärung agreement, declaration of consent
Einwand argument, defenc(s)e, exception, objection, plea, protest, traverse
— erheben (vorbringen) enter (present) (put in) a plea, raise an objection
Einwanderer immigrant
einwandern immigrate
Einwanderung immigration
Einwanderungs-
—beschränkungen immigration restrictions
—bewilligung (—erlaubnis) immigration permit
—gesetz immigration law
—sperre immigration stoppage
—verbot immigration ban
einwandfrei accurate, blameless, beyond doubt, faultless, impeccable, incontestable, irreproachable, perfect, unexceptionable, unobjectionable
einwechseln cash, change, convert, exchange
Einwechselung change, conversion, exchange
einweihen dedicate, inaugurate, open
— in admit in(to), initiate in(to), instruct, let into
Einweihung dedication, inauguration, initiation, opening
—srede inauguration address (speech)
einweisen assign into, brief, direct, induct in(to), initiate into, install in, introduce into
Einweisung assignment, briefing, direction, installation, introduction
einwenden argue, demur, object, oppose, plead, protest
Einwendung argument, defence (se), demurrer, exception, objection, plea, protest
— erheben (machen) argue against, demur to, oppose, raise an objection to
einwerfen interpose, put in
einwilligen accede to, acquiesce in, agree (to), approve of, assent to, comply with, consent to, subscribe to
Einwilligung acquiescence, agreement, approval, assent, authorization, consent, compliance, permission
Einwilligungs-
—erklärung deed of consent
einwirken auf affect, have an effect on, influence, operate on, work (up)on
Einwirkung effect, influence, impingement, impression, operation
Einwohner citizen, inhabitant, native, population, resident
Einwohner-
—meldeamt registration office
—meldepflicht compulsory registration
—schaft inhabitants, population
—zahl number of inhabitants, (total) population
—zählung census
Einwurf demurrer, interposition, objection
— machen demur
einzahlen deposit, lodge, pay in(to) (up)
Einzahler depositor, payer
Einzahlung deposit, paying in, payment
Einzahlungs
—schein deposit receipt (slip), pay-in slip
—tag (-termin) day (date) of payment
Einzel
—angaben particulars
—arrest (—haft) solitary confinement
—fall individual (isolated) case
—handel retail (trade)
—händler retail dealer, retailer

—heiten data, details, particulars
einzeln detached, individual, isolated, particular, separate, several, single, solitary, special
— angeben detail, particularize, specify
einzelnen, im in detail
Einzelner (Einzelperson) individual (person)
Einzelrichter judge sitting alone
einziehbar cashable, collectible, confiscable, forfeitable, recoverable, redeemable, seizable
einziehen call in, cash, collect, confiscate, forfeit, gather, induct, redeem, seize, withdraw
Einziehung calling in, cashing, collection, confiscation, forfeiture, induction, seizure, withdrawal
—sspesen collection charges
einzig only, single, singular, sole, solitary, unique
einzigartig remarkable, singular, unique
Einzug cashing, collection
—sstelle collection office
Element element
elementar elementary, primary, primitive, rudimentary
Elend destitution, distress, misery, need, poverty, wreched-ness
elend miserable, poor, wreched
eliminieren eliminate
Eliminierung elimination
elterlich parental
—es Erbteil patrimony
—e Gewalt parental authority (power)
Eltern parents
elternlos parentless, orphaned
Elternteil parent
Emanzipation emancipation
emanzipieren emancipate
Embargo embargo
— auferlegen embargo, lay an embargo on, lay under an embargo
— aufheben take off an embargo
emeritieren discharge from, pension off, retire
emeritiert emeritus, pensioned, retired
Emigrant emigrant, émigré, exile, refugee
Emigration emigration
emigrieren emigrate
eminent distinguished, eminent, outstanding
Emission emission, issue
—sbank bank of issue, issuing bank
emissionsfähig issuable
Emissions-
—geschäft issuing transaction
—jahr year of issue
Emittent emitter, issuer
emittierbar issuable
emittieren emit, issue
Empfang receipt, reception
empfangen accept, conceive, get, obtain, receive, welcome
Empfänger acceptor, addressee, consignee, payee, receiver, recipient, transferee
Empfängnis conception
—verhütung contraception
empfängnisverhütendes Mittel contraceptive
Empfängniszeit conception period
Empfangs-
—anzeige notice of receipt
—bescheinigung (-schein) acquittance, (certificate of) receipt
—bestätigung acknowledgement (confirmation) of receipt
empfehlen advise, commend, recommend
empfehlenswert advisable, recommendable, suitable
Empfehlung advice, commendation, recommendation
—sschreiben letter of recommendation (introduction), credentials
Empfinden feeling, perception
empfinden experience, feel, perceive, realize, sense
empfindlich considerable, delicate, heavy, irritable, perceptible, sensible, sensitive, serious, severe, touchy, vulnerable
Empfindlichkeit delicacy, heaviness, irritability, sensibility, sensitiveness, sensitivity, severity

Empfindung feeling, perception, sensation, sense, sentiment
emporarbeiten, sich work one's way up
emporkommen rise
Emporkömmling parvenue, upstart
empören disgust, enrage, exite, offend, rouse, scandalize, shock, stir
sich — gegen insurge, rebel against, revolt against, rise against
sich — über be disgusted at, resent at, be scandalized at, be shocked at
empörend disgusting, revolting, shocking, outrageous
Empörer insurgent, mutineer, rebel
empörerisch mutinous, rebellious
Empörung disgust, indignation, insurrection, mutiny, rebellion, resentment, revolt
Ende close, conclusion, death, end(ing), expiration, outcome, result, termination, upshot
enden break up, cease, close, (come to an) end, expire, finish, result, stop, terminate, wind up
End-
—ergebnis (—resultat) final result, upshot
endgültig conclusive, definite, definitive, final
Endgültigkeit finality
endlich final, last, ultimate
endlos boundless, endless, infinite, perpetual
End-
—lösung final solution
—termin dies ad quem, final (latest) date, termination date
—ursache final cause
—urteil final decision (decree)
—verfügung final order
—ziel (-zweck) end, final aim (purpose), ultimate target
Energie drive, energy, force, power, push, vigour
energisch energetic, enterprising, forceful, powerful, strong
— vorgehen take a strong line
eng close, firm, intimate, narrow, small, tide
Engagement commitment, employment, engagement
engagieren employ, engage, hire, take in (on)
—, sich bind oneself, commit oneself, engage in
Enge
in die — treiben (drive into a) corner, nonplus, stalemate
Engpaß bottleneck, defile, notch, pass
en gros wholesale
Engrosgeschäft (—handel) wholesale business (trade)
Engroshändler wholesale dealer, wholesaler
Enquete (official) inquiry, investigation
entäußern, sich discard, dispose of, divest of, get rid of, give up, part with, resign
Entäußerung discarding, divesting, getting rid of, giving up, parting with
entbehren lack, miss, spare, be void of, want
entbehrlich dispensable, unnecessary, superfluous
entbinden absolve from, disengage, dispense from, excuse from, exonerate from, release from, relieve from, set free, suspend
Entbindung confinement, dispensation, exemption, exoneration, release, relief
entblößen denude, deprive of, dismantle, divest of, strip of, uncover
Entblößung denudation, deprivation
entdecken ascertain, descry, detect, disclose, discover, expose, find out, pick up, recognize, reveal, spot
Entdecker discoverer
Entdeckung detection, disclosure, discovery, exposure, finding (out), spotting
entehren deflower, degrade, disgrace, dishono(u)r, ravish
entehrend degrading, disgraceful, dishono(u)rable

Entehrung defloration, degradation, disgrace, dishono(u)r, ravishing
enteignen dispossess, expropriate, forjudge
Enteignung dispossession, expropriation, forjudgement
—sverfahren expropriation proceedings
enterben disinherit
Enterbung disinheritance
entfallen cease, drop out, be dropped, escape, slip from
— auf be apportioned to, fall upon, fall to the share of
entfalten develop, display, evolve, exhibit, reveal, unfold
Entfaltung development, display, unfolding
entfernen dismiss, do away with, put aside, remove, strike out, take away (out), withdraw
—, sich absent oneself, draw away, leave, remove oneself, retire, withdraw
entfernt distant, remote
— verwandt distantly related
—er Verwandter distant relative
Entfernung departure, deviation, discharge, dismissal, distance, range, removal, withdrawal
entflechten decartelize, decentralize, deconcentrate, disentangle
Entflechtung decartelization, decentralization, deconcentration, disentanglement
entfremden alienate, estrange
Entfremdung alienation, estrangement
entführen abduct, carry off, elope with, kidnap
Entführer abductor, kidnapper
Entführung abduction, elopement, kidnapping
entgegen adversely to, against, contrary to, in the face of, in opposition to
entgegen
—arbeiten counteract, counterplot, counterwork, oppose, work against
—bringen grant, meet with, offer, show
—gehen approach, confront, face
— —, dem Ende come to an end, draw to a close
—gesetzt antagonistic, contrary, opposed, opposite
—halten confront with
— —, die Hand hold out (extend) one's hand to
—handeln act against (in opposition to), contravene, infringe
Entgegenkommen concession, cooperation, courtesy, obligingness
— zeigen make advances (compromises)
entgegen
—kommen comply with, compromise, cooperate, be obliging (accommodating), meet
— —, auf halbem Weg meet a person half-way
—kommend accommodating, compliant, cooperative, obliging
— —erweise accommodatingly, obligingly, in an obliging manner (way)
—setzen contrast with, meet, object, oppose, put up
—stehen bar, conflict, contradict, controvert, be opposed to, preclude, prevent, stand in the way
—stehend conflicting, contrary, contradictory
—treten confront, contradict, counter, face, meet, oppose
—wirken antagonize, counter (act), oppose, work against
entgegnen answer, make a replication, rejoin, reply, respond, retort, return
Entgegnung answer, rejoinder, replication, reply, retort
entgehen avoid, elude, escape, evade, fail, get off, miss, slip away
Entgelt compensation, consideration, equivalent, indemnification, payment, recompense, remuneration, reward
—, als in return
—, gegen against consideration, subject to payment, for reward
—, ohne free of (without) charges, gratis, gratuitously

entgelten compensate, indemnify, pay for, suffer for
entgeltlich against (for) consideration (payment), onerous
un— free of (without) charges, gratis, gratuitous
entgleisen fail, make a faux pas (slip)
Entgleisung faux pas, lapse, slip
enthalten comprehend, comprise, contain, cover, embody, hold, include
— sein in be included in
—, sich abstain from, forbear, refrain from
—, sich der Stimme abstain from voting
enthaltsam abstemious, abstinent, continent, temperate
Enthaltsamkeit abstemiousness, abstinence, continence, temperance
Enthaltung abstention, forbearance, refraining from
Stimm— abstention (from voting)
enthaupten behead, decapitate
Enthauptung beheading, decapitation
entheben dismiss, dispense, excuse, exempt, free, oust, release, relieve, remove, suspend
Enthebung deposition, discharge, dismissal, exemption, release, relief, removal, suspension
entheiligen desecrate, profane
Entheiligung desecration, profanation
enthüllen bring to light, disclose, divulge, expose, reveal, uncover, unveil
Enthüllung disclosure, discovery, exposure, revelation, uncovering, unveiling
entjungfern deflower, ravish
Entjungferung defloration
entkartellisieren decartelize
Entkartellisierung decartelization
entkleiden divest, strip of
Entkommen escape, get-away
entkommen break loose, escape, flee, get (run) away
entkräften annul, debilitate, exhaust, invalidate, nullify, refute, weaken
Entkräftung debilitation, exhaustion, invalidation, nullification, refutal, refutation, weakening
entlarven expose (for), unmask
Entlarvung exposure, unmasking
entlassen disband, discharge, dismiss, fire, oust, part with, pay out, pension off, release, remove, retire, sack, set free, suspend
Entlassung cashierment, disbandment, discharge, dismissal, release, removal, retirement
Entlassungs-
—befehl order of release
—bescheid notice of dismissal
—gesuch (—schreiben) petition for release, (letter of) resignation
—papiere discharge papers
—schein certificate of discharge (release)
—zeugnis certificate of discharge, testimonial
entlasten clear, credit (for), discharge, disencumber, exculpate, exonerate, release, relieve, unburden
entlastend exculpatory, exonerating(ive)
—es Beweismaterial evidence for the defenc(s)e
Entlastung credit, discharge, disencumbering, exculpation, exoneration, release, relief
Entlastungs-
—beschluß (—verfügung) order of discharge
—beweis evidence for the defenc(s)e, exculpatory (exonerating) evidence
—klausel exoneration (relieving) clause
—material evidence (documents) for the defenc(s)e
—zeuge witness for the defenc(s)e
entlaufen elope, escape, run away
entledigen, sich acquit oneself of, carry out, discharge, execute, perform
entlegen distant, remote

Entlegenheit distance, remoteness
entlehnen (entleihen) borrow from
Entlehner borrower
Entlehnung borrowing
entleiben, sich commit suicide
entloben break off an engagement
Entlobung disengagement
entlohnen compensate, pay (off), remunerate
Entlohnung compensation, consideration, pay, payment, remuneration
entmachten deprive of power
Entmachtung deprivation of power
entmannen castrate, emasculate, unman
Entmannung castration, emasculation
entmündigen incapacitate, place under guardianship, put under tutelage
entmündigt (legally) incapacitated, under restraint
Entmündigter tutelee, incapacitated person
Entmündigung (legal) incapacitation
entmutigen discourage, dishearten
Entmutigung discouragement, disheartenment
Entnahme drawing, taking out, withdrawal
entnehmen draw, learn from, quote from, remove, take out (from), withdraw
Entnehmer drawer, taker
entrechten deprive of rights, disfranchise
Entrechtung deprivation of rights, disfranchisement
entrichten discharge, pay (off)
Entrichtung discharge, payment
entrinnen elude, escape (from), evade
entrüsten anger, enrage, exasperate, incense, infuriate, make angry, pique, provoke, scandalize
entrüstet
— **sein** be angry about (at, with), be indignant at, be outraged at, be scandalized at, be shocked at
Entrüstung anger, exasperation, indignation, resentment
entsagen abandon, abdicate, abjure, abstain, desist from, disclaim, discontinue, dispose of, forsake, give up, refrain from, relinquish, renounce, resign, waive
Entsagung abandonment, abdication, abjuration, abnegation, relinquishment, renunciation, resignation, restraint
entsagungsvoll full of resignation, resigned
entschädigen compensate, indemnify, make good, recompense, recoup, redeem, reimburse, repair, repay, remunerate
Entschädigung allowance, compensation, consideration, damages, indemnification, indemnity, recoupment, reimbursement, remuneration, reparation
—, **gegen** for a compensation (consideration)
—, **Klage auf** action for damages, damage suit
— **verlangen** claim compensation (damages)
Entschädigungs-
—**anspruch** claim for compensation (damages)
—**antrag** action for damages
—**betrag** amount of compensation (damages), indemnity
—**gesetz** compensation law
—**kasse** indemnity fund
entschädigungspflichtig liable to compensation (damages)
Entschädigungs-
—**summe** compensation, damages, indemnity
—**verfahren** compensation proceedings
—**zahlung** payment for compensation (damages)
Entscheid award, decision, decree, finding, order, ruling, verdict
entscheiden adjudge, arbitrate, decide, decree, determine, judge, order, resolve, rule

— **über** pass sentence (judgement) on
entscheidend conclusive, critical, crucial, deciding, decisive, definite, definitive, essential, final
Entscheidung decision, decree, determination, finding, judgement, resolution, ruling, sentence, verdict
— **herbeiführen** bring about a decision
— **treffen** take a decision, decide
Entscheidungs-
—befugnis competence, jurisdiction
—freiheit discretion
—grund decisive factor
—gründe arguments, grounds (reasons) of judgement
—sammlung case book, law reports, summary of leading cases and decisions
entscheidungsreif ready (ripe) for judgement
entscheidungsvoll critical, crucial, decisive, fateful
entschieden clear, decided, definite, determined, distinct, firm, peremptory, resolute, steadfast, unquestionable
—er Gegner declared (unyielding) adversary (enemy)
Entschiedenheit decisiveness, definiteness, determination, firmness, peremptoriness, resoluteness, resolution
—, mit (aller) categorically, decidedly, peremptorily, resolutely
entschließen (sich) decide, determine, make up one's mind, resolve
sich — für decide for (in favo[u]r of)
Entschließung decision, determination, order, resolution, resolve, ruling
—sentwurf draft resolution
entschlossen decided, determined, energetic, resolute, resolved, steadfast
Entschlossenheit determination, energy, firmness, resoluteness, resolution
Entschluß decision, determination, resolution, resolve
— **fassen** decide (determine) (resolve) on
zu einem — kommen arrive at (come to) a decision (determination, decide (determine) (resolve) on
entschlußfassend decision-making
Entschluß-
—freiheit free determination, freedom of decision
—kraft determination, initiative, strength of purpose, resolution
— **— beweisen** show initiative
entschlüsseln decipher, decode
Entschlüsselung deciphering, decoding
entschuldbar excusable, pardonable
Entschuldbarkeit pardonableness
entschulden disencumber
entschuldigen apologize for, excuse, justify, pardon
Entschuldigung apology, excuse
Entschuldigungs-
—grund excuse
—schreiben (—brief) letter of apology (excuse), written apology
Entschuldung disencumbrance
—sverfahren debtor relief proceedings
Entsetzen dismay, fright, horror, terror
entsetzen dismiss, displace, dispossess, eject, evict, frighten, oust, relieve, remove, shock, suspend
entsetzlich disastrous, dreadful, frightful, horrible, shocking, terrible
Entsetzlichkeit atrocity, dreadfulness, frightfulness, terribleness
entsetzt sein über be frightened (horrified) at
Entsetzung dismissal, dispossession, ejection, eviction, ouster, relief, removal, suspension
entsichern unblock, unlock, set out of operation
entsiegeln unseal
entspannen ease, relax, release, relieve, slacken

Entspannung relaxation, release
entsprechen answer (to), be in accordance with, coincide with, comply with, correspond to, grant, meet
entsprechend according to, adequate, analogical, analogous, answerable, appropriate, commensurate, in conformity with, corresponding, equivalent, proportional, proportionate, respective, suitable
entstaatlichen denationalize, disestablish
Entstaatlichung denationalization, disestablishment
entstammen arise from, be born of, derive from, be due to, be native from, originate from, result from
entstehen arise, come into being, emerge, originate from
Entstehung birth, emergence, formation, origin, rise
Entstehungs-
—geschichte genesis
—lehre genetics
entstellen deform, disfigure, distort, misinterpret, misrepresent, pervert
Entstellung deformation, disfiguration, distortion, misinterpretation, misrepresentation, perversion
entthronen depose, dethrone
Entthronung deposition, dethronement
entvölkern depopulate, dispeople, unpeople
entvölkert depopulated, deserted
Entvölkerung depopulation
entwaffnen disarm
entwaffnend disarming
entwaffnet disarmed
Entwaffnung disarmament, disarming
entweder ... oder either ... or
entweichen abscond, elude, escape, evade
entwenden abstract, misappropriate, pilfer, purloin, steal
Entwendung abstraction, misappropriation, pilferage, purloining, stealing, theft
entwerfen chart, design, draft, draw up, frame, lay out, outline, plan, project, sketch
entwerten cancel, demonetize, depreciate, devaluate, devalue, obliterate, reduce in value, withdraw
Entwertung cancellation, demonetization, depreciation, devaluation, decline (reduction) in value, obliteration, withdrawal
Entwertungsklausel depreciation clause
entwickeln develop, display, elaborate, evolve, form, grow up, set forth, unfold, work out
Entwicklung development, elaboration, evolution, formation, growth, unfolding, working out
entwicklungsfähig capable of development, developable, promissing
entwischen elude, escape, evade, steal away
Entwicklungs-
—gang course of development (evolution)
—grad degree of development
—tendenz (—trend) tendency (trend) of development
entwürdigen abase, degrade, disgrace, dishono(u)r
entwürdigend degrading, disgraceful
Entwürdigung abasement, degradation, derogation, disgrace
Entwurf blueprint, copy, design, draft, drawing, model, outline, plan, project, scheme, sketch
entziehen cancel, deprive of, dispossess, divest of, forbid, evict, exclude from, oust, revoke, rule out, suspend, strip of, take away from, withdraw from
entziehen
—, Staatsangehörigkeit denaturalize
—, Wahlrecht disfranchise
—, sich elude, evade, get off
sich der Beurteilung — be beyond judgement
sich einer Gefahr — escape a danger

sich dem Gericht — flee from justice
sich einer Pflicht — evade (shirk) a duty
Entziehung deprivation, dispossession, eviction, forfeiture, oust, removal, revocation, suspension, taking away, withdrawal
— der bürgerlichen Ehrenrechte civil degradation, deprivation of civil rights
— der Staatsangehörigkeit denaturalization, expatriation
— des Wahlrechts disfranchisement
entzifferbar decipherable
entziffern decipher, decode
Entzifferung deciphering, decoding
Entzug s. Entziehung
Epoche age, epoch, era, period
— machen make (mark) an epoch
Erachten consideration, judgement, opinion, view
erachten consider, deem, esteem, hold, judge, regard as, think
Erb
—anfall inheritance, legacy
—anlage hereditary (innate) disposition
—anspruch hereditary title
—anteil hereditary share, portion (share) of inheritance
—antritt assumption of succession
—auseinandersetzung conflict of heirs
—ausschlagung renunciation of inheritance
—ausschluß exclusion from inheritance
—baurecht hereditary building right
erbberechtigt having a hereditary title, inheritable
Erb-
—berechtigter heir
—berechtigung right of inheritance (succession)
—besitz hereditary possession
Erbe heir, inheritor, legate, successor (in right, in title)
Mit— co-heir
—, alleiniger sole (universal) heir
—, gesetzlicher (gesetzmäßiger) (rechtmäßiger) heir-at-law, lawful (legal, statutory) heir, heir apparent
—, mutmaßlicher heir presumptive
Erbe estate, heirdom, heirship, hereditament, heritage, inheritance, legacy
—, väterliches patrimony
— antreten enter into heritage
erbeigen inherited, possessed by inheritance
Erbeinsetzung appointment (institution) of heirs, entailment, hereditary appointment
erben be (fall) heir to, inherit, succeed to
—, Geld come in for money
—, Vermögen come (drop, step) into fortune
Erbengemeinschaft community of heirs
erbenlos heirless
erbfähig capable of inheriting (succeeding), inheritable
Erb
—fähigkeit capability of inheriting
—fehler hereditary defect
—feind sworn enemy
—folge entail, hereditary succession, succession of inheritance
— —krieg war of succession
— —ordnung order of succession
— —recht hereditary right (title), law (right) of inheritance (succession)
—gut estate, heritage, inheritance
—hof hereditary farm
erbieten, sich offer, volunteer
Erbin heiress, inheritrix
Mit— co-heiress
erbitten ask for, beg for, request, solicit
Erb-
—krankheit hereditary disease
—lasser bequeather, devisor, legator, testator
—lasserin testatrix
—lehn entail

erblich hereditable, hereditary, heritable, inheritable
Erblichkeit hereditability, hereditariness, heritability
Erb-
—linie line of succession
—masse assets, estate, heritage
—pacht hereditary lease (tenure)
—pächter hereditary tenant
erbrechen break (open), unseal
Erbrecht law (right) of inheritance (succession), hereditary right (title)
erbringen, Beiweis furnish (produce) evidence, offer proof
Erbschaft estate, heirdom, heirship, hereditament, heritage, inheritance, legacy
Mit— co-inheritance
Erbschafts-
—anspruch claim to inheritance, hereditary title
—klage (—prozeß) inheritance action
—masse estate
—steuer death (legacy) (succession) duty, inheritance tax
Erb-
—schein certificate of inheritance, heir's certificate
—schleicher legacy hunter
—stück heirloom
—teil portion (share) of inheritance, hereditary portion
— —, väterliches patrimony
—teilung division of inheritance
erbunfähig incapable of inheriting (succeeding)
Erbunfähigkeit incapacity of inheriting (succeeding)
erbunwürdig unworthy of inheritance
Erbunwürdigkeit unworthiness of inheritance
Erb
—vergleich settlement of inheritance
—vertrag inheritance (testamentary) contract
—vertretung substitution of an heir
—verzicht waiver of hereditary titles, renunciation of inheritance
erdenken conceive, devise, invent, think out
erdenklich conceivable, imaginable, possible
erdolchen poniard, stab
erdreisten, sich dare, presume, venture
erdrosseln gar(r)otte, strangle, throttle
Erdrosselung gar(r)otte, strangulation, throttling
erdrückend overwhelming
—es Beweismaterial cumulative (damning) evidence
erdulden endure, suffer
Erduldung endurance, sufferance
ereignen, sich happen, occur, take place
Ereignis affair, event, happening, incident, occurrence
—, zufälliges coincidence, contingency
ererben inherit
erfahren come to know, experience, go through, hear, learn, meet with, suffer, undergo, understand
erfahren experienced, expert, practised, skilful, skilled, versed
— sein be expert at (in), be familiar with, be versed in
un- unexperienced, unskilled, unversed
— — sein lack experience
Erfahrenheit experience, skilfulness, skill
Erfahrung experience, practice
aus — from (by) experience
in — bringen ascertain, learn
— haben have experience
keine — haben lack experience
—en machen experience
—saustausch exchange of experiences
erfahrungsgemäß according to (by) experience, empiric(al)
erfassen comprehend, comprise, cover, include, list, record, register, size
Erfassung coverage, listing, recording, registration, seizure
—, steuerliche taxation
erfinden devise, invent
Erfinder inventor

Erfinderin inventress
erfinderisch constructive, creative, imaginative, ingenious, inventive
Erfindung device, invention
Erfolg achievement, consequence, effect, end, hit, issue, outcome, result, success
erfolgen arise, come on, ensue, follow, happen, occur, take place
erfolglos abortive, fruitless, ineffective, ineffectual, unsuccessful, vain
Erfolglosigkeit failure, ineffectiveness
erfolgreich effective, successful
erfolgversprechend hopeful, promising
erforderlich essential, imperative, indispensable, necessary, required, requisite
erforderlichenfalls if necessary (required), in case of need
erfordern call for, demand, exact, necessitate, need, require, take, want
Erfordernis demand, exigence(cy), necessity, qualification, requirement, (pre)requisite
erforschen examine into, explore, inquire into, investigate, penetrate, research, search into (out), sound
Erforscher explorer, investigator
Erforschung examination, exploration, inquiry, investigation, research, sounding
erfragen ascertain, inquire
erfüllen accomplish, answer, carry out, come up to, complete, comply with, discharge, execute, fulfil, keep, meet, perform, realize, satisfy, serve
—, sich be fulfilled (realized), come true, materialize
—, sich nicht fail
Erfüllung accomplishment, completion, compliance, discharge, fulfilment, performance, realization
Erfüllungs-
—gehilfe agent, servant
—klage action (suit) for contractual performance
—ort place of performance
—tag settling day
—zeit time of performance
ergänzen complement, complete, fill up, make up, replace, replenish, substitute, supplement
ergänzend additional, complementary, subsidiary, supplemental, supplementary
Ergänzung complement, completion, making up, replacement, replenishment, restoration, supplement(ation)
Ergänzungs-
—antrag application (motion) for amendment, supplement bill
—anweisungen supplementary regulations
—bestimmungen supplementary provisions
ergänzungsfähig amendable
Ergänzungs-
—gesetz supplemental bill (act)
—statut by-statute
—steuer additional (supplementary) tax
—vertrag supplementary agreement
—vorschlag amendment
—wahl by-election
ergattern get hold of, secure, snatch
ergaunern obtain by false pretenses, receive by unlawful practices, swindle (out of)
ergeben amount to, produce, recoup, result in, total, yield
—, sich arise, capitulate, emerge, ensue, follow, rise, surrender
sich — aus accrue (arise) (result) from
sich — in acquiesce in, put up with, resign to, submit to
ergeben addicted to, attached to, devoted to, resigned to
Ergebenheit attachment, devotion, submission
Ergebnis consequence, effect, finding, issue, outcome, result, upshot
—, ohne (ergebnislos) fruitless, ineffective, ineffectual, resultless, unsuccessful, without result

Ergebnislosigkeit failure, fruitlessness, futility, ineffectiveness, uselessness
ergebnisreich fructuous, fruitful, resultful
Ergebung capitulation, resignation, submission, surrender
ergehen be issued (passed) (published)
— lassen issue, pass, pronounce
sich — in indulge in
über sich — lassen acquiesce in, bear, endure, put up with, submit, suffer, undergo
ergiebig abundant, fertile, fructuous, fruitful, lucrative, (out) paying, productive, profitable, remunerative, rich, yielding
Ergiebigkeit abundance, fertility, fruitfulness, lucrativeness, productiveness, productivity, richness
ergreifen adopt, affect, apprehend, arrest, assume, catch, get (lay) hold of, grasp, grip, move, pick up, seize, take up (over), thrill, touch
ergreifend affecting, impressive, moving, pathetic, stirring, thrilling, touching
Ergreifung apprehension, arrestment, assumption, capture, picking up, seizure, taking
Ergriffenheit emotion
erhaben
— sein über be above (beyond)
Erhalt obtaining, receipt
erhalten be awarded, come in for, continue, fetch, keep, maintain, obtain, preserve, receive, retain, secure, support, sustain, uphold
Erhalter maintainer, preserver, supporter
erhältlich available, obtainable, procurable
nicht — non-obtainable, unavailable
Erhaltung conservation, maintenance, preservation, retention, support, sustenance, upkeep
—skosten cost of maintenance
erhängen (sich) hang (oneself)
erhärten affirm, confirm, corroborate, harden, substantiate
Erhärtung confirmation, corroboration, substantiation
erhebbar collectible
erheben ascertain, bring, charge, collect, elevate, enter, exalt, hear, levy, lift, lodge, make, impose, investigate, put forward (in), present, raise, record, set up, take
—, sich get up, revolt, rise, stand up against
erheblich considerable, grave, heavy, important, large, material, relevant, serious, significant, weighty
erheblich
un- irrelevant, unimportant
Erheblichkeit consequence, considerableness, importance, relevance, weight(iness)
Erhebung collection, elevation, entering, exaltation, filing, imposition, inquiry, insurrection, investigation, levy, lodging, mutiny, promotion, raising, rebellion, rising, revolt, upheaval
erhellen clarify, clear up, elucidate, illuminate, light up, shed light upon
erhöhen advance, enhance, enlarge, improve, increase, raise
Erhöhung advance, enhancement, enlargement, improvement, raising, rise
erholen, sich recover
Erholung recovery, recreation
erinnern recall to, remind of
—, sich remember
Erinnerung memory, recollection, remembrance, reminder, reminiscence
—en memoirs, reminiscences
—sschreiben reminder
erkennen adjudge, appreciate, decide, detect, discern, discover, find (out), identify, judge, perceive, realize, recognize
zu — geben indicate, show
erkenntlich grateful, perceptible, thankful
sich — zeigen acknowledge, appreciate, reciprocate for (with)

Erkenntlichkeit acknowledgement, gratefulness, gratitude, thankfulness
Erkenntnis comprehension, decision, judgement, knowledge, perception, realization, recognition, sentence
Erkennung comprehension, detection, identification, perception, realization, recognition
Erkennungs-
—dienst criminal identification department
—karte identity (identification) card
—marke identity (identification) disk (tag)
—wort catchword, password, test word, watchword
—zeichen distinctive (identification) mark
erklärbar explainable, explicable, interpretable
un- inexplicable
erklären declare, define, demonstrate, describe, enter, explain, expound, illustrate, interpret, specify
—d declaratory, explanatory, explicative
Erklärer commentator, declarant, expounder, interpreter
erklärlich accountable, explainable, explicable, evident, obvious
—erweise as a matter of course
erklärt avowed, declared, professed
Erklärung announcement, comment, declaration, definition, entry, explanation, interpretation, proclamation, profession, pronouncement, statement
—, eidesstattliche affidavit
erkunden explore, locate, reconnoitre, scout, search out, spot, spy out
erkundigen, sich ask, inquire (about, for), gather (seek) information, make inquiries (about, on)
Erkundigung information, inquiry
—en einholen s. erkundigen
— sbrief (—sschreiben) letter of inquiry
Erkundung exploration, location, reconnaissance, reconnoitre
erlangen achieve, acquire, attain (to), gain, get, obtain, procure, reach
Erlangung achievement, acquisition, attainment, getting, obtaining, procurement, reaching
Erlaß abatement, cancellation, decree, deduction, discharge, dispensation, edict, enactment, exemption, granting, issue, order, ordinance, promulgation, pronouncing, reduction, release, remission, rescript, writ
erlassen abate, cancel, decree, deduct, dispense, excuse, give, issue, order, pass, promulgate, pronounce, publish, put through, release
—, Gesetz enact
—, Schuld remit
—, Strafe pardon
erlauben admit, allow, authorize, permit, suffer, tolerate
Erlaubnis authorization, concession, consent, grant, leave, licenc(s)e, permission, permit
—erteilung grant of permission
—schein certificate, licenc(s)e, permit
erlaubt allowed, lawful, legal, permissible, permitted
un- illegal, inadmissible, not permitted, unlawful
erläutern annotate, clear up, comment, elucidate, exemplify, explain, expound, illustrate, interpret, make clear
—d elucidative, elucidatory, explanatory, illustrative
Erläuterung annotation, comment(ary), declaration, elucidation, exemplification, explanation, illustration, interpretation
mit —en versehen annotate
erleben experience, go (pass) through, meet with, see, witness
Erlebnis episode, event, experience, occurrence

erledigen adjust, answer, arrange, attend, comply with, deal with, dispose of, effect, execute, finish (off, with), get (go) through, handle, manage, settle
Erledigung answer, arrangement, attending, compliance, disposal, execution, finishing off, handling, management, settlement
erleichtern alleviate, deprive of, ease of, facilitate, lighten, relieve from
Erleichterung alleviation, ease, facilitation, facility, relief, respite
erleiden bear, endure, experience, incur, suffer, sustain, undergo
erliegen fall a victim to, succumb to, yield to
erlogen false, untrue
Erlös(e) proceeds, takings
erloschen expired, extinct, extinguished, lapsed
Erlöschen expiration, extinction, lapse
erlöschen be extinguished, become extinct, expire, lapse, terminate
erlösen deliver, redeem, release, rescue, save (from)
Erlöser deliverer, redeemer
Erlösung deliverance, release
ermächtigen authorize, empower, license
ermächtigt authorized, empowered, having authority
Ermächtigung authority, authorization, permission, permit, power, warrant
—sschreiben letter of authority
ermahnen admonish, exhort, expostulate, warn
ermahnend admonitory, (ex)hortative, (ex)hortatory, monitorial
Ermahner admonisher, monitor
Ermahnung admonition, exhortation, warning
ermangeln be short (void) of, fail, lack, want, be lacking (wanting) in
Ermangelung
in — von failing, in the absence of, in default of, in lack of, for want of
ermäßigen abate, cut (down), diminish, lower, reduce
Ermäßigung abatement, allowance, cut, decrease, lowering, reduction, remission, relief
Ermessen discretion, estimate, estimation, judgement
nach eigenem — at one's own discretion
ermessen calculate, compute, estimate, judge
Ermessens-
—entscheidung discretionary decision
—irrtum error of judgement
—mißbrauch abuse of discretion
—recht discretionary power
ermitteln ascertain, detect, determine, discover, establish, find (out), identify, inquire (about, into), investigate into, locate, trace
Ermittler investigator
Ermittlung ascertainment, calculation, computation, detection, determination, discovery, information, inquiry, investigation, research
—en facts, findings, inquiries, investigations
—en anstellen make inquiries (investigations) about
—en einleiten institute investigations
Ermittlungs-
—ausschuß fact-finding committee
—beamter investigator
—verfahren preliminary proceedings
ermöglichen enable, make (render) possible (feasible)
ermorden assassinate, murder
Ermordeter killed person, murderee
Ermordung assassination, murder
ermutigen countenance, encourage
—d encouraging
Ermutigung countenance, encouragement
ernähren keep, maintain, support

Ernährer bread-winner, maintainer, supporter
Ernährung food, maitenance, support
ernannt appointed, nominated
Ernannter appointee, nominee
ernennen appoint, constitute, designate, name, nominate
Ernenner nominator
Ernennung appointment, call, designation, nomination
Ernennungs-
—recht right of appointment (nomination)
—urkunde certificate (deed, letter) of appointment
erneuern prolong, refresh, renew, renovate, repair, repeat, restore, revive
Erneuerung prolongation, renewal, renovation, repair, repetition, restoration, revival
Erneuerungs-
—antrag petition for revival
—schein renewal coupon, talon
—vertrag renewal (revival) agreement
—wahl by-election
erneut fresh, new, renewed, repeated
—e Verhandlung rehearing
erniedrigen abase, degrade, humble, humiliate, lower, reduce
—, sich demean (degrade) (lower) oneself
Erniedrigung abasement, degradation, humiliation, lowering, reduction
Ernst gravity, importance, seriousness, severity, solemnity
ernst critical, earnest, genuine, grave, important, serious, severe, solemn, weighty
Ernstfall, im in case of emergency (need, war)
ernstgemeint meant in earnest, serious(ly meant)
ernsthaft earnest, genuine, grave, serious
Ernsthaftigkeit earnestness, seriousness
ernstlich earnest, genuine, serious
Eroberer conqueror
erobern acquire, capture, conquer, gain, take, win
Eroberung acquisition, capture, conquest, gain(ing)
—skrieg war of conquest
eröffnen communicate, dedicate, disclose, establish, inaugurate, institute, launch, notify, open, set up, start
Eröffnung beginning, communication, disclosure, establishment, inauguration, notification, opening, setting up
Eröffnungs-
—ansprache (—rede) inaugural (opening) address (speech)
—protokoll opening protocol
—sitzung initial meeting, opening session
erörtern argue, comment on, debate, discuss, examine, review
Erörterung argument, debate, discussion
erpressen blackmail, extort, squeeze
Erpresser blackmailer, extortioner, racketeer
—brief blackmailing letter
Erpressung blackmail, extortion, racket, squeezing
—sversuch attempted blackmail (extortion)
erproben prove, test, try
erprobt approved, experienced, proved, tested, tried
Erprobung proof, test, trial
errechnen calculate, compute, work out
Errechnung calculation, computation
erregbar excitable, irritable, nervous
Erregbarkeit excitability, irritability, nervousness
erregen agitate, arouse, cause, excite
Erregung agitation, excitation, excitement
— öffentlichen Ärgernisses excitation of public scandal
erreichbar achievable, approachable, attainable, available, securable, within reach

un— out of reach, unattainable
erreichen achieve, arrive at, attain, catch, come up, draw up, get (to), obtain, reach
Erreichung accomplishment, achievement, attainment, reaching
erretten deliver, rescue, save
Erretter deliverer, rescuer, saviour
Errettung deliverance, rescue, salvation, saving
errichten build, constitute, construct, create, draw up, erect, establish, found, open, raise, set up
Errichtung building, construction, erection, establishment, foundation, institution
erringen achieve, acquire, gain, secure, win
Erringung achievement, acquisition, gaining, winning
Errungenschaft accomplishment, achievement, acquisition, attainment, improvement
Ersatz alternative, amends, compensation, damages, equivalent, indemnification, indemnity, recompense, redress, reimbursement, reparation, replacement, restitution, substitute, substitution, surrogate
als — für as compensation for, by way of compensation, in exchange (return) for, in substitution of
Ersatz-
—anspruch claim for compensation (damages)
—erbe substituted (representative) heir
—forderung compensation claim
—leistung compensation, indemnification, indemnity
—lieferung replacement
—mann substitute
—pfand collateral
ersatzpflichtig liable to compensation (damages)
—wahl by-election
ersatzweise in default of, as a substitute, by way of substitution
Erscheinen appearance, publication
—, persönliches appearance in person, personal appearance
Nicht- absence, default, nonappearance
erscheinen appear (before, in), be issued (published), come along (forth, forward, out), emerge, turn up
nicht — be absent, default
Erscheinung appearance, aspect, attendance, manifestation, phenomenon, publication, spectacle, vision
Erscheinungs-
—jahr year of publication
—tag day of issue (publication)
Erschienener appearer, party (person) present
erschießen shoot
Erschießung shooting
erschlagen kill, slay
Erschlagung slaying
erschleichen obtain surreptitiously
—, Gunst creep (insinuate) into the favo(u)r of, ingratiate oneself with
erschlichen surreptitious
erschließbar developable
erschließen develop, disclose, open (up), reveal, unfold
Erschließung development, disclosure, opening (up)
erschöpfen deplete, drain, exhaust
—d complete, comprehensive, exhaustive
Erschöpfung depletion, drain, exhaustion
erschrecken alarm, dismay, frighten, shock, startle
—, sich be alarmed (frightened) (startled)
erschreckend alarming, startling, terrible
erschüttern agitate, shake, shock, stagger, thrill
—d impressive, moving
Erschütterung agitation, convulsion, emotion, shock, thrill
erschweren aggravate, complicate, embarrass, handicap, impede, render difficult

—d aggravating, complicating
—e Umstände aggravating circumstances
Erschwerung aggravation, complication, embarrassment, handicap, impediment
erschwindeln obtain by swindling, swindle out of
ersetzbar (-lich) reparable, replaceable, retrievable
ersetzen compensate, cover, fill, make amends for, recompense, recoup, recover, refund, reimburse, repair, repay, replace, restore, restitute, retrieve, substitute, supersede
Ersetzung compensation, displacement, reimbursement, replacement, substitution, supersession
ersichtlich clear, evident, obvious
ersinnen contrive, devise, excogitate, invent, think out
ersitzen acquire by prescription, usucapt
Ersitzung prescription, usucaption
—sfrist prescriptive limitation, usucaption period
ersparen save, spare
Ersparnis(se) economy(ies), saving(s)
erstatten compensate, give, make, recompense, refund, reimburse, render, repay, restitute, restore, return
—, Anzeige denounce, inform against, lay (prefer) an information against
—, Bericht give (render) an account of, give (make) a report of, report on
Erstattung compensation, refund, reimbursement, remission, repayment, restitution, return
— eine Anzeige information
Erstattungs-
—anspruch claim for reimbursement
—pflicht reimbursement obligation, restitutional liability
—verfahren restitution proceedings
erstehen acquire, buy, purchase
Ersteher buyer, purchaser
Erstehung acquisition, purchase
Ersteigerer auction buyer, highest bidder, purchaser
ersteigern buy (purchase) at (in) auction
Ersteigerung purchase at (by, in) auction
erstellen build, construct, erect, put (set) up, institute
Erstellung construction, erection, putting up
erstgeboren first-born
Erstgebot first bid
Erstgeburt first-born (child)
Erstgeburt(srecht) primogeniture, priority of birth
erstklassig first-class, first-rate, prime
erstrangig first(-rate)
erstrecken
sich — auf apply to, concern, cover, range to, refer to, relate to, spread over
Ersuchen demand, petition, request, solicitation
auf — von at (on) the request of
ersuchen ask, call upon, demand, request, solicit
ertappen catch, detect, seize, surprise
—, auf frischer Tat catch in the (very) act, take a person redhanded
erteilen allocate, bestow, confer, furnish, give, grant, place
Erteilung allocation, conferring, giving, grant(ing), placing
—sbeschluß granting order
Ertrag earnings, gain(ings), output, proceeds, produce, profit, receipts, result, return, revenue, yield
ertragbringend (-fähig, -reich) lucrative, productive, profitable
ertraglos nonproductive, unproductive, unprofitable
Ertraglosigkeit unproductivity
Ertrags-
—grenze limit of productiveness, profit margin
—lage earnings, returns

—rechnung profit and loss account
ertragen bear, endure, put up with, stand, suffer, tolerate
erträglich bearable, endurable, passable, supportable, tolerable
Ertragfähigkeit productiveness, productivity
ertränken (sich) drown (oneself)
Ertrinken, Tod durch death by drowning
ertrinken drown, be (get) drowned
Ertrinkender drowning man (person)
Ertrunkener drowned man (person)
erübrigen save, spare
—, sich be not necessary, be useless
erwachsen accrue, arise, develop, incur, involve, result
— sein be grown-up
Erwachsener adult, grown-up
erwägen consider, contemplate, deliberate, examine, take into account (consideration), think over, weigh
Erwägung consideration, deliberation, reflection
in — ziehen take into consideration
erwähnen mention, refer to
—swert worth mentioning, worthy of note
Erwähnung mention, reference
erwarten anticipate, await, expect, look for(ward), wait for
Erwartung anticipation, expectance (cy), expectation, hope
erweisen bestow, do, establish, prove, render, show, turn out to be
—, sich als wahr be verified, come true, prove (to be) true, turn out to be true
erweislich demonstrable, proveable
erweitern aggrandize, dilate, enlarge, expand, extend, improve, widen
Erweiterung aggrandizement, dilation, enlargement, expansion, extension, improvement, increase, widening
erweiterungsfähig expansible, expansive
Erwerb acquisition, earnings, gain, income, living, profit, purchase
erwerben acquire, buy, earn, gain, make, purchase, secure, win
Erwerber acquirer, buyer, purchaser, transferee, vendee
erwerbs
—behindert disabled, incapacitated
—fähig capable of earning, fit for work
Erwerbsfähigkeit earning capacity, fitness
—genossenschaft cooperative society
—gesellschaft trading company (corporation)
erwerbslos out of work (employment), unemployed
Erwerbs
—loser unemployed
—losigkeit unemployment
—quelle source of income
—steuer profit tax
—tätigkeit productive activity
—titel transfer (title) deed
erwerbsunfähig disabled, incapable of earning, unfit for work
Erwerbs
—unfähigkeit disability, disablement, incapacity
—urkunde title deed
—zweig branch of industry (trade), line, profession
Erwerbung acquisition, purchase
erwidern answer, reciprocate, rejoin, reply, retort, return
Erwiderung answer, reciprocation, rejoinder, replication, reply, return, retort
erwiesen established, proved
erwiesenermaßen according to evidence, evidently, obviously, as proved, provedly
erwirken apply for, bring about, effect, obtain, petition for, procure (for), recover, take out
erwischen catch, detect, get hold of, surprise

erwürgen scrag, strangle, throttle
Erwürgung strangling, strangulation
erzählen give an account of, narrate, relate, report, tell
Erzählung account, narration, narrative, relation, report, story, tale
erzeugen bring forth, cause, generate, make, manufacture, originate, produce
Erzeuger maker, manufacturer, originator, producer
Erzeugnis creation, manufacture, produce, product
Erzeugung creation, generation, manufacture, origination, output, production
erziehen bring up, cultivate, educate, train, tutor
Erzieher educator, instructor, pedagogue, teacher, tutor
erzieherisch educational, educative, instructional, pedagogical
Erziehung bringing up, cultivation, education, instruction, manners, training
Erziehungs
—anstalt educational establishment (institution), reformatory
—berechtigter guardian
erzielen achieve, arrive at, attain, come to, get, obtain, reach, realize, secure
Erzielung achievement, attainment, realization
erzogen, gut well-bred, well-educated
—, schlecht ill-bred, ill-educated
erzwingbar enforceable
Erzwingbarkeit enforceability
erzwingen compel, enforce, exact, extort, force
Eskalationsklausel escalation clause
Eskorte convoy, escort
eskortieren escort
etablieren establish, found, set up, settle down, start
Etablierung establishment, settlement, setting up
Etat budget, estimates
—, außerordentlicher extraordinary budget
—, ordentlicher ordinary budget
—, aufstellen draw (make) up the budget
Etikett docket, label, tag, ticket
Etikette ceremony(ies), etiquette, formalities
etikettieren docket, label, tag, ticket
evakuieren evacuate, remove
Evakuierung evacuation
Eventual
—antrag secondary motion
—fall contingency
—forderung contingent claim
—haftung contingent liability
(—verbindlichkeit,
—verpflichtung)
Eventualität contingency, eventuality
eventuell contingent, eventual, possible, potential
evident clear, evident, manifest, obvious
Evidenz clearness, evidence, obviousness
exakt accurate, exact
Exaktheit accuracy, exactitude, exactness
Examen examination
  Schluß— final examination
  Staats— state examination
  Zulassung zum — admission to the examination
Examinant candidate, examinee
Examinator examiner
examinieren catechize, examine, question
exekutieren execute
Exekution execution
Exekutions
—befehl death warrant, execution order
—verfahren distress, execution
—verkauf forced sale
exekutiv executive
Exekutive executive
Exekutivgewalt executive power
Exekutivorgan law enforcement authority, executive body

Exempel example, instance
ein — statuieren make (set) an example
Exemplar copy, number, pattern, sample, set, specimen
exemplarisch by way of example, exemplary
exhumieren exhume
Exhumierung exhumation
Exil banishment, exile
ins — gehen go into exile
im — leben live in exile
ins — schicken banish, exile, send into exile
Exilregierung government(-)in(-) exile
Existenz existence, livelihood, living, subsistence
Existenz
—bedingungen living conditions
—berechtigung right to exist
existenzfähig capable to exist
Existenz
—grundlage basis of existence, livelihood
—kampf struggle for life (existence)
—lohn living (subsistence) wage
—minimum living wage, minimum of existence, subsistence minimum
existieren be (in existence), exist, live, subsist
exklusiv exclusive, select
exklusive excluding, exclusive, to the exclusion of
Exklusivität exclusiveness
Exkommunikation excommunication
exkommunizieren excommunicate
Exmission ejectment, eviction
exmittieren eject, evict
Expansion expansion
—spolitik expansionism, policy of expansion
expansiv expansive
expatriieren expatriate
Expatriierung denaturalization, expatriation
expedieren consign, despatch, dispatch, expedite, forward, send
Expedition consignment, dispatch, expedition, forwarding, sending
Experiment experiment
experimentell experimental
experimentieren experiment
Experte expert
Expertise expertise
explizieren explain
explizite explicitly
Export export(ation)
—abgabe export duty
—agent export agent
—artikel export article
—beschränkungen export restrictions
—bestimmungen export regulations
—deklaration export declaration (specification)
—erlaubnis (-bewilligung, -genehmigung) export permit (licence)
Exporteur exporter
Export
—handel export trade
—händler exporter, export trader
exportieren export
Export
—überschuß export surplus
—verbot export embargo
—zoll export duty
Expreß, per by express, by special delivery
—brief express (special-delivery) letter
—zustellung express (special) delivery
Expropriation expropriation
expropriieren expropriate
extern external
exterritorial ex(tra)territorial
Exterritorialität ex(tra)territoriality
extra additional, extra, in addition, special(ly)
Extrem extreme
extrem extreme
Extremismus extremism
exzerpieren excerpt, extract
Exzerpt excerpt, extract
Exzeß excess, outrage, riot, violation, violence

F

Fabrik factory, mill, plant, works
Fabrikant factory owner, maker, manufacturer, producer
Fabrikarbeiter (factory) hand, (industrial) labo(u)rer, (industrial) worker, workman
Fabrikat article, fabric, make, manufacture, product
Fabrikation fabrication, manufacture, production
Fabrikbesitz factory property
Fabrikbesitzer factory owner, manufacturer
Fabrikmarke brand, trademark,
fabrizieren fabricate, make, manufacture, produce
Fach business, branch, compartment, department, division, field, line, partition, profession, province, subject, trade
Fach
—arbeit expert (skilled) labo(u)r (work)
—arbeiter skilled (expert) worker, specialist
—ausbildung professional (special, technical) education (training)
—ausdruck technical term
—gebiet special field (branch), speciality
—kenner expert
—kenntnis expert (professional, special, technical) knowledge
—kräfte qualified personnel, skilled (trained) workers, specialists, technical staff
—kreise experts, specialists
in — —n among experts (specialists)
fachkundig competent, expert, specialized
fachlich professional, technical
Fachmann authority, expert, professional, specialist
fachmännisch competent, expert, professional, specialistic, specialized, technical
Fach
—schaft trade association
—sprache technical language (terms), terminology, nomenclature
—welt experts
—wissen expert (special, professional, technical) knowledge
fadenscheinig poor, sham, thin
fähig able, capable, competent, qualified
Fähigkeit ability, capability, capacity, competence, faculty, power, qualification
fahnden nach investigate, search for
Fahndung investigation, search
Fahndungs
—abteilung search department
—buch wanted persons file
—gesuch search warrant
—dienst (—stelle) (criminal) investigation service
Fahnenflucht desertion
fahnenflüchtig deserting
fahnenflüchtig werden desert (from)
Fahnenflüchtiger deserter
fahren drive
Fahrer driver
Fahrer
—flucht hit-and-run offence (driving)
— — begehen be a hit-and-run driver
Fahr
—erlaubnis driving licence
—geschwindigkeit speed
fahrlässig careless, negligent
—, grob grossly negligent, by gross negligence
Fahrlässigkeit carelessness, negligence
—, grobe gross negligence
— —sklausel negligence clause
Fahrnis goods and chattels, movables
—hypothek chattel mortgage
Fahrprüfung driving test
Faksimile facsimile
— herstellen (make a) facsimile
Fakten data, facts

faktisch actual, effective, de facto, factual, in fact, practical, real
Faktor element, factor
—, bestimmender determinant
Faktum fact
Faktur(a) bill, invoice
fakturieren bill, invoice
Fakultät faculty
—, juristische law faculty, faculty of law
fakultativ facultative, optional
Fakultativklausel optional clause
Fall affair, case, decline, fall, matter
auf jeden — at any rate, in any case (event)
auf keinen — by no means, on no account
im —e in case, in the event of
im anderen —e otherwise
Fall, zu — bringen defeat, ruin, wreck
Fallbeil guillotine
Falle deadfall, trap
in die — gehen fall (walk) into (be caught by) the trap
eine — stellen lay (set) a trap for
fallen be defeated (killed), decline, decrease, drop, fall
—lassen discontinue, drop, waive, withdraw
fällen deliver, give, make, pass, pronounce
fällig collectible, due, mature, payable
längst — (über-) overdue
— sein be due
— werden become (fall, grow) due, expire, be mature
Fälligkeit due date, expiration, maturity
—sdatum (—stermin) (—stag) due date, date (day) of maturity
Fallmethode case method
falls in case, in the event of (that)
falls nicht unless
Fallsammlung table of cases
Fallstricke pitfalls
Fallstudium case study
falsch bogus, counterfeit, deceptive, erroneous, fake, false, falsified, faulty, feigned, forged, fraudulent, incorrect, sham, spurious, wrong
Falschbeurteilung misjudgement
fälschen adulterate, counterfeit, fabricate, fake, falsify, forge
Fälscher adulterator, counterfeiter, fabricator, faker, falsifier, forger
fälschlich
(—erweise) deceitfully, erroneous(ly), falsely, fraudulently, incorrect(ly), by mistake, wrong(ly)
Falsch
—geld counterfeit (forged) money
—heit deceit, duplicity, falseness, falsity
—meldung bogus message, false news (report)
—münzer (false) coiner, counterfeiter, forger
—münzerei counterfeiting, false coining
Fälschung adulteration, counterfeit(ing), fabrication, fake, faking, falsification, forgery, forging, sham
Falsifikat counterfeit, fake, falsification, forgery, sham
Familie family
Familien
—angehöriger (-mitglied) member of the family
—angelegenheit family affair
—beihilfe family allowance
(—unterstützung,
—zulage)
—name family name, surname
—oberhaupt head of the family
—rat family council
—recht family law
—stand family (marital) status
fassen apprehend, arrest, catch, comprehend, draft, draw up, express, grasp, include, seize, understand, word
Fassung composure, countenance, draft, tenor, text, version, wording
—svermögen capacity, comprehensive faculty

faul bad, foul, idle, lame, lazy, shady, unfair, unreliable, unsound, worthless
—e Ausrede lame (poor, thin) excuse
Faulheit badness, idleness, laziness, shadiness, unsoundness
Faust, auf eigene — handeln act on one's own (account)
Faustpfand lien, pawn, pledge
—gläubiger lien holder, lienor, pawnee, pawnholder, pledge holder, pledgee
Faust
—recht fist law, club law, law of the jungle
—regel rule of thumb
Fehde feud, quarrel
—brief challenge
—handschuh gauntlet, gage, glove
— — aufnehmen take up the gauntlet
— — hinwerfen throw down the gauntlet to
Fehlanzeige negative report, nil return
fehlbar fallible
Fehlbarkeit fallibility
Fehlbetrag deficiency, deficit, difference, shortage
Fehlen absence, lack, nonappearance, nonattendance, want
fehlen be absent, be lacking, be missing, be short of, be wanting, fail, lack, miss
Fehler defect, error, fault, mistake
—breite error band
fehlerfrei (—los) correct, faultless, flawless, perfect
Fehlerfreiheit (—losigkeit) faultlessness, flawlessness, perfection
Fehlergrenze margin of error, tolerance
fehlerhaft defective, deficient, faulty, incorrect
Fehlerhaftigkeit defectiveness, faultiness
Fehlerquelle source of error (mistake)
Fehlgeburt miscarriage
Fehlgewicht short weight, underweight
fehlleiten miscarry, misdirect, mislead
Fehlmenge deficiency, deficit, shortage
Fehlschlag failure, miscarriage, setback
fehlschlagen fail, fall flat, go wrong, miscarry, prove a failure
Fehlschluß false conclusion (reasoning)
Fehlspruch (-urteil) error of judgement, erroneous (false) judgement, judicial error, miscarriage of justice, misjudgement
Fehltritt false step, fault, (moral) lapse, offence, slip, trip
feierlich ceremonial, ceremonious, festive, formal, impressive, solemn
— begehen (feiern) celebrate, solemnize
Feierlichkeit ceremoniousness, ceremony(ies), impressiveness, solemnity
Feiertag holiday
—, gesetzlicher legal (official, public) holiday
National— national holiday
Feind adversary, antagonist, enemy, opponent
feindlich adverse, antigonistic, enemy, hostile, inimical, unfriendly
Feindschaft animosity, antagonism, aversion, enmity, hatred, hostility
feindschaftlich hostile, unfriendly
feindselig adverse, hostile, malevolent, malignant, unfriendly
Feindseligkeit enmity, hatred, hostility, malevolence
Feldzug campaign
Ferien holidays, leave, recess, vacation
Fernbleiben absence, absenteeism, nonappearance, nonattendance
—, unentschuldigtes absenteeism, absence without leave

fernbleiben (be) absent, not to come, keep (stay) away, remain absent
fertig accomplished, complete(d), finished, perfect, ready
— **werden mit** get along with, manage
fertigstellen accomplish, arrange, complete, finish, manufacture, prepare
Fertigstellung accomplishment, completion, finishing, perfection
Fesseln bonds, chains, fetters, irons, shackles
fesseln attract, bind, (en)chain, hand cuff, (put in) iron(s), fetter, shackle
fest binding, constant, durable, firm, fixed, hard, inflexible, permanent, resolute solid, stable, steadfast, steady, strong
fest anstellen appoint a person during good behavio(u)r, give a permanent position
Festhalten adherence, attachment
festhalten arrest, detain, keep in custody, retain, seize
— **an** abide by, adhere (keep, stick) to, observe
festigen cement, consolidate, establish, fortify, harden, settle, solidify, stabilize, steady, stengthen
Festigkeit constancy, firmness, resistance, resoluteness, solidity, stability, steadiness, strength
Festigung cementation, consolidation, establishment, fortification, stabilization, strengthening
festlegen adjust, assign, determine, establish, fix, lay down, lock up, mark out, prescribe, schedule, set, settle, state, tie (up, down)
—, **gesetzlich** regularize
—, **vertraglich** stipulate
sich — bind (commit) oneself, tie oneself down to
Festlegung adjustment, determination, establishment, fixation, regularization, stipulation
Festnahme apprehension, arrest, arrestment, detention, seizure
festnehmen apprehend, (place under) arrest, take into custody
festsetzen appoint, arrange, assess, confine, determine, establish, fix, imprison, lay down, prescribe, provide, regulate, schedule, set, settle
—, **vertraglich** agree upon, stipulate
Festsetzung agreement, oppointment, arrangement, assessment, determination, establishment, fixation, imprisonment, provision, regulation, settlement
feststehen be certain, be established (settled), be a fact
feststehend established, fixed, positive, settled
feststellbar ascertainable, detectable, determinable, identifiable
feststellen ascertain, assess, declare, detect, determine, discover, establish, find out, identify, locate, make out, prove, record, register, spot, state, trace
Feststellung ascertainment, assessment, comment, conclusion, detection, determination, discovery, establishment, finding, identification, location, observation, proof, statement, tracing
Feststellungs-
—**beschluß** declaratory decree
—**klage** declaratory action
—**prozeß** declaratory proceedings
—**urteil** declaratory judgement
Festtag holiday
festverzinslich fixed-interest bearing
Festwert standard value
Feudal
—**herr** feudal lord, liege
— —**schaft** feudalism, feudality
—**recht** feudal law (right)

—system feudal system, feudalism
Fideikommiß entail, estate in tail, feoffment in trust, trust
Fideikommiß-
—auflösung disentailment
—erbe feoffee in trust
—inhaber tenant in tail
fiduziarisch fiduciary
Fiktion (legal) fiction
fiktiv fictitious, fictive
Filiale agency, branch (establishment, office)
Finanz-
—abkommen financial (monetary) agreement
—abteilung financial (finance) department (division)
—amt finance (revenue, tax) authority (board, office)
—ausschuß finance committee
—beamter finance (revenue) officer, fiscal
—behörde finance (fiscal) authority
—bericht financial statement, fiscal report
Finanzen finances
Finanz
—gericht Court of Claims (USA), Court of Exchequer (GB), finance (fiscal) court
— —shof finance court of appeal
—gesetz bill, finance act
—gesetzgebung financial legislation
finanziell financial, fiscal, monetary, pecuniary
— unterstützen subsidize
finanzieren finance, provide money for
Finanzierung financing
Finanz
—jahr financial (fiscal) year
—lage financial position
—politik financial (fiscal) policy
—wechsel financial (accommodation, bank, finance) bill
Findelkind foundling
finden find, meet with, obtain
Finder finder
—lohn (finder's) reward
Finger
—abdruck dactylogram, finger impression (mark), fingerprint
—zeig cue, hint, index, indication, suggestion, tip
fingieren feign, pretend, sham, simulate
fingiert assumed, feigned, fictitious, pro forma, imaginary, sham
Fingierung simulation
finster dark, grim, obscure
—e Angelegenheit grim business
Finte feint, pretence, subterfuge, tergiversation, trick
Firma business, company, enterprise, firm, house
fiskalisch financial, fiscal
Fiskaljahr fiscal year
Fiskus fisc, finance (fiscal) authorities, fisk, government, Exchequer, Treasury
fix firm, fixed
fixieren fix, settle
Fixierung fixation, fixing
Fixum fixed sum (salary)
flehen beg, implore, plead, supplicate
—, um Frieden sue for peace
—, um Gnade plead for mercy
—, um Verzeihung crave (supplicate) pardon
Fleiß assiduity, diligence, hard work, industry
fleißig active, assiduous, busy, diligent, hard-working, industrious
fliehen abscond, avoid, desert, escape, flee, refuge, run away
Fliehender fugitive
Fluch anathema, blasphemy, curse, imprecation, malediction
fluchen curse, execrate, swear
Flucht escape, flight, run
—, auf der flying, on the run
— ergreifen take (to) flight
Flucht-
—verdacht suspicion of absconding (escape)
—versuch attempt to escape
flüchten abscond, escape, flee, run away
flüchtig absconding, careless, casual, fugitive, runaway, superficial
— werden abscond, take (to) flight, run away

Flüchtiger fugitive, runaway
Flüchtigkeit carelessness, superficiality
—sfehler oversight, slip
Flüchtling expellee, fugitive, refugee, runaway
Flugblatt (-schrift) broadsheet, handbill, leaflet, pamphlet
flüssig available, easy, fluid, liquid
— machen convert into cash, liquidate, make available, mobilize, realize
— sein be financially sound
Flüssigmachung liquidation, realization
Flüsterpropaganda underground propaganda, whispering compaign
föderal federal
Föderalismus federalism
Föderalist federal(ist)
föderalistisch federal(ist)
Föderation federation, federacy
föderieren (con)federate
Folge consequence, effect, issue, order, outcome, result, sequence, sequel, series, succession
als — von because of, in consequence of, on account of
zur — haben bring about, call forth, entail, involve, lead to, originate, result in
— leisten accept, answer, comply with, follow, obey
keine — leisten disobey
—n tragen take the consequences
Folgeerscheinung outcome, result, sequel
folgen comply, follow, obey, succeed (to)
— aus ensue (result) from, be a consequence of
folgend consequent, ensuing, following, next, resultant, resulting, subsequent
im —en below, in the following (sequel)
folgendermaßen (-weise) as follows, in the following way, like this
folgenlos resultless, without consequences (effect, result)
folgenreich effective, resultful
folgenschwer grave, momentous, weighty, with grave (heavy) consequences
folgerichtig coherent, consequent, consistent, logical
Folgerichtigkeit consistency, logic, logical consequence, sequence
folgern conclude, deduce, gather, infer
Folgerung conclusion, deduction, inference
folgewidrig illogical, inconsequent(ial), inconsistent
Folgewidrigkeit inconsequence, inconsistency
Folgezeit following period, future time, sequel, time to come
folglich as a consequence, consequently, hence, therefore
folgsam obedient
Folgsamkeit obedience
Folter rack, torment, torture
foltern excruciate, lacerate, rack, torment, torture
Fonds foundation, fund(s)
forcieren force
Forderer claimant, demandant
Förderer advocate, patron, promoter, sponsor, supporter
förderlich beneficial, helpful, serviceable, useful
fordern ask (for), call for, challenge, charge, cite, claim, demand, exact, postulate, request, require, summon
fördern advance, aid, assist, benefit, develop, encourage, foster, further, improve, increase, patronize, promote, stimulate, subserve, support
Forderung call, challenge, charge, claim, debt, demand, dictate, exaction, matter (chose) in action, postulation, requirement, requisition, title
—en accounts receivable, outstanding debts, outstandings, receivables
—sabtretung (—sübertragung) assignment (transfer) of a claim (title)
forderungsberechtigt entitled to a claim

Forderungs-
—berechtigter (rightful) claimant, obligee
—recht legal claim, chose in action
—verzicht remission of a claim
Förderung advancement, aid, assistance, benefit, encouragement, furtherance, promotion, subservience, support
forensisch forensic
Form appearance, condition, cut, design, fashion, figure, form, formality, frame, manner, mode, model, shape, style, usage
formal formal, technical
Formalien formalities
Formalität form, formality
Format capacity, format, range, size, shape, stature
Formation formation
Formblatt blank, form
Formel form, formula, wording
formell formal, functional
formen construct, fashion, form, frame, model, shape
Formfehler error, flaw, formal defect, informality
Formfrage matter of form
formgerecht accurate, duly, in due (proper, regular) form
förmlich absolute, ceremonial, ceremonious, downright, formal, literal, outright, pedantic, precise, punctilious, regular, veritable
Förmlichkeit ceremoniousness, ceremony, conventionality, formality
formlos amorphous, crude, formless, informal, rude, shapeless, unceremonious, unconventional, unorganized
Formlosigkeit amorphism, crudeness, formlessness, informality, rudeness, shapelessness, unconventionality
Formmangel defect (lack) of form, formal defect, informality
Formsache formality, matter of form, procedural matter
Formular blank, form, schedule
formulieren define, draft, draw up, enunciate, formularize, formulate, frame, state, word
Formulierung definition, enunciation, formulation, statement, wording
Formung formation
Formverletzung breach of form
Formvorschrift formal requirement, formality
formwidrig informal
Formwidrigkeit informality
forschen examine, inquire, look for, research, search, scrutinize, seek
forschend inquiring, scrutinizing, searching, studious
Forscher inquirer, (re)searcher, seeker, research worker
Forschung investigation, research
Fortbestand continuance, survival
Fortbestehen continuance, persistence (cy)
fortbestehen be (remain) in existance, continue, perpetuate, persist, subsist, survive
Fortdauer continuance, continuation, duration, permanence, perpetuance, perpetuation, perpetuity
Fortdauern persistence
fortdauern continue (to exist), endure, last, linger on, persist, subsist
fortdauernd constant, continual, continuous, endless, incessant, lasting, permanent, persistent, recurrent
fortfahren continue, go on, keep (on), proceed
fortführen carry on, continue, extend, go on with, keep up, proceed, pursue, resume
Fortführung carrying on, continuation, pursuance, resumption
fortgesetzt constant, continual, continuous, uninterrupted
fortlaufen abscond, (be) continue(d), escape, run away (on)
fortlaufend consecutive, continual, continuous, current, regular, running, serial, successive

fortschaffen carry (clear, take) away, eliminate, get rid of, remove, transport
Fortschaffung elimination, removal, transportation
fortschicken dismiss, despatch, dispatch, send away (off)
fortschreiten advance, proceed, progress
fortschreitend onward, progressive, progressional
Fortschritt advance(ment), improvement, progress
—e machen advance, improve, (make) progress
fortschrittlich advanced, future-minded, modern, progressive, up-to-date
Fortschrittlichkeit progressivity
fortsetzen carry on, continue, proceed, pursue, resume
Fortsetzung carrying on, continuation, pursuit, resumption, sequel
fortstehlen, sich steal away (off)
fortwährend constant, continual, continuous, incessant, permanent, perpetual
Forum forum, panel, tribunal
Fracht cargo, carriage, freight, freightage, lading, load, shipment
Fracht-
—brief bill of lading, consignment note, freight (shipping) bill, waybill
—gebühr (—geld, —kosten, —spesen) carriage, cartage, freight (charges), freightage
—empfänger consignee
frachtfrei carriage-free, freight free (paid)
Fracht-
—gut cargo, freight, load
—papiere (—urkunden) shipping documents
—nota (—rechnung) freight account (bill, note)
—satz (—tarif) freight rate (tariff)
—stück package, parcel
—versicherung freight insurance
—vertrag charterparty, freight (shipping) contract
Frage inquiry, interest, interrogation, issue, matter, point, problem, query, question
Haupt— (Kern—) point
Fragebogen question form, questionnaire
— ausfüllen complete (fill in, up) a questionnaire
fragen ask, inquire, interrogate, query, question
—, um Rat consult, seek advice
Frage-
—recht right to interrogate (cross-examine)
—steller interrogator, querist, questioner
—stellung interrogation, questioning
fraglich doubtful, in question, problematic(al), questionable, referred to, uncertain, under discussion
fraglos indisputable, unquestionable
fragwürdig doubtful, dubious, equivocal, questionable, shady
Fraktion fraction, group
Fraktions-
—beschluß fractional motion
—führer fraction leader
—vorsitzender floor leader
franko carriage paid, free (of charges), freight free (paid), post-free (-paid), postage free (paid), prepaid
Frau female, lady, mistress, wife, woman
—, geschiedene feme discovert
—, unverheiratete (—, ledige) feme sole, unmarried woman
—, verheiratete feme covert, married woman
Frauen-
—rechte women's rights
—stimmrecht (—wahlrecht) female (woman, women's) suffrage
Fräulein girl, miss, young (unmarried) lady (woman)
frei blank, frank, free (of charges), gratis, gratuitous, independant, liberal, open, outspoken, unhampered, unrestrained, unrestricted, vacant
frei von clear from (of), exempt from, free from (of), void of

freier Beruf free-lance (liberal) profession
auf freiem Fuß at large
auf freien Fuß setzen free, release, set free
freie Hand haben be at liberty to, have a free hand
freie Hand lassen give a free hand
aus freien Stücken spontaneously, voluntarily
freie Wahl free choice, liberty
freier Wille free will
aus freiem Willen of one's own free will
Freibetrag free (exempt) amount, exemption, tax-free income
freiberuflich free-lance
Freibeuter buccaneer, filibuster, freebooter
Freibeuterei freebooting
freibeutern buccaneer, filibuster, freeboot
Freibrief charter, passport, patent, privilege
Freidenker freethinker
Freigabe clearance, decontrol, emancipation, release
freigeben decontrol, release, set free, unblock, unlock
freigebig generous, liberal, openhanded
Freigebigkeit generosity, liberality, openhandedness
freigeboren free-born
Freihafen free port
freihalten keep clear (free, open)
Freihandel free trade
Freihandelszone free trade area
freihändig by private contract, privately
Freiheit exemption, franchise, freedom, immunity, independence, liberty, privilege
—, in free, at large
in — setzen release, set free
freiheitlich free, independent, individualistic, liberal
Freiheits-
—beraubung confinement without authority, deprivation of liberty, duress, false imprisonment, unlawful detention
—beschränkung restraint (restriction) of liberty
—bewegung movement of (struggle of) independence
—entzug detention, imprisonment
—krieg war of independence (liberation)
—strafe confinement, (sentence to) imprisonment
freilassen discharge, free, liberate, release, set free
—, gegen Sicherheitsleistung (Bürgschafts-) release on bail
Freilassung discharge, liberation, release
— gegen Sicherheitsleistung (Bürgschafts-) release on bail
— anordnen order release (a person released)
freisprechen absolve, acquit, discharge, exonerate
Freisprechung (Freispruch) absolution, acquittal, discharge, exoneration, verdict of not guilty
Freistaat free state, republic
freistehen be free for (to), be open to, be left to (within) one's discretion, be vacant (unoccupied)
freistellen discharge, exempt, leave to (up to), leave to a person's option, release from
Freistellung exemption, release
Freitod suicide
freiwillig free (-will), optional, private, spontaneous, voluntary
—e Gerichtsbarkeit non-contentious jurisdiction
un— involuntary
Freiwilliger volunteer
Freiwilligkeit free will, spontaneity, voluntariness
Freizeit free (leisure, spare) time, time off, vacancy
Freizone free zone
freizügig free to move, unhampered, unrestricted
Freizügigkeit free movement, freedom (of movement)
fremd alien, extraneous, foreign, heterogeneous, outside, strange, unfamiliar, unknown
Fremdarbeit outside labo(u)r
Fremdarbeiter foreign labo(u)r(er) (worker)

Fremder alien, foreigner, stranger
Fremdkapital debts (and liabilities), outside (loan) capital
Fremdsprache foreign language
Fremdwort foreign word
Freund comrade, friend
gut — sein mit be on friendly terms with, be well acquainted with
freundlich amicable, friendly
Freundschaft amity, friendly relations, friendship
freundschaftlich amicable, friendly
Freundschafts-
—dienst good offices (turn)
—pakt (—vertrag) friendship pact, treaty of amity (friendship)
Frevel crime, desecration, misdeed, offence, outrage, profanation, sacrilege
— begehen commit sacrilege on, desecrate, outrage, profane, violate
—tat enormity, outrage, outrageous crime, wicked act
frevelhaft atrocious, criminal, outrageous, sacrilegious, wicked
Frevler criminal, malefactor, offender, outrager
Frieden harmony, peace, quiet, tranquillity
Arbeits— industrial peace
Welt— world peace
— halten (wahren) keep the peace
— schließen conclude (make) peace
— stiften appease, pacify
— stören break (disturb) the peace
Friedens-
—angebot peace offer
—appell appeal for peace
—bedingungen terms of peace
—brecher peacebreaker
—bruch breach (violation) of the peace
—erklärung declaration of peace
—konferenz peace conference
—politik peace (pacific) policy
—richter Justice of the Peace (GB), arbitrator, magistrate
—schluß conclusion of peace
—stifter pacifier, peacemaker
—verhandlungen peace negotiations
—vertrag (—pakt) peace treaty (pact), treaty of peace
—zeit peace time, time of peace
friedfertig peaceable
Friedfertigkeit peaceableness
friedlich amicable, pacific, peaceable, peaceful, quiet, tranquil, untroubled
friedliebend peaceable, peace-loving
Frist delay, grace, limitation, limited period, period (allowed, of time), prescribed period, respite, term, time (allowed, limit)
Gnaden— reprieve, respite
Kündigungs— [period (term) of] notice
Frist-
—ablauf end of the term, expiration of period (term), lapse of time
—beginn beginning of term, commencement of period
fristgemäß in (due) time, punctual, within a given time, within the period allowed (prescribed)
fristgerecht in due course (time), on the appointed day, in season (time)
Fristgesuch petition for respite
fristlos at a minute's warning, immediate, instant, without notice
Fristverlängerung delay, extension of time, prolongation, respite
Fristversäumnis default
Front front (line)
Früchte benefits, products, profits, results
fruchtbar (fruchtbringend) fructuous, fruitful, pregnant, productive, profitable, prolific
Fruchtbarkeit fruitfulness, pregnancy, productivity, prolificacy, prolificity

fruchtlos fruitless, effectless, ineffective, ineffectual, profitless, unsuccessful, useless, without effect (result)
Fruchtlosigkeit fruitlessness, ineffectiveness, uselessness
früher earlier, former, late, past, previous, prior
fügen, sich accommodate (adapt) oneself to, compromise with, conform to, defer to, give in, give way, refrain, yield
sich — in acquiesce in, put up with, reconcile oneself with, resign (submit) oneself to
fügsam compliant, obedient
Fügung dispensation, providence
fühlbar appreciable, considerable, great, serious
fühlen be aware (sensible) of, feel, have a sense of, sense
Fühlung contact, touch
— nehmen get into touch, make contact with
Fühlungnahme approach, communication, contact, getting into touch with, taking contact, understanding
führen be in charge of, carry (on), command, conduct, direct, drive, guide, head, hold, keep, lead, operate, manage, run
—, schlecht misdirect, mismanage
— zu lead to, result in
—, sich bear (conduct) oneself, behave
sich gut — behave (conduct) well
sich schlecht — misbehave, misconduct
führend at the top, controlling, directing, first-rate, leading, prominent, top-ranking, uppermost
Führer commander, conductor, director, guide, head, leader, manager, ringleader
führerlos leaderless
Führerschein driving (driver's) licenc(s)e
Führung bearing, behavio(u)r, command, conduct, direction, guidance, guidership, keeping, lead, leadership, management
—, gute good behavio(u)r (conduct)
—, schlechte bad conduct, misbehavio(u)r, misconduct
— übernehmen take charge (the lead)
Führungszeugnis certificate of character (good behavio[u]r) (good conduct)
Fund (Fundgegenstand) find(ing), lost property, object found
Fundament basis, foundation, ground, groundwork
fundamental basic, fundamental
Fundbüro lost property office
fundieren consolidate, establish, fund
fundiert consolidated, funded
—, gut solid, sound, well-established, well-grounded
Fundierung consolidation, funding
Fundort place of discovery (finding), finding place
fungieren als act (function, officiate, sit) as
Funktion action, activity, charge, duty, function, office, role
Funktionär functionary, official
funktionell functional, official
funktionieren act, function, operate, run, work
Für und Wider pros and cons
Fürbitte intercession
— einlegen intercede, plead
Fürbitter intercessor
Fürsorge assistance, care, provision, solicitude, welfare
—, soziale social welfare, welfare work
Fürsorge-
—anstalt reformatory
—behörden welfare authorities
—einrichtung social (welfare) institution, social services
Fürsorger social (welfare) worker
Fürsorge-
—erziehung correctional (trustee) education
—zögling ward
Fürsprache intercession, mediation
— einlegen intercede

Fürsprecher advocate, intercessor, mediator, sponsor
Fusion amalgamation, confusion, consolidation, fusion, merger
fusionieren amalgamate, combine, consolidate, fuse, merge
Fuß
auf freiem —e at large
auf freien — setzen set at liberty
auf gutem —e stehen mit be on good terms with
auf eigenen Füßen stehen be independent, stand on one's own legs
fußen auf be based on, rely on, rest on
Fuß-
—gänger pedestrian
— —überweg pedestrian crossing (lines)
—note footnote
mit —n versehen footnote
—spur footmark, footprint, track

G

Gabe donation, endowment, faculty, gift, present, skill, talent
—, milde alms, charity
Gage pay, remuneration, salary
Galgen gallows, gibbet
an den — bringen bring to (hang on) the gallows
am — enden end on the gallows
dem — entrinnen cheat the gallows
an den — kommen come to the gallows
Galgen
—frist last respite, short grace (shrift)
—gesicht hangdog (gallows) face (look)
—humor grim humour
—strick (—vogel) gallows bird, hangdog, good for nothing
Gang action, aisle, commission, corridor, course, errand, gangway, motion, operation, passage, process, round, running
in — setzen (bringen) launch, put (set) in motion, set going, start
gangbar current, feasible, marketable, merchantable, passable, possible, practicable, sal(e)able, workable
Gangbarkeit currency, feasibility, marketability, merchantableness, passableness, practicability, practicableness, sal(e)ability, sal(e)ableness, workableness
gängig current, marketable, practicable, sal(e)able, workable
Gangster gangster, racketeer
—bande gang (of criminals), group of gangsters
—tum racketeering
Ganove hoodlum
ganz all, complete, entire, full, total, whole
Ganzes entity, total(ity), whole
als — in the aggregate, in its entity, at (in) large, as a whole
im großen — on the whole
gänzlich absolute(ly), entire(ly), complete(ly), fully, total(ly), utter(ly), wholly
ganztägig all-day, full(-)time, whole-time
— arbeiten work full time
Ganztagsbeschäftigung full-time job
Garant bail, guarantee, guarantor, surety, warrantor
Garantie guarantee, guaranty, security, surety(ship), warranty
Garantie-
—abkommen (—vertrag) guarantee (warranty) contract

—erklärung declaration of guarantee, letter of guarantee (indemnity), bond of indemnity, deed of suretyship
—frist term of guarantee (warranty)
garantieren guarantee, vouch for, warrant, be bail for
Garantierung guaranty
Garantie-
—schein bond, guaranty, certificate of suretyship
—verpflichtung guarantee obligation, indemnity (surety) bond
—wechsel security bill
Garnison garrison
Gast client, customer, guest, frequenter, tourist, visitor
—freiheit hospitality
gastfreundlich generous, hospitable
Gast-
—freundschaft generosity, hospitality
—geber host
—geberin hostess
—geberstaat host nation
—hörer auditor, guest student
—recht hospitality law, right to hospitality
— — gewähren accord hospitality, receive as a guest
—vorlesung guest lecture
Gatte husband, spouse
Gatten husband and wife, married couple, spouses
Gattin spouse, wife
Gattung class, kind, sort, species, type
Gau country, district, province, region
Gauner cheat, knave, rascal, rogue, rook, sharp(er), shark,
—bande gang of swindlers (sharpers)
Gaunerei cheat(ing), knavery, swindle, swindling, trickery
geächtet outlawed, proscribed
Geächteter outlaw
Gebärde gesticulation, gesture
gebärden, sich act, behave, gesticulate
Gebaren act, behavio(u)r, demeanour, gesture
Gebäude building, edifice, frame, structure
—steuer (inhabited) house duty (tax)
Gebeine boons, (mortal) remains
geben give, grant, hand over, offer, present
Geber donor, giver
— und Nehmer seller and buyer
Gebiet area, district, domain, field, ground, jurisdiction, province, range, region, scope, sphere, territory, zone
gebieten command, dictate, direct, govern, impose, order, require, rule (over), sway (over)
—d commanding
Gebieter governor, lord, master, ruler
gebieterisch authoritative, categoric, dictatorial, imperative, imperious, peremptory
Gebiets-
—abkommen regional pact
—abtretung cession of territory
—anspruch (—forderung) territorial claim
—aufteilung distribution of territory, dismemberment
—austausch exchange of territory
—beauftragter regional commissioner
—hoheit territorial juridiction (sovereignty)
—körperschaft territorial authority
—streifen zone
—streitigkeit territorial dispute
—verletzung territorial violation
Gebilde entity, formation, institution, thing
gebildet cultivated, civilized, educated
geboren born
  erst— first-born
  frei— free-born
  neu— new-born
  tot— still-born
—, ehelich born in wedlock, legally born
—, unehelich born out of wedlock
—, im Ausland foreign-born
geborene born, neé

Gebot bid(ding), command (ment), dictate, offer, percept, rule
Gebote, die Zehn the Ten Commandments
Gebrauch application, custom, employment, exercise, practice, usage, use
gebrauchen apply, employ, make use of, need, use, want
—, falsch misuse
Gebraucher consumer, user
gebräuchlich common, customary, current, ordinary, in use, usual
un— not customary, out of use, unusual
Gebrauchs-
—anmaßung illicit (unauthorized) use
—anweisung (—vorschrift) direction (instruction) for use
—gegenstand article for daily (everyday) use, commodity, requisite, utensil
—muster design, patent, pattern, sample
— —, eingetragenes registered design
— —schutz legal protection of pattern and designs
—recht right of (to) use, user
—wert present (use) value, value in use
Gebrechen affliction, ailment, defect, frailty, handicap, infirmity, weakness
gebrechlich disabled, frail, invalid, weak
Gebrechlichkeit debility, disability, infirmity, invalidity
Gebrüder brothers
Gebühr charge, commission, due, duty, fee, rate, retainer, royalty, scale, tax, toll
gebühren be due to
—d adequate, appropriate, becoming, due, fit, proper, seemly, suitable
—einheit tariff unit
—erhebung collection of charges (fees)
—erlaß remission of charges (fees)
Gebühren-
—ermäßigung reduction of fees
gebührenfrei duty-free, exempt from duty, free [of charge(s), from duty]
Gebühren-
—freiheit exemption from charges (duties)
—ordnung regulation (scale) (schedule) of charges (fees), tariff
—pflicht obligation to pay fees
gebührenpflichtig chargeable, dutiable, liable to fees (duties), subject to charges, taxable
Gebührenvorschuß retainer, retaining fee
gebunden bound, confined, controlled, directed, fixed, limited, prescribed, subject to, tied (up)
—, vertraglich bound by contract, under contract
Gebundenheit confinement, dependence, restraint, restriction, subordination
Geburt birth, descent, extraction
Erst— first-born
Fehl— miscarriage
Tot— still-born
—, eheliche legitimate birth, legitimacy
Geburten-
—beschränkung (—kontrolle, —regelung) birth control
—häufigkeit (-ziffer) birth rate, number of births
—register register of births
gebürtig born, by birth, native (of)
Geburts-
—jahr year of birth
—land birthland, country of birth, native country
—mal birthmark
—name maiden name, name of birth, birth name
—ort birthplace, native place
—recht birthright
—schein (—urkunde) birth certificate
—stadt native town
—tag anniversary, birthday
Gedächtnis memory, mind, remembrance, recollection
—, gutes good memory

—, schlechtes defective memory
— verlieren lose one's memory
Gedächtnis-
—fehler slip of memory
—rede commemoration speech, memorial address
—schwäche weakness of memory
—verlust amnesia, loss of memory
Gedanke idea, notion, reflection, thought
Gedanken-
—austausch exchange of ideas (thoughts) (views)
—freiheit freedom of thought
—gang drift, reasoning, train of thought
—gut ideas, thoughts
—losigkeit thoughtlessness
—übertragung telepathy
—verbindung association of ideas, combination of thoughts
—vorbehalt mental reservation
—welt (range, scope, world of) ideas, intellectual world, thought
gedanklich ideal, immaginary, intellectual, mental
—, rein abstract, ideal, rational, speculative
Gedeih
auf — und Verderb for better or for worse, for good and evil
Gedeihen growth, progress, prosperity, success, thriving
gedeihen blossom, get on, grow, flourish, (make) progress, succeed, thrive
Gedenk-
—protokoll memorandum
—rede commemorative (memorial) address
Gedinge (tut-)bargain, contract work, piecework
Geduld forbearance, lenience, patience, perseverance
—sprobe trial of patience
gedulden, sich have patience, wait
geduldig patient, with patience
geeignet applicable, appropriate, convenient, eligible, fit, proper, qualified, suitable
Gefahr danger, hazard, jeopardy, peril, risk
gefährden compromise, endanger, expose to danger, imperil, menace, jeopardize, prejudice, risk
gefährdet endangered, imperiled, in danger (jeopardy) (peril)
Gefährdung endangering, jeopardy, menace, prejudice, threat
—shaftung absolute liability
Gefahren-
—bereich danger area
—zone danger zone
—zulage danger allowance
gefährlich critical, dangerous, hazardous, perilous, risky, serious
Gefährlichkeit danger(ousness), peril, risk(iness)
gefahrlos harmless, riskless, safe, secure, without danger (risk)
Gefahrlosigkeit risklessness, safety
gefahrvoll dangerous, full of danger, perilous, riskful, risky, venturesome
Gefallen delight, favo(u)r, kindness, pleasure
um einen — bitten ask a favo(u)r of
— erweisen do a favo(u)r
gefallen be pleased with, please, suit
gefällig accommodating, agreeable, complaisant, kind, obliging, pleasing
Gefälligkeit accommodation, agreeableness, complaisance, courtesy, favo(u)r, kindness, obligingness, service
Gefälligkeit
—, als (aus) as a favo(u)r, in order to oblige
— erweisen accommodate with, do a favo(u)r (good turn)
Gefälligkeits-
—akzept (—wechsel) accommodation bill
gefälscht counterfeit, false, falsified, forged
gefangen captivated, captive, captured, caught, imprisoned, in prison

—halten detain, hold, imprison, keep captive (imprisoned) (a prisoner)
—nehmen (setzen) apprehend, arrest, captivate, capture, get hold of, imprison, put in prison, take in custody (a prisoner), seize
Gefangenen-
—arbeit prison labo(u)r
—austausch exchange of prisoners
Gefangener captive, detained person, prisoner
Gefangen-
—haltung arrest, confinement, detention
—nahme apprehension, arrest, caption, capture, imprisonment, seizure
Gefangenschaft captivity, custody, detention, imprisonment
in — geraten be taken prisoner
Gefängnis goal, imprisonment, jail, prison, penitentiary
Gefängnis, im — in prison
ins — werfen imprison, put in prison, send to prison
mit — bestrafen sentence to imprisonment
Gefängnis-
—arbeit prison labo(u)r
—aufseher (-wächter, -wärter) gaoler, jailer, jailor, prison guard, warder
—hof prison court (yard)
—strafe (penalty of) imprisonment
— — verhängen inflict imprisonment
bei — — under penalty of imprisonment
—verwaltung prison administration
—wesen prison system
Gefecht action, combat, encounter, engagement, fight(ing)
außer — setzen put out of action
gefeit sein gegen be fortified (proof) against, be immune (protected) from (against), be invulnerable to
geflissentlich deliberate, intentional, wilful
Gefolge attendants, escort, suite, train
Gefolgschaft adherents, attendants, employees, followers, personnel, staff
Gefüge fabric, framework, make(-up), structure
gefügig compliant, submissive
gegebenenfalls if necessary, if the case arises, possibly, when occasion arises
Gegebenheit condition, datum, fact, factor, reality
—en data
gegen against, contrary, in exchange (return) for, re, versus
Gegen-
—aktion counteraction, counterblast, counteroperation
—angebot counteroffer
— — machen offer in return
—angriff counterattack
—anklage countercharge
— — erheben countercharge
—anspruch counterclaim, cross claim (demand)
—antrag countermotion, counterpetition
—antwort rejoinder, replication, reply
—anwalt opposing counsel
—argument counterargument
—aufstellung counterstatement
—auftrag countermandate, counterorder
—aussage counterevidence, deposition (statement) to the contrary
—bedingung countercondition, counterstipulation
—befehl countermand, counterorder
—behauptung counterstatement, denial, traverse
—beschuldigung countercharge, cross charge
—bewegung counterblast, countermovement, reaction
—beweis counterevidence, evidence to the contrary, rebuttal
—blockade counterblockade
—bündnis opposition league
—bürgschaft countersecurity, countersurety

Gegend area, country, district, environs, neighbourhood, part, quarter, region, section, surroundings, zone
Gegen-
—dienst return, return (reciprocal) service
— — erweisen do a service in return, reciprocate (return) a service
gegeneinander against one another, mutually, reciprocally
Gegen-
—forderung counterclaim, counterdemand, cross claim, cross demand
— — erheben counterclaim
—frage counterquestion
—gesuch counterpetition, cross petition
—gewicht balance, counterbalance, counterweight
—gift antidote, remedy
Gegen-
—grund counterargument
—kandidat opposition (rival) candidate
—klage countercharge, counterplea, countersuit, cross action
—kläger counterclaimant, counterpleader
—leistung compensation, consideration, equivalent, return
—maßnahme counteraction, countermeasure, preventive measure
—mittel antidote, remedy
—partei opponent, opposite party
—probe control test, countertest
—rede contradiction, counterplea, counterdeclaration
—regierung counter- (opposite) government
—revolution counterrevolution
—satz antagonism, contrast, difference, opposition
im — — zu contrary to, in contrast (opposition) to
im — — stehen zu be in contrast to, contradict
gegensätzlich antagonistic, contrary, hostile, opposing, opposite
Gegen-
—sätzlichkeit antagonism
—schlag counterblow, counterstroke, retaliation
zum — — ausholen prepare for a counterblow
—seite adverse party, counterside, other side, opposite party (side)
gegenseitig mutual, reciprocal
Gegenseitigkeit mutuality, reciprocity
Gegenseitigkeits
—abkommen reciprocal agreement, treaty of mutual assistance
—klausel reciprocity clause
—prinzip principle of reciprocity
Gegen-
—spieler adversary, antagonist, counterpart, opponent
—spionage counterintelligence, counterespionage
—stand affair, article, issue, item, matter, object, point, subject, substance, theme, thing, topic
gegenständlich concrete, objective
gegenstandlos baseless, groundless, immaterial, invalid, irrelevant, unfounded, unnecessary
als — erweisen prove unfounded
Gegen-
—stimme adverse vote, dissentient voice
—stück counterpart, equivalent
—teil contrary, opposite, reverse
gegenteilig (to the) contrary, opposite
gegenüberstellen compare, confront, contrast with, oppose
Gegenüberstellung comparison, confrontation
gegenübertreten confront, face
Gegen-
—unterschrift countersignature
—untersuchung counterinquiry
—verpflichtung counterobligation
—versprechen counterbond
—vormund supervising (joint) guardian, counterguardian
—vorschlag counterproposal
—wart presence, present (time)
— —swert actual (present) value
gegenwärtig actual, current, imminent, (at) present

Gegen-
—wechsel counterbill
—wert countervalue, equivalent (value)
—wirkung counteraction, countereffect, reaction
gegenzeichnen countersign
Gegen
—zeichner countersigner
—zeichnung countersignature
—zeuge counterwitness, witness for the opposing party
—zug countermove
Gegner adversary, antagonist, enemy, opponent, opposing party, rival
gegnerisch adverse, antagonistic, enemy, hostile, opposing
Gehalt capacity, compensation, consideration, content, pay, percentage, proportion, salary, standard, strength, substance, tonnage, volume
Gehalts-
—abzug deduction from (reduction of) salary
—anspruch (—forderung) salary claim (demand)
—bezüge emoluments
—empfänger salaried employee, salariat, salary earner
—erhöhung increase of salary
—gruppe (—klasse, —stufe) salary bracket (class, group)
—liste payroll
—pfändung attachment of salary
—scheck pay cheque (check)
—vorschuß salary advance
—zahlung salary payment
—zulage bonus, extra pay, increase of salary
gehalten sein zu be bound (obliged, required) to
geheim clandestine, confidential, hidden, (in) private, (in) secret
—, streng top secret
geheimhalten conceal, keep private (secret)
Geheim-
—abkommen secret agreement
—agent secret agent
—dienst intelligence (secret) service
—haltung concealment, discretion, secrecy
— —spflicht secrecy
—klausel secret clause
Geheimnis mystery, secret
—, offenes open secret
Geheim-
—polizei secret police
—polizist detective
—sache secret matter
—vertrag secret treaty
Gehilfe accessory, accomplice, aid, aider and abettor, assistant, associate, attendant, clerk, employee, helper
Gehör audience, hearing
—, rechtliches due process of law
um — bitten ask for attention
— schenken give a hearing, listen to
gehorchen follow, be obedient, obey
—, nicht be disobedient, disobey
gehören (zu) appertain to, belong to, be (form) part of, be owned by, be the property of, rank among, rest with
—, sich be fit (proper, right, seemly)
gehörig appertaining to, belonging to, due, incidental, proper,
—, zur Sache pertinent, relevant, to the point
—, nicht zur Sache beside the point, irrelevant
Gehorsam obedience
Un— s. —sverweigerung
—, blinder blind obedience
—, unbedingter implicit obedience
— verweigern refuse obedience, disobey
—sverweigerung disobedience, insubordination
gehorsam obedient, submissive
— sein be obedient, obey
Geisel hostage
als — behalten keep as hostage
—n stellen give hostages
Geist esprit, ghost, intellect, intelligence, mind, spirit
geistesabwesend absent-minded, absent of mind
Geistesabwesenheit absence of mind, absent-mindedness
Geistesarbeit brain (head, intellectual) work

— **—er** brain (intellectual) worker
Geistesgegenwart presence of mind
geistesgestört (be) of unsound mind, (mentally) deranged, insane, mentally disturbed (unsettled)
Geistes-
—gestörter person of unsound mind, insane person
—gestörtheit alienation of mind, (mental) derangement, insanity, lunacy, mental disorder
—größe greatness of mind, intellectual greatness
—haltung attitude of mind, mental attitude, mentality
geisteskrank insane, mentally defective (deranged), of unsound mind
Geistes-
—kranker insane (person), lunatic, mental patient, person of unsound mind
—krankheit insanity, lunacy, mental alienation (disease, disorder)
—leben intellectual life
geistesschwach feeble-minded, imbecile, weak-minded
Geistes-
—schwacher imbecile, mental defective
—schwäche feeble-mindedness, imbecility, mental infirmity, weak-mindedness
—störung aberration, mental alienation (derangement, disorder)
—tätigkeit brain work, mental activity
—trägheit mental indolence
—verfassung mentality, frame (state) of mind
—verwirrung (—zerrüttung) aberration, insanity, mental alienation (derangement)
—zustand mental state, state of mind
geistig immaterial, intellectual, mental, spiritual

Gelände area, ground(s), (piece of, tract of) land, lot, site, terrain
—abtretung cession of land
gelangen zu attain (to), gain, reach
zum Abschluß — be settled, reach a conclusion
zur Macht — come into power
geläufig common, current, fluent, usual
— **sein** be current (in use), be familiar to (with)
Geld bid, capital, cash, money
Hart— coin
Klein— change
Papier— paper money
Geld-
—abfindung cash settlement, financial arrangement, monetary (pecuniary) compensation
—angelegenheiten money (pecuniary) matters (affairs)
—anlage investment
—anleihe (money) loan
—anweisung money (postal) order, remittance
—aufnahme raising of money
—ausleiher money lender
—bedarf need (want) of money, pecuniary requirements
—bestand cash on hand
—buße fine, penalty
— **— auferlegen** fine a person
—entschädigung indemnity, pecuniary compensation
Gelder means, money(s), funds
Geld-
—forderung money (pecuniary) claim (demand)
—geber financier, money lender
—geschäft financial operation, money transaction
—geschenk gratuity, money gift, tip
—heirat money match
—herrschaft plutocracy
—hilfe pecuniary aid, subsidy
—hinterlegung cash deposit, deposit of money
—institut credit (financial) institution
—knappheit (—mangel, —not) lack (scarcity, shortage) of money

—leistung payment
geldlich financial, monetary, pecuniary
Geld-
—makler money broker
—markt money market
—mittel funds, (financial) means, (pecuniary) resources
—schein bank note (bill)
—schrank safe
— —knacker safebreaker, safeblower, safecracker
—schuld money debt
—schwierigkeiten monetary (pecuniary) difficulties
—sendung remittance
—spende money gift
—strafe fine, penalty
zu einer — — verurteilen fine a person
—stück coin, piece of money
—summe sum of money
—überweisung remittance, transfer
—unterschlagung embezzlement
—unterstützung pecuniary aid (assistance, support)
—verlegenheit (pecuniary) embarrassment
—verleiher money lender
—verlust loss of money, pecuniary loss
—verschwendung waste of money
—versorgung money supply
—vorschuß cash (money) advance
—währung currency
—wechsel exchange (of money)
—wechsler money changer
—wert monetary (money) value
—wesen finance, monetary system (matters)
—wirtschaft money economy
—wucher usury
gelegen convenient, opportune, proper, suitable
Gelegenheit chance, facility, occasion, opportunity
Gelegenheits-
—arbeit casual employment (job, labo[u]r)
—arbeiter casual hand (labo[u]rer, worker), casual
—kauf bargain sale, chance bargain
gelegentlich casual, chance, incidental, irregular, occasional, temporary
Geleit conduct, convoy, escort
—, freies (sicheres) safe-conduct
freies — gewähren give safe-conduct
geleiten accompany, conduct, convoy, escort
Geleit-
—brief letter of safe-conduct, pass(port), safeguard
—schein navicert, pass (bill), permit, transire
—schutz convoy
—zug convoy, escort
gelernt
—er Arbeiter skilled worker
gelingen achieve, be successful, succeed, work
—, nicht fail
geloben promise, vow
Gelöbnis promise, vow
— ablegen make (take) a vow
gelten be current (effective, operative, valid), be in force (operation), hold, operate, prevail, rule
— als be considered (regarded as), be deemed (to, as), pass for
— für apply to, be applicable to, be meant (intended) for
gelten lassen allow, approve (of), (let) pass
nicht — lassen disallow, disapprove of
geltend accepted, acknowledged, applicable, current, effective, existing, in force (operation), lawful, legal, operative, prevailing, ruling, valid
— machen advance, assert, bring to bear, constitute, enforce, exercise, exert, file, insist on, lodge, maintain, plead, prefer, put forward, raise, use, urge, vindicate
Geltendmachung assertion, enforcement, exercise, insistence, vindication
Geltung acceptation, authority, consequence, credit, currency, effect, force, importance, prevalence, reputation, standing, validity, value, weight, worth

— **erlangen (zu — kommen)** become effective, take effect
— **haben** be current (valid), be in force, prevail
— **verschaffen** enforce
sich — verschaffen assert oneself
Geltungs-
—**bedürfnis** egomania, egotism, self-assertion, craving for admiration, sense of importance
—**bereich** authority, control, jurisdiction, power, purview, scope (of application)
—**dauer** duration of validity, life, (valid) period, term (of validity)
Gelübde pledge, vow
— **ablegen** make (take) a vow
— **brechen** break the pledge
— **halten** keep the pledge
Gemahl consort, husband, spouse
Gemahlin consort, spouse, wife
Gemarkung boundary, (land) mark
gemäß according to, appropriate to, conformable to, corresponding to, in accordance with, in compliance with, in conformity with, in pursuance of, pursuant to
gemäßigt common, public
gemein caddish, common, dirty, general, low, mean, ordinary, public, sordid, universal, vile, vulgar
Gemeinde borough, commune, community, parish
Stadt— municipality
Gemeinde
—**abgaben** (borough, local, municipal) rates
—**ausschuß** borough (municipal, parish, town) council, local board
—**beamter** municipal officer
—**behörde** municipal authority
—**betrieb** municipal enterprise (service)
—**bezirk** borough
—**einnahmen** local revenue
—**einrichtung** communal organization
—**haus** town hall
—**haushalt** communal (municipal, local) budget
—**land** common
—**mitglied** citizen, parishioner
—**ordnung** communal (local) statute, municipal regulations (code)
—**rat** borough (local, parish, town) council
—**recht** municipal (local) law
—**steuern** s. —abgaben
—**verwaltung** local government, municipal administration
—**vorstand** local board
—**vorsteher** chairman of the municipal (parish) council, chief communal officer, town council
—**wahl** local (municipal) election
Gemein-
—**eigentum** common property
—**gebrauch** common use
gemeingefährlich constituting a public danger, dangerous to the public weal
— **sein** be a public danger
Gemein-
gläubiger bankrupt's (general) creditor, creditor at large
gemeingültig generally acknowledged (admitted, applicable)
Gemeingut common property
Gemeinheit base (low, mean) action, baseness, meanness, sordidness, vulgarity
gemeinhin commonly, currently, generally
Gemein-
—**kosten** general expenses, fixed (overhead) costs
—**last** common burden
—**nutz** common (public) weal
gemeinnützig nonprofit, public (-spirited)
gemeinsam (in) common, joint (ly), together, mutual, united
Gemeinsamkeit association, commonness, community, union, unity
Gemeinschaft community, joint ownership, partnership
— **zur gesamten Hand** co-ownership
—, **eheliche** conjugal community
gemeinschaftlich common, joint(ly), in union, united

Gemeinschaftsarbeit teamwork, cooperation
Gemein-
—schuldner declared (abjudicated) bankrupt, common debtor
—sinn public spirit
—wesen commonwealth, community, polity
—wirtschaft social economy
—wohl common (public) weal (welfare)
genannt aforesaid, above-mentioned, nominal, surnamed
genau accurate, careful, close, correct, in detail, detailed, due, exact, intimate, minute, nice, particular, precise, punctilious, specified, strict, true
un— inaccurate, inexact
Genauigkeit accuracy, closeness, exactitude, exactness, minuteness, niceness, particularity, precision, puntiliousness, strictness
Un— inaccuracy, inexactitude, lack of precision
Gendarm country policeman (constable), rural police, gendarme
Gendarmerie country constabulary, rural police, gendarmerie
genehmigen agree to, approve (of), assent to, authorize, consent to, grant, license, pass, permit, ratify, sanction
—, nicht disapprove
Genehmigung acceptance, approbation, approval, assent, authority, authorization, consent, grant, licence(se), permission, permit, ratification, sanction
genehmigungspflichtig subject to approval (authorization) (a licenc(s)e)
General-
—amnestie (—pardon) amnesty, general pardon
—bevollmächtigter (fully) authorized representative, general agent
—direktor director general, general manager, managing director
—gouverneur governor general
Generalisation generalization
generalisieren generalize
General-
—sekretär secretary general
—streik general strike
—versammlung general assembly, general meeting
—vollmacht general power of attorney, full power (authority)
generell general
genießen enjoy, have
Genosse accomplice, associate, companion, colleague, comrade, fellow, partner
Genossenschaft association, campanionship, company, cooperation, cooperative, (cooperative) society, fellowship, partnership
Genossenschafts-
—bank cooperative bank
—gesetz cooperative law
—wesen cooperative system
genug enough, sufficient
Genüge sufficiency
— tun give satisfaction, satisfy
zur — enough, sufficiently
genügen be enough (sufficient), comply with, meet, satisfy, suffice
genügend enough, satisfactory, sufficient
genügsam contented, moderate, modest, easily satisfied
Genugtuung gratification, redress, reparation, satisfaction
— geben give satisfaction
— erhalten be satisfied
— leisten make reparation
sich — verschaffen obtain redress
Genuß benefit, consumption, delight, enjoyment, exercise, gratification, indulgence, pleasure, use, usufruct
—aktie (—schein) bonus share (stock), bonus certificate
gerade direct, downright, exact, frank, honest, straight, straightforward, upright
Geradheit straightforwardness, straightness, rectitude, uprightness
geraten in get (come, run) into
gerecht equitable, fair, impartial, just, justified, legitimate,

right, righteous, rightful, unbiassed, well-deserved (-founded)
— **werden** do justice (to), meet
gerechtfertigt justifiable, justified, warrantable
Gerechtigkeit equity, equitableness, fairness, impartiality, justice, justification, justness, legitimacy, right, righteousness, rightfulness
Gerechtigkeits
—**gefühl** sense of justice
—**liebe** love of justice
gerechtigkeitsliebend equitable, fair-minded
Gerechtigkeitssinn sense of justice
Gerechtsame franchise, prerogative, privilege, right
gereuen regret, repent of
Gericht bar, bench, court (of justice), forum, judicature, law court, tribunal
—, **vor** in court
— **halten** hold court
vor — bringen bring into (up before) the court
vor — gehen go to law, take legal action
vor — kommen go on trial, come into court
vor — laden cite, summon
zu — sitzen über sit in judgement (up)on, try
vor — stellen bring to (on) trial, prosecute, try (for)
gerichtlich forensic, judicial, judiciary, juridical, legal, in (by the) court, by order of the court, by process of law, at law
—**e Urkunde** legalized document
— **vorgehen** prosecute, take proceedings (an action at law) against
Gerichts-
—**akten** court files (records)
gerichtsanhängig pending
Gerichts-
—**arzt** legal medical officer, medical examiner (expert of the court)
gerichtsbar justiciable
Gerichts-
—**barkeit** judicature, jurisdiction
— —, **streitige** contentious jurisdiction
— —, **freiwillige** noncontentious jurisdiction
—**beamter** court official (officer), law officer
—**befehl** court order, decree of the court, warrant, writ, order of the court
—**behörde** judicial (legal) authority
—**beisitzer** assessor, assistant (associate) judge
gerichtsbekannt judicially known, known to the court
Gerichts-
—**beschluß** court decision (order), decree of the court
—**bezirk** (court) circuit, judicial district, jurisdiction
—**bote (—diener)** court messenger, marshall, usher
—**entscheidung** court (legal, judicial) decision, court judgement, judicial ruling
—**ferien** recess, vacation of the courts
—**gebäude** courts of justice (law), law courts
—**gebühren (—kosten)** court (legal) fees, (court) costs, law (legal) charges
—**hof** bar, court (of justice, of law), judicature, law court, tribunal
—**instanz** court instance
—**kanzlei** record office, law-court offices
gerichtskundig (—notorisch) known to the court, of common knowledge
Gerichts-
—**medizin** forensic medicine, medical jurisprudence
—**ordnung** rules of the court
—**ort** venue
—**periode** law-sitting, session, (trial) term
—**person** law officer, court official
—**perücke** forensic wig
—**polizei** court (judiciary) police
—**präsident** presiding judge

—praxis court (law) practice
—protokolle court rolls (records), minutes
—saal court room
—schranke bar
—schreiber clerk of the court, keeper of the records, registrar, recorder
—siegel court seal
—sitzung hearing, session, sitting (of a court)
— —, in öffentlicher in open court
—sprache law language, legal terminology
—stand (place of) jurisdiction, (legal) domicile, venue
—tag court day
—termin day of hearing (trial)
— — ansetzen assign a day of hearing
—urteil court decision (order), judgement, sentence, verdict
—verfahren court procedure, judicial process, lawsuit, legal proceedings, trial
—verfassung court (judicial) system, judiciary, judicial organization
— —sgesetz Judicature Act (GB)
—verfügung court order, warrant, writ
—verhandlung hearing, court (legal) proceedings, pleadings, trial
—vollzieher bailiff, marshall, sheriff's officer
—vorsitzender presiding judge
—weg beschreiten go to law, initiate (conduct) legal proceedings, proceed by law, take legal steps
—wesen judicial (court) system, judiciary, judicature
gering few, inferior, insignificant, little, low, mean, minor, poor, scanty, small, trivial
geringfügig insignificant, little, minor, negligible, of little importance, petty, slight, small, trifling, trivial, unimportant
Geringfügigkeit insignificance, slightness, smallness, trifle, unimportance
Gerücht report, rumo(u)r
Gerüchtemacher rumour-monger
gerüchtweise as report (rumo[u]r) has it, as the story goes, by hearsay, by rumo(u)r, reportedly
gesamt aggregate, all, collective, complete, entire, general, overall, total, whole
zur —en Hand in common, jointly
Eigentum zur —en Hand joint property
Gesamt-
—ausgaben total expenditure (expenses)
—betrag total (amount), sum total
—bevölkerung total population
—eigentum collective ownership, joint property
—eindruck general impression
—einkommen total income
—einnahmen total receipts
—erbe universal (sole) heir
—forderung total claim
—gläubiger general (joint) creditor
—haftung joint liability
—hand joint ownership, co-ownership
—heit aggregate, entirety, totality, whole
—kapital total capital
—masse total assets (estate)
—schaden general damage, total loss
—schuld general (joint, total) debt
—schuldner co-debtor, general (joint) debtor
—strafe collective (total) penalty (punishment)
—summe (sum) total
—verantwortung joint responsibility
—verlust overall (total) loss
—vermögen general property (estate), total assets
—wert total value
—wohl public weal (welfare)
Gesandter envoy, minister
Gesandtschaft legation, mission
geschädigt damaged, injured
Geschädigter damaged (injured, harmed) party (person)
Geschäft affair, bargain, business, calling, concern, deal(ing),

duty, employment, enterprise, establishment, firm, house, job, line, occupation, operation, shop, store, trade, transaction, work
—**e** dealings, operations, pursuits, transactions
geschäftlich (on) business, commercial
Geschäfts-
—**abschluß** (business) transaction, deal
—**adresse** business address
—**angelegenheiten** business matters
—**anteil** (—**einlage**) business interest (share)
—**bedingungen** terms of trade, trading conditions, business conditions (terms)
—**bereich** business line, competence, field of activity, jurisdiction, portefolio, scope (sphere) of business
—**bericht** annual (business) report
—**beziehung** business (commercial) relation
—**bücher** (account) books, ledgers
geschäftsfähig capable of contracting, legally capacitated
—, **beschränkt** of limited capacity, limited in legal capacity
—, **nicht** incompetent
Geschäftsfähigkeit legal capacity
—, **beschränkte** limited capacity
geschäftsführend executive, managing
Geschäfts-
—**führer** agent, director, manager
— — **ohne Auftrag** agent of necessity
—**führung** administration, agency, conduct of business, direction, management
— — **ohne Auftrag** agency of necessity
—**geheimnis** business (trade) secret
—**interessen** business concerns (interests)
—**jahr** business (financial, fiscal) year
—**kapital** (—**vermögen**) business (trading, working) capital
—**leiter** director, manager
—**leitung** board of directors, management
—**mann** business man, tradesman
—**ordnung** agenda, business rules, order of the day, standing orders, rules of procedure
—**partner** (—**teilhaber**) (business) partner, (business) associate
—**sitz** domicile, place of business, registered (principal) office
—**stelle** bureau, office, secretariate
Haupt— — head office, headquarters
—**stunden** (—**zeit**) business (office) hours
geschäftsunfähig legally incapacitated, incompetent
Geschäfts-
—**unfähigkeit** incompetence, legal incapacity
—**verbindungen** business (commercial) relations
—**zweig** branch (line) of business
geschehen be done, come to pass, happen, occur, take place
Geschehnis event, happening, incidence, occurrence
Geschenk donation, gift, gratuity, present
— **machen** make a donation (gift)
Geschenk-
—**geber** donor
— **nehmer** donee
geschieden divorced
Geschlecht birth, class, family, generation, kind, lineage, race, **sex**
geschlechtlich sexual
Geschlechts-
—**beziehungen** (—**verkehr**) sexual intercourse
—**krankheit** sexual (veneral) disease
geschlossen closed, private
Geschmacksmuster design (patent)
Geschwindigkeit speed
Geschwindigkeits-
—**begrenzung** (—**beschränkung**) speed restriction
—**grenze** speed limit

— — überschreiten exceed the speed limit
—kontrolle speed control
Geschwister brother(s) and sister(s)
Geschworenen, die jury, panel
Geschworenen-
—bank jury box
—gericht assizes, jurors, jury (court), court of assizes
—liste panel
—spruch verdict
Geschworener assize, juror, juryman
Gesellschaft association, body, community, companionship, company, corporation, fellowship, partnership, society
—, eingetragene incorporated company, registered corporation
—, rechtsfähige incorporated company (society), legal corporation
—, nicht rechtsfähige unincorporated society
— mit beschränkter Haftung limited (liability) company
Gesellschafter associate, companion, partner, shareholder, stockholder
—, stiller dormant (secret, silent, sleeping) partner
Gesellschafter-
—anteil interest, share
—versammlung stockholders' (company) meeting
gesellschaftlich corporate, social
Gesellschafts-
—anteil interest, share, stock
—bank joint-stock bank
—kapital company('s) capital, capital stock
—klasse social class
—ordnung social order
—recht company law, corporation act
—satzung (—statut[en]) articles of association (incorporation, partnership)
—sitz domicile, registered office, residence (of a company)
—urkunde charter of incorporation, partnership deed
—vertrag articles of association, firm's contract, partnership agreement (contract)
Gesetz act, bill, law, statute
kraft —es by act (virtue) of law, by operation of law
Gesetz-
—blatt law (official) gazette
—buch code (of laws), law book, statute book
— —, Bürgerliches Civil Code
Straf— — Penal Code
—entwurf bill
Gesetzes-
—absicht intention of law
—anwendung application of law
—artikel section of an act
—auslegung (—interpretation) interpretation of law
—bestimmung legal regulation, provision of law, rule of law, statute
—brecher law breaker
—bruch breach of the law, law breaking
—entwurf bill
—fiktion legal fiction, fiction of law
—formel legal formula
—kenntnis familiarity with (knowledge of) the law, legal knowledge
—konflikt conflict of law, conflicting laws
—kraft force (strength) of law, legal force (power), statutory effect
— —, durch by operation of law
— — erlangen become law
gesetzeskundig knowing the law
Gesetzes-
—kundiger lawyer
—lücke gap in the law, legal defect, loophole
—periode legislative period
—recht statutory (statute, written) law
—sammlung codification, compendium of laws, digest, statute book
—statut articles of association
—stelle passage in the law
—text text (wording) of the law
gesetzestreu law-abiding

Gesetzes-
—treue law-abidingness
—übertreter law breaker, offender
—übertretung contravention (violation) of the law, law breaking
—umgehung evasion of the law
—verletzung breach (infringement, violation) of the law, law breaking
—vermutung legal presumption, presumption of law
—verordnung decree law, statutory order
—verstoß law breaking
—vorlage bill
—vorschrift legal regulation, rule of law, statute
gesetzgebend law-giving, law-making, legislative
—e Gewalt legislative power, legislature
Gesetzgeber lawgiver, lawmaker, legislator
gesetzgeberisch legislative
Gesetzgebung law-giving, legislation, legislature
Gesetzgebungs-
—akt act of legislation, legislative act
—funktion legislative function
—gewalt (—recht) legislative authority (power)
—periode legislature
gesetzlich lawful, legal, legitimate, statutory
— geschützt registered
Gesetzlichkeit lawfulness, legality, legitimacy
gesetzlos anarchic(al), lawless
Gesetzlosigkeit anarchism, anarchy, lawlessness
gesetzmäßig lawful, legal, legitimate, regular, statutory
Gesetzmäßigkeit lawfulness, legality, legitimacy, regularity
gesetzwidrig illegal, illicit, unlawful, contrary to the law
Gesetzwidrigkeit illegality, unlawfulness
Gesichtspunkt aspect, point of view, viewpoint
gesondert separate(ly)
Gespräch conversation, discourse, discussion, interview, talk
—e führen mit converse with, have a conversation (talk) with, talk with
Gestalt appearance, condition, figure, form, frame, kind, manner, shape, statute
gestalten arrange, create, fashion, form, frame, model, organize, shape
Gestaltung arrangement, condition, creation, formation, make-up, organization, production, state, structure
geständig confessing, pleading guilty
— sein confess, make a confession, plead guilty
nicht — sein plead not guilty, refuse to make a confession
Geständnis admission, avowal, confession
— ablegen make a confession
gestatten admit, allow, approve of, authorize, consent to, grant, permit, tolerate
Geste gesture
gestehen admit, avow, confess
Gesuch application, petition, request, suit
—steller applicant, petitioner
gesucht (steckbrieflich) wanted
—, von der Polizei wanted by the police
gesund healthy, sound
—, geistig sane
Gesundheit health, soundness
—, geistige sanity
—, öffentliche public health
Gesundheits-
—amt health (medical) board, health office (department), sanitary authority (board)
—attest (—papiere) (—zeugnis) health certificate
—beamter health officer
—behörden health authorities
—bestimmungen sanitary regulations
—dienst public health service
—einrichtungen public health institutions (service)
—kontrolle sanitary control
—polizei sanitary police
gesundheitsschädlich insanitary, unhealthy

Gesundheits
—verordnungen (—vorschriften) health prescriptions, sanitary regulations
—wesen health service
—zustand (state of) health
Getöteter dead (killed) person
getrennt detached, separate
— leben live apart (separate, in separation)
Getrenntleben separation
Gewähr guarantee, guaranty, security, warranty
—, ohne subject to correction, without guarantee
gewähren accord, afford, allow, concede, fulfil, furnish, grant, offer, permit, yield
gewährleisten ensure, give security for, guarantee, vouch for, warrant
Gewährleistung guarantee, guaranty, warranty
Gewährleistungs-
—klage action for warranty, redhibitory action
—klausel warranty clause
—pflicht warranty obligation
—vertrag warranty deed (contract)
Gewahrsam care, charge, control, custody, detention, imprisonment, safe keeping (custody)
Gewahrsam
in — haben be in charge of, have the care of, have in (under) custody, have in safe keeping
in — nehmen take charge of, take into custody, place under detention
sich in — befinden be in custody (safe keeping)
Gewährsmann authority, informant, guarantee, guarantor, warrantor
Gewalt authority, command, control, dominion, force, grip, hold, influence, might, power, sway, violence
mit (durch) — by force, forcibly, with violence
mit aller — at all costs

Gewalt
—, ausübende executive
—, elterliche parental authority
—, gesetzgebende legislative (power), legislature
—, höhere Act of God, force majeure
—, höchste (oberste) supremacy, supreme power, sovereignty
—, richterliche judicial power
—, unumschränkte absolute (sovereign) power
Gewalt
— antun do violence to, offend against, outrage
— anwenden employ force, use violence
in seine — bringen bring under one's sway, conquer, overrule, overwhelm
— haben über control, have authority (power) over, sway
in der — haben have a grip on, have in one's power
sich in der — haben have command of oneself, keep oneself under control
— verlieren lose control of (one's grip on)
der — weichen yield to force
Gewalt-
—akt (—handlung, —maßnahme, —tat) act of violence (force), (act of) outrage
—anwendung (durch) (by) use of force
—enteilung distribution of power
—entrennung separation of power
—herrschaft despotism, tyranny
—herrscher despot, tyrant
—mensch brute, rowdy
gewaltsam by force, forceful, forcible, violent, with violence
—er Tod violent (unnatural) death
gewalttätig brutal, outrageous, violent
Gewalt-
—tätigkeit (act of) outrage, act of violence (force)
—verbrecher cutthroat, gangster, racketeer
Gewand, amtliches gown, robe
Gewehr gun, rifle
—schein gun licenc(s)e

Gewerbe business, craft, industry, occupation, profession, trade
—, dunkles (schmutziges) shady (dirty) business
—, ehrliches honest trade
— anmelden register a trade (business)
— ausüben (betreiben) carry on (exercise, follow, pursue) a trade, run a business
Gewerbe-
—anmeldung registration of trade
—aufsicht trade (factory) inspection
—aufsichtsamt industrial inspection board, trade board
—bank industrial (trade) bank
—erlaubnis trade licence
—freiheit freedom of trade
—gericht court of trade, industrial court
—gerichtsbarkeit industrial arbitration, trade jurisdiction
—gesetze industrial (trade) laws, factory act (law)
—gesetzgebung industrial legislation
—kapital trading capital
—ordnung trade regulations
—polizei trade police, factory inspection
—recht industrial (trade) law
—schein trade (trading) certificate (licenc[s]e)
—stand trade, trading class
—steuer trade tax
gewerbetreibend industrial, trading
Gewerbe-
—treibender tradesman
gewerblich business, commercial, industrial, trade
gewerbsmäßig for gain, habitual, professional
Gewerbszweig branch (line) of industry (trade)
Gewerkschaft trade (labo[u]r) union
Gewerkschaftler **(trade)** unionist, union member, organized workman
Nicht— non-unionist, non-union workman
gewerkschaftlich (trade-)unionist
— organisiert unionized
Gewerkschafts-
—führer union (labo[u]r) leader
—führung union leadership
—funktionär union officer (official)
—mitglied union member, unionist
—mitgliedschaft union membership
—verband federation of trade unions
—vorschriften union regulations
—wesen (trade) unionism
Gewicht consequence, importance, weight
— beimessen (legen auf) attach great importance (weight) to
ins — fallen count, be important, matter
Gewichts-
—bescheinigung (—zeugnis) weight certificate
—differenz (—unterschied) weight difference
—manko deficiency in (shortness of) weight, shortweight, underweight
—maß weight
—schein weight note
—verlust loss of weight
Gewinn advantage, benefit, earnings, gain(ings), income, increment, issue, prize, profit(s), proceeds, receipts, return, surplus, win(nings), yield (in profits)
—anteil bonus, dividend, share in profits
—anteilschein dividend coupon (warrant)
—ausfall loss of earnings
—ausschüttung distribution of profits, dividends
gewinnberechtigt (-beteiligt) participating, profit-sharing
Gewinn-
—beteiligung profitsharing, participation, share in profits
gewinnbringend advantageous, gainful, lucrative, paying, profitable, remunerative
gewinnen, acquire, extract, gain, get, mine, obtain, produce, win
Gewinner gainer, winner

Gewinn
—rechnung, Verlust und profit and loss account, income statement
—spanne profit margin
—steuer profits tax
—sucht covetousness, greed, lucre
gewinnsüchtig covetous, greedy, profit-seeking
Gewinnung acquisition, extraction, mining, production, winning
Gewinn-
—verteilung distribution of profits
Gewissen conscience
—, gutes good conscience
—, reines clear conscience
—, ruhiges peaceful conscience
—, schlechtes bad conscience
—, schuldbeladenes guilty conscience
gegen Recht und — contrary to right and morals
nach bestem Wissen und — conscientiously
—, ohne without conscience
wider besseres Wissen und — contrary to the dictates of conscience
auf dem — haben have on one's conscience
gegen sein — handeln act against the dictates of conscience
ins — reden appeal to conscience
gewissenlos conscienceless, reckless, unconscientious, unscrupulous
gewissenhaft conscientious, scrupulous
Gewissens-
—angst (—not) anguish, anxiety, qualms of conscience
—bisse compunction, conscientious scruples, pricks of conscience, qualms, remorse
—frage question of conscience
—freiheit freedom (liberty) of conscience
—klausel conscience clause
—konflikt conflict of conscience
—pflicht commands (dictates) of conscience
—sache matter of conscience
—zwang pressure (restraint) of conscience
—zweifel conscientious scruples
Gewißheit certainty, certitude, conviction, security
—, mit with certainty
sich — verschaffen make sure of
Gewohnheit convention, custom, habit, practice, usage, use, wont
—, aus from (out of) habit
—, Macht der force of habit
gewohnheitsmäßig conventional, customary, formal, habitual, mechanical, normal, routine, usual
Gewohnheits-
—recht common (conventional, customary) law, customary (right), prescriptive right
—trinker habitual drunkard
—verbrecher habitual criminal, hoodlum, gaol bird
gewöhnen
sich — an acclimatize (accustom, habituate) oneself to, get accustomed (used) to
gewöhnlich common, customary, general, habitual, ordinary, usual, vulgar
Gewöhnung acclimatization, accustoming, habituation
geziemen, sich be fitting, be fit and proper
sich — für become, befit
geziemend convenient, decent, due, fitting, proper, seemly
gezwungen constrained, forced, formal, stiff, strained, unnatural
gezwungenermaßen forced, perforce, under coercion (compulsion, duress)
Gezwungenheit constraint, formality, stiffness, unnaturalness
Gier cupidity, greed(iness), rage
gierig covetous, greedy
Gift poison, toxicant
Gegen— antidote, remedy
Rausch— dope, drug, narcotic
—, schleichendes slow poison
—, schnell wirkendes rapid poison, toxicant
—, tierisches venom

giftig poisonous, toxic(al), venomous
Giftigkeit poisonousness, venomousness, virulence
Gift-
—mischer poisoner
—mischerei poisoning
—mord (murder by) poisoning
—mörder poisoner
Gilde corporation, g(u)ild, trade
Gipfel acme, climax, culmination, peak, summit, top
—abkommen summit agreement
—gespräche summit talks
—konferenz summit conference
—punkt culminating point
—treffen summit meeting
Girant endorser, indorser
Girat(ar) endorsee, indorsee
girierbar assignable, endorsable, indorsable, negotiable, transferable
girieren assign, endorse, indorse, transfer
—, blanko endorse (indorse) in blank
Giro assignment, endorsement, indorsement, transfer
Blanko— blank endorsement (indorsement), endorsement in blank
Glaube belief, confidence, creed, faith, trust
—, blinder implicit faith
—, öffentlicher public faith, prima facie evidence
—, religiöser religious belief, persuasion
auf Treu und —n on trust
in gutem Glauben in good faith, bona fide
in schlechtem —n in bad faith, mala fide
glauben believe, credit, give credit to, suppose, think, trust
— an believe in, have confidence in, trust
— machen make believe
—, nicht misbelieve
Glaubens-
—bekenntnis confession (of faith), credo, creed
— —, politisches political credo
—freiheit freedom of faith (religion), religious liberty
glaubhaft authentic, believable, credible, faithful, plausible, prima facie (evidence), veracious
— machen establish the credibility of, establish a prima facie case, give prima facie evidence, make appear credible, render believable, substantiate
Glaubhaftigkeit authenticity, credibility
Glaubhaftmachung authentication, establishing the credibility, making credible, prima facie evidence, satisfactory proof, substantiation
Gläubiger creditor, guarantor, mortgagee, obligee
—staat creditor nation
glaubwürdig authentic, credible, reliable, trustworthy, worthy of belief, veracious
Glaubwürdigkeit authenticity, credibility, credit, reliability, trustworthiness, veracity
gleich equal, equivalent, even, identical, like, same
—altrig of the same age
—artig homogeneos, of the same kind
Gleichartigkeit equality in kind, homogeneity, homogeneousness, similarity
gleichbedeutend (mit) equivalent (to), interchangeable, synonymous (with)
gleichberechtigt having (enjoying) equal rights, on equal terms
— sein be equal, have the same rights, rank equally
Gleichberechtigung equality (of rights, status), parity, equal rights (status)
gleichbleibend constant, invariable, stable, steady, unvarying
gleichen be like, resemble
gleichförmig equable, equal, in conformity, monotonous, uniform
Gleichförmigkeit conformity, equality, monotony, uniformity
gleichgestellt coordinate, equal, on the same level
Gleichgewicht balance, equilibrium, (equi)poise

—, **mangelndes** disequilibrium, lack of balance
—, **moralisches** equipoise
—, **politisches** balance of power, political equilibrium
—, **seelisches** mental equilibrium, poise of mind
Gleichgewichtsstörung disturbance of equilibrium
Gleichheit conformity, equality, identity, likeness, monotony, parity, sameness, uniformity
gleichkommen be equivalent to, be (come) up to, equal, match
—, nicht fall short of
gleichlautend concurrent, conformable, identical, unisonant, in conformity with, to the same effect, of the same tenor
gleichmachen equalize (to, with), level (with), make equal, put on an equality with, settle
gleichmäßig equal, regular, steady, uniform
Gleichmäßigkeit equality, regularity, uniformity
gleichnamig of (having) the same name
gleichrangig equivalent, ranking equally, of equal rank
— **sein** be of the same standing, rank equally
gleichschalten bring into line, coordinate, streamline, unify
Gleichschaltung bringing into line, coordination, unification
gleichsetzen equate with
gleichstehen equal, be on par (an equality) with
gleichstellen equalize, equate, level, assimilate in status, put on a par with, treat as an equal
sich — mit put oneself on a par with
Gleichstellung comparison, emancipation, equal treatment, equalization, levelling
gleichteilig of equal parts
gleichtun come up to, equal, match
gleichwertig equal, equipollent, equivalent, of the same value
— **sein** be on a par with, be in the same class with
Gleichwertigkeit equal value, equivalence
gleichzeitig at the same time, coincident(al), contemporaneous, contemporary, simultaneous
Gleichzeitigkeit coexistence, coincidence, contemporaneity, contemporaneousness, simultaneity, simultaneousness
gleitend sliding
—**e Preise** sliding scale prices
Gleitklausel escalation clause
Glied link, member
gliedern arrange, articulate, class, classify, dispose, divide, group, joint, organize
sich — in be divided into, consist of
Gliederung arrangement, articulation, break-down, classification, disposition, division, grouping, organization, structure
glimpflich forbearing, gentle, indulgent, mild
— **davonkommen** come (get) off lightly (easily)
—**e Behandlung** gentle treatment
global global, overall, worldwide
Gnade clemency, favour, grace, mercy, pardon
ohne — mercilessly, without mercy
um — bitten beg for pardon, sue for mercy
— **erweisen** do a favour, pardon
— **finden** be pardoned, find favour
— **vor Recht ergehen lassen** be merciful, show mercy, temper justice with mercy
Gnaden-
—**akt** act of grace
—**erlaß** act of grace, amnesty, general pardon
—**frist** days of grace, reprieve, respite
—**gesuch** petition for pardon (clemency, grace, mercy, reprieve), plea for clemency
—**recht** power (right) of pardon (grace), prerogative of mercy

—stoß finishing stroke, coup de grâce
—tod mercy killing
gnädig clement, favo(u)rable, gracious, lenient, merciful, mild
Gönner benefactor, patron, protector, sponsor
gönnerhaft patronizing
Gotteslästerer blasphemer
Gotteslästerung blasphemy
Gouvernement government
Gouverneur governor
Grab grave, tomb
—schändung desecration of (outrage on, sacrilege on, violation of) a grave
Grad degree, grade, rank
—einteilung graduation, scale
graduell gradual
graduieren graduate
Graduierung graduation
Grafschaft county
Gratifikation bonus, gratification, gratuity
gratis free of charge, gratis, gratuitous
Gratisaktie bonus share (stock)
grausam atrocious, brutal, cruel, fierce, hard, inhuman
Grausamkeit atrocity, atrociousness, atrocious act, brutality, cruelty, ferocity
greifbar available, seizable, tangible
greifen zu have recourse to, resort to, take (up)
Gremium board, body, committee, corporation, group
Grenze border, boundary, bound, confines, frontier, limit, margin
Grenz-
—abkommen border treaty
—bestimmung boundary settlement, fixation of boundaries (frontiers)
—bezirk (—gebiet, —zone) borderland, border (frontier) area (district, zone)
grenzen an adjoin, be adjacent (adjoining) to, border on, be bounded by, verge on
grenzenlos boundless, excessive, immense, limitless, unbounded, unlimited
Grenz-
—enlosigkeit boundlessness, excessiveness, immensity, unboundedness
—fall borderline (limiting) case
—festlegung delimitation, determination of frontiers, fixation of boundaries
—kampf border fighting
—konflikt border (frontier) zone
—kontrolle border (frontier) control, customs inspection
—land borderland
—linie borderline, boundary line, demarcation line
—mal landmark
—polizei border (frontier) police
—schutz border protection, frontier defenc(s)e (guards), protection of frontiers
—staat border (frontier) state
—station border (frontier) station
—stein (—zeichen) boundary (border) stone (mark), landmark
—streifen border (frontier) zone
—streit(igkeit) border (frontier, boundary) dispute
—übergang (—übertritt) border (frontier) crossing
—übergangsstelle checkpoint, crossing point
—übertritt, unerlaubter unlawful crossing of the frontier
—verkehr border traffic
—verlauf course of frontier
—verletzung violation of the frontier (border)
—wache frontier guard
—zeichen boundary mark, landmark
—ziehung delimitation
—zwischenfall border (frontier) incident (trouble)
Greuel abomination, atrocity, horror
—tat (act of) atrocity, atrocious crime (deed)
grob brutal, crass, crude, gross, rough, rude
— fahrlässig grossly negligent
—e Fahrlässigkeit gross negligence
Grobheit crudeness, crudity, grossness, roughness, rudeness

gröblich crass, flagrant, gross, shameless
Größe bulk, dimension, extent, greatness, height, largeness, magnitude, quantity, range, size, volume
—nangabe statement of size
—nordnung dimension, order, scale
—nverhältnis proportion, scale
Groß-
—handel wholesale (trade)
—händler (Grossist) wholesale dealer, wholesaler
großjährig of (full) age
— werden come of age
Großjähriger major
Großjährigkeit full age, majority
Großmacht great power
großzügig generous, liberal, broad-minded
Großzügigkeit generosity, liberality, breadth of mind
Grund account, argument, base, basis, bottom, cause, foundation, ground(s), land, motive, occasion, reason, soil, territory
— und Boden land (property), real estate (property), landed (real) property
Grund-
—bedeutung basic (original) meaning
—bedingung basic (main, principal) condition, fundamental term, prerequisite
—begriff basic (fundamental) concept (idea)
—begriffe fundamentals, principles
—belastung land charge
—besitz landowning, landed property, real estate (property)
— —, freier freehold property (estate), realty
—besitzer (—eigentümer) landed (real estate) proprietor, landowner
—buch land (real estate, real property) register
—buchamt land office (registry), real estate recording office
—dienstbarkeit easement, landed (real) servitude
—eigentum landed (real) property, real estate, realty
gründen build up, constitute, create, establish, float, form, found, institute, launch, open, organize, promote, set up, start
— auf base (found) on
sich — auf rest on
Gründer builder, creator, founder, institutor, originator, promotor
Grund-
—erwerb acquisition (purchase) of land
—fläche acreage
—gebühr basic fee (rate)
—gedanke (—idee) basic (fundamental, leading) idea (notion), keystone
—gehalt basic salary
—gesetz basic (fundamental) law, constitution
—herr landlord
—kapital capital (original) stock
—kenntnisse fundamental knowledges
—kredit mortgage loan, real estate credit
—lage base, basis, element, foundation, fundament, groundwork
—lagen rudiments
grundlegend basic, constitutive, fundamental
Grundlegung establishment, foundation
gründlich careful, complete, profound, solid, thorough
Gründlichkeit carefulness, profundity, solidity, thoroughness
Grundlohn basic wage
grundlos baseless, groundless, unfounded, unreasonably, without reason
Grundlosigkeit baselessness, groundlessness
Grund-
—pfand real estate mortgage
— — brief mortgage bond
—pfandgläubiger mortgagor
—pfeiler keystone
—prinzip basic (fundamental, guiding) principle, keystone
—recht basic (fundamental) right
—regel basic principle (rule)

—satz axiom, maxim, principle, rule
grundsätzlich as a general principle, as a matter of principal, as a rule, fundamental, on principle
Grund-
—schuld land charge
—steuer land tax, property tax
—stück land, piece (plot) of land, plot, premises, (real) property, real estate
—tarif basic rate
—tatsache basic (fundamental, ground) fact
—tendenz tenor
—übel basic evil, root (source) of evil
Gründung creation, establishment, formation, foundation, institution, promotion, setting up
—svertrag (—surkunde) articles (memorandum) of association, foundation charter, articles (certificate, charter) of incorporation
Grund-
—ursache primary (prime) cause
—vermögen capital stock, land(ed) property, real estate
—zins ground rent
—zug basic concept, distinctive mark, main (chief, fundamental) feature
Gruppe category, class, cluster, crew, crowd, gang, group, section, series, squad, team
gruppieren arrange in groups, group
—, sich cluster, gather
Gruppierung arrangement in groups, grouping
Guillotine guillotine
guillotinieren behead, decapitate, guillotine
gültig admissible, available, current, effective, good, in force, lawful, legal, valid
für — erklären validate
— sein be current (in force, valid)
Gültigkeit admissibility, availability, currency, effectiveness, force, lawfulness, legality, validity
— aufheben invalidate
— erlangen become effective
— haben be valid, run
— verleihen legalize, authenticate
— verlieren expire
Gültigkeits-
—bereich scope of validity
—dauer life, (duration, term of) validity
—erklärung legalization, validation
Gunst favo(u)r, goodwill, grace, kindness, partiality, patronage
— erweisen do a favo(u)r
in — stehen be in good graces
zu —en von in favo(u)r of, in (on) behalf of, for the benefit of, to the credit of
Gunstbezeigung (—bezeugung) favo(u)r, kindness
günstig advantageous, auspicious, beneficial, convenient, favo(u)rable, opportune, promissing, propitious
—e Bedingungen easy (favo(u)rable) terms
—e Gelegenheit chance, facility, opportunity
un— unfavo(u)rable, unpropitious
günstigst
im —en Fall at (the) best
Günstling favo(u)rite
—swirtschaft favo(u)ritism
Gut belongings, commodity, estate, farm, good(s), merchandise, property
—, Hab und goods and chattels
gut advantageous, favo(u)rable, good
Gutachten award, expertise, opinion, report
— abgeben deliver (render) an opinion
— einholen take an opinion, take expert opinion
Gutachter arbitrator, expert, umpire, surveyor
gutachtlich expert
gutartig harmless
Gutartigkeit harmlessness
Gutdünken discretion, judgement
—, nach at discretion

Güte benevolence, benignity, friendliness, good nature, goodness, kindness, quality
—, in amicably, in a friendly way
—, Vorschlag zur conciliatory proposal
Güte-
—antrag petition for amicable settlement
—grad grade, standard
—prüfung (—überwachung) quality control
—schutz quality protection
—stelle conciliatory court
—termin day of reconciliation hearing
—verfahren amicable settlement, conciliation, conciliatory proceedings
—zeichen brand, quality mark (label)
Güter goods, commodities, merchandise
Güter-
—austausch exchange of goods
—gemeinschaft community of property, joint ownership (property)
— —steilung dissolution of the community of property
—recht property law
—trennung separate ownership (property), separation of property
in — — leben have separate property
gutgläubig bona fide, (in) good faith, credulous
Guthaben credit (balance)
Bank— bank account (balance)
gutheißen approve, countenance, sanction
nicht — disapprove
gütig benevolent, benignant, good, kind
gütlich amicable, friendly, out-of-court
sich — einigen come to an amicable arrangement
—e Einigung amicable (friendly) arrangement (settlement)
gutmachen compensate (for), make good, make up for, make amends for
gutsagen answer (vouch) for, be security (surety) for, stand bail for, warrant
Gutsbesitzer farmer, farmholder, landowner, landed proprietor
Gutschein coupon, credit note (entry), ticket, voucher, warranty
gutschreiben credit to (with)
Gutschrift credit entry (item)
—sanzeige credit note
gutstehen für answer for, be security (surety) for, guarantee, stand bail for

H

Hab und Gut goods and chattels
Habe belongings, effects, goods, property
—, bewegliche (fahrende) chattels, movables, movable property
—, persönliche personal effects (things)
—, unbewegliche immovables
Haben credit
—, Soll und assets and liabilities, debit and credit
haben be in possession of, have, hold, possess
—, unter sich be in charge (control) of, command, control
Habenichts have-not
habhaft werden get hold of
habilitieren habilitate
Habilitierung (Habilitation) habilitation
habituell habitual

Habitus bearing, deportment, habit
Habseligkeiten belongings, effects, goods, things
Haft arrest, confinement, custody, detention, imprisonment
Schutz— protective custody
aus der — entlassen discharge, release
in — under arrest
in — halten detain
in — nehmen (setzen) arrest, place under confinement, take into custody (charge)
zu — verurteilen condemn to imprisonment
Haftanordnung committal order
haftbar answerable, liable, responsible
— machen hold (make) liable (responsible) for
— sein be liable for, be responsible for
voll — fully liable (responsible)
Haftbarkeit liability, responsibility
Haftbefehl capias, warrant (writ) of arrest, writ of attachment
— erlassen issue (make out) a warrant of arrest
Haftbestätigungsbefehl (— — ausweis) (writ of) detainer
haften answer for, bail for, be answerable (liable, responsible) for, guarantee, stand (be) security for, vouch for, warrant for
Haftentlassung release from custody
—, vorläufige conditional (preliminary) release
—sbefehl order of release
Häftling detainee, prisoner
Haftpflicht liability, responsibility
—, beschränkte limited liability (responsibility)
—, gemeinsame joint liability (responsibility)
—, unbeschränkte unlimited liability (responsibility)
haftpflichtig answerable, liable, responsible
Haftpflichtversicherung liability (third-party) insurance
Haftung liability, responsibility
—, beschränkte limited (restricted) liability (responsibility)
—, unbeschränkte unlimited (unrestricted) liability (responsibility)
Gesellschaft mit beschränkter — limited (liability) company
Haftungs-
—ausschluß exclusion (exemption) from liability, nonliability
—begrenzung (—beschränkung) limitation of liability
—beschränkungsbestimmung limiting clause
—gemeinschaft collective (joint) liability (responsibility)
—übernahme assumption of liability
—umfang extent (scope) of liability (responsibility)
Haft
—vollzug arrest, imprisonment
—verlängerungsbefehl (writ of) detainer
halbamtlich (—dienstlich) semi-official, officious
Halbblut half-blood (-caste)
halbblütig half-blooded (-caste)
halber for the sake of, on account of, owing to
beispiels— by way of example
ehren— honorary, honoris causa
Halbheit half-measure, imperfection, incompleteness, insufficiency
halbieren halve
Halbjahr half(-)year
—esbericht half-yearly (six-months') report
halbjährlich every six months, half-yearly, semi-annual
halbtägig half-day (-time), part-time
— arbeiten work half-day (-time)
Halbtags
—arbeit (—beschäftigung) part-time employment (job)
—arbeiter half-time worker, half-timer
Halb-
—waise fatherless (motherless) child

—welt semi-monde, half(-)world
—wissen half-knowledge
—zeit half(-)time
Hälfte half, moiety
Halsabschneider cutthroat
Halt footing, grip, halt, hold, stop(page), support
— finden an find support in (from)
— gebieten call a halt to, stop
keinen festen — haben be of no standing, have no permanency
— suchen seek support
— verlieren über lose one's grip on
haltbar durable, justifiable, lasting, solid, stable, strong, valid
Haltbarkeit consistence (cy), durability, solidity, stability
halten deliver, entertain, give, have, hold, keep, make, observe, take (in)
— für believe, consider, deem, hold, regard as, take as
auf dem laufenden — keep informed (up-to-date)
für richtig — approve of
in Gang — keep going
sich — an have recourse to, keep to, stick to
Halter holder, keeper, owner, supporter
Halte
—schild stop sign
—signal (—zeichen) block (stop) signal
haltlos baseless, boneless, groundless, irresolute, unfounded, unmaintainable, unmotivated, unprincipled, unstable, unsteady, unsubstantial, untenable, without backbone
Haltlosigkeit baselessness, groundlessness, irresoluteness, unfoundedness, unstableness, unsteadiness
Haltung approach, attitude, bearing, carriage, deportment, mind, position, posture
— einnehmen assume (take up) an attitude
Haltungsänderung change of attitude (mind)
Halunke blackguard, rascal, rogue, scoundrel, scamp
Hammelsprung division
Hand hand
an — von based on, in the light of
— legen an attempt at a person's life, lay hands on
freie — haben have a free hand
freie — lassen give a free hand
in der — haben have in hand
in die — nehmen take in hand (up)
unter der — privately, secretly, underhand
von der — weisen refuse, reject
zu treuen Händen in trust
Hand
—akten files, papers
—arbeit handwork, manual labo(u)r (work)
—arbeiter manual labo(u)rer (worker)
—ausgabe pocket (small) edition
—buch guide, handbook, manual, reference book
Handel agreement, bargain, business, commerce, dealings, trade, transaction
Handel
— abschließen come to terms, do a deal with, strike a bargain
— treiben carry on commerce, deal, trade
Handel und Gewerbe commerce and trade
Handel und Industrie trade and industry
Handel und Wandel trade and traffic
Handel conflict, dispute, quarrel
Handeln action, doings, trading
handeln act, bargain, carry on a trade, deal, do business, function, handle, operate, proceed, take action, trade
— gegen act contrary to, infringe, violate
— nach act upon
— von be concerned with, deal with, treat of
mit sich — lassen be open to conviction (an offer)
schlecht — an do a bad turn
sich — um be a case (matter) of, be in question, concern

Handels-
—abkommen commercial treaty, trade agreement
—abordnung (—delegation) trade delegation
—agent commercial agent
—amt board of trade
—artikel article (of merchandise), commodity
—ausschuß trade committee
—bank commercial bank
—bedingungen trading terms, terms of trade
—befugnis (—bewilligung) trading licenc(s)e
—bestimmungen trade regulations
—beziehungen commercial relations
—bilanz balance of trade, trade balance
—blockade blockade of commerce, commercial barriers, restraint of trade, trade restrictions
—brauch trade custom (usage)
—buch ledger, trade book
handelseinig werden come to terms (an agreement), strike a bargain
Handels-
—erlaubnis trading licenc(s)e
—erleichterungen trade facilities
handelsfähig marketable, negotiable
Handels-
—firma (commercial) firm, commercial establishment (house)
—freiheit free trade, freedom (liberty) of trade
—genosse partner
—genossenschaft company, partnership
—gericht commercial court, court of trade
handelsgerichtlich eingetragen incorporated, registered
—e Eintragung incorporation, registration
Handels-
—gesellschaft (business) corporation, (trading) company, trade association
—gesetz commercial (business, mercantile, trade) law
— —buch commercial code
— —gebung commercial legislation
—gewerbe trade
—gewohnheitsrecht law merchant
—güter commodities, goods, merchandise
—innung guild
—kammer board of trade, chamber of commerce
— —, Industrie- und Chamber of Commerce (and Industry)
—kapital trading capital
—konferenz trade conference
—konzession trading licenc(s)e
—korrespondenz commercial correspondence
—makler commercial (mercantile) broker
—marke brand, trademark
—minister Minister of Commerce, President of the Board of Trade (GB), Secretary of Commerce (USA)
—ministerium Board of Trade (GB), Department of Commerce (USA), Ministry of Commerce
—mission trade mission
—monopol trade monopoly
—name trade name
—nation trading nation
—papiere negotiable instruments, commercial papers
—partner (business) partner
—preis market price
—recht commercial (business, mercantile, trade) law, law merchant
—register commercial (trade) register
—richter commercial judge
—sache commercial affair (matter, case)
—schranken trade barriers
—spanne margin
—sperre embargo
—streitigkeit trade dispute
handelsüblich customary (usual) in trade
Handels-
—verband (—vereinigung) trade association
—verbot embargo, prohibition of trade

—vertrag commercial treaty, trade agreement
—vorschriften business (trade) regulations
—ware article (of merchandise), commodity
—waren merchandise
—wechsel trade (commercial) bill
—wert market value
—zeichen brand, trademark
—zweig brand of trade
handeltreibend commercial, trading
Handeltreibender dealer, merchant, trader, tradesman
Handgeld earnest (imprest, press) money
Handgemenge handbill
handgeschrieben handwritten, in long-hand, written by hand
Handhabe charge, dodge, possibility, pretext
—, gesetzliche legal grounds
— bieten give a handle (against, to)
handhaben administer, deal with, handle, manage, manipulate, operate, run, work
Handhabung administration, handling, management, manipulation
Händler dealer, merchant, trader, tradesman
Handlung act, action, deed, proceeding
—, strafbare offence, penal (punishable) act
—, unerlaubte tort, tortuous (unlawful, wrongful) act
Handlungs-
—beauftragter agent
—bevollmächtigter attorney, proxy, authorized agent (representative)
—freiheit free scope, freedom (liberty) of action
—gehilfe clerk
—vollmacht authority (to act), power (of attorney)
—weise attitude, behavio(u)r, conduct, dealing, manner of acting, method, practice, procedure, proceeding
Handschelle handcuff, manacle
—n anlegen handcuff, manacle
Handschrift hand, handwriting, manuscript
handschriftlich hand-written, in handwriting, in long-hand, in writing, manuscript, written
Handwechsel handbill, promissory note
Handwerk craft, handicraft, trade
— legen put a stop to a person's plans
— treiben carry on a trade
sein — verstehen know one's job
Handwerker craftsman, handicraftsman, tradesman
Handzeichen hand signal, manual sign
Handzettel handbill
hängen hang
hängig pending
harmlos harmless, innocent, insignificant, simple, small
Harmlosigkeit harmlessness, innocence
hart difficult, hard, harsh, heavy, ligid, rigorous, severe, solid, stiff, strong, vehement
Härte hardness, hardship, harshness, rigidity, rigour, severity
—fall case of hardship
—klausel hardship clause
Hartgeld coins, hard cash (money)
hartnäckig obstinate, persistent, pertinacious, stubborn, unyielding
Hartnäckigkeit obstinacy, persistence (cy), pertinacity, stubbornness
Haß hatred
hassen hate
hauen beat, hit, strike
häufen, sich accumulate, aggregate, increase, multiply, be spreading
häufig frequent
Häufigkeit frequency
Häufung accumulation, increase, multiplication, spreading
Haupt boss, chief, head, leader, principal

—aktionär leading (principal) shareholder (stockholder)
—angeklagter (—angeschuldigter) main defendant (accused)
—anspruch main claim
—bedeutung primary meaning
—bedingung main condition
—belastungszeuge principal witness for the prosecution, star prosecution witness
—beruf chief occupation, main profession
—berufung main appeal
—beschäftigung full-time job, main (principal) occupation
—bestandteil main part, chief constituent
—beteiligter principal party (person)
—beweggrund leading (main) motive
—buch (general) ledger
—eigenschaft principal quality
—entlastungszeuge principal witness for the defenc(s)e
—erbe chief (principal) heir
—faktor major factor
—fehler chief mistake, main (principal) defect
—feind chief enemy
—frage chief question, main issue
—gedanke chief thought, fundamental idea, keynote, keystone
—gegenstand principal subject
—geschäft(sstelle) head office, headquarters
—gläubiger principal creditor
—grund chief (main) reason
—kartei master file
—klage main action
—kläger principal plaintiff
—merkmal main (characteristic) feature, chief mark
—person chief, principal person
—punkt chief (main) point
—sache chief (principal) matter, main issue (point, thing), substance
in der — in the main, mainly, on the whole, principally
in der — entscheiden give judgement on the main case
Hauptsache
sich zur — einlassen join issue
zur — verhandeln plead the main issue
hauptsächlich chief, main, principal, primary
Haupt-
—schuld main (principal) fault
—schuldiger principal
—schuldner principal debtor
—sitz head office, headquarters
—sorge chief concern
—stadt capital, metropolis
—täter principal
—tatsache leading fact
—teil main (major) part
—umstand main circumstance
—ursache main (principal) cause
—verfahren (—verhandlung) trial
—versammlung general meeting
— —, ordentliche annual general meeting
— —, außerordentliche extraordinary general meeting
—zeuge material (principal) witness
—ziel (—zweck) main objective, principal aim
—zug characteristic (main) feature
Haus firm, home, house
—arbeit domestic work, homework, housework
—besitz house property (ownership)
—besitzer (—eigentümer) house owner, landlord
—frieden domestic peace
—friedensbruch breach of domestic peace (domicile), disturbance of domestic peace and security, trespass
—halt budget, estimates, household
— —sjahr fiscal year
— —splan budget, estimates
—herr host, landlord, householder
Hausieren hawking, peddling
hausieren hawk, peddle
Hausierer canvasser, hawker, pedlar
Hausierschein pedlar's licenc(s)e
Hausierwaren pedlary
häuslich domestic, family
Haus-
—meister caretaker, house steward, janitor, porter

Haus-
—**ordnung** house regulations, rules of a house
—**recht** domestic right
—**stand** household
—**suchung** domiciliary visit, search(ing) of a house
— — **vornehmen** search a house
—**suchungsbefehl** search warrant
—**wirt** landlord
—**wirtin** landlady
Haverie average, sea damage
hehlen receive stolen goods
Hehler receiver of stolen goods, accessory after the fact
Hehlerei receiving of stolen goods
heilig holy, inviolable, sacred, solemn, venerable
heiligen justify, sanction, sanctify
Heiligkeit inviolability, sacredness, sanctity
Heiligtum sanctuary, shrine
Entweihung (Raub) eines —s sacrilege
Heilmittel remedy
Heim home, house, residence
Heimarbeit homework, outwork
Heimarbeiter homeworker, outworker
Heimat country of birth (origin), domicile, home (country), homeland, native place (country)
—**adresse (anschrift)** home address
heimatberechtigt having right of residence
Heimatland country of birth (origin), homeland, native country (land), mother country
heimatlos homeless, stateless
Heimat-
—**ort** birth place, native place (town)
—**recht** domestic law, right of domicile (residence, settlement)
—**schein** certificate of domicile (citizenship, origin)
—**schutz** home defenc(s)e
—**staat** country (state) of origin, home country, native country
—**stadt** home (native) town
—**urlaub** home leave
Heimfall devolution, escheat, reversion
—**berechtigter** reversioner
heimfallen devolve (on), (revert by) escheat, revert (to)
heimfällig escheatable, reversionary, revertible
Heimfälligkeit revertibility
Heimfallrecht escheatage, reversionary right, right of escheat (reversion)
Heimfallsgut escheat
heimführen repatriate
Heimführung repatriation
heimisch domestic, home, native
heimlich clandestine, concealed, hidden, secret, surreptitious, underhand
Heimlichkeit secrecy, secret, secretiveness
Heimtücke foul play, insidiousness, malice, treachery
heimtückisch foul, insidious, malicious, perfidious, treacherous, underhand
heimzahlen pay back, repay, requite (for), retaliate
Heimzahlung repayment, requital, retaliation
Heirat marriage
  Geld— money marriage
  Liebes— love match
  Vernunfts— convenience (prudential) match
heiraten get married, marry
Heirats-
—**antrag** marriage offer (proposal)
—**anzeige** marriage announcement
—**aufgebot** (marriage) banns
—**erlaubnis (—genehmigung)** marriage licenc(s)e
heiratsfähig eligible, marriageable, nubile
Heirats-
—**fähigkeit** marriageable age, nubility
—**gut** dowry, marriage portion
—**register** marriage register
—**schein (—urkunde)** marriage certificate
—**vermittler** marriage broker (agent)
—**vermittlung** marriage agency

—vermittlungsgebühr marriage brokerage
—versprechen promise of marriage, marriage promise
—vertrag marriage contract (articles, settlement)
helfen assist, help, relieve
Helfer assistant, helper
Helfershelfer abettor, accomplice, confederate
hemmen block, check, delay, hamper, handicap, hinder, impede, obstruct, restrain, retard, suspend
hemmend hampering, hindering, impeding, obstructive
Hemmung blocking, delay, hindrance, obstruction, retardation, retraint, suspension
Hemmung blocking, delay, hindrance, obstruction, retardation, retraint, suspension
Hemmungen inhibitions
(keine) Hemmungen haben feel (no) inhibitions
hemmungslos uninhibited, unrestrained, unscrupulous, reckless
Hemmungslosigkeit lack of restraint, recklessness
Henker executioner, hangman
Henkers-
—beil executioner's axe
—knecht hangman's assistant
—lohn hangman's fee
—mahlzeit farewell dinner, last meal
herabsetzen abate, belittle, cut, curtail, decrease, degrade, depreciate, disparage, lower, reduce
Herabsetzung abatement, belittlement, curtailment, cut, depreciation, disparagement, lowering, reduction
herantreten an approach
heranwachsen adolesce, grow (up, to)
Heranwachsender adolescent
heranziehen cite, consult, draw upon, enlist, mobilize, quote
Heranziehung consultation, enlistment, mobilization
heraufarbeiten work (fight) one's way up
heraufsetzen increase, mark up, raise
Heraufsetzung increase, rise
herausarbeiten elaborate, work out
herausbekommen discover, elicit, find (get, make) out, puzzle out, trace
herausbringen bring (get, turn) out, edit, elicit, extract, produce, publish
herausfinden ascertain, discover, establish, find out, spot, trace
Herausforderer challenger
herausfordern challenge, provoke
herausfordernd defiant, provocative
Herausforderung challenge, provocation
Herausgabe bringing out, delivery, editing, handing over, issue, publication, restitution, restoration, return
—anspruch claim for restitution (return), claiming back, revendication
—klage action for restitution (return), action of detinue, revendication action
—pflicht obligation to return
herausgeben deliver, edit, hand over, issue, publish, restitute, restore, return
Herausgeber editor, publisher
Herausgeberin editress
herauspressen extort, extract, press out, squeeze out
herausreden, sich invent excuses
herausstellen emphasize, point (put) out, set forth, stress
—, sich prove (to be), be proved, turn out
herausziehen disengage, disentangle, extract, extricate, get out, withdraw
herbeiführen bring about, cause, effect, lead to
herbeischaffen bring (forward), procure, produce, provide
Herbeischaffung procurement, production
Herberge accommodation, hostel, inn, lodging, refuge, shelter
Jugend— youth hostel

Herde crowd, herd, mass, multitude
Herden-
—geist herd instinct (mentality, mind)
—mensch gregarious person, one of the general herd
—trieb gregariousness, herd instinct
Hergang circumstances, course of events, details, facts, happening, occurrence, proceedings
hergebracht conventional, customary, established, traditional, usual
Herkommen birth, convention, custom, descent, extraction, practice, tradition, usage, use
herkömmlich conventional, customary, ordinary, traditional, usual
Herkunft birth, derivation, descent, extraction, origin, provenance, source
Herkunfts-
—angabe (—bezeichnung) indication of origin
—bescheinigung (—nachweis, —zeugnis) certificate of origin
—land country of origin
herleiten date from, deduce, derive (from), draw, go back to, infer, originate from
Herleitung deduction, derivation, inference
Herr boss, gentleman, governor, lord, master, mister, monarch, principal, ruler, sovereign
— werden bring under control, master, overcome, rule
herrenlos abandoned, derelict, masterless, ownerless, unappropriated, unclaimed, unowned, vacant
Herrin lady, mistress
Herrschaft authority, command, control, domination, dominion, empire, government, grip, mastery, power, reign, rule, sovereignty, supremacy, sway
—sbereich (—sgebiet) empire, jurisdiction, power, sway
herrschen control, dominate, govern, prevail, reign, rule, sway
herrschend controlling, dominating, (pre)dominant, prevailing, prevalent, ruling
Herrscher boss, monarch, potentate, ruler, sovereign
—geschlecht dynasty
herrühren arise (come, derive, proceed, result) from, be due (owing) to, originate from (with)
herstellen create, establish, fabricate, make, manufacture, produce, turn out
wieder— re-establish, renovate, repair, restore
Hersteller maker, manufacturer, producer
Herstellung creation, establishment, fabrication, making, manufacture, preparation, production
Wieder— re-establishment, renovation, restitution, restoration
Herstellungs-
—kosten (—preis) cost price
—recht manufacturing (production) right (licenc[s]e)
—verfahren production process (method)
heruntersetzen s. herabsetzen
Heruntersetzung s. Herabsetzung
herunterwirtschaften deteriorate, dilapidate, mismanage, ruin, run down
hervorbringen bring about (forth), cause, create, effect, generate, give birth (rise) to, produce
Hervorbringung creation, generation, production
hervorgehen aus arise (emerge, follow, result) from, come out
hervorheben accentuate, emphasize, insist on, point out, set out, stress
Hervorhebung accentuation, emphasis, insistence
hervorragen be conspicuous (preeminent, prominent), distinguish oneself, exceed, excel, stand out
hervorragend conspicuous, distinguished, eminent, first-class (-rate), outstanding, prominent

hervorrufen bring about, call forth, cause, create, evoke, generate, give rise to, produce, raise
Hervorrufung causation, creation, evocation, generation, production
hervorstehend (hervortretend) conspicuous, (pre)dominant, outstanding, paramount, striking
hervortun, sich distinguish oneself, excel, put oneself forward
Hetze agitation, chase, instigation
hetzen chase
— gegen agitate against
Hetzer agitator, inciter, instigator
hetzerisch inflammatory, sensational
Heuchelei dissembling, dissimulation, hypocrisy
heucheln counterfeit, dissemble, dissimulate, fake, feign, hypocritize, stimulate
Heuchler counterfeiter, dissembler, hypocrite
heuchlerisch deceitful, dissembling, feigning. hypocritical
Heuer hire, rent, wages
heuern charter, engage, hire, ship
Heuerlohn wages
Heuervertrag charter party, shipping articles
Hieb blow, cut, hit, stroke
— versetzen deal a blow to, have a fling at, strike
Hierarch hierarch
Hierarchie hierarchy
hierarchisch hierarchic(al)
Hilfe (—leistung) aid, assistance, help, relief, support
—, erste first aid
Hilfe
— leisten assist, help, support
— suchen seek help
Hilfe-
—leistung s. Hilfe
—ruf call (cry) for aid (help), distress call
hilflos defenceless, destitute, forlorn, helpless
Hilflosigkeit defencelessness, helplessness
hilfreich helpful
Hilfs-
—aktion relief work
—arbeiter assistant, helper, subsidiary, unskilled worker
hilfsbedürftig indigent, needy, requiring help
Hilfs-
—bedürftiger destitute, needy, poor
—bedürftigkeit distress, indigence
hilfsbereit cooperative, helpful, ready to help
Hilfs-
—bereitschaft helpfulness
—maßnahme emergency measure, relief action
—mittel remedy, resource
—quelle resource
—richter assistant judge
—schöffe talesman, sessioner
hilfsweise in default
Hilfswerk relief work
hinauslaufen auf amount to, come to, result in
hinausschieben defer, delay, postpone, prolong, protract, put off
Hinausschiebung delay, postponement, prolongation, protraction
hinaustreiben eject, evict, expel
hinausziehen delay, extend, protract
Hinblick
im — auf considering, in consideration (view) of, in the face (light) of, with a view to, with regard (respect) to
hinderlich embarrassing, inconvenient, obstructive
hindern check, estop from, hamper, handicap, hinder, interfere with, obstruct, prevent from
Hindernis check, handicap, hindrance, impediment, obstacle, obstruction
—, gesetzliches legal impediment
Hinderung estoppel, hindrance, obstruction
—sgrund cause of impediment, obstacle

hindeuten auf hint at, indicate, intimate, point at (to), suggest
Hindeutung hint, indication, intimation, suggestion
hinfällig futile, ineffective, invalid, untenable, void, voidable, weak
— werden be annulled, become void, elapse, expire
Hinfälligkeit futility, weakness
hinkend defective, lame, limping, poor
hinlänglich adequate, enough, satisfying, sufficient
Hinlänglichkeit sufficiency
hinreichend ample, sufficient
hinrichten behead, execute, put to death
Hinrichtung execution
— —sbefehl death warrant
Hinsicht
in — auf (hinsichtlich) as to, concerning, in consideration of, in regard (respect) of, with regard to
hintansetzen disregard, ignore, neglect, set aside
Hintansetzung disregard, neglect
Hinterbliebener bereaved, survivor
hintereinander one after another (the other), in succession
hintergehen cheat, circumvent, deceive, doublecross, impose upon
Hintergehung deception, fraud
Hinterhalt ambush, reserve
— bereiten lay an ambush (a trap) for
hinterhältig foul, insidious, perfidious, underhand
Hinterhältigkeit insidiousness, perfidiousness, perfidy
hinterlassen bequeath, devise, leave (behind)
Hinterlassenschaft estate, inheritance, property left
hinterlegen consign, deposit, give in trust, lodge
Hinterleger depositor
Hinterlegung consignment, deposit, depositing, lodgement, lodging
Hinterlegungs-
—erklärung trust declaration
—gelder deposit(ed) funds, deposits, trust money
—schein (—urkunde) certificate of deposit
—stelle depositary, depository
Hinterlist furtiveness, insidiousness, malice
hinterlistig foul, furtive, insidious, underhand
Hintermann backer, coverer, subsequent endorser, supporter
hinterrücks from behind, behind one's back, insidiously
hintertreiben circumvent, counteract, frustrate, hinder, obstruct, prevent, torpedo
Hintertreibung circumvention, frustration, hindrance, obstruction, prevention
hinterziehen defraud
Hinterzieher defrauder
Hinterzienhung defraudation
hinweggehen über (sich hinwegsetzen über) dismiss, disregard, ignore
Hinweis allusion, hint, index, indication, reference, suggestion
unter — auf referring to, with reference to
hinweisen auf allude to, hint at, indicate, point out, refer to, suggest
hinziehen delay, lengthen, prolong, protract
hinzufügen add, annex, append, attach, enclose, join, subjoin
Hinzufügung addition
hinzuziehen call in, consult
Hinzuziehung calling in, consultation
hochachten esteem (respect) highly
Hochachtung esteem, estimation, regard, respect
hochachtungsvoll respectful
hochangesehen (hochgeachtet) of high repute (standing), high esteemed, highly respected
hochgestellt high-ranking, of high rank
Hochstapelei confidence trick, imposture, sharping, swindle, swindling, tricking

Hochstapler crook, impostor, sharper, swindler, confidence man
hochstehend distinguished, high-ranking
Höchst-
—betrag maximum (amount), limit
—bietender highest bidder
—dauer maximum duration
—gebot highest bid (offer)
—geschwindigkeit maximum (top) speed, speed limit
—gewicht maximum weight
—grenze (upper) limit
— — für Löhne wage ceiling
—lohn ceiling (maximum) wage
—löhne wage ceilings
—maß maximum
—preis ceiling (maximum) price
—stand peak
—strafe maximum penalty (punishment)
Hochverrat high treason
Hochverräter high treasoner, traitor
hochverräterisch treasonable, traiterous
Hochverratsprozeß treason trial
Hochzeit marriage, wedding
Hof court, courtyard, farm, yard
Gerichts— court of justice (law), law court, tribunal
Gefängnis— prison court
Hofamt court office
Hofbeamter court official
höflich civil, courteous, polite
Höflichkeit civility, courtesy, politeness
Höhe amount, extent, height, importance, level
in der — von to the amount of
Hoheit jurisdiction, sovereignty
Hoheits-
—akt act of sovereignty (state)
—gebiet (—bereich) jurisdiction, national (sovereign, state) territory
—gewässer territorial waters
—rechte sovereign rights
Höhepunkt climax, culminating point, culmination, peak, summit
— erreichen culminate
höhergestellt higher (superior) in rank

Höllenmaschine time bomb
Holschuld debt collectible at debtor's domicile
Homosexualität homosexuality
homosexuell homosexual
Honorar fee, gratification, honorarium, honoration, payment, remuneration, reward
honorieren accept, discharge, fee, hono(u)r, meet, pay, protect, remunerate
—, nicht dishono(u)r
Honorierung acceptance, discharge, payment, protection, remuneration
honorig hono(u)rable, respectable
Hörensagen, vom by hearsay
Hörer auditor(s), hearer, listener
hörig dependent, subject, subordinate, submissive
Höriger dependent, subordinate
Hörigkeit dependence, subordination
horten accumulate, hoard
Hortung hoarding
Hospital hospital
Hospiz asylum, home, hospice, hostel
huldigen do (pay, render) homage (obeisance) to, give an ovation to
Huldigung homage, obeisance, ovation
—seid oath of allegiance
human humane
Humanität humanity
—sverbrechen offence against humanity
Hunger hunger
—lohn pittance, starvation wage
—snot famine, starvation
—streik hunger strike
in den — treten (go on) hunger-strike
—tod death from starvation
hüten guard, keep, look after, protect, watch over
sich — vor be aware of
Hüter custodian, guardian, keeper, protector, warden
— des Gesetzes policeman
Hypothek mortgage
— aufnehmen raise a mortgage

Hypothekar-
—gläubiger mortgage creditor, mortgagee
—kredit (—darlehn) mortgage loan
hypothekarisch hypothecary, by (on) mortgage
Hypotheken-
—anlage mortgage bond (security)
—anleihe mortgage loan
—bank mortgage bank
—brief mortgage bond (deed, note)
—buch mortgage register
—darlehen mortgage loan
—eintragung mortgage registration
—forderung mortgage claim
hypothekenfrei free of mortgages, unencumbered
Hypotheken-
—gläubiger mortgage creditor, mortgagee
—kredit mortgage credit
—last mortgage charge
—löschung mortgage cancellation
—obligation (—pfandbrief) mortgage bond (debenture, note)
—pfandrecht mortgage lien
—register mortgage register
—register(amt) mortgage registry
—schein mortgage bond (deed, note)
—schuld mortgage debt
—schuldner mortgager, mortgagor
—schuldverschreibung mortgage bond (debenture)
—tilgung mortgage redemption
—titel (—urkunde) mortgage bond (deed)
Hypothese hypothesis

I

Idee conception, idea, notion
identifizierbar identifiable
identifizieren identify
Identifizierung identification
—szeichen identification mark
identisch identic(al)
Identitäts-
—karte identity (identification) card
—nachweis identity certificate, proof of identity
—zeichen identification mark
ignorieren ignore, take no notice of
illegal illegal, unlawful
Illegalität illegality, unlawfulness
illegitim illegitimate
Illegitimität illegitimacy
Illusion delusion, illusion, misleading impression
sich —en hingeben (machen) be under an illusion, delude oneself
sich keine —en machen have no illusion
illusorisch deceptive, illusive, illusory
Illustration explanation, illustration
illustrieren explain, illustrate
imaginär imaginary
Imitation copy, counterfeit, fake, forgery, imitation, sham
imitieren copy, counterfeit, fake, forge, imitate, sham
immateriell immaterial, intangible, nominal
Immatrikulation enlistment, enrolment, matriculation
immatrikulieren enlist, enrol, matriculate, register
Immigrant immigrant
Immission appointment, immission, installation

Immobiliar-
—klage real action
—kredit mortgage credit, real estate credit
—vermögen real estate, real property, realty
Immobilien immovables, real estate, real property, realty
immun immune, privileged, proof (against)
Immunität exemption, immunity, privilege
imperativ imperative
Imperialismus imperialism
Imperialist imperialist
imperialistisch imperialist(ic)
Imperium empire
implizieren imply
implizit(e) implicit(ly)
Import import(ation)
—abgabe import duty
—agent import agent
—artikel import article
—beschränkungen import restrictions
Importeur import dealer, importer
Import
—handel import trade
—händler import dealer, importer
importierbar importable
importieren import
Import-
—kontingent import quota
—kontrolle import control
—lizenz import licenc(s)e
—monopol import monopoly
—überschuß import surplus
—verbot import embargo
—zoll import duty
Improvisation extemporization, improvisation
improvisieren extemporize, improvise
Impuls impetus, impulse, stimulus
impulsiv impulsive
Impulsivität impulsiveness
imstande sein zu be able to, be capable of
nicht — sein zu be incapable of, be unable to
inadäquat inadequate
inakkurat inaccurate
Inangriffnahme beginning, coping, embarking, entering, start(ing), tackling, undertaking
Inanspruchnahme absorption, claiming, drain, employment, engrossment, laying claim to, resort to, strain, use
Inaussichtstellung promise
Inbegriff aggregate, entirety, essence, quintessence, substance
inbegriffen included, including, inclusive of
Inbesitznahme appropriation, occupation, taking possession
Inbetriebnahme (Inbetriebsetzung) initiation, opening, putting into operation, starting
Index index
auf den — setzen ban, interdict
indirekt indirect
indiskret indiscreet, tactless
Indiscretion indiscretion
— begehen be indiscreet, commit indiscretion
indiskutabel indiscussible, out of court (question)
Individual-
—eigentum personal (private) property
—rechte individual (personal) rights, titles in personam
individualisieren individualize, individuate, particularize, specify
Individualismus individualism
Individualist individualist
individualistisch individualist(ic)
Individualität individuality
Individualversicherung individual (personal) insurance
individuell individual, particular
Individuum individual (person), person
Indiz evidence, indicium
Indizien indicia
—beweis circumstantial (presumptive) evidence
indizieren indicate
indossabel endorsable, indorsable
Indossament endorsement, indorsement

Indossant (Indossent) endorser, indorser
Indossat(ar) endorsee, indorsee
indossierbar endorsable, indorsable
indossieren endorse, indorse
Industrie industry
—abkommen industrial agreement
—aktie industrial share (stock)
—anleihe industrial loan (bond)
—arbeiter factory worker, industrial labo(u)rer (worker)
—bank industrial bank
—beteiligung industrial participation
—bezirk (—gebiet) industrial area (region), manufacturing district
—emissionen industrial issues
—gericht industrial court
—gesellschaft industrial company
—gesetze factory acts
—gesetzgebung factory legislation
—gewerkschaft industrial union
Industrie- und Handelskammer Chamber of Commerce (and Industry)
—kredit industrial credit
—land industrial(ized) country
industriell industrial
Industrieller industrial(ist), manufacturer
Groß— big manufacturer (industrial)
Industrie-
—obligation industrial bond
—spionage industrial espionage
—staat industrial country (state)
—verband industrial (trade) association (organization)
—zentrum industrial centre
—zweig branch of industry
Inempfangnahme receipt, reception
inexakt inaccurate, inexact
infam atrocious, dirty, foul, infamous, shameless
Infamie infamy, shamelessness
in flagranti in flagrante delicto
Inflation inflation
inflationistisch inflationary
Inflationspolitik inflationary policy
infolge on account of, in consequence of, due to, owing to, as a result of, on the strength of
infolgedessen consequently, in consequence, as a consequence (result)
Information advice, (piece of) information
—sbüro information bureau, inquiry office
informativ (informatorisch) exploratory, informative, informatory
informieren advise, inform, instruct, notify
—, sich gather information, inquire, make inquiries
Infrastruktur infrastructure
Ingangsetzung beginning, putting into operation, start(ing)
Inhaber bearer, holder, keeper, occupant, occupier, owner, possessor, proprietor, tenant
—aktie bearer share
—obligation (—schuldverschreibung) bearer bond (debenture)
—scheck bearer cheque
—wechsel bearer bill
inhaftieren arrest, imprison, incarcelate, put in prison
Inhaftierung imprisonment, incarcelation
Inhalt capacity, content(s), essence, purport, subject, substance, summary, tenor, volume
Inhalts-
—angabe statement of contents, summary
—verzeichnis (table of) contents, docket, index, register
Initiative activity, energy, initiative, push
— ergreifen take the initiative
Inkasso cashing, collection, encashment
—wechsel bill for collection
inklusive included, including, inclusive
inkognito incognito
inkompetent incompetent
Inkompetenz incompetence(cy)
Inkorporation incorporation
inkorporieren incorporate

inkorrekt inaccurate, inappropriate, incorrect
Inkorrektheit inaccuracy, incorrectness
Inkrafttreten coming (entry) into force
Tag des —s effective date
Inland, im at home
im — und im Ausland at home and abroad
Inländer native
inländisch domestic, home, inland, native
Inlands-
—handel domestic (home) trade
—wechsel inland (domestic) bill
inliegend enclosed
innehaben hold, keep, occupy, own, possess, be in possession of
innehalten adher to, cease, halt, keep (to), observe, pause, stop
Innehaltung observance
Innendienst home service, office work
Innenminister Home Secretary (GB), Minister of the Interior, Secretary of the Interior (USA)
Innenministerium Home Office (GB), Department of the Interior (USA), Ministry of the Interior
Innenpolitik domestic (home) policy
Innung association, corporation, guild
Innungs-
—brief corporation (guild's) charter
—satzung corporation articles
—wesen guild system
inoffiziell informal, inofficial
inoffiziös informal, inofficious
inopportun inopportune, unseasonable
Insasse inhabitant, inmate, lodger, occupant, passenger, resident
insbesondere especially, in particular, particularly, principally
Inschrift inscription
insgeheim in private, privately, in secret, secretly
insgesamt altogether, in the aggregate
insolvent bankrupt, insolvent
Insolvenz bankruptcy, insolvency
Inspektion examination, inspection, survey
Inspektor inspector, superintendent
Inspiration inspiration
inpirieren inspire
inspizieren examine, inspect, superintend, survey
instand halten keep up, maintain
Instandhaltung maintenance, upkeep
inständig earnest, instant, urgent
instand setzen repair, restore
Instandsetzung repair, restoration
— bitten beseech, implore, supplicate (for)
Inständigkeit earnestness, instancy, urgency
Instanz authority, instance, resort
—, erste first instance
—, höhere higher instance, superior court
—, letzte last instance
in letzter — in the last resort, without further appeal
Instanzenweg official channels, stages of appeal
—, auf dem through the official channels
den — einhalten go through (keep) the channels
Instanzenzug appeal, sequence of authorities (instances), successive stages of appeal
Institut establishment, institute, institution
Institution institution
instruieren brief, direct, instruct, teach
Instruktion brief, direction, instruction, order
instruktionsgemäß according to (in conformity with) instructions
Instrument deed, document, legal instrument
Integration integration
integrieren integrate
Integrität integrity

intelligent intelligent
Intelligenz intelligence
intensiv intense, intensive
intensivieren intensify
Intensivierung intensification
Intention intention
Interesse concern, interest
—, berechtigtes legitimate interest
Interessen-
—gebiet domain, field (sphere) of interest (influence)
—gegensatz clashing of interests
—gemeinschaft community (union) of interests, pool
—gruppe interest group, pressure group
—kollision (—konflikt) collision (conflict) of interests
Interessent interested (concerned) party (person)
Interessenverband combine, pool, syndicate
interessieren interest (in)
—, sich be interested in, have an interest in
interimistisch interim, provisional, temporary
Interims-
—regierung provisional government
—wechsel interim (provisional) bill
intern internal, interior, private
international international
internationalisieren internationalize
Internationalisierung internationalization
Internationalität internationality
internieren intern
Internierter interned, internee
Internierung internment
—slager internment camp
Interpellation interpellation, question
—srecht right of interpellation
interpellieren address (ask) a question, interpellate
Interpretation interpretation, reading
interpretieren interpret
Intervenient interpleader, intervener
intervenieren interfere, interplead, interpose, intervene
Intervention interference, interpleading, interposition, intervention
Interventions-
—klage litigation of interference
—prozeß interference proceedings
—recht right of interference
Intestat intestate
—erbe(in) intestate heir(ess), heir(ess)-at-law
—erbfolge intestate succession
intim intimate
Intimität intimacy
intolerant intolerant
Intoleranz intolerance
Intrigant intriguer, plotter, schemer
intrigant intriguing, plotting, scheming
Intrige intrigue, plot, scheme
intrigieren intrigue, plot, scheme
invalide disabled, invalid
Invalidenversicherung invalidity (disability, disablement) insurance
Invalider disabled (person), invalid
Invalidität disability, disablement, invalidity
—sversicherung invalidity (disability, disablement) insurance
Invasion invasion
Inventar inventory, stock
Inventur inventory, stocktaking
— machen take stock (inventory)
investieren invest
Investierung investment
Investition investment
—sgüter capital goods
Investitur investiture
Inzucht endogamy, inbreeding
irreführen (—leiten) deceive, delude, dupe, lead astray, misdirect, misguide, mislead
sich — lassen be misled
irreführend deceitful, false, misleading
Irreführung deceit, deception, misguidance, misleading statement, mystification
irrelevant irrelevant, trifling
irremachen bewilder, confound, confuse, perplex, puzzle

irren, sich be in error, be mistaken (wrong), commit an error, make a mistake
sich — in misjudge, misunderstand
Irrenanstalt (Irrenhaus) lunatic asylum, madhouse
Irrenarzt alienist, mental specialist, psychopathist
Irrenhäusler lunatic, madman
Irrer insane (person), lunatic
irrig erroneous, false, incorrect, inexact, wrong
irritieren irritate, provoke, puzzle
Irrsinn absurdity, alienation of mind, insanity, lunacy, madness, mental alienation (derangement)
irrsinnig insane, lunatic, mad, (mentally) deranged
Irrtum error, fault, mistake, misconception, misunderstanding
— begehen commit an error, make a mistake, misunderstand
irrtümlich erroneous(ly), faulty, mistaken, by mistake
isolieren isolate
Isolierung isolation

J

Jagd chase, hunt(ing), pursuit, shooting
— machen auf chase, hunt after, pursue, persecute
Jagd
—aufseher game keeper
—berechtigung hunting right, shooting licenc(s)e
—bezirk hunting (shooting) ground, hunt
—frevel poaching
—frevler poacher
—gesetz game law
—polizei game police
—recht game laws, hunting (shooting) right, shooting licenc(s)e
—revier hunt, hunting (shooting) ground
—schein (—erlaubnis) hunting (shooting) licenc(s)e (permit)
jagen chase, drive, hunt, pursue
Jäger hunter
Mitgift— dowry hunter
Jahr year
—buch almanac, annual (register), year book
jahrelang for (since) years
Jahres-
—abonnement annual subscription
—abrechnung annual settlement
—abschluß annual settlement (statement) of accounts, annual balance sheet
—ausweis annual return (statement
—bericht annual report
—bilanz annual balance sheet
—einkommen annual income
—rente annuity
—versammlung annual meeting
—zahlung annual payment
Jahrgang age group, annual set, class, vintage, year
jährlich annual, per annum, yearly
Jahrzehnt decade, ten years
Jawort geben accept, consent
jedenfalls at all events, at any rate, however it is, in any case
jederzeit at any time
jedesmal as often as, each (every) time, whenever
jetzig actual, current, existing, present
jetzt at present, now
von — ab from now on, from this time, henceforth
jeweilig in charge (office), on duty, specific, for the time being

Jugend youth
—amt youth (welfare) office
—arbeit juvenile labo(u)r (work)
—arrest arrest for juveniles, juvenile detention
—erziehungsheim institution of reform
—fürsorge (—pflege) juvenile care, youth welfare
—gefängnis juvenile detention home
—gericht juvenile court
—heim youth centre
—herberge youth hostal
—kriminalität juvenile delinquency
jugendlich juvenile, youthful
Jugendlicher juvenile
Jugend
—recht juvenile law
—verbrechen juvenile crime
—verbrecher juvenile offender, youthful criminal
Jungfrau virgin
jungfräulich virginal
Jungfräulichkeit virginity
Junggeselle bachelor
—nsteuer bachelor's tax
Junior junior
Jura law
—studieren study law(s)
—student law student, student of law
Jurisdiktion jurisdiction
Jurisprudenz legal science, jurisprudence
Jurist jurist, lawyer
juristisch juridical, legal, of law
—e Person juridical (artificial, legal) person, legal entity, body corporate
Jury jury(men)
Justiz administration of justice, judicature, judiciary, justice
—beamter law (legal) (court) officer, officer of justice (the law)
—behörde legal (court) (judicial) authority
—gebäude (—palast) Law Courts
—gewalt judicature, judiciary (power)
—irrtum judicial error, miscarriage of justice
—minister Attorney General (USA), Lord Chancellor (GB), Minister of Justice
—ministerium Department of Justice (USA), Ministry of Justice
—mord judicial murder
—reform judicial reform
—verfassung judicial (court) system, judiciary, system of judicature
—verwaltung administration of justice
—wesen judiciary, law (judicial) affairs

K

Kabinett cabinet, government
Kabinetts
—ausschuß cabinet committee
—befehl (—order, —verfügung) order in council, cabinet decision
—chef head of the government (cabinet)
—frage cabinet issue (question)
—krise cabinet crisis
—liste list of cabinet members
—minister cabinet minister
—mitglied cabinet member, member of the government
—rat cabinet council, council of ministers, Privy Council, Privy Councillor (GB)
—sitzung cabinet meeting
Kadaver cadaver, corpse, (dead) body
Kader cadre, skeleton
—einheit cadre unit

Kaiser emperor
Kaiserin empress
Kaiserkrone imperial crown
kaiserlich imperial
Kaiserreich (-tum) empire
Kalender almanac, calendar
—jahr calendar year
Kalkulation calculation, computation
—sfehler miscalculation
kalkulieren calculate, compute, reckon
—, falsch miscalculate
kaltblütig cold-blooded, cool
Kaltblütigkeit cold-blood(edness), coolness
Kammer board, cabinet, chamber, court, house
  Rechtsanwalts— Bar, Bar Association
  Handels— (Industrie- und —) chamber of commerce (and industry)
Kammergericht supreme court (of justice), highest (supreme) court of appeal
Kammerrichter judge of the supreme court
Kämmerei board of finances, Exchequer (GB), finance department, Treasury (USA), treasurer's office
  Stadt— city treasury, municipal board of finances
Kämmerer treasurer
  Stadt— city (municipal) treasurer
Kampagne campaign
Kampf action, battle, combat, conflict, encounter, engagement, fight(ing), struggle, war
kämpfen battle, combat, fight, struggle
Kämpfer battler, combatant, fighter
kämpferisch combative, militant, pugnacious
Kandare curb
  an die — nehmen put the curb on
  an der — halten keep in check
Kandidat applicant, aspirant, candidate, claimant, examinee, nominee
— aufstellen nominate a candidate
Kandidatenliste list of candidates (nominees), party list, slate, ticket
Kandidatur candidacy, candidature
kandidieren candidate, contest, run for, stand for, stand (offer oneself) as candidate
Kannvorschrift discretionary clause
kanonisch canon, canonic(al), church, ecclesiastical
—es Recht canon (church, ecclesiastical) law
Kanton canton
kantonal cantonal
Kanzlei chambers, chancellery, chancery, office, secretariate
  Anwalts— chambers, law office
  Gerichts— record office
  Präsidential— presidential bureau (office)
—gericht Court of Chancery
Kanzler chancellor
—amt chancellery(ory), chancellorship
Kapazität authority, capacity, expert, specialist
Kaper captor, corsair, pirate
Kaperbrief letter of marque
Kaperei capturing, privateering
kapern capture, seize
Kaperer freebooter, privateer
Kaperung capture
Kapital assets, capital, funds, means, resources, substance, stock
  Aktien— share (stock) capital
—abfindung cash (lump-sum) settlement, financial (monetary) compensation
—abgabe capital levy
—abschöpfung depletion of capital
—abwanderung outflow of capital
—abzug withdrawal of capital (funds)
—anhäufung (—ansammlung, —schöpfung) accumulation of capital (funds)
—anlage (capital) investment, capital spending, employment (investment) of funds

—**anlagen** —**anlagegüter)** capital assets
—**anlagegesellschaft** investment company (trust)
—**anteil** capital share (holding), investment
—**anteilschein** stock certificate
—**aufbau** capital structure
—**aufnahme** raising of capital (funds)
—**aufstockung** capital increase
—**aufwand** capital expenditure
—**ausfuhr** capital export
—**bedarf** capital demand, capital (financial, pecuniary) requirements, want of money
—**belastung** capital charge
—**beschaffung** provision of capital (funds)
—**betrag** capital amount
—**bewegung** capital movement
—**bewertung** capital valuation
—**bildung** accumulation of capital (funds)
—**einbringung (—einlage, —einzahlung)** capital invested (paid in), investment
—**einkommen** income from capital (investments), unearned income, capital gain, investment income
—**emission** capital issue
—**erhöhung** capital increase
—**ertrag** capital yield, return on capital
—**ertragssteuer** capital gains tax, withholding tax
—**export** capital export
—**fehler** capital fault
—**flucht** flight of capital
—**gesellschaft** (stock) company, (stock) corporation
—**güter** capital goods
—**herabsetzung** capital reduction
—**herrschaft** capitalism
Kapitalien capital, funds, means, resources
Kapitalimport capital import
Kapitalinteressen capital interests
kapitalisierbar capitalizable, fundable
kapitalisieren capitalize, finance, fund, realize
Kapitalisierung capitalization
Kapitalismus capitalism
Kapitalist capitalist, financier
Groß— big capitalist
Groß—en big capitalists, high finance
kapitalistisch capitalistic
Kapital-
—**knappheit (—mangel)** capital shortage, scarcity (want) of funds
—**kosten** capital expenditure (cost)
kapitalkräftig financially strong (sound), moneyed, wealthy, well-founded
Kapital-
—**lenkung** investment control
—**markt** capital (money) market
—**quelle** (capital) resources, source of funds
kapitalschwach financially weak
Kapital-
—**schwund** dwindling (of) assets
—**steuer** capital tax (levy)
—**struktur** capital structure
—**umsatz (—umschlag)** capital turnover
—**verbrechen** capital crime
—**verbrecher** capital criminal
—**verkehr** capital movement (transaction)
—**vermögen** capital assets, funded property
—**verteilung** distribution of capital
—**verwendung** allocation (application, employment) of funds
—**wert** capital value
—**zufluß** influx of capital
Kapitel chapter, head(ing)
Kapitulation capitulation, surrender
—, **bedingungslose** unconditional surrender
kapitulieren capitulate, surrender
—, **bedingungslos** surrender unconditionally
Kardinal
—**fehler** cardinal error
—**frage** cardinal question
—**punkt** cardinal point
—**tugend** cardinal virtue
—**zahl** cardinal number
Karenzzeit waiting period (time)

Karriere career
— **machen** get on, be successful, have a good career, work one's way up
Karrieremacher careerist
Karte bill, card, form, map, note, ticket
Kartei (Kartothek) card catalogue (index), register, filing cabinet
—**karte** index (file, record) card
Kartell cartel, combination, combine, pool, ring, syndicate, trust
—**abkommen** pooling agreement (contract)
—**absprache (—vereinbarung)** cartel agreement
—**behörde** antitrust division, cartel bureau
—**bestimmungen** cartel regulations
—**entflechtung** decartelization
—**gericht** cartel court
—**gesetz** anti(-)cartel law, Antitrust Act (Law) (USA), Statute of Monopolies (GB)
—**gesetzgebung** antitrust legislation
kartellisieren cartelize, concentrate
Kartellisierung cartelization
Kartell-
—**klage** antitrust action (suit)
—**vertrag** cartel (trust) agreement, pooling agreement (contract)
—**wesen (-system)** cartelism
Kassation annulment, cancellation, cassation, discharge, dismissal, quashing
Kassations-
—**gericht (—gerichtshof, —hof)** court of cassation, (supreme) court of appeal
—**gesuch** application for (petition of) appeal
Kasse cash, cash (pay) office, chest, fund, till
Kassen-
—**anweisung (—schein)** cash order, bank (treasury) bill (note), pay voucher
—**beamter** cashier, teller
—**beleg** cash voucher
—**bestand** cash (on hand), cash balance, balance in hand
—**buch** cash book
—**dieb** peculator
—**diebstahl** peculation
—**führer** cashier, teller, treasurer
—**führung** cash keeping
—**konto** cash account
—**revision** cash audit(ing)
—**revisor** cash auditor
—**schrank** safe
—**zettel** cash (check, sales) slip, coupon
Kassette casket, cash (deed, money, strong) box
kassieren annul, cancel, cash, cashier, collect, discharge, dismiss, put (set) aside, invalidate, quash, rescind
Kassierer cash keeper, cashier, collector, paymaster, teller, treasurer
Kaste caste
—**ngeist** caste consciousness (feeling)
Katalog catalog(ue), list
katalogisieren catalog(ue), list
Kataster cadastral survey, cadastre, land register, register of assessment
Grundsteuer— land tax register
—**amt** land register (survey) office, land registry
—**beamter** land surveyor
katastrophal catastrophic, devestating, disastrous, overwhelming
Katastrophe catastrophe, disaster
Kategorie bracket, category, class, group, order
kategorisch absolute, categorical, flat
kategorisieren categorize
Kategorisierung categorization
Kauf acquisition, bargain, purchase
—**abschluß** bargain, completion (conclusion) of purchase, deal, purchase
—**auftrag** buying (purchase) order
—**bedingungen** purchase terms (conditions)

—brief bill of sale, title deed
kaufen acquire, buy, purchase
—, jemanden buy, bribe, corrupt
—, Zeugen subborn
Käufer acquirer, bidder, buyer, customer, demander, purchaser, taker, vendee
Kaufleute merchants, tradesmen
käuflich buyable, bribable, corrupt, corruptible, marketable, purchasable, by purchase, for sale, to be sold, venal
käuflich erwerben acquire by purchase
—e Justiz venal justice
Käuflichkeit corruptibility, venality
Kaufmann dealer, merchant, trader, tradesman
kaufmännisch business(like), commercial, mercantile, trading
—er Angestellter commercial clerk (employee)
Kaufmanns-
—brauch commercial usage, trade
—gericht trade (commercial) court, court of trade
—gericht trade court
Kauf-
—preis purchase price, price of acquisition
—urkunde bill (deed) of sale, title deed
—vertrag purchase (sales) contract
kaufweise by (way of) purchase
Kaufwert acquisition (purchase) value
kausal causal, causative
Kausalität causality
Kausalzusammenhang causal connection, causality
Kaution bail, bailment, bond, caution (money), guarantee, security (bond), surety (bond)
—, gegen against security, on bail
Kaution leisten (stellen) give bail, provide (stand) security
Kautions-
—betrag caution money
—höhe amount of security
—leistung bailment
—summe caution money, amount of security
kennen be acquainted with, be aware of, know
Kenner connoisseur, expert, judge, specialist
Kennkarte identity card
Kennmarke identification mark
kenntlich conspicuous, distinguishable, recognizable
— machen mark
Kenntnis acquaintance, cognizance, information, knowledge, note, notice
Sach— expertise, factual knowledge, knowledge of the fact
— nehmen von note, take note (notice) of
in — setzen von advise of, inform of, notify of
Kenntnisnahme cognizance, information, notice
Kenntnisse accomplishments, acquirements, attainments, knowledge
Kennwort cipher (code) word, password
Kennzeichen brand, earmark, label, (characteristic, distinctive) mark, sign
—(tafel) licence plate
—, polizeiliches registered (registration) number, identification (registration) plate
kennzeichnen characterize, distinguish, mark
kennzeichnend characteristic, typical
Kennzeichnung characterization, marking
Kennziffer code (index, key, reference) number
Kerker gaol, jail, imprisonment, prison
—meister jailer
in den — werfen throw into prison
Kern core, essence, gist, heart, main point (issue)
Ketten
in — legen chain, put into chains (fetters), shackle
Kind child, infant, issue, minor, offspring, progeny

Adoptiv— adopted (adoptive, foster) child
Findel- foundling
Kinderbeihilfe children's (family) allowance
Kinderfürsorge child welfare
kinderlos childless, without issue
Kinderlosigkeit childlessness
Kindes-
—alter child's age, infancy, tender age
—annahme adoption
—aussetzung exposure of a child
—entführung (—raub) kidnapping
—mißhandlung ill-treatment of a child
—statt
an — — annehmen adopt
—mord (—tötung) child murder, infanticide
—mörder infanticide
Kindheit childhood, infancy
Kirche church
Kirchen-
—ältester church warden, elder
—amt church office, ecclesiastical function
—ausschuß church committee
—bann excommunication, interdict
—behörde church authority
—buch (—register) church register
—dieb (—räuber) church thief (robber)
—diebstahl (—raub) church robbery, sacrilege
—gemeinde parish
—gericht church (ecclesiastical) court
—gut (-vermögen) church property
—jahr ecclesiastical year
—kalender church almanac (calendar)
—rat church assembly, (member of) consistory
—recht canon (canonical, church, ecclesiastical) law
—staat papal (pontifical) state
—steuer church tax (rate)
—strafe ecclesiastical punishment
—streitigkeit religious controversy
—versammlung church assembly, synod
kirchlich canonical, clerical, ecclesiastical, ritual, spiritual
Kirchspiel diocese, parish
klagbar actionable, enforceable, suable, recoverable
— — vorgehen bring in (enter) an action, take legal action, file a suit, go to law, initiate legal proceedings, sue
Klagbarkeit enforceability, suability
Klage action, charge, claim, complaint, grievance, lawsuit, petition, suit
— abweisen dismiss an action
— beantworten file an answer (a replication, a replique)
— einbringen (einreichen, erheben) bring in (enter) an action, institute legal proceedings, sue
— führen complain, make complaints
— stattgeben allow (grant) an action
— zurückziehen withdraw an action
Klage-
—abweisung dismissal of action, nonsuit
—anspruch (—grund) cause of action, title
—beantwortung defendant's answer, plea, statement of defence, answer to a charge
—begründung responsive pleading, statement (substantiation) of claim
—erhebung (—einreichung) filing of an action
—frist limitation
—gegenstand subject of an action
klagen bring in an action against, complain about, go to law, sue (for), take legal action
Kläger claimant, complainant, petitioner, plaintiff
Klagerecht right of action (to sue)
Klagesache cause, law action, action at law, lawsuit

Klageschrift bill of complaint, legal action, plaint, statement of claim, writ
Klagezustellung notice of action, service of process
Klammer bracket, parenthesis
—n, in in brackets (parenthesis)
klären clarify, clear (up), settle
Klärung clarification, clearing up, eludication, settling
klarstellen clarify, clear up, explain, settle
Klarstellung clarification, clearing up, explanation, settlement
Klasse bracket, category, class, degree, division, form, grade, order, quality, rank, type
Klassen-
—bewußtsein class consciousness
—einteilung classification
—haß class hatred
—justiz class justice
—kampf class conflict (struggle, warfare)
—unterscheidung class distinction
—wahlrecht class voting
klassifizieren classify
Klassifizierung classification
Klausel article, clause, condition, provision, proviso, rider, stipulation
Klausur seclusion, written examination, examination paper
—, in under supervision
klein insignificant, little, petty, small, trifling
Kleinigkeit bagatelle, petty, matter, trifle
kleinlich narrow-minded, petty
Klemme difficulty, dilemma, embarrassment, trouble
Kleptomane cleptomaniac, kleptomaniac
Kleptomanie cleptomania, kleptomania
klerikal clerical
Klerikaler churchman, clerical(ist), clergyman, ecclesiastic
Klerikalismus clericalism
Klerus clergy
Klient client, customer
Klientel (Klientschaft) clientele, clients, customers
Klub club
knapp concise, insufficient, narrow, scanty, scarce, scare, short, small, stringent, terse, tight
Knappe miner, mine worker, pitman
Knappheit conciseness, deficiency, hardness, lack, narrowness, scantiness, scarcity, shortage, shortness, stringency, tightness
Knappschaft body (corporation, society) of miners
—sverband miner's union
Knebel gag
knebeln gag
Knecht labo(u)rer, servant, slave
knechten enslave, oppress, subjugate
Knechtschaft serfdom, servitude, slavery, vassalage
Knechtung enslavement, oppression, subjugation
Kniff artifice, dodge, trick, strategem
Koalition coalition, combination, fusion
Koalitions-
—recht freedom of association
—regierung coalition government
Kode(x) code, codex
Kodifikation codification
kodifizieren codify
Kodizill codicil
Koexistenz coexistence
Kollaboration collaboration
kollaborieren collaborate
Kollaborator collaborator
kollateral collateral
Kollege colleague, fellow-worker
Kollegium assembly, board, body, committee, council, court, faculty, staff
kollektiv collective, joint
kollektivieren collectivize
Kollektivierung collectivization
Kollektivismus collectivism
Kollektivität collectivity
Kollektiv-
—besitz (—eigentum) collective ownership
—haftung joint liability (responsibility)

—schuld collective guilt (liabilities)
—strafe collective penalty (punishment)
—versicherung group insurance
—vertrag collective contract (treaty, agreement)
—vollmacht collective (joint) power
—zeichnung joint signature
kollidieren clash, collide, conflict
Kollision clash(ing), collision, conflict
—sklausel collision clause
Kollusion collusion, complicity, connivance, criminal collusion, secret understanding
kolonial colonial
Kolonial-
—besitz colonial possessions
—macht colonial power
—politik colonial policy
—verwaltung colonial administration
—wesen colonialism
Kolonie colony, settlement
Kron— crown colony
Straf— penal colony (settlement), convict settlement
Kolonisation colonization
kolonisieren colonize
Kolonist colonist, settler
Kombination combination
kombinieren combine, conclude, deduce, infer
Komitee committee
— einsetzen set up a committee
Kommandant commander, commanding officer, governor
Kommandeur commander, commanding officer
kommandieren (be in) command (of)
Kommandit-
—gesellschaft limited partnership
— — auf Aktien limited partnership on shares
Kommanditist limited partner
Kommando command, order
Kommentar annotation, comment, commentary, textbook
Kommentator annotator, commentator
kommentieren annote, comment
Kommilitone comrade, fellow-student
kommerzialisieren commercialize
Kommerzialisierung commercialization
kommerziell commercial
Kommissar commissary, commissioner, police inspector, superintendent
Kommissariat commissionership, commissioner's (superintendent's) office
kommissarisch on commission, provisional, temporary
Kommission brokerage, commission, committee, consignment, order
—, in on commission, on consignment
in — geben consign
in — nehmen take on commission (consignment)
Kommissionär agent, commissioner, factor
Kommissionsagent commission agent
Kommissionsgebühr commission
kommissionsweise on commission (consignment)
Kommittent consigner, employer, principal
kommunal communal, local, municipal
Kommunal-
—abgaben rates, local taxes
—anleihe (—darlehen) municipal loan
—beamter municipal (town) officer
—behörde municipal authority
—betrieb municipal enterprise
—kredit municipal credit
—obligation (—schuldverschreibung) municipal bond
—steuer local (municipal) rate (tax), rate
—verwaltung local (municipal) administration
Kommune commune, community, municipality
Kommunismus communism
Kommunist communist
kommunistisch communist(ic)
kommunizieren communicate

Kompagnon associate, partner
Kompanie company
Kompensation (Kompensierung) compensation
Kompensations-
—abkommen barter (compensation) agreement
—geschäft barter (compensation) transaction
—zoll compensatory duty
kompensieren adjust, compensate, counterbalance, offset
kompetent cognizant, competent, expert, reliable, responsible
Kompetenz cognizance, competence, competency, jurisdiction
—konflikt (—streit, —streitigkeit) concurrence of jurisdiction, conflict of authority, dispute of competence
Komplementär general partner
komplett complete, entire, whole
Komplex aggregate, block, body, complex, fixation, group, plot of land
Fragen— group of questions
Minderwertigkeits— inferiority complex
Komplikation complication
Komplize accessory, accomplice, confederate, partner in crime
komplizieren complicate, embarrass
kompliziert complex, complicated, difficult, intricate, perplexed
Kompliziertheit complexity, difficulty, intricacy
Komplott conspiracy, intrigue, plot
— schmieden conspire, intrigue, plot
Komposition composition, layout, make-up
Kompromiß agreement, arrangement, compromise, settlement
— schließen come to an agreement (arrangement), (make a) compromise, reach a settlement (an agreement)
kompromißbereit ready to compromise
Kompromißbereitschaft conciliatory spirit, spirit of conciliation
kompromißlos uncompromising
kompromittieren compromise, expose
—, sich commit (compromise) oneself
Kondition condition, state, term
Konferenz conference, congress, convention, meeting, parley, talks
— abhalten hold a conference (meeting)
— einberufen convoke a conference (meeting)
konferenzieren confer, deliberate, hold a conference
Konferenz-
—teilnehmer conferee, conference member
—tisch conference table
—zimmer conference room
Konfession confession, denomination, faith, religion
konfessionell confessional, denominational
über— interdenominational
konfessionslos creedless, undenominational
Konfiskation (Konfiszierung) condemnation, confiscation, seizure
konfiszieren confiscate, seize
Konflikt clashing, conflict, dispute
in — geraten mit come into conflict with, get mixed up with
Konföderation confederacy
konform conformable, in accordance (conformity) (with)
— gehen mit be in accordance (conformity) with, correspond to
Konformität conformity
Konfrontation confrontation
konfrontieren confront
konfus confused, in confusion, perplexed
Konfusion confusion, perplexity
kongenial congenial
Kongenialität congeniality
Kongregation congregation
Kongreß assembly, conference, congress, convention, meeting
—abgeordneter delegate

—mitglied congressman, member of Congress (USA), congress member
—wahlen congressional elections
König king
Königin queen
königlich regal, royal
Königreich kingdom, realm
Königtum kingdom, kingship, realm, royalty
Königs-
—krone royal crown
—mord regicide
—mörder regicide
—sitz royal residence
königstreu loyal, royalistic
Königs-
—treuer royalist
—treue loyalty
Konklave conclave
Konkordat concordat(e)
konkret actual, concrete, material, practical, tangible
konkretisieren itemize, realize, reify
Konkubinat concubinage
Konkurrent competitor, contestant, rival
Konkurrenz competition, rivalship, rivalry
— machen compete with
—angebot competitive bid (offer)
—bedingung competitive condition
—beschränkung (—verbot) restraint of trade
konkurrenzfähig competitive, marketable
Konkurrenz-
—kampf competition, competitive struggle, trade rivalry
—klausel competition clause
—lohn competitive wage
konkurrenzlos matchless, unrivalled, without competition
Konkurrenz-
—neid professional (trade) jealousy
—preis competitive price
—tarif competitive rate
—verbot s. —beschränkung
konkurrieren be in competition with, compete with, rival

Konkurs bankruptcy, failure, insolvency
— anmelden declare bankruptcy, file one's bankruptcy petition
— eröffnen become a (go) bankrupt, institute bankruptcy proceedings
in — gehen (geraten) become a (go) bankrupt, fail
—machen become a (go) bankrupt, fail
in — treiben (make) bankrupt, force into bankruptcy
Konkurs-
—anmeldung (—antrag) petition in bankruptcy
—anzeige bankruptcy notice
—beschluß receiving order, winding-up order
—bestimmungen bankruptcy regulations
—erklärung abjudication (declaration) of bankruptcy (insolvency)
—eröffnung abjudication (declaration) of bankruptcy, institution of bankruptcy proceedings
—fall bankruptcy case
—gericht court of bankruptcy, bankruptcy court
—gesetz Act of Bankruptcy (USA), Bankruptcy Act (GB)
—gesetzgebung bankruptcy legislation
—gläubiger creditor in bankruptcy
—masse bankrupt's estate
—ordnung s. —gesetz
—pfleger s. —verwalter
—recht bankruptcy law
—richter magistrate in bankruptcy
—sache s. —fall
—schuldner bankrupt
—verfahren bankruptcy proceedings, proceedings in bankruptcy
— — eröffnen (einleiten) institute bankruptcy proceedings
—verwalter administrator of bankrupt's estate, custodian (trustee) in bankruptcy, official receiver

—verwaltung administration of bankrupt's estate, receivership, trusteeship in bankruptcy
—verzicht withdrawal of bankruptcy
Können ability, efficiency, faculty, power, skill
nach bestem — to the best of one's ability
können be able to, be capable of, know, understand
—, nicht be unable to, be incapable of
Konnossement bill of lading, shipping bill (note)
Konsens consent
konsequent consequent(ial), consistent, in consequence, logical
Konsequenz consequence, consistency, determination, resolution
—en haben be followed by consequences
—en ziehen face (put up with) (take) the consequences
konservativ conservative
Konservativer conservative
Konservatismus conservatism
Konsignant consignor
Konsignatar consignee
Konsignation consignment
konsignieren consign
konsolidieren consolidate, fund
Konsolidierung consolidation, funding
Konsortium association, gang, group, syndicate
konspirieren conspire, plot
konstant constant, fixed, stable, standing
Konstanz constancy, stability
konstatieren establish, find out, notice, observe, state, verify
Konstatierung statement, verification
Konstellation constellation, position, situation, state
konsternieren consternate, dismay
konstituieren appoint, constitute, form, organize, set up
konstituierend constituent
Konstitution constitution, fundamental law, habit
konstitutionell constitutional
konstruieren build, construct, construe, design, erect
Konstrukteur designer
Konstruktion construction, design
Fehl— defective construction, faulty design, misconstruction
—sfehler constructional defect, defect of construction, fault in design (construction)
konstruktiv constructive, positive
Konsul consul
konsularisch consular
Konsulat consulate, consulship
General— consulate general
Konsulent (legal) adviser, advocate, barrister, consultant, counsel, solicitor
Konsultation consultation, deliberation
konsultieren consult, deliberate
Konsum consumption
Konsument consumer
konsumieren consume
Konsum-
—güter consumer goods
—steuer excise duty
—verein cooperative society
Kontakt contact
— aufnehmen (enter into) contact
— verlieren lose contact
Kontaktmann contact man
Konterbande contraband (goods)
Kontingent allocation, allotment, contingent, contribution, proportion, quota, share
kontingentieren apportion pro rata, fix contingents, fix a proportion(quota), ration
Kontingentierung allotment, fixing of contingents (quota) (a proportion), limitation, pro rata apportionment, quota system, restriction
kontinuierlich continuous
Kontinuität continuity
Konto account
—auszug statement of account
—buch account book
—inhaber account holder, depositor
—sperre blocking of account

kontradiktorisch contentious, contested, contradictory, defended
—, nicht non-contentious
Kontrahent contracting party, contractor, party to the contract
kontrahieren (make a) contract
Kontrakt agreement, bargain, contract, covenant
—bruch breach of contract
kontraktlich by contract, contractual, stipulated
konträr contrary
Kontroll-
—ausschuß control (supervisory) committee
—beamter control officer, controller, inspector, supervisor
—behörde board of control
—gebiet controlled area, area of control
—gesellschaft holding company
Kontrolle check(ing), checkup, control, examination, inspection, supervision, verification
—, behördliche regimentation
—, staatliche state control
Kontrolleur auditor, controller, examiner, inspector, superintendent, supervisor
kontrollieren audit, check, control, examine, inspect, supervise, verify
Kontroll-
—maßnahme control(ling) measure
—organ control organ, controlling (supervisory) board
—recht right of control (supervision)
—schein (—zettel) counterfoil
—system control sytem
Kontroverse controversy
Konvention agreement, convention, treaty
Konventionalstrafe stipulated penalty, penalty (for nonperformance of a contract)
konventionell conventional contract
Konversation conversation, talk
Konversion conversion
konvertierbar convertible
—, nicht inconvertible
Konvertierbarkeit (Konvertibilität) convertibility
konvertieren convert
Konvertierung conversion
Konvertit convert
Konvoi convoy
konzedieren concede
Konzentration concentration
—slager concentration (detention) camp
konzentrieren centre (upon), concentrate on (upon)
Konzept concept, foul (rough) copy, draft, sketch
aus dem — bringen confuse, perplex, upset
aus dem — kommen break down
Konzern combination, combine, concern, group, pool, trust
—abkommen (—vertrag) trust agreement
—entflechtung decartelization, deconcentration of trust, detrust
—verflechtung business concentration, interlocking combination (combine)
Konzession charter, concession, franchise, grant, licenc(s)e, patent, permit, privilege, right
— erteilen give an licenc(s)e, license
—en machen make concessions
Konzessionär concessionary, concessionaire, licensee, licenc(s)e holder, patentee
konzessionieren give a licenc(s)e, grant a concession, license
Konzessions-
—entsetzung revocation (withdrawal) of concession (licenc[s]e)
—erteilung granting of concession (licenc[s]e)
—gebühr licenc(s)e fee
—inhaber (—nehmer) s. Konzessionär
Konzil council, synod
konzipieren conceive, draft, draw up, formulate, imagine, outline
Konzipierung conception
Kooperation cooperation
kooperativ cooperative
kooperieren cooperate

Koordination (Koordinierung) coordination
koordinieren coordinate
Kopf head(ing), title
—, pro per capita (head)
—arbeit brain (head, mental) work
—arbeiter brain worker
Kopie copy, duplicate, imitation
kopieren copy, imitate
Kopist copyist
Körper body
körperlich bodily, corpor(e)al, material, physical, solid, substantial, tangible
Körperschaft artificial person, body (corporate), corporation, legal entity, organization
— des öffentlichen Rechts public body (corporation), body corporate
Körperschaftsteuer corporation tax
Körper-
—strafe corporal punishment
—verletzung bodily injury
Korporation corporation
korporativ corporate
Korps corps
—, diplomatisches diplomatic corps
Korpus body
— delicti tangible proof, convicting (convincing) object
— juris law code
korrekt accurate, correct
Korrektheit accuracy, correctitude, correctness, exactitude
Korrektur adjustment, correction, proof(-sheet), rectification, revisal, revise, revision
Korrespondent correspondent
Korrespondenz correspondence (cy), letters, papers
korrespondieren correspond (to, with), exchange letters
korrigieren adjust, correct, rectify, revise
korrumpieren bribe, corrupt
korrupt corrupt(ed)
Korruption bribery, corruption, graft
kostbar costly, expensive, precious, valuable
Kostbarkeit preciousness, valuableness
Kostbarkeiten valuables
Kosten charges, cost(s), expense(s), fees
Anwalts— lawyer's fees
Gerichts— court costs, law (legal) charges, court (legal) fees
Verwaltungs— administrative costs (expenses)
kosten cost
Kosten-
—anschlag estimate (of costs)
—aufwand expenditure, expenses
—beschluß decree of costs
—erstattung compensation, indemnification, refund (reimbursement) of expenses
Kostenfestsetzung assessment (determination) of costs
kostenfällig with costs
— abweisen dismiss with costs
kostenfrei free of charge(s) (cost, expense)
Kostenfreiheit exemption from charges
kostenlos free of charge(s) (cost), gratis, gratuitous, without cost
kostenpflichtig with costs
— verurteilen sentence with costs
Kosten-
—preis cost price
—punkt matter (question) of expenses
—rechnung bill of costs, cost account
—urteil judgement of costs, order to pay the costs
—voranschlag estimate (of costs)
—vorschuß advence(d costs, expenses), retainer, retaining, fees
Kostgeld (board) allowance, board wages, boarding money
kostspielig costly, dear, expensive
Kostspieligkeit costliness, dearness, expensiveness
Krach collapse, crash, debacle, failure, panic, quarrel, row, smash

Kraft ability, capacity, energy, force, might, power, strength, vigour
Beweis— probative weight, conclusive (probatory) force, conclusiveness
Gesetzes— legal force (power), statutory effect, force (strength) of law
Körper— physical strength
Rechts— (legal) validity, legal effect (force), effectiveness, force of law
Kraft, außer repealed
—, in in force, valid
in — bleiben remain in force
in — sein be effective (in force)
in — setzen give effect to, put into force
außer — setzen abolish, annul, cancel, declare invalid, invalidate, repeal, rescind
in — treten become effective (operative), come into effect (force) (operation), take effect
außer — treten become invalid, expire, cease to have effect (force), lapse, lose force
kraft according to, by operation (virtue) of, on the strength of
— Gesetzes by (operation of) law
—anstrengung effort, exertion
—ausdruck forcible (vigorous) expression
—ausdrücke strong language
—fahrer driver, motorist
—fahrzeug automobile, motor vehicle, motor car
— —brief motor vehicle registration certificate
— —halter motor vehicle holder
— —steuer motor vehicle tax
— —versicherung motor car (automobil, motor vehicle) insurance
— —zulassung motor vehicle licence
Kräfte forces, powers
—gleichgewicht equilibrium of forces (powers)
—verhältnis proportion of forces (powers)
—verteilung distribution of forces (powers)
kräftig efficacious, energetic, forcible, powerful, solid, strong, valid, vigorous
kräftigen invigorate, strengthen
Kräftigkeit energy, powerfulness, strength, validity, vigour
Kräftigung invigoration, strengthening
kraftlos faint, feeble, ineffective, inefficient, inoperative, invalid, null and void, powerless, void, weak, without strength
für — erklären abolish, annul, cancel, declare (null and) void, invalidate
— werden become invalid, cease to be valid (have force)
Kraftloserklärung abolishment, annulment, cancellation, declaration of invalidity, invalidation
Kraftlosigkeit feebleness, lack of strength (vigour)
krank sick
— melden report sick
kranken an suffer from
kränken afflict, annoy, grieve, humble, injure, irritate, offend, mortify, vex, wound
Kranken-
—bericht bulletin, sick report
—geld sick allowance (benefit) (pay)
—kasse sick(ness) fund
—urlaub sick leave
—versicherung health (sick) (sickness) insurance
Kranker sick (person), patient
krankhaft abnormal, diseased, insane, morbid, pathological
Krankhaftigkeit abnormality, morbidness
Krankheit disease, illness, malady, sickness
Geistes— insanity, mental disease
krankheitshalber because of (on account of, owing to, through) illness
Krankheitsurlaub sick leave
Kränkung annoyance, grievance, injury, mortification, offence, vexation
kraß awful, blatant, crass, crude, direct, flagrant, gross, marked

krasser Widerspruch direct (flagrant) contradiction
Kreatur creature
Kredit advance, belief, credence, credit, loan, reputation, trust
—, auf on credit (trust)
— aufnehmen borrow money, raise (take up) a credit
— einräumen (gewähren) give (grant, open) a credit
Kredit-
—abkommen loan (credit) agreement
—anstalt credit institution
—aufnahme raising of credit
—bank loan bank
—beschaffung credit supply
—brief letter of credit
kreditfähig (-würdig) creditable, good, reliable, sound, trustworthy, worthy of credit
Kredit-
—fähigkeit creditability, reliability, soundness, trustworthiness
—geber borrower, creditor, lender
—geschäft credit transaction
—gewährung granting of credits
—grenze credit line (limit)
kreditieren (give) credit, trust
Kreditinstitut credit institution
Kredit-
—linie credit line (limit)
—nehmer borrower, lender
—note credit note
Kreditor creditor
Kredit-
—papier (—dokument) credit instrument
—risiko credit risk
—sicherheit collateral, security
—sperre loan embargo
—system (—wesen) credit system
—überschreitung overdraft
—überwachung credit control
kreditunwürdig not worthy of credit, unreliable
—würdig s. —fähig
Kredit-
—würdigkeit s. —fähigkeit
Kreis borough, circle, circuit, county, district, group, quarter, range, sphere, scope
Wahl— constituency, (election) district
Kreis-
—amt district office
—ausschuß district committee
—beamter district officer
—behörde district (local) authority (board)
—gericht county (district) court
—ordnung district regulations
—richter district judge
—stadt county (district) town
—tag county (district) council, district assembly
Kreuzverhör cross-examination
ins — nehmen cross-examine
Krieg armed conflict, contest, quarrel, strife, war, warfare
— erklären declare war
— führen make war against, fight
im — liegen mit be at war with
kriegerisch armed, bellicose, belligerent, hostile, martial, warfaring, warlike
kriegführend at war, belligerent
Kriegführung belligerence(cy), conduct of war, strategy, warfare
Kriegs-
—anstrengungen war efforts
—artikel articles of war
—beute loot, war booty
kriegsbeschädigt (war-)disabled
Kriegs-
—dienst (military) service
—erklärung declaration of war
—fuß
auf dem — — stehen mit be at war with
—gebiet war zone
—gebrauch (—brauch) custom (usage) of war
—gefangener prisoner of war
—gefangenschaft captivity
in — — sein be a prisoner of war
—gericht court(-)martial
vor ein — — bringen (bring before a) court(-)martial
—gesetz martial law
—handlung act of war
—hetze war agitation
—hetzer war agitator
—invalide war invalid

—**klausel** war clause
—**macht** military power (forces)
—**minister** Minister of War, Secretary of State for War (GB), Secretary of War (USA)
—**ministerium** Ministry of War, War Office (GB), War Board (Department) (USA)
—**rat** war council
—**recht** articles of war, martial law, laws of warfare, military law
—**schaden** war damage
—**schuld** war guilt
—**steuer** war tax
—**verbrechen** war crime
—**verbrecher** war criminal
—**versehrter** war disabled
—**vorbereitungen** war preparations
—**wirtschaft** war (wartime) economy
—**zeit** war time(s), time(s) of war
—**zone** war zone
—**zustand** state of war

kriminal criminal

Kriminal-
—**abteilung** criminal department (office), criminal investigation department
—**beamter (—kommissar)** criminal investigator, (official) detective, officer of the criminal (investigation) department
—**film** crime film
—**gericht** court of criminal jurisdiction, criminal court

kriminalgerichtlich criminal, penal

Kriminal-
—**gerichtsbarkeit** criminal (penal) jurisdiction
—**gesetz** criminal (penal) law
—**gesetzbuch** criminal (penal) code

Kriminalist criminal expert, criminalist, detective, specialist on criminal law

kriminalistisch criminal

Kriminalität crime rate, criminality
 Jugend— juvenile (youth) delinquency

Kriminal-
—**polizei** criminal police, Criminal Investigation Department (C. I.D.) (GB), Federal Bureau of Investigation (F.B.I.) (USA)
—**polizist** s. —beamter
—**prozeß** criminal procedure
—**psychologe** psychologist of crime
—**pschologie** psychology of crime
—**recht** criminal (penal) law
—**roman** crime novel, detective story
—**sache** criminal case
—**statistik** criminal statistics
—**strafkunde** criminology, penology
—**verfahren** criminal proceedings

kriminell criminal

Kriminologe criminologist

Kriminologie criminal sociology, criminology

kriminologisch criminological
—**es Institut** criminological institute

Krise crisis

krisenfest stable

Kriterium criterion, test

Kritik censure, criticism, critique, review(al)

Kritiker critic, reviewer

kritisch critical, crucial, dangerous, decisive, precarious

kritisieren censure, criticize, review

Krone crown
 der — entsagen (die — niederlegen) abdicate the throne

Kron-
—**amt** crown office
—**anwalt** General Attorney (USA), Solicitor General (GB), public prosecutor
—**beamter** crown officer, officer of the crown
—**erbe** heir to the crown
—**gut** crown property, royal domain (demesne)
—**juwelen** crown jewels
—**kolonie** crown colony
—**land** crown estate (land)
—**rat** crown council
—**recht** royal prerogative
—**zeuge** approver, king's evidence, principal (chief) (crown)

witness, witness of the first class
krönen crown
Krönung coronation
Krönungs-
—akt (—feierlichkeit) coronation ceremony
—eid coronation oath
kulant accommodating, easy, fair, obliging
Kulanz fair dealing, fairness, obligingness
Kulisse coulisse
hinter den —n behind the scenes, underhand
Kult cult
kultisch cultic
kultivieren cultivate
Kultur civilization, cultivation, culture
—abkommen cultural convention (agreement)
—austausch cultural exchange
—geschichte history of civilization, social history
—staat civilized country
—volk civilized nation
kulturell cultural
kumulativ (ac)cumulative
kumulieren accumulate
Kunde client, customer, information, intelligence, knowledge, notice, science
Kunden-
—dienst service
—kreis clientele, customers
—wechsel trade (customer's) bill
Kundgabe announcement, proclamation, publication
kundgeben (-machen, -tun) give notice, make known (public), manifest, notify, publish
Kundgebung (-machung) declaration, demonstration, manifestation, notice, proclamation, publication, statement
kundig acquainted with, expert, familiar with, knowing, skilled in, skilful, versed in
kündbar at call (notice), callable, redeemable, subject to call (notice), terminable
kündigen abrogate, call in, cancel, denounce, dissolve, foreclose, give notice (warning), quit, recall, rescind, revoke, sign off, terminate, withdraw
Kündigung abrogation, calling in, cancellation, denunciation, foreclosure, notice, recall, revocation, termination, warning, withdrawal
Kündigungs-
—frist period (term) of notice
—grund ground (argument, reason) of notice
—klausel cancellation (termination) clause
—recht right of cancellation (notice)
—schreiben written notice
—termin date (term) of cancellation (notice)
Kundschaft clientele, connection (xion), custom(ers), good will, information, intelligence
Kundschafter emissary, scout, spy
künftig coming, future, next, prespective
—hin for the (in) future, henceforth
Kunst art, skill
— und Gewerbe arts and crafts
Künste practices, tricks
Künstler artist, performer
künstlich artificial, false, imitated
Kupon coupon, counterfoil, divident (interest) coupon (warrant)
—inhaber coupon holder
—steuer coupon (dividend) tax
Kuppelei matchmaking, pandering, procuring
kuppeln make a match, pander, procure
Kuppler matchmaker, pander, procurer
Kupplerin pandress, procuress
Kuratel guardianship, trusteeship, tutelage
unter — stehen be under trusteeship (in ward)
unter — stellen appoint a guardian (trustee) for, put under guardianship (trusteeship)
Kurator administrator, curator, guardian, trustee, warden
Kuratorium curators, (board of) **trustees**

Kurpfuscher charlatan, quack
Kurpfuscherei charlatanism, charlatanry, quackery
Kurs circulation (price), course, currency, current price (rate), exchange rate, market price (rate), orientation, quotation, rate, value
kursieren be current (in circulation), circulate
kursierend current, in circulation
Kurs-
—makler exchange broker
—notierung (market, price) quotation
—parität exchange parity
—schwankungen exchange fluctuations
—spekulant market manipulator (operator)
—spekulation exchange manipulation (speculation)
—wechsel alteration (change) of course, reorientation, turnabout
—wert markt price (rate, value)
—zettel (—bericht) exchange (price, quotation, stock) list, market report
Kursus class, course (of lectures)
kurz brief, concise, short, small
Kurz-
—arbeit part-time (short-time) work
—arbeiter part-time (short-time) worker, part timer
—bericht (—fassung) summary (report)
Kürze brevity, briefness, shortness
—, in briefly, in brief (short), in a nutshell, in a word
kürzen abridge, curtail, cut (down), reduce, shorten, simplify, slash
kurzfristig at short notice, short-term
Kurz
—schrift shorthand (writing), stenography
—urlaub short leave, pass
Kürzung abridgement, curtailment, cut, cutting down, deduction, reduction, retrenchment, slashing
Küste coast, shore
Küsten-
—gebiet (—zone) coastal area (district, region)
—gewässer coastal waters
—polizei (—wache) coast guard, coastal patrol
—schutz coastguards, coastal defence
Kux mining share (stock)

L

labil labile, unstable, weak
Labilität instability, insteadiness, lability
laden ask, call, charge, cite, freight, invite, lade, load, summon
—, Zeugen summon a witness
—, unter Strafandrohung subpoena
—, Schuld auf sich become guilty, burden oneself with guilt
als Zeuge — call as witness
vor Gericht — cite (summon) before the court
Laden shop, store
—besitzer s. —inhaber
—dieb shoplifter
—diebstahl shoplifting
—einbruch shopbreaking
—inhaber shopkeeper, storekeeper
—kasse till
—schluß closing time (hour)
—stunden shop hours
Lade-
—papiere shipping documents
—schein (—brief) bill of lading, shipping bill (note)

Ladung cargo, citation, consignment, freight, invitation, load, shipment, subpoena, summons
— ergehen lassen issue a summons (a subpoena), serve somebody with a summons, take out a summons against
Ladung
— erhalten be summoned, be served with a summons
— nachkommen answer (comply with) a summons
lädieren damage, injure
Lage circumstances, condition, locality, location, position, site, situation, state (of affairs)
in der — sein be able to, be in a condition (situation, position) to
in die — versetzen enable
Lage-
—bericht background (situation) report
—besprechung briefing
—plan layout, site (ground) plan, survey
Lager assortment, camp, depot, stock, store, storehouse, supply, warehouse
—bestand inventory, stock (on hand)
— —saufnahme inventory, stock taking
—geld (—miete, —spesen) storage warehouse charges
—halter (—verwalter) storekeeper, stock (warehouse) keeper
—haltung stock keeping
—haus storehouse, warehouse
—kontrolle inventory (stock) control
lagern store, warehouse
Lagerschein warehouse receipt (certificate, warrant)
Lagerung storage, storing, warehousing
Lager
—verzeichnis inventory record
lahm flagging, lame, paralyse
lahmlegen obstruct, paralyse
Laie dilettante, layman, nonexpert
Laien (—schaft, —stand) laity
Laien-
—beisitzer juror, lay assessor
laienhaft lay
Laienrichter lay judge
Laiin laywoman
Land country, ground, land, land(ed) propery, lot, piece of land, plot, region, soil, state, territory
—es, außer abroad
außer —es gehen go abroad, leave the country
Land-
—adel (landed) gentry
—arbeit agricultural labo(u)r (work), farm work
—arbeiter farm hand, agricultural (farm, land) labo(u)rer (worker)
—besitz landowning, real estate, realty, land(ed) (real) property
—besitzer landowner, real estate owner
—bevölkerung rural population
—bezirk rural district
—eigentümer land(ed) (real estate) proprietor (owner)
Ländereien land(s), land(ed) property, (real) estates, grounds
Landes-
—arbeitsamt labour (industrial) court of appeal
—bank national (regional) bank
—brauch national (general) custom
—fürst (—herr) monarch, sovereign
—gebiet national (state) territory
—gesetz common law, national (state) law, law of the country (land)
—gesetzgebung national, legislation
—grenze frontier, national boundary, state border
—hauptstadt capital
—herrschaft (—hoheit) sovereignty, supremacy
—recht national (territorial) law
—regierung central (national, land) government
—sitte national custom
—sozialgericht social (welfare) court of appeal
landesüblich customary, usual

Landes-
—verrat (high) treason
—verräter traitor
landesverräterisch treasonable
Landes-
—verteidigung home (national) defence
—verweisung banishment, deportation, exile, expatriation
—währung legal (national) currency
—zentralbank national (regional) central bank, Bank of England (GB), Federal Reserve Bank (USA), national state bank
Land-
—frevel trespass
—frieden public peace
— —sbruch breach (violation) of the public peace
—gericht high court, district (provincial) court, Quarter Sessions (GB)
— —srat district (provincial) judge
landkundig notorious
landläufig conventional, current, customary, general, generally accepted, usual
ländlich rural
Land-
—pacht lease
—polizei rural police
—recht common law
—smann compatriot, fellow countryman
—steuer land tax
—streicher tramp, vagabond, vagrant
—streicherei vagabondism, vagrancy
—tag diet
Landtags-
—abgeordneter member of a diet
—sitzung diet
Land-
—verteilung distribution of land
—wirtschaft agriculture
landwirtschaftlich agricultural
lange long, for a long time
Länge duration, length, longitude
in die — ziehen protract
sich in die — ziehen last long, take a long time
langfristig long, long-dated, long-term
langjährig of long standing, long
Lärm, nächtlicher disorder by night
Lärm, ruhestörender disturbance
Last burden, cargo, charge, duty, encumbrance, freight, load, onus, tax, trouble, weight
Beweis— burden (onus) of evidence (proof)
zur — fallen be blamed on, be encumbered on, be(come) a burden to, be imputed to
zur — legen blame for, charge with, impute to, lay to the charge of
zu —en von at the cost (expense) of
lasten auf be burdened (encumbered, mortgaged) with, press upon, weigh upon
Lasten-
—ausgleich equalization of burdens, restitution
— —sgesetz Equalization of Burdens Act (Law)
— —svermögensabgabe equalization of burdens property levy
lastenfrei free from debts (mortgage, taxes), free of charges (encumbrance), unencumbered
Laster depravity, vice, viciousness
dem — verfallen sink into vice
Lästerer backbiter, calumniator, defamer, slanderer
lasterhaft corrupt, depraved, dissolute, lascivious, profligate, vicious, wicked
Lasterhaftigkeit corruptness, depravity, dissoluteness, lasciviousness, profligacy, viciousness, wickedness
Gottes— blasphemer
lästern abuse, backbite, blaspheme, defame, malign, slander
Lästerung abuse, calumniation, calumny, defamation, slander
Gottes— blasphemy
Läster-
—rede defamatory (slanderous) language
—schrift libel

—wort blasphemy, slander
lästig annoying, bothersome, burdensome, cumbersome, importunate, incommodious, irksome, onerous, troublesome, uncomfortable, undesirable
— werden become (fall) a burden (trouble) to
— sein be a burden (nuisance)
Lastschrift debit entry (item)
—anzeige debit note
latent dormant, hidden, latent, potential, secret
Latenz latency
Latifundien large estates
Lauer ambush, lurking place
auf der — liegen lie in ambush (wait)
lauern lie in wait for, (be in the) lurk, watch for
lauernd creeping, cunning, searching
Lauf course, run(ning)
— lassen let something take its course
im — von in the course (process) of, within
Laufbahn career
— einschlagen enter upon a career
laufen be in process, function, operate, run, rush, work
laufend consecutive, continuous, current, daily, pending, present, regular, routine, running
auf dem —en halten keep informed of
auf dem —en sein be up-to-date
Lauf
—paß dismissal, sack
— — geben dismiss
—zeit currency, due date, duration, life, maturity, period, term, validity
—zettel circular (letter), tracer
lauschen eavesdrop, listen
Lauscher eavesdropper, listener
laut — according to, as per, in accordance (conformity) with, in pursuance of
lauten read, run
— auf be made out in (to), be payable to
dahin —, daß be to the effect that
lauter candid, clear, genuine, honest, pure, sincere, transparent, true
—e Wahrheit very (unvarnished, plain) truth
Lauterkeit candour, clearness, honesty, integrity, pureness, purity, righteousness, sincerity, transparency, uprightness, veracity
Leben existence, life, living
am — bleiben escape, remain alive, survive
ums — bringen kill, murder, put to death
ums — kommen lose one's life, be killed
— führen live a life
am — lassen (— schenken) spare a person's life
sich das — nehmen commit suicide
ins — rufen bring forth, bring into existence, call into being, create, generate, give life to, originate, produce
am — sein be alive, exist
sein — aufs Spiel setzen risk one's life
nach dem — trachten make an attempt at somebody's life, seek (attempt) a person's life
leben be alive, exist, live, subsist
—, getrennt be separated from, live apart from
— nach live up to, follow
— von be supported by, live on, subsist on (upon)
über seine Verhältnisse — live beyond one's means
Lebender living person
Über— survivor
unter Lebenden inter vivos
lebendig active, alive, animated, lively, living, vivid
Lebendigkeit aliveness, liveliness, vitality
Lebens-
—abschnitt period of life
—alter age
—anschauung (—auffassung) concept (philosophy, view) of life, outlook on life
—art behavio(u)r, manner of life, manners, way of living

—aufgabe life task
—aussichten expectancy (prospects) of life
—bedingungen living conditions
—bedürfnisse necessaries (necessities) of life
—beschreibung biography, life
—dauer durability, duration of life, life span, life(time)
—ende end of life
bis ans — — until death, to the end of one's days
—erfahrung life (practical) experience
—erwartungen expectations (expectancy) of life
lebensfähig capable of living, viable
Lebens-
—fähigkeit viability, vitality
—frage vital question
—gefahr danger of life
in — — schweben go in fear of one's life, be in danger (of one's life)
unter — — at the risk of one's life
lebensgefährlich dangerous to (endangering) life, mortal, perilous
Lebens-
—gefährte partner for life, life companion
—gemeinschaft community of life
—haltung living standard, mode of life, standard of living
— —skosten cost of living
—kampf struggle for existence (life)
lebenslänglich for (during) life, lifelong
Lebens-
—lauf course of life, curriculum vitae
—licht
— — auspusten take a person's life
lebens
—müde weary of life
—notwendig essential, vital
Lebens-
—notwendigkeit vital necessity
—raum living space
—recht right of existence (to exist)
—regel maxim, rule of life
—rente life annuity
—retter live saver
—spanne life span
—standard living standard, standard of living
—stellung life-time job, permanent position (employment, situation), social position (status)
—strafe capital punishment
—unterhalt livelihood, living, maintenance, subsistence, sustenance
—verhältnisse living conditions
—vermutung presumption of life
—versicherung life insurance (assurance)
—wandel behavio(u)r, conduct (course) of life, way of living
— —, schlechter misconduct
—weise mode of living
—werk life work
lebenswichtig essential, vital
Lebens
—wichtigkeit vital importance
—zeichen sign of life
—zeit lifetime, (term, time of) life
auf — — for (during) life, lifelong
bei — — in one's lifetime
lebhaft active, animated, busy, full of life, keen, lively, vivacious
Lebhaftigkeit animation, liveliness, vivacity
leblos dull, inanimate, lifeless, stagnant
Leblosigkeit dullness, impassiveness, stagnation
Lebzeiten, zu (bei) in one's lifetime
ledig discovert, exempt, free, illegitimate, single, sole, unoccupied, vacant
Ledigensteuer bachelor's tax
leer blank, empty, free, idle, lame, unoccupied, vacant, vain
—stehend empty, tenantless, uninhabited, unoccupied, vacant
legal lawful, legal, rightful
Legalisation (Legalisierung) authentication, certification, legalization, legitimation, validation

legalisieren authenticate, legalize, legitimate, render valid, validate
Legalität lawfulness, legality, validity
Legat bequest, devise, legacy, legate
Legatar devisee, legatee
Legation embassy, legation
Legislative legislature, legislative body (power)
Legislaturperiode legislature, legislative period (session), parliamentary session
legitim lawful, legitimate
Legitimation identification, legitimation, proof of identity
Aktiv— power to act, right (power) to sue
Passiv— capacity to be sued
Aktiv- und Passiv— power to sue and to be sued
Legitimations-
—karte identity card
—nachweis proof of identity
—papier identification paper
legitimieren authorize, identify, legitimate, legitimize
—, sich prove (establish) one's identity
legitimiert authorized, legitimated
aktiv — entitled to sue
passiv — capable to be sued
Legitimierung s. Legitimation
Legimität legitimacy
Leh(e)n fee, fief, tenure
Leh(e)ns-
—besitz feudal tenure
—brief bill of feoffment
—eid oath of allegiance
—gut feud, (estate in) fee
— —, freies freehold
—erbe feudal heir
—herr feoffor, feudal lord, liege lord
leh(e)nsherrlich seignorial
— —e Rechte seignorial rights
Leh(e)ns-
—mann feoffee, feudal tenant, liege, vassal
—pflicht fealty, feudal duty
—recht feudal law
leh(e)nsrechtlich under feudal law
Leh(e)ns-
—verhältnis tenure
—wesen feudal system, feudalism
Lehr-
—amt professorship, teachership
—anstalt academy, school
—auftrag lecturership
—brief apprentice certificate, indenture
Lehre advice, apprenticeship, doctrine, hint, instruction, lesson, rule, science, system, teaching, theory, training, tution
— erteilen teach a lesson
— ziehen aus draw a lesson from
lehren give lessons (lectures), inform, instruct, teach, train
Lehrer instructor, lecturer, master, professor, schoolmaster, teacher, tutor
—schaft body of teachers
Lehr-
—gang class, course
—geld apprentice fee
— — zahlen by experience, learn it the hard way
—herr (—meister) boss, employer, master, principal
Lehrling apprentice
Lehr-
—verhältnis apprenticeship
—vertrag apprenticeship contract, articles of apprenticeship, indenture
—zeit (time of) apprenticeship
Leibes-
—strafe corporal punishment
—visitation bodily search
leiblich bodily, corporal, full, natural, physical
Leibrente life annuity
Leibrenten-
—versicherung annuity insurance
—vertrag annuity contract
Leiche corpse, dead body
Leichen-
—ausgrabung exhumation
—begängnis burial, funeral
—beschauer coroner
—besorger (—bestatter) undertaker
—halle (—haus) morgue, mortuary
—öffnung autopsy, post-mortem examination, section

—schändung desecration of a dead body
—schau (coroner's) inquest, postmortem examination
—verbrennung cremation
leicht easy, light, slight
—fertig careless, frivolous, irresponsible, light-minded, reckless, thoughtless, volatile
Leichtfertigkeit carelessness, frivolity, levity, recklessness, thoughtlessness, volatility
leichtgläubig credulous
Leichtgläubigkeit credulity
Leichtsinn carelessness, frivolity, levity, recklessness
leichtsinnig careless, flighty, frivolous, irresponsible, light-minded, reckless
Leidenschaft emotion, passion
Leih-
—amt loan office, pawnshop, pawnbroker's office
—bank loan bank (office)
Leihe loan (for use) (of goods), lending
Leihen borrowing, lending, loan
leihen advance, accommodate with, borrow, hire, lend, loan, rent
Leiher borrower, lender
Pfand— pawnbroker
Leih-
—gabe loan
—gebühr lending fee, rental
—haus loan office, pawnbroker's shop, pawnshop
—pacht lend-lease
—schein pawn ticket
—vertrag loan contract
leihweise as a loan, by way of a loan, on credit (hire, loan)
leisten accomplish, carry out, do, effect, execute, fulfil, furnish, perform, realize, render
—, sich afford
leisten
—, Abbitte apologize, ask somebody's pardon
—, Anzahlung make a deposit
—, Arbeit perform work
—, Beihilfe render assistance
—, Beitrag make a contribution
—, Bürgschaft go (stand) bail, give security
—, Dienst render a service
—, Eid deliver (swear, take) an oath
—, Ersatz make restitution, pay compensation
—, Folge accept, comply with
—, Garantie guarantee, warrant
—, Gehorsam yield obedience
—, Genugtuung give satisfaction
—, Hilfe render assistance
—, Kaution become a (go) bail
—, Schadenersatz pay damage
—, Schwur swear an oath
—, Sicherheit give security
—, Verzicht disclaim, give up, renounce, waive
—, Vorschuß advance money
—, Widerstand offer resistance, resist
—, Zahlung make payment, pay
Leistung accomplishment, achievement, attainment, capacity, contribution, effect, efficiency, execution, output, payment, performance, power, production, proficiency, rendering, result, service, taking
leistungsfähig able, capable, efficient, powerful, productive, serviceable, solid, solvent
Leistungsfähigkeit ability, capability, capacity, efficiency, output, performance, power, productiveness, productivity, proficiency, serviceableness, solvency
Leistungs-
—klage action for performance
—ort place of performance
—vermögen capacity, productivity
leiten be at the head of, be in charge of, conduct, control, direct, govern, guide, have in charge, lead, manage, operate, preside over, rule, superintend
leitend chief, conducting, directing, dominant, executive, governing, guiding, key, leading, managing
Leiter chief, conductor, director, guide, head, leader, manager, president

Leitgedanke guiding principle, leading (directive, governing) idea
Leitung administration, chairmanship, conduct, control, direction, government, guidance, lead(ing), leadership, management, operation, presidency, superintendence
unter — von under the control (direction, management) of
Leitwort keyword
Lektion lecture, lesson
— erteilen give a lecture, lecture, teach a lesson
Lektor lecturer
lenken control, direct, drive, guide, govern, manage, rule
Lenker controller, driver, governor, ruler
Lenkung control, direction, driving, governing, government, guiding, leadership, management, ruling
lernen learn, study
Lesart interpretation, reading, version
lesbar legible, readable
Lesbarkeit legitibility, readableness, readability
lesen give lectures, lecture on, read
Leser reader
leserlich legible
un— illegible
Leserlichkeit legibility
Un— illegibility
Lesung reading
—, in erster at the first reading
letzt bottom, extreme, final, last, latest, lowest, ultimate
letzt-
—es Angebot final offer (proposal)
—er Ausweg last resource (resort)
—es Gebot last (highest) bid
—e Instanz last instance
—er Versuch last attempt, supreme effort
—er Wille last will and testament
Letztbietender last and highest bidder
letzterwähnt last mentioned
letztwillig by testament (will), testamentary
—e Verfügung last will and testament, testamentary disposition, will
—e Zuwendung testamentary gift
Leugnen abnegation, denial, disavowal
leugnen abnegate, contest, deny, disavow, disclaim, disown, gainsay, recant, retract, traverse
nicht zu — sein be undeniable, not to be denied
—, Schuld deny the charge(s), plead not guilty
Leugner denier
Leumund character, renown, reputation, repute, standing
—, guter good reputation
—, schlechter bad reputation
Leumundszeugnis certificate of good behavio(u)r (character), character
Leute men, people, persons
Lexikon dictionary, lexicon
Rechts— law dictionary
Liaison liaison
liberal liberal
liberalisieren liberalize
Liberalisierung liberalization
Liberalismus liberalism
Liebes-
—affäre intrigue, love affair
—antrag love suit
—beteuerung protestation of love
—bezeigung love making
—brief love letter
—dienst favour, good turn, kind office, kindness
— — erweisen do a good turn
—erklärung declaration of love
—geständnis confession of love
—heirat love match, marriage in love
—paar couple (pair) of lovers
—werk charity work
Liebhaber admirer, amateur, dilettante, fancier, lover
—preis fancy price
—wert amateur (fancy, sentimental) value
Liefer-
—abkommen delivery (supply) contract

Lieferant (Lieferer) contractor, deliverer, furnisher, purveyor, supplier
lieferbar available, deliverable
Liefer-
—bedingungen terms of delivery
—fähigkeit (—möglichkeit) delivery power
—frist delivery term (period)
liefern deliver, furnish, procure, produce, provide, purvey, supply, yield
Liefer-
—ort place of delivery
—preis delivery price
—schein bill of delivery, delivery (supply) note, docket
—tag day of delivery
—termin delivery date
Lieferung delivery, supply
Liefer-
—vertrag delivery (supply) contract
—verzögerung deferred delivery
—verzug default of delivery
—zeit time of delivery
Liegenschaften immovables, land(ed) (real) property, real estate(s)
Liegenschaftsrecht real property law
Liege-
—gebühren demurrage
—tage (—zeit) lay days
Liga league
liieren, sich ally with, associate with, enter an alliance, join, unite
Liierung alliance
Limit limit
limitieren limit, fix a limit
Limitierung limitation
lindern alleviate, mitigate, relieve, soften
Linderung alleviation, mitigation, relief
Linie branch, course, descent, line, lineage, policy, route, tendency, trend
—, in direkter in the direct line
Linke, die the left
Anhänger der —en leftist
—, äußerste the extreme left
linksgerichtet leftist
Links-
—koalition left-wing (leftist) coalition
—partei leftist (left-wing) party
—presse leftist press
linksradikal of the extreme left
Linksverkehr left-hand traffic
liquid available, liquid, ready, solvent
nicht — illiquid, insolvent, not liquid
Liquidation bill, charge, dissolution, fee, liquidation, settlement, winding up
—, gerichtliche (zwangsweise) compulsory liquidation (winding up)
Liquidations-
—anordnung dissolution order, liquidation order
—antrag application (petition) for liquidation (winding up)
—bedingungen settlement terms
—beschluß dissolution (liquidation) order
—datum day of settlement
—preis settling (winding up) price
—quote (—rate) liquidation dividend
—tag day of settlement
—verfahren liquidation (winding up) proceedings
—wert liquidation (realization) value
Liquidator liquidator, receiver
liquidieren charge, dissolve, finish off, liquidate, realize, settle, wind up
Liquidierung bill, dissolution, liquidation, settlement, winding up
Liquidität liquidity, solvency
List artifice, cunning, ruse, stratagem, trick, trickery
Liste bill, calendar, catalogue, docket, file, inventory, list, manifest, panel, register, roll, schedule, scheme, specification, ticket
listenmäßig erfassen catalogue, empanel, list, register, schedule
literarisch
—er Diebstahl plagiarism
Literatur literature
—, juristische legal literature

—, **unzüchtige** indecent (obscene) literature
Literatur-
—**angabe** (—**verzeichnis**) bibliography
Lizenz licence, license
— **erteilen** give (grant, issue) a licence, license
— **erwerben** take out a licence
Lizenz-
—**abgabe** licence fee, royalty
—**abkommen** licence agreement
—**bedingungen** terms of licence
—**geber** licencer
—**gebühr** licence fee, royalty
—**inhaber** licence holder, licensee
lizenzieren approbate, license
Lizenz-
—**nehmer** (—**träger**) licensee
—**vertrag** licence contract
—**zahlung** royalty
lockern loosen, relax, slacken
Lockerung derestriction, relaxation
logieren accommodate, lodge, room, stay
Logik logic
logisch consistent, logical
Lohn compensation, consideration, fee, gratification, hire, pay, payment, rate, recompense, remuneration, return, reward, salary, wage
—**abbau** wage deflation (cut, reduction)
—**abkommen** wage agreement
—**ansprüche** wage claims (demands)
—**anstieg** wage increase
—**arbeit** paid (hired) labo(u)r
—**arbeiter** hired man (labo[u]rer), paid labo(u)rer (worker), wage earner
—**ausfall** dead time, lost pay
—**ausgleich** wage adjustment
—**auszahlung** wage payment
—**büro** payroll department, pay (payroll) office
—**einkommen** earned (wage) income
—**empfänger** wage earner
lohnen compensate, recompense, repay, reward
—, **sich** be profitable, be worth (-while), pay out
lohnend advantageous, gainful, lucrative, paying, profitable, remunerative, worth-while
Lohn-
—**erhöhung** wage increase
—**forderungen** wage claims (demands)
—**kürzung** wage cut (reduction)
—**pfändung** wage garnishment
—**satz** wage rate
—**skala** wage scale
—**spirale** wage spiral
—**steigerung** wage increase
—**steuer** wage (salary, withhold) tax
—**stopp** wage stop (freeze)
—**streit** wage dispute, labo(u)r conflict
—**stufe** wage bracket
—**tag** pay day
—**tarif** wage rate (scale, schedule)
—**tüte** pay envelope
—**zahlung** wage payment
—**zettel** payroll (voucher), wage (pay) slip
—**zugeständnisse** wage concessions
—**zuschlag** extra pay
Lokal inn, locality, office, place, premises, public house, restaurant, room, station
lokal local
Lokal-
—**behörde** local authority
—**kenntnis** local knowledge
lokalisieren localize, locate
Lokalisierung localization
Los allotment, destiny, fate, lot, portion, share, ticket
durch — entscheiden decide by lot
lösbar extinguishable, soluble, solvable
löschen cancel, close, delete, discharge, efface, erate, expunge, extinguish, land, lighten, liquidate, pay off, put out, strike out, unload, unship
Löschung cancellation, discharge, dissolution, effacement, expunction, extinguishment, landing, release, satisfaction, striking out, unloading, unshipping

Lösegeld ransom
— **zahlen** ransom
losen um cast (draw lots) for
lösen annul, break off, buy, cancel, clear up, detach, discontinue, dissolve, loosen, redeem, relax, release, rescind, set aside, sever, settle, solve, terminate, untie, unknot, unravel, withdraw
losgehen begin, go off
losgehen auf attack
Loskauf buying off, ransom, ransoming, redemption
loskaufen buy off, ransom, redeem
löslich dissolvable
Löslichkeit dissolvability
loslösen (lostrennen) detach, sever
—, **sich** break with, disengage from, disaffiliate, separate, sever oneself
Loslösung (Lostrennung) detachment, disaffiliation, separation
Losnummer ticket number
lossprechen absolve, acquit, free
Lossprechung absolution, acquittal
Losung password, slogan, watchword
Lösung annulment, breaking off, cancellation, discontinuance, key, rescission, settlement, solution, termination
Lotse pilot
lotsen pilot
Lotsen
—**gebühr** pilotage
—**zwang** compulsory pilotage
loyal loyal
Loyalität loyalty
Lücke blank, breach, deficiency, gap, omission
Gesetzes— gap in the law, loophole
Lückenbüßer makeshift, makeweight, stopgap
lückenhaft defective, fragmentary, imperfect, incomplete
lückenlos without a gap (gaps), airtight, uninterrupted
Luft-
—**abkommen** air pact
—**abwehr** air (anti-aircraft) defence
—**angriff** air raid
—**aufsicht** air traffic control
—**brücke** air lift
—**fahrt** aeronautics, air navigation, aviation
— —**sabkommen** air navigation (aviation) agreement
—**gewehr** air gun
—**herrschaft** air supremacy
—**hoheit** air sovereignty
—**kampf** air combat (fighting)
—**pistole** air pistol
—**polizei** air police
—**post** air mail
— —, **durch** by air mail
—**raum** air space
—**recht** air law
—**weg** air route
— —, **auf dem** by air
lüften drop, reveal, unveil
Lüge falsehood, lie
lügen lie, tell a falsehood (a lie) (lies) (stories)
Lügner liar
lügnerisch lying, mendacious
lukrativ lucrative, paying, profitable, remunerative
Lump blackguard, knave, rotter, scoundrel
Lustmord rape and murder
luxuriös luxurious, sumptuous
Luxus luxury, sumptuousness
—**artikel (—güter, —waren)** luxuries
—**steuer** luxury tax
lynchen lynch
Lynchjustiz lynch law

M

machen cause, construct, create, effect, fabricate, form, make, manufacture, prepare, produce, raise, take
bekannt— advertise, announce, make known (public), promulgate, publish
haftbar — hold (make) liable for
verantwortlich — hold (make) responsible for
Machenschaften doings, intrigues, machinations, manoeuvres, practices
Macht authority, capacity, command, control, domination, force, grip, hold, influence, might, power, strength, sway
— ausüben exercise power, hold sway
— ergreifen (— übernehmen) assume (seize) power
zur — gelangen come into power
— an sich reißen usurp power
an der — sein be in power, be in (hold) office
Macht-
—befugnis authority, competence, power(s)
—bereich orbit, sphere of influence
—ergreifung assumption (seizure) of power
—gruppe pressure group
—haber dictator, lord, potentate, ruler
—kampf struggle for power
mächtig considerable, enormous, great, huge, immense, massive, mighty, potent, powerful
machtlos helpless, impotent, powerless
Macht-
—losigkeit impotence, powerlessness, weakness
—politik power politics
—probe trial of strength
—sphäre orbit
—spruch authoritative decision, fiat, peremptory order
—staat totalitarian state
—stellung ascendency, power, powerful position, predominance
—übernahme accession to (assumption of, seizure of) power
—verhältnis balance of power
machtvoll impressive, powerful
Macht-
—wort absolute command
— — sprechen interpose one's authority, speak a decisive word
Mädchen
—handel girls slavery, pimping
—händler bawd, pimp
—name maiden name
Magazin depot, magazine, store, storehouse, warehouse
—verwalter storekeeper, warehousekeeper
Magistrat municipal (town) council, municipal board
Magistrats-
—beamter (—personal) magistrate, municipal officer
—mitglied (town) councillor, municipal officer
—rat town council, town councillor
—wahlen municipal elections
Magistratur magistracy
Mahnbrief (—schreiben) (letter of) reminder, dunning (admonition, hortatory, monitory) letter
mahnen admonish, demand, dun, press, remind, request, urge, warn
Mahner admonisher, creditor, dun(ner), monitor
Mahnung admonition, demand, dunning, exhortation, monition, notice, reminder, request (of payment), warning
Mahn
—verfahren collection proceedings, hortatory procedure
—zettel reminder
Majestät majesty
—sbeleidigung lese majesty

Majorat entail, (right of) primogeniture
majorisieren beat by majority, outvote, vote down
Majorität majority
—, absolute absolute majority
—, einfache bare (simple) majority
—, qualifizierte qualified majority
—, relative relative majority
—sabstimmung majority vote
—sbeschluß majority vote, decision (resolution) of the majority
Makel blame, blemish, blot, defect, fault, flaw, odium, spot, stain, stigma
—, ohne immaculate, without blame (blemish)
makellos blameless, immaculate, spotless, stainless, unblemished, without blemish
Makellosigkeit immaculateness, purity, spotlessness
Makler agent, broker, factor, jobber, middleman, solicitor
—gebühr brokerage
maliziös malicious, spiteful
malträtieren ill-treat
Mandant client, customer, mandator
Mandat authority, authorization, brief, decree, mandate, order, power, seat, warrant, writ
Straf— summons, penalty
Mandatar authorized agent, mandatary, mandatory, proxy, representative
—macht mandatary (mandatory) power
Mandats-
—gebiet mandate, mandated territory
—macht mandatary (mandatory) power
—regierung mandatory government
Mangel absence, default, defect, deficiency, deficit, fault, lack, need, scarcity, shortage, shortness, vice, want
mangelfrei faultless, free from defects
mangelhaft defective, deficient, faulty, imperfect, incomplete
Mangel-
—anzeige demonstration of defect(s)
—haftigkeit defectiveness, faultiness, imperfection
Mängelhaftung express warranty, warranty (for defects, of fitness)
mangeln be in want of, be lacking (deficient, wanting), be short of, fail, lack, want
mangelnd absent, lacking, missing, wanting
mangels failing, for lack (want) of, in the absence of, in default of
— Beweisen in default of evidence
Mängelrüge complaint, deficiency claim, disapproval, notification of defect(s)
Mangelware deficiency (scarce, shortage) goods
Manifest manifesto, (public) statement
Manifestation demonstration, manifestation
manifestieren manifest
Manipulation handling, manipulation
manipulieren handle, manage, manipulate
Manko defect, deficiency, deficit, shortage, shortness
Mann gentleman, husband, man
Ehren— man of hono(u)r
Fach— expert, specialist
Stroh— dummy, man of straw
männlich male, masculine
Mannschaft company, crew, gang, men, personnel, staff, team
—sgeist team spirit
Manöver manoeuvre(s), politics, strategem, trick
manövrieren manoeuvre, practise
Manteltarif skeleton agreement
—vertrag basic wage(s) agreement
Mantelvertrag covering agreement

Manual manual, note book
Manuskript copy, manuscript, matter
Marge margin
Mark border(land), boundary
Marke badge, brand, check, chip, counter, coupon, label, make, mark, quality, sort, stamp, ticket, token, trademark, type
Marken-
—artikel branded (patent, proprietary) article (goods)
—name brand (trade) name
—schutz trademark protection
—ware branded (patent, trademark) articles (goods)
markieren brand, label, mark, pretend, put a mark on
Markierung marking
Markstein boundary stone, landmark, milestone
Markt market
—abgaben (—gebühren) market dues
—abrede (—absprache) marketing arrangement (agreement)
—analyse market analysis
—bericht market report
marktfähig marketable, negotiable, saleable
Markt
—fähigkeit marketability, saleability
—forschung (—untersuchung) market research
—freiheit free market
marktgängig current, marketable, saleable
Markt-
—gängigkeit marketability, saleability
—gefüge market structure
—kurs market price
—notierung market quotation
—ordnung market regulations
—organisation (—ordnung) market organization (system)
—polizei market police
—preis market (current) price
—recht market regulations
—sachverständiger marketing expert
—schutzabkommen marketing (market protection) agreement
—wert market (marketable) value
—wirtschaft (— —, freie) free-enterprise (-market) economy
— —, soziale social market economy
Maschine apparatus, engine, machine(ry)
Höllen— time bomb
Maß dimension, extent, gauge, measure, measurement, moderation, proportion, quantity, rate, standard, size, volume
Straf— sentence
Masse assets, bulk, crowd, estate, lump, mass, multitude, quantity, substance, volume
Maßeinheit standard (unit) of measure
Massen-
—bewegung mass movement
—demonstration mass demonstration
—entlassungen mass dismissals
—erhebungen mass risings
—flucht stampede
—grab common grave
—mord mass murder, massacre, slaughter
—mörder mass murderer
—verhaftungen mass arrests
—versammlung mass meeting
Maßgabe measure, proportion
maßgebend (maßgeblich) authentic, authoritative, competent, decisive, determining, dispositive, essential, governing, influential, leading, relevant, standard
mäßig moderate, reasonable
mittel— average, fair, mediocre, medium, middling, moderate
über— beyond (without) measure, excessive, exorbitant, immoderate, undue
mäßigen mitigate, moderate, temper
Mäßigkeit moderateness, moderation, reasonableness, temperance
Mittel— mediocrity, moderateness
Über— excess, immoderateness

Mäßigung mitigation, moderateness, moderation, restraint
maßlos beyond all bounds, beyond (without) measure, excessive, exorbitant, extravagant, immoderate, measureless, reckless
Maßlosigkeit boundlessness, extravagance, immoderateness, want of moderation
Maßnahme action, arrangement, measure, move, step
Abhilfs— remedy
Dringlichkeits— urgency measure
Gegen— countermeasure
Gewalt— act of force
Hilfs— emergency measure
Ordnungs— safety (precautionary) measure
Sofort— emergency measure
Straf— punitive measure, sanction
Sühne— sanction
Vergeltungs— reprisal, retaliatory, measure
Vorsichts— precaution(ary) measure
Zwangs— compulsory (coercive) measure
Maßnahmen
— ergreifen (treffen) adopt measures, take measures (steps)
die äußersten — ergreifen go (proceed) to extremes, take extreme measures
Maßregel measure, step
—n treffen take measures (steps)
maßregeln censure, discipline, inflict disciplinary punishment on, reprimand, take measures (steps) against
Maßregelung disciplining, disciplinary punishment
Maßstab criterion, measure, rule, scale, standard
maßvoll discreet, lenient, moderate, temperate
Material equipment, material, matter, stock, stuff, substance, supply
Beweis— evidence (material)
Materialismus materialism
materialistisch materialistic
Materie (subject) matter, substance, stuff
mit der — vertraut sein be familiar with the matter
materiell actual, financial, intrinsic, material, pecuniary, physical, substantial, substantive, tangible
—es Recht substantive law
Matrikel register, roll
Maut custom(s), duty, excise, toll
maximal maximum
Maxime maxim, principle
Maximum maximum
Mäzen patron, protector
Medizin medicine, remedy
Gerichts— forensic (legal) medicine, medical jurisprudence
Institut für Gerichts— institute for forensic medicine, medicolegal institute
medizinisch medical
gerichts— forensic, medicolegal
medizinisch
—es Gutachten medical opinion
—er Sachverständiger medical expert
Meeres
—grenze sea frontier
—grund sea bottom (floor)
Mehr addition, excess, increase, majority, surplus
—arbeit extra work, overtime
—betrag excess, surplus (amount), overplus
—bietender (—bieter) higher bidder, outbidder
mehrdeutig ambiguous, equivocal, of double meaning
Mehrdeutigkeit ambiguity, equivocation
mehrfach manifold, multiple, multiplex, repeated
Mehr-
—gebot higher bid, outbid(ding)
—gewicht excess (surplus) weight, overweight
Mehrheit majority, plurality
Zweidrittel— two-thirds majority
—, absolute absolute majority
—, einfache simple (bare, mere) majority

—, geringe small majority
—, qualifizierte qualified majority
—, relative relative majority
—, schwache narrow majority
Mehrheits-
—abstimmung (—wahl) majority vote
—beschluß (—entscheidung) majority vote (decision, resolution)
—beteiligung majority (controlling) interest
—partei majority party
—system majority rule
Mehrparteiensystem multiple party system
mehrseitig multilateral, multipartite
Mehrstimmenwahlrecht multiple (plural) vote
Mehrstimmrechtsaktie multiple share
Mehrwert surplus (value), overvalue
—steuer surplus (added) value tax
Mehrzahl majority
Mehrzahlung extra pay(ment)
Meilenstein milestone
Meineid false oath, forswearing, perjury
— leisten commit perjury, forswear, perjure oneself, swear falsely
Meineidiger perjurer
meinen assert, believe, be of the opinion (that), have in view, imagine, intend, mean, purpose, suppose, think
Meinung belief, conviction, idea, intention, judgement, meaning, mind, notion, opinion, significance, (point of) view
—, nach meiner in my opinion (view)
seine — ändern change one's opinion
seine — äußern express (put forward) one's opinion
um eine — bitten ask somebody's opinion, consult
eine — haben have an opinion
seine — sagen say one's say, let somebody know one's opinion
die — sagen give a bit (piece) of one's mind
seine — sagen dürfen have one's say
der — sein, daß be of the opinion that, hold that
eine — teilen agree with (a person's opinion), share a person's opinion
eine — verfechten advocate (defend) an opinion
einer — zustimmen agree with an opinion, share (endorse) a view (an opinion)
Meinungs-
—änderung change of opinion
—äußerung expression (statement) of opinion
—austausch exchange of views
—freiheit liberty of opinion
—umfrage (opinion) poll, public opinion research
—umschwung change (reversal) of opinion
—verschiedenheit controversy, difference (disparity, divergence) of opinion (views), disagreement, dissent
—wechsel change of opinion
meistbegünstigt most favo(u)red
Meistbegünstigung most-favo(u)red treatment, preference
Meistbegünstigungsklausel most-favo(u)red clause
Meistbietender highest bidder
Meister champion, master
—arbeit master work
—brief master's certificate
—schaft championship, mastership
—stück (—werk) masterpiece
meistern govern, master
Meistgebot best offer, highest bid
Meldeamt registration office
melden advise, announce, inform, notify, report, return
—, der Polizei report to the police
—, sich apply for, enter (one's name) for, present oneself, register
sich polizeilich — register (one's address) with the police

Melde-
—frist registration period
—liste entry (list), registration list
—pflicht compulsory registration, obligation to notify (register)
meldepflichtig declarable, notifiable, subject to registration
Melde-
—schein (—zettel) registration form
—stelle registration office
—vorschriften notification orders
Meldung advice, announcement, application, entry, information, message, notice, notification, registration, report, return
—, polizeiliche registration with the police
Memoiren memoirs
—schreiber memoirist
Memorandum memo, memorandum
Menge amount, crowd, mass, multitude, plenty, quantity, volume
Mengeneinheit quantity unit
Mengenkontrolle quantitative control
mengenmäßig quantitative
Mensch human being, individual, man, person
Menschen- humanity, mankind, men, people, world
—kenner judge of character
—kenntnis judgement of character
—material man power
—menge crowd
—mord homicide, murder
—raub kidnapping
—räuber kidnapper
—recht(e) law of man, human rights, rights of man
—tötung homicide
—verstand, gesunder common sense
Menschheit human race, humanity, mankind
menschlich decent, human, humane, tolerable
Menschlichkeit human nature, humaneness, humanity
—, Verbrechen gegen die crime against humanity
merkbar marked, noticeable, perceptible
Merkblatt instructional pamphlet, instructions, leaflet, memorandum, supplement
Merkbuch memorandum (note) book
merken notice, perceive, realize
—, sich note, remember, retain, make note of
merklich considerable, evident, marked, noticeable, obvious, preceptible, visible
Merkmal attribute, characteristic, criterion, feature, mark, particularity, peculiarity, sign, speciality, token
meßbar measurable
Messe exhibition, fair
messen gauge, measure
messen, mit zweierlei Maß judge by two different standards
sich — mit match, measure oneself with (against)
Messung measurement
Methode line, manner, method, mode, policy, process, system, technique, way
methodisch methodical, systematic
Metier business, calling, profession, trade, vocation
Meuchelmord (foul) assassination, murder
Meuchelmörder (foul) assassin, murderer
meuchelmörderisch insidious, murderous, treacherous, assassin-like
meuchlings insidiously, treacherously
Meute gang, pack
Meuterei mutiny, sedition
Meuterer mutineer
meuterisch mutinous, seditious
meutern mutineer, mutiny
Mietausfall loss of rent
Mietbesitz tenancy
Miete hire, lease, rent, rental, tenancy
Mieteinnahmen rentals, rental income

mieten charter, engage, hire, lease, rent, take
Mietentschädigung rent allowance
Mieter charterer, hirer, leaseholder, lessee, lodger, roomer, tenant
Unter— sublessee, subtenant, underlessee
Mieterhebung rent collection
Mieterschutz rent control (restrictions), tenants protection
—gesetz Rent Restriction Act (GB)
Miet-
—ertrag rental
—erträge (—einkommen) rentals, rental income
—forderung rent claim
mietfrei rentfree
Miet
—rückstand rent arrears
—verhältnis tenancy, tenure
—verlust loss of rent
—vertrag charterparty, hire contract, lease (contract), tenancy agreement
—vorauszahlung advance rental
—zahlung rent(al) payment
—zins rent, rental
mild benevolent, charitable, gentle, indulgent, lenient, light, mild, slight
— urteilen give a lenient judgement, judge leniently
—e Gaben alms, charity
Milde benevolence, charitableness, gentleness, indulgence, leniency, mildness
mildern alleviate, assuage, extenuate, mitigate, relax, soften, soothe
mildernd
—e Umstände extenuating (mitigating) circumstances
Milderung alleviation, extenuation, mitigation, moderation, relaxation
Milderungs-
—antrag mitigation plea
—grund extenuating cause, reason for mitigation
—mittel lenitive
mildtätig benevolent, charitable, munificent
Mildtätigkeit charitableness, charity, liberality, munificence
Milieu environment, milieu, (social) surroundings
Militär army, military, soldiery
—behörde military authority
—bündnis military alliance
—dienst military service
— —pflicht compulsory (military) service
—gericht military court (tribunal), court martial
—gerichtsbarkeit military jurisdiction
—gerichtsverfahren military legal procedure
—gesetz military law
—gesetzbuch military code
—herrschaft militarism
militärisch military
militarisieren militarize
Militarisierung militarization
Militarismus militarism
Militarist militarist
militaristisch militarist
Militär-
—macht military power
—mission military mission
militärpflichtig liable to military service
Militär
—polizei military police
—regierung military government
—strafgesetzbuch military penal code
—verwaltung military administration
—zeit time of service
Miliz militia
Minder-
—betrag deficit, shortage
—gebot lower bid (offer), underbid
—gewicht short weight, underweight, weight deficiency
Minderheit minority
Minderheiten-
—kabinett minority party cabinet
—schutz minority protection
Minderheits-
—beteiligung minority interest
—regierung minority government

minderjährig minor, under age
Minderjähriger infant, minor, person under age
Minderjährigkeit infancy, minority, minor age
mindern abate, decrease, depreciate, diminish, impair, lessen, lower, reduce
Minderung abatement, decrease, depreciation, diminution, reduction
—sklage action for reduction (abatement)
Minderwert depreciation, undervalue
minderwertig base, inferior, low-grade, second-rate, substandard, of inferior value
Minderwertigkeit defectiveness, inferior quality, inferiority
Minderwertigkeits-
—komplex inferiority complex
—klausel depreciation clause
Minderzahl minority
Mindest-
—alter minimum age
—betrag minimum (amount)
—bietender lowest bidder
—einkommen minimum income
—gebot lowest bid, put-up price
—gehalt minimum salary, lowest percentage
—gewicht minimum weight
—grenze minimum limit
—kapital minimum capital
—lohn minimum wage (pay)
—maß minimum
—preis minimum price
—reserve minimum (statutory, lawful, legal) reserve
—strafe minimum penalty
minimal insignificant, minimum, trifling
Minimum minimum
Existenz— living wage, minimum of existence, subsistence level
Minister minister, Secretary (USA), Secretary of State (GB)
Ministerial-
—beamter ministerial officer
—erlaß (—entscheid, —verfügung) ministerial decree (order)
ministeriell ministerial
Ministerium board, cabinet, department, government, ministry, office
Minister-
—konferenz conference of ministers
—krise ministerial crisis
—präsident Prime Minister
—rat cabinet council, council of ministers
—verantwortlichkeit ministerial responsibility
Minorität minority
—sbeteiligung minority interest
Minus (—betrag) deficiency, deficit, shortage
Mischehe mixed marriage
Mischling half-breed (-caste), hybrid
mißachten despise, disdain, disregard, neglect
Mißachtung contempt, disdain, disregard
— des Gerichts contempt of court
unter — von in defiance of
mißbilligen deprecate, disapprove of, object to, reprobate
Mißbilligung deprecation, disapprobation, disapproval, reprobation
Mißbrauch abuse, misapplication, misappropriation, misuse
Amts— misfeasance, abuse (misuse) of authority (power)
mißbrauchen abuse, misapply, misuse
mißbräuchlich abusive, improper
mißdeuten misconstrue, misinterpret, misrepresent
Mißdeutung misconception, misconstruction, misinterpretation, misrepresentation
Mißerfolg failure, ill success
Missetat crime, misdeed, offence
Missetäter criminal, delinquent, evil-doer, felon, malefactor, malignant, offender
Mißgeschick adversity, bad luck, disaster, misadventure, mischief, misfortune, mishap

mißglücken fail, miscarry, not to succeed
mißgönnen envy, grudge
Mißgriff blunder, lapse, mistake
Mißgunst disfavour, envy, grudge, ill-will, jealousy, malevolence
mißhandeln brutalize, ill-treat, maltreat, mishandle
Mißhandlung ill-treatment, maltreatment
—, tatsächliche assault and battery
Mißhelligkeit difference, difficulty, disagreement, discord, dissension, misunderstanding
Mission delegation, mission
in geheimer — on secret mission
Mißkredit discredit, disrepute
in — bringen bring into disrepute, discredit
in — kommen become discredited, fall into discredit (disrepute)
Mißlingen failure, ill success
mißlingen fail, miscarry, prove a failure
Mißstand abuse, defect, grievance, injustice, nuisance
— abhelfen remedy (redress) an abuse (a grievance)
Mißtrauen distrust, lack of confidence, mistrust, suspicion
mißtrauen distrust, have no confidence, mistrust, suspicion
Mißtrauens-
—antrag motion of censure
— — einbringen propose a vote of censure
—votum vote of censure (no-confidence)
mißtrauisch diffident, distrustful, mistrustful, suspicious
Mißverhalten misbehavio(u)r, misconduct
Mißverhältnis disproportion, incongruity
mißverständlich erroneous, misleading
Mißverständnis dissension, misapprehension, misconception, mistake, misunderstanding
mißverstehen misapprehend, misconceive, misconstrue, mistake, misunderstanding
Mißwirtschaft maladministration, mismanagement
Mißzustände abuses, calamity
Mitangeklagter co-accused, co-defendant
Mitarbeit assistance, collaboration, contribution, cooperation
mitarbeiten assist, collaborate, contribute (to), cooperate
Mitarbeiter assistant, collaborator, colleague, contributor, co-worker, fellow labourer (worker)
Mitbegründer co-founder
Mitbeklagter co-defendant
mitbenutzen use jointly
Mitbenutzung joint use
—srecht common right, right of common
Mitbesitz joint possession
mitbesitzen possess in common
Mitbesitzer joint holder (possessor, owner), copartner
Mitbestimmung codetermination, co-voting, participation
—srecht right of codetermination (codecision, participation)
Mitbeteiligter accomplice, associate, interested party, partner
Mitbeteiligung participation, partnership
Mitbewohner co-inhabitant, fellow lodger
Mitbürge joint bail (security)
Mitbürger fellow citizen
Miteigentum joint ownership (property)
Miteigentümer co-owner, co-proprietor, joint holder (owner, proprietor)
miteinander jointly, together
Miterbe coheir, joint heir
Miterbin coheiress, joint heiress
miterben inherit jointly
Miterbschaft coheritage, co-inheritance
Mitgebrauch joint use
Mitgefangener fellow prisoner
Mitgefühl sympathy
Mitgift dowry, (marriage) portion
—jäger dowry (fortune) hunter

Mitgläubiger co-creditor, joint creditor
Mitglied fellow, member
Mitglieder-
—versammlung general meeting, meeting of members
—verzeichnis (—liste) membership list
—zahl membership
Mitglieds-
—ausweis (—karte) membership card (ticket)
—beitrag membership dues (fee, contribution)
Mitgliedschaft fellowship, membership
Mitglieds-
—land member country
—nummer membership number
—staat member state
Mitgründer co-founder, joint founder
mithaften be jointly liable
Mithaftung joint liability
mithelfen assist, help
Mithelfer accomplice, aider, assistant, helper
Mitherausgeber coeditor, joint editor
Mitherrscher co-regent
Mitherrschaft co-regency, co-rule, joint rule
Mithilfe aid, assistance, cooperation, help
mithören listen in, tap
Mitinhaber co-owner, copartner, joint holder (owner, partner)
Mitkläger co-plaintiff, joint plaintiff
Mitläufer fellow traveller, follower, nominal member
Mitleid compassion, pity
Mitleidenschaft
in — ziehen affect, interfere with
in — gezogen werden be adversely affected by
mitmachen join in, take part in
Mitpächter co-lessee, co-tenant, joint lessee (tenant)
Mitschuld accessoriness, complicity, joint guilt (debt), participation in guilt
mitschuldig sein be an accomplice in (an accessory to)
Mitschuldiger accessory, accomplice, associate in guilt
Mitschuldner co-debtor, joint debtor
Mittäter accessory, accomplice, co-actor, joint tortfeasor
Mittäterschaft complicity
Mitte center, centre, middle
mitteilen advise, communicate, inform, intimate, let know, make known, notify
Mitteilhaber copartner, joint partner
Mitteilung advice, communication, information, intimation, message, notice, notification, report
— machen von communicate, give information about, advise (inform, notify) of
Mitteilungs-
—pflicht obligation to notify
Mittel average, funds, instrument, means, measure, method, resources
mittelbar indirect, mediate
mittelfristig medium-term
Mittelklasse middle classes
mittellos destitute, impecunious, needy, penniless, without means
Mittellosigkeit destitution, lack of means, poverty
mittelmäßig average, fair, mediocre, middling, moderate
Mittelmäßigkeit mediocrity, moderateness
Mittelpunkt central point, centre, focus, heart
mittels by means (way) of, with the assistance of
Mitelsmann (-person) agent, go-between, intermediary, mediator, middleman
Mittelstand middle classes
Mittelweg compromise, middle course
Mittelwert mean (average) value
Mittler agent, intermediary, mediator, middleman
—amt mediatorship
mitunterschreiben (mitunterzeichnen) countersign
Mitunterschrift (Mitunterzeichnung) joint signature

Mitunterzeichner cosignatory, joint signatory
Mitverantwortung joint responsibility
Mitverwaltung coadministration, joint administration
—srecht right of coadministration
Mitvormund co-guardian, joint guardian
Mitvormundschaft co-guardianship, joint guardianship
mitwirken assist, collaborate, contribute, cooperate, take part in
Mitwirkung assistance, collaboration, cooperation, participation
Mitwissen (Mitwisserschaft) (joint) knowledge, privity
mitwissen know of, be privy of
Mitwisser accessory, confidant, party
—schaft collusion, complicity
Mitzeuge fellow witness
Mobilien movables, personal property (estate)
mobilisieren (mobil machen) mobilize
Mobilisierung (Mobilmachung) mobilization
Modell design, model, pattern, type
Modifikation modification
modifizieren modify
Modus manner, method, mode, way
möglich contingent, eventual, feasible, possible, potential, practicable
Möglichkeit chance, contingency, eventuality, feasibility, opportunity, possibility, potentiality, practicability
Monarch monarch
Monarchie monarchy
Monat month
monatlich monthly
Monats-
—abschluß monthly settlement (statement)
—ausweis monthly return (statement)
—bericht monthly report (statement)
—gehalt monthly salary
—lohn monthly wage (pay)
—rate monthly instalment
—zahlung monthly payment
Monopol- monopoly
—gesellschaft monopoly company
Monopolist monopolist
Moral ethics, moral(s), morality
moralisch moral
  unmoralisch immoral
Moralist moralist
Mord assassination, murder
  Bruder— fratricide
  Gift— poisoning
  Kindes— infanticide
  Königs— regicide
  Lust— rape and murder
  Meuchel— assassination
  Mutter— matricide
  Raub— murder and robbery
  Selbst— suicide
  Vater— patricide
Mord begehen commit murder
Mord-
—anklage charge for (on) murder
— —, unter accused of (charged with) murder
  unter — — stehen be (stand) indicted for murder, be under murder charge
—anschlag attempt at life, attempted assassination, murderous assault (plot)
morden assassinate, murder
Mörder assassin, murderer
  Meuchel— assassin
  Raub— robber and murderer
  Selbst— suicide
Mörderin murderess
mörderisch cutthroat, homicidal, murderous, slaughterous
Mord-
—kommission homicide squad
—nacht night of murder
—plan assassination plot
—prozeß murder trial
—tat murder(ous deed)
—verdacht suspicion of murder
—versuch attempt at (attempted) murder, murderous attempt
—waffe murderous weapon
Motiv ground, motive, reason
motivieren account for, explain, give reasons for, justify, motivate
Mühe effort, pains, trouble

Mündel pupil, ward
—geld trust (ward) money
—gut ward's property
mündelsicher gilt-edged, trust, trustee
Mündelstand pupilage
Mündelvermögen trust fund
mündig of (full) age
für — erklären declare of age
— werden attain majority, come of age
Mündiger major
Mündigkeit full age, majority
mündlich oral, parol, verbal, vocal, by word of mouth
Mundraub theft of food
Münze coin, mint
Münzamt (-anstalt) mint
—beamter mint official
münzen coin, mint
Münzer coiner, minter
Falsch— false coiner, money forger
Münz-
—fälscher false coiner
—fälschung false coining
—gesetz coinage act
—herr master of the mint
—hoheit right of seignorage
—presse coining press
—recht right of coinage
—verbrechen (—vergehen) coinage offence, false coining
Muster design, model, pattern, sample, standard
—beispiel example, model
mustern examine, inspect, muster, review
Musterung examination, inspection, muster(ing), review
Mut boldness, bravity, courage
mutig bold, brave, courageous
mutmaßen assume, conjecture, guess, presume, suppose, surmise
mutmaßlich apparent, assumed, conjectural, hypothetical, presumable, presumptive, probable, putative, supposed
Mutmaßung conjecture, guess, presumption, supposition, surmise
—en anstellen form conjectures, conjecture
Mutter mother
Adoptiv— foster mother
Stief— stepmother
Mutter-
—gesellschaft parent company
mütterlich maternal, motherly
mütterlicherseits maternal ,on the mother's side
mutterlos motherless
Mutter-
—mord matricide
—mörder matricide
—sprache mother tongue, native language
Mutwille malice, mischief, wantonness
mutwillig deliberate, malicious, mischievous, wanton, wilful
mysteriös mysterious

N

nachahmen adulterate, copy, counterfeit, imitate
nachahmenswert exemplary, worthy of imitation
Nachahmer copyist, counterfeiter, forger, imitator
Nachahmung copy, counterfeit, forgery, imitation, replica
Nachbar fellow lodger, neighbo(u)r
—grundstück (—eigentum) adjoining (neighbo[u]ring) property (estate)
—haus adjoining house
—land neighbo(u)ring country
nachbarlich neighbo(u)rly

Nachbar-
—recht neighbo(u)r law
—schaft neighbo(u)rhood, proximity, vicinity
—staat neighbo(u)ring state
—volk neighbo(u)ring nation (people)
Nachbezahlung additional (subsequent) payment
nachbilden copy, counterfeit, forge, imitate, reproduce
Nachbildung copy, counterfeit, facsimile, forgery, imitation, replica
Nachbürge second (counter) bail, collateral security
Nachbürgschaft collateral security
nachdatieren postdate
nachdenken cogitate, consider, mediate, reflect, think
Nachdruck emphasis, reprint, reproduction, stress
—, mit emphatically, energetically, vigorously
— verleihen emphasize, reinforce, stress, urge
nachdrucken reprint
nachdrücklich emphatic, energetic, expressive, firm, vigorous
Nachdrucksrecht copyright
nacheinander alternately, by turns, in succession, one after another (the other), successively
Nacherbe reversionary (second) heir
Nacherb-
—folge reversionary succession
—recht right of reversion, reversionary succession
—schaft remainder(ship)
Nachfahre(n) descendant, offspring
Nachfolge sequence, succession
nachfolgen follow, succeed
nachfolgend following, subsequent, succeeding
Nachfolger follower, successor
als — von in succession to
Nachfolgestaat succession state
Nachforderung afterclaim, additional (supplemental) claim, extra charge
nachforschen inquire, investigate, search
Nachforschung examination, inquiry, investigation, research, search
—en anstellen inquire, investigate, make inquiries, search
Nachfrage call, demand, inquiry, market, need
nachfragen demand, inquire
Nachfrist extension of time, period of grace (grant), respite
nachgeben comply with, decline, give in, give way, make concessions, yield (to), recede, relax, relent, slacken, surrender
nachgebend complying, indulgent
nachgeboren afterborn, junior, later born, posthumous, younger
Nachgebot later bid
Nachgebühr excess postage, surcharge, postage due
nachgehen follow (up), indulge in, investigate, pursue, seek
nachgemacht artificial, copied, counterfeit, false, forged, imitated, sham
nachgeordnet inferior, lower, secondary, subordinate
nachgewiesenermaßen as has been proved (shown)
nachgiebig acquiescent, compli(s)ant, declining, forbearing, indulgent, yielding, receding
Nachgiebigkeit complaisance, compliance, indulgence, yieldingness
nachhaltig enduring, lasting
nachholen make good, make up fort, recover
Nachkomme descendant, offspring
Nachkommen descendants, issue, offspring, progeny
—, ohne without issue
nachkommen accede to, come up to, discharge, follow, fulfil, keep, meet, obey
Nachkommenschaft s. Nachkommen
Nachkömmling descendant
Nachkriegszeit post-war period
Nachlaß abatement, allowance, assets, deduction, discount, estate, heritage, inheritance, property left, rebate, reduc-

tion, relaxation, relief, remission, residue
nachlassen abate, bequeath, leave, make an allowance, grant (make) a reduction, mitigate, reduce, relax, remit, slacken
Nachlaß-
—begünstigter residuary beneficiary
—forderung demand on an estate
—gegenstand (—gut) heritable estate
—gericht probate (surrogate's) court
—klage testamentary cause
—kosten charges on an estate
—ordnung probate code
—pfleger (—verwalter) administrator (curator) of an estate
—pflegschaft (—verwaltung) administration (curatorship) of an estate
—register probate registry
—regulierung settlement of an estate
—richter probate judge, surrogate
—sache testamentary cause
—steuer death (estate) duty, estate (inheritance) tax
— —amt estate duty (tax) office
— —satz estate tax rate
—verfahren probate proceedings
nachlässig careless, derelict, indolent, neglectful, negligent, remiss
Nachlässigkeit carelessness, indolence, neglect, negligence, remissness
nachmachen copy, counterfeit, fake, forge, imitate
Nachmacher forger, imitator
Nachnahme (gegen, per) cash (collect) on delivery (C.O.D.), to be paid for on delivery (P.O.D.)
—gebühr collection fee
Nachname family name, surname
Nachporto additional charge (postage), surcharge
nachprüfbar verifiable
nachprüfen check, control, inspect, investigate, make sure, recheck, reconsider, re-examine, review, scrutinize, verify
Nachprüfung check(ing), control, inspection, reconsideration, recount, re-examination, review, revision, scrutiny, verification
Nachprüfungs-
—antrag petition for review
—recht right of review
—stelle control office
Nachrede epilogue
—, mündliche slander
—, schriftliche defamation, libel
—, üble defamation of character, evil (ill) report, libel and slander, slander
in üble — bringen injure a person's reputation, slander
Nachricht account, advice, communication, information, intelligence, message, (piece of) news, notice, report
— geben advise, give advice (information, notice), inform, let know, send word
—enaustausch exchange of information
Nachruf obituary (notice)
Nachschlagebuch (-werk) reference book
nachschlagen consult, look up, refer to
Nachschlüssel false (duplicate, master, skeleton) key, picklock
Nachsicht clemency, forbearance, indulgence, leniency, patience, respite
— haben be indulgent towards, be patient with, excuse
um — bitten ask a person's indulgence
nachsichtig forbearing, gentle, indulgent, lenient, mild, patient
— sein be indulgent (lenient) towards
Nachsichtigkeit forbearance, indulgence
Nachsichts-
—frist period of grace (respite)
—tage days of grace
Nachspiel aftermath, consequences, sequel, subsequent, results
ein gerichtliches — haben have a judicial sequel, have a sequel in court

nachstehend (mentioned) below, following, hereinafter (set forth), herewith, in the following, subjoined, thereinafter
Nachsteuer additional (supplementary) tax, extra duty
Nachsuchen petition, request, suit
nachsuchen apply for, petition for, request, solicit
Nacht-
—arbeit night work
—dienst night duty (service)
Nachteil damage, detriment, disadvantage, drawback, handicap, injury, loss, prejudice, shortcoming
zum — von to the detriment (injury, loss, prejudice) of
zum — gereichen be detrimental
nachteilig adverse, derogatory, detrimental, disadvantageous, injurious, prejudicial, prejudicious, unfavo(u)rable
— sein be a disadvantage for
nächtlich
—e Ruhestörung disorder by night
Nachtrag addendum, addition, amendment, annex, appendix, postscript, supplement
Testaments— codicil
nachtragen add, append, make an addition, resent, supplement
nachträglich additional, afterwards, later, subsequent, supplementary
Nachtschicht night shift
Nachtwächter watchman
nachversichern insure for a larger amount, reinsure
Nachversicherung reinsurance, additional insurance
Nachwahl by-election, second ballot
Nachweis certificate, demonstration, evidence, information, proof, record, voucher
nachweisbar (-lich) ascertainable, demonstrable, provable, traceable, verifiable
nachweisen authenticate, demonstrate, establish, identify, prove, show
—, Verbrechen convict of a crime
Nachweisung demonstration, information, intelligence, proof
Nachwirkung after-effect, aftermath, consequences
Nachwort epilogue
nachzahlen make an additional payment, pay in addition
Nachzahlung additional (extra, subsequent, supplementary) payment
nahelegen advise, give to understand, urge (on), intimate
naheliegend obvious
Name appellation, denomination, designation, name, renown, reputation, title
Deck— code name, psydonym
Eigen— (Familien—) family name
Geburts— birth name
Handels— brand, trade name
Mädchen— maiden name
Vor— Christian name
Zu— family name, surname
Vor- und Zu— full name
im —en von in the name of, on behalf of
namenlos anonymous, boundless, indescribable, inexpressible, nameless
namens named, in the name of, on behalf of
Namens-
—änderung change of name
—angabe indication of name
—aufruf roll call
—bezeichnung denomination, name
—liste list of names, roll, roster
—unterschrift signature
—verwechs(e)lung confusion of names, mistake in name
—verzeichnis index, list of names, roll
—zug signature, initials
namentlich by name, especially, individually, namely, nominal, in particular, particularly
—e Abstimmung division, voting by call
namhaft considerable, distinguished, large, notable, noted, renowned, substantial, well-known

nämlich namely, that is (to say), to wit
Nation nation, people
national national
nationalisieren nationalize
Nationalisierung nationalization
Nationalismus nationalism
Nationalist nationalist
nationalistisch nationalist
Nationalität nationality
— entziehen expatriate, withdraw (renounce) national citizenship
Nationalvermögen national property
—versammlung national assembly
Natur character, constitution, disposition, nature, temperament
Natural-
—abgabe levy in kind
—ausgleich settlement in kind
—bezüge remuneration in kind
—entgelt consideration in kind
—entschädigung indemnity in kind
—ersatz reparation in kind
—leistung payment in kind
—lohn wage in kind
—vergütung allowance in kind
—wert value in kind
Naturalisation (Naturalisierung) naturalization
naturalisieren naturalize
Natur-
—ereignis Act of God, catastrophe, phenomenon
—gesetz natural law
—recht natural law (right), right of nature
naturgetreu realistic
natürlich constitutional, genuine, illegitimate, innate, native, natural, normal, rational, simple
un— abnormal, unnatural
Neben-
—arbeit extra (spare-time) work
—bedeutung secondary meaning
—bedingung additional (secondary) condition
—beklagter co-defendant
—beruf (—beschäftigung) additional occupation, avocation, by-job, by-occupation, by-work, extra job, side-line
nebenberuflich avocational, part-time, side-line
Neben-
—beweis additional (collateral) proof, secondary evidence
—buhler rival
—bürge collateral bail, co-surety
—bürgschaft collateral security, co-surety
—einanderstellung comparison, juxtaposition, opposition
—einkommen (—einnahmen) additional (casual, incidental, subsidiary) income, perquisites
—erbe co-heir
—forderung accessory (secondary) claim
—frage secondary question, side issue
—klage incidental action
—kläger co-plaintiff, intervener
—kosten additional (extra, incidental) charges, extras
—produkt by-product
—sache incident, incidental (minor, secondary, subordinate) matter
nebensächlich immaterial, incidental, irrelevant, minor, negligible, secondary, subordinate, subsidiary, unimportant
Neben-
—sächlichkeit triviality
—sächlichkeiten irrelevancies
—schuldner co-debtor
—sicherheit collateral security
—stelle agency, branch (office), suboffice
—strafe additional penalty, secondary punishment
—straße by-road, by-street, secondary road, side-street
—titel subtitle
—umstände accessory circumstances, collateral facts
—ursache secondary (collateral) cause
—verdienst additional (incidental) income, perquisites
—vereinbarung collateral (sub-) agreement
—verpflichtung collateral obligation

—versicherung collateral insurance
—vertrag collateral agreement (contract), sub-agreement, subcontract
—vormund co-guardian, joint (ancillary) guardian
—wirkung incidental consequence, secondary (side-) effect
—zweck by-end, secondary object
Negation negation
negativ negative
negieren deny, ignore, negate, reject
nehmen accept, buy, capture, deprive of, engage, free from, grasp, lay hold of, purchase, receive, retain, seize, steal, take (away, from), use
Nehmer buyer, payee, purchaser, taker
Neid envy, grudge, jealousy
neiderfüllt envious
neiden envy, grudge
Neider envious person, grudger
neidisch envious, grudging, jealous
— sein envy, grudge
Neigung inclination, liking, preference, proneness, propensity, tendency, trend
Nennbetrag face (nominal) amount
nennen call, cite, denominate, designate, enter for, mention, name, nominate, quote, style, term
nennenswert considerable, worth mentioning
Nennung calling, denomination, designation, entry, mentioning, naming, nomination
Nennwert face (nominal) value, par (value)
—, zum at par
Nerven
—anstalt (-heil-) mental (nerve) hospital
—arzt mental specialist
nervenkrank nervous, neurotic
Nerven-
—kranker mental patient
—krankheit nervous disorder (disease)
—probe test of nerves
—zusammenbruch nervous breakdown
netto net
Netzwerk network
Neu-
—abschluß new (fresh) contract
—anmeldung new application (registration)
—anschaffung accession, new acquisition
—auflage (—ausgabe) new edition, reprint
—bearbeitung revised edition
—bewertung reappraisal, revaluation
—bildung new formation
—druck reprint
—einstufung (—einteilung) reclassification
—entdeckung rediscovery
Neuerung change, innovation, reform
Neu-
—erwerb accession, new acquisition
—fassung amendment, revision
—gestaltung modification, reconstruction, reorganization
—gründung reconstruction, reestablishment, reorganization
—gruppierung reclassification, regrouping
Neuheit newness, novelty
Neuigkeit (piece of) news
Neuling beginner, greenhorn, new hand, newcomer, novice
Neu-
—ordnung rearrangement, reform, reorganization
—regelung rearrangement, reorganization
neutral neutral
neutralisieren neutralize
Neutralität neutrality
Neutralitäts-
—abkommen neutrality treaty
—erklärung declaration of neutrality
—gesetz neutrality act (law)
—gesetzgebung neutrality legislation
—politik neutrality policy
—rechte rights of neutrality

—verletzung violation of neutrality
Neu-
—veranlagung reassessment
—wahl by-election, new election
—wert original value
Nicht-
—achtung disregard, disrespect
— —des Gerichts contempt of court
—anerkennung disavowal, nonrecognition, repudiation
—angriffspakt non-aggression pact
—annahme nonacceptance, refusal of acceptance
—anwendung nonapplication
—anwesenheit absence, absenteeism, nonattendance, nonpresence
—ausführung nonexecution, nonperformance
—ausübung nonexercise, nonusage, nonuse(r)
—beachtung disregard, nonobservance
— — des Gesetzes noncompliance with the law
—befolgung noncompliance, nonobservance
nichtberechtigt unauthorized, unqualified
Nicht-
—berechtigter unauthorized person
—bestehen nonexistence
—beteiligung nonparticipation
—bezahlung nonpayment
—duldung intolerance
—einhaltung noncompliance, nonobservance
—einmischung noninterference, nonintervention
— —sabkommen (— —spakt) nonintervention agreement (pact)
—erfüllung default, failure, noncompliance, nonexecution, nonfulfilment, nonperformance
—erneuerung nonrenewal
—erscheinen absence, default, failure to appear, nonappearance, nonattendance, nonpublication
—erscheinender (—erschienener) defaulter, nonattendant
—fachmann nonexpert
—handeln inaction
nichtig empty, futile, ineffectual, invalid, nugatory, null, null and void, vain, void
—, null und null and void
für — erklären abolish, annul, declare (null and) void, invalidate, make void, nullify, quash
Nichtigkeit futility, invalidity, nullity, vanity, voidness
Nichtigkeits-
—beschwerde plea of nullity
—erklärung annulment, cancellation, decree of nullity, invalidation, nullification, reversion
—klage action for annulment, nullity suit
—klausel cancellation clause
—prozeß (—verfahren) nullity proceedings
—urteil decree of nullity
Nicht-
—mitglied nonmember
— —schaft nonmembership
— —staat nonmember state (country)
nichtöffentlich closed, in camera, in chambers, private
nichtorganisiert non-society, nonunion(ist)
nicht rechtsfähig unincorporated, without legal capacity
Nichtsachverständiger nonexpert
nichtssagend empty, futile, inexpressive, insignificant, meaningless, trivial, vague, vain, void
nichtstreitig noncontentious, nonlitigious
nichtswürdig base, contemptible, infamous, vile, worthless
Nicht-
—übereinstimmung discrepancy, dissenting opinion, nonagreement, nonconcurrence
—vorbestrafter first offender
—verantwortlichkeit (—haftbarkeit) irresponsibility
—vorhandensein absence, nonexistence
—wählbarkeit ineligibility
—wissen ignorance, absence (want) of knowledge
—wollen unwillingness

—zahlung default (of payment), nonpayment
—zulassung nonadmission
—zuständigkeit incompetence
nicht zutreffend inapplicable
nieder base, common, inferior, low, lower, mean, minor, vulgar
Niedergang decadence, decline, fall
niederknallen shoot (down)
Niederlage branch, defeat, establishment, failure, overthrow
Wahl— defeat at the polls
— erleiden be defeated, suffer a defeat
niederlassen
—, sich establish oneself, set up (in business), settle (down), take up one's domicile
Niederlassung branch, colony, domicile, establishment, settlement
Haupt— head office
Zweig— agency, branch (office)
Niederlassungs-
—freiheit freedom of domicile (settlement)
—recht right of domicile (settlement)
niederlegen abandon, abdicate, deposit, formulate, give up, lay down, put down, resign, retire, set forth, vacate
—, Arbeit cease (suspend, stop) work, down tools, go on strike, strike, walk out
Niederlegung abdication, resignation, retirement
Arbeits— cessation (stoppage, suspension) of work, strike, walk-out
niedermetzeln butcher, kill, massacre, slaughter
niederschießen shoot down
niederschlagen beat down, cancel, crush, defeat, knock down, quash, quell, remit, stop, strike down, waive
Niederschlagung cancellation, quashing, suppression
niederschreiben note, make a minute of, put down (in writing), put into the minutes, record, take (note of), write down
Niederschrift copy, minutes, record, report
niederstimmen outvote, vote down
niederträchtig base, dirty, insidious, low, mean, sordid, vile
Niederträchtigkeit base action, baseness, meanness
niedrig base, cheap, dirty, humble, inferior, low, mean, moderate, short, vile
Niedrigkeit baseness, humbleness, lowness, meanness, moderateness, vulgarity
Nießbrauch enjoyment, beneficial interest, usufruct
—, lebenslänglicher life interest
Nießbraucher beneficial owner, usufructuary
Nießbrauchrecht usufructuary right, right of usufruct (enjoyment)
Niveau level, standard
nominal nominal
Nominal-
—betrag nominal (face) amount
—einkommen nominal income
—kapital nominal capital
—lohn nominal wage
—preis nominal price
—wert nominal (face) value, par (value)
nominell nominal, titular, by name
nominieren nominate
Nominierung nomination
Norm norm, quota, rate, rule, standard
Rechts— rule of law
als — gelten serve as a standard
normal normal, ordinary, regular, standard
unter —en Umständen under ordinary circumstances
—erweise normally, in the ordinary course
Normal-
—bedingungen standard terms
—blatt standard sheet
—größe standard (regular) size
normalisieren (normen, normieren) normalize, standardize

Normalisierung (Normierung, Normung) normalization, standardization
Normal-
—lohn regular pay (wage)
—maß standard (measure)
—satz standard rate
—zeit standard time
normativ normative
Not affliction, agony, anguish, anxiety, compulsion, danger, destitution, difficulty, distress, emergency, exigency, extremity, indigence, misery, necessity, need, stress, trouble, urgency, want
— leiden be in necessity, be short of, suffer want
in — sein be destitute, be in distress (trouble, want)
Nota bill, invoice, memorandum, note
Notar conveyancer, notary (public), solicitor
Notariat notary's office
Notariats-
—bescheinigung notarial certificate
—gebühren (—kosten) notarial (notary's) fees (charges)
—siegel notarial seal
—stil notarial style
—urkunde notarial deed (document)
notariell notarial
— beglaubigen certify, legalize, notarize
— beglaubigt certified, notarized
Notausgang emergency exit
Notbehelf expedient, makeshift, stopgap
notdürftig needy, poor, scanty, temporary
Note account, annotation, banknote, bill, mark, memorandum, note
Fuß— footnote
Verbal— memorandum
Noten-
—ausgabe issue of banknotes (notes)
—austausch exchange of notes
—bank bank of issue, issuing bank
Not-
—erbe lawful (legitimate) heir
—fall case of necessity (need), emergency, exigency
—, im (notfalls) in case of need (emergency, necessity), if necessary
Notfrist peremptory term
notieren book, enter, list, note, put down, quote, record, take a note of
Notierung entry, quotation
notifizieren notify
Notifizierung notification
nötig essential, indispensable, necessary, needed, needful, required, requisite
nötigen compel, force, necessitate, oblige, press, urge
nötigenfalls in case of need, if necessary
Nötigung compulsion, constraint, duress, force, physical coercion, undue influence
Notiz announcement, memorandum, note, notice, quotation
—en machen make a note of, take notes
— nehmen take notice of
keine — nehmen ignore
Notizbuch memorandum book, notebook
Notklausel emergency (escape) clause
Notlage calamity, difficulty, distress, emergency, misery, need
sich in einer — befinden be in difficulties
notleidend destitute, dishono(u)red, distressed, in need, indigent, necessitous, needy, poor
Notlüge white lie
Notmaßnahme emergency measure
notorisch known, notorious
Notstand (state of) distress, (state of) emergency, need
Notstands-
—bestimmungen emergency provisions
—gesetz emergency law (act), Emergency Powers Act (GB)
—gesetzgebung emergency legislation

—maßnahme emergency measure
—verordnung emergency decree
Notwehr self-defence
—, in in self-defence, se defendendo
notwendig essential, imperative, indispensable, inevitable, mandatory, necessary, needful, required, requisite
notwendig
— machen necessitate, require
— sein be necessary (required)
notwendigenfalls in case of need
notwendigerweise necessarily
Notwendigkeit necessity, need, needfulness, requirement, urgency
Notzucht (—sverbrechen) criminal (indecent) assault, rape, violation
— begehen commit a rape upon
notzüchtigen assault, commit rape, outrage, ravish, violate
Notzuchtsversuch attempted rape
Novelle amending (supplementary) law, amendment
nüchtern calm, dry, sensible, sober, temperate, unemotional
Nüchternheit dryness, sobriety, temperance
null und nichtig nil, null and void
für null und nichtig erklären declare null and void, annul, invalidate
numerieren label, number, ticket
numerisch numerical
Nummer copy, edition, issue, mark, number, size
—nschild licence (number) plate
Nutzanwendung (practical) application, utilization
nutzbar effective, productive, profitable, remunerable, serviceable, useful, utilizable
— machen turn to account (one's advantage), utilize
Nutzbarmachung employment, use, utilization
nutzbringend advantageous, productive, profitable, remunerative
Nutzeffekt effective power, efficiency, practical (useful) effect
Nutzen advantage, benefit, gain, interest, proceeds, profit, return, service, use, usefulness, utility
nutzen (nützen) avail oneself of, be of advantage (use), be useful, benefit, profit, put to account, serve for, use, utilize
—, nichts be of no avail, be useless
—, wenig avail (help) little, do little (good)
Nutzleistung effective power
nützlich advantageous, beneficial, helpful, profitable, serviceable, useful
Nützlichkeit advantage, advantageousness, profitableness, serviceableness, usefulness, utility
nutzlos futile, needless, of no use, unavailing, unprofitable, useless
Nutzlosigkeit uselessness
nutznießen (hold in) usufruct
Nutznießer beneficial owner, beneficiary, user, usufructuary
Nutznießung enjoyment, use, usufruct
—, lebenslängliche life interest
—srecht right of usufruct, usufructuary right
Nutzung benefit, enjoyment, proceeds, produce, profit, return, revenue, use, using, usufruct, utilization, yield
Nutzungs-
—berechtigter beneficiary, usufructuary
—entgelt hire, rental, compensation for use
—recht beneficial interest (employment), right of use (usufruct), usufructuary right

O

Obacht attention, care
— geben pay attention (to), take care of
Obdach asylum, cover, dwelling, home, lodging, shelter
— gewähren give cover (shelter), grant asylum, harbour, put under shelter
obdachlos homeless, unhoused, unsheltered, without shelter
Obdachloser casual, homeless (person)
Obdachlosigkeit homelessness
Obduktion autopsy, post-mortem examination
obduzieren hold an inquest (post-mortem examination) on
obenerwähnt (—genannt) above-mentioned (-cited, -named, -quoted), aforesaid
Ober
—aufseher superintendent
—aufsicht superintendence, supervision
—befehl supreme command
—befehlshaber commander-in-chief
—finanzgericht high finance court
oberflächlich casual, rough, shallow, superficial
Oberflächlichkeit shallowness, superficiality
Ober-
—gericht superior court
—gewalt supreme authority, sovereignty, supremacy
—hand superiority, upperhand
— — gewinnen conquer, prevail, win the upperhand
— — haben predominate, prevail
—herrschaft hegemony, sovereignty, supremacy, suzerainty
—hoheit sovereignty, supremacy
—kommando chief (high) command
—landesgericht (provincial) court of appeal, provincial supreme court
—richter chief justice
—staatsanwalt attorney general
oberst chief, guiding, highest, maximum, principal, supreme, top, topmost, uppermost
Oberverwaltungsgericht high administration (administrative) court
Obhut care, charge, custody, guard, guardianship, keeping, protection
der — anvertrauen (in — geben) commit to the care (charge) of, give into the charge of, put (place) in (under) the care of
in — nehmen take care (charge) of, take in custody, take under one's wings
obig above, above-mentioned (-said), foregoing
Objekt object, project, property
objektiv actual, detached, impartial, material, objective, practical, unbiassed
Objektivität detachment, impartiality, objectiveness, objectivity
obliegen attend (to), be duty of, be incumbent on, study
Obliegenheit duty, function, incumbency, obligation, office
obligat compulsory, customary, indispensable, inevitable, obligatory
Obligation bond, debenture (bond), obligation
Obligations-
—anleihe debenture loan
—gläubiger bond creditor, obligee
—schein bond
—schuld bond debt
—schuldner bond debtor, obligor
obligatorisch compulsory, consensual, mandatory, obligatory
Obligo commitment, engagement, liability
Obmann chairman, foreman, umpire
Betriebs— shop (works) steward

Obrigkeit authorities, (public) powers, government, magistracy
obrigkeitlich by authority, magisterial, official, public
obsiegen carry the day, conquer, be successful (victorious), gain one's cause, triumph over, win
obsiegende Erkenntnis favo(u)rable decision
obsiegende Partei successful party
obsiegendes Urteil favo(u)rable judgement
obskur obscure
Obstruktion obstruction, filibuster(ing)
Obstruktions-
—methoden obstructive measures
—taktik obstructive tactics, obstructionism
obszön obscene
Obszönität obscenity
obwalten control, exist, prevail, rule (over)
offen blank, candid, clear, current, downright, frank, free, not shut, open, outspoken, pending, running, sincere, unaffected, unclosed, unlimited, unsettled, vacant
offenbar apparent, clear, evident, manifest, obvious, open, public
— werden become known (evident)
offenbaren disclose, make known, manifest, reveal
Offenbarung disclosure, manifestation, revelation
—seid oath of manifestation
— — leisten take the oath of manifestation
offenhalten reserve
Offenheit candidness, candour, directness, frankness, openness
—, in aller in all honesty
offenkundig blatant, established, evident, manifest, notorious, public, spectacular, well-known
Offenkundigkeit notoriousness, publicity
offenlegen disclose, expose, lay open
Offenlegung disclosure, exposure
offensichtlich apparent, evident, manifest, obvious
Offensichtlichkeit evidence, notoriousness, obviousness
offensiv offensive
Offensive offensive
— ergreifen take the offensive
offenstehen be open (for), be due (outstanding, owing), be pending
offenstehend open, outstanding, unliquidated, unsettled
öffentlich civil, public, in open court, in public
—e Abbitte apology
—es Amt public (government) office
—es Amt bekleiden hold a public office
—e Angelegenheit public matter
—er Ankläger public prosecutor
—es Ärgernis public nuisance
—e Aufforderung public summons
—er Aufruf public proclamation
—e Beglaubigung legalization, official confirmation
—e Bekanntmachung manifesto, proclamation, public notice (notification)
—er Dienst civil (public) service
—e Gelder public funds
—e Gewalt public authority (power)
—e Hand fisc, public purse, state
—es Interesse public interest
—e Körperschaft (public) corporation
—e Ladung public summons
—es Leben public life
—e Meinung public opinion
—e Mittel public funds
—es Recht public law
Anstalt des —en Rechts public corporation
—e Schuld public debt
—e Sicherheit public security
—e Sitzung open (public) session
in —er Sitzung in open court, in full session
—er Skandal public scandal
—e Verhandlung public trial

—e Versammlung open (public) meeting
—e Versteigerung public auction
Öffentlichkeit publicity, (general) public
in der — (in aller —) openly, in public
— von Verhandlungen proceedings in public
—, Ausschluß der exclusion of the public
unter Ausschluß der — in camera, in chambers, in private, in closed session
— ausschließen exclude the public
— wiederherstellen restore the public
Öffentlichkeits-
—arbeit public relations, publicity
—prinzip principle of publicity
öffentlich-rechtlich under public law, public
offerieren offer, tender
Offerte bid, offer, tender
Offizialverteidiger counsel assigned by the court
—verteidigung assigned counsel, official defence
offiziell official
Offizier officer
offiziös inofficial, officious, semi-official
Ohrenzeuge ear witness
Okkupation occupation
okkupieren occupy
Operation operation, transaction
operieren operate, transact
Opfer immolation, sacrifice, victim
— bringen make a sacrifice
zum — fallen be (become, fall) a victim of
opfern immolate, (make a) sacrifice
Opponent adversary, opponent
opponieren offer resistance, oppose, resist
opportun convenient, expedient, opportune
Opportunismus opportunism
Opportunist opportunist
Opposition opposition
in — stehen be in opposition, oppose
in — treten go into opposition
Optant optant
optieren choose, decide for, opt for, vote in favo(u)r of
optimal maximum, optimum
Optimum maximum, optimum
Option option
— ausüben exercise an option
optionell optional
Options-
—anleihe optional bond
—ausübung exercise of option
—klausel optional clause
—recht (right of) option, optional right
—vertrag option (agreement)
ordentlich careful, decent, full, good, orderly, in good order, ordinary, proper, regular, respectable, sound, steady
Ordentlichkeit good (proper) order, regularity, respectability, steadiness
Order command, order
ordinär common, inferior, mean, ordinary, regular, vulgar
ordnen adjust, arrange, classify, dispose, order, organize, put (set) in order (to rights), regulate, settle
Ordnung arrangement, class, classification, code, disposition, division, formation, order, pattern, rank, regime, regimentation, regulation(s), regularity, rules, succession, system
—, öffentliche public order, law and order
in — bringen adjust, order, put to rights (straight), rectify, repair
zur — rufen call to order
ordnungsgemäß (—mäßig) due, lawful, in due order, orderly, proper, regular
ordnungshalber for regularity's sake, for the sake of (good) order
Ordnungs-
—mäßigkeit regularity
—maßnahme safety (precautionary) measure

—ruf call to order
—strafe disciplinary fine (penalty)
mit einer — — belegen fine
ordnungswidrig against the rules (regulations), contrary to order, illegal, irregular
Ordnungswidrigkeit breach of the rules, irregularity
Organ agency, agent, authority, body, element, institution, instrument, officer, organ
Organisation organization
Organisator organizer
organisieren arrange, organize
orientieren find out, guide, inform, instruct, locate, orientate
Orientierung guidance, information, instruction, orientation
original original
Original original
—ausgabe first edition
—fassung original version
originaltreu in accordance with the original
Originalurkunde original (document)
Ort lieu, locality, place, point, position, site, spot
an — und Stelle on the (very) spot
  Leistungs— place of performance
  Tat— lieu (scene) of the crime
  Ursprungs— place of origin
  Wohn— domicile, residence
örtlich local
Örtlichkeit locality, place
ortsansässig local, resident
Ortsansässiger resident, residential citizen
Orts-
—beschreibung topography
—besichtigung local inspection
—behörde local authority (government)
Ortschaft locality, place
Orts
—gebrauch local custom
—kenntnis knowledge of a place, local knowledge
ortskundig having knowledge of a place
Orts-
—polizei local police
—recht local law
ortsüblich according to local usage, in accordance with local custom, customary in a place, usual at a place
Orts-
—verwaltung local administration
—verweis local banishment
—vorsteher chief magistrate, mayor
—zeit local time

P

Pacht lease, rent, rental, tenancy, tenure
  Erb— hereditary lease
  Jagd— shooting lease
  in — geben let on (put out to) lease, farm (let) out
  in — haben have on lease
  in — nehmen farm, take on lease
Pacht-
—ablauf expiration of lease
—abtretung assignment of lease
—bedingungen leasehold condition. terms of lease
—besitz leasehold (possession), tenancy
—brief lease
—dauer tenancy, duration (life, term) of lease (tenancy)
—einnahme rent, rental
pachten farm, lease, take a lease of, take on lease, rent
Pächter farmer, leaseholder, lessee, tenant

Pacht-
—ertrag rental
pachtfrei rent-free
Pacht-
—geld rent, rental
—grundstück (—gut) farm, holding, leasehold (estate)
—herr landlord, lessor
—inhaber tenant
—preis rent, rental
—rückstand rent arrears
—schein (—urkunde) lease
Pachtung estate, farming, holding, leasehold, taking on lease, tenancy, tenement
Pacht-
—verhältnis lease, tenancy, tenure
—verlängerung extension (renewal) of lease
—vertrag lease (contract)
pachtweise on lease
Pacht-
—wert rental value
—zeit term of lease
—zins rent, rental
Pakt agreement, compact, covenant, pact, treaty
Beistands— mutual assistance pact
— schließen covenant, make (sign) a pact
paktieren agree, come to terms, make a compact (agreement), make (sign) a pact
Pamphlet lampoon, pamphlet
Panik panic, scare, stampede
in — versetzen stampede
panisch panic
Panne breakdown, failure
— erleiden (haben) break down, have a breakdown
panschen adulterate, water
Panscher adulterator
Papier bill, bond, document, draft, instrument, paper, share, stock
auf dem — on paper, theoretically
zu — bringen commit to (put down on) paper
Papiere bonds, documents, identity papers, papers, passport, securities, shares, stocks
Papier-
—geld paper money, bills, notes
—währung paper currency
—wert paper value
—werte paper securities
Paragraph article, clause, paragraph, section
Parallele parallel
eine — bilden form a parallel
eine — ziehen draw a parallel (between, with)
Parallelfall parallel case
Pardon forgiveness, mercy, pardon, quarter
pardonieren pardon, give quarter to
pari, al at par (parity)
parieren obey
Parikurs par of exchange
Parität parity, equality
paritätisch at par (parity), on the basis (on a footing) of equality
Pariwert par value
Parlament parliament
— einberufen convoke (summon) parliament
Parlamentarier member of parliament, parliamentarian
parlamentarisch parliamentary
Parlamentarismus parliamentarism
Parlaments-
—akte act of parliament
—ausschuß parliamentary committee
—beschluß vote of parliament
—ferien recess
—mehrheit majority in parliament
—mitglied member of parliament, parliamentarian
—ordnung parliamentary regulations
—wahlen general (parliamentary) elections
Partei faction, part, party, side
—gericht party court (tribunal)
—gerichtsbarkeit party jurisdiction
parteiisch (parteilich) biassed, interested, one-sided, partial, prejudiced
Parteilichkeit bias, partiality
parteilos impartial, independent, neutral, non-party

Partei-
—losigkeit impartiality, independence, neutrality
—mitglied party member
—nahme partisanship
—tag party conference (congress)
—versammlung party meeting
—vorbringen pleadings
—wesen party system
Partie company, line, lot, match, part, party, passage
partiell partial, in part
Partikularismus particularism, sectionalism, separatism
Partikularist particularist, sectionist
partikularistisch particularistic
Partisan guerilla, halberd, partisan
—enkrieg guerilla (partisan) warfare
Partizipation participation
partizipieren have an interest (a share) in, participate in, take part in
Partner associate, copartner, partner, party
Partnerschaft association, copartnership, partnership
—sverhältnis partnership relation
Parzelle allotment, lot, parcel, plot (of land)
parzellieren divide into lots, parcel (out), partition, plot
Paß papers, pass, passage, passport, permit
passabel passable, tolerable
Passage passage
Passagier fare, passenger
—, blinder deadhead, stowaway
Paßamt (-büro) passport office
Paßantrag passport application
passen agree, be befitting (fit, fitting, convenient, proper, suited), fit, harmonize, meet, suit
passend adapted, appropriate, apt, becoming, convenient, fit, fitting, good, harmonizing, opportune, proper, right, seasonable, seemly, suitable
Paßfälschung passport falsification
passierbar passable, traversable
Passierbarkeit passableness, traversableness
passieren come to pass, cross, go through, happen, occur, pass, take place
Passierschein docket, pass (bill, check), permit
passiv adverse, indolent, passive, unfavo(u)rable
— legitimiert capable to be sued
—e Handelsbilanz adverse (unfavo[u]rable) balance of trade
—es Mitglied associate (paying) member
—er Teilhaber dormant (silent, sleeping) partner
—es Wahlrecht eligibility
—er Widerstand passive resistance
Passiva debts, liabilities
Passivität passiveness, passivity
Passiv-
—legitimation capacity to be sued
—masse liabilities
Paßkarte certificate of identity, identity card, pass, passport, permit
Paßkontrolle examination of passport, pass(port) control
Paßstelle passport office
Paßvermerk visa
Paßvorlage submission of passport
Paßwesen passport system
Passus article, clause, passage
Patent licenc(s)e, patent
— anmelden apply for a patent
— besitzen hold a patent
— erlangen obtain a patent
— erteilen grant (issue) a patent
Patent-
—abgabe licence (patent) fee, royalty
—ablauf expiration of patent
—abteilung patent department
—amt patent office
—anmelder applicant for a patent
—anspruch patent claim
—antrag patent application
—anwalt patent agent (attorney, lawyer, solicitor)
— —sbüro patent agency
—brief letters patent
—bruch patent infringement

—dauer duration (life, term) of patent
—erteilung grant (issue) of a patent
—erträge royalties
patentfähig patentable
Patent-
—fähigkeit patentability
—geber patentor
—gebühr licence (patent) fee, royalty
—gegenstand patented article
—gesetz patent act (law)
—gesetzgebung patent laws (legislation)
patentierbar patentable
Patentierbarkeit patentability
patentieren grant (issue) a patent, patent
— lassen take out a patent for
patentiert patented, proprietary, registered
Patentierung grant (issue) of a patent, patenting
Patent-
—inhaber patent holder (owner), patentee
—klage patent action (suit)
—prozeß patent trial
—recht patent law (right)
patentrechtlich geschützt patented, proprietary, patent right reserved
—register patent rolls
—sachen patent matters
—schrift patent specification
—schutz patent protection
— —gesetz patent law
—träger patent holder (owner), patentee
—verletzung patent infringement
—verzeichnis patent register
Patient invalid, patient
Patrimonial-
—gericht patrimonial jurisdiction
—güter patrimonial estate
Patrimonium patrimony
Patriot patriot
patriotisch patriotic
Patriotismus patriotism
Patron patron, protector
Patronat patronage
Patronin patroness, protectress
pauschal all-included, all-inclusive, in the lump (bulk), lump-sum, overall
Pauschal-
—abfindung (**—entschädigung**, **—regelung**, **—regulierung**) lump-sum settlement
—betrag global amount, lump sum
—besteuerung taxation in bulk
Pauschale all-inclusive price, global amount, lump sum
Pauschal-
—gebühr flat rate, lump-sum charge
—honorar general retainer, lump-sum fee
—kauf purchase in bulk
—police general (open, unvalued) policy
—preis flat price (rate), lump-sum price
—satz flat rate
—steuer comprehensive (lump-sum) tax
—summe flat sum, lump sum
—tarif flat rate
—versicherung blanket (overall) insurance
—wert flat (overall) value
—zahlung lump-sum payment
Pause break, intermission, interval, pause, recess, rest, stop
Pein agony, pain, torment, torture
peinigen rack, torment, torture
Peiniger tormentor, torturer
Peinigung torment(ing), torture
peinlich awkward, criminal, capital, delicate, painful, penal
—e Gerichtsbarkeit criminal jurisdiction
Peinlichkeit agony, criminality, painfulness
pekunär financial, monetary, pecuniary
Pension boarding house, half-pay, old-age pension, pension (allowance), retired pay(ment), retirement
—, in pensioned off, retired
in — gehen retire (on a pension)
in — sein be retired, board (at, in, with)
Pensionär boarder, pensionary, pensioner

Pensionat boarding school
pensionieren pension off, superannuate
sich — lassen retire
pensioniert in retirement, pensioned off, retired, superannuated
— werden be pensioned off, be superannuated, retire on a pension
Pensionierung pensioning off, retirement, retiring, superannuation
—salter age of retirement, pensionable (retirement, retiring) age
das — — erreichen reach the age limit, superannuate
Pensions-
—anspruch pension claim
pensionsberechtigt entitled to pension, pensionable
Pensions-
—berechtigter pensionary, pensioner, person entitled to a pension
—berechtigung pension claim, pensionary right, right to pension
—bestimmungen pension provisions
—empfänger pensionary, pensioner
—fonds (—kasse) pension (superannuation) fund
—leistung pension payment, retirement allowance (benefit)
—liste retired list
—versicherung (old-age) pension insurance
—zahlung pension payment, retirement pay
per as of, by, per
peremptorisch peremptory
perfekt accomplished, concluded, perfect, settled
perfektionieren consummate, bring to perfection, make perfect
Pergament document, parchment
Periode cycle, period, term
Amts— term (tenure) of office
Gerichts— trial term
Legislatur— legislative term
Sitzungs— session
periodisch periodic(al)
permanent permanent
Permanenz permance, permanency
Person body, figure, individual, party, person, personage, personality
Privat— individual, private person
Vertrauens— person of confidence, trustee
—, dritte third party
—, juristische body corporate, corporate body, legal entity, artificial (juridical, juristic, legal) person
—, natürliche natural person
Person, in in person, in personam, oneself, personally
Personal attendants, employees, personnel, servants, staff
Personal-
—abbau reduction of staff
—abteilung personnel (staff) department (division)
—akten personnel files
—angaben personnel data
—ausbildung staff training
—ausweis identity (identification) card
—beschreibung description
—bestand personnel, staff
—büro personnel department (division, office)
—gesellschaft partnership
Personalien particulars of a person, personal data
Personal-
—kredit personal (private) credit
—steuer personal tax
—union personal union
—unterlagen personnel records
—verzeichnis staff register
Personen-
—beschreibung description
—schaden personal injury
—stand civil (family, personal) status
— —sregister register of births, deaths and marriages
—vereinigung association, society
—versicherung casual (personal accident) insurance
—verzeichnis register of persons

Personifikation (Personifizierung) embodiment, impersonation, personification
personifizieren embody, impersonate, personify
persönlich in person, in personam, personal, private
— haften be personally liable (responsible)
Persönlichkeit leading figure, personage, personality
pervers abnorm, degenerate, invert, invested, perverse
Perversität abnormality, perverseness, perversity
Petent petitioner
Petition petition
petitionieren petition, submit a petition for
Petitions-
—recht right of petition
—weg, auf dem by way of petition
Petschaft seal, signet
Pfand collateral, deposit, earnest money, forfeit, gage, mortgage, pawn, pledge, security, surety
—einlösen redeem a pledge, take out a pawn
Pfandauslösung redemption of a pledge, replevin
pfandbar mortgageable
pfändbar attachable, distrainable, mortgageable, seizable
—, nicht not attachable, not distrainable
Pfändbarkeit attachability, seizableness
Pfand-
—besitzer pawnee, pledgee, pledge holder
—bestellung mortgaging, pawning, pledging
—brief bond, debenture (bond), mortgage bond (deed)
— —anstalt (— —institut) land (mortgage) bank
— —gläubiger (— —inhaber) bond creditor, bondholder, debenture holder, hypothecary, mortgage holder
— —schuldner bond debtor
—darlehen collateral loan, loan on pawn (against security)
pfänden attach, distrain (upon), distress, garnish, impound, levy, levy distress (execution), seize
Pfänder bailiff, distrainer, executor
Pfand-
—forderung hypothecary claim, secured debt
pfandfrei pledge-free
Pfand-
—freigabe replevin
—geber mortgagee, mortgagor, pawner, pledger, pledgor
—gläubiger (—halter, —inhaber, —nehmer) hypothecary, mortgagee, pawnee, pledgee, pledge holder
—gegenstand (—objekt) pawn, pledge, pawned (pledged) article
—gut pledged property
—haus pawnshop
—hinterlegung deposit
—leihanstalt loan (pawn) office, pawnshop
—leihe pawnbroking
—leiher pawnbroker
—recht law of distraint and mortgage, lien, mortgage, pawn, pledge
— —sgläubiger lienor
pfandrechtlich hypothecary, pawnable
Pfand-
—schein certificate of pledge, mortgage document, pawn ticket
—schuld debt on pawn, hypothecary debt, mortgage debt
—schuldner distrainee, lienee, mortgager, mortgagor, pawner, pledger, pledgor
—sicherheit (collateral, hypothecary) security
—stück pawn, pledge
Pfändung attachment, distraint, distress, execution, garnishment, seizure
— vornehmen distrain, levy distress
Pfändungs-
—beamter executioner
—befehl warrant of distress

—beschluß distraint (distress, garnishment) order, order of attachment
Pfändungs- und Überweisungsbeschluß decree of seizure and assignment
pfändungsfrei exempt from execution (seizure)
Pfändungs-
—freiheit exemption from execution (seizure)
—gläubiger attachment creditor, distrainer
—kosten costs of levy
—pfandgläubiger garnisher
—pfandrecht execution lien, lien by distraint
—schuldner distrainee
—verfahren attachment (execution) proceedings
—verfügung distraint (garnishee) order, warrant of distress
Pfand-
—urkunde deed of security, letter of hypothecation, mortgage deed
—verkauf distress sale
—verleiher pawnbroker, pawnee, pledgee
—verschreibung s. -brief
—vertrag deed of security, mortgage deed, pledge
pfandweise by way of pledge, as collateral, on mortgage (pawn)
Pflege administration, care, direction, guardianship, nursing, superintendence, tutelage
  in — geben give at nurse, put (out) to nurse, place under the care of
  in — nehmen take care (charge) of
  in — sein be in (under) the care of
Pflege-
—amt board of guardians, guardianship
pflegebefohlen committed to charge
Pflege-
—befohlener charge, ward
—bestellung appointment of a guardian (trustee)
—eltern foster parents
—heim nursing house, charity
—kind foster (nurse) child, nursling, ward
—mutter foster mother
pflegen apply oneself to, attend (to), be used (accustomed) to, care for, carry on, conduct, cultivate, exercise, foster, have, keep up, look after, maintain, nurse, perform, take care of, tend, use, wait upon
Pfleger administrator, curator, custodian, fosterer, guardian, nurse, patron, promoter, trustee
  Abwesenheits- curator absentis
  Erbschafts- (Nachlaß-) administrator (curator) of an estate
Pflege-
—sohn foster son
—tochter foster daughter
—vater foster father
pfleglich careful, gentile
Pflegling charge, foster child, ward
Pflegschaft curatorship, guardianship, trusteeship
Pflicht duty, function, liability, obligation, office, responsibility, task
—, eheliche conjugal (matrimonial) duty
—, moralische moral duty
—, staatsbürgerliche civic duty
—, erfüllen — nachkommen, tun) do (fulfil) one's duty
— sein be obligatory
Pflicht-
—anteil contingent, quota
—beitrag compulsory contribution
pflichtbewußt conscious, responsible
Pflicht-
—bewußtsein sense of duty
—eifer zeal
pflichteifrig zealous
Pflicht-
—enkreis duties, responsibilities
—erfüllung performance of duty
—gebot moral duty (obligation)
—gefühl sense of duty
pflichtgemäß (—mäßig) due, duly, dutiful, faithful, loyal, (as) in

duty bound, in conformity with duty
Pflicht-
—gesetz moral law
pflichtig liable, obligatory, obliged, in duty bound
Pflichtiger contributory
Pflicht-
—mitglied compulsory member
—mitgliedschaft compulsory membership
—reserve legal (lawful, statutory) reserve
pflichtschuldig duly. in duty bound, obligatory
Pflicht-
—teil legal (legitimate) portion
auf — setzen give a person his legal portion
Pflichtteils-berechtigter compulsory beneficiary, forced heir
pflichttreu devoted, dutiful, faithful
Pflichttreue devotion, dutifulness, faithfulness, loyalty
pflichtvergessen disloyal, undutiful
Pflicht-
—vergessenheit dereliction of duty, disloyalty
—verletzung breach (infringement, violation) of duty
—vernachlässigung dereliction (neglect) of duty
—versäumnis neglect of duty
—versicherung compulsory insurance
—verteidigung assigned counsel, official defence
pflichtwidrig contrary to duty, disloyal, undutiful
Pfründe benefice, living, prebend, sinecure
Phase phase, stage
Phrase phrase
Pirat pirate
Piraterie piracy
Pistole gun, pistol
placieren place, negotiate
Placierung placing, position
plädieren argue, plead
Plädoyer address, pleading(s), speech
Plagiat plagiarism
— begehen commit a plagiarism, plagiarize
Plagiator plagiarist
plagiieren plagiarize
Plakat bill, placard, poster
Plan blueprint, chart, design, device, draft, idea, intention, layout, map, plan, plot, project, schedule, scheme, table
planen conceive, design, devise, envisage, intend, plan, plot, project, propose, schedule, scheme, time
planlos aimless, at random, desultory, planless, purposeless, unmethodical, unsystematic, without a fixed plan
Planlosigkeit aimlessness, desultoriness
planmäßig according to plan, designed, methodical, planned, regular, (as) scheduled, systematic
Planmäßigkeit methodicalness, systematic arrangement
Planung planning
Planwirtschaft planned economy
Platz city, ground, locality, lot, place, plot, point, position, post, room, seat, site, space, spot, square, town
fehl am — e misplaced, out of place
nicht am — e impertinent, irrelevant, out of place, unwanted
plausibel plausible
Plebiszit plebiscite
Pleite bankruptcy, failure
pleite bankrupt
—gehen (machen) fail, go bankrupt
Plenar-
—ausschuß plenary committee
—sitzung full (plenary) session, session in pleno
—versammlung plenary assembly (meeting)
in pleno in full court
Plenum full assembly (session), full court, plenum
Plombe seal
plombieren seal

Plünderer looter, pillager, plunderer
plündern despoil, loot, pillage, plunder, raid, ransack, ravage, rifle, rob, sack, strip
Plünderung looting, pillage, plundering, robbery, sack(ing), spoliation
Pluralwahlrecht plural vote
Police policy
—nbesitzer (—ninhaber) policy holder
Politik policy, politics
Politiker politician
politisch politic(al)
—e Einstellung political opinion
—er Gefangener political prisoner
—e Maßnahme political action
—e Rechte political liberties (rights)
—es Verbrechen political offence (crime)
—er Verbrecher political offender
Polizei police
—agent police agent
—aktion police action
—amt police station
—arzt police surgeon
—aufgebot police detachment, posse (of constables)
—aufsicht police control (supervision, surveyance)
unter — — stellen place under police control
—ausweis police pass
—beamter constable, police officer, policeman
—beamtin police woman, woman police officer
—bedeckung police escort
—behörde police
—bericht police report
—boot police boat
—büro police office
—gefängnis lock-up, police prison
—gericht police court
—gesetz constable act, police law
—gewalt (—macht) police power
—hund police dog
—knüttel espantoon, truncheon
—kommissar police inspector

polizeilich (of the, to the) police
—e Anmeldung registration with the police
—e Anordnung police regulation
—e Anzeige notification to the police
—e Aufsicht (unter) (under) police control (supervision)
—e Bestimmungen police regulations
—es Einschreiten police intervention
—es Führungszeugnis certificate of good conduct; police attestation of good behavio(u)r, conduct and moral
—e Maßnahme police measure
—e Meldung notification to the police
—e Meldepflicht obligatory registration
—e Untersuchung police investigation
—es Verbot police ban
—e Verordnung police ordinance
polizeilich verboten contrary to police regulations
Polizei
—maßnahme police measure
—ordnung police regulations
—präsidium police office (headquarters)
—razzia police raid
—register police register, charge sheet
—revier police station
—richter police magistrate
—sache police matter
—spitzel police spy
—staat police state
—strafe police penalty
—streife patrol, police picket (squad), (police) raid
—stunde closing hour (time)
—truppe police force
—verbot police ban
—vergehen offence against the police
—verordnung police ordinance
—vorschriften police regulations
—wache police station
polizeiwidrig contrary to police regulations

Polizist bobby, constable, patrolman, policeman
Verkehrs— traffic policeman
— in Zivil plain-clothes policeman
Polizistin police woman, woman police officer
Polygamie polygamy
Pool combination, combine, pool
—vertrag pooling agreement
populär popular
popularisieren popularize
Popularisierung popularization
Popularität popularity
Portefeuille portfolio
Portion allowance, portion, share
Position item, place, position, post, situation, standing, station
Post letters, mail, post, post office
—, mit der by mail (post)
postalisch postal
Post
—amt post (office)
—anweisung money order, post-office order, postal (money) order
—beamter post clerk (official)
—behörde postal authority
—diebstahl mail robbery, post-office theft
Posten amount, article, berth, entry, item, lot, office, picket, place, position, post, situation, station, sum
Post
—fach post-office box
—gebühren postal charges, postage
—geheimnis postal secrecy, secrecy of letters
postlagernd general delivery, poste restante, to be called for
Post
—raub mail robbery
—recht post(al) law
—sache postal matter
—sachen letters
—scheck postal check (cheque)
—schein post-office receipt
—schließfach post-office box
—stempel postmark
—tarif postal rate
—tarif postal rate (tariff)
—verein, Weltpostverein World Postal Union
—vertrag postal convention
—verwaltung postal administration, postal authorities
postwendend by return of mail (post)
Post
—zeichen postmark
—zensur postal censorship
Postulat postulate
postulieren postulate
Potential capacity, potential, power
potential potential
Präambel introduction, preamble, preface, recital
prädominieren predominate
Präfekt prefect
Präfektur prefecture
Polizei— police headquarters
Prägeanstalt mint
prägen coin, mint, stamp
Präger coiner, stamper
Präge
—ort place of coinage
—presse coining (minting) press
—recht seignorage
—stempel coin stamp, die
Prägung coinage, mintage, stamping
Präjudiz precedent, prejudice
—recht case law
präjudizieren prejudge, prejudice
präkludieren exclude, foreclose
Präklusion foreclosure
Praktikant assistant, practitioner, probationer
Praktiken contrivances, dodges, machinations, practices, tricks
Praktiker expert, practical man, practician, practitioner
Praktikum practices
praktisch practical, in (by) practice, practised, pragmatic, sensible, serviceable, useful, working
praktizieren exercise, practice, practise
Präliminarien preliminaries
Prämie award, bonus, bounty, consideration, premium, prize, remuneration, reward

prämiieren place (grant) a premium on, award a prize to
Prämisse premise
Präsent gift, present
Präsentant bearer, presenter
Präsentation (Präsentierung) presentation
präsentieren offer, present
Präservativ preservative
Präsident chairman, president, speaker
Präsidenten
—amt (-stelle) chairmanship, presidency, presidentship
—stuhl presidential chair
— — einnehmen take the chair
—wahl presidential election
Präsidentschaft chairmanship, presidency, presidentship
Präsidentschafts
—kandidat presidential candidate
—wahlen presidential elections
—zeit presidential term
präsidieren be in the chair, preside (over)
Präsidium board (of directors), chairmanship, presidency
— übernehmen take the chair
— abtreten leave the chair
präsumieren presume
Präsumtion presumption
Präsumtiverbe heir presumptive
Prätendent claimant, pretender
Prätention claim, pretension
prätentiös pretentious
Präventiv
—krieg preventive war
—maßnahme preventive measure
Praxis application, clientele, clients, custom, exercise, experience, patients, practice, usage
—, in der in practice, practically
in die — umsetzen put into practice
Präzedenzfall leading case, precedent
— schaffen set a precedent
Präzedenz
—recht case law
—streit precedent question
präzis exact, precise, punctual
präzisieren define exactly, specify
Präzision accuracy, exactitude, exactness, precision
Preis award, charge, cost, fare, fee, price, prize, rate, reward, value
Preis
—abbau price cut (reduction)
—abkommen price agreement
—abschlag abatement, allowance, discount, price deduction
—änderung price change
—angabe price mark, quotation
—aufschlag extra charge
—aufsicht (-kontrolle, -lenkung, -überwachung) price control
—angleichung (-anpassung) price adjustment
—behörde price control authority (board)
—bericht market report
—beschränkung price limit
—bestimmung price regulation, price-fixing clause (agreement)
—bildung price formation
—differenz price difference
—diskreminierung price discrimination
—erhöhung price increase, rise in price
—ermäßigung abatement, allowance, price cut (reduction)
—gabe abandonment, disclosure, give-away, revelation
preisgeben abandon, disclose, expose, give up (away), part with, prostitute, relinquish, reveal, surrender
Preis
—gebung abandonment, prostitution, surrender
—gefüge (-struktur) price structure
—gericht jury
—gesetzgebung price legislation
—gleitklausel escalation clause
—grenze (-limit) price limit
—liste price list, rate book
—nachlaß abatement, allowance, discount, price deduction (reduction), rebate
—niveau price level
—regelung price regulations
—richter arbiter, judge, umpire
als — fungieren abjudicate

—senkung price cut (decrease, reduction)
—skala price range (scale)
—spanne price margin (range)
—steigerung price increase
—überschreitung exceeding of the lawful price
—unterbietung dumping
—vereinbarung price (-fixing) agreement
—vergehen (-verstoß) offence against price regulations
—vorschriften price regulations
prekär equivocal, precarious
prellen bambozzle, cheat, defraud, dupe, trick out
Prellerei cheat(ing), fraud, imposition
Premierminister premier, prime minister
Presse press
—bericht press report
—fehde press feud
—feldzug press campaign
—freiheit freedom (liberty) of the press
—gesetz press law
—knebelung muzzling of the press
—konferenz press conference
—ordnung press regulations
—vergehen offence against the press laws
—zensur press censureship
—zwang restriction (suppression) of the freedom of the press
Prestige face, prestige, reputation
sein — wahren save one's face
Prestigeverlust loss of face (prestige)
primär primary
Primawechsel first of exchange, original (first) bill
primitiv primitive, rough, rude, simple
Primogenitur primogeniture, priority of birth, right of primogeniture
Prinzip principle, rule
—, im (prinzipiell) in principle, principally
Prinzipienfrage question of principle
Prinzipal boss, chief, employer, head, master, principal
Priorität precedence, preference, priority
— genießen enjoy preference (priority)
Prioritäts
—aktie preference share, preferred share (stock)
—anspruch priority claim
—gläubiger preferential (preferred) creditor
—papiere preference (preferred) stock
—recht preference, priority
Prise capture, prize
Prisen
—anteil (—geld) prize money
—gut prize goods
—gericht (— —shof) prize court
—ordnung prize code
—recht prize law
privat confidential, individual, personal, private
Privat
—abkommen private agreement
—abmachung private arrangement
—adresse (—anschrift) home (private) address
—angelegenheit private affair (matter)
—besitz personal (private) possession (property)
— —, im privately owned
—betrieb private establishment
—brief private letter
—detektiv (private) detective, private investigator
—eigentum personal (private) property (ownership)
—eigentümer private proprietor
—gebrauch private use
— —, (nur) zum for private use (only)
—interesse private interest
—klage private action (charge, complaint, prosecution)
—kläger complainant, private accusant
—kredit personal credit
—leben private life
—mann (—person) private person (individual)
—post private mail

—recht civil (private) law
privatrechtlich according to private law, under civil law
Privat
—sache private affair (matter)
—unternehmen private enterprise
—urkunde private deed (document)
—verkauf private sale
—vermögen personal (private) property (fortune)
—versicherung private insurance
—vertrag private agreement (contract)
—wirtschaft private economy
Privileg benefit, charter, licen(s)e, patent, preference, prerogative, priority, privilege
privilegieren charter, license, privilege
privilegiert chartered, preferential, preferred, privileged
Probe example, exhibition, experiment, pattern, probation, proof, sample, specimen, test, trial, tryout
Blut— blood test
Gegen— control test
Stich— random test
— —en machen make tests at random
Unterschrifts— specimen signature
Zerreiß— endurance test
Probe
— bestehen stand the test (trial)
auf die — stellen test, try
Probe
—angestellter probationary employee
—anstellung probationary employment
—auftrag (—bestellung) trial order
—bogen proof sheet
—exemplar specimen copy
—fall test (trial) case
—gehalt probationary wage
—jahr year of probation, trial year
—kauf purchase on approval
—zeit (period of) probation, probationary term, trial period
probeweise on probation (trial) (approval), as a specimen
probieren test, try
Problem problem
problematisch problematic(al), uncertain
Produkt outcome, produce, product(ion), result
Produktion output, production
—sausfall (—sverlust) production loss
produktiv fecund, paying, productive, profitable, prolific
Produktivität efficiency, productive capacity, productiveness, productivity
Produktivitätsgrenze limit of productivity, marginal productivity
Produzent maker, manufacturer, producer
produzieren furnish, make, manufacture, produce, turn out
Profession business, profession, trade, vocation
—, von by profession (trade)
professionell professional
Profit advantage, benefit, gain, profit
profitabel advantageous, lucrative, profitable
profitieren benefit, gain, profit (by), take advantage of
pro forma as a matter of form, proforma, feigned, sham, simulated
Prognose forecast, prognosis
prognostizieren forecast, predict, prognosticate
Programm plan, platform, program(me), schedule, ticket
Progression progression
progressiv progressive
Progressivität progressiveness, progressivity
Progressivsteuer progressive duty (tax)
prohibitiv prohibitive, prohibitory
Prohibitiv
—gesetze prohibitory laws
—maßnahme prohibitive measure
—steuer prohibitive tax
—system prohibitionism

—zoll prohibitive duty
Projekt design, plan, project, scheme
projektieren plan, project, schedule
Proklamation proclamation
proklamieren proclaim
Prolongation carry(ing) over, continuation, extension, prolongation, renewal
prolongierbar continuable, renewable
prolongieren carry over, continue, extend, prolongate, renew
Promesse promissory note
Promille per thousand
prominent prominent
Promotion graduation
promovieren graduate
prompt immediate, prompt, punctual, quick, ready
Promptheit promptitude, promptness, punctuality
Propaganda advertising, propaganda, publicity
Flüster- whispering campain (propaganda)
— machen canvass, make propaganda, propagandize, propagate
Propagandafeldzug propaganda (publicity) campaign
prophylaktisch preventive, prophylactic
Prophylaxe prophylaxis
Proportion proportion, ratio
proportional proportional, pro rata
prostituieren (sich) prostitute (oneself)
Prostituierte prostitute
Prostitution prostitution
Protegé favo(u)rite, protégé
protegieren favo(u)r, patronize, protect, sponsor
Protektion patronage, protection, sponsorship
Protektionismus favo(u)ritism
Protektor patron, protector, sponsor
Protektorat patronage, protectorate
Protest protest(ation), remonstrance
—, ohne without protest
—, unter under protest
— einlegen (erheben) (enter a) protest (against)
zu — gehen lassen dishono(u)r, get (have) protested, protest
Protest
—anzeige note (notice) of protest (dishono(u)r)
—erhebender protester
—erhebung protestation
—frist limitation of protest
—gebühren protest fees
protestieren dishono(u)r, object, protest (against), take exception to
Protestierender protester
Protestierung protestation
Protest
—kosten (—spesen) protest charges
—kundgebung remonstrance
—schreiben remonstrative letter
—urkunde deed of protestation
Protokoll minutes, protocol, record, register
— aufnehmen draft (draw up) the minutes of, (draw up a) protocol, take down
— führen keep the minutes (register), protocol, record
zu — geben depose, have a record made of, place on record
zu — nehmen record, take down
protokollarisch by (entered in) the minutes, on record, recorded
Protokoll
—buch minute book
—eintragung entry, minute
—führer (Protokollant) clerk, recorder, registrar
protokollieren enter into the minutes, minute, (draw up a) protocol, put down to record, (draft a) record, register, take down
Protokollierung entry, registration, registry
protokollmäßig according to the minutes
Provenienz origin, provenance
Provinz province
provinziell provincial

Provision brokerage, commission, percentage, provision
provisionsweise on commission
provisorisch interim, makeshift, provisional, provisory, temporary
Provisorium makeshift, provisional (temporary) arrangement
Provokation provocation
provozieren challenge, provoke
provozierend provocative
Prozedur procedure, proceeding
Prozent per cent, percentage
—satz percentage, proportion, rate of interest
prozentual percentage, percentage, proportional
Prozeß action, case, cause, law case, lawsuit, legal proceedings, litigation, plea, procedure, proceeding(s), process, suit, trial
— androhen threaten a suit (with legal proceedings)
— anfangen (anhängig machen) bring an action (a lawsuit) against, institute legal proceedings against
— anstrengen bring an action against, institute legal proceedings against, have recourse to the law
— führen carry on a lawsuit, conduct a case (suit)
— gewinnen win a case
— haben mit have a lawsuit with
— machen prosecute, put on trial
zu einem —
kommen lassen let a matter come to legal proceedings
der —
schwebt the case is pending
in einem — unterliegen (— verlieren) lose a case
Prozeßakten minutes (of a case), records (of a lawsuit)
prozeßfähig having legal capacity
Prozeßfähigkeit legal capacity
prozeßführend litigant
—e Partei litigant(s)
Prozeß
—führender litigant, plaintiff, suitor
—führung conduct of a case, litigation
—gebühr legal cost, trial fee
prozessieren be at (go to) law, carry on a lawsuit, institute legal proceedings, litigate
Prozeß
—kosten law costs, legal costs, litigation fees
—ordnung rules of the court, rules of procedure
—partei litigant party, party to a case (suit)
—pfleger guardian ad litem
—recht procedural law
—sache cause, law (legal) case, lawsuit
—sucht litigiousness
prozeßsüchtig litigious
Prozeß
—verfahren legal proceedings, procedure
—vollmacht letter (power) of attorney
—vorschriften procedural rules, rules of procedure
—weg, auf dem by legal process
—wesen legal procedure
prüfen audit, check (up), control, examine, inspect, investigate, look into (over), probe, prove, review, scan, screen, scrutinize, study, survey, test, try, verify
Prüfer auditor, checker, examiner, inspector, investigator, scrutineer, scrutinizer, tester
Prüfling candidate, examinee
Prüfung audit(ing), check(ing), examination, inspection, investigation, probation, reconcilement, review, revisal, scrutiny, studies, supervision, temptation, test, trial, verification
Abschluß- (Schluß-) final examination
Aufnahme- entrance examination
Eignungs- aptitude test
Intelligenz- intelligence test
Staats- state examination
Vor- preliminary examination
Zulassungs- admission test, entrance examination

Zwischen- intermediate examination
—, mündliche oral examination
—, schriftliche written examination
Prüfung
— abhalten hold an examination
— ablegen go in for (make, sit for, undergo) an examination
— bestehen pass an examination
— nicht bestehen fail in an examination
sich zur — melden enter for an examination
Prüfungs
—amt (—stelle) control (inspection) office, examining board, testing authority
—ausschuß (-kommission) board of examination, examining (testing) board, review board
—bedingungen testing conditions
—bericht audit (examination, investigation) report
—gebühren audit (examination, inspection) fees
—kandidat candidate, examinee
—ordnung (-bestimmungen) examination regulations
—recht right of control (examination)
—verfahren auditing (examination, test) procedure
—vermerk audit certificate, test note
—zeit testing time, time of examination
—zeugnis attestation, certificate, diploma
Prügelei brawl, fight, row, scuffle
prügeln beat, flog, thrash
prügeln, sich (have a) fight
Prügelstrafe corporal punishment
Pseudonym assumed name, pen name, pseudonym
pseudonym pseudonymous
psychisch psychic(al)
Psychoanalyse psycho-analysis
Psychologie psychology, psychics
psychologisch psychological
publik public
Publikation publication
—srecht right of publication
Publikum audience, public, readers
publizieren publish, promulgate
Publizist journalist, publicist
Publizität publicity
Pufferstaat buffer state
Punkt article, charge, clause, item, mark, order, place, point, respect, spot, topic
Anklage- charge, count
Ausgangs- starting point, point of departure
Gesichts- (Stand-) point of view
Höhe- culminating point
Streit- point in dispute (of issue)
Stütz- base
pünktlich accurate, exact, in time, precise, prompt, punctual, strict
Pünktlichkeit accuracy, exactitude, promptitude, promptness, punctuality, strictness
pur genuine, mere, pure, unvarnished
Putsch coup de main, insurrection, putsch, rebellion, revolt, riot
putschen insurrect, revolt, riot

Q

Qualifikation capacity, eligibility, fitness, qualification
qualifizieren fit, modify, qualify
—, sich qualify (for), be suitable for
qualifiziert capable, eligible, fitted, qualified
Qualifizierung qualification
Qualität brand, class, description, grade, kind, mark, quality, sort, type
qualitativ qualitative, in quality
Qualitäts-
—bescheinigung (-zeugnis) quality certificate
—differenz (-unterschied) difference of quality
—fehler defect of quality
—kontrolle (-prüfung) quality control
—muster (-probe) quality sample, representative sample
Quantität amount, lot, quantity
quantitativ quantitative, as to quantity
Quantum amount, portion, quantity, quantum, quota, ration, share
Quarantäne quarantine
in — legen (unter — stellen) quarantine
Quarantäne
—beamter quarantine officer
—bestimmungen (-vorschriften) quarantine regulations
—flagge quarantine (yellow) flag
—station quarantine station
—zeit quarantine period
Quartal quarter, three months
quartalsweise quarterly
Quartier accommodation, district, lodging(s), quarters
quartieren be quartered (on, with)
Quelle authority, origin, source
—, an der at first hand
—, sichere (zuverlässige) good authority, reliable source
Quellen
—angabe (-nachweis) indication of authorities, reference, source documentation
—steuer withholding tax
Querulant litigious (querulous) person
querulieren be litigious (querulous)
quitt even, square
— sein mit be even (quits, square) with
quittieren abandon, acknowledge receipt of, give a receipt for, leave, quit, receipt, sign (for)
Quittung acknowledgement, (ac) quittance, receipt, voucher
—, gegen against (on) receipt
— ausstellen give (make out) a receipt, receipt
Quote contingent, dividend, portion, quota, rate, ratio, share
quotieren quote
Quotierung quotation

R

Rabatt abatement, allowance, deduction, discount, rebate, reduction
— gewähren allow an abatement (a discount), grant a reduction, make an allowance
Rabattmarke discount ticket, trading stamp
Rache retaliation, revenge, vengeance
— brüten plan vengeance
— nehmen take revenge

— **schwören** vow revenge
Racheakt act of revenge
rächen avenge
—, **sich** revenge oneself, take revenge (on, for)
Rächer avenger
racherfüllt full of resentment
Rachgefühl resentment
Rachsucht revengefulness, vindictiveness
rachsüchtig resentful, revengeful, vindictive
Radau racket, row
Radaubruder rowdy, tough
Rädelsführer ringleader
radikal extreme, radical
Radikaler extremist, radical
Radikalismus radicalism
Rahmen background, border, bound, frame, framework, limit, scope, setting, skeleton, structure, surroundings
—**abkommen (-vertrag)** basic agreement (contract), skeleton agreement
—**gebühr** basic charge, skeleton fee
—**gesetz** basic act, skeleton law
—**organisation** skeleton organization
—**tarif** skeleton wage agreement
Rand border, brink, edge, fringe, margin, outskirts, periphery, side
—**bemerkung** gloss, marginal note, side note
—**gebiet** borderland
—**staat** border state
Rang class, degree, dignity, grade, order, position, quality, rank, rate, rating, standing, state, station, status
—**folge** order, priority, sequence
—**gleichheit** equal rank, equality of rank (of rights)
rangieren class, classify, range, rank, rate
Rang
—**klasse** category, class
—**liste** ranking list, list of precedence (priorities)
—**ordnung** classification, gradation, hierarchy, order of rank (precedence), ranking, social scale
—**stufe** class, degree, grade, order, range, rank
—**unterschied** distinction of rank
—**verhältnis** order of priority, ranking
—**verlust** degradation, loss of rank
Räson reason
— **annehmen** listen to reason
Rasse blood, breed, race
rassebewußt race-conscious
Rassebewußtsein race consciousness, racialism
rassemäßig racial
Rasseminderheit racial minority
Rassen
—**frage** colo(u)r (race, racial) question
—**haß** race hatred
— —, **Aufhetzung zum** racial incitement
—**kampf** racial (race) conflict, struggle of races
—**kunde** ethnology
—**pflege** eugenics, race culture
—**politik** racial policy
rassenpolitisch racial-political
Rassen
—**schranke** colo(u)r bar
—**theorie** racial theory
—**trennung** (racial) segregation
Rat advice, (legal) adviser, board, consultation, council, councillor, counsel, counsellor, deliberation, expedient, means, recommendation, remedy, suggestion
—, **juristischer** legal advice
Ältesten- alderman, council of elders (aldermen)
Arbeiter- workers' council
Aufsichts- supervisory board
Bei- advisory board
Betrieb- firm's council, factory (shop, works) committee (council)
Bezirks- county (district) council
Bundes- federal council
Familien- family council
Gemeinde- borough, (local, parish, town) council

Stadt- city (municipal, town) council (councillor), alderman
Treuhand- trusteeship council
Verwaltungs- board of directors (managers), governing board, managing board
Vormundschafts- board of guardians
— **befolgen** follow (take) an advice
— **einholen** ask for (seek somebody's) advice, ask consultation of, consult
— **erteilen (geben)** advise, counsel, give an advice
Rate dividend, instalment, part payment, proportion, rate, ratio
auf Raten by (on) instalments, on hire purchase
in Raten by (in) instalments
raten advise, counsel, give advice, guess, recommend
Raten
—**kauf** hire purchase, purchase on instalments
ratenweise by instalments
Raten
—**zahlung** instalment, part payment, payment by (in) instalments
Ratenzahlungs-
—**system** instalment (hire-purchase) system
—**vertrag** hire-purchase agreement (contract)
Ratgeber adviser, advisor, counsel, counsellor
Rathaus town (city) hall
Ratifikation (Ratifizierung) ratification
Ratifikationsurkunde ratification document
ratifizieren ratify
Ration allowance, portion, ration, share
rational rational
rationalisieren rationalize
Rationalisierung rationalization
Rationalismus rationalism
Rationalist rationalist
rationalistisch rationalist(ic)
rationell economical, efficient, rational, reasonable
rationieren allowance, ration
Rationierung rationing
Rationierungs-
—**maßnahme** rationing arrangement
—**system (—wesen)** rationing system
—**vorschriften** rationing regulations
ratlos helpless, perplexed, without advice
Ratlosigkeit embarrassment, helplessness, perplexity
ratsam advisable, commendable, expedient, useful
Ratschlag advice, counsel
Rats
—**herr** alderman, councillor, counsellor, senator
—**mitglied** councilman, councillor, counsellor, member of the council
—**versammlung** (meeting of the) council
— — **abhalten** hold a council
—**wahlen** council elections
Raub booty, loot, looting, pillage, pillaging, piracy, plunder(ing), prey, rape, robbery, sacking, spoil(s), stolen goods
Bank- bank robbery
Kindes- (Menschen-) kidnapping
Mund- theft of food
Straßen- highway robbery
—, **gewaltsamer** theft with violence
— **begehen** commit a robbery
rauben kidnap, pillage, plunder, rob (and murder), steal, take by force
—, **die Ehre** calumniate, defame
—, **die Unschuld** deflower
Räuber brigand, highwayman, pirate, robber, thief
Räuberbande gang of robbers (thieves)
Räuberei brigandage, depredation, pillage, robbery
räuberisch predatory, rapacious
Raub
—**mord** murder and robbery
—**mörder** murderer and robber, cutthroat
—**tat** robbery with violence
—**gut** booty, stolen goods

—überfall hold-up, robbery (with violence), armed robbery
—zug raid
Raufbold (Raufer) brawler, rough, rowdy, ruffian
raufen, sich fight, scramble, scuffle
Rauferei brawl, fight, row, scuffle
Raufsucht pugnacity
raufsüchtig brawling, pugnacious, quarrelsome
Raum accommodation, area, capacity, chamber, locality, margin, occasion, place, room, scope, space, territory, volume
räumen abandon, clear off, evacuate, give up, leave, quit, remove, sell off, vacate
Räumlichkeit accommodation(s), locality, premises, room
Räumung clearance, clearing (off), ejection, evacuation, eviction, quitting, removal, removing, vacating
Räumungs-
—befehl eviction notice (order), order to evacuate (quit)
—klage action of ejectment (eviction)
—urteil eviction order, writ of ejectment
—(aus)verkauf clearance sale
Rausch delirium, drunkenness, ecstasy, inebriation, intoxication
Rauschgift- dope, drug, narcotic
—handel drug traffic
—händler drug peddlar, dope smuggler (trafficker)
—vergehen offence against narcotic regulations
Razzia raid, razzia, round-up
Polizei- police raid
— halten (machen) make a raid
reagieren react, respond
Reaktion reaction, response
Reaktionär reactionary, reactionist
reaktionär reactionary
real actual, material, real, substantial
real denkend objective
Realeinkommen real income
Realien real facts, realities
Realinjurie assault and battery
Realisation (Realisierung) liquidation, realization, sale
realisierbar convertible, liquidatable, marketable, realizable
—, sofort (leicht) fluid, liquid
—, nicht sofort frozen
Realisierbarkeit realizability
realisieren carry into effect, cash, convert, effect, execute, perform, realize
Realismus realism
Realist realist
realistisch realistic
Realität reality
realiter in reality
Real
—konkurrenz concurrence of (actual) offences, concurrent offences, cumulation (of facts)
—kredit credit on real estate (real property), real estate loan
—last land charge, real burden
—lohn real wage
—servitut easement, real servitude, real property mortgage
—sicherheit real security
—steuer property tax
—vermögen real estate, real property
—wert actual (real) value
Rebell insurgent, mutineer, rebel
rebellieren mutiny, rebel, revolt, rise
Rebellion insurrection, mutiny, rebellion, revolt
rebellisch insurrectional, mutinous, rebellious, revolutionary, seditious
Rechenschaft account
— ablegen account for, answer for, give (render) an account of
— fordern call to account for
— schuldig sein be accountable (responsible)
zur — ziehen bring to book, call to account for
Rechenschafts-
—bericht account (rendered), report, statement (of accounts)
—legung rendering of account
—pflicht accountability, responsibility

rechenschaftspflichtig accountable, responsible
Recherche inquiry, investigation
—n anstellen make inquiries (investigations)
recherchieren inquire, investigate, make inquiries
rechnen calculate, compute, count, estimate, reckon, valuate
— auf count on, expect, reckon (up)on, rely on
— mit calculate on, consider, contemplate, face, reckon on (with), take into account
— zu be classed with (included in, reckoned among), number among
Rechnung account, bill, calculation, check, computation, invoice, note, opinion, reckoning, score, supposition
auf — von for (on) account of
— ablegen account, give (render) account, report
— (ab)schließen close (settle, wind up) an account
— ausstellen (schreiben) make out an invoice
— begleichen clear (settle) an account, pay the reckoning (one's score), square accounts, strike a balance
— bezahlen clear (pay) an account, pay a bill (the reckoning)
in — bringen carry (pass, put) to account, take into account
— führen keep account(s)
— legen render (an) account of
in — stellen bill, charge, debit, invoice, carry (pass, place) to account, put into account
— tragen accommodate oneself to, comply with, make allowance for, take into account
in — ziehen take into account (consideration)
Rechnungs-
—beamter accountant, auditor
—beleg voucher
—bericht auditor's report
—buch account book, ledger
—datum date of invoice
—empfang receipt of invoice
—führer accountant, bookkeeper
—führung accounting, keeping of accounts
—hof (—kammer) audit office, court of audit
—jahr financial (fiscal) year
—legung rendering of account
—nummer invoice number
—posten entry, item
—prüfer auditor, controller
—prüfung audit, auditing, checking (examination) of accounts
—wert invoice value
Recht authority, claim, interest, jurisprudence, justice, law, power, privilege, right, title
Abbau— mining right
Ablehnungs— right of refusal
Absonderungs— preferential right
Allein— exclusive (sole) right
Anfechtungs— right of avoidance
Anklage— right of accusation (to prosecute)
Anlieger— neighbo(u)r right
Arbeits— labo(u)r (industrial) law
Armen— poor law
Asyl— right of asylum (sanctuary)
Ausbeutungs— right of exploitation
Auswahl— option, right of choice
Ausweisungs— right of expulsion
Begnadigungs— power (right) of pardon (grace)
Benutzungs— right of use, user
Berufungs— right of appeal
Beschlagnahme— right of seizure (confiscation)
Beschwerde— right of complaint
Besitz— right of possession
Billigkeits— (law of) equity
Bürger— civic right, (right of) citizenship
Durchfahrts— (Durchgangs—) right of passage (way)
Durchsuchungs— right of search
Ehe— marriage law

Ehescheidungs— divorce law
Ehren— law of honour
Ehren—e, bürgerliche civil rights
Ehrenbürger— freedom of the city, honorary citizenship
Eigentums— ownership, (right of) property
Einspruchs— right of protest, veto
Erb(folge)— hereditary right, law (right) of inheritance (succession)
Ernennungs— right of appointment
Erstgeburts— primogeniture
Familien— family law
Faust— fist law
Feudal— feudal law (right)
Frauenwahl— (Frauenstimm—) women's suffrage
Gemeinde— municipal law
Gesellschafts— company law, corporation act
Gesetzes— statute (statutory) law
Gesetzgebungs— legislative power (authority)
Gewohnheits— common (customary) law, usage
Gnaden— s. Begnadigungs-
Handels— business (commercial, mercantile, trade) law, law merchant
Heimfall— right of reversion
Herstellungs— right of production
Hoheits— sovereign right
Interpellations— right of interpellation
Jagd— game laws
Jugend— juvenile law
Klage— right to sue
Konkurs— bankruptcy law
Kontroll— right of control (supervision)
Kriegs— laws of warfare, martial law, military law
Landes— national (territorial) law
Lehns— feudal law
Luft— air law
Menschen—e human rights
Münz— right of coinage
Natur— law of nature, natural law (right)
Nutzungs— right of use (usufruct)
Pfand— lien
Präzedenz— case law
Prioritäts— (right of) priority
Privat— civil (private) law
Prozeß— rules of procedure
Rückfall— right of reversion
Sachen— real right
Scheidungs— divorce law
See— maritime (naval) law
Selbstbestimmungs— right of self-determination
Selbstverwaltungs— autonomy, self-government
Sonder— privilege, special right
Stadt— town law
Stand— martial law
Stimm— suffrage, right to vote
Straf— criminal (penal) law
Streik— right to strike
Un— injustice, tort, wrong
Untersuchungs— s. Durchsuchungs-
Urheber— copyright
Veräußerungs— right of alienation
Verfassungs— constitutional law
Verfügungs— right of disposal
Verjährungs— statute of limitation
Verkaufs— right to sell
Vermögens— property right
Versammlungs— right of meeting (assembly)
Vertrags— contractual right
Verwaltungs— administrative law
Veto — (right of) veto
Völker— international law, law of nations
Vorfahrts— right of way
Vorkaufs— option, (right of) preemption
Vorschlags— right of nomination
Vor(zugs)— preferential right, privilege, (right of) preference
Wahl— electoral law, suffrage, right to vote
—, passives eligibility

Wechsel— bill of exchange act (law)
Wege— right of passage (way)
Widerspruchs— right of objection
Wohn— right of domicile (residence)
Zeichnungs— subscription right (privilege)
Zivil— civil law
Zutritts— (Zugangs—) easement, right of access

Recht
—, absolutes absolute (peremptory) right
—, abtretbares (übertragbares) transferable right
—, alleiniges (ausschließliches) exclusive (sole) right
—, angeborenes inherent right
—, angestammtes birthright
—, bedingtes contingent interest, qualified title
—, bürgerliches civil law (code)
—e, bürgerliche civil (civic) rights
—, dingliches real right, right in rem
—, eheliches conjugal (marital) right
—, eingetragenes registered claim (title)
—, erworbenes vested interest
—, vertraglich festgelegtes contractual right
—, geltendes existing law, law in force
—, gemeines common law
—, geschriebenes statute (statutory, written) law
—, gültiges law in force
—, internationales international law, law of nations
—, materielles substantive law
—, nationales national law
—, öffentliches public law
—, persönliches personal claim (right, title)
—, positives positive law
—, privates civic (personal, private) right
—, römisches Roman law
—e, staatsbürgerliche civil (political) rights
—, strittiges litigious right
—, unabdingbares peremptory right
—, unangreifbares unimpeachable right
—, unantastbares indefeasible interest (right)
—, unbestrittenes clear title
—, ungeschriebenes unwritten (customary, oral) law
—, unübertragbares inalienable (non-transferable) right
—, veräußerliches alienable right
—, verbrieftes chartered (vested) right
—, verwirktes forfeited right

Recht, mit deservedly, justifiably, legitimately, rightly, with justice
—, ohne unjustly

von —s wegen according to law (justice), by force of law, by law (right), de jure, in justice, ipso jure

Recht
— und Billigkeit (right and) equity
—e, Doktor der doctor of law (L. L. D.)
—e, Student der law student, student of law
—e, Studium der law studies, studies of law

Recht
— aberkennen deprive (divest) of a right
— abtreten assign (cede) a right
— anmaßen usurp a right
— anwenden administer justice
— ausüben exercise a right
— durchsetzen assert (enforce) a right
— erwerben acquire a right

sich eines —es begeben abandon (surrender) a right
sein — fordern claim one's rights
— geltend machen assert (establish, enforce) a right
— genießen enjoy a right
— haben be justified (to do), have the right (to do)
zu seinem — kommen be granted one's rights, come into one's rights (own)

im — sein be in the right, have the law on one's side

— **sprechen** administer justice, judge
— **streitig machen** contend a right
— **studieren** study law(s)
— **übertragen** transfer a right
— **verdrehen** pervert the course of justice
— **verletzen** infringe a right
— **vorbehalten** reserve a right
— **wahren** maintain a right
— **widerfahren lassen** do justice (to)
recht accurate, correct, genuine, just, lawful, legitimate, proper, real, right, true
un— unjust, wrong, wrongful
— **haben** be right
recht und billig equitable, fair and just, just and equitable (due), right and correct (proper)
Rechte the right
—, äußerste extreme right
Rechtens sein be according to law, be lawful (legal), be the law
rechtfertigen defend, exculpate, excuse, justify, vindicate, warrant
—, nicht zu indefensible, unjustifiable
rechtfertigen, sich clear (exculpate) oneself, plead
Rechtfertigung clearing, defence (se), exculpation, excuse, justification, vindication, warranty
Rechtfertigungs
—grund justification
—schrift apology
rechtlich judicial, juridical, lawful, legal, legitimate, valid
bürgerlich— civil-law, under civil law
gemein— at common law
straf— under criminal (penal) law
völker— under international law
wider— unlawful
zivil— under civil law
Rechtlichkeit honesty, judicialness, lawfulness, legality, legitimacy, probity, rectitude, uprightness

rechtlos illegal, lawless, outlawed, unlawful, without rights
Rechtloser outlaw
Rechtlosigkeit absence of right, illegality, lawlessness, outlawry, unlawfulness
rechtmäßig just, lawful, legal, legitimate, proper, rightful, of right, true
Rechtmäßigkeit lawfulness, legality, legitimacy, rightfulness, validity, warrantableness
Un— illegality, unlawfulness
Rechts-
—abteilung law (legal) department, law office, legal branch
—abtretung assignment, cession
—änderung change of title, legal alteration
—angelegenheit law affair, legal matter
rechtsanhängig pending at law
Rechts
—anmaßung usurpation of a right
—anspruch (legal, legitimate) claim, (legal) demand, (legal) right, (good, just) title
—anwalt advocate, attorney (at law), barrister (at law), counsel, counsellor (at law), lawyer, solicitor
—anwältin advocatress, woman barrister
Rechtsanwalts
—beruf bar, legal profession
— — ausüben practise law
—büro (—kanzlei) law (laywer's) office
Rechtsanwaltschaft attorneyship, bar, legal profession, solicitorship
—, Zulassung zur admission (call) to the bar
von der — ausschließen disbar
Rechtsanwalts
—gebühren (—kosten) counsel's (lawyer's) fees, legal charges, retaining fees
—kammer bar (council)
Rechts
—anwendung application of law, dispensation of justice
—auffassung judicial conception, legal concept(ion)

—ausdruck legal term
—ausführungen legal arguments, pleadings
—auslegung interpretation of law, legal interpretation
—ausschuß judicial committee
—ausübung exercise of a right
—befugnis competence(cy)
—begehren petition
—begriff legal term
—behelf benefice of the law, defense, demurrer, legal remedy, plea, protest, remonstrance
—beistand (—berater) attorney (at law), counsel, counsellor (at law), legal adviser, solicitor
—beistand (—beratung) legal advice (aid, assistance)
—belehrung law instruction, legal direction (information), summing up
—bestand validity
rechtsbeständig valid
Rechts
—bestimmungen provisions of the law
—beziehung law (legal) relation
—brauch legal custom
—brecher criminal, offender
—bruch breach (infringement) of the law
rechtschaffen honest, righteous, straight, upright
Rechtschaffenheit honesty, integrity, probity, righteousness, uprightness
Rechts
—einrichtung legal institution
—einwand demurrer, legal estoppel, objection, plea, traverse
— — erheben demur, present a plea, raise an objection, traverse
rechtserheblich relevant in law
Rechts
—erheblichkeit relevance in law
rechtsfähig competent, having legal capacity, incorporated, legally capable, personable, registered
Rechts
—fähigkeit legal capacity
—fakultät faculty of law, law faculty
—fall case in law, cause, law (legal) case, suit
—fiktion fiction of law, legal fiction
—folge legal effect (consequence), operation of law
—folgerung conclusion of law, legal conclusion
—form form of law, legal form
—formalität legal formality
rechtsförmig in due form, judicial, legal
Rechts
—frage issue of law, law (legal) question, question of law
—gang course of law, lawsuit, legal procedure, procedure at law
—gefühl sense of justice
—gelehrsamkeit jurisprudence
rechtsgelehrt learned in the law
Rechts
—gelehrter jurist, lawyer
—gemeinheit community of rights
—genuß enjoyment of a right
—geschäft law business, legal act (transaction)
—geschichte jurisprudence, legal history
—gewohnheit judicial (legal) custom
—gleichheit equal rights, equality of law
—grund legal argument (ground, title)
—grundlage legal basis
—grundsatz legal principle, maxim (principle) of law
rechtsgültig effective, good in law, lawful, legal, valid (in law)
für — erklären validate
Rechts
—gültigkeit lawfulness, legality, legal validity, validity (in law)
—gut protected interest
—gutachten counsel's (legal) opinion, counsel's expertise
—handel action, case, cause, lawsuit, legal case, litigation
—handlung juristic (lawful, legal) act, legal transaction
rechtshängig in litigation, litigious, pending in court (at law), sub judice

Rechts
—hängigkeit litispendence, pendency
—hilfe legal aid (assistance, remedy), judicial assistance, relief
—hilfeersuchen letters rogatory
—inhaber holder of a right
—irrtum judicial error, miscarriage of justice, mistake in law
—kenntnis legal knowledge
—kniff chicane, lawyer's trick
—konsolent legal adviser, solicitor
—korrespondenz legal correspondence
—kosten legal costs
—kraft effectiveness, force of law, legal effect (force), (legal) validity
— — erlangen become effective (final, valid), become law, enter into effect
— — erteilen make valid
rechtskräftig absolute, effective (in law), final, legal, legally binding (effective), of legal effect (force), (legally) valid
—es Urteil absolute (final) decision (judgement)
— werden become absolute (effective, final, valid), become (pass into) law
Rechtskunde jurisprudence
rechtskundig having legal knowledges, knowing the law
Rechts
—kundiger lawyer
—lehre jurisprudence, legal science
—lage (-position, -stellung) legal position (situation, status)
—literatur legal literature
—mangel defect of (deficiency in, failure of) title, defective title
—maxime legal maxim, maxim of law
—mißbrauch abuse of rights
—mittel appeal (at law), legal measure (redress, remedy), (means of) redress, relief, remedy (at law)
— — einlegen appeal, enter (file, lodge, prefer) an appeal
Rechtsmittel
—begründung reasons for an appeal
—beklagter respondent
—entscheidung appeal decision, decision upon appeal
—frist limitation of appeal
—gericht (-instanz) appellate court
—kläger appellant
—schrift notice (petition) of appeal
—verfahren appeal procedure
Rechts
—nachfolge legal succession, succession in right
—nachfolger assign, assignee, cessionary, legal (personal) representative, legal successor, successor in title
—nachteil legal prejudice (detriment)
—nachweis proof of a right
—nießbrauch legal usufruct
—norm law, legal rule, principle of law
—ordnung law and order, legal order
—person artificial (legal) person, body corporate, legal entity
—pflege administration of justice, judicature
— — ausüben administer (dispense) justice
—pflicht judicial duty, legal duty (obligation)
—position s. -lage
—praxis law (practice), practice of law (the court)
—quellen sources of law
Rechtsprechung administration of justice, judicature, judiciary, jurisdiction
rechtsradikal rightist
Rechts
—radikaler rightist
—regel legal rule
—sache action, case (in law), cause, law affair, lawsuit, legal case (matter)
—sachverständiger legal expert
—satz law, legal axiom
—satzung enactment

—schutz legal protection
—sprache law language, legal terminology
—spruch abjudication, award, legal decision, judgement, sentence, verdict
—staat constitutional state
—standpunkt legal point of view
—stellung s. —lage
—streit action, cause, (legal) contest, dispute (at law), law case, lawsuit, legal procedure, litigation, plea, suit
—streitigkeit action, case, cause, lawsuit, suit
—student law student, student of law
—studium law studies, study of law
—system court (judicial, legal) system
—titel legitimate claim, (good, just, legal) title, title deed
—tod civil death
—träger legal entity
—übertragung assignment (cession, transfer) of a right
rechtsunfähig legally incapacitated, having no (without) legal capacity
Rechts
—unfähigkeit legal incapacity
rechtsungültig illegal, invalid (at law), void
Rechts
—ungültigkeit illegality, legal invalidity
rechtsunwirksam (legally) ineffective, invalid (at law), without legal force
Rechts
—unwirksamkeit (legal) ineffectiveness (invalidity)
—urkunde legal document (instrument)
rechtsverbindlich binding in law, legally binding, obligatory
Rechts
—verbindlichkeit legal obligation
—verdreher chicaner, pettifogger
—verdrehung chicanery, legal quibble (trickery), pettifogging
—verfahren court procedure (proceeding), judicial proceeding(s), legal procedure (proceedings)
—verfahrensregeln forms of legal procedure
—verfassung judicature, judicial system, judiciary
—verfolgung enforcement of right, litigation, prosecution, law enforcement
—vergleich legal settlement
—verhältnis legal relation(ship)
—verhandlung legal (judicial) proceedings
—verkehr right-hand traffic
—verletzer infringer, lawbreaker
—verletzung infringement (violation) of law (right), lawbreaking
—verlust loss of a right
—vermutung legal presumption, presumption of law
—verordnung statutory order (rule)
—verpflichtung legal liability (obligation)
rechtsverständig skilled in law
Rechts
—verständiger jurist, legal authority
—verteidigung defence
—vertreter attorney (in fact), counsel, law agent, legal representative, proxy, statutory agent
—verweigerung denial (refusal) of justice
—verweser administrator of justice
—verwirkung forfeiture of a right
—vorbehalt legal reservation, reservation of title
—vorgänger assignor, predecessor in title
—vorschrift legal regulation, provision of law, rule of law
—weg course (process) of law
— —, auf dem by legal proceedings, by suit, by process of law
— —, auf dem ordentlichen in due course (process) of law
unter Ausschluß des — —es admitting of no appeal
— — ausschließen bar legal proceedings

— — beschreiten go to law, initiate legal proceedings, proceed by law, take legal action (measures, steps)
Rechtswesen judicature, judiciary, jurisdiction, juridical system
rechtswidrig against the law, contrary to law, false, illegal, illicit, tortuous, unlawful, wrongful
Rechtswidrigkeit illegality, unlawfulness
rechtswirksam effective in law, final, legally effective (valid), of legal effect (force), operative, valid (in law)
Rechts
—wirksamkeit force of law, legal effect (force, validity), operation, validity (of law)
—wirkung legal effect
—wissenschaft jurisprudence, law, legal science
rechtswissenschaftlich jurisprudential
Rechts
—wohltat benefit of law, legal remedy
—zug instance, legal process
—zustand s. —lage
—zuständigkeit competence, jurisdiction
—zwang legal compulsion
rechtzeitig duly, in due course, opportune, seasonable, in (good) time, timely, at the right time
Rechtzeitigkeit opportuneness, punctuality
Redakteur editor
Rede address, conversation, discourse, oration, speech, talk
— halten deliver (give) an address, deliver (make) a speech
— und Antwort stehen answer for, give an account of
zur — stellen call to account
Rede
—freiheit free speech, freedom (liberty) of speech
—gabe eloquence
redegewandt eloquent
Rede
—gewandtheit eloquence
—kunst rhetoric
reden converse, discourse, plead, speak, talk
— über discuss
redigieren draw up, edit
Redigierung drawing up, editing
Rediskont rediscount
rediskontieren rediscount
redlich candid, in good faith, honest, hono(u)rable, sincere, upright
Redlichkeit candour, honesty, integrity, probity, sincerity, uprightness
Redner orator, speaker
reduzierbar diminishable, reducible
reduzieren cut, decrease, diminish, limit, lower, reduce
Reduzierung cut, decrease, reduction
Reede road(s), roadstead
Reeder shipowner
Reederei shipping company (business)
reell bona fide, clear, fair, genuine, good, honest, real, reasonable, reliable, respectable, solid, sound
Referat department, division, lecture, paper, report, review
— halten give (present, read) a lecture, give (make) a report, read a paper
Referendar junior barrister
Referendum plebiscite, referendum
Referent adviser, consultant, departmental chief (head), expert, referee, reporter, reviewer, speaker
Referenz information, reference
referieren give a lecture, read a paper, report
Reflektant applicant, inquirer, intending purchaser, interested party, prospect, prospective buyer
reflektieren auf have in mind (view), intend, reflect upon, think of
Reform reform
—bestrebungen reformatory efforts
—bewegung reform movement
reformieren reform

Reformprogramm reform program
Regel precept, principle, regulation, rule, standard
—, als (in der —) as a rule, generally, in general, ordinarily, usually
regellos irregular, lawless, without rule
Regellosigkeit irregularity
regelmäßig generally, normal, orderly, ordinary, regular
Regelmäßigkeit normality, regularity
regeln adjust, arrange, control, direct, manage, meet, order, pay, provide, put in order, regularize, regulate, settle, wind up
Regelung adjustment, arrangement, control, determination, ordering, provision, regulation, ruling, settlement, winding up
regelwidrig abnormal, against the rules (regulations), contrary to rule, foul, irregular
Regelwidrigkeit abnormality, foulness, irregularity
Regent regent, ruler, sovereign
Regentschaft regency, reign
Regie (public) administration, commission, control, direction, management, government (state) monopoly
regieren govern, hold office, predominate, prevail, reign, rule
Regierung cabinet, government, reign
—, an der in power
an die — gelangen come to the throne, come into power
Regierungs
—amt government office
—antritt accession (to the throne)
—ausschuß government (cabinet) committee, state commission
—beamter civil servant, government (state) official (employee), governmental officer
—betrieb government enterprise
—bezirk administrative (governmental) district
—chef head of the government
—erklärung (cabinet, government) communiqué
—form form of government
—gewalt governmental power
—koalition government coalition
—kreise government(al) circles
—krise cabinet (government) crisis
—mehrheit government majority
—organ government organ
—partei government party
—paß government pass(port)
—sitz seat of the government
—stelle government(al) agency
—system system of government
—tätigkeit government(al) action
—truppen government forces
—umbildung change in cabinet (of government), governmental change
—verlautbarung s. —erklärung
—verordnung government decree
—vertreter governmental representative
—vorlage government bill
—wechsel change in cabinet (of government)
—zeit reign
Regiment government, regiment, rule
— führen command, govern, rule
Region district, region
regional regional
Regional
—abkommen regional pact
—bank regional bank
Register catalog(ue), index, list, record, register, roll, table of contents
Registeramt public records (registration, registry) office
Registrator filer, recorder, registrar
Registratur files, filing cabinet, records, record (registrar's, register) office, registry
registrieren enter, file, index, list, record, register, tally
Registrierung filing, recording, registration
Reglement by-laws, regulations, rules
reglementieren order, regiment, regularize

Reglementierung regimentation
Regreß recourse, regress, remedy
— nehmen have (seek) recourse, recur
—, mit (ohne) with(out) recourse
Regreß
—anspruch claim to damages, recourse
—klage action for recourse
—nehmer claimant, person (party) seeking recourse, recoverer
—pflicht liability to recourse
regreßpflichtig liable to recourse (remedy)
— machen have recourse against
Regreß
—pflichtiger (—schuldner) party (person) liable to recourse, recoveree
—recht recourse, right of recovery
regulär regular
Regularität regularity
Regulation regularization
regulierbar adjustable, controllable
regulieren adjust, control, regulate, settle, square
Regulierung adjustment, regulation, settlement
Regung emotion, impulse, motion, movement, rising, stirring(s)
—, menschliche humanity
regungslos immovable, motionless, unmoving
rehabilitieren discharge, rehabilitate, whitewash
—, sich rehabilitate oneself, recover one's reputation, right oneself
Rehabilitierung discharge, rehabilitation, white wash(ing)
Rehabilitierungs
—antrag application for discharge
—bescheinigung bankrupt's certificate
Reibung clash, collision, difference, dissension, friction
reibungslos easy, frictionless
Reibungspunkt point of friction
Reich empire, kingdom, realm
reich ample, fertile, generous, great, large, moneyed, opulent, rich, wealthy, well-to-do, wide
reichen bis extend to, range (from) to, reach
— für be sufficient for, cover, suffice
Reicher rich man, well-to-do person
Reichtum fortune, opulence, riches, richness, wealth
Reichweite range, reach, scope
reif mature, mellow, ripe
Reife maturity, ripeness
reifen grow ripe (to maturity), mature, ripen
Reife
—prüfung leaving (final) examination
—zeugnis leaving certificate, certificate of maturity
reiflich careful, mature
Reihe file, line, number, order, queue, range, rank, row, series, succession, turn
Reihenfolge order (of succession), sequence, series, succession
rein blank, chaste, clean, clear, correct, downright, genuine, faultless, free (from), mere, net, pure, real, true
ins reine bringen arrange, clear, set in order, settle, square, straighten out
ins reine kommen arrange with, come to an understanding with, get even with
Reinertrag net proceeds (income)
Reinfall failure, fiasco
reinfallen come down, fail
reinlegen deceive, let down, take in
Reingewinn net profit
Reinheit chastity, cleanness, clarity, genuineness, innocence, purity
reinigen clear, purge, purify
—, sich clear oneself (of)
Reinigung purgation, purification
— durch Eid compurgation
Reinigungseid oath of purgation
Reinverlust net loss
Reinvermögen net (actual) assets, net property

Reise journey, passage, tour, travel, trip, voyage
Reisender commercial traveller, passenger, tourist, travel(l)er, travelling agent, voyager
Reisepaß passport
Reisescheck traveller's cheque (check)
reizen attract, entice, exasperate, excite, incite, instigate, interest, irritate, provoke, work up
Reizung enticement, incitement, instigation, irritation, provocation
Rekapitulation recapitulation, summary
rekapitulieren recapitulate, sum up
Reklamant claimant
Reklamation claim, complaint, objection, protest, reclamation
Reklamations
—frist limitation of complaint
—schreiben letter of complaint
Reklame advertisement, advertising, propaganda, publicity
— machen advertise, publicize
Reklamefeldzug publicity (advertising) campaign
reklamieren claim (back), complain (about), demand, object (to), protest (against), reclaim
Rektifikation (Rektifizierung) correction, rectification
rektifizieren correct, rectify
Rekurs appeal
— einlegen (nehmen) appeal
Rekursverfahren procedure of appeal
Relation relation
relativ comparative, relative
Relegation expulsion
relegieren expel, send down
Religion confession, creed, denomination, faith, religion
Religions
—ausübung, freie freedom of worship
—bekenntnis (religious) profession
—freiheit freedom of religion (faith), religious liberty
—gemeinschaft religious community
—gesellschaft religious society
—krieg religious war
—streit religious war
—system religious system
—zwang religious compulsion
Remittent consignor, payee, remitter, sender
remittieren remit, return, send back
Rendite profitability, yield, return
Renommee fame, renown, reputation
renommiert famous, of good repute, renowned
renovieren recondition, renew, renovate, repair, restore
Renovierung renovation
rentabel lucrative, paying, productive, profitable, remunerative
Rentabilität productiveness, profitability, profitableness
Rentamt revenue office, board of revenue
Rente annuity, income, interest, pension, rent, revenue
— beziehen draw a pension
Renten
—ablösung liquidation of an annuity
—anleihe annuity bond
—anspruch right to pension
—bank annuity bank
—basis annuity basis
rentenberechtigt entitled to pension
Renten
—berechtigter annuitant, beneficiary, person entitled to pension
—bezieher (—empfänger) annuitant, pensioner
—brief annuity bond
—einkommen rental income
—empfänger s. —bezieher
—papiere bonds
—schein annuity bond
—schuld annuity charge
—titel annuity bond
—versicherung annuity insurance, pension insurance fund
— —sanstalt annuity insurance office
—vertrag annuity contract
—zahlung annuity payment
Rentier (Rentner) annuitant, pensionary, pensioner, rentier,

person of independent (private) means
rentieren, sich be profitable, leave a margin, pay, yield a profit (goods profits)
Reparationen reparations
— leisten make reparations
Reparations
—abkommen reparation agreement
—anleihe reparation loan
—ausschuß reparation committee
—forderung reparation claim
—leistung payment of reparations
—verpflichtung reparation obligation
—zahlungen reparation payments, reparations
Reparatur repair
—kosten repair costs
reparierbar repairable
reparieren mend, repair
repatriieren repatriate
Repatriierung repatriation
—sabkommen repatriation agreement
repetieren repeat
Repetition repetition
Replik counterplea, replication, rejoinder, reply, retort
replizieren make a replication, reply
Report report
Repräsentant agent, exponent, representative
Repräsentation representation
repräsentativ representative
repräsentieren represent
Repressalie reprisal, retaliation, retortion
—n ergreifen make reprisals, retaliate (on)
Reproduktion reproduction
reproduzieren reproduce
Republik republic
Republikaner republican
republikanisch republican
Reputation renown, reputation, repute
requirieren requisition
Requisition requisition
Requisitions
—amt requisition office
—recht right of requisition
—verfahren requisitioning procedure
Reservat reservation
—recht reserved right
Reserve reserve
—, offene open (declared) reserve
—, gesetzliche statutory reserve
—, stille hidden (secret) reserve
Reservefond reserve fund
reservieren book, earmark, reserve, secure, set aside
Reservierung reservation
Resident resident
—schaft residentship
Residenz residence(cy)
residieren reside
Resignation resignation
resignieren resign
resistent resistant
Resistenz resistance
Resolution resolution
— einbringen move (offer) a resolution
Respekt regard, respect
— verschaffen command (enforce) respect, make oneself respected
respektabel hono(u)rable, repectable
respektieren hono(u)r, respect
—, nicht dishono(u)r
respektive respectively (resp.)
respektlos disrespective, irreverent, without respect
Respektlosigkeit disrespect, irreverence
Respekttage days of grace (respite)
respektvoll deferential, respectful
respektwidrig disrespectful
Respektwidrigkeit disrespect, disrespectfulness, irreverence
Ressort department, division, province, purview
ressortmäßig departmental
Rest arrears, balance, hangover, remainder, remains, remnant, residual, residue, rest, surplus, survival
Restbestand remainder, remaining stock
Restbetrag remainder, remaining amount, residual

restituieren refund, restitute, restore
Restitution restitution, restoration
Restitutions
—anspruch restitution(al) claim
—klage action for restitution
—recht restitution right
restlich remaining
restlos complete, final, in full, without a remainder (leaving anything)
Resultat answer, finding, issue, outcome, result, return, showing, upshot
resultieren result
Resümee recapitulation, resumé, summary
resümieren make a resumé of, recapitulate, sum up, summarize
Retorsion retortion
Retorsions
—maßnahme retaliatory measure
—zoll retaliatory duty
retten deliver, free, preserve, recover, rescue, salvage, save
—, seine Ehre vindicate one's honour
—, sein Leben run for one's life
Retter deliverer, rescuer
Rettung deliverance, escape, recovery, rescue, salvage, salvation
—, ohne past help
Rettungs
—maßnahme salvage operation
—mittel expedient, remedy
—versuch attempt at rescue
rettungslos irrecoverable, irremediable, irretrievable, past help
Reue remorse, repentance
Reuegefühl remorse
reuelos remorseless
reuevoll repentant
reuen be (feel) sorry for, repent
Reugeld atonement (conscience, forfeit, smart) money
reumütig repentant
Revanche return, revenge
— geben give a person his revenge
revanchieren, sich get one's own back, make up for, have one's revenge on, repay
revidieren audit, check, correct, examine, inspect, investigate, reconsider, re-examine, review, revise
Revier district, estate, quarter
Jagd- shooting ground
Polizei- police station
Revision appeal, audit, checking, examination, inspection, investigation, re-examination, rehearing, review, reviewal, revise, revisal, revision, verification
Anschluß- cross-appeal
— einlegen appeal, give notice of appeal, lodge (institute) an appeal
— stattgeben allow (grant) an appeal
einer — unterziehen review
— verwerfen dismiss an appeal
Revisions
—begründung reasons of appeal
—beklagter respondent
revisionsfähig reviewable, revisable
Revisions
—frist limitation of appeal
—gericht (-hof) appellate court, court of revision
—instanz appellate instance
—kläger appellant
—verfahren appellate procedure
Revisor auditor, controller, examiner, inspector, reviser
Revolte rebellion, revolt, riot
revoltieren revolt, rise
Revolution revolution
Revolutionär revolutionary, revolutionist
revolutionär revolutionary
revolutionieren revolutionize
Revolutionsgericht revolutionary tribunal
Revolver revolver
Rezensent critic, reviewer
rezensieren criticize, review
Rezension critique, review
reziprok reciprocal
Reziprozität reciprocity
richten condemn, criticize, execute, judge, pronounce sentence, sentence, try

— **über** pass sentence on, sit in judgement on
— **an** direct (put) to
—, **sich selbst** commit suicide, pass judgement on oneself
sich — nach accommodate oneself to, be determined (guided) by, conform with, depend on, follow, go by, take as a lead
Richter judge, justice
—, **die** judiciary, judicature
Richter
Berufungs- appellate judge
Ferien- vacation judge
Friedens- justice of the peace
Hilfs- assistant judge
Laien- lay judge
Nachlaß- surrogate
Polizei- police magistrate
Preis- arbiter, judge, umpire
Schieds- arbitrator
Straf- criminal (puisne) judge
Untersuchungs- investigating judge, screening-court judge
Vormundschafts- judge of a guardianship court
Richter
—**amt** judgeship, judicature, judicial office (function), justiceship
—**bank** bench, judges, judicial bench, magistrates
—**kollegium** bench, body of judges
richterlich as a judge, judicial, judiciary, magisterial
Richter
—**spruch** decision, judgement, sentence, legal (judicial) decision (judgement), court decision (judgement, sentence)
—**stand** bench, judges, judgeship, judicature, judicial calling, judiciary, justiceship
richtig accurate, adequate, appropriate, correct, due, exact, fair, genuine, good, just, own, proper, real, regular, right, suitable, true
Richtigbefund acknowledgement, approval, verification
Richtigkeit accuracy, conformity, correctitude, correctness, exactitude, exactness, fairness, justice, justness, regularity, rightness, soundness, truth
richtigstellen adjust, correct, put (set) right, rectify
Richtigstellung adjustment, correction, dementi, reclamation, rectification
Richt
—**linien** (general) directions, directives, (general) instructions, lines, guiding principles (rules), regulations, rules of conduct
—**maß** gauge, standard
—**preis** basic (standard) price
—**satz** basic (standard) rate
—**schnur** direction, guidance, (guiding) line, guiding principle, precept, rule(s), rules of conduct, standard
Richtung aim, course, direction, drift, line, movement, route, tendency, trend, turn, way
richtunggebend (—weisend) constitutive, directive
Rimesse remittance
— **machen** make remittance, remit
Ring circle, combine, pool, ring, syndicate, trust
Risiko danger, hazard, jeopardy, peril, risk, venture
—, **ohne (risikolos)** without risk
—, **auf eigenes** at one's own risk
sich einem — aussetzen incur (run) a risk
— **eingehen** incur (run, take) a risk
— **laufen** run a risk
— **tragen** bear (entertain, take) a risk
— **übernehmen** accept (assume, undertake) a risk
riskant adventurous, hazardous, perilous, risky
riskieren hazard, jeopardize, risk, run (take) a risk, venture
Rivale competitor, rival
rivalisieren compete (with), rival
Rivalität competition, rivalry, rivalship
Robe dress, gown, robe
roh brutal, coarse, crude, gross, raw, rough, rude, vulgar
Roh
—**ertrag** gross income
—**gewinn** gross profit

Rohheit brutal act(ion), brutality, coarseness, crudeness, rawness, roughness, rudeness
Rohling rowdy
Rolle list, part, register, rôle, roll
Rotes Kreuz Red Cross
Rotkreuzflagge Red Cross flag
Routine (daily) practice, routine
—arbeit routine work
—aufgabe routine duty
—bericht routine report
routinemäßig as a matter of routine
routiniert experienced, practised, skilled, smart, versed
Rubrik category, class, column, head, heading, rubric, title
Rück
—abtretung reassignment, reconveyance, retrocession
—anspruch counterclaim
—antwort reply
—berufung recall
—bleibsel remainder, remnant, residue, rest
—blick retrospect
—bürge (-bürgschaft) counter-security
rückdatieren date back, postdate
Rückendeckung aid, assistance, background, backing, cover, support
rückerstatten give (pay) back, refund, reimburse, repay, replace, restitute, restore, return
Rückerstattung refund, reimbursement, repayment, restitution, restoration, return
Rückerstattungs
—anspruch claim for restitution (repayment), restitution(al) claim
—pflicht obligation of repayment
—verpflichteter restitutor
Rückfall relapse, reversion, setback, recidivism
—, im in case of recidivism
Rückfall
—anspruch (—recht) reversionary interest, right of reversion
—gut reversion estate
rückfällig recidivous, relapsing, revertible
— werden become recidivous, have a relapse, revert
rückfälliger Verbrecher recidivist
Rückfälligkeit relapse
Rückfall
—recht s. -anspruch
Rückfalls
—strafe penalty in case of repetition
—verbrecher recidivist
—vergehen second offence
Rückforderung counterclaim, counterdemand, reclamation
Rückfrage counterquestion, inquiry, query
Rückgabe restitution, restoration, retrocession, return
rückgabepflichtig returnable
Rückgang decline, decrease, downward movement, drop, fall(ing), retrocession, recession, regress, retrogradation, retrogression, return
rückgängig declining, falling, retrograde
— machen annul, break off, call off, cancel, countermand, rescind, retract, revoke, undergo
Rückgängigmachung annulment, cancellation, rescission, withdrawal
Rückgriff indemnity, recourse
— nehmen have recourse
Rückgriffs
—anspruch claim for indemnification (indemnity)
—klage action for recourse
—recht right of recourse
Rückhalt backing, reserve, stay, support
rückhaltlos frank, reserveless, unconditional, unqualified, unreserved, unrestricted, without reserve (restraint)
Rückhaltlosigkeit unreservedness
Rückhaltung retention
Rückkauf redemption, repurchase
Rücklage reserve(s), reserve fund
rückläufig declining, downward, falling, recurrent, retroactive, retrograde, retrogressive
rücklings from behind

Rücknahme revocation, taking back, withdrawal
Rückporto return postage
Rückschau retrospect
rückschauend in retrospect, retrospective
Rückschluß conclusion
Rückschreiben answer, reply, rescript
Rückschritt reaction, regress, retrocession, retrograde step, retrogression, setback
rückschrittlich retroactionary, retrograde, retrogressive
Rücksicht consideration, regard, respect
— **nehmen** consider, have regard for, pay attention to, take into account, take notice of
Rücksichtnahme consideration, regard
rücksichtslos inconsiderate, reckless, regardless
Rücksichtslosigkeit inconsiderateness, lack of consideration, recklessness
rücksichtsvoll considerate, regardful, thoughtful
Rücksprache conference, consultation
—, **nach** after conferring (consultation, consulting) (with)
— **nehmen** confer (with), consult
Rückstand arrears, balance, remainder, remnant, residue, rest, outstanding debts
in — geraten fall behind, fall (get) into arrears, get behindhand
im — sein be in arrears, be behindhand (behind in)
rückständig antiquated, in arrears, back, backward, behind, behind the time, delinquent, obsolete, old-fashioned, outstanding, overdue, underdeveloped, unpaid
— **sein** be in arrears, be behind (the time)
— **werden** fall behind, fall into (get in) arrears
Rücktritt abdication, cancellation, rescission, resignation, retirement, retreat
seinen — erklären tender (hand in, send in) one's resignation, declare one's withdrawal, resign
Rücktritts
—**alter** age of retirement, retiring age
—**bestimmung** escape clause
—**erklärung** declaration of withdrawal, resignation
—**frist** limitation of withdrawal, escape period
—**gesuch** resignation
— — **einreichen** hand in (send in, tender) one's resignation
—**klage** rescissory action
—**klausel** cancellation (escape) clause
—**recht** right of cancellation
—**schreiben** (letter of) resignation
—**termin** retiring date
rückumwandeln reconverse
Rückumwandlung reconversion
rückvergüten refund, reimburse, repay, replace
Rückvergütung drawback, refund, reimbursement, repayment, return
rückversichern reassure, reinsure
Rückversicherung reassurance, reinsurance
rückwirken be retroactive, react (on)
rückwirkend reacting, retroactive, retrospective
Rückwirkung reaction, repercussion, retroaction, retroactive, effect, retrospectiveness
rückzahlbar redeemable, reimbursable, repayable, returnable, terminable, to be paid back (redeemed)
Rückzahlbarkeit redeemability, repayability
rückzahlen redeem, refund, reimburse, repay
Rückzahlung amortization, redemption, refund, reimbursement, repayment, return
Rückzahlungs
—**bedingungen (-bestimmungen)** terms of redemption (repayment)
—**tag** day of repayment (redemption)

—termin date of repayment (redemption)
—wert redemption value
—zoll drawback

Rückzug retreat, return
— machen beat a retreat

Ruf appointment, call(ing), character, credit, cry, fame, name, record, renown, report, reputation, repute, respect, shout, signal, standing, summons, vocation
um den guten — bringen bring in disrepute, ruin a person's reputation
einen guten — genießen (besitzen) be of good report, bear a good character
in üblen — bringen bring disrepute upon, defame
in gutem (schlechtem) — stehen be well (ill) reputed

rufen call, cry, shout, summon
— lassen send for
—, um Hilfe call (cry, shout) for help
—, zur Ordnung call to order

Ruf
—mord smearing campaign
— — begehen ruin a person's good reputation
—name Christian (first) name
—nummer call number

Rüge admonition, blame, censure, claim, denunciation, reprimand, reproach, reproof
— bekommen (erhalten) be reprimanded
— erteilen reprimand, reprove

Rügefrist limitation of claims

rügen blame, censure, find fault with, make a claim, reprehend, reprimand, reprove

Ruhe balance, calm, composure, imperturbability, leisure, peace, quiescence, quiet, recreation, repose, rest, silence, tranquillity
sich zur — setzen retire
die öffentliche — stören break the public peace
die öffentliche — wiederherstellen restore the public peace

Ruhegehalt (retiring) pension, retired (retirement) pay, superannuation

Ruhegehalts
—alter retiring age
—empfänger pensionary, pensioner

Ruhen abeyance, repose, rest, resting, stay, suspension

ruhen be in abeyance, be interrupted (suspended), be at a standstill, be in suspense, cease, repose, rest, stay

ruhen auf be based (founded) on, be supported by, rest on

Ruhestand pension, retirement
—, im pensioned off, retired
im — leben live in retirement (retired)
in den — treten retire
in den — versetzen pension off, retire, superannuate

Ruhestifter peace maker

Ruhestörer disturber of the peace

Ruhestörung breach (disturbance) of the peace, disorderly conduct, nuisance, riot(ing)

Ruhetag day of rest, day off, holiday, rest day
—, öffentlicher public holiday

Ruhezeit (time of) rest

ruhig calm, composed, cool, dull, easy, lifeless, peaceful, quiescent, quiet, at rest, retired, silent, smooth, steady, still, taciturn, tranquil

Ruhm fame, glory, honour, praise, renown, reputation

Ruin decay, fall, ruin, undoing

ruinieren be ruinous to, cause ruin, destroy, dilapidate, mar, ruin, spoil, wreck

Ruinierung ruination

ruinös ruinous

Rund
—erlaß circular (note, notice), inter-office memo
—frage inquiry (by circular), poll, questionnaire
—gang beat, round, tour
—schreiben circular (letter, note, notice)

S

Saal hall, room
Gerichts- court room
Sabotage sabotage
— treiben sabotage
—abwehr countersabotage
—akt (act of) sabotage
—prozeß sabotage trial
—recht right of sabotage
—versuch attempt at sabotage
sabotieren frustrate, sabotage, torpedo
Sach
—angabe statement of facts
—anlagen (—anlagevermögen) tangible fixed assets
—bearbeiter appointed agent, competent clerk (official, person), expert, official (person) in charge, referee
—beschädigung damage to property, wilful destruction
—beweis objective proof, material evidence
—bezüge payment (remuneration) in kind, perquisites
—darstellung statement of facts, stated case
— —, falsche misstatement of facts
sachdienlich appropriate, helpful, pertinent, practical, relevant, serviceable, suitable, to the purpose, useful
Sachdienlichkeit pertinence, relevance, relevancy
Sache action, affair, business, case, cause, circumstance, concern, event, fact, issue, item, job, lawsuit, matter, object, point, thing
Ansichts- matter of opinion
Bagatell- petty case (cause)
Ehe- marriage matter
Ehren- matter of honour
Form- matter of form, procedural matter
Haupt- principal (chief, essential) matter
Neben- incident, incidental (minor, secondary, subordinate) matter
Privat- private matter
Streit- (matter at) issue
Straf- criminal case, penal matter
Zivil- civil matter (case)
Sache
zur — gehörig pertinent, relevant, to the point
nicht zur — gehörig beside the mark, irrelevant, off the point
— aufrufen call a case (cause)
bei der — bleiben keep (stick) to the point
— führen plead a cause
sich an die — halten keep to the facts
zur — kommen come to the point, get down to business
gemeinsame — machen mit make common cause with
die — schwebt matter is in abeyance
zur — sprechen speak to the point
seiner — gewiß sein feel sure about the matter
— verfechten defend a cause
— verfolgen follow up (proceed with) a matter
— verhandeln hear (proceed with, sit on, try) a case
— verlieren lose a case
seine — verstehen know one's job
sich aus der — ziehen draw out of the affair
Sach
—eigentum tangible property (assets)
—einlage contribution in kind
—einwand plea, material allegation
Sachen belongings, chattels, effects, goods, objects, things
—, in concerning, in matters of, in the matter of, in re, regarding
in — gegen in re (the case, lawsuit) versus

Sachenrecht law of objects (property), real estate law, real right
Sach
—entscheidung decision on the facts
—erklärung definition
—gebiet field, province, subject
—gegenstand subject matter
sachgemäß appropriate, pertinent, proper, suitable, to the purpose
Sach
—güter material goods
—kenner (—kundiger) authority, connoisseur, expert, specialist
—kenntnis (—kunde) expert (factual, special) knowledge, expertise, experience, knowledge of the facts (subject)
sachkundig acquainted (familiar) with the matter, competent, experienced, expert, skilled, specialist, versed
Sach
—lage circumstances, facts, position, situation, state of affairs (things)
—leistung payment (performance) in kind
sachlich actual, detached, essential, factual, impartial, material, matter-of-fact, non-personal, pertinent, practical, objective, real, realistic, relevant, substantial, technical, to the point, unbiassed, unprejudiced
Sach
—lichkeit detachment, essentiality, impartiality, matter-of-factness, objectiveness, objectivity, practicality, reality, realism, relevance(cy)
—register (subject) index, table of contents
—schaden damage to property, material damage
—spende donation (gift) in kind
—verhalt bearings, circumstances, facts
— —, wahrer actual state of affairs, true facts
— — darlegen give (present, state) the facts
—vermögen tangible property (assets)
sachverständig expert
Sachverständigen
—ausschuß committee of experts, expert (standing) committee
—bericht (—gutachten) expert (expert's) opinion, expertise
— — einholen take an opinion
—beweis expert evidence
—erklärung sworn statement
—gebühr expert's fee
—gremium group of experts
—untersuchung expert inquiry
—urteil award
—vermögen material assets
Sachverständiger authority, expert, specialist
—, beeidigter (vereidigter) sworn expert
—, medizinischer medical expert
—, juristischer legal expert
Sach
—verständnis experience, knowledge of the facts (subject)
—verzeichnis index, inventory, schedule, table of contents
—walter administrator, agent, attorney, councellor, counsel, legal adviser, (legal) representative, solicitor, trustee
—waltung administration, management
—wert real value
—werte material (tangible) assets
—zusammenhang actual (factual) relation, connexity of facts
saldieren balance, clear, offset, set off, settle, square
Saldo balance
Sammelbegriff comprehensive term
Sammelklausel general clause
sammeln accumulate, amass, canvass, collect, compile, concentrate, gather, heap, hoard, mass, pile, store, treasure up
—, sich concentrate, compose oneself, recover (oneself), regain one's composure
Sammel
—name collective name
—paß collective passport

—platz depot, meeting place
—stelle collecting station (point), depot
Sammler amasser, collector, compiler, gatherer, hoarder
Sammlung accumulation, assembly, balance of mind, collectedness, collection, compilation, composure, concentration, gathering, hoarding, selection
Dokumenten— (Urkunden—) collection of documents
Entscheidungs— law reports
Gesetzes— compendium of laws, digest
sanieren clear, cure, reconstruct, reorganize, restore, sanitate
Sanierung reconstruction, reorganization, restoration, sanitation
sanitär sanitary
Sanitäts
—beamter sanitary officer
—behörde board of health
—polizei sanitary police
—wesen sanitary matters, medical service
Sanktion sanction
sanktionieren sanction
Satisfaktion satisfaction
— geben give satisfaction
— fordern demand satisfaction
Satz amount, article, assortment, clause, copy, fee, limit, lot, phrase, price, proposition, rate, sentence, set, thesis
Satzung articles (memorandum) of association, by(e)laws, charter, institution, regulations, (standing) rules, statute(s)
satzungsgemäß (—mäßig) constitutional, statutory
satzungswidrig against the rules (articles, regulations), contrary to the statute, ultra vires
säubern clean, clear, mop up, purge, purify
Säuberung cleaning, clearing, mopping up, purge, purification
—saktion cleaning action, mopping-up operation
säumen delay, hesitate
Säumer defaulter
säumig behindhand, defaulting, delinquent, dilatory, in default, negligent, remiss, slow, tardy
Säumnis default, delatoriness, delay
—gebühr default fee
Schaden damage, defect, detriment, disadvantage, handicap, harm, hurt, infirmity, injury, loss, mischief, prejudice, tort
zum — von to the detriment of
— abschätzen appraise (assess, estimate, value) damages
— anrichten cause damage, damage, do harm (damage)
vor — bewahren protect from damage
für einen — einstehen be answerable (responsible) for a damage
— erleiden become damaged, suffer damage
— ersetzen (wiedergutmachen) make good a loss, pay damages, repair the damage
für einen — haften be liable for damage
— nehmen get damaged, suffer damage
— regeln settle for losses
— tragen bear the loss
— verursachen cause damage
— zufügen bring harm to, do damage to, harm, hurt, inflict injury upon, wrong
schaden be derogatory (an injury, prejudicial), damage, do harm to, harm, hurt, injure, prejudice
Schadens
—abschätzung (—berechnung, —feststellung) appraisal (assessment) of damages
—abfindung compensation, indemnification, indemnity
—anspruch (—forderung) claim for damages, claim in tort
—anzeige notice of damage, damage report
—ausmaß extent of damages
—bericht damage report, statement of damages (losses)

—ersatz amends, compensation, damages, indemnification, indemnity, payment of damages

Schadensersatz

— beanspruchen (fordern, verlangen) claim damages (compensation)

— erhalten (erlangen) recover damages

— leisten allow compensation, compensate, indemnify, make amends, pay damages

Schadensersatz

—anspruch action in tort, claim for damages (compensation), damage claim, right of indemnity (compensation)

—bestimmungen compensation provisions

—klage action for damages

—leistung compensation, indemnification, recovery of damages

—pflicht liability (obligation) to pay damages

schadensersatzpflichtig liable for damages (to pay damages)

Schadensersatz

—prozeß damage suit

—regelung (—regulierung) adjustment of damages (losses)

—versicherung liability insurance

Schadens

—fall, im in case of loss

—festsetzung damage assessment

—forderung claim for damages

—höhe amount (extent) of damages (losses)

—meldung damage report, notice of damage

—nachweis proof of loss

—ort (—stelle) place of loss

—umfang extent of damages

—ursache cause of loss

—verhütung loss prevention

—versicherung casualty (indemnity) insurance, insurance against damages (losses)

schadhaft damaged, decayed, defective, dilapidated, faulty, hurt, imperfect, injured, ruinous, spoiled, spoilt, worn out

Schadhaftigkeit damaged condition (state), defectiveness, faultiness

schädigen damage, damnify, do harm, harm, hurt, impair, infringe, injure, let down, prejudice, worry

Schädigung damage, damnification, derogation, detraction, detriment, impairment, infringement, injury, prejudice

schädlich bad, deleterious, detrimental, disadvantageous, harmful, hurtful, injurious, mischievous, noisome, noxious, pernicious, prejudicial, unwholesome

Schädlichkeit harmfulness, injuriousness, malignity, noisomeness, noxiousness, perniciousness

schadlos harmless, indemnified, without damage (loss)

— halten compensate, indemnify, refund, recoup

sich — halten indemnify (recoup, reimburse, repay) oneself

sich — halten bei hold responsible for

sich — halten für recover damages (one's loss)

Schadloshaltung compensation, indemnification, indemnity, recoupment

Schadlosigkeit harmlessness, hurtlessness

schaffen bring about (forth), call into life (existence), cause, constitute, create, establish, furnish, make, manage, procure, produce, provide, set up, work

schaffend active, creative, producing, productive, working

Schaffung creation, establishment, formation, organization, production, provision, setting up

Schafott scaffold

das — besteigen mount the scaffold

auf dem — enden end on the gallows

Schande discredit, disgrace, dishonour, ignominy, infamy, outrage, shame

schänden bring disgrace upon, deflower, deform, desecrate, disfigure, disgrace, dishonour, profane, ravish, spoil, violate
Schänder defamer, detractor, profaner, ravisher, slanderer, violater
schändlich abominable, atrocious, base, disgraceful, foul, ignominious, infamous, low, outrageous, scandalous, shameful. vile
Schändlichkeit atrociousness, baseness, disgrace(fulness), ignominousness, infamousness, shamefulness
Schandtat (disgraceful) crime, foul deed, infamous (shameful) action, iniquity
Schändung desecration, disfigurement, profanation, prostitution, rape, ravishing, sacrilege, violation
Scharfrichter executioner, hangman
Scharfsinn acuteness, discrimination, ingenuity, penetration, power of discernment, sagacity
scharfsinnig acute, discerning, ingenious, penetrating, sagacious, sharp-witted, shrewd
Scharfsinnigkeit acuteness, sagacity
Scharlatan charlatan, humbug, quack
Scharlatanerie charlatanry, humbug, quackery
Schatz treasure
Schatzamt Exchequer (GB), Treasury (USA)
Schatz
—anleihe treasury loan
—anweisung exchequer (treasury) bill (bond)
schätzbar appreciable, estimable, rat(e)able, valuable
Schätzbarkeit estimableness, rat(e)ability, valuability
Schätze riches, wealth
schätzen appraise, appreciate, assess, calculate, compute, esteem, estimate, evaluate, guess, judge, rate, reckon, respect, think, value
—, gering hold in low esteem
—, hoch have a great regard for, hold in high esteem
—, zu hoch overestimate, overrate, overvalue
—, zu niedrig underestimate, underrate, undervalue
Schätzer appraiser, appreciator, assessor, estimator, valuator, valuer
Schatz
—kammer s. —amt
—kanzler Chancellor of the Exchequer (GB), Secretary of the Treasury (USA)
—meister treasurer
— —amt treasurership
Schätzung appraisal, appraisement, appreciation, assessment, calculation, computation, esteem, estimate, estimation, guess, rating, regard, respect, valuation
schätzungsweise approximately, roughly
Schatzwechsel exchequer (treasury) bill (bond)
Schätzwert appraised (estimated) value
Scheck check, cheque
— annehmen accept a cheque
— ausstellen make out a cheque
mit — bezahlen pay by cheque (in cheques)
— einlösen cash a cheque
— fälschen forge a cheque
— zurückweisen reject (return) a cheque
Scheck
—betrug cheque fraud
—buch cheque book
—fälscher cheque forger
—fälschung cheque forgery
—zahlung cheque payment
scheiden depart, divide, divorce, part, separate, withdraw
—, aus dem Amte resign, retire from office
sich — lassen divorce, sue for a divorce
Scheidung divorce, separation
— aussprechen grant a divorce
— beantragen sue for a divorce
— einleiten start divorce proceedings

— **einreichen** file a petition for divorce
— **erlangen** get a divorce
auf — klagen sue for a divorce
in — liegen be in the divorce courts, have taken divorce proceedings against
Scheidungs-
—**begehren** application (petition) for divorce
—**erkenntnis** decree nisi
—**grund** cause (ground) for a divorce
—**klage** action for divorce, divorce suit
— — **einreichen** sue for a divorce
—**kläger** divorce petitioner, divorcer
—**material** divorce evidence
—**prozeß** divorce suit
—**recht** divorce act (law)
—**richter** divorce judge
—**urteil** divorce decree, decree nisi
— —, **provisorisches** decree nisi
— —, **absolutes** decree absolute
—**verfahren** divorce proceedings
Schein air, appearance, attestation, bill, blank, certificate, deed, document, fake, form, instrument, label, look, note, paper, pretence, receipt, semblance, sham, slip, ticket
Anmelde- application (registration) form
Antwort- reply coupon
Empfangs- acquittance, receipt
Entlassungs- certificate of discharge
Erlaubnis- certificate, permit
Führer- driving licence
Geld- bank bill, banknote
Gewerbe trade (trading) licence
Lager- warehouse warrant
Jagd- hunting licence
Schuld- bond, debenture
Tauf- baptismal certificate, certificate of baptism
Toten- death certificate
Trau- marriage certificate
Waffen- gun licence
dem — nach apparently
zum — for form's sake, pro forma
Scheinangebot sham offer
scheinbar apparent, fictitious, likely, plausible, quasi, ostensible, seeming, specious
Scheinbeweis delusive (specious) proof
scheinen appear to be, seem
Schein
—**geschäft** fictitious (sham, simulated) transaction
—**tod** apparent death, semblance of death
scheintot seemingly dead
Schein
—**toter** apparently dead
—**vertrag** fictitious (sham, simulated) contract
—**wechsel** accommodation (fictitious, pro forma) bill
Scheiterhaufen stake
Scheitern breakdown, failure, ill success, miscarriage, shipwreck
zum — bringen defeat, foil, frustrate, shipwreck, wreck
scheitern be frustrated (lost, wrecked), fail, fall through, go to pieces, miscarry, split
Schema diagram, model, pattern, plan, schedule, scheme, sketch, system
systematisch schematic, systematic
systematisieren schematize
schenken acquit, bestow (upon), donate, endow (with), give, grant, make (give) a present, present with
—, **eine Strafe** remit a sentence
Schenker (Schenkgeber) donor, giver
Schenknehmer donee
Schenkung bequest, bestowment, donation, endowment, gift, grant, presentation
— **machen** donate
—, **durch** by free gift, by way of donation
Schenkungs
—**brief (-urkunde)** deed of gift (donation)

—empfänger donee, presentee
Schenkungssteuer gift tax, duty (tax) on donations inter vivos
schenkungsweise as a gift, by way of donation
Scherbengericht ostracism
Schicht break, class, gang, mass, pause, rank, rest, shift, turn
schicken consign, convey, dispatch, forward, mail, post, remit, send, transmit, transport
— nach send for
—, sich be becoming (fit, proper, suitable), come to pass, fit, happen, suit
sich — in accommodate (adapt, resign) oneself to, conform to, get accustomed to, put up with, yield to
schicklich appropriate, becoming, convenient, decent, proper, seemly, suitable
Schicklichkeit becomingness, convenience, decency, decorum, propriety, suitability
Schicksal destiny, fate, fortune, lot
schicksalhaft fateful
schieben graft, manipulate, move, profiteer, push, sell illicitly (on the black market), shift, smuggle, traffic, wangle
Schieber black marketeer, grafter, jobber, profiteer, racketeer, smuggler, trafficker, wangler
Schiebergeschäft graft, illegal transaction, profiteering (job), racket
—e machen graft, profiteer
Schiebertum (-unwesen) profiteering, trafficking
Schiebung job, graft, manipulation, profiteering, put-up job, racket, sharp practices, trafficking, underhand dealings, wangling
Schieds
—abkommen arbitration agreement
—amt arbitration board, board of conciliation
—ausschuß arbitration committee
—gericht arbitration court (committee), court of arbitration, tribunal
schiedsgerichtlich arbitral, by arbitration, arbitrational
Schiedsgerichts
—barkeit arbitration, arbitral jurisdiction
—gebühren (-kosten) arbitration charges
—hof court of arbitration
—klausel arbitration clause
—spruch (-urteil) award, arbitrament, arbitration
—verfahren arbitration (procedure)
—vertrag arbitration agreement
Schieds
—klausel arbitration clause
—mann arbitrator, umpire
—richter arbiter, arbitrator, referee, umpire
—richteramt arbitrationship, umpirage, umpireship
—richterin arbitress
schiedsrichterlich arbitral, arbitrational, by arbitration
Schieds
—sache arbitral case
—spruch (-urteil) award, arbitrament, arbitration
— — fällen arbitrate, make an award
—verfahren arbitration (procedure)
—vertrag (-vereinbarung) arbitration agreement
Schieß
—affäre shooting affair
—befehl order to shoot (fire)
schießen fire, shoot
Schießer shooter
Schießerei shooting
Schieß
—recht right to shoot
—vorschriften shooting regulations
—zeit shooting season
Schiffbruch failure, shipwreck, wreck
— erleiden be shipwrecked (wrecked)
Schikane annoyance, chicanery, trick, vexation
schikanieren annoy, chicane, vex

schikanös vexatious
Schild label, plate, sign, tag, ticket
schildern delineate, depict, describe, outline, portray, represent
Schilderung account, delineation, description, picture, portrait, recital, representation
— **geben** give an account of, recite
Schirmherr patron, protector, sponsor
Schirmherrin patroness, protectress
Schirmherrschaft patronage, protectorate, protectorship, sponsorship
Schlag beat, blow, coup, knock, smack, stroke, swipe
Schlagbaum toll gate, turnpike
schlagen beat, dash, defeat, hit, knock, smack
schlagend conclusive, convincing, striking
Schläger brawler, fighter
Schlägerei affray, brawl, fight (ing), fray, row, scuffle
Schlagwort catchword, slogan
Schlagzeile headline
schlecht amiss, bad, base, common, decayed, dubious, foul, hard, ill, incorrect, inferior, low, ordinary, poor, rotten, spoiled, spoilt, vile, wicked, wretched
— **behandeln** ill-treat, maltreat
— **beraten** ill-advised
schlechtgläubig in bad faith, mala fide
schlechtmachen backbite, malign
Schlechtigkeit badness, base (evil) deed, baseness, meanness, vile action, wickedness
schleichen creep, slink, sneak
sich davon— steal away (off)
sich hinein— steal in
schleichend creeping, furtive, lingering, prowling, slow, sneaking
Schleicher creeper, intriguer, prowler, sneak
Schleich
—handel black market, clandestine (illegal, illicit) trade, contraband (trade), smuggling, underhand dealings
— — **treiben** carry on an illicit trade, run contraband, smuggle
—händler black marketeer, contrabandist, illicit (clandestine) trader, smuggler, trafficker
—ware smuggled goods
schleppend dragging, flagging, heavy, languid, slow, wearisome
schlichten accommodate, adjust, arbitrate, arrange, compose, compromise, make up, mediate, reconcile, settle
Schlichter arbiter, arbitrator, conciliator, mediator, peacemaker, referee
Schlichtung accommodation, adjustment, arbitration, arrangement, composition, conciliation, mediation, settlement
Schlichtungs
—amt (-stelle) arbitration board, board of conciliation
—ausschuß arbitration committee
—verfahren arbitration (procedure)
—versuch attempt at reconciliation
—wesen arbitration system
schließen argue, arrive at, close, come to, conclude, consummate, contract, end, enter into, finish, form, lock, make, negotiate, reason, shut (down), sign, wind up
— **von (auf)** conclude (infer) from (to)
Schließfach lockbox, safe
Bank- safe (deposit box)
Post- post office box
Schließung breaking up, closing, closure, conclusion, shutdown, shutting
Schloß lock, padlock
— **erbrechen** pick a lock
hinter — und Riegel under lock and key
Schluß breaking up, close, closing, closure, conclusion, consequence, deduction, end, inference, issue, resolution, result, shutting, upshot, winding up

— **ziehen aus** conclude, draw a conclusion from
Schluß
—**abrechnung (-rechnung)** final account (settlement)
—**abstimmung** final vote (passage)
—**ansprache (-rede)** closing address (speech)
—**antrag** motion for closure
—**bemerkung** final observation, concluding remark
—**bestimmung** concluding (final) clause
— —**en** concluding (final) provisions
—**bilanz** final balance (sheet)
—**effekt (-ergebnis)** final result, upshot
Schlüssel cipher, code, index, key, quota
Code- cipher key
Nach- duplicate (skeleton) key, picklock
Schlüssel
—**frage** key question
—**gewalt** power of the keys
—**position (-stellung)** key (leading) position
—**wort** code (key) word
—**zahl** code (key) figure, index number
Schluß
—**examen** final examination
—**folgerung** argument(ation), conclusion, inference, reasoning
— — **ziehen (aus)** draw a conclusion (from)
schlüssig certain, conclusive, convincing, determined, logical, resolved, well-grounded
sich — werden make up one's mind, resolve
—, **nicht** inconclusive
Schlüssigkeit conclusiveness
Schluß
—**protokoll** final protocol (record)
—**punkt** last point
—**rechnung** s. -abrechnung
—**rede** s. ansprache
—**satz** concluding sentence
—**sitzung** closing (final) session, final meeting, last sitting
—**strich** final stroke
— — **ziehen** draw the line, put an end to
—**tag** last day
—**termin** final (latest) date, final hearing
—**urteil** final judgement
—**verfügung** final decree (order)
—**verhandlung** final hearing
—**wahl** final vote
Schmähbrief defamatory (insulting) letter
schmähen abuse, calumniate, defame, insult, libel, revile, slander
Schmäher calumniator, detractor, reviler
Schmähschrift lampoon, libellous pamphlet (publication)
—**schreiber** libeller
Schmähung abuse, calumny, defamation, libel, slander
schmälern belittle, curtail, cut down, derogate, detract, diminish, encroach upon, impair, lessen, retrench
Schmälerung belittlement, curtailment, cut, defamation, derogation, detraction, diminution, encroachment, impairment, lessening, retrenchment
Schmerzensgeld smart money
schmieren bribe, fee, grease a person's palm
Schmier
—**gelder** bribe (hush, slush) money, bribes, fee, graft, grease, palm oil, illicit (secret) commissions
—**unwesen** corruption, grafting
Schmuck (-sachen) jewelry, jewels
Schmuggel(-ei) contraband, illegal trade, smuggling, traffic
Alkohol- bootlegging, liquor smuggling
Devisen- currency smuggling
Waffen- arms smuggling, gun running
schmuggeln (Schmuggel treiben) bootleg, contraband, run contraband (hot, smuggled) goods
Schmuggelware contraband, contraband (hot, smuggled) goods
Schmuggler contrabandist, smuggler

Alkohol- bootlegger, rumrunner
—bande gang (ring) of smugglers
Schnell
—gericht summary court
——sbarkeit summary jurisdiction
—schrift shorthand, stenography
—verfahren summary proceedings
—verhör rapid trial
Schöffe alderman, juror, juryman
Schöffen
—gericht jury, jury court, court of aldermen
—liste (jury) panel
schonen look after, preserve, save, spare, take care of
schonend careful, considerate, forbearing, indulgent, lenient
Schonfrist days of grace
Schonung careful treatment, forbearance, good care, indulgence, preservation, protection
schonungs
—bedürftig convalescent, in want of rest
—los merciless, relentless, unsparing
—voll full of consideration
Schonzeit close(d) time (season)
schöpfen, Verdacht become suspicious, conceive a suspicion
Schöpfer author, creator, maker, originator
schöpferisch creative, inventive, productive
Schöpfung creation, production
Schranke bar, barrier, gate
Zoll- custom barrier, toll gate, tariff wall
Schranken bounds, limits
Handels- trade barriers
Schranken
— errichten errect barriers
in — halten hold in check, keep within bounds (the limits), restrain
— setzen check, limit, set bounds to
schrankenlos boundless, unbounded, unlimited
Schrankenlosigkeit boundlessness
Schreiben letter, note, writ, writing
Beglaubigungs- credentials, letter of credence
Ermächtigungs- letter of authority
Rund- circular (letter)
schreiben write
Schreiber author, clerk, secretary, writer
Schrift book, character(s), deed, document, hand, handwriting, letters, paper, publication, record, text, type, work, writ, writing
Ab- copy
Anklage- charge sheet
Beschwerde- (Klage-) bill of complaint
Denk- memorandum
Hand- hand, handwriting, manuscript
Schmäh- lampoon, libellous pamphlet (publication)
Unter- signature
Zweit- duplicate
Schrift
—führer secretary
—leiter editor
—leitung editorship
schriftlich by letter, in writing, written
hand- hand-written
Schrift
—probe specimen of handwriting (type)
—sache writing, written matter
—sachverständiger graphologist, handwriting expert
—satz file, pleadings, statement, writ
—sprache literary language
—steller author, publicist, writer
schriftstellerisch literary
Schrift
—stück deed, document, instrument, paper, record, writ, writing
—wechsel correspondence, exchange of letters
—zeichen character, letter
—zug character
Schritt action, footstep, measure, move, pace, step

— **halten mit** keep in step with, keep up with
gerichtliche —e ergreifen take legal proceedings against
den ersten — tun make the first move, take the initiative
—e unternehmen take action (measures, steps)
Schul
—abgangsalter school-leaving age
—alter school age
—anstalt college, school
—besuch attendance at school
—bildung education
Schuld blame, cause, debt, fault, guilt, indebtedness, liability, obligation, offence, sin, wrong (-doing)
— **ablösen (abtragen)** redeem a debt
— **begleichen (bezahlen, tilgen)** discharge (pay, settle) a debt
— **einklagen** sue for a debt
für eine — einstehen answer for a debt
— **erlassen** release from (relinquish) a debt
— **geben** ascribe (impute) the fault to, blame
— **haben** be guilty (liable, responsible), be to blame for
— **leugnen** plead not guilty
— **löschen** cancel a debt
— **auf sich nehmen** take the blame
in der — stehen von be in the debt of, be indebted to
— **tragen** be responsible (to blame) for, bear the blame
Schuld
—anerkenntnis acknowledgement of debt
—ausschließungsgrund defence
—bekenntnis admission (confession) of guilt, plea of guilty
schuldbeladen guilty, laden with crime
Schuldbeweis proof of guilt
schuldbewußt conscious of guilt
Schuld
—bewußtsein conscience of guilt
—brief bond, deed (document, instrument) of debt
—buch debt book (register), ledger
— **—forderung** registered debt
Schulden debts, indebtedness, liabilities
in — geraten get (fall, run into) debt, incur debts
sich etwas zu — kommen lassen become (make oneself) guilty of, commit a fault (crime, misdemeanour)
— **machen** contract (incur) debts, run into debt
in — stecken be in debt
schulden be indebted (to), owe
schulden
—belastet burdened with debts, deep in debt
—frei free from debt, unencumbered
—halber owing to debts
Schulden
—last burden of debts, encumbrance, indebtedness, liabilities
—macher contractor of debts
—masse liabilities, total indebtedness
—nachweis proof of debt
—tilgung discharge (payment, redemption, sinking) of debts
— **—sfond** sinking fund
Schuld
—erlaß release from (remission of) debt
—forderung claim, debt, demand
—frage question of fact (guilt)
— **—, Entscheidung über die** finding
—gefangener prisoner for debt
—haft imprisonment (detention) for debt
schuldhaft culpable, guilty, wrongful
Schuldherr creditor
schuldig culpable, due, guilty (of), owing, payable
un- guiltless, innocent, not guilty
für — befunden werden be found guilty
sich — bekennen acknowledge one's guilt, enter a plea of guilty, plead guilty
sich nicht — bekennen plead not guilty, enter a plea of not guilty

— bleiben remain due (in a person's debt)
auf — erkennen bring in a verdict of guilty
für — erklären (-sprechen) find (pronounce) guilty
für — erklärt werden be found (pronounced) guilty
für — halten account to be guilty
sich — machen commit, make oneself guilty of
— sein be (in duty) bound, be obliged (under an obligation), be guilty of, be indebted to, owe
Schuldiger convict, culprit, delinquent, guilty (party, person)
Mit- accessory, accomplice, associate in guilt
Schuldigerklärung (-sprechung) conviction, verdict of guilty
Schuldigkeit debt, duty, obligation
seine — tun do one's duty
Schuldklage action for debt
schuldlos blameless, guiltless, innocent, not guilty
Schuldlosigkeit guiltlessness, innocence
Schuldner debtor, obligator, obligor
Schuldnerland (-staat) debtor nation
Schuldrecht contractual law, law of contract
schuldrechtlich contractual, obligatory
Schuld
—schein bond, debenture, handbill, obligation, note of hand, promissory note, I.O.U. („I owe you")
—spruch verdict of guilty
—titel instrument of indebtedness
—übernahme assumption of debt
—übertragung transfer of debt
—verhältnis obligation
—verpflichtung liability, obligation
—verschreibung bond, debenture, handbill, obligation
—versprechen promise (of debt), promissory note
schuldvoll guilty
Schuldwechsel bill (note) payable
Schule academy, college, institute, school
Hoch- academy, college, university
schulen discipline, instruct, teach, train, tutor
Schüler pupil, scholar, schoolboy, student
Schülerin schoolgirl
Schul
—ordnung school regulations
—pflicht (-zwang) compulsory education
schulpflichtig schoolable, of school age
Schulprüfung school examination
Schulung education, instruction, schooling, training
—, berufliche professional training
Schulzeugnis school certificate, report
Schurke blackguard, rascal, scoundrel, villain
Schuß shot
— abgeben fire a shot
—bereich zone of fire, range
schußbereit ready to fire
Schuß
—feld zone of fire
—waffe fire arm
—weite range
— —, auf within range
— —, außer out of shot
—, in within shot
Schutz care, cover, custody, defence, escort, guardianship, protection, refuge, safeguard, safety, shelter, support
Feuer- protective fire
Schutz
unter dem — von under the protection of
sich in den — begeben von seek shelter with, take refuge with
um — bitten ask for protection
— gewähren afford (give) refuge (shelter)
in — nehmen defend, support, vindicate

unter seinen — nehmen take under one's protection
— suchen seek shelter
Schutz
—amt guardianship, protectorship
—befohlener charge, protégé, ward
—brief charter, (letter of) safe conduct
—bündnis defensive alliance
Schütze gunner, rifleman, shot
schützen defend, guard, honour, protect, safeguard, secure, shelter, vindicate
schützend protective, tutelary
Schützer guardian, protector
Schutz
—gebiet colony, preserve, protectorate
—geleit convoy, escort, safe conduct
—gesetz protective act (law)
—haft protective custody
—herr patron, protector
—herrschaft protectorate
Schützling charge, protégé, ward
schutzlos defenceless, unprotected
Schutz
—macht protecting power
—mann constable, policeman
—marke trademark
— —ngesetzgebung trademark legislation
— —nrechte trademark rights
—maßnahme (-maßregel) precaution, preventive (protective) measure
—mittel preservative, preventive
—polizei security police
—polizist s. -mann
—recht protective right
—rechte patent rights, trademark rights
— —, gewerbliche industrial rights
—verfügung order of protection
—verordnung protective statute
—vorrichtung (safe)guard, safety device
—wache escort, safeguard
—waffe defensive weapon
—zoll protective duty
schwach bad, feeble, infirm, low, moderate, poor, slack, slight, small, weak
geistes- feeble-minded, imbecile, weak-minded
Schwäche debility, feebleness, infirmity, weakness
Geistes- feeble-mindedness, imbecility, mental infirmity, weak-mindedness, weakness of mind
schwächen debilitate, diminish, enfeeble, lessen, weaken
Schwachsinn feeble-mindedness, imbecility, weak-mindedness, weakness of mind
schwachsinnig feeble-minded, imbecile, weak-minded
Schwachsinniger feeble-minded person, imbecile
Schwächung debilitation, diminution, weakening
schwanger expectant, pregnant
Schwangerschaft pregnancy
—sunterbrechung abortion
schwängern impregnate
Schwängerung impregnation
schwanken fluctuate, hesitate, vary, wave
Schwankung fluctuation, variation
schwarz black, dark, illicit, unlawful
— hören tap
—er Markt black market
—e Ware smuggled goods
Schwarz
—arbeit illicit work
—brennerei black distillation
—handel black marketing, illicit trade
—händler black marketeer (merchant), blacketeer, illicit trader, profiteer, trafficker
—hörer pirate
—markt black market
Schwebe dependence, pendency, suspense
in der — sein be pending (in suspense, undecided)
schweben be pending (in suspense, suspended)
schwebend floating, pending, in suspense, suspended, undecided

Schwebe
—zeit suspension period
—zustand abeyance, dependence, suspense
Schweigen silence
— gebieten impose silence
— bewahren keep silence
zum — bringen silence
schweigen be silent, keep silence, say nothing
Schweige
—geld hush money
—pflicht professional discretion (secret), secrecy
schweigsam discreet, quiet, silent, taciturn
Schweigsamkeit discretion, taciturnity
schwer bad, difficult, grave, great, grievous, gross, hard, heavy, onerous, ponderous, serious, severe, weighty
Schwer
—arbeit heavy work, hard working
—arbeiter hard (heavy) worker
schwerbewaffnet heavy-armed
Schwere gravity, heaviness, import, ponderousness, pregnancy, seriousness, severity, weight
Schwergewicht (-punkt) emphasis, stress
schwerbeschädigt badly injured, seriously disabled
Schwer
—beschädigter invalid
—verbrecher criminal, felon, gangster
schwerverletzt seriously wounded
Schwerverletzter (-verwundeter) major casualty, seriously injured (wounded) person
schwerwiegend pregnant, serious, weighty
schwierig arduous, awkward, complicated, delicate, difficult, hard, intricate, precarious, stiff, tough, troublesome, trying
Schwierigkeit arduousness, awkwardness, delicacy, difficulty, intricacy, precariousness, problem, trouble
Schwierigkeitsgrad degree of difficulty

Schwindel bubble, cheat, fraud, humbug, swindle
Schwindelei bubble, cheat, swindle, swindling
schwindeln cheat, humbug, sharp, swindle
Schwindler cheat, crook, grafter, imposter, sharper, trickster
Heirats- wedding hoaxer
—bande gang of swindlers (sharpers)
schwören swear, take an oath
—, Rache swear revenge, vow vengeance
—, Treue swear fidelity
—, falsch commit perjury, forswear (oneself), perjure, swear falsely
Schwörer swearer
Schwund decay, decline, diminution, disappearance, dwindling, falling, leakage, loss, shrinkage
Schwur oath, vow
— ablegen (leisten) swear (take) an oath, make a vow
Schwur
—formel wording of an oath
—gericht (court of) assizes, jury (court)
—gerichtsverfahren trial by jury (assizes)
—zeuge sworn witness
See
—amt Court of Admiralty (GB), maritime (naval) court
seefahrend sea-going, seafaring
seefest sea-proof, seaworthy
See
—gebrauch maritime custom, custom at sea
—gericht s. -amt
— —sbarkeit maritime jurisdiction
—gesetz maritime (naval, sea) law
—handel maritime (oversea) trade
— —srecht merchant shipping act (law)
—herrschaft command (control) of the sea, naval supremacy
—kontrolle naval control
—krieg naval war(fare), war at sea

— **—srecht** articles of war at sea, law of naval warfare
—macht maritime (naval, sea) power, power at sea, naval force, navy
—mann mariner, seaman, sailor
— **—sbrauch** seamen's custom (usage)
—not distress (at sea)
—offizier naval officer
—paß sea letter (pass), ship's passport, shipping permit
—räuber buccaneer, pirate
—räuberei piracy
—recht maritime (naval) law
—sache naval affair
—schaden average, sea damage
—streitkräfte naval forces
—stützpunkt naval base
—transport sea transport, shipment by sea
seetüchtig seaworthy
Seetüchtigkeit seaworthiness
Seeunfall accident at sea
seeuntauglich (seeuntüchtig) unseaworthy
See
—untüchtigkeit unseaworthiness
—versicherung marine insurance
—vertrag marine contract
—wechsel sea bill
—weg sea route
—wesen marine, maritime (naval) affairs, shipping concerns
—zeichen sea mark
Seite aspect, direction, face, flank, page, party, side, wing
Gegen- adverse party, counterside, other side, opposite party (side)
seitens by, on the part (side) of
Sekretär clerk, secretary
General- secretary general
Sekretariat secretariat(e), secretary's office
Sekretärin lady clerk, secretary
Sektion autopsy, branch, dissection, paragraph, post mortem, section
—schef departmental chief (head)
Sektor sector
Sekundant second
sekundär secondary
Sekundawechsel second (of exchange)
sekundieren accompany, second
Sekundogenitur right of the younger son
selbst in person, personally, oneself
—, von automatically, mechanically, of itself, of one's own accord, spontaneously, voluntarily
Selbst
—achtung self-esteem (-estimation, -respect)
selbständig autonomous, independent, individual, original, self-reliant, self-supporting, separate, sovereign, unaided, unassisted
Selbständigkeit autonomy, independence, sovereignty
Selbst
—anklage (-beschuldigung, -bezichtigung) self-accusation, self-incrimination
—beherrschung self-command (-control, -possession)
—bestimmung autonomy, independence, self-determination, sovereign right
— **—srecht** right of self-determination
—betrug self-deceit (-deception, -delusion)
—disziplin self-discipline
—einschätzung self-assessment
—erhaltung self-preservation
— **—srecht** right of self-preservation
— **—strieb** instinct of self-preservation
selbstgerecht self-righteous
Selbst
—gerechtigkeit self-righteousness
—herrschaft autocracy, self-command
—herrscher autorat
—hilfe self-aid (-defence, -help, -redress)
—interesse self-interest
—kosten (— —preis) cost price, prime cost
—kritik self-criticism
—mord suicide

— — **begehen** commit suicide
Selbstmordabsicht suicidal intent
Selbstmörder suicide
selbstmörderisch suicidal
in —er Absicht with the intent to commit suicide
Selbstmord
—klausel suicidal clause
—versuch attempted suicide
Selbst
—rechtfertigung self-justification
—regierung autonomy, self-administration (—government)
—schuldner original (principal) debtor
als — — haften be liable as original (principal) debtor
—schuß spring-gun
—schutz self-protection
—täuschung self-deception (—delusion)
—vernichtung self-destruction
—verschulden one's own fault
—versorger self-supporter
—versorgung autarchy, self-sufficiency (-support)
selbstverständlich natural, obvious, of course, self-evident
Selbst
—verständlichkeit matter of course
—verstümmelung autotomy, self-mutilation
—verteidigung self-defence
—verwaltung autonomy, local government, self-administration (-government)
Selbst
—zensur self-censorship
—zerstörung self-destruction
Senat senate
Senator senator
senatorisch senatorial
Senats
—ausschuß (—kommission) senate, committee, senatorial commission
—beschluß senatorial decree (vote)
—bezirk senatorial district
—mitglied senate member, senator
—präsident president of the senate
—sitz senatorial seat
—sitzung senate session
—wahlen senatorial elections
senden broadcast, consign, dispatch, forward, mail, post, remit, send, transmit
Sender broadcasting station, sender, transmitter
Geheim— mystery station
Schwarz— pirate station
Sendung cargo, consignment, delivery, dispatch, forwarding, mailing, mission, posting, remittance, sending, shipment, transmission
Senkung cut(ting), lowering, reduction
senken cut, drop, lower, reduce
Sensation sensation, thrill
sensationell sensational, thrileing
Sensationslust sensationalism
separat apart, particular, separate, special
Separat
—abkommen (—vertrag) separate (special) agreement (contract, treaty)
—frieden separate peace
Separatismus separatism
Separatist separatist
separatistisch separatist
Sequester compulsory administration, (official) receiver, sequestration, sequestrator, trustee
Sequestration attachment, compulsory administration, sequestration, seizin
sequestrierbar attachable, seizable
sequestrieren attach, put in trust, seize, sequester, sequestrate
Serie issue, series
seriös reliable, respectable, serious, sound
Servitut easement, servitude
seßhaft domiciled, established, permanent, resident, sedentiary, settled, stationary
— werden settle
Sexual
—erziehung sexual education
—verbrechen (—vergehen) indecent assault, sexual offence

Sexualität sexuality
sexuell sexual
Sezession secession
—skrieg war of secession
sezieren dissect
Sezierung dissection
sicher certain, confident, good, positive, proof, reliable, safe, secure, in security, sound, steady, sure, trustworthy
Sicherheit assurance, bail, certainty, collateral, confidence, cover, guarantee (ty), positiveness, reliableness, safeguard, safety, security, surety, trustworthiness, warranty
—, öffentliche public safety
mit — annehmen take for granted
— bieten give security, offer security (a guarantee)
als — dienen serve as security (cover)
— geben (leisten, stellen) become (stand) surety, give security, guarantee
als (zur) — für as (in) security for
in — secure, in safety (security)
ohne — without guarantee (security)
Sicherheits
—abkommen security agreement
—arrest precautionary (preventive) custody (detention)
—ausschuß safety (vigilance) committee
—beamter police officer, security agent, vigilante
—behörde safety board
—bestimmungen safety regulations
—dienst secret service
—empfänger security holder, warrantee
—faktor safety factor
—fonds guarantee (security) fund
—garantie guarantee, guaranty, security
—geber warrantor
—geleit safe conduct
—gründe safety reasons
sicherheitshalber for safety, for safety's sake
Sicherheits
—kette safety chain
—klausel escape (safety) clause, safeguard
—kontrolle safety control
—leistung bail, bond, guarantee, security
— —, gegen on bail (security)
—maßnahme (—maßregel) precaution, precautionary (protective, safety) measure, safeguard
— —n treffen take precautions
—pakt security pact
—pfand deposit, guarantee, pawn, pledge, security
—polizei security police
—rat security council
—schloß safety lock
—vertrag security agreement (treaty)
—verwahrung preventive detention
—vorkehrung precaution, protective (safety) measure
—vorrichtung safety device
—vorschrift precaution, precautionary (safety) provision
—zone safe(ty) zone
sichern (sicherstellen) cover, guarantee, make safe, protect, safeguard, secure, seize
Sicherung (Sicherstellung) cover, guarantee (ty), protection, safeguard, security
Sicherungs
—fonds guarantee fund
—klausel safeguard
—übertragung protective conveyance
—verwahrung preventive custody (detention)
Sicht
—tage days of grace
—vermerk visa
—wechsel sight bill
Sieg conquest, mastery, success, victory
— davontragen (erringen) gain the victory, win (carry) the day
Siegel seal
— anbringen affix a seal to, seal

— **erbrechen** break a seal
unter dem — von under the seal of
Siegel
—**anbringung** affixing of a seal
—**bewahrer** keeper of the seal
—**bruch** breaking of a seal
siegeln seal
siegen be victorious, conquer, gain the victory, prevail, triumph (over), win (carry) the day
Sieger conqueror, victor, winner
siegreich conquering, triumphant, victorious
Signal mark, sign, signal
— **geben (signalisieren)** give a mark (sign), signal
Signatar signatory
—**macht** signatory power
—**staat** signatory nation
Signatur brand, mark, signature, stamp
signieren brand, designate, initial, mark, sign
Simulant malingerer
simulieren feign, malinger, pretend, sham, simulate
simultan simultaneous
Sinn faculty, import, intention, liking, meaning, mind, opinion, purport, sense, significance, signification, spirit, taste, tenor
sinngemäß analogous, correspondent
sinnlos absurd, brainless, futile, meaningless, senseless
sinnvoll pregnant, significant, suggestive
sinnwidrig absurd, preposterous
Sinnwidrigkeit absurdity, paradox, preposterousness
Sippe clan, consanguity, kin, kindred, kinship, tribe
sistieren apprehend, arrest, inhibit, nonsuit, stay, stop, summon, suspend
Sistierung apprehension, arrest, cessation, inhibition, nonsuit, stay, stoppage, summons, suspension
Sitte custom, fashion, habit, practice, tradition, usage
Sitten manners, morality, morals
Sittengesetz moral law
Sittenkodex moral code
Sittenlehre ethics, moral philosophy
sittenlos immoral, licentious, profligate
Sitten
—**losigkeit** immorality, licence, profligacy
—**polizei** vice squad
—**regel** moral precept, rule of conduct
—**richter** censor
sittenwidrig against good morals, contra bonos mores, immoral
Sittenzeugnis certificate of (good) conduct
sittlich decent, ethical, moral, respectable
un— immoral, indecent
Sittlichkeit morality, morals
Sittlichkeits
—**delikt (—verbrechen, —vergehen)** indecent assault, sex crime , sexual (immoral) offence
—**gefühl** moral feeling (sense)
—**verbrecher** sex criminal (offender)
Situation condition, occasion, opportunity, position, situation
—**splan** site plan
Sitz abode, chair, domicile, head office, headquarters, place, residence, seat
Amts— official residence
Haupt— head office, headquarters
Wohn— abode, domicile, residence
sitzen
— **(im Gefängnis)** be in prison, do time, sit in jail
—, **zu Gericht** sit in judgement on
Sitzstreik sit-down strike, stay-in strike
Sitzung conference, hearing, meeting, session, sitting
—, **in öffentlicher** in full session, in open court
— **abhalten** hold a conference (meeting), sit, be sitting, be in session

— **einberufen** convoke a meeting, summon a conference
— **eröffnen** declare a court in session, open a meeting
— **leiten** preside a conference
— **schließen** close (dissolve) a conference (meeting)
— **unterbrechen** adjourn a meeting
Sitzungs
—**bericht** (—**protokoll**) minutes (of a meeting, of proceedings), record (report) of a meeting (of proceedings)
—**pause** recess
—**periode** session, term
—**tag** day of sitting, meeting day
Skala scale
—, **gleitende** sliding scale
Skandal disturbance, noise, riot, row, scandal
—**fall** scandalous matter
skandalös outrageous, scandalous, shocking
Skizze rough draft (drawing), outline, sketch
skizzieren draft, draw, outline, sketch
Skonto (cash) discount
Skrupel scruple
skrupellos unscrupulous
sofort at once, directly, forthwith, immediately, prompt, right (straight) away
— **tot** killed on the spot
Sofort
—**hilfe** immediate aid
—**maßnahme** emergency (urgent) measure
—**programm** emergency programme
—**sache** urgent case
sogenannt so-called
Solawechsel promissory note, single (sole) bill
Sold pay, wages
Soldat soldier
— **werden** enlist, enter the army, join up
Solidar
—**bürge** joint surety (warrantor)
—**bürgschaft** joint surety (warranty)
—**gläubiger** cocreditor, joint creditor
—**haftung** joint liability
solidarisch joint (and several), jointly and severally
Solidarität solidarity
aus — streiken strike in sympathy
Solidaritäts
—**erklärung** declaration of solidarity
—**streik** sympathetic strike
Solidar
—**schuld** joint debt
—**schuldner** joint debtor
—**verpflichtung** joint obligation
solide durable, good, of good standing, reliable, respectable, safe, solid, solvent, sound, steady, strong, trustworthy
Solidität firmness, reliability, respectability, solidity, solvency, soundness, stability, steadiness, trustworthiness
Soll debit, target
— **und Haben** debit and credit
solvent able to pay, solvent, sound
Solvenz ability to pay, solvency, soundness
Sonder
—**abkommen** (—**vereinbarung**) separate (special) agreement (arrangement)
—**ausgabe** extra (separate, special) edition
—**ausgaben** extras, special expenditure
—**ausschuß** select (special) committee
—**ausweis** special pass
—**beauftragter** special commissioner
—**behandlung** special treatment
—**bericht** special report
—**bestimmung** saving clause, special provision
—**bestrebung** particularism, separatism
—**fall** exceptional (special, particular) case
—**friede** separate peace
—**gericht** special court
—**gerichtsbarkeit** special jurisdiction

—gesetz special act (law)
—interesse special interest
—kosten extra charges
—leistung extra performance
—nummer special edition
—recht liberty, privilege, preferential (special) right
—regelung separate settlement (treatment), special arrangement (regulation)
—sitzung extra session
—stellung exceptional (privileged, special) position
—tarif preferential (special) tariff
—vereinbarung s. —abkommen
—vertrag separate (special) agreement (contract, treaty)
—vollmacht special authority (power)
—vorrecht special privilege
—zoll specific duty
—zulage special bonus
sondieren sound
Sorge alarm, anxiety, care, concern, grief, solicitude, sorrow, troubles
— tragen attend to, see (to it) that, take care
Sorgeberechtigter curator, guardian, tutor
sorgen arrange for, attend to, care for, lock after, provide for, see to, take care of (that)
Sorgerecht curatorship, custody, tutorship
Sorgfalt accuracy, attention, care, carefulness, conscientiousness, diligence, exactness, precision
sorgfältig accurate, attentive, careful, caretaking, exact, painstaking, precise, with care
Sorte brand, description, grade, kind, species, sort, type
Sorten foreign currency, foreign notes and coins
—zettel bill (list) of specie
sortieren arrange, assort, classify, grade, shift, sort
Sortiment assortment, collection, range, set
Sortimentenhändler retail seller
Souverän sovereign
souverän sovereign, supreme
Souveränität sovereignty
sozial social
Sozial
—abgaben social (social service) contributions, social security taxes, old-age benefit taxes
—amt social welfare office
—aufwendungen social expenditure
—einrichtungen social services, welfare (social) institutions
—fürsorge social service, social welfare, welfare (social) work
—fürsorger welfare (social) worker
—gericht social (welfare) court
—gesetzgebung social legislation
sozialisieren communize, nationalize, socialize
Sozialisierung communization, nationalization, socialization
Sozialismus socialism
Sozialist socialist
sozialistisch socialist(ic)
Sozial
—kredit social credit
—lasten social charges (cost)
—löhne social wages
—ordnung social order
—partner employers and employees, social partners
—politik social policy
sozialpolitisch social-political, socio-political
Sozial
—versicherung social (social security) insurance
— —sgesetz National Insurance Act (GB), Social Security Act (USA)
— —sgesetzgebung social security legislation
—wissenschaft sociology
—zulage family allowance (benefit), social allowance
Sozietät company, partnership, society
Sozius associate, partner
spalten split
—, sich divide, split up
Spaltung cleavage, dissension, disunion, division, rupture, split(ting)
Spanne margin, span, spread

Spannung strain, strained relations, tension, tightness
Sparbuch savings (—bank) book
Spareinlagen savings (deposits)
sparen economize, save, spare
Sparer depositor, economizer, saver
Spar
—guthaben savings account (balance), credit balance
—kasse savings bank
—konto savings (—bank) account
—maßnahme economy measure
sparsam economical, frugal, parsimonious, saving, sparing, thrifty
Spar
—samkeit economy, frugality, parsimony, thrift, thriftiness
—vertrag savings agreement (contract)
Sparte branch, department, division, field, section, sector
Spekulant gambler, jobber, operator, speculator
Spekulation gamble, gambling, jobbing, speculation, venture
spekulativ speculative
spekulieren gamble, operate (for), reckon (on), speculate (on, upon)
Spende alms, charity, contribution, dole, donation, gift, present
spenden bestow, contribute, deal out, distribute, donate
Spender contributor, dispenser, distributor, donor, giver
Sperr
—auftrag stop order (payment)
—betrag blocked amount
Sperre ban, bar, barricade, barrier, barring, blockade, blocking, bolt, closing, closure, embargo, gate, inhibition, interdiction, obstacle, obstruction, shutting, stop, stoppage
Ausfuhr— export embargo
Ausgeh— curfew
Einfuhr— import embargo
Gesundheits— quarantine
Handels— embargo
Sperre
—aufheben lift a ban (an embargo)
— verhängen closure, impose a ban (an embargo)
sperren bar, barricade, block (up), blockade, bolt, close, closure, cut off, embargo, lay an embargo on, lock (up), obstruct, put a stop on, shut, stop, suspend
Sperr
—frist restrictive (waiting) period
—gebiet (—zone) prohibited (restricted) area, forbidden zone
—geld entrance money, tolerance
—konto blocked account
—stunde closing hour
—zeit closing time
—zoll prohibitive duty
Sperrung ban, barring, block, blockade, blocking, closing, embargo, obstruction, prohibition, stop, stoppage, stopping
—svermerk non-negotiability notice
Spesen charges, costs, expenses, fees
spezial particular, special
Spezial
—fall special case
—gebiet special branch (subject)
spezialisieren specialize, specify
—, sich specialize (in, on)
Spezialisierung specialization
Spezialist expert, specialist
Spezialität specialty
Spezial
—kenntnisse special knowledge
—vollmacht special authority (power)
speziell particular, special
Spezifikation itemization, particularization, specification
spezifizieren itemize, particularize, specify
Sphäre domain, sphere, zone
Spiel game, gambling, play
—, falsches cheating, foul play
aufs — setzen hazard, jeopardize, risk, stake, venture
spielen gamble, play, pretend
—, falsch cheat
Spieler gambler, player
Falsch— cheat, card-sharper, foul player

Spiel
—raum free play, latitude, margin, range, scope
— — gewähren leave a margin
freien — — haben have full scope
—regel rule of a game
—schuld gambling debt
—verbot disqualification, suspension
—verlust gambling loss

Spion plant, spy
Spionage espionage, intelligence
—abwehr counter espionage, counter intelligence
—dienst intelligence service
spionieren spy
Spitzel informer, police spy

Sprache diction, expression, language, parlance, speech, style, tongue
Amts— official language
Fach— technical language
Fremd— foreign language
Geheim— code language
Gerichts— law language, legal terminology
Geschäfts— business language
Handels— commercial language
Mutter— mother tongue, native language
Rechts— law language, legal terminology
Umgangs— colloquial language, slang
Zeichen— sign (symbolic) language

Sprach
—gebiet language area
—gebrauch linguistic usage, parlance, usage (of a language)
—kenntnis knowledge of a language
—studium study of a language

Sprechchor speaking chorus
—, im in unisono
sprechen consult, see, speak, talk
— für plead for
—, vor Gericht plead
—, Urteil pronounce judgement
frei— absolve, acquit, discharge, exonerate
schuldig — find (pronounce) guilty

Sprecher announcer, foreman, orator, speaker, spokesman
Sprechstunde calling (business, consultation, office) hour
Sprengbombe high explosive bomb

Sprengel parish

sprengen blast, blow up, break (up), burst (open), disperse, disrupt, dissolve, force

Sprengstoff blasting agent, explosive
—attentäter dynamiter

Sprengung break-up, dispersal, disruption, explosion

Spruch aphorism, award, dictum, judgement, maxim, passage, ruling, saying, sentence, text, verdict
Frei— verdict of not guilty
Richter— court decision (judgement, sentence)
Schieds— award
Schuld— verdict of guilty

Spruch
einen — fällen give a verdict, make an award, pronounce a sentence

Spur footprint, footstep, hint, lead, mark, print, remains, scent, sign, trace, track, trail

Staat commonwealth, country, fisc, government, nation, public, state
Angreifer— aggressor state
Anlieger— border (bordering, neighbouring) country (state)
Bundes— federal state
Frei— free state
Gläubiger— creditor nation
Heimat— home country
Kultur— civilized country
Mitglied— member country (state)
Nachbar— neighbouring country (state)
Polizei— police state
Puffer— buffer state
Rechts— constitutional state
Schuldner— debtor nation
Signatar— signatory nation
Stadt— city state
Volks— people's state

Staaten
—bund commonwealth, confederacy, confederation, federacy, federation
—kunde politics
staatenlos stateless, without a nationality
Staaten
—loser stateless person
—losigkeit statelessness
staatlich fiscal, government(al), national, political, public, state
Staats
—abgaben government (state) taxes
—akt act of state, governmental act
—akten state records (papers)
—amt public authority (office), government appointment
—angehöriger citizen, national, subject
—angehörigkeit citizenship, nationality, national status
—angelegenheit matter of state, state affair
—angestellter government employee, state employee
—anleihe government (public) loan
—anstellung government appointment (employment)
—anwalt district attorney, public prosecutor
—anwaltschaft public prosecution, public prosecutor's office
—anzeiger official gazette
—archiv Public Records (USA), Public Record Office (GB)
—aufträge government (public) orders
—aufsicht government (state) control, state supervision
—ausgaben public expenditure
—bank national bank, state bank
—beamter civil servant, civil officer, government (public, state) officer, state official
—beauftragter public agent
—behörde public authority (office)
—besitz government (state) ownership (property)
— —, im government-owned, state-owned
—betrieb government (state) enterprise
—bürger citizen, national, subject
— —kunde civics
staatsbürgerlich civic, civil, political, public
Staats
—bürgerrecht (— —schaft) citizenship, nationality
—chef head of the state
—dienst civil (government, public) service, public employment
staatseigen government-owned, state-owned
Staats
—eigentum public property
—einkünfte inland revenue, public revenue (income)
—examen government (state) examination
—feind anarchist, public enemy
staatsfeindlich anarchic(al), subversive
Staats
—form form of government
—gebiet state territory
—gefangener state prisoner
—gefängnis state prison
—geheimnis state (official) secret
—gelder public funds (money), state funds
—gericht state court
—geschäft state affair (business)
—gesetz state (statute) law
—gewalt public (state) authority, supreme power
—gläubiger public creditor
—grenze (state) border, frontier
—gut public property
—hilfe state aid
—hoheit sovereignty
—interesse public interest
—kosten, auf at public expense
—kredit public loan, government credit
—kunde politics
—mann politician, statesman
staatsmännisch statesmanlike
Staats
—minister minister, secretary of state
—notstand national emergency

—oberhaupt head of the state, sovereign
—papiere public bonds (securities) (stocks)
—polizei state (secret) police
—präsident president of the state
—prozeß state trial
—prüfung government (state) examination
—rat state council, Privy Council (Counsellor) (GB)
—recht political (public, state) law
—regierung (national) government, state government
—religion state religion
—sache state affair
—schuld national (public) debt
— —verschreibung state (treasury) bond
—sekretär secretary of state
—sicherheit public security
—siegel great (official, public) seal
—stelle public office
—stellung government employment
—steuern government (state) taxes
—streich coup d'état
—unternehmen government (state) enterprise
—unterstützung state aid (subsidy)
—verbrechen political crime
—verbrecher political criminal, state criminal
Staats
—verfassung (political) constitution
—vertrag convention, treaty
—verwaltung public (state) administration, government
—wissenschaft political science
—wohl public weal
—zuschuß state aid (subvention)
Stab corps, headquarters, number, staff
stabil solid, stable, steady
stabilisieren stabilize
Stabilisierung stabilization
Stabilisierungs
—anleihe stabilization loan
—fonds stabilization fund
Stabilität firmness, fixity, stability, steadiness
Stadium phase, stage, state
Stadt city, town
Stadt
—abgaben rates, municipal taxes, town dues
—amt (—behörde) municipal office (authority)
—anleihe corporation (municipal) loan
—archiv town records
—bank city (municipal) bank
—beamter municipal officer
—behörde municipal authority
—bezirk municipal (urban) district, ward
—gemeinde municipal borough, municipality, township
—gericht city (municipal) court
—halle city (town) hall
städtisch municipal, town
Stadt
—rat alderman, city (municipal, town) council (councillor)
—recht city (municipal, town) law, freedom of a city
—richter city magistrate
—schreiber town clerk
—staat city state
—verwaltung city (local, municipal, town) administration
Staffelpreis sliding scale price
Stamm blood, clan, family, house, line, race, skeleton, stock, tribe
Stamm
—aktie common share (stock), ordinary (original) share (stock)
—aktionär ordinary stockholder
—buch album, register
stammen (aus, von) be of, be derived (descended) from, come from, date from, descend from, originate from, spring off, have been written by
Stamm
—kapital capital stock, original (ordinary) stock (capital)
Stand caste, class, condition, level, order, position, profession, rank, rate, situation, standing, state, station, status
Ehe- married state, matrimony, wedlock
Familien- family status

Ruhe- retirement
Zeugen- witness box
Standard level, standard
standardisieren standardize
Standardisierung standardization
Standesamt register (office), registrar's (registration, registry) office
standesamtlich civil, common law, before the registry
Standes
—beamter registrar
—bewußtsein class-feeling
—register register of births, deaths and marriages
Standgericht court martial
standhaft constant, firm, persevering, pertinacious, steady, unyielding
Standhaftigkeit constancy, firmness, perseverance, steadfastness
ständig continuous, fixed, permanent, regular, standing, stationary, steady
Standpunkt point of view, position, standpoint, station, viewpoint
Standrecht martial law
standrechtlich under (according to) martial law
stark big, considerable, good, great, heavy, large, numerous, powerful, strong, strong-minded, vigorous, violent
Stärke force, fortitude, largeness, potency, potential, power, size, strength, vigour, violence
stärken stimulate, strengthen
Stärkung fortifying, invigoration, strengthening
Station station
stationär stationary
stationieren station
Statistik statistics
statistisch statistical
statt in lieu of, instead of
Stätte place
stattfinden come off (to pass), happen, occur, take place
stattgeben admit, allow, give way to, grant
statthaft admissible, allowable, competent, lawful, legal, legitimate, permissible, permitted, valid
Statthaftigkeit admissibility
Statthalter governor
statuieren enact, establish, decree, ordain
—, ein Exempel make (set) an example
Status state (of affairs), status
— quo actual state
Statut charter, regulation, statute
Statuten articles (memorandum) of association, regulations, rules, statutes
—recht statutory law
Steckbrief description, tipstaff's warrant, wanted circular, warrant of apprehension (arrest), writ of attachment
— erlassen take out a warrant against
steckbrieflich by (tipstaff's) warrant
— verfolgen search for a person by (tipstaff's) warrant
— verfolgt werden be wanted by the police
Stegreif (aus dem —) ex-tempore, off-hand
aus dem — sprechen extemporize, improvise, speak off-hand
stehen
in Beziehung — mit be in touch with
—, Bürge go security
—, zur Debatte be at issue
—, vor Gericht take one's trial
—, Rede answer
—, in Verdacht be suspected
stehend regular, standing
Stehlen pilfering, stealing, theft, thieving
stehlen commit larceny (theft), kidnap, misappropriate, pilfer, purloin, steal, take away, thieve
Stehler stealer, thief
Stehlsucht cleptomania, thievishness
steigen advance, improve, increase, mount, move up, rise
steigend advancing, growing, increasing, mounting, rising, upward

Steigerer auctioneer, bidder
steigern aggravate, augment, bid, enhance, improve, increase, intensify, outbid, raise, rouse, strengthen
Steigerung advance, aggravation, augmentation, development, enhancement, improvement, increase, intensification, raising, rise
Stelle agency, appointment, authority, bureau, charge, department, employment, job, office, passage, place, position, post, site, situation, spot, stand
an — von in lieu of, in (the) place of, instead of, vice
—, freie vacancy
an die — treten von replace, substitute, supersede, take the place of

stellen allocate, assign, bring in (forward), challenge, contribute, file, find, fix, furnish, give, lay, locate, make, place, post, produce, propose, provide, put (up), set, stop, submit, supply

stellen, jemanden bring to the police, catch
—, Bedingungen condition, stipulate
—, unter Beweis prove
—, vor Gericht bring to (up for) trial, produce to the court
—, in Rechnung charge, debit, put to account

stellen, sich appear, feign, present oneself, pretend
—, sich dem Gericht give oneself up to the law, surrender to the court
—, sich der Polizei give oneself up to the police

Stellen
—angebot employment (position) offered, offer of a post, vacancy
—angebote vacancies, want ad(vertisement)s, wanteds
—bewerber (employment) applicant, applicant for a post
—gesuch employment application, application for a post
—inhaber occupant (of a post), officeholder

stellenlos jobless, out of work (employment, job), unemployed, unengaged

Stellen
—markt employment (labo(u)r) market
—nachweis employment agency, labo(u)r exchange
—vermittler employment agent
—vermittlung employment agency

Stellung arrangement, attitude, capacity, character, disposition, employment, engagement, filing, footing, formulation, function, furnishing, giving, (foot) hold, job, level, line, occupation, place, placing, position, post, posture, putting, rank, regulation, situation, standing, state, station, status
Dauer- permanent position
Frage- interrogation, questioning
Lebens- permanent position, life-time job
Rechts- legal position (situation, status)
Sonder- exceptional (special) position
Vertrauens- confidential position

Stellung
—, ohne s. stellenlos
— bekleiden (innehaben) hold (occupy) a position
— nehmen comment on, take up a position on
— verlieren lose one's job (position)

Stellungnahme answer, attitude, comment, decision, declaration, endorsement, (statement of) opinion, point of view, reaction, statement

stellungslos s. stellenlos

stellvertretend acting, assistant, deputy, representative, vicarious, vice

Stellvertreter agent, attorney in fact, delegate, deputy, locum

tenens, proxy, representative, substitute
als — handeln act as deputy (substitute), deputize for, stand proxy for
zum — ernennen appoint as substitute, deputize
Stellvertretung agency, deputyship, proxy, representation, substitution
—, in by proxy
Stempel brand, die, impress, mark, stamp
Amts- official stamp
Unterschrifts- signature stamp
Stempel
—abgabe (—gebühr) stamp duty (tax)
—amt (—büro) stamp office
stempelfrei free from stamp duty
Stempel
—freiheit exemption from stamp duty
—gesetz Stamp Act (GB)
—marke duty stamp
stempeln mark, stamp
— gehen be on the dole
stempelpflichtig subject (liable) to stamp duty
Stempel
—steuer stamp duty (tax)
—steuergesetz Stamp Act (GB)
Stenogramm shorthand notes (report)
Stenograph shorthand writer, stenographer
Stenographie shorthand, stenography
stenographieren write (take down in) shorthand
stenographisch in shorthand, stenographic(al)
Sterbe
—beihilfe (—geld) death benefit
—fall death
—kasse burial fund
sterben (an) decease, die (from)
sterben
eines gewaltsamen Todes — die a violent death
eines (un)natürlichen Todes — die a(n) (un)natural death
—, bei einem Unfall be killed by an accident

Sterbe
—register register of deaths
—stunde dying hour
—tag dying day, day of death
—urkunde death certificate
—versicherung death insurance
Sterblichkeit death rate, mortality
stetig constant, continual, perpetual, stable, steady, undeviating, uninterrupted
Stetigkeit constancy, continuity, steadiness
Steuer assessment, customs, duty, imposition, impost, levy, rate, tax
Ausfuhr- export tax
Benzin- gasoline (petrol) tax
Börsenumsatz- stock exchange tax
Dividenden- dividend tax
Einfuhr- import duty
Einkommen- income tax
Erbschafts- death duty, inheritance tax
Gebäude- housing tax (duty)
Gemeinde- (borough, local, municipal) rate
Getränke- beverages tax
Gewerbe- trade tax
Gewinn- profits tax
Grund- land (property) tax
Hunde- dog licence (tax)
Hypotheken- mortgage duty
Junggesellen- bachelor's tax
Kapital- capital tax
Kapitalertrags- capital gains tax, withholding tax
Kirchen- church tax
Konsum- excise (duty), indirect tax
Kopf- personal tax, poll tax
Körperschafts- corporation tax
Kraftfahrzeug- automobile (motor vehicle) tax
Lohn- salary (wage, withhold) tax
Luxus- luxury tax
Mehrwert- surplus value tax
Nachlaß- s. Erbschafts-
Personal- s. Kopf-
Schenkungs- donation (gift) tax
Sonder- special tax, surtax
Stempel- stamp duty (tax)

Umsatz- sales (turnover) tax
Verbrauchs- s. Konsum-
Vergnügungs- entertainment tax
Vermächtnis- legacy duty
Vermögens- property tax
Wechselstempel- s. Stempel-
Steuer
—, direkte direct tax
—, indirekte excise (duty), indirect tax
Steuern
— auferlegen tax
— erheben collect (impose, levy) taxes
— berechnen (— festsetzen) assess taxes
— bezahlen pay taxes
— hinterziehen defraud the revenue
Steuer
—abgabe levy
—abkommen tax treaty
—abteilung tax division
—abzug tax deduction
—amnestie tax amnesty
—amt board of assessment, fiscal (tax[ation]) authority, inland revenue office, tax office
—angelegenheit tax matter
—anschlag assessment
—ausschuß tax committee
steuerbar assessable, dutiable, rat(e)able, taxable
Steuer
—barkeit rat(e)ability, taxability
—beamter revenue officer, tax assessor (official)
steuerbefreit tax-exempt (—free)
Steuer
—befreiung exemption from taxation (taxes), tax exemption
—begünstigung tax privilege
—behörde s. -amt
—belastung tax burden (charge)
—berater fiscal adviser, tax counsellor (adviser, expert)
—bescheid notice of assessment, tax assessment, tax bill
—betrag tax amount
—betrug tax fraud (offence)
—einnehmer tax collector (receiver)
—einspruch tax appeal
—einziehung tax collection
—erhebung levying of taxes, tax collection, taxation
—erhöhung increase in taxes
—erklärung tax return
—erlaß (—erleichterung, —ermäßigung) tax abatement (reduction, remission)
—erstattung tax refund
— —sverfahren tax refund proceedings
steuerfähig s. —bar
Steuer
—fachmann tax expert
—festsetzung tax assessment
—flucht flight from taxation, tax evasion
—forderung tax claim
steuerfrei duty-free, exempt from taxation (taxes), free of duty, tax-exempt (-free)
Steuer
—freiheit exemption from taxation (taxes)
—fuß (—grundlage) basis of taxation, tax rate
—gesetz finance bill, revenue act (law), tax law
— —gebung revenue laws, tax legislation
—gruppe tax bracket
—herabsetzung tax reduction
—hinterziehung tax evasion
—hinterzieher tax dodger
—hoheit power of taxation, tax jurisdiction
—jahr financial (fiscal) year
—klasse tax bracket
—last tax burden
steuerlich fiscal, tax
steuern control, direct, guide, pilot, steer
Steuer
—marke tax (revenue) stamp
—maßnahme tax measure
—nachlaß tax abatement (reduction)
—periode fiscal period
—pflicht tax liability
steuer
—pflichtig assessable, rat(e)able, taxable
Steuer
—pflichtiger ratepayer, taxpayer

—pflichtigkeit rat(e)ability, taxability
—prüfer tax inspector
—prüfung tax inspection
—recht revenue (tax) law
steuerrechtlich financial, fiscal
Steuer
—rückerstattung tax refund
—sache tax matter
—sachverständiger tax expert
—satz tax rate, rate of assessment
—schuld tax liability
—schuldner tax debtor
—senkung tax reduction
—strafe fine, tax penalty
—streit tax litigation (dispute)
—stufe tax bracket
—stundung tax deferral (respite)
—system financial (fiscal, tax, taxation) system
—tabelle tax schedule
—umgehung tax evasion (dogding)
Steuerung control, direction
Steuer
—veranlagung tax assessment
—vergehen revenue (tax) offence
—vergünstigung tax privilege
—vergütung tax refund
—verwaltung fiscal (tax) administration
—wesen finances, fiscal matters, taxation
—zahler ratepayer, taxpayer
—zahlung rate paying, tax payment
—zuschlag additional tax, extra duty, surcharge, surtax
stichhaltig plausible, proof, solid, sound, standing the test, valid
Stichhaltigkeit soundness, validity, weight
Stichprobe chance control, random test, sample (spot) check
Stichtag deadline, appointed (critical, crucial, decisive, fixed) date, key (target) date, term
Stickwaffe stabbing (thrusting) weapon
Stichwahl second ballot
Stichwort catchword, code (key) word, test word
Stichwunde stab, thrust(-wound)
Stief
—bruder half-brother, stepbrother
—eltern stepparents
—kind stepchild
—mutter stepmother
—schwester half-sister, stepsister
—sohn stepson
—tochter stepdaughter
—vater stepfather
Stift apprentice, convent, foundation, institution
stiften bequeath, cause, create, donate, endow, establish, found, give, institute, make, originate, produce, set up, start, subscribe
Stifter author, donor, founder, originator
Stifterin foundress
Stiftung bequest, donation, endowment, establishment, foundation, institution, trust
Stiftungs
—brief (—urkunde) charter of foundation, deed of donation, foundation deed
—fonds endowment fund
Stil manner, style
Gerichts- (Kanzlei-) law (legal) style
stilisieren compose, draft, formulate, frame, stylize, word
Stilisierung wording
still calm, dead, dull, dormant, flat, liveless, motionless, peaceable, peaceful, quiet, secret, silent, slack, sleeping, stagnant, still, tacit, tranquil, wordless
—er Teilhaber dormant (silent, sleeping) partner
stillegen close (down), shut down, stop
Stillegung closing (down), shutdown, stoppage
Stillhalteabkommen standstill agreement
Stillschweigen secrecy, silence
— auferlegen enjoin secrecy on
— bewahren keep quiet, keep (observe) secrecy (silence), maintain secrecy
stillschweigen be silent, keep silence

stillschweigend implicit, implied, silent, tacit
Stillstand stagnation, standstill, stop, stoppage
zum — bringen halt, shut down, stop
zum — kommen come to a standstill (deadlock), stop
stillstehen be at a standstill, be stagnant, stand still, stop
Stimmabgabe vote, voting
stimmberechtigt (—fähig) enfranchised, entitled to vote
—e Aktie voting share
Stimm
—berechtigter elector, voter
—berechtigung franchise, (right to) vote, suffrage
—bezirk constituency, electoral district
Stimme call, comment, suffrage, voice, vote
—n, abgegebene votes polled (cast)
—, ausschlaggebende casting vote
seine — abgeben cast (give) one's vote
—n sammeln collect votes
um —n werben canvass for votes
stimmen be correct (in order, right, true), cast (give) one's vote, poll, vote
— für give one's vote to, vote in favour of
Stimmen
—abgabe vote, voting
—gleichheit equality (parity) of votes
—mehrheit majority of votes
—minderheit minority of votes
Stimmenthaltung abstinence (abstention) from voting
Stimmen
—zahl number of votes
Stimm
—recht franchise, right to vote, suffrage
— —saktien voting shares (stocks)
stimmrechtslos non-voting
Stimmung atmosphere, disposition, feeling, frame of mind, humour, mood, temper, tendency
Stimmzettel ballot, voting paper
Stipendiat scholar, stipendiary
Stipendium bursary, exhibition, foundation, scholarship
Stipulation clause, stipulation
stipulieren stipulate
Stoff material, matter, subject (matter), substance, topic
Stopp ban, freeze, stop
stoppen freeze, interrupt, stop
stören annoy, bother, cause trouble, discommode, disturb, inconvenience, interfere with, interrupt, trespass, trouble
—, den Frieden break the peace
Störer disturber, intruder
Friedens- breaker of the peace, peacebreaker
stornieren annul, cancel, reverse
Stornierung (Storno) annulment, cancellation, reversal
Störung disturbance, encroachment, infringement, interference, interruption, intrusion, nuisance, obstruction, trespass
Straf
—akten criminal records
—änderung commutation of sentence
strafandrohend comminatory
Straf
—androhung penalty clause, (punitive, vindicative) sanction, threat of punishment
— —, unter under penalty
unter — — vorladen subpoena
—anstalt house of correction, penitentiary
—anwendung application of penalties
—antrag charge, request for prosecution, sentence demanded
— — stellen file a request for prosecution, bring a charge against
—anzeige charge, denouncement, report to the police
— — erstatten bring a charge against, denounce, report to the police
—aufschub delay, reprieve
—ausschließungsgründe legal reasons for exemption

—aussetzung remission of sentence
strafbar against the law, criminal, culpable, liable to punishment (prosecution), punishable
sich — machen be liable to prosecution, render oneself liable to punishment
—e Handlung offence (se), malfeasance, unlawful (wrongful) act
Straf
—barkeit criminal nature, criminality, culpability, guilt, punishability
—befehl (—entscheid) order of punishment, summons
—befugnis penal authority (power), power of sentence
—bestimmungen penal clause (statute), penal provisions, penalty clause
Strafe correction, fine, penalty, punishment, retribution
Disziplinar- disciplinary punishment
Freiheits- (Gefängnis-) imprisonment
Geld- fine, penalty
Höchst- maximum penalty
Konventional- stipulated penalty
Körper- corporal punishment
Mindest- minimum penalty
Ordnungs- disciplinary fine (penalty)
Prügel- flogging, corporal punishment
Todes- capital punishment, death penalty
— —, bei (unter) under penalty of death
Vor- previous conviction
Zuchthaus- penal servitude
Strafe
als — für as a punishment for
bei — von on pain of, under penalty of
— abbüßen (verbüßen) serve a sentence, undergo punishment
— absitzen do one's time, expiate one's crime in prison
— auferlegen impose a sentence
— bekommen be punished
— erhöhen increase a sentence
— erlassen let off, remit a sentence
— festsetzen determine (fix) a penalty
— herabsetzen decrease a sentence
— umwandeln commute a sentence
— verhängen impose (inflict) a sentence
— vollstrecken (vollziehen) complete (execute) a sentence
bei — vorladen subpoena
— zahlen pay a fine
strafen chastise, correct, punish
Straf
—erkenntnis sentence
—erlaß pardon, release of sentence, remission of penalty (punishment)
— —, allgemeiner amnesty
—ermäßigung reduction of penalty
straferschwerend aggravating
Straf
—erschwerungsgründe aggravating reasons (for punishment)
—fall criminal case
straffällig culpable, liable to punishment, criminal
— werden incur a penalty
Straf
—fälligkeit culpability, punishability, punishableness
straffrei exempt from punishment, unpunished
Straf
—freiheit exemption from punishment, immunity, impunity
—gefangener prisoner, convict
—gefängnis convict prison, house of correction, penitentiary
—geld fine, penalty
—gericht criminal court, tribunal
strafgerichtlich criminal
Straf
—gerichtsbarkeit criminal (penal) jurisdiction
—gerichtshof criminal court
—gesetz criminal (penal) law
—gesetzbuch criminal (penal) code

—gesetzgebung criminal (penal) legislation
—gewalt s. —befugnis
—haft detention, penal confinement
—herabsetzung reduction of a sentence
—justiz criminal (penal) jurisdiction, punitive justice
—kammer criminal court
—klage criminal (penal) action
—klausel penal clause (statute), penalty clause
—kolonie penal colony (settlement), convict settlement
sträflich criminal, culpable, punishable
Sträfling convict, prisoner
Strafliste criminal record
straflos s. straffrei
Straf
—losigkeit s. —freiheit
—mandat penalty, summons
—maß sentence
—maßnahme sanction, punitive, measure
strafmildernd extenuating, mitigating
Straf
—milderung mitigation of a penalty (of punishment)
strafmündig accountable, responsible
Straf
—mündigkeit accountability, responsibility, age of discretion
—porto extra postage
—prozeß criminal procedure (proceedings), penal suit, trial
— —ordnung criminal procedure code, rules of criminal procedure
—recht criminal (penal) law
strafrechtlich criminal, penal, under criminal (penal) law
— verfolgen prosecute
Strafrechts
—pflege (—sprechung) criminal (penal) jurisdiction
—praxis criminal practice
—reform penal reform
—wissenschaft criminology
Straf
—register criminal record, register of former convictions
—richter criminal judge, puisne judge
—sache criminal case, penal matter
—sanktion punitive sanction
—summe fine, penalty
—tat crime, felony, misdemeanour, offence, punishable act, tort, tortious act
—täter criminal, offender
—umwandlung commutation of punishment
strafunmündig unaccountable
Straf
—untersuchung criminal investigation
—urlaub leave from jail
—urteil judgement, sentence
—verfahren criminal procedure (proceedings), penal suit, prosecution
—verfolgung prosecution
strafverschärfend aggravating
Straf
—verschärfung aggravation of punishment
—versetzung disciplinary transfer
—verteidiger attorney, counsellor for the defence
—verteidigung defence in a criminal case
—vollstreckung (—vollzug) completion (execution) of a sentence
—vorschrift penal statute, penalty clause
strafwürdig penal, punishable
Straf
—zeit term (of confinement, of imprisonment)
—zoll penal duty
—zumessung award of punishment, fixing of penalty
—zweck punishment purpose
Strand
—gut flotsam, jetsam, stranded goods
—recht right of salvage
stranden be stranded (wrecked), founder, strand
Strang halter, rope
zum — verurteilen condemn to be hanged

Strangulation (Strangulierung) strangulation
strangulieren strangle
Straßen gleicher Ordnung streets (roads) of equal priority
Straßen
—handel hawking, street trade
—händler hawker
—kampf street fighting
—raub highway robbery
—räuber highwayman
—sperre barricade
—verkauf hawking
—verkehrsordnung rules of the road
Stratege strategist
Strategie strategy
strategisch strategic(ally)
streichen cancel, cross out, cut, delete, erase, expunge, obliterate, strike off (out)
Streichung cancellation, deletion, expurgation, obliteration, striking out
Streik stoppage of work, strike, walkout
—, wilder illegal (outlaw, wildcat) strike
General- general strike
Hunger- hunger strike
Protest- protest strike
Sitz- sit-down (stay-in) strike
Sympathie- sympathetic strike
Warnungs- warning strike
Streik, im on strike, striking
— abbrechen (einstellen) call off a strike
— ausrufen call a strike
sich im — befinden (be on) strike
— brechen break a strike
in — treten come out (go) on strike, down tools, stop work, strike
Streik
—ankündigung strike notice
—anweisungen strike orders
—aufhebung (—einstellung) calling off a strike
—ausschuß strike committee
—befehl strike order
—brecher strikebreaker
—drohung strike threat
streiken be (come out, go) on strike, down tools, stop work, strike
streikend on strike, striking
Streikender striker, walkout
Streik
—fonds (—kasse) strike fund
—führer strike leader
—geld (—lohn) strike pay
—klausel strike clause
—recht freedom of (right to) strike
—termin strike date
—verbot ban on a strike, injunction
—versicherung strike insurance
—welle strike wave
—zahlung strike pay(ment)
Streit argument, combat, conflict, contention, controversy, debate, difference, dispute, fight, quarrel, row, squabble
Grenz- frontier dispute
Kompetenz- conflict of authority
Rechts- dispute at law, lawsuit, litigation
Wett- competition
streitbar aggressive, argumentative, belligerent, combative, fighting, martial, militant, pugnacious, quarrelsome, valiant, warfaring, warlike
Streitbarkeit aggressiveness, combativeness
streiten altercate, argue, be at issue with, be at variance, combat, contend, dispute, fight, litigate, quarrel, struggle
streitend beligerent, contending, disputing, in dispute, litigant, militant
—e Parteien litigants
Streiter champion, combatant, disputant, fighter, quarreller, warrior
Streit
—fall action, case (at law), contest, controversy, dispute, (case at) issue, lawsuit, litigation, matter in dispute
—frage argument, contention, contentious issue, controversial question, point at issue, question

—gegenstand debating point, matter at issue (in controversy, in dispute)
streitig at issue, contentious, contestable, contested, controversial, debatable, disputable, disputed, in dispute (litigation), doubtful, litigious, pending
—, nicht incontestable, indisputable, noncontentious, noncontroversial, nonlitigous
streitig machen contend (for, with), contest, dispute
Streitigkeit argument, combat, conflict, controversy, difference, disagreement, dispute, litigation, quarrel, struggle
Streit
—kräfte (—macht) armed forces
—objekt s. —gegenstand
—punkt s. —frage
—rede dispute
—sache case under dispute, controversial matter, lawsuit, litigation, (matter at) issue
—schrift controversial (polemic[al]) treatise, disputation, pamphlet
—sucht litigiousness, quarrelsomeness
streitsüchtig litigious, quarrelsome
Streit
—verfahren contentious proceedings
—verkündung third-party notice
—wert value of the matter in controversy (dispute)
streng austere, close, harsh, precise, rigid, rigorous, severe, stern, strict, stringent, strong, uncompromising
— vertraulich strictly confidential
Strenge austerity, intensity, rigour, severity, sternness, strictness, stringency
strikt strict
strittig s. streitig
Strittigkeit contentious nature
Strohmann dummy, man of straw
Struktur make, structure
strukturell structural
Stück copy, extract, part, passage, piece, portion, unit
Beleg- voucher copy
Beweis- exhibit, piece of evidence
Bruch- fragment
Geld- coin, piece of money
Grund- (piece of) land, plot (of land)
Muster- sample
Schrift- document, paper
Student student, undergraduate
Jura- law student, student of law
Studentin girl undergraduate, woman student
Studie analysis, essay, sketch, study, survey
studieren mediate (upon), read (for), reflect, study
—, Jura study law(s)
Studium pursuit, reading, studies, study
Stufe bracket, degree, footing, grade, level, order, rank, rung, schedule, standard, step
stunden allow (give) time for, defer, delay, grant a respite (delay) for (payment), respite
Stunden
—arbeiter hourly worker
—geschwindigkeit speed per hour
—lohn wage per hour, time wage
—lohnarbeit time work
—plan schedule, time table
Stundung delay, extension of time, respite (for payment)
Stundungs
—antrag (—gesuch) request for respite
—frist delay granted for payment, respite
—vertrag letter of respite
Sturz abolition, collapse, comedown, crash, downfall, failure, fall, overthrow, overturn, ruin
stürzen collapse, fail, overthrow, overturn, ruin, subvert, upset
Stütze support
stützen back (up), base (on), countenance, found (on), retain, support
sich — auf be based on, rely on, rest upon
Stützpunkt base
subaltern subaltern, subordinate

Subalternbeamter subordinate official
Subjekt individual, subject
subjektiv personal, subjective
Subjektivität subjectivity
Submission (contract by) tender
Submissions
—angebot tender
—bedingungen terms of tender
—preis contract price
—vertrag contract by tender
Submittent contractor
Subordination subordination
subordinieren subordinate
Subsidien subsidies
— zahlen subsidize
substantiell substantial
Substanz body, capital, material, principal, substance
substanzieren particularize, substantiate
substituieren act as substitute for, replace by, substitute (for)
Substituierung replacement, substitution
Substitut substitute
Substitution substitution
subsumieren sum up, summarize
Subsumption summarizing, summary
Subvention bonus, bounty, financial aid, grant, subsidy, subvention
subventionieren grant financial aid, subsidize, subvention
Suchaktion search
Suchanzeige want ad, wanted
Suche inquiry, quest, search
suchen look for, search, seek
Sucht disease, mania, passion, rage
Stehl- kleptomania
süchtig addicted to, diseased, having a mania for
suggerieren influence by suggestion, prompt with, suggest
suggestiv suggestive
Suggestivfrage leading question
sühnbar expiable
Sühne atonement, expiation
Sühne
—maßnahme sanction
sühnen atone for, expiate
Sühne
—termin conciliation hearing
—verfahren conciliatory proceedings
—versuch attempt at reconciliation
—vorschlag conciliatory proposal
sukzessiv gradual, in stages, successive
summarisch summary
—es Verfahren summary proceedings
Summe aggregate, amount, sum (total), (sum) total
summieren sum up
Summierung addition, summing up
Surrogat substitute
suspendieren abolish, suspend
Suspendierungsbefehl suspendeas
Suspension abolition, suspension
Sympathiestreik sympathetic strike
in einen — treten strike in sympathy
Syndikat association, combine, ring, syndicate, trust
Syndikats
—anteil underwriting share
—mitglied member of a syndicate, underwriting member
—vertrag underwriting agreement (contract)
System plan, system
systematisch methodical, systematic
systematisieren systematize
Systematisierung systematization
systemlos without system

T

Tabelle chart, diagram, graph, index, scale, schedule, table, tabulation
tabu taboo
Tadel admonition, blame, censure, criticism, fault, rebuke, reprimand, reproach, reproof
—, ohne blameless, faultless, spotless
tadellos blameless, excellent, faultness, first-class, immaculate, irreproachable, perfect
Tadellosigkeit blamelessness, faultlessness
tadeln admonish, blame, censure, criticize, disapprove, find fault with, rebuke, reprimand, reprove, take exception to
tadelnswert blamable, blameworthy, censurable, faulty, objectionable, reprehensible, reproachable
Tadelsantrag motion of censure
Tadler censurer, fault-finder
Tafel bill board, board, chart, counter, hoarding, panel, plate, poster, scale, schedule, table
  Warnungs— notice board
Tag date, day
  Achtstunden— eight-hour day
  Anfangs— initial date
  Arbeits— workday, working day
  Fälligkeits— day (date) of maturity, due date
  Feier— (Fest—) holiday
  Geburts— anniversary, birthday
  Gerichts— court day
  Partei— party congress (conference)
  Ruhe— rest day, day of rest, day off, holiday
  Stich— deadline, appointed (critical, crucial, decisive, fixed) date, key (target) date, term
  Verfall— s. Fälligkeits—
  Werk— s. Arbeits—
  Wochen— weekday
  Zahl— day of payment, pay day
Tage
—buch daybook, diary, journal, log
—geld daily allowance
—lohn day's pay (wage), daily pay (wage)
—löhner day labo(u)rer
tagen be in session, confer, deliberate, hold a meeting, meet, sit
Tages
—ablauf daily routine
—angabe date
—arbeit day's work (labo[u]r)
—befehl order of the day
—bericht bulletin, daily report
—entgelt daily pay
—kurs current rate, rate (quotation) of the day
—ordnung agenda, order of the day
  an der — — sein be the order
  auf der — — stehen be on the agenda
  zur — — übergehen pass (proceed) to the order of the day
— — verlesen read the agenda
—preis current price, price of the day
—presse daily press
—satz daily rate, per diem equivalent
—stempel date stamp
—wert actual (current, present) value
—zeit daytime, time of day
—zeitung daily (newspaper, paper)
Tagewerk day's work, routine
täglich at call, day-to-day, daily, from day to day, every day, per day, per diem, ordinary
Tagung conference, congress, convention, gathering, meeting, session, sitting
Tagungs
—bericht conference paper
—leiter conference leader
—ort meeting place

—raum conference (meeting) room
—teilnehmer conferee, conference, member
Takt tact
Taktik politics, tactics
taktisch tactical
taktlos ill-judged, indelicate, indiscreet, injudicious, tactless
Taktlosigkeit indelicacy, indiscretion, injudiciousness, tactlessness
taktvoll delicate, discreet, judicious, tactful
Talar gown, robe
Talon counterfoil, dividend warrent, renewal coupon, stub, talon
—steuer coupon tax, talon tax
Tantieme bonus, fee, gratuity, percentage, premium, royalty, share in profits
Tarif rates, tariff
—abbau cut in rates
—abkommen tariff agreement (contract, treaty), collective agreement
—änderung tariff amendment
—bestimmungen tariff regulations
—bruch tariff violation
—erhöhung increase in rates
—ermäßigung rate (tariff) reduction
—frage tariff question
—gruppe wage class
tarifieren tariff
Tarif
—kampf (—krieg) rate (tariff) war
—klasse tariff schedule, wage class
—klausel wage clause
—konferenz tariff conference
—lohn tariff wage
tariflich (—mäßig) according to tariff, by tariff
Tarif
—ordnung tariff regulations
—politik rate (tariff) policy
—reform tariff reform
—regelung tariff treatment, collective wage agreement
—satz tariff rate
—senkung tariff reduction
—streitigkeit tariff dispute
—stufe tariff bracket
—system tariff system, wage schedule
—verband tariff syndicate
—verhandlungen collective (wage) negotiations
—vertrag collective agreement, tariff agreement (contract, treaty)
—vorschriften tariff provisions
—zoll tariff duty
—zugeständnis tariff concession
Tarnbezeichnung code word
tarnen camouflage, cover up, hide, mask, screen, veil
Tarnung camouflage, hiding, masking, screening
Taschen
—ausgabe pocket edition
—buch notebook, pocketbook
—dieb pickpocket
—diebstahl pocket-picking
Tat act, action, deed
—, auf frischer in flagranti, in the very act (fact), red-handed
—, Mann der man of action
Gewalt— act of violence (force)
Straf— crime, felony, misdemeanour, offence, punishable act, tort
Un— atrocity, crime, misdeed, outrage
Tat
—bericht charge report, statement of facts, summary of evidence
—bestand actual circumstances, facts (of the case), matter of fact, state of affairs
— —, objektiver material facts
—bestandsaufnahme factual statement, finding of the facts, statement of facts
—beweis practical proof
—einheit coincidence
in — — mit in coincidence with
Täter actor (of the crime), author, committer, criminal, culprit, delinquent, doer, inflictor of the law, perpetrator, tortfeasor
Haupt— principal

Mit— accessory (in the fact), accomplice, co-actor, joint tortfeasor
Straf— criminal, offender
Täterschaft guilt
Tatfrage matter (issue, question) of fact
tätig acting, active, busy, operative, working
— sein als act (function) as
— sein für work for
tätigen bring off, carry out, conclude, effect, execute, make, transact
Tätigkeit action, activity, business, function, job, occupation, operation, profession, vocation
Erwerbs— productive activity
Geistes— brain work
Gewalt— act of violence, (act of) outrage
Wohl— charity
Tätigkeits
—bereich (—feld, —gebiet, —kreis) field (scope) of activity, sphere of action, field of operation
tätlich violent
— angreifen (beleidigen) assault, commit an assault on
—er Angriff (—e Beleidigung) assault (and battery)
Tätlichkeit (act of) violence, assault (and battery)
Tat
—ort scene (place) of the crime
—ortbesichtigung visit to the scene
—sache fact, matter (issue) of fact
— —, festgestellte accomplished fact
— —, feststehende established fact
— —, gegebene data
— —, vollendete accomplished fact, fait accompli
— —n, Vorspiegelung falscher false pretences, misrepresentation of facts
auf — —n beruhen be founded on facts
bei den — —n bleiben stick to the fact
den — —n entsprechen be in accordance with fact
falsche — —n vorspiegeln make false pretences
—sachensinn factual sense
—sachenvermutung presumption of fact
tatsächlich actual, as a (matter of) fact, based (founded) on fact, factual, in fact, real, true
Tat
—umstände actual circumstances, facts (of the case)
—verdacht suspicion to be the offender
Tauf
—name Christian name
—pate godfather
—patin godmother
—schein certificate of baptism, baptismal certificate
taugen zu be fit (good, of use) for
tauglich able, able-bodied, appropriate, apt, capable, fit, good, proper, qualified, serviceable, sufficient, suitable, useful
Tauglichkeit ability, aptitude, capacity, fitness, qualification, serviceableness, usefulness
—szeugnis certificate of qualification, fitness (qualifying) certificate
Tausch barter, exchange, swap, truck
—abkommen barter agreement
tauschen barter, change, exchange, swap, truck
täuschen belie, cheat, deceive, defraud, delude, disappoint, dupe, fraud, mislead, trick
täuschen, sich be deceived (deluded, mistaken)
täuschend deceptive, delusive, illusory, striking
Tauscher barterer
Täuscher cheat, deceiver
Täuscherei deception, delusion
tauschfähig barterable
Tausch
—gegenstand exchange article
—geschäft barter (transaction), exchange (transaction)
—handel barter, exchange, truck

—händler barterer, trucker
—mittel medium of exchange
Täuschung deceit, deception, delusion, error, fraud, illusion, imposition, imposture, misrepresentation, mystification, trick
—, arglistige fraud, wilful deceit
—, optische optical delusion
Täuschungs
—absicht intentional deceit
—manöver (—unternehmen) diversion
—versuch attempted deceit, attempt to deceive
Tausch
—vertrag barter agreement (contract), exchange agreement
tauschweise by way of exchange
Tauschwert exchange(able) value
Taxation appraisal, appraisement, taxation, valuation
Taxator appraiser, assessor, valuer
Taxe charge, duty, estimate, fee, rate, tariff, tax
taxfrei free from taxation
Taxgebühr valuer's fee
taxierbar appreciable, assessable, rat(e)able
taxieren, appraise, appreciate, assess, estimate, rate, tax, value
Taxierer s. Taxator
Taxierung s. Taxation
Tax
—ordnung assizement, scale of fees, tariff
—preis appraised price
—wert appraised (assessed, estimated) value
Technik execution, skill, technics, technique, workmanship
technisch special, technical
Teil assortment, lot, part, party, piece, portion, section, share, side, volume
  An— allotment, interest, part, percentage, portion, quota, share
  Bestand— component, constituent, element, ingredient, part
  Bruch— fraction
  Erb— hereditary portion, portion (share) of inheritance
  Pflichtan— contingent, quota
teilbar divisible, partable, separable
Teil
—barkeit divisibility, separability
—bereich (—gebiet) branch, section
—besitz part ownership
—besitzer part owner
—betrag instalment, part, partial amount, quota
teilen apportion, distribute, divide, participate, partition (off), portion out, separate, share, split
teilhaben have an interest (a share (in), partake (of), participate (in), share (in)
Teilhaber associate, participant, participator, partner, joint owner (proprietor)
—, stiller dormant (secret, silent, sleeping) partner
Teilhaberschaft partnership
Teilhaftung partial liability
Teilnahme attendance, complicity, concern, cooperation, interest, participation, share, sympathy
teilnehmen assist at, attend (at), be interested (involved) (in), be present (at), contribute (to), cooperate, partake (in), participate (in), share (in), sympathize (with), take part (in)
Teilnehmer accomplice, attendant, competitor, contestant, member, participant, subscriber
teils in part, partly
Teil
—schaden partial damage (loss)
—schuldschein partial bond
—summe subtotal
Teilung dismemberment, distribution, division, partition, separation, sharing, splitting
  Arbeits— division of labo(u)r
  Auf— allocation, allotment, dismemberment, distribution, division, parcelling, partition
  Ein— arrangement, classification, division

Ver— allotment, apportionment, distribution, division, repartition
Zu— abjudication, allotment, allowance, apportionment, assignment
Teilungs
—vertrag treaty of partition
Teil
—urteil partial judgement (verdict)
—verlust partial loss
teilweise in part, partial, partly
Teil
—wert partial value
—zahlung instalment, part payment
Teilzahlungs
—kauf hire purchase
—verkauf instalment sale
—vertrag hire purchase agreement, instalment contract
Telefon telephone
—anruf (Telefonat) telephone call
—buch telephone directory (book)
—gebühren telephone charges
—gespräch telephone call (conversation)
telefonieren telephone
telefonisch telephonic, (by) telephone
Telefon
—leitung telephone line
— — anzapfen tap telephone wires
—nummer call (telephone) number
—zelle call-box, phone-booth
Telegramm cable(gram), telegram, wire
Antwort— reply telegram
Brief— letter telegram
Code— (Chiffre—) code (cipher) telegram
Dienst— service (official) telegram
Telegramm
—adresse cable (telegraphic) address
—code cable code
—formular telegraph form
—schlüssel telegram code (key)
Telegraphenamt (—station) telegraph office
telegraphieren cable, telegraph, wire
telegraphisch by cable (telegram), telegraphic
Tempo pace, speed
temporär temporary
Tendenz tendency, trend
tendenziös biassed, prejudiced, tendentious
tendieren zu incline to, tend to (wards)
Tenor substance, tenor, wording
Termin appointed (fixed) day (date, time), day, date, delay, hearing, respite, summons, term, time
Ablauf— day of expiration, expiration date
Abschluß— closing date, settling day
Anfangs— initial date
Beweis— date for evidence
End— dies ad quem, final (latest) date
Fälligkeits— due date, date (day) of maturity
Kündigungs— date of cancellation (notice)
Liefer(ungs)— delivery date
Schluß— final (latest) date, final hearing
Sühne— conciliation hearing
Versand— shipping date
Versteigerungs— auction day
Wahl— election day
Zahlungs— date (time) of payment
Termin
—, abgelaufener expired term
—, äußerster deadline, final term, time limit
—, fester fixed date
—, verstrichener due date
— anberaumen set a day
— ansetzen appoint time, assign a date for, fix a date (time)
— einhalten keep one's time
— festsetzen decide upon a day, fix a date
— haben be (summoned) to appear (in court)
— setzen fix a time
— wahrnehmen attend a hearing

termingerecht according to schedule, in due time, on the due date
Termin
—kalender (—liste) calendar, cause list, schedule
Terminologie nomenclature, technical language, terminology
Termin
—verlängerung extension (of period, term)
—versäumnis default(ing), failure to appear, nonappearance
—wechsel dated bill
territorial territorial
Territorial
—gerichtsbarkeit territorial jurisdiction
—gewässer territorial waters
—rechte territorial rights
—regierung territorial government
Territorium territory
Terror terror, terrorism
terrorisieren terrorize
Terrorisierung terrorization
Terrorist terrorist
terroristisch terrorist
Tertiawechsel third of exchange
Test test
Testament testament, (last) will
— anfechten (bestreiten) contest (dispute, oppose) a will
— aufheben (umstoßen, widerrufen) revoke a will
im — bedenken remember in a (mention in one's) will
— eröffnen open a testament, read out a will
— errichten (machen) make (set up) a will
sein — machen make one's testament (will)
— vollstrecken execute a will
testamentarisch by testament (will), testamentary
— bestimmen will
— hinterlassen bequeath, devise by will
— verfügen (dispose by) will
—e Erbfolge testamentary succession
—e Verfügung testamentary disposition
—e Zuwendung bequest, legacy
Testaments
—anfechtung contesting (of) a will, will contest
—anhang codicil
—bestätigung probate
—erbe devisee, testamentary heir
—erbin testamentary heiress
—erbfolge testamentary succession
—eröffnung opening (reading) of a will
—klausel testamentary clause
—kosten testamentary charges
—nachtrag (—zusatz) codicil
—urkunde testamentary document (instrument)
—verwalter administrator
—vollstrecker executer (of a will)
—vollstreckerin executress, executrice
—vollstreckung execution (of a will)
—widerruf revocation of a will
—zeuge testamentary witness, witness to a will
—zusatz s. —nachtrag
Testat certificate (of attendance)
Testator bequeather, devisor, testator
testen test
testieren attest, bequeath, certify, dispose by will, make a (one's) will, testify
testierfähig having testamentary capacity
Testierfähigkeit testamentary capacity, power of testation
testierunfähig without testamentary capacity
Testierunfähigkeit testamentary incapacity
Testimonium certificate, testimonial
Text book, context, tenor, text, wording, words
Text
—ausgabe text (edition)
—stelle (text) passage
—vergleich text comparison
Thema subject, theme, topic
thematisch thematical, topical
Theoretiker theorist
theoretisch in the abstract, in theory, theoretic(al)

Theorie theory
— aufstellen evolve a theory
thesaurieren accumulate, amass, hoard, store (up)
Thesaurierung accumulation, amassing, hoarding, storing
These thesis
Thron throne
— besteigen mount the throne
auf den — setzen enthrone, raise to the throne
vom — stoßen depose, dethrone
Thron
—anwärter heir to the throne
—besteigung accession to the throne
—bewerber aspirant (claimant) to the throne, pretender
—bewerbung pretendership
—entsagung (—verzicht) abdication (of the throne)
—erbe heir (successor) to the throne, heir apparent
—folge succession (to the throne)
—folger heir (successor) to the throne
—prätendent pretender to the throne
—rede King's (Queen's) speech, royal speech, speech from the throne
Tierquälerei cruelty to animals
tilgbar amortizable, extinguishable, redeemable, repayable
un— (nicht —) irredeemable
Tilgbarkeit amorizableness, extinguishableness, redeemableness
tilgen abolish, amortize, annihilate, annul, cancel, clear off, compound, delete, destroy, discharge, efface, expunge, extinguish, extirpate, liquidate, pay (off, up), redeem, retire, return, strike out, wipe out
Tilgung abolition, amortization, annulment, cancellation, deletion, destruction, discharge, effacement, erasure, expiation, extinction, extirpation, liquidation, obliteration, payment, redemption, repayment, settlement, striking out, wiping out
Tilgungs
—abkommen redemption agreement
—anleihe (—darlehen) amortization (redemption) loan
—bescheinigung acquittance, certificate of redemption
—bestimmungen terms of redemption
—betrag redemption amount
—dauer redemption (repayment) period
—fonds (—kasse) sinking (redemption) fund
—frist limitation of redemption
—klausel redemption clause
—last redemption charge
—plan redemption plan
—quote (—satz) redemption rate
—rate instalment, amortization rate
—schein bill of amortization, redemption certificate
—termin redemption date
—wert redemption value
Titel caption, character, claim, heading, rank, style, title, title deed
Besitz— titel (deed)
Eigentums— deed of property, title
Erwerbs— title deed
Hypotheken— mortgage bond (deed)
Schuld— instrument of indebtedness
Titulatur titles
titulieren address, call, give the title of, style, title
Tochtergesellschaft affiliate, affiliated company, subsidiary (company)
Tod death, decease
Schein— apparent death, semblance of death
Unfall— death by accident
mit dem —e bestrafen punish with death
eines (un)natürlichen —es sterben die a natural (violent) death
zum —e verurteilen sentence to death
von —es wegen mortis causa
todähnlich death-like

todbringend deadly, fatal
Todes
—ahnung presentiment of death
—anzeige announcement (notice) of death, orbituary (notice)
—art manner of death
—fall (case of) death, decease
—fälle casualties, deaths
—gefahr danger of (to) life, deadly peril, peril of (to) life
in — — schweben be in mortal danger
—nachweis death certificate, proof of death
—stoß death (finishing, mortal) blow
— — versetzen deal (deliver) the death blow
—strafe capital punishment, death penalty
— —, bei under penalty of death
— — erleiden be executed
— — verhängen impose the death sentence, pronounce sentence of death
—stunde hour of death
—tag day of death
—urkunde death certificate
—urteil sentence of death
— — fällen pronounce sentence of death
— — vollstrecken carry out sentence of death
—verbrechen capital crime
—vermutung presumption of death, presumptive death
—wunde mortal wound
Todfeind deadly (mortal, sworn) enemy
tödlich complete, deadly, fatal, mortal
—er Unfall accidental death
— verunglücken be killed in an accident, have a fatal accident
Tödlichkeit deadliness, fatal nature
tolerant tolerant
Toleranz margin, tolerance, toleration
tolerieren tolerate
tot dead, deceased, defunct, extinct, inanimate, lifeless
für — erklären declare dead
total altogether, complete, entire, total, whole
Totalbetrag (sum) total, total amount (sum), whole amount
totalitär totalitarian
Totalität totality
Totalverlust total loss
töten destroy, kill, put to death, slay
Toten
—schau coroner's inquest
—schauer coroner
—schein death certificate
totgeglaubt supposed to be dead
Toter dead (body, person)
Schein- apparently dead
Tot
—schlag homicide, manslaughter, second-degree murder
—schläger blackjack, homicide, life preserver, manslayer
totstellen, sich feign death
Tötung destruction, homicide, kill(ing), slaying
—, auf Verlangen manslaughter on request
—, fahrlässige manslaughter (by carelessness)
—, vorsätzliche murder
Tötungsabsicht intent to kill
trachten aim (at), aspire (to), endeavour, strive (after, for), try (to)
—, nach dem Leben attempt (seek) a person's life
Tradition custom, tradition
traditionell traditional
tragbar appropriate, bearable, sustainable, tenable, tolerable
tragen bear, bring (in), carry, convey, endure, meet, produce, profit, run, stand, suffer, support, take, transport, uphold, wear, yield
Träger bearer, holder, representative, wearer
Tragweite bearing, consequence, import(ance), magnitude, range, reach, scope, significance
Transaktion operation, transaction
Transfer transfer
—abkommen transfer agreement
Transferent transferor
transferierbar (-fähig) transferable

transferieren transfer
Transferierung transfer
Transfer
—gebühr transfer fee
—steuer transfer tax
—zahlung transfer payment
Transformation transformation
transformieren transform
Transport carriage, conveyance, dispatch, forwarding, freightage, shipment, shipping, transport, transportation
transportabel (transportierbar, transportfähig) transportable
Transport
—anweisungen forwarding (shipping) instruction
—auftrag shipping order
—bedingungen shipping terms
—gesellschaft forwarding (shipping, transport) company, transportation agency
Transporteur transport agent, transportation carrier, transporter
transportieren carry, convey, forward, move, ship, transport
Transport
—kosten carriage, shipping (transport, transportation) charges
—papiere (-unterlagen) shipping documents
—risiko risk of carriage, transportation risk
—schaden transport damage (loss)
—schwierigkeiten transport difficulties
—spesen s. -kosten
—steuer transportation tax
—unternehmen s. -gesellschaft
—versicherung transport(ation) (shipping) insurance
—vertrag shipping contract
—verzögerung delay in transit
—vorschriften s. -anweisungen
Tratte bill of exchange, draft
trauen believe (in), confide, marry, trust
—, nicht distrust
sich — lassen get married, marry
Trauschein marriage certificate (licence)
Trauung marriage
Trauzeuge marriage witness, witness to a marriage
Treffen conference, convention, gathering, meeting, rally
treffen affect, beat, come to, effect, encounter, hit (the mark), make, meet (with), pass, strike, take
—, nicht miss
—, sich assemble, gather, meet, rally
treffend appropriate, apt, felicitous, pertinent, proper, right, striking, to the point (purpose)
Treffpunkt meeting place, rendez-vous
treiben carry on, cultivate, do, drive, exercise, follow, impel, incite, move, practise, press, pursue, rush, urge (on)
treibend driving, motive
Treiber driver, instigator, oppressor
trennbar dissoluble, divisible, separable
Trennbarkeit dissolubility, divisibility, separability
trennen break, cut off, detach, disconnect, disjoin, dissolve, disunite, divide, divorce, isolate, part, segregate, separate, sever, split, sunder
—, sich be(come) divorced, part, separate
Trennung disconnection, disjoining, dissolution, division, divorce, parting, segregation, separation, severance
Güter- separate ownership (property), separation of property
— von Bett und Tisch separation from bed and board
Trennungs
—zulage (-entschädigung) separation allowance, severance benefit (pay)
Tresor safe (deposit), treasury
—raum strong room
Treu
— und Glauben (loyalty and) good faith, faith and trust, trust

auf — und Glauben on trust
nach — und Glauben in good faith
treu devoted, faithful, firm, loyal, reliable, sincere, staunch, true, trustworthy, upright
un- disloyal, unfaithful
zu -en Händen in (on) trust
Treubruch breach of faith (trust), disloyalty, faithlessness, perfidy
treubrüchig disloyal, faithless, perfidious
Treue faith, faithfulness, fidelity, loyalty
— brechen break faith
— geloben declare one's loyalty to
Treueid oath of allegiance
treuergeben loyal
Treu
—gut trust property
—hand trust
—handabkommen trust agreement
—händer custodian, executor, fiduciary, official receiver, sequester, trustee
treuhänderisch fiduciary, in trust, under trusteeship
Treuhand
—geschäft (-verwaltung) trusteeship
—gesellschaft trust company
—gut trust estate (property)
—rat trusteeship council
—verhältnis trust (relationship)
—vermögen trust property
—vertrag trust agreement
—verwahrung, in in trust
—verwaltung trust administration, trusteeship
treulos disloyal, faithless, false, perfidious, treacherous
Treulosigkeit faithlessness, infidelity, perfidy, perfidiousness, treachery, treacherous deed
Tribunal tribunal
Tribut tribute
tributpflichtig tributory
Trick trick
Trieb appetency, desire, impetus, impulse, inclination, instinct, propensity
triftig cogent, conclusive, convincing, plausible, pleadable, sound, strong, urgent, valid, weighty, well-founded
Trinker alcoholic, drinker, drunkard
Trinkgeld gratuity, tip
Triplikat triplicate
Triplik surrejoinder
Triptyk triptique
Trug deceit, deception, delusion, fraud, imposition
trügen be deceitful (deceptive), deceive, delude
trügerisch deceitful, deceptive, delusive, fallacious, illusive, illusory, misleading, treacherous
Trugschluß fallacy, false conclusion, false (unsound) reasoning
trunken drunk(en), inebriated, intoxicated
Trunken
—bold drunkard, inebriate
—heit drunkenness, inebriation, inebriety, intoxication
— — am Steuer drunken driving
Trunksucht alcoholism, dipsomania, (habitual) drunkenness, inebriety, intemperance, mania for drinking
trunksüchtig addicted (given) to drinking, dipsomaniac
Trunksüchtiger alcoholic, dipsomaniac, drunkard
Trust cartel, combine, ring, syndicate, trust
Tumult commotion, disturbance, racket, riot, row, tumult, uproar
tun do, effect, make, perform
an- harm, injure, (hurt)
—, Abbitte apologize, excuse
tunlich convenient, feasible, opportune, possible, practicable, suitable
Turnus rotation, turn
turnusmäßig by (in) rotation, by turns

Typ character, design, model, type
typisch typical
typisieren standardize
Typisierung standardization
Tyrann despot, tyrant
Tyrannei despotism, tyranny
Tyrannenherrschaft despotism, tyranny
Tyrannenmord tyrannicide
tyrannisch despotic, tyrannical, tyrannous
tyrannisieren domineer (over), oppress, tyrannize (over)

U

Übel abuse, evil, grievance, ill, malady, mischief, trouble, wrong
übel bad, black, disastrous, evil, foul, ill, unfair
Übel
—stand abuse, drawback, grievance, inconvenience
—tat crime, misdeed
—täter criminal, evil-doer, malefactor, offender, wrongdoer
— wollen bear a person a grudge, bear malice (ill-will) to(wards), wish ill (to)
übelwollend malevolent, spiteful
überaltert obsolete, superannuated
überantworten deliver up, surrender
Überantwortung delivery, surrender
überarbeiten do over again, revise, work over
Überarbeitung revision
überbeanspruchen overstrain, overstress
Überbeanspruchung overstrain, overstress
überbewerten overestimate, overvalue
Überbewertung overestimation, overvaluation
überbieten bid higher, outbid, outdo, overbid, surpass
Überbietender higher bidder, outbidder
Überbietung higher bid, outbidding
überbleiben be left, remain
Überbliebener survivor
Überbleibsel leavings, remainder, remains, remnant, residue, rest
Überblick control, outline, review, sketch, summary, survey
überblicken control, overlook, survey
überbringen bring (carry, take) to, deliver, hand over, present, transmit
Überbringer bearer, bringer, carrier, conveyer, deliverer, presenter
Überbringung delivery, surrender, transmission
überbrücken bridge, tide over
Überbrückungs
—hilfe interim aid (assistance), readjustment allowance, stopgap aid (relief)
—kredit interim (stopgap) loan
überdurchschnittlich above average (normal, standard), outstanding
übereignen assign, convey, transfer
Übereignung assignment, conveyance, transfer
Übereinandergreifen overlapping
übereinandergreifen overlap
Übereinkommen agreement, arrangement, composition, compromise, convention, settlement, understanding
übereinkommen agree, arrange, come to (enter into, make an)

aggreement, come to terms (an understanding), compromise, meet, settle, understand
Übereinkunft s. Übereinkommen
übereinstimmen agree (on, with), answer, be conform (correspondent) to, be in accordance (agreement, keeping, line) with, be of the opinion of, coincide, concur (with), conform (to), harmonize, square, tally
—, nicht differ, disagree
übereinstimmend accordant (to, with), concurring, conformable, consistent, consonant, corresponding, identical, in accordance (conformity) (with), unanimous
Übereinstimmung accord, agreement, concurrence, conformity, correspondence, harmony, understanding
in — mit according to, in accordance (answer, concert, conformity, keeping, line) with
Überfall assault, (sudden) attack, hold-up, inroad, invasion, onslaught, racket, raid, robbery, surprise
—kommando flying squad
überfallen assault, attack (suddenly), invade, raid, surprise
überfällig belated, overdue
überfordern overcharge, overstrain, overwork, surcharge
Überforderung excessive demand, overcharge, overstrain, surcharge
überführen carry over, convey, convict of, find guilty of, transfer, transport
Überführung conveyance, conviction, transfer, transport, transportation
Übergabe capitulation, consignment, delivery, handing in (over), submittal, surrender, transfer
—, bedingungslose unconditional surrender
Übergabe
—bedingungen terms of surrender
—bescheinigung delivery receipt
Übergang assignment, change, crossing, devolution, passage, passing, transfer, transmission, transition, turn
— für Fußgänger crossing for pedestrians, pedestrian lines
Übergangs
—abkommen (-vereinbarung) transitional arrangement
—bestimmungen provisional (temporary, transitional) regulations
—gesetz transitional law
—hilfe interim (stopgap) aid
—maßnahme transitory measure
—periode (-zeit) transitional period, period of transition
—regelung temporary arrangement
—regierung provisional government
—stadium stage of transition, transitional stage
—vorschriften transitional provisions
—zustand transitional stage
übergeben abandon, commit, deliver (up), entrust, give (in, up), hand in (over), present, surrender, transfer
—, sich surrender
—, dem Gericht take legal proceedings against
Übergebot higher bid, overbid (ding)
übergehen be passed (transferred) to, be taken over by, change into, devolve to (upon), drop out, leave out, merge into, move, omit, overlook, override, pass into (over, to), proceed to, turn into
—, zum Feind go over to the enemy
—, in andere Hände change hands
Übergehung omission, passing over
übergeordnet higher, senior, superior, superordinate
Übergewicht extra (surplus) weight, overweight, predominance, superiority
— gewinnen prevail
— haben predominate

im — sein preponderate
übergreifen overlap
— auf encroach (up)on, spread to, trench (up)on
Übergriff encroachment, impingement, infringement, inroad, invasion, trespass
überhöht excessive
überholen fetch (haul) over, overhaul, overtake, recondition
überholt antiquated, obsolete, outdated, reconditioned
Überholung overhaul
überhören lose, miss, not to hear
überkonfessionell interdenominational
überlassen abandon, assign, cede, commit, entrust, give up, leave, let (have), relinquish, remit, resign, transfer, yield (up)
—, käuflich sell
Überlassung abandonment, assignment, cession, leaving, relinquishment, resignation, transfer, yielding
überlasten overburden, overcharge, overload
Überlastung overcharge, overload, overstress, overwork
Überläufer deserter, runaway, turncoat
Überleben survival
überleben last, live out, outlast, outlive, survive
überlebend remaining, surviving
Überlebender survivor
Überlebensvermutung presumption of survival
überlegen consider, deliberate, ponder, reflect, think over
—, vorher premeditate
— sein be superior to, outdo, surpass (in)
Überlegenheit odds, preponderance, superiority, supremacy
überlegt careful, considerate, considered, deliberate, premeditated, prudent
un- inconsiderate, unpremeditated
Überlegung cogitation, consideration, deliberation, judgement, premeditation, reflection, thought
überleiten lead over (up to), transfer
Überleitung delivery, transfer, transition
Überleitungs
—bestimmungen transitional regulations
—vertrag transitional agreement
überliefern commit, deliver, entrust, give up, hand over, surrender, transmit
Überlieferung delivery, surrender, tradition, transmission
Überliegegeld (—tage, —zeit) demurrage
überlisten circumvent, defraud, dupe, outsmart, outreach, outwit
Überlistung circumvention, deception, fraud, outwitting
übermachen make over
Übermacht odds, superior force (numbers, power), superiority, supremacy
Übermaß excess, exorbitance, intemperance
übermäßig exaggerated, excessive, exorbitant, immoderate, undue
Übermäßigkeit excess, immoderateness
übermitteln communicate, convey, deliver, hand over, remit, transfer, transmit
Übermittlung conveyance, delivery, passage, remittance, transfer, transmission
Übernahme acceptance, acquisition, adoption, assumption, entrance, seizure, taking over, taking charge (possession) of, undertaking
Amts- accession to (entrance into) office
Macht- accession to (assumption, seizure of) power
Übernahme
—bedingungen terms of acceptance
—schein (certificate of) receipt
übernational supranational
übernehmen accept, assume, enter into (upon), overcharge,

receive, take charge (possession) of, take in hand, take over, undertake
Überpreis excessive price, overprice, premium
überprüfen audit, check, control, examine, inspect, investigate, overhaul, reconsider, review, revise, screen, scrutinize, study, test, verify
Überprüfung audit, check-up, checking, control, examination, inspection, investigation, overhaul, review, revision, testing, screening, verification
überqueren cross
Überquerung crossing
überreden persuade
Überredung persuasion
überreichen deliver, hand in, hand (pass) over, present
Überreichung delivery, handing over, presentation
Überrest remainder, remains, remnant, residue, rest
überschätzen overestimate, overrate, overvalue
Überschätzung overestimation, overestimate, overvaluation
Überschlag computation, estimation, rough calculation (estimate), sketch
überschlagen calculate, compute, estimate (roughly)
Überschlagsrechnung rough estimate
überschneiden, sich (mit) overlap (with)
Überschneidung overlapping
überschreiben address, convey, entitle, head, superscribe, transcribe, transfer, transmit
Überschreibung conveyance, superscription, transcription, transfer
überschreiten cross, exceed, go across (beyond), infringe, overdraw, override, overrun, overstay, overstep, pass across (over), surpass, transgress, trespass (up)on
Überschreitung abuse, crossing, excess, exceeding, infringement, overdraft, transgression, trespass
Überschrift address, caption, heading, headline, inscription, title
Überschuß balance, excess, profit, remainder, residue, surplus
überschüssig abundant, exceeding, (in) excess, left over, spare, surplus
übersenden consign, convey, forward, remit, send, transmit
Übersendung consignation, consignment, conveyance, dispatch, forwarding, remittance, sending, transmission
übersetzbar translatable
übersetzen translate
Übersetzer translator
—, beeidigter sworn translator
Übersetzung translation
—srecht right of translation
Übersicht account, control, outline, prospect, review, schedule, sketch, summary, survey, view
übersiedeln emigrate, move, remove
Übersiedlung emigration, removal
überstaatlich supranational
überstehen endure, get over, overcome, pass, surmount, survive, tide over
übersteigen exceed, go beyond, pass, surpass
übersteigern exaggerate, outbid, overbid
Übersteigerung exaggeration, outbidding
überstimmen defeat, outvote, vote down
Überstunden extra hours, overtime
— machen work extra hours, do (make, work) overtime
Überstunden
—arbeit extra working hours, overtime work
—bezahlung (-gelder) overtime pay(ment)
—verbot prohibition of overtime
Übertrag assignment, transfer

übertragbar alienable, assignable, cessible, negotiable, transferable, transmissible
übertragbar, nicht (un-) inalienable, nonassignable, nontransferable, unassignable, untransferable
Übertragbarkeit alienability, assignability, negotiability, transferability
übertragen alienate, assign, cede, charge with, commission with, commit, communicate, confer (up)on, convey, copy, delegate, endorse, entrust, hand (make) over, sign away, transcribe, transfer, transmit, turn over, vest (in)
Übertragender assigner, transferor
Übertragung alienation, assignation, assignment, cession, conveyance, delegation, endorsement, handing over, transcription, transfer, transference, transmission
Übertragungs
—brief deed of conveyance
—erklärung declaration of assignment, transfer deed
—papier transfer paper
—urkunde deed of assignment (conveyance), transfer deed
—vertrag contract of conveyance, transfer contract
übertreiben exaggerate, overdo, overstate
Übertreibung exaggeration, excess, overstatement
übertreten act contrary to, break, contravene, convert, exceed, go (pass, step) over to, infract, infringe, transgress, trespass, violate
Übertreter breaker, contravener, infringer, transgressor, trespasser, violator
Übertretung breach, contravention, infraction, infringement, misdemeanour, transgression, trespass
übertrieben exaggerated, excessive, exorbitant, extreme, immoderate, unreasonable
Übertritt change (of), conversion (to), going over (to)
übervorteilen cheat, circumvent, defraud, impose upon, overcharge, overreach
Übervorteilung cheat, overcharging, overreaching, imposition
überwachen control, inspect, shadow, superintend, supervise, watch over
überwacht werden, polizeilich be under police supervision
Überwachung control, inspection, observation, superintendence, supervision, surveillance, watching over
Überwachungs
—ausschuß board of control, control board (commission), supervisory board (committee)
—recht right of control
—stelle board of control, supervisory agency
—system supervisory system
überwältigen overcome, overmaster, overpower, overwhelm, subdue
überwältigend imposing, overwhelming, sweeping
überweisen assign, commit, refer, remit, transfer
—, einem Gericht commit for trial
Überweisung assignment, commitment, conveyance, reference, remittance, remittal, transfer, transmission
überwiegen preponderance
überwiegen predominate, preponderate, prevail
überwiegend paramount, predominant, preponderant, prevailing, vast
überwindbar conquerable, superable, surmountable
überwinden conquer, control, overcome, override, surmount
Überwindung conquest, overcoming, passage, self-command (-control, -restraint)
überzeichnen oversubscribe
Überzeichnung oversubscription
überzeugen carry, convince, persuade, satisfy
—, sich satisfy oneself

sich — lassen be open to conviction
—, vom Gegenteil disconvince, persuade to the contrary
überzeugend cogent, compelling, conclusive, convincing, forcible, satisfactory
Überzeugung conviction, persuasion, principles, satisfaction
—, aus by conviction
—, politische political opinion
überziehen overdraw
Überziehung overdraft, overdrawing
üblich accustomed, common, conventional, customary, ordinary, normal, prevailing, routine, standard, usual
Übung custom, discipline, exercise, experience, practice, routine, usage, usance, use, training
ultimativ as an ultimatum
Ultimatum ultimatum
— stellen deliver (issue) an ultimatum
umändern alter, change, rearrange, revise, transform
Umänderung alteration, change, rearrangement, revision, transformation
umarbeiten recast, recondition, remake, remodel, revise, transform, work over
Umarbeitung recast, revision, transformation
umbenennen rename
umbilden rearrange, recast, reform, remodel, reorganize, reshuffle, transform
Umbildung rearrangement, recast, reform, reorganization, transformation
Umbruch upheaval, revolution
umdatieren change the date
Umfang amount, domain, extent, range, scale, scope, size, sphere, volume
umfassen comprehend, comprise, contain, cover, embrace, include
umfassend ample, capacious, complete, comprehensive, embracing, extended, extensive, large, overall, sweeping, wide-reaching
umformen recast, recondition, remodel, reshape, transform
Umformung recast, transformation
Umfrage inquiry
Umgang acquaintance, association, dealing, intercourse
Umgebung environment, environs, neighbo(u)rhood, surroundings, vicinity
umgehbar avoidable, evadable
umgehen avoid, bypass, elude, evade, shirk
umgehend immediate, prompt, without delay
Umgehung avoidance, elusion, evasion, shirking
umgekehrt contrary to, opposite, reciprocal, reverse(d)
umgestalten recast, reform, remodel, reorganize, transform
Umgestaltung recast, reform, reorganization, transformation
umgruppieren rearrange, recompose, regroup, reshuffle, shift
Umkehr conversion, return, reversal, turnabout
umkehrbar convertible, reversible
—, nicht irreversible
umkehren convert, invert, overturn, pervert, reverse, upset
Umkehrung conversion, inversion, overturning, reversal, subversion
umkommen die, fall, perish, spoil
Umlauf circulation, currency
im — befindlich afloat, circulating, current, floating, in circulation
in — bringen (setzen) circulate, emit, float, issue, put into circulation, spread
im — sein be in circulation, circulate
Umorganisation reorganization
umorganisieren reorganize
umrechnen convert, reduce
Umrechnung conversion, reduction

Umrechnungs
—kurs (-satz) exchange rate
Umriß outline, (rough) sketch
Umsatz returns, sale(s), turnover
—steuer turnover (sales) tax
umschreiben convey, paraphrase, rewrite, transcribe, transfer
Umschreibung conveyance, paraphrase, transcription, transfer
umschulden convert a debt
Umschuldung conversion of a debt
umschwenken turn round, veer round (from, to)
Umschwung change(-over), reaction, reversal, revolution, turn
umsetzbar convertible, marketable, negotiable, realizable, saleable
umsetzen convert, realize, rearrange, return, sell, shift, turn into (over)
Umsicht care, circumspection, deliberation, discretion, precaution, prudence, vigilance
umsichtig careful, cautious, circumspect, with deliberation, discreet, prudent
umsiedeln resettle, transplant
Umsiedlung resettlement, transplantation
—sbeihilfe resettlement allowance
umsonst gratis, gratuitous, for nothing, to no purpose, unavailing, useless, in vain, without charge (costs, payment)
Umstand circumstance, fact
Umstände circumstances, conditions, details, facts, factors, particulars, position, situation, state (of affairs)
Begleit- attendant (accessory, concomitant) circumstances, res gestae
—, belastende incriminating circumstances
—, erschwerende aggravating circumstances, complications
—, mildernde extenuating circumstances
umstellen readjust, adapt, convert, enclose, reduce, reorganize, round up, shift, surround, transpose
—, sich accommodate (adapt) oneself to, change one's attitude
Umstellung adaption, changeover, conversion, readjustment, reorganization, transposition
umstoßen abolish, annul, countermand, invalidate, make void, overthrow, overturn, quash, rescind, reverse, revoke, set aside, undo, unmake, upset
Umstoßung annulment, invalidation, overthrow, overturning, quashing, rescission, reversal, revocation, upsetting
umstritten contested, controversial, disputed, open
— sein be in controversy
Umsturz overthrow, overturn, revolution, subversion, upheaval
umstürzen overthrow, overturn, upset
umstürzlerisch revolutionary, subversive
umtaufen change a person's name, rechristen, rename
Umtausch change, conversion, exchange
umtauschbar commutable, convertible
Umtauschbarkeit convertibility
umtauschen change, commute (for), convert, exchange
umtauschfähig convertible, exchangeable, returnable
—, nicht inconvertible, not returnable
umwälzen revolutionize
Umwälzung change-over, revolution
umwandelbar commutable, convertible, transformable
—, nicht inconvertible
Umwandelbarkeit commutability, convertibility
umwandeln alter, change (into), commute, convert, transform
Umwandlung change, commutation (to), conversion, transformation
umwechseln change, exchange (for)

Umwechslung change, exchange
—skurs exchange rate
Umwelt environment, milieu
umweltbedingt conditional on the surroundings, environmental
umwerfen overthrow, overturn, reverse, subvert
umziehen change one's residence, move, remove
umzingeln encircle, encompass, round up, surround
Umzug move, removal
unabänderlich immutable, incommutable, irrevocable, unalterable, unchangeable
Unabänderlichkeit irrevocability, unalterableness
unabdingbar inalienable, inevitable, peremptory, unavoidable
unabhängig independent
Unabhängigkeit independence
unabkömmlich indispensable
Unabkömmlichkeit indispensability
unabsichtlich inadvertent, involuntary, unintended, unintentional
unabtretbar inalienable, unassignable, untranferable
Unabtretbarkeit inalienability
unabwendbar inevitable, irremediable
unachtsam absent-minded, careless, inattentive, negligent
Unachtsamkeit absent-mindedness, carelessness, inadvertency, inattention, negligence
unanfechtbar inappealable, incontestable, indisputable, nonappealable, unassailable, unchallengeable
Unanfechtbarkeit incontestability, indisputability
unangefochten unchallenged, uncontested, undisputed, unhindered, unmolested
unangemeldet unannounced, without announcement (notice)
unangemessen improper, inadequate, inappropriate, unsuitable
Unangemessenheit inadequacy, inappropriateness, unsuitableness
unangreifbar indisputable, unassailable
unannehmbar unacceptable
Unannehmbarkeit unacceptableness
Unannehmlichkeit annoyance, difficulty, drawback, inconvenience, trouble
unanständig improper, indecent, shocking
Unanständigkeit indecency
unantastbar intangible, inviolable, taboo, unassailable, unimpeachable
Unantastbarkeit inviolability, taboo, unimpeachableness
unanwendbar inapplicable
Unanwendbarkeit inapplicability
unauffällig inconspicuous, unobtrusive
unauffindbar indiscoverable (un-), untraceable
unaufgefordert of one's own accord, spontaneously, unasked, unbidden, uncalled
unaufgeklärt mysterious, unexplained, unexperienced, unsolved
unaufhaltsam irresistible, resistless, unavoidable
unaufhebbar uncancellable
unauflösbar indissoluble, inexplicable, insoluble
Unauflösbarkeit indissolubility
unaufmerksam absent-minded, inattentive
Unaufmerksamkeit absent-mindedness, inattention, inattentiveness
unaufrichtig deceitful, insincere
Unaufrichtigkeit insincerity
unaufschiebbar imperative, not to be delayed (postponed), pressing, urgent
Unaufschiebbarkeit urgency
unausbleiblich certain, inevitable, infallible, unfailing
Unausbleiblichkeit infallibility
unausdenkbar unimaginable, unthinkable
unausführbar impossible, impracticable, impractical, unfeasible, unworkable
Unausführbarkeit impossibility, impracticability, unfeasibility

unauslöschlich indelible, inextinguishable, lasting
unaussöhnlich irreconcilable
unaussprechlich indescribable, inexpressible, unmentionable, unspeakable
unausweichlich inescapable, inevitable, unavoidable
unbeabsichtigt inadvertent, unintentional
unbeachtet disregarded, unnoticed
— lassen ignore, neglect, pay no attention to
unbedacht imprudent, inconsiderable, indiscreet, rash, thoughtless
unbedenklich harmless, unhesitating, unobjectionable, unscrupulous, without hesitation
unbedeutend immaterial, inferior, insignificant, minor, negligible, petty, trifling, trivial, unimportant
unbedingt absolute, by all means, implicit, peremptory, unconditional, unlimited, unqualified, without reserve
unbeeidigt not sworn, unsworn
unbeeinflußt unaffected, unbiassed, uninfluenced, unprejudiced
unbeeinträchtigt undisturbed, unimpaired, uninjured
unbefähigt incompetent, unqualified
unbefangen frank, impartial, ingenuous, natural, open, unaffected, unbiassed, unprejudiced
Unbefangenheit impartiality, openness, unaffectedness
unbefriedigend insufficient, unsatisfactory
unbefriedigt dissatisfied, not contented (with), unappeased, unsatisfied
unbefristet perpetual, unlimited
unbefugt improper, incompetent, unauthorized, without permission
—es Betreten trespass(ing)
unbefugterweise without authority
Unbefugter unauthorized person
unbeglaubigt uncertified, unsealed
unbeglichen outstanding, unliquidated, unpaid, unsettled
unbegreiflich incomprehensible, inconceivable, mysterious
Unbegreiflichkeit incomprehensibility, inconceivability, mystery
unbegrenzbar illimitable
unbegrenzt boundless, indefinite, limitless, unbounded, unlimited
unbegründet groundless, ill-founded, unbased, unfounded, unsupported
unbegütert having no property, impecunious, not rich (well off), without means
unbehelligt undisturbed, unmolested
unbeherrscht unbalanced, uncontrolled, unrestrained
unbehindert unimpeded, unopposed
unbekannt ignorant (of), obscure, unacquainted (with), unfamiliar (with), unidentified, unknown
Unbekannter unknown person
unbekehrbar callous, unconvinceable
— sein not listen to reason
unbelastet carefree, clear, unencumbered
unbelästigt unmolested
unbelehrbar unconvincible
— sein take no advice
unbemerkbar imperceptible
unbemerkt unnoticed, unperceived, unseen
unbemittelt impecunious, necessitous, poor, without means
unbenannt anonymous, unnamed
unbenutzt idle, unemployed, unused
unberechenbar erratic, incalculable, incomputable, unreliable
Unberechenbarkeit incalculability, unreliability
unberechtigt illicit, incompetent, misplaced, not entitled, unauthorized, unfounded, unjustified, unlawful, unqualified, un-

reasonable, unwarranted, without authority, wrongful
Unberechtigter unauthorized person
unberücksichtigt disregarded, unconsidered, unnoticed
— lassen ignore, leave out of account (consideration), make no allowance for, neglect
unbeschadet apart from, irrespective, notwithstanding, without detriment (prejudice) (to)
unbeschädigt in good condition, intact, undamaged, unhurt, unimpaired, uninjured, unspoilt
unbeschäftigt at leisure, disengaged, out of work, unemployed, unoccupied
unbescheiden exacting, immodest, insolent, presumptuous, unreasonable
Unbescheidenheit exaction, immodesty, insolence, presumption
unbescholten blameless, irreproachable, of stainless (unblemished) character, of good reputation
— sein have an honourable record
Unbescholtenheit blamelessness, integrity, good name
unbeschränkt absolute, unbounded, uncontrolled, unlimited, unrestricted, without limitation (restriction)
— haften be fully liable
unbeschreiblich indescribable, inexpressible
unbesetzt unoccupied, vacant
unbesonnen inconsiderate, indiscreet, rash, reckless, thoughtless
unbeständig inconstant, unstable, unsteady
Unbeständigkeit inconstancy, instability, unsteadiness
unbestätigt unconfirmed
unbestechlich incorruptible, unbribable
Unbestechlichkeit incorruptibility
unbesteuert untaxed
unbestimmbar indeterminable, undefinable
unbestimmt indefinite, indeterminate, irresolute, uncertain, undecided, undetermined, unsettled
Unbestimmtheit indefiniteness, indetermination, irresolution, uncertainty, vagueness
unbestraft unpunished
unbestreitbar incontestable, incontrovertible, unchallengeable, indisputable, unquestionable
Unbestreitbarkeit indisputability
unbestritten unchallenged, uncontested, undisputed, without doubt
unbeteiligt disinterested, impartial, not involved, unbiassed, unconcerned, uninterested, unprejudiced
Unbeteiligter disinterested party
unbeträchtlich inconsiderable, insignificant, trifling
unbewacht unguarded, unwatched
unbewaffnet unarmed
unbeweglich callous, fixed, immovable, impassive, inflexible, motionless, real
—es Gut real estate
—e Sachen (Güter) immovables
—es Vermögen real property, realty
unbeweisbar undemonstrable, unprovable
unbewiesen not proved (proven), unproved
unbewohnbar uninhabitable
unbewohnt desert, uninhabited, unoccupied, vacant
unbewußt automatical, instinctive, involuntary, mechanical, unconscious, unknown
Unbewußtheit unconsciousness
unbezahlt outstanding, unpaid, unsettled, without pay(ment)
Unbill hardship, injury, injustice, insult, wrongs
unbillig inequitable, unfair, undue, unjust, unreasonable
Unbilligkeit inequity, injustice, unfairness, unreasonableness
unbrauchbar inefficient, of no use, unavailable, unfit, unserviceable, unsuitable, useless

Unbrauchbarkeit unserviceableness, uselessness
Undank ingratitude
undankbar thankless, ungrateful, unthankful
Undankbarkeit ingratitude, thanklessness, ungratefulness
undatiert undated
undefinierbar undefinable
undeklariert undeclared, unentered
undenkbar inconceivable, unimaginable, unthinkable
undeutlich indistinct, obscure, unintelligible, vague
Unding absurdity, impossibility
undiszipliniert undisciplined
unduldsam intolerant
Unduldsamkeit intolerance
undurchdacht ill-considered, immature
undurchführbar impracticable, impractical, unfeasible, unworkable
Undurchführbarkeit impracticability, impracticableness
unecht artificial, counterfeit, false, imitated, not genuine, sham
Unechtheit falsehood, falsity
unehelich illegitimate
Unehelichkeit illegitimacy
unehrenhaft disgraceful, dishonourable, indecent
unehrlich dishonest, false, foul, insincere, unfair
Unehrlichkeit dishonesty, bad faith, disgrace, improbity, infamy, insincerity
uneingelöst dishonoured, unpaid, unredeemed
uneingeschränkt unconditional, unlimited, unqualified, unreserved, unrestrained, unrestricted, without restriction
uneinheitlich irregular, non-uniform
uneinig disagreeing, disunited, divided
— sein be at variance (with, on), disagree
Uneinigkeit disagreement, discord, disharmony, dissention, disunion, division
uneinlösbar (-lich) irredeemable
uneintreibbar irrecoverable, not enforceable (recoverable), unenforceable
unentbehrlich indispensable, irreplaceable, necessary
Unentbehrlichkeit indispensableness
unentgeltlich free (of charge), gratis, gratuitous, voluntary, without consideration (recompense)
unentlastet undischarged
unentrinnbar unescapable
unentschieden dependent, doubtful, in dispute, open, pending, undecided, undetermined, unsettled
— lassen leave in suspence
Unentschiedenheit doubtfulness, indecision, pendency, suspense, undecided state
unentschlossen hesitating, irresolute, undecided, undetermined, wavering
Unentschlossenheit irresolution, lack of decision, undecision
unentschuldbar inexcusable, unpardonable, without excuse
unentschuldigtes Fehlen absenteeism, absence without leave
unerbittlich harsh, implacable, inexorable, stern, subborn, unrelenting
unerfahren innocent, unexperienced
Unerfahrenheit inexperience, lack of experience
unerfüllbar unrealizable
unergiebig unproductive
unergründlich impenetrable, inscrutable
unerheblich immaterial, inconsiderable, insignificant, irrelevant, minor, negligible, slight, small, trifling, trivial, unimportant
Unerheblichkeit inconsiderableness, insignificance, irrelevance(cy), slightness
unerkannt incognito, unrecognized
unerklärlich inaccountable, inexplicable

unerläßlich essential, imperative, indispenspensable, irremissable
Unerläßlichkeit indispensability
unerlaubt forbidden, illegal, illicit, not allowed, prohibited, tortious, unauthorized, unlawful, wrongful
—e Handlung tort, unlawful (wrongful) act
unerledigt undischarged, unsettled
unermeßlich boundless, immense, immeasurable, incalculable, infinite
Unermeßlichkeit immensity, immeasurableness
unerreichbar inaccessible, out of reach, unattainable
unerreicht unequalled, unrivalled
unerschöpflich inexhaustible
unerschütterlich unassailable, unshakeable
unerschwinglich enormous, exorbitant, prohibitive
unersetzlich irrecoverable, irrepairable, irreplaceable
unerträglich insufferable, intolerable
unerwähnt unmentioned, unnoticed
unerwartet unexpected, unforeseen
unerweichlich unrelenting
unerweislich indemonstrable, unprovable
unerwiesen unproved
unfähig disabled, disqualified, incapable, incompetent, inefficient, unable, unfit
Unfähigkeit disability, disqualification, inability, incapability, incapacity, incompetence (cy), unfitness
Unfall accident, casualty, mishap
—, durch by accident, accidentally
—, tödlicher accidental death, fatality, fatal accident
— erleiden (haben) meet with an accident
Unfall
—anzeige notice of accident
—entschädigung accident benefit (indemnity), (workmen's) compensation
unfallfrei accident-free
Unfall
—meldung accident report
—rente accident annuity
—schaden accidental damage
—tod casualty, accidental death, death by accident
—ursache cause of accident
—verhütung accident prevention
—versicherung accident insurance
— —sgesetz Workmen's Compensation Act (GB)
—zeuge witness of an accident
unfaßbar incomprehensible, inconceivable
unfehlbar infallible, safe, unfailing, unmistakable
Unfehlbarkeit infallibility
unfertig immature, unfinished
unfreiwillig compulsory, involuntary, unwilling
unfreundlich unfriendly
Unfug disorderly conduct, mischief, misdemeanour, nuisance
—, grober gross misdemeanour, public nuisance
ungeachtet despite (regardless) of, not esteemed (respected), notwithstanding
ungebräuchlich obsolete, not used, uncommon, unusual
Ungebühr abuse, contempt, excess, improperty, impropriety, indecency, injustice, misconduct, unseemliness
— vor Gericht contempt of court
ungebührlich improper, indecent, unbecoming, undue, unjust, unseemly, unwarrantable
ungebunden free, unbound, unconventional, unlimited, unrestrained
Ungebundenheit freedom, unrestraint
ungedeckt uncovered, unprotected, unsecured, without cover (security)
ungeeignet inappropriate, inopportune, unavailable, unfit, unsuitable, unsuited

ungefährdet out of danger, unendangered
ungefährlich harmless, not dangerous, safe
ungefälscht pure, unadulterated
ungehindert without hindrance
ungehörig foul, impertinent, improper, undue, unfair, unseemly
Ungehörigkeit impropriety
Ungehorsam default, disobedience
ungehorsam disobedient, insubordinate
— sein disobey
ungekürzt unabridged, unexpurgated, in entirety
ungelegen inconvenient, inopportune, unseasonable, untimely
Ungelegenheit inconvenience, inopportunity, trouble
ungelernt unskilled
ungenannt anonymous, unnamed
ungenau inaccurate, incorrect, indefinite, inexact, vague
Ungenauigkeit inaccuracy, incorrectness, inexactness, vagueness
ungenügend inadequate, insufficient, unsatisfactory
ungeordnet confused, unarranged, unsettled
—e Verhältnisse disorder
ungerecht inequitable, unfair, unjust, wrongful
ungerechtfertigt unjust, unjustified, unreasonable, unwarrantable, unwarranted
Ungerechtigkeit iniquity, injustice, tort, unfairness, unwarrantableness, wrong
— begehen commit an injustice
ungeschrieben unwritten
—es Gesetz (Recht) unwritten law
ungeschützt exposed (to), unprotected
ungesetzlich against (contrary to) the law, illegal, illegitimate, illicit, lawless, unlawful, wrongful
Ungesetzlichkeit illegality, unlawfulness
ungesichert uncovered, unsecured
ungestört undisturbed, unmolested
ungestraft unpunished, with impunity
ungetilgt unredeemed
ungetreu faithless, perfidious, treacherous, unfaithful
ungewiß doubtful, dubious, precarious, problematic(al), uncertain, undecided, vague
Ungewißheit doubt, doubtfulness, incertitude, suspense, uncertainty
ungewöhnlich exceptional, extraordinary, remarkable, strange, uncommon, unusual
ungewohnt unaccustomed, unusual
ungewollt unwilled
ungezeichnet unmarked, unsigned
ungeziemend improper, indecent, unbecoming
unglaubhaft discreditable, incredible, unauthenticated, unreliable, untrustworthy, unworthy of belief
unglaublich extraordinary, incredible, unbelievable
unglaubwürdig s. unglaubhaft
Unglaubwürdigkeit untrustworthiness
ungleich different, disproportionate, dissimilar, inconsistent, inconstant, irregular, unbalanced, unequal, uneven, unlike, varying
Ungleichgewicht disequilibrium
Ungleichheit disparity, dissimilarity, inequality, irregularity, unevenness, unlikeness, variation
ungleichmäßig disproportionate, irregular, non-uniform, unequal
unglimpflich harsh, rigorous
Unglück accident, adversity, calamity, catastrophy, disaster, distress, ill luck, misadventure, misery, misfortune, mishap
Unglücksfall accident, casualty, misadventure, misfortune
Ungnade disfavour, disgrace
in — fallen fall into disgrace

(with), fall out of favour (grace) (with)
ungültig inoperative, invalid, not current, null, unavailable, (null and) void
für — erklären (—machen) annul, cancel, declare invalid, declare (null and) void, invalidate, nullify, quash, rescind
— werden become invalid
Ungültigerklärung (Ungültigmachen) annulment, cancellation, invalidation, nullification, rescission
— von Urkunden notice of legal extinction
Klage auf — nullity action (suit), action for annulment
Ungültigkeit invalidity, nullity, unavailableness, voidness
Ungültigwerden extinction, nullification
Ungunst disadvantage, disaffection, disfavour, ill will, unpropitiousness
zu —en von against
ungünstig adverse, disadvantageous, unfavourable, unpropitious
unhaltbar indefensible, unbearable, unmaintainable, unsustainable, untenable, unwarrantable
Unhaltbarkeit untenability, untenableness
Unheil calamity, disaster, evil, frustration, harm, mischief, ruin, trouble
— anrichten cause (do, make) mischief
unheilbar incurable, irremediable, irreparable
Unheilstifter mischief-maker
unheilvoll calamitous, destructive, disastrous, fatal, malefic, malign, unfortunate
Uniform uniform
—, in in full-dress (uniform)
—, nicht in in plain clothes
uniform uniform
uninteressant incurious, unattractive, uninteresting
uninteressiert disinterested, indifferent, uninterested
Uninteressiertheit disinterestedness, indifference, lack (want) of interest
Union convention, union
Unions
—land member country, union state
—mitglied union member
—vertrag convention agreement, convention of the union
universal universal
Universalerbe sole (universal) heir, residuary legatee
universell universal
Universität university, college
Universitäts
—bibliothek university library
—bildung academical training, university education
—examen academic qualification
—stadt university town
—studium university studies
—zeit college years
unkenntlich indiscernible, not to be identified, unrecognizable
— machen camouflage, deface, disguise, obliterate
Unkenntlichkeit disguise, indiscernible (unrecognizable) condition
—, bis zur past recognition
Unkenntlichmachung defacement, obliteration
Unkenntnis absence of knowledge, ignorance, unawareness
—, aus out of (through) ignorance
in — von ignorant of
in — lassen keep in the dark about
in — sein be ignorant (unaware) of
unklagbar not actionable, unactionable, unenforceable
unklar abstruse, ambiguous, dark, indistinct, not clear (evident), obscure, unapparent, unclear, unintelligible, vague
Unklarheit ambiguity, ambiguousness, lack (want) of clearness, obscurity, unclearness, vagueness
unklug impolitic, imprudent, injudicious, thoughtless, unwise

Unklugheit imprudence
unkollegial disobliging, unlike a colleague
unkompliziert clear, simple, uncomplicated
unkontrollierbar uncontrollable
unkontrolliert uncontrolled
unkonvertierbar inconvertible
Unkosten charges, cost(s), expenses
Unkosten
—anteil cost rate, share of expenses
—aufstellung statement of expenses
—beitrag contribution to expenses
—bericht cost report
—betrag amount of charges (expenses)
—verteilung allocation of expenses, cost distribution
unkündbar interminable, irredeemable, irrevocable, permanent, perpetual, not subject to notice, not to be foreclosed
Unkunde ignorance
unkundig having no knowledge of, ignorant (of), unacquainted (with), unfamiliar (with)
unlauter impure, mean, shady, sordid, squalid, unfair
Unlauterkeit unfairness
unleserlich illegible
— machen blot, deface, obliterate
Unleserlichkeit illegibility
unleugbar evident, incontestable, indisputable, irrefutable, undeniable
Unlogik inconsequence, inconsistency
unlogisch illogical, inconsequent, inconsistent
unlösbar indissoluble, inexplicable, inextricable, insoluble, unsolvable
unlöschbar inextinguishable
Unmaß excess, immensity
unmaßgeblich unauthoritative
unmäßig excessive, immoderate, inordinate, intemperate
Unmäßigkeit excess, immoderateness, intemperance
Unmensch brute, fiend, monster
unmenschlich brutal, cruel, degrading, inhuman, superhuman
Unmenschlichkeit brutality, cruelty, inhumanity
unmerklich inperceptible, insensible
unmeßbar immeasurable
unmethodisch casual, unmethodical
unmißverständlich unequivocable, unmistakable
unmittelbar direct, immediate
— bevorstehen be imminent, impend
— bevorstehend immediate, imminent
Unmittelbarkeit directness, immediacy, immediateness
unmöglich impossible, impracticable
Unmöglichkeit impossibility, impracticability
unmoralisch immoral
unmotiviert groundless, unmotivated, without motive
unmündig minor, not of age, under age
Unmündiger infant, minor, person under age
Unmündigkeit infancy, minor age, minority
unnachahmlich inimitable
unnachbarlich unneighbourly
unnachgiebig inflexible, intransigent, relentless, stubborn, uncompromising, unyielding
unnachsichtig hard, relentless, severe, strict, unrelenting
unnatürlich affected, non-natural, unnatural
unnennbar inexpressible, unmentionable, unnamable, unutterable
unnotiert unquoted
unnötig needless, superfluous, unnecessary
unnütz fruitless, idle, unprofitable, useless, vain
unordentlich careless, confused, disorderly, irregular, negligent
Unordnung confusion, disarray, disorder
unparlamentarisch unparliamentary

unparteiisch (unparteilich) impartial, unbiassed, unprejudiced
Unparteiischer arbiter, referee, umpire
Unparteilichkeit fairness, impartiality
unpassend improper, inappropriate, inopportune, misplaced, out of place, unreasonable, unsuitable
unpersönlich impersonal
unpfändbar exempt (from execution), not attachable, unseizable
Unpfändbarkeit exemption from seizure
unpolitisch impolitic, imprudent, non-political, unpolitical
unpraktisch impracticable, unpractical
unproduktiv unproductive
Unproduktivität unproductiveness
unpünktlich inexact, irregular, unpunctual
Unpünktlichkeit unpunctuality
unqualifizierbar unqualifiable
unqualifiziert unqualified
unquittiert unreceipted, without receipt
unratsam inexpedient, unadvisable
Unrecht injury, injustice, tort, unlawfulness, wrong
—, mit (zu) unfairly, unjustly, wrongfully, wrongly
— begehen commit an injustice
— haben (im — sein) be mistaken, be (in the) wrong
ins — setzen get (put) in the wrong
— zufügen (tun) do an injustice to, do wrong, wrong
unrecht improper, incorrect, unfair, unjust, unlawful, unsuitable, wrong, wrongful
unrechtlich illegal, unjust, unlawful, wrongful
unrechtmäßig false, illegal, illegitimate, lawless, unlawful, without authority, wrongful
Unrechtmäßigkeit illegality, illegitimacy, lawlessness, unlawfulness, wrongfulness
unredlich dishonest, underhand, unfair
Unredlichkeit dishonesty, unfair dealing
unreell dishonest, unfair, unreliable, unsound
Unregelmäßigkeit irregularity
unrein impure, unclean
unrentabel not paying, unprofitable, unremunerative
Unrentabilität unprofitableness
unrichtig erroneous, false, inaccurate, incorrect, inexact, by mistake, unjust, untrue, wrong
Unrichtigkeit error, fallacy, falsehood, fault(iness), inaccuracy, incorrectness, inexactitude, inexactness
Unruhe agitation, alarm, connotion, disorder, disturbance, riot, trouble, unrest
Unruhestifter agitator, disturber (of the peace), troublemaker
unsachgemäß careless, faulty, improper
unsachlich biassed, impertinent, irrelevant, not objective, partial, personal, prejudiced, off the point
unsauber dishonest, impure, unclean, underhand, unfair, unsound
unschadhaft intact, sound
unschädlich harmless, innocuous, innoxious
— machen get out of the way, neutralize, render harmless
unschätzbar incalculable, inestimable, invaluable, priceless
unscheinbar insignificant, trifling, trivial
unschicklich improper, indecent, out of place, unbecoming, unseemly
Unschicklichkeit impropriety, indecency, unseemliness
unschlüssig irresolute, undecided, undetermined, wavering
— sein hesitate, waver
Unschlüssigkeit indecision, irresolution
Unschuld chastity, innocence purity
seine — beteuern assert (insist

upon, protest) one's innocence, plead not guilty
unschuldig chaste, guiltless, harmless, innocent, not guilty, pure, virgin
für — erklären acquit, declare innocent, plead not guilty
für — halten hold guiltless
unselbständig dependent, irresolute
Unselbständigkeit dependence (cy)
unsicher doubtful, dubious, erratic, insecure, precarious, uncertain, unsafe, unstable, unsteady
Unsicherheit insecurity, instability, precariousness, uncertainty, unsteadiness
unsichtbar hidden, imperceptible, invisible, latent, obscure
Unsitte abuse, bad custom (habit), nuisance
unsittlich immoral, indecent, licentious
Unsittlichkeit immoral (indecent) act, immorality, indecency
unsolid unreliable, untrustworthy
Unsolidität unreliability, untrustworthiness
unstatthaft contrary to the rules, forbidden, foul, illegal, illicit, inadmissible, invalid, not allowed (permitted), unlawful, unsuitable
Unstatthaftigkeit illegality, inadmissibility
unsterblich immortal
Unsterblichkeit immortality
unstet(ig) inconstant, not fixed, restless, unsettled, unstable, unsteady
Unstetigkeit inconstancy, instability, restlessness, unsteadiness
Unstimmigkeit disagreement, discrepancy, dissention, friction, inconsistency
unstreitig beyond dispute, incontestable, indisputable, noncontentious, non-litigious, uncontested, undisputed, unquestionable
untad(e)lig blameless, faultless, immaculate, irreproachable, unimpeachable, unobjectionable
Untadeligkeit blamelessness
Untat atrocity, crime, misdeed, outrage
untätig idle, inactive, indolent
Untätigkeit idleness, inaction, inactivity
untauglich disabled, incompetent, unapt, unfit, unqualified, unserviceable, unsuitable, useless
Untauglichkeit disqualification, unfitness, unserviceableness, unsuitability, unsuitableness, uselessness
unteilbar indivisible
Unteilbarkeit indivisibility
untenbenannt (—erwähnt, —genannt, —stehend) as hereunder, mentioned below, undermentioned
Unter
—absatz subparagraph
—abschnitt subsection, subsector
—abteilung, branch, department, subdivision
—amt inferior office
—ausschuß subcommittee
—bau basis, groundwork
—behörde inferior authority
unterbewerten underestimate, underrate, undervalue
Unterbewertung underestimation, undervaluation
Unterbewußtsein subconsciousness
Unterbezahlung underpayment
Unterbezirk subdistrict
unterbieten dump, underbid, undercut, undersell
Unterbietung dumping, undercutting, underselling
unterbinden call a halt to, cut off, forestall, neutralize, obviate, stop
Unterbleiben cessation, discontinuance, nonperformance, omission
unterbleiben be discontinued, be left undone, cease, not to happen, not to take place, remain undone
unterbrechen adjourn, break (off), cut off (short), discon-

nect, discontinue, intercept, interrupt, stay, stop, suspend
Unterbrecher interrupter
Unterbrechung adjournment, break, disconnection, discontinuance, intermission, interruption, recess, rest, stay, stoppage, suspension
unterbreiten lay (place) before, present, submit
Unterbreitung presentation, submission, submittal
unterbringen accommodate, dispose of, lodge, negotiate, place
Unterbringung accommodation, disposal, negotiation, placing
Unterdelegierter subdelegate
unterdrücken check, conceal, crush, curb, oppress, override, quell, repress, suppress
Unterdrücker oppressor
Unterdrückung concealment, oppression, repression, suppression
—smaßnahme repressive measure
unterdurchschnittlich below average (normal, standard), subaverage, subnormal
Untereinheit subunit
Untereinteilung subdivision
unterentwickelt backward, developing, subnormal, underdeveloped
Unterlangen attempt, enterprise, venture
unterfangen, sich attempt, dare, undertake, venture
Untergang destruction, downfall, end, extinction, failure, fall, loss, ruin, shipwreck, sinking
untergeben inferior, subaltern, subordinate
— sein be under the care (control) of
Untergebener inferior, subaltern, subordinate
untergehen be destroyed (ruined), become extinct, fall, founder, perish, sink
untergeordnet ancillary, base, inferior, lower, minor, secondary, subaltern, subordinate
Untergericht inferior court
Untergewicht underweight, short weight
untergliedern subdivide
Untergliederung subdivision
Untergrund underground
—bewegung underground movement
Untergruppe subgroup
Unterhalt alimony, keep, livelihood, living, maintenance, subsistence, support, sustenance, upkeep
unterhalten carry on, keep (up), maintain, run, support
Unterhalts
—anspruch claim for (right to) alimony (maintenance)
—beihilfe maintenance allowance
—beitrag (—betrag) alimony, allowance
unterhaltsberechtigt entitled to alimony (maintenance)
Unterhalts
—berechtigter beneficiary, dependent
—beschluß maintenance order
—forderung claim for maintenance
—klage action (suit) for maintenance
—kosten cost of maintenance
—leistung alimony, allowance
—pflicht maintenance obligation, obligation to pay alimony
unterhaltspflichtig liable to pay alimony
Unterhalts
—prozeß (—verfahren) alimentary proceedings
—urteil maintenance order
—verpflichtung maintenance obligation
—zahlung alimony payment
—zuschuß s. —beitrag
Unterhaltung conversation, interview, keep, maintenance, support, sustenance, talk, upkeep
— führen carry on a conversation
Unterhaltungskosten cost of maintenance
unterhandeln negotiate, parley, tamper, transact, treat

Unterhändler agent, broker, commissioner, go-between, mediator, negotiator
Unterhandlung negotiation, parley, transaction, treaty
unterjochen subdue, subjugate
Unterjochung subjugation
Unterkommen accommodation, employment, lodging, place, shelter, situation
Unterkontrahent subcontractor
Unterkonzession subconcession, sublicence
Unterkunft accommodation
Unterlage base, datum, document, evidence, foundation, groundwork, proof, record, voucher
Unterlagen data, documents, information, material, records, references, sources
unterlassen abstain from, drop, fail (to), forbear, miss, neglect, omit, refrain from, stop
Unterlassung abstention, default, failure, forbearance, neglect, nonperformance, omission, oversight
— begehen do an act of omission
Unterlassungs
—befehl injunction
—fall case of omission
— —, im in default thereof
—klage action for injunction, injunction suit
unterliegen be defeated (overcome, overthrown, unsuccessful), be liable (subject) to, be open to, be governed by, come (fall) within, fail, fall into (under), lose, succumb
Unterlizenz sublicence
— erteilen sublicense
Unterlizenznehmer sublicencee
Untermiete sublease, underlease, undertenancy
untermieten sublease
Untermieter lodger, roomer, sublessee, subtenant, undertenant
Unternehmen adventure, business, concern, establishment, enterprise, firm, house, operation, project, transaction, undertaking, venture
Privat— private enterprise
Staats— government (state) enterprise
unternehmen attempt, engage in, execute, face, make, take in hand, undertake, venture
—, Versuch (make an) attempt
Unternehmer contractor, employer, enterpreneur, enterpriser, industrialist, manufacturer, operator, principal, undertaker
Unternehmertum employers, industrialists
—, freies free enterprise
Unternehmerverband employers (trade) association (federation)
Unternehmung s. Unternehmen
unterordnen subordinate
Unterordnung subordination
Unterorganisation suborganization
Unterpacht sublease, subtenancy, underlease
Unterpächter sublessee, subtenant, underlessee, undertenant
Unterpfand pawn, pledge, security
unterreden, sich confer, converse, talk
Unterredung conference, conversation, interview, speech, talk
Unterricht classes, education, instruction, lessons, tuition
— erteilen give lessons, instruct, teach, train
— nehmen take lessons
unterrichten advise, give lessons, inform, instruct, teach, train
—, falsch misinform
Unterrichtung advice, information, instruction, notice
untersagen forbid, inhibit, not to allow, prohibit, restrain
—, gerichtlich enjoin, grant an injunction
Untersagung interdiction, prohibition
unterschätzen underestimate, underrate, undervalue
Unterschätzung underestimation, undervaluation
unterscheidbar discernible, distinguishable
—, nicht indiscernible, indistinguishable

unterscheiden differentiate, discern, discriminate, distinguish
—, sich differ
unterscheidend characteristic, discriminatory, distinctive
Unterscheidung differentiation, discrimination, distinction
Unterscheidungs
—merkmal characteristic (distinctive) feature, criterion
—vermögen discernment, judicial faculty, power of distinction
—zeichen distinctive mark
—zoll differential duty
unterschieben attribute (falsely), impute, insinuate, substitute
Unterschiebung imputation, insinuation, substitution
Unterschied difference, distinction
—, ohne indifferently, indiscriminately
unterschiedlich different(ial), discriminating, discriminatory, diverse
— behandeln discriminate
—e Behandlung discrimination
unterschiedslos indiscriminate, undiscriminatory, without distinction (exception)
unterschlagen defraud, embezzle, intercept, misappropriate, peculate, suppress
Unterschlager defaulter
Unterschlagung defraudation, embezzlement, interception, misappropriation, peculation, suppression
Unterschlupf refuge, shelter
unterschreiben approve of, sign, subscribe, underwrite
Unterschrift signature, subscription
mit einer — versehen sign
Unterschriften
—sammlung signature collection
—verzeichnis signature book
Unterschrifts
—beglaubigung attestation (legalization, verification) of signature
unterschriftsberechtigt authorized (empowered, entitled) to sign
Unterschrifts
—berechtigter authorized signer
—muster (—probe) specimen signature
—recht authority to sign
—stempel signature stamp
—vollmacht authority (power) to sign
unterstehen be (come) under, be under the control of, be subject (subordinate) to
unterstellen assume, impute, insinuate, place (put) under, suppose
Unterstellung assumption, implication, imputation, insinuation, supposition
unterstreichen emphasize, punctuate, stress, underline
unterstützen abet, advocate, aid, assist, back (up), countenance, endorse, favour, further, give support to, pratronize, relieve, second, strengthen, subsidize, subvention, support, sustain
Unterstützer backer, patron, promoter, supporter
Unterstützung aid, allowance, assistance. benefit, contribution, furtherance, maintenance, relief, subsidy, support
— erhalten draw support (from)
Unterstützungsanspruch claim to benefit, right of support
unterstützungsbedürftig in need, indigent, needy
Unterstützungs
—fonds (—kasse) provident (relief) fund
—gelder subsidies, subventions
—gesuch application for relief
—zahlungen maintenance (relief) payments
untersuchen analyse, check, examine, explore, go into, inquire (into), inspect, investigate, look into, make an inquiry into, scrutinize, search into, test
Untersuchung analysis, check-up, examination, exploration, inquest, inquiry, inspection, in-

vestigation, research, scrutiny, treatise
—, **gerichtliche** judicial inquiry, trial
Untersuchungs
—**ausschuß (—kommission)** board of inspection, committee of inquiry, investigating committee
—**befehl** search warrant
—**bericht** research report
—**gefangener (—häftling)** prisoner on remand (upon trial)
—**gefängnis** remand prison
—**gericht** court of inquiry, screening court
—**haft** detention on remand, custody upon trial, imprisonment, pending trial, pre-trial custody
in — — nehmen commit for trial
in — — sein be kept on remand
—**recht** right of search
—**richter** examining (investigating) judge, screening court judge
Untertan citizen, subject
untertan subject (to)
unterteilen subdivide
Unterteilung subdivision
Untertitel subhead(ing), subtitle
untervermieten sublease, sublet, underlease, underlet
Untervermieter sublessor, subletter, underlessor
Untervermietung sublease, subleasing, subletting, underletting
unterverpachten s. untervermieten
Unterverpächter s. Untervermieter
Unterverpachtung s. Untervermietung
unterversichern underinsure
Unterversicherung underinsurance
unterweisen instruct, teach, train
Unterweisung instruction, teaching, training, tuition
Unterwelt gangsters, underworld
unterwerfen subdue, subject, subjugate
—, **sich** abide by, accept, acquiesce in, comply with, obey, submit, yield
Unterwerfung acquiescence, conquest, resignation, subjection, subjugation, submission
unterworfen addicted to, exposed to, liable to, subject to
unterzeichnen ratify, sign, subscribe, underwrite
Unterzeichner signatory, signer, subscriber, underwriter
Unterzeichneter undersigned
Unterzeichnung ratification, signature, subscription
unterziehen subject (to), submit
—, **einer Prüfung** review, revise
—, **sich** go in for, make, sit for, take, undergo, undertake
untilgbar indelible, inextinguishable, irredeemable, not payable
untragbar intolerable, prohibitive, unbearable, unmaintainable, unwarrantable
untrennbar inseparable
untreu dishonest, disloyal, faithless, false, perfidious, unfaithful, untrue
Untreue breach of trust, dishonesty, disloyalty, faithlessness, infidelity, perfidy, unfaithfulness
untrüglich certain, infallible, sure, unerring, unfailing, unmistakable
Untrüglichkeit infallibility
untüchtig incapable, incompetent, inefficient, unfit, unqualified, useless
Untüchtigkeit incapacity, incompetence, unefficiency, unfitness
untunlich impossible, impracticable, impractical, inopportune, unfeasible
unüberlegt inconsiderate, indiscreet, injudicious, rash, thoughtless, unreflecting, unwise, without consideration
Unüberlegtheit absence of consideration, inconsideration, thoughtlessness
unübertragbar inalienable, not negotiable (transferable), non-

negotiable, non-transferable, unassignable
Unübertragbarkeit inalienability, unassignability
unüberwindlich impregnable, insuperable, insurmountable, invincible, unconquerable
unumgänglich indispensable, inevitable, necessary, unavoidable
unumschränkt absolute, autocratic, sovereign, unlimited
Unumschränktheit absoluteness
unumstößlich incontestable, incontrovertible, irrefutable, irrevocable
unumstritten uncontested
ununterbrochen continuous, incessant, unintermitted, uninterrupted, without intermission (interruption)
ununterscheidbar indiscernible, indistinguishable
ununterrichtet uninformed
ununtersucht unexamined
unveränderlich constant, immutable, invariable, stable, unalterable, unchangeable
unverändert (the same) as before, unaltered, unchanged
unverantwortlich inexecusable, injustifiable, irresponsible, unwarrantable
Unverantwortlichkeit irresponsibility
unveräußerlich entailed, inalienable, unassignable, unsaleable
Unveräußerlichkeit inalienability, unassignability, unsaleableness
unverbesserlich confirmed, hopeless, incorrigible, inveterate, irreclaimable, unmendable
unverbindlich disobliging, free, informal, noncommittal, not binding (compulsory, obligatory), without commitment (engagement, guarantee, obligation)
unverbrieft not bounded, unchartered, unsecured
unverbürgt unauthentic, unconfirmed, unvouched, unwarranted
unverdächtig not suspect, trustworthy, unsuspected, unsuspicious
unverderblich incorruptible
unverdient undeserved, unearned, unmerited
unverdorben innocent, pure, uncorrupted, unspoilt
unvereidigt unsworn
unvereinbar conflicting, incompatible, incongruous, inconsistent, irreconcilable, out of keeping (with), repugnant (with)
— sein mit be at variance with
Unvereinbarkeit incompatibility, inconsistency, irreconcilability, repugnancy
unverfälscht genuine, pure, real, unadulterated, undiluted
Unverfälschtheit genuineness
unverfänglich harmless, not captious, not insidious
unvergänglich everlasting, immortal, imperishable
unverhältnismäßig disproportionate, excessive, inadequate, out of proportion, unreasonable
unverheiratet single, unmarried
Unverheirateter single person
unverjährbar imprescriptible, not subject ot the statute of limitations
Unverjährbarkeit imprescriptibility, imprescriptibleness
unverjährt not forfeited by prescription
unverkäuflich not for sale (to be sold), unmarketable, unmerchantable, unsaleable
Unverkäuflichkeit unsaleableness
unverkennbar evident, obvious, unmistakable
unverkürzt unabridged, uncurtailed
unverlangt not asked for, not ordered, unsolicited
unverletzlich imprescriptible, inviolable, invulnerable, sacred
Unverletzlichkeit inviolability. invulnerability, invulnerableness

unverletzt intact, safe (and sound), undamaged, unharmed, unhurt, uninjured
unverlöschlich unextinguishable
unvermeidbar (unvermeidlich) inevitable, unavoidable
unvermietet unlet, untenanted, vacant
unvermindert unabated, undimished
Unvermögen disability, disqualification, impotence, inability, incapacity, incompetence, insolvency
unvermögend impecunious, impotent, incapable (of), incompetent, insolvent, penniless, powerless, unable, without means
Unvernunft absurdity, senselessness, unreason, unreasonableness, want of reason
unvernünftig absurd, irrational, senseless, unreasonable, void of reason
unveröffentlicht unpublished
unverrichtet unperformed
—er Dinge unsuccessfully, with empty hands, with nothing achieved
unverrückbar immovable, steadfast, unremovable, unshak(e)able
unverschämt exorbitant, impertinent, impudent, insolent, shameless, unconscionable
Unverschämtheit impertinence, impudence, insolence, shamelessness
unverschlossen unclosed, unlocked
unverschuldet not in debt, undeserved, unencumbered, unindebted
unversehrt intact, safe (and sound), undamaged, unharmed, unhurt, uninjured
Unversehrtheit integrity
unversichert uninsured
unversiegelt unsealed
unversöhnlich implacable, irreconcilable
Unversöhnlichkeit implacability, implacableness, intransigency, irreconcilability, irreconcilableness
unverständlich incomprehensible, inconceivable, mystic, obscure, unintelligible
unversteuert duty unpaid, before taxes, taxe-exempt (-free), tax unpaid
unverwechselbar non-interchangeable, unmistakable
unverwendbar unemployable
unverwundbar invulnerable
unverzeihlich inexcusable, unpardonable
unverziehen unpardoned
unverzinslich bearing no interest, free of interest, interest-free, non-interest bearing
unverzollt bonded, in bond, duty-free, duty unpaid, exempt from duty, unentered
unverzüglich forthwith, immediate, instant, instantaneous, at once, prompt, on the spot, without delay
unvollendet unaccomplished, unfinished
unvollkommen defective, imperfect
Unvollkommenheit imperfection, incompleteness
unvollständig defective, incomplete
Unvollständigkeit imperfection, incompleteness, insufficiency
unvollstreckt unexecuted
unvollzählig incomplete
unvorbedacht undesigned, unpremeditated, without premeditation
unvorbereitet extempore, spontaneous, unprepared
unvoreingenommen impartial, unbiassed, unprejudiced
Unvoreingenommenheit impartiality
unvorhergesehen unexpected, unforeseen
unvorhersehbar fortuitous, unforeseeable
unvorsätzlich undeliberate, undesigned, unintentional, unpremeditated

unvorschriftsmäßig against (contrary to) regulations (rules), improper, irregular
unvorsichtig careless, imprudent, incautious, inconsiderate
Unvorsichtigkeit carelessness, imprudence, incautiousness
unvorstellbar unimaginable
unvorteilhaft disadvantageous, unbecoming, unfavo(u)rable, unprofitable
unwahr false, fictitious, untrue, untruthfull
Unwahrheit falsehood, lie, mendacity, trustlessness, untruth-(fulness)
— sagen tell a lie (an untruth)
unwahrscheinlich improbable, unlikely
Unwahrscheinlichkeit improbability, unlikelihood, unlikeliness
unwandelbar immutable, unalterable, unchangeable, undeviating, unshak(e)able
Unwandelbarkeit immutability
unweigerlich certain, undeniable, unhesitating, unquestioning, unrefusable, unresisting
Unwesen disorder, excesses, nuisance
— treiben be up to (do) mischief
unwesentlich accidental, immaterial, irrelevant, unessential, unimportant
unwichtig insignificant, of no consequence, trifling, unessential, unimportant
Unwichtigkeit insignificance, unimportance
unwiderlegbar (-lich) incontestable, incontrovertible, irrefutable, unanswerable
Unwiderlegbarkeit irrefutability
unwiderlegt unrefuted
unwiderruflich beyond recall, irreversible, irrevocable
Unwiderruflichkeit irrevocability
unwidersprechlich incontestable
unwidersprochen uncontradicted
unwiderstehlich compelling, irresistible, overpowering
Unwiderstehlichkeit irresistibility
unwiederbringlich irrecoverable, irreparable, irretrievable
Unwille anger, animosity, displeasure, exasperation, indignation, unwillingness
unwillig angry, displeased, indignant, reluctant, unwilling
unwirksam inactive, ineffective, ineffectual, inefficacious, inefficient, inoperative, invalid, null, void, without effect
— machen frustrate, neutralize, nullify
Unwirksamkeit inactivity, inefficacy, inefficiency, inoperativeness, invalidity, nullity
unwirtschaftlich uneconomic(al), unproductive, unprofitable, unremunerative
unwissend ignorant, ill informed (of), illiterate, not cognizant (of)
Unwissender ignorant person
Unwissenheit absence of knowledge, ignorance, illiteracy
unwissentlich s. unwissend
unwürdig discreditable, disgraceful, undignified, undeserving, unseemly, unworthy
Unwürdigkeit unworthiness
Unzahl immense (vast) number
unzählbar countless, innumerable, numberless
unzensiert uncensored
unziemlich improper, indecent, unbecoming, unseemly
Unzucht immorality, impudicity, indecency, indecent act, lewdness, sexual offence, unchastity
—, gewerbsmäßige prostitution
—, widernatürliche sodomy
unzüchtig indecent, lascivious, lewd, libidinous, obscene, unchaste
—e Handlung lewd act
Unzüchtigkeit obscenity, unchastity
unzufrieden discontented, dissatisfied
Unzufriedenheit disaffection, discontent, dissatisfaction
—, soziale social unrest

unzugänglich inaccessible, intractable, proof against, reserved, unapproachable, unsusceptible
unzulänglich deficient, inadequate, insufficient
Unzulänglichkeit deficiency, disability, inadequacy, insufficiency, unsatisfactoriness
unzulässig illegal, inadmissible, outlaw, not permissible (permitted), prohibited, undue, unlawful
Unzulässigkeit inadmissibility
unzumutbar unimputable, unreasonable
unzurechnungsfähig imbecile, insane, irresponsible, mentally defective, of unsound mind, non compos (mentis), weakminded
Unzurechnungsfähigkeit imbecility, incapability, insanity, irresponsibility
unzureichend deficient, inadequate, insufficient
unzuständig incompetent, unqualified, without jurisdiction
Unzuständigkeit incompetence (cy), want of jurisdiction
unzustellbar undeliverable
Unzustellbarkeit nondelivery
unzuträglich disadvantageous, inconvenient, prejudicial
unzutreffend false, inapposite, incorrect, unfounded, wrong
unzuverlässig doubful, elusive, inaccurate, incalculable, inexact, treacherous, uncertain, unreliable, untrustworthy
Unzuverlässigkeit uncertainty, unreliability, untrustworthiness
unzweckmäßig inappropriate, inexpedient, not to the purpose, unsuitable
Unzweckmäßigkeit inexpedience, unsuitableness
unzweideutig clear, explicit, plain, self-evident, simple, unambiguous, unequivocal
Unzweideutigkeit clearness, unambiguousness
unzweifelhaft beyond (without) doubt, decided, doubtless, established, indubitable, undoubted, unquestionably, unquestioned
Unzweifelhaftigkeit certainty
Urabstimmung (original) vote
Urbedeutung original meaning, primitive signification
Urfassung original version
Urheber artificer, author, creator, founder, originator
Urheberrecht copyright
urheberrechtlich geschützt copyright
Urheberrechts
—anspruch claim to copyright
—behörde copyright office
—gebühren copyright fees
—gesetz copyright act (law)
—klage copyright case
—register register of copyrights
—schutz copyright protection
—verfahren copyright procedure
—verletzung copyright infringement
—vermerk copyright notice
Urheberschaft authorship
Urkunde certificate, charter, copy, deed, document, evidence, (legal) instrument, licence, paper, proof, record, roll, title, voucher, writ
Abdankungs- deed (document, instrument) of abdication
Abtretungs- deed of assignment
Anerkennungs- deed of acknowledgement (recognition)
Beitritts- deed of accession (consent)
Besitz title deed (document)
Bestallungs- certificate, commission, deed of appointment, diploma, letters-patent, patent
Beweis- piece of evidence, proof, voucher
Erwerbs- title deed
Geburts- birth certificate
Gesellschafts- charter of incorporation, partnership deed
Gründungs- articles (memorandum) of association, foundation charter
Heirats- marriage certificate
Hypotheken- mortgage bond (deed)

Privat- private deed (document)
Protest- deed of protestation
Schenkungs- deed of donation (gift)
Sterbe- (Todes-) death certificate
Stiftungs- charter of foundation, deed of donation
Übertragungs- deed of assignment (conveyance), transfer deed
Verfassungs- charter of the constitution
Verkaufs- bill of sale
Urkunden
—bewahrer keeper of the records, Master of the Rolls (GB)
—beweis documentary evidence (proof)
—buch record, register
—fälscher forger (falsifier) of documents
—fälschung falsification (forgery) of documents
—material documentary evidence (material)
—prozeß trial by record
—rolle roll
—sammlung archives, collection of documents (records)
—unterschlagung suppression of documents
—vernichtung (-beseitigung) spoliation (of documents)
urkundlich authentic, by documents, documental, documentary
— belegen document, support by documents (records)
— belegt documented, supported by documents
—e Belegung documentation
—es Beweismaterial documentary evidence (material)
Urlaub furlough, holidays, leave, vacation
Krankheits- sick leave
—, bezahlter paid holidays (leave, vacation)
—, unbezahlter leave without pay, unpaid holidays (leave, vacation)
Urlaubs
—anspruch (-recht) vacation privilege (right)
—bestimmungen vacation provisions
—geld holiday (leave, vacation) pay
—gesuch application for leave
—schein certificate of leave, pass, permit
—sperre stoppage of leave
—überschreitung leave breaking
Urne urn
Wahl- ballot box, polls
Ursache cause, ground, motive, occasion, reason
ursächlich causal
Ursächlichkeit causality
Urschrift autograph, first draft (sketch), original (text)
urschriftlich autografic, (in the) original
Ursprung extraction, origin, primal cause, provenience, source
Ursprung haben (in) come (from), descend (from), originate (in)
ursprünglich at first, in the beginning, initial, original, primal, primary, primitive
Ursprungs
—angabe indication of origin
—attest (-bescheinigung, -schein, -zeugnis) certificate of origin
—bezeichnung (-vermerk) mark of origin
—land country of origin
—nachweis certificate (proof) of origin
—ort place of origin
—stand primitive state
Urteil adjudgement, award, decision, decree, finding, judg(e)ment, opinion, order, sentence, verdict
Anerkenntnis- consent decree (judgement), decree (judgement) by confession, judgement by admission (consent)
Berufungs- appellate judgement, judgement of appeal
Ehescheidungs- decree of divorce
— —, provisorisches decree nisi
— —, endgültiges decree absolute

End- final decision (decree, judgement)
Gerichts- court decision (judgement, order, sentence, verdict)
Gottes- ordeal
Kosten- judgement of costs
Nichtigkeits- decree of nullity
Präzedenz- precedent
Sachverständigen- award
Scheidungs- s. Ehescheidungs-
Schieds- award
Straf- judgement, sentence
Teil- partial judgement (verdict)
Todes- sentence of death
Versäumnis judgement by default
Vollstreckungs- enforceable judgement
Vor- prejudice
Vorbehalts- provisional judgement
Zivil- (civil) judgement
Zwischen- interim judgement, interlocutory decree
Urteil
— **abgeben** express an opinion
sein — **abgeben** give one's opinion
— **anerkennen** confess a judgement
— **anfechten** appeal against (attack) a judgement
— **annehmen** acquiesce in a judgement
— **aufheben** quash a sentence, annul (quash, recall, reverse, set aside) a judgement
— **aussetzen** arrest a judgement
— **begründen** motify a judgement, set forth the reasons for a judgement
— **fällen** pass (pronounce, deliver) a judgement (sentence) (upon), abjudicate, judge
— **sprechen** award (deliver, give, pass) judgement
— **verkünden** deliver (pass, pronounce) judgement
— **vollstrecken** carry out a judgement, execute a sentence
— **zustellen** notify of decision
urteilen decide, decree, give one's opinion (about, on), judge, pass judgement (on)
— **nach** judge by (**from**)
Urteils
—**abfassung** wording of a decision
—**anerkennung** confession of judgement
—**aufhebung** reversal of judgement
—**aussetzung** arrest of judgement
—**begründung** grounds of judgement, opinion
—**eröffnung** publication of a judgement
urteilsfähig competent, discriminating, judicious
Urteils
—**forderung** judgement claim (debt)
—**fällung** deliverance (passing) of judgement
—**gebühr** judgement fee
—**gläubiger** judgement creditor
—**gründe** reasons for judgement, opinion
—**kraft** discernment, [faculty (power) of] judgement, judiciousness
—**register** judgement book (docket)
—**schuldner** judgement debtor
—**spruch** decree, judgement, sentence, verdict
—**verkündung** announcement (pronouncement) of judgement
—**vermögen** discernment, faculty (power) of judgement, judicial faculty, judiciousness
—**vollstreckung** carrying out (execution) of a judgement (sentence)
—**zustellung** notice of judgement
Urtext original (text)
Urwahl preliminary (primary) election
Urwähler primary elector (voter)
Urzustand original condition
Usance custom, practice, usage
usancemäßige according to custom, customary
Usurpation usurpation
Usurpator usurper
usurpieren usurp
Usus custom, practice, usage
Utensilien implements, requisites, utensils

V

Vagabund tramp, vagabond, vagrant
Vagabundentum vagrancy, vagabondage
vagabundieren tramp about, vagabond, vagabondize
vakant unoccupied, vacant
Vakanz vacancy
Valuta consideration, (foreign) currency, equivalent, (foreign) exchange, exchange rate, value
Valuta
—klausel currency (exchange) clause
—kurs exchange rate
—notierung quotation of exchange rates
—regulierung currency regulation
Valuten foreign exchange
valutieren value
variabel fluctuating, variable
variieren vary
Vasall retainer, vassal
Vasallenschaft vassalage
Vasallenstaat satellite (tributary, vassal) state
Vater father
  Adoptiv— adoptive father
Vater
—haus (parental) home, paternal roof
—land native (parent) country, fatherland
vaterländisch national, patriotic
Vaterlandsliebe patriotism
väterlich ancestral, fatherly, paternal
—es Erbteil patrimony
väterlicherseits by (on) the father's side
vaterlos fatherless
Vatermord parricide
—mörder parricide
—recht patriarchate
—schaft fatherhood, fathership, paternity
Vaterschafts
—anerkenntnis acknowledgement of paternity
—feststellung (-ermittlung) affiliation
—klage affiliation case, paternity suit
—prozeß affiliation (paternity) procedure
—urteil affiliation order
—vermutung presumption of paternity
Vater
—stadt home (native) town
—teil patrimony
verabfolgen deliver, give, hand over, pass, provide, remit, serve
Verabfolgung administration, delivery, handing over, provision
verabreden agree upon, appoint, arrange, fix, set, settle, stipulate
—, sich make an appointment (a date) (with)
Verabredung agreement, appointment, arrangement, clause, conspiracy, engagement, stipulation
verabscheuen abhor, abominate, detest
verabschieden discharge, dismiss, pass, pension off, retire
—, sich take one's departure (leave)
Verabschiedung discharge, dismissal, passage, passing
verachten be contemptuous (of), despise, disdain, scorn
Verachtung contempt, disdain, scorn
verallgemeinern generalize
Verallgemeinerung generalization
veraltet antiquated, obsolete, old-fashioned, out of date
veränderlich alterable, changeable, fluctuating, inconstant, unsettled, variable
Veränderlichkeit changeableness, inconstancy, instability, variability, variableness
verändern alter, change, modify, vary

—, **sich** alter, change, fluctuate, vary
Veränderung alteration, change, fluctuation, modification, shift, turn, variation
veranlagen assess, rate
Veranlagung assessment, disposition, gift, rating, talent, taxation
Veranlagungs
—**beamter** assessor
—**zeitraum** assessment (taxable) period
veranlassen arrange for, bid, bring about, call forth, cause, direct, dispose, give rise to, induce, lead (to), make, order, provoke
Veranlassung arrangement, cause, direction, inducement, initiative, motive, occasion, order, reason, request, suggestion
auf — von at the suggestion (orders, request) of, on the initiative of, by the direction (orders) of
ohne jede — without any provocation
veranschaulichen illustrate
Veranschaulichung demonstration, illustration
veranschlagen appraise, assess, estimate, evaluate, rate, value
Veranschlagung assessment, calculation, estimate, estimation, rating, taxation, valuation
veranstalten arrange, give, make, manage, organize
Veranstalter host, manager, organizer
Veranstaltung arrangement, event, management, meeting, organization, performance
—**skalender** calendar of events
verantworten account for, answer for, be liable (responsible) for, stand for
—, **sich** defend (justify) oneself
verantwortlich accountable, answerable, justifiable, liable, responsible
—, **nicht** irresponsible
—, **voll** fully responsible
— **machen** hold (make) accountable (liable, responsible) for
Verantwortlichkeit accountability, answerableness, liability, responsibility
—, **gegenseitige** solidarity
Verantwortung defence, justification, liability, responsibility, vindication
—, **auf eigene** on one's own responsibility
— **tragen** be responsible for
— **übernehmen** accept liability for, assume responsibility for
zur — ziehen call to account, hold liable (responsible)
verantwortungsbewußt responsible
Verantwortungsbewußtsein (-gefühl) sense of responsibility
verantwortungslos irresponsible
verantwortungsvoll responsible
Veräußerer alienator, seller, transferrer
veräußerlich alienable, assignable, negotiable, sal(e)able, transferable
—, **nicht (un-)** entailed, inalienable, not transferable, unassignable, unsal(e)able
Veräußerlichkeit alienability, negotiability, transferability
veräußern alienate, assign, dispose of, sell, transfer
Veräußerung alienation, disposal, negotiation, sale, transfer
Veräußerungs
—**recht** right of disposal (alienation), right to alienate (sell)
—**verbot** prohibition of sale, restraint on alienation
Verbal
—**injurie** (verbal) insult
—**note** verbal note, memorandum
Verband association, combine, commonwealth, federation, formation, group, syndicate, union, unit
Arbeitgeber- (Unternehmer-) employers' (trade) association (federation)
Arbeiter- workers' union (association)

Arbeitnehmer- employees' association, workers' (labo(u)r, trade) union
Berufs- professional union, trade association
Gewerkschafts- federation of trade unions
—, öffentlicher body corporate, public body (corporation)
Verbandssatzung articles of association
verbannen banish, deport, expel, exile, outlaw, send into exile
Verbannter exile, outlaw
Verbannung banishment, deportment, exile, expulsion
in die — gehen be exiled
in der — leben live in exile
in die — schicken (send into) exile
verbergen conceal, hide, secrete
—, sich abscond, hide
Verbergung concealment
verbessern (a)meliorate, (a)mend, better, correct, improve, rectify, reform, revise
Verbesserung (a)melioration, amendment, betterment, correction, improvement, rectification, reform, revisal, revision
Verbesserungs
—antrag amendment
— — einbringen move an amendment
—vorschlag proposal for (of) improvement
verbieten ban, forbid, inhibit, interdict, outlaw, prohibit, rule out, suppress
verbinden add (to), ally, attach, bind (up), combine, connect, consolidate, engage, incorporate, join, link up (with), pledge, unite
—, sich affiliate (with), ally, associate (with), combine, confederate, enter into partnership, form an alliance, join, link up (with), unite
—, die Augen blindfold
verbindlich binding, compulsory, obligatory, obliging
un- disobliging, free, informal, noncommittal, not binding (compulsory, obligatory), without commitment (engagement, guarantee, obligation)
Verbindlichkeit binding force, commitment, engagement, favo(u)r, kindness, liability, obligation, obligingness
Gesamt- joint liability
Verbindlichkeit
—, mit gegenseitiger mutually binding
—, ohne without commitment (engagement, liability, obligation)
Verbindlichkeiten accounts payable, debts, indebtedness, liabilities, payables
seinen — nachkommen meet one's liabilities (engagements)
Verbindung alliance, amalgamation, association, coalition, combination, communication, connection, connexion, contact, fusion, junction, juncture, liaison, merger, nexus, relation(ship), society, union
in — mit in conjunction (connection) with, together with
—en abbrechen break off (discontinue) relations
— aufnehmen communicate (with), (establish) contact
in — bringen mit associate (connect, link up) with, put in touch with
— eingehen enter into relation (to)
— haben mit be in touch with
sich in — setzen mit communicate with
in — stehen mit be connected with, be in touch with, correspond with
in — treten contact, enter into relation, take up with
— verlieren mit lose touch with
Verbindungsmann contact man, liaison man (officer)
Verbleib whereabouts
verbleiben be left, continue, persist in, remain, stay
verborgen concealed, hidden, latent, secret
im —en in secret, secretly

— **halten** keep a secret from
Verborgenheit concealment, secrecy
Verbot ban, inhibition, injunction, interdiction, prohibition, suppression
Aufenthalts- local banishment
Ausfuhr- (Export-) export embargo
Ausgeh- confinement, curfew
Einfuhr- (Import-) import embargo
Handels- embargo, prohibition of trade
—, **amtliches** (official) ban
—, **gerichtliches** (court) injunction
—, **gesetzliches** interdiction
—, **polizeiliches** police ban
— **aufheben** lift a ban
— **erlassen** impose a ban (on), issue a prohibition
verboten forbidden, illegal, illicit, prohibited, unlawful
Verbrauch consumption, expenditure
verbrauchen consume, exhaust, expend, spend, use (up)
Verbraucher consumer
—**schaft** consumers
Verbrauchs
—**artikel (-güter)** articles of consumption, commodities, consumer goods
—**genossenschaft** consumers' union, cooperative society
—**steuer** excise (duty), indirect tax
Verbrechen crime, delinquency, felony, (criminal) offence, outrage, treason
— **begehen (verüben)** commit (perpetrate) a crime
eines —s überführt werden be convicted of a crime
eines —s schuldig sein be guilty of a crime
verbrechen commit, perpetrate
Verbrechensbekämpfung (-verhütung) crime prevention
Verbrecher criminal, delinquent, felon, gangster, offender
Berufs- (Gewohnheits-) habitual (profession) criminal
Gewohnheits- gaol bird
Kriegs- war criminal
Schwer- criminal
Sittlichkeits- sex criminal (offender)
Verbrecher
—, **erstmaliger** first offender
—, **jugendlicher** juvenile offender
—, **politischer** political offender
—, **überführter** convict
—**album** collection of criminals' portraits, rogues' gallery
—**bande** criminal organization, gang (of criminals)
—, **Mitglied einer** gangster
verbrecherisch criminal, felonious
Verbrecher
—**jagd** man hunt
—**kolonie** convict colony (settlement), penal colony (settlement)
—**laufbahn** criminal career
—**tum** criminality, outlawry
—**welt** crime world, gangland, underworld
verbreiten circulate, diffuse, disseminate, divulge, propagate, spread
Verbreiter disseminator, divulger, propagator, spreader
Verbreitung circulation, diffusion, dissemination, distribution, divulgation, extension, propagation, spreading
verbriefen charter, convey, confirm by document, promise by writ, secure by charter, transfer by deed
—, **sich** bind oneself by deed, stand security
verbrieft bonded, chartered, conveyed, guaranteed, transferred, vested
—**er Anspruch** title
—**es Recht** chartered (vested) right
Verbriefung conveyance (transfer) of property (title), documentation, acknowledgement in writing
verbringen pass, spend
verbuchen book, enter (into the books), record, register, secure

Verbuchung entry, registration
verbünden ally, unite
—, sich ally oneself (with), confederate (with), enter into a confederation (league), form an alliance, league oneself (with)
verbündet allied, confederate
Verbündeter ally, confederate
verbürgen guarantee, warrant
sich — für answer for, bail for, be (become, stand) surety for, furnish (give) security for, go (stand) bail for, pledge oneself for, undertake, vouch for
verbürgt authentic, well-founded
verbüßen atone for
—, seine Strafe complete (serve) one's sentence, do (serve) one's time
Verbüßung completion
Verdacht suspicion
auf den — hin on the strength of, on the suspicion (that)
unter — suspect(ed)
unter dem — under suspicion (of)
— ablenken divert (remove) suspicion from
— beseitigen (zerstreuen) dispel suspicions
— bestätigen confirm suspicion
in — bringen cast (throw) suspicion upon
in falschen — bringen slander
— erregen (erwecken) arouse (exite) suspicion, become suspect
in — haben suspect (of)
— hegen attach suspicion to, entertain a suspicion (of), have suspicions about
in — kommen excite suspicion
— schöpfen become suspicious
in (im, unter) — stehen be suspected (of)
verdächtig doubtful, questionable, suspect(ed), suspicious, untrustworthy
verdächtig
— sein be suspected of, be under suspicion
— machen cast (throw) suspicion on
— werden fall under suspicion
verdächtigen cast (throw) suspicion on, hold suspect, suspect
—, einer Sache impute a thing to
Verdächtigkeit suspiciousness
Verdächtigter suspect
Verdächtigung casting suspicion on, insinuation
Verdachts
—grund cause (ground) of suspicion, reason for suspicion
—moment suspicious fact
—person suspect
verdammen condemn
verdammenswert condemnable
Verdammung condemnation
—surteil sentence of condemnation
verdanken be intebted (to, for), derive (from), owe (to)
Verderb decay, destruction, ruin
Verderben corruption, decay, destruction, ruin
ins — stürzen ruin, undo
verderben be damaged (ruined), corrupt, debase, decay, deprave, destroy, perish, pervert, ruin, spoil
Verderber corrupter, destroyer, spoiler
verderblich dangerous, demoralizing, destructive, fatal, perishable, pernicious, ruinous
Verderbnis corruption, depravity, perversity
verderbt corrupt(ed), demoralized, depraved, perverse, vicious
Verderbtheit corruption, corruptness, depravity, perversion
Verderbung corruption, depravation, perversion
verdeutlichen illustrate, make clear (plain)
Verdeutlichung elucidation, illustration
verdienen be worth, deserve, earn, gain, get, make, merit, win
Verdiener earner, gainer, winner
Verdienst desert, earnings, gain, merit, profit, worth
Verdienst
—ausfall broken time, loss of earnings

—spanne (profit) margin
verdientermaßen deservedly
verdingen contract for, hire out, let out
—, sich engage oneself, enter service (with), hire oneself out
Verdingung contract, hire, hiring out
verdorben corrupt(ed), damaged, decayed, depraved, spoiled, spoilt
Verdorbenheit s. Verderbtheit
verdrängen dislodge, displace, drive (push) away, extrude from, oust, repress, supercede, supplant
—, aus dem Besitz dispossess
Verdrängung dislodgement, displacement, supplantation
—, aus dem Besitz dispossession
verdrehen distort, misinterpret, misrepresent, pervert, twist, wrench, wrest
—, Recht pervert justice, pettifog
Verdreher
Rechts- lawmonger, pettifogger
Verdrehung distortion, misinterpretation, misrepresentation, perversion
Rechts- pettifoggery, pettifogging
verdunkeln black-out, camouflage, darken, obscure
Verdunkelung black-out, collusion, darkening, obscuration, obscuring
Verdunkelungs
—gefahr danger of collusion (of obscuring the traces)
—manöver collusion
vereiden (vereidigen) administer (tender) an (the) oath to, put (up) on (one's) oath, swear (in)
vereidet (vereidigt) sworn (in)
vereidigt werden be sworn in
Vereidigung administration of an oath, attestation, swearing (in)
Verein association, club, league, society, union
—, eingetragener registered (incorporated) association (club)
—, nichtrechtsfähiger unincorporated association
vereinbar compatible, consistent
nicht — (unvereinbar) conflicting, incompatible, incongruous, inconsistent, irreconcilable, out of keeping (with), repugnant (with), at variance
Vereinbarkeit compatibility
Un- incompatibility, inconsistency, irreconcilability, repugnancy
vereinbaren agree upon, appoint, arrange, come to (make) an arrangement (agreement), concert, covenant, fix, reconcile, set, stipulate
sich — lassen mit be consonant with
vereinbart agreed upon, concerted, stipulated
—, wie (vereinbarungsgemäß) as agreed upon, as per agreement
Vereinbarung agreement, appointment, arrangement, contract, covenant, convention, engagement, provision, settlement, stipulation
—, laut as agreed upon (arranged)
—en treffen come to (make, reach) an agreement, come to (make) an arrangement
vereinfachen simplify
Vereinfachung simplification
vereinen (vereinigen) add (to), amalgamate, assemble, combine, concentrate, consolidate, coordinate, fuse, incorporate (with), integrate, join, merge, pool, reconcile (with), unite
vereinigen, in sich embody
—, sich associate, combine, conspire, join, meet, merge, rally
sich — lassen mit be compatible with
Vereinigung alliance, amalgamation, assembly, association, club, coalition, combination, concentration, confederacy, consolidation, corporation, federation, fusion, gathering, group, junction, meeting, merger, organization, pool, society, union

vereinnahmen cash, receive, take in
Vereinnahmung cashing, receipt
Vereins
—freiheit freedom of association
—recht right of association
—register register of association
—satzung articles of association, association law, club laws
vereiteln baffle, defeat, disappoint, foil, frustrate, kill, repel, shatter, thwart
Vereitelung defeat, frustration
vererben bequeath, leave, transfer by will
—, sich be hereditary
sich — auf be handed down, descend, devolve (up)on, transmit (to)
vererbbar devisable, hereditable, heritable
vererblich hereditary, inheritable, transmissible
Vererblichkeit inheritableness
Vererbung heredity, leaving, transmission
Vererbungs
—gesetz law of heredity
—theorie theory of heredity
Verfahren dealing(s), method, proceeding(s), procedure, process
Anklage— procedures of indictment, prosecution
Aufgebots— public citation, (procedure [proceedings] by) public summons
Auslieferungs— extradition procedure (proceedings)
Berufungs— appellate proceedings, procedure of appeal
Beschwerde— procedure of complaint
Beweis— (—aufnahme—) rules of evidence
Disziplinar— disciplinary action (proceedings)
Ehescheidungs— divorce proceedings (suit)
Einspruchs— opposition proceedings
Enteignungs— expropriation proceedings
Gerichts— court procedure, lawsuit, legal proceedings
Güte— amicable settlement, conciliation, conciliatory proceedings
Haupt— trial
Konkurs— bankruptcy proceedings
Revisions— appellate procedure
Schiedsgerichts— arbitration (procedure)
Straf— criminal procedure (proceedings), penal suit, prosecution
Verwaltungs— administrative procedure
Wiederaufnahme— rehearing, retrial
Zivil— civil procedure
Zwischen— interlocutory proceedings
Verfahren
—, anhängiges pending proceedings
—, beschleunigtes summary procedure
Verfahren
— einleiten institute (take) proceedings, proceed
— einstellen stay (quash) proceedings
— eröffnen initiate proceedings
— niederschlagen quash proceedings
— unterbrechen interrupt (suspend) proceedings
— vertagen adjourn proceedings
— wiederaufnehmen reinstall (reinstitute, reopen) proceedings
verfahren act, handle, proceed
— gegen prosecute, take legal proceedings against
— mit deal with
Verfahrens
—einstellung stay of proceedings
—frage matter of form
—kosten law costs
—ordnung (—regeln, —vorschriften) rules of procedure, procedural rules
—recht law of procedure, procedural law
verfahrensrechtlich procedural
Verfahrensweise method, process

Verfall corruption, decadence, decay, decline, depravity, dilapidation, downfall, expiration, expiry, extinction, foreclosure, forfeiture, lapse, maturity, nonsuit, ruin, termination
—datum date of expiration (maturity), due date, expiry date
verfallen become (fall) due, become extinct (forfeited, payable), decay, decline, degenerate, dilapidate, due, expire, lapse, mature
— an devolve on, become the property of
verfallen addicted to, decayed, dilapidated, forfeited, ruinous
für — erklären foreclose, forfeit
— lassen abandon, drop
Verfall
—erklärung cancellation, confiscation, foreclosure
—frist maturity, period (term) of expiration
—klausel forfeit clause
—tag day of expiration (maturity), due date, day of payment, expiration (maturity) date
—zeit maturity, time of payment
verfälschen adulterate, debase, falsify, forge
Verfälscher adulterator, adulteror, falsifier, **forger**
Verfälschung adulteration, falsification, forgery
verfassen compile, compose, draft, draw up, write
Verfasser author, compiler, composer, draftsman, writer
—schaft authorship
Verfassung charter, condition, constitution, organization, state, structure, system
Geistes— frame (state) of mind, mental condition
Gemüts— frame (state) of mind, disposition
verfassunggebend constituent
Verfassungs
—änderung amendment of the constitution
—bestimmung constitutional provision
—bruch breach (violation) of the constitution
verfassungsgemäß (—mäßig) according to (in accordance with) the constitution, constitutional
Verfassungs
—mäßigkeit constitutionality
—recht constitutional law
verfassungsrechtlich constitutional, under the constitutional law
Verfassungs
—reform constitutional reform
—staat constitutional state
verfassungstreu loyal to the constitution
Verfassungsurkunde charter of the constitution, constitutional charter (document)
verfassungswidrig against the constitution, unconstitutional
Verfassungswidrigkeit unconstitutionality
verfechten advocate, argue, assert, defend, fight, maintain, stand up for
Verfechter advocate, apostle, champion, defender, exponent
verfehlen fail, miss
Verfehlung breach, delinquency, failure, lapse
verfemen boycott, ostracize, outlaw, proscribe
verflechten (in) entangle (in), involve (in)
Verflechtung entanglement, interdependence, involving, nexus
— von Umständen coincidence
verfließen elapse, expire, pass
Verfolg continuation, progress
im — von in the course of, in pursuance of
verfolgbar actionable, indictable, punishable, suable
Verfolgbarkeit suability
verfolgen chase, follow (up), persecute, proceed with, prosecute, pursue, shadow, trace (back), track
—, gerichtlich institute legal proceedings against, prosecute
Verfolger persecutor, pursuer

Verfolgter persecutee
Verfolgung chase, persecution, prosecution, pursuance, pursuit
—swahn obsession, persecution mania
verfrüht premature
verfügbar at one's disposal, available, disposable, in hand, liquid
—, nicht unavailable
Verfügbarkeit availability, availableness, liquidity
verfügen decree, enact, order, prescribe, provide
— über be in control of, dispose of, have at one's disposal
—, letztwillig dispose by will
Verfügung command, decree, direction, disposal, disposition, enactment, injunction, instruction, order, ordinance, regulation, rule, ruling
—, einstweilige injunction, temporary decree
—, gerichtliche injunction, judicial order
—, letztwillige last will, testamentary disposition
Verfügung
— erlassen decree, enter (issue) an order, issue (pass) a decree, order
zur — haben have at hand (on one's hands)
zur — halten hold to the order of
sich zur — halten stand by
zur — stehen be available (in attendance, on hand), be at one's disposal, stand by
zur — stellen place at one's disposal, offer
—en treffen give orders, make arrangements
verfügungsberechtigt authorized (entitled) to dispose (of), having the right to dispose (of)
Verfügungs
—befugnis (—berechtigung) power of disposal (disposition), right of disposal (to dispose)
—beschränkung (—verbot) restraint on disposal
—freiheit discretion
—gewalt (—macht) power of disposal (disposition), control, disposal, disposition
—recht right of disposal (disposition)
verführen corrupt, induce, misdirect, seduce, suborn, tempt
Verführer corrupter, seducer, tempter
Verführung corruption, seduction, subornation
Vergangenheit antecedents, history, past, record
—, einwandfreie clean record
vergebbar pardonable
vergeben allocate, award, bestow (on), cede, confer (on), dispose of, forgive, give (away), place
vergebens to no purpose, of no use, in vain, vainly
vergeblich abortive, fruitless, futile, idle, ineffectual, needless, useless, vain
Vergebung bestowal, cession, conferment, forgiveness, pardon, pardoning, placing
Vergehen delict, felony, offence (se), tort, trespass, violation
—, geringfügiges petty offence
—, politisches political offence
—, strafrechtliches crime, criminal offence
vergehen cease, disappear, elapse, end, go by, pass, run, vanish
—, sich commit an offence, fail in one's duty
sich — an assault, violate
—, gegen break, infringe, injure, insult, offend, trespass against, violate
vergelten pay back, recompense, remunerate (for), repay, requite, retaliate, return, reward
Vergelter avenger, rewarder
Vergeltung recompense, reprisal, requital, retaliation, retribution, return, reward
— üben exercise retaliation, make reprisals (on), retaliate (on)
Vergeltungs
—angriff reprisal (retaliation) attack

—maßnahme (—maßregel) reprisal, retaliatory measure
— — ergreifen make reprisal (on)
—recht right of reprisal (retaliation)
—zoll retaliatory duty (tariff)
vergewaltigen coerce, commit an assault on, distort, do violence to, force, oppress, rape, ravish, terrorize, twist, use force on, violate
Vergewaltigung outrage, rape, violation, violence
vergewissern assure of, convince of
—, sich ascertain, make sure (of)
Vergewisserung assurance
vergiften contaminate, envenom, poison
—, sich poison oneself, take poison
Vergiftung poisoning
Vergleich accommodation, accord, adjustment, arrangement, collation, comparison, composition, compromise, contract, settlement
im — zu in comparison with, (as) compared to (with)
— anstellen draw a parallel
— aushalten bear comparison (with)
zu einem — kommen (einen — schließen) come to terms, come to (make) an agreement (an arrangement, a settlement), make a composition (with)
vergleichbar comparable (to)
Vergleichbarkeit comparability
vergleichen adjust, collate, compare (with), draw a parallel (between), reconcile, settle
sich — mit come to terms with, come to (make) an agreement (an arrangement, a compromise), compound with, compromise
vergleichend comparative
Vergleichs
—bedingungen terms of arrangement (settlement)
—friede peace by agreement
—mittel means of reconciliation
—summe compensation
—termin day of settlement
—urkunde (—vertrag) composition deed, deed of settlement
—verfahren arbitration, conciliatory (settlement) proceedings
vergleichsweise comparatively, by (way of) agreement (comparison)
Vergleichs
—wert comparative (relative) value
—zahlen comparative figures
—zeitraum comparative period
Vergleichung adjustment, collation, comparison, settlement
vergreifen
sich — an lay hands on, steal, violate
vergrößern add, aggrandize, augment, enlarge, exaggerate, expand, increase
—, sich increase
Vergrößerung addition, aggrandizement, augmentation, enlargement, exaggeration, expansion, increase
Vergünstigung allowance, benefit, deduction, favour, permission, preference, preferential treatment, privilege
Vergünstigungs
—klausel preferential clause
—tage days of grace, respite
—zoll preferential duty (tariff)
vergütbar remunerable
vergüten allow, compensate (for), indemnify (for), make good, make up for, pay, refund, reimburse, remunerate, restore, temper
Vergütung allowance, bonus, compensation, consideration, fee, indemnity, indemnification, payment, refund, reimbursement, remuneration
verhaften apprehend, arrest, attach, imprison, put under arrest, take into custody
verhaften
— lassen give in charge
verhaftet in custody, under arrest
Verhafteter prisoner
Verhaftung apprehension, arrest (ment), capture, imprisonment

Massen—en mass arrests
— durchführen s. verhaften
Verhaftungs
—befehl capias, warrant (writ) of arrest
— — erlassen issue (make out) a warrant of arrest
—ort place of arrest
—welle wave of arrests
Verhalt state of affairs
—, wahrer real facts
Verhalten attitude, behavio(u)r, conduct, dealing, demeanour, deportment, procedure, manner (mode, way) of acting
—, schlechtes misbehaviour, misconduct, misdemeanour
verhalten, sich act, be, behave, comport oneself, conduct oneself, demean oneself
Verhältnis condition, dividend, intercourse, liaison, position, proportion, quota, rate, ratio, relation(ship), standard
Verhältnisse circumstances, condition(s), matters, means, position, situation, state
Verhältnisanteil dividend, quota, share
verhältnismäßig comparative, in comparison (proportion), proportional, proportionate, relative
Verhältniswahl proportional ballot (representation)
—system proportionalism, proportional representation
verhältniswidrig disproportionate
Verhaltungs
—art conduct
—anweisung letter of instruction
—befehl direction, instruction
—maßregeln directions, instructions, orders, rules of conduct
verhandeln argue, confer (with), debate (upon), discuss, hear, negotiate, plead, transact, treat (about, with), try
— gegen try (for)
—, vor Gericht plead before the court
Verhandler negotiator
Verhandlung case, conference, debate, discussion, hearing, negotiation, parley, pleading, proceeding, talk, transaction, treaty, trial
—en abbrechen break (cut) off negotiations
—en abschließen terminate negotiations
—en aufnehmen enter into negotiations
— eröffnen open the case (trial)
— führen conduct (hold) a trial
—en führen carry on (conduct) negotiations, negotiate
zur — kommen be up for trial
Verhandlungs
—bericht (—protokoll) minutes (of proceedings), trial record
verhandlungsfähig negotiable
Verhandlungs
—fähigkeit negotiability
—friede peace by negotiation
—ort conference place, place of hearing (negotiations, trial), venue
—partner partner, party
—raum (—saal) court room
—tag juridical day, day of hearing (negotiation)
—termin date of hearing (negotiation), day fixed for trial
—vollmacht negotiating power, power of negotiation
—weg, im by negotiations
verhängen decree (against), impose (on), inflict (up)on, ordain, proclaim, send
Verhängnis destiny, doom, fate
zum — werden be one's doom
verhängnisvoll fatal, fateful, ominous
verharren persist (in), remain
verhehlen conceal, hide, suppress
Verhehlung concealment, hiding, suppression
verheimlichen conceal (from), disguise, dissemble, hide, hush up, keep a secret from, pocket, suppress
Verheimlichung concealment, hiding, suppression

verheiratet married
un— not married, single, unmarried
Verheirateter married person
verhelfen help (to)
verhindern block, hinder, obstruct, prevent (from), stop
verhindernd prohibitive
Verhinderung disability, frustration, hindrance, impediment, obstacle, prevention
Verhinderungs
—fall, im in case of prevention
—grund cause of impediment (prevention)
Verhör examination, hearing, interrogation, questioning, trial
Kreuz— cross-examination
ins — — nehmen cross-examine
ins Verhör nehmen (einem — unterziehen) (cross-)examine, question
verhören (cross-)examine, hear, interrogate, question
—, sich misunderstand
verhüten avert, avoid, obviate, prevent
verhütend preservative, preventive, prophylactic
Verhütung averting, avoidance, precautions, prevention, prophylaxis
Empfängnis— contraception
Verhütungs
—maßregel preventive measure
—mittel contraceptive, preservative, preventive, prophylactic
verifizieren verify
verjagen dispel, expel
verjährbar prescriptible, subject to the statute of limitations
verjähren be in lapse, become barred (invalid, prescriptive, stale), come under (fall under, be lost by) the statute of limitations, grow obsolete
verjährt antiquated, barred (cancelled) by the statute of limitations, obsolete, out of date, outdate, outlawed, prescribed, prescriptive, stale, statute-barred, superannuated
Verjährung limitation, prescription, superannuation, statute of limitations
— geltend machen plead limitation
Verjährungs
—bestimmungen (—recht) statute of limitations
—frist limitation period, period (term) of limitation (prescription)
Verkauf disposal, realization, sale, selling
—, zum on sale
zum — stehen be for sale
zum — stellen put up for sale
verkaufen dispose of, market, realize, sell, vend
—, sich prostitute oneself
—, zu be for sale, to be sold
Verkäufer bargainor, retailer, seller, vendor
verkäuflich by (for) sale, marketable, mercenary, merchantable, negotiable, realizable, sal(e)able, to be sold, venal, vendible
— überlassen sell
Verkäuflichkeit marketability, merchantableness, negotiability, sal(e)ability, sal(e)ableness, vendibility
Verkaufs
—auftrag sales (selling) order
—bedingungen terms of sale, sales (selling) conditions
—berechtigung power of sale
—bescheinigung sales sheet (ticket)
—beschränkung restraint on sale
— —en sales (selling) restrictions
—buch sales book
—erlaubnis (—lizenz) selling licence
—kontrolle sales control
—methode sales (selling) method
—organisation sales organization
—preis market value, sales (selling) price
—recht right to sell, selling right (licence)
—urkunde bill (deed) of sale
—verbot prohibition of (restraint on) sale

—vereinbarung selling agreement
—vertrag sales agreement (contract)
—vollmacht power of sale
—wert sales (selling) value
Verkehr circulation, commerce, communication, communion, dealings, intercourse, market, service, trade, traffic, transaction, transport(ation)
Grenz— border traffic
Zahlungs— money transfer, payment transactions
verkehren mit associate with, have intercourse with, have relations to, trade (traffic) with
Verkehrs
—abgabe traffic duty
—abkommen traffic arrangement
—ampel (—licht) traffic light
—bestimmungen (—ordnung, —vorschriften) traffic regulations
—gesetz traffic law
—kontrolle traffic control
—polizei traffic (road) police
—polizist (—schutzmann) traffic constable (policeman)
—posten traffic post
—regeln traffic rules
—regelung traffic regulations
—schild traffic sign
verkehrssicher road-worthy
Verkehrs
—signal traffic signal
—steuer (property) transfer tax
—strafe traffic fine
—streife traffic patrol
—sünder violator, jaywalker
—unfall traffic accident
—vergehen (—delikt) violation of traffic regulations
—verordnung (—vorschrift) traffic ordinance
verkehrswidrig contrary to traffic regulations
Verkehrszeichen traffic sign(al)
verkennen misapprehend, misjudge, mistake, misunderstand, fail to recognize
Verkennung misapprehension
Verkettung connection, enchainment
— von Umständen chain of events
verklagbar actionable, indictable, suable
verklagen accuse (of), go to the law (with), bring an action against, sue (for), take legal proceedings against
Verklagter accused, defendant
verkleinern belittle, depreciate, derogate (from), detract (from), diminish, disparage, lessen, reduce
Verkleinerung belittlement, derogation, detraction, diminution, reduction
verkommen decay, go to ruin
verkommen decayed, degenerate, demoralized, depraved, disreputable, profligate
Verkommenheit demoralization, depravity
verkörpern embody, impersonate, incarnate, personify, represent
Verkörperung embodiment, impersonation, incarnation, personification
verkünden announce, deliver, give notice, make known (public), proclaim, promulgate, pronounce, publish, render
Verkündung announcement, deliverance, proclamation, promulgation, pronouncement, publication
—stermin date of decision
verkürzen abridge, beguile, curtail, cut, diminish, lessen, reduce, shorten, stint
Verkürzung abridgement, cut, curtailment, reduction, shortening
Verlade
—bestimmungen loading regulations
—gebühr (—kosten, —spesen) loading (shipping) charges
—papiere shipping documents
—schein bill of loading, shipping bill
—vertrag shipping contract

Verlag publication, publisher(s), publishing firm (house)
Verlagsrecht copyright
verlagsrechtlich geschützt copyright
Verlagsvertrag publishing contract
Verlangen demand, desire, request
—, auf at call, on command, on demand, by one's desire, at request, by request
verlangen apply for, ask (for), call for, claim, command, compel, demand, desire, dictate, require, want
verlängern continue, extend, lengthen, prolong, prolongate, renew
Verlängerung extension, lengthening, prologation, protraction, renewal
Verlängerungs
—abkommen prolongation agreement
—antrag application for extension (renewal)
verlängerungsfähig renewable
Verlängerungs
—klausel renewal clause
—zeitraum extension period (term)
Verlassen abandonment, desertion
—, böswilliges malicious abandonment
verlassen abandon, desert, forsake, leave, let down, quit, relinquish, run away from
sich — auf count on, depend upon, rely (up)on, reckon (up)on, trust
verläßlich certain, reliable, trustworthy
Verläßlichkeit reliability
Verlauf course, development, expiration, lapse, process, progress
im — von in the course of
verlaufen (e)lapse, expire, go (off), pass (off), proceed, progress
verlautbaren disclose, divulge, make known, report, state
Verlautbarung bulletin, communiqué, disclosure, publication, report, statement
verlauten be reported (spread about), transpire
— lassen give to understand, hint (that), intimate (that)
verleben pass, spend
verlegen adjourn, edit, mislay, misplace, move, postpone, publish, remove, shift, transfer
sich — auf apply oneself to, devote oneself to, (take) resort to
Verlegenheit difficulty, dilemma, embarrassment, inconvenience, perplexity, predicament
—, finanzielle financial straits
in — bringen baffle, embarrass, inconvenience, puzzle
in — kommen get embarrassed
Verleger editor, publisher
Verlegung adjournment, postponement, publication, publishing, removal, transfer
verleihen appoint (to), award (to), bestow (on), confer (up) on, give, grant, hire out, invest with, lend (out), let out, loan, put out, tender
Verleiher bestower, grantor, jobber, lender
Geld— moneylender
Verleihung award(ing), bestowal, bestowment, concession, conferment, endowment, grant(ing), hiring out, investiture, lending out, letting out
Verleihungs
—urkunde lending (loan) document
verleiten entice, incite, induce, inveigle, lead astray, mislead, seduce, suborn
Verleitung inducement, misleading, seduction, subornation
verlesen read (out), recite
Verlesung reading, recital
verletzbar damageable, sensitive, violable, vulnerable
verletzen break, contravene, damage, encroach upon, hurt, infringe, injure, neglect, offend (against), outrage, transgress, violate, wound, wrong

Verletzer breaker, infringer, transgressor, violator
Verletzter injured person (party)
Verletzung breach, contravention, damage, encroachment, hurt, infraction, infringement, injury, insult, neglect, offence, outrage, transgression, violation, wound, wrong
Grenz— violation of the border (frontier)
Pflicht— breach (infringement, violation) of duty
Rechts— infringement of law (right), lawbreaking
Vertrags— breach of agreement (contract), breach (infringement, violation) of a treaty
verleugnen abnegate, act against, belie, deny, disavow, disown, ignore
Verleugner abnegator, denier, disowner
Verleugnung denial, disavowal
verleumden backbite, calumniate, defame, libel, malign, slander, traduce
Verleumder backbiter, calumniator, libeller, slanderer
verleumderisch calumnious, defamatory, libellous, slanderous
Verleumdung calumniation, calumny, defamation, detraction, libel, slander
—, mündliche slander
—, schriftliche libel
Verleumdungs
—feldzug smearing campaign
—klage action for libel, libel suit
verlieren lose
Verlierer loser
verloben, sich become engaged (to), engage oneself (to)
Verlobte betrothed, fiancée
Verlobter, betrothed, fiancé
Verlobung betrothal, engagement
verlocken allure, entice, inveigle, seduce, tempt
verlockend inviting, tempting
Verlocker misleader, seducer
Verlockung allurement, enticement, seduction, temptation
verlöschbar extinguishable
verlöschen efface, extinguish, obliterate
Verlust damage, deficit, disappearance, forfeiture, loss, broken time
—e casualties
— erleiden suffer (incur) a loss
Verlust
—anzeige loss report, notice of loss
—fall, im in case of loss
—liste casualty list, (list of) casualties
—meldung loss (casualty) report
—nachweis proof of loss
—rechnung, Gewinn- und profit and loss account, income statement
verlustig deprived of
— gehen forfeit, lose, miss
vermachen bequeath, devise, leave
Vermächtnis bequest, devise, legacy, trust, will
—erbe (—nehmer) devisee, legatee
—geber legator
—steuer legacy duty
vermehren (sich) add (to), augment, enlarge, increase, multiply
Vermehrung addition, augmentation, enlargement, increase, multiplication
vermeidbar (—lich) avoidable
vermeiden avoid, elude, escape, eschew, evade, shirk, steer clear of
Vermeidung avoidance
bei — von under pain of
vermeintlich alleged, imaginary, presumed, presumptive, pretended, putative, reputed, supposed
vermelden announce, inform, mention, notify
Vermerk docket, endorsement, entry, mark, memorandum, note, notice, remark
Sicht- visa
vermerken enter, make (take) note of, note (down), record, remark
vermietbar hireable, rentable

vermieten hire out, job, lease, let out, let on hire (lease), rent
—, zu on hire, for rent
Vermieter hirer out, jobber, landlord, lessor, letter, renter
Vermieterin landlady
Vermietung hiring out, lease, leasing, letting (out)
vermindern curtail, cut (back, down), decrease, diminish, impair, lessen, lower, reduce, retrench
—, sich decline, decrease, fall, go down
Verminderung cut, decrease, diminution, impairment, lessening, reduction, retrenchment
vermischen amalgamate, mingle, mix (up)
vermissen miss
vermißt
— werden be missed (missing)
als — melden report missing
Vermißter missing person
vermitteln act as intermediary, arrange, convey, effect, go between, intercede, interpose, intervene (in, with), mediate, negotiate, pass on (to), procure, reconcile, settle, transmit
vermittelnd conciliating, conciliatory, intercessory, intermediary, mediating, mediatory
Vermittler agent, arbitrator, broker, conciliator, go-between, interceder, intercessor, intermediary, intermediator, mediator, middleman, negotiator
Vermittlerin mediatress, mediatrix
Vermittlerprovision (-vergütung) (agency, broker's) commission
Vermittlung accommodation, adjustment, agency, arrangement, brokerage, conciliation, exchange, intercession, intermediation, interposition, intervention, mediation, negotiation, settlement
Vermittlungs
—amt exchange
—ausschuß mediation committee (board)
—büro broker's (registry) office
—gebühr (-provision) brokerage, commission
—stelle agency
—versuch attempt at reconciliation, attempted settlement
—vorschlag conciliatory proposal, offer of mediation, proposal for arrangement (settlement)
Vermögen ability, assets, capability, capacity, capital, estate, faculty, fortune, funds, means, money, power, property, riches, substance, wealth
Anlage- fixed assets, invested capital, investments
Bar- cash (assets)
Betriebs- trading (business) capital
Grund- capital stock, land(ed) property, real estate
National- (Volks-) national property
Privat- personal (private) property
Sach- tangible assets (property)
Treuhand- trust property
Umlauf- circulating assets (capital)
—, bewegliches goods and chattels, movables, personal chattels (property), personalty, movable property
—, persönliches individual assets, personal assets, personal (private) property
—, unbewegliches immovables, land(ed) property, real estate, real property, realty
— erwerben make a fortune
vermögend capable, moneyed, opulent, powerful, rich, wealthy, well-off, well-to-do
Vermögens
—abgabe capital (property) levy
—abtretung assignment of property
—angabe (-anmeldung) declaration of property
—angelegenheiten financial affairs
—anlage (capital) investment
—anteil proprietary interest, share in property
—aufsicht financial (property) control

—aufstellung financial (property) statement, statement of affairs
—beschlagnahme distraint (attachment, seizure) of property
—besteuerung taxation of property
—bewertung valuation of property
—bildung formation of property
—erklärung property statement
—freigabe release of property
—gegenstand asset
—lage financial position
—masse assets, estate
—nachweis property statement
—pfleger s. —verwalter
—recht property (real) right, law of property
vermögensrechtlich financial, pecuniary, under the law of property
Vermögens
—sperre blocking of property
—steuer capital (property) tax
—stück asset
—übertragung transfer of property
—umstände (-stand, -verhältnisse) assets, financial position, means
—verwalter administrator (of an estate), (official) receiver, steward (of an estate), trustee
—verwaltung administration (of property, an estate), stewardship, trust administration, trusteeship
—werte assets, effects, property, resources
—zuwachssteuer capital gains tax
vermuten assume, conjecture, expect, fancy, guess, imagine, presume, suppose, surmise, suspect
vermutlich assumable, likely, presumable, presumptive, probable, supposed
Vermutung conjecture, expectation, guess, idea, guess, presumption, supposition, surmise
Abwesenheits- presumption of absence
Ehelichkeits- presumption of legitimacy
Gesetzes- legal presumption, presumption of law
Lebens- presumption of life
Rechts- legal presumption, presumption of law
Tatsachen- presumption of fact
Todes- presumption of death, presumptive death
Überlebens- presumption of survival
vernachlässigen be derelict in, fail, ignore, neglect, slight, waste
Vernachlässigung careless treatment, dereliction, neglect
Vernehmen
dem — nach according to accounts (information, report, rumour), by all accounts
vernehmen cross-examine, examine, hear, interrogate, learn, perceive, question, understand
Vernehmer (cross-)examiner, interrogator
Vernehmung (cross-)examination, hearing, interrogation, questioning, trial
vernehmungsfähig in a condition (state) to be examined (interrogated)
verneinbar deniable
verneinen answer (reply) in the negative, contradict, deny, disavow, gainsay, negative, say no
verneinend negative
Verneinung denial, negation, negative
vernichtbar destructible, voidable
vernichten abolish, annihilate, annul, avoid, destroy, destruct, disappoint, eradicate, exterminate, extirpate, kill, obliterate, nullify, overthrow, undo, unmake
vernichtend annihilating, destructive, devastating
Vernichter annihilator, destroyer
Vernichtung abolition, annihilation, annulment, avoidance, destruction, extermination, overthrow
Vernunft intellect, judgement, reason, understanding

— **annehmen** listen to reason
vernünftig acceptable, judicious, logical, rational, reasonable, sensible, wise
un- absurd, irrational, senseless, unreasonable, void of reason
Vernunfts
—**ehe (-heirat)** marriage of convenience, prudential match
—**gründe** reason
vernunfts
—**gemäß** logical, rational, reasonable
—**los** irrational, senseless, unreasonable
—**widrig** contrary to reason, illogical, irrational, unreasonable
veröffentlichen advertise, announce, edit, make known (public), promulgate, publish
veröffentlicht published
—, **nicht** unpublished
Veröffentlichung advertisement, announcement, edition, promulgation, publication
Veröffentlichungs
—**datum** date of publication
—**recht** copyright, right to publish
verordnen decree, enact, establish, institute, issue an order, ordain, order, pass a decree, prescribe
Verordnung decree, direction, edict, enactment, institution, order, ordinance, prescription, regulation, rescript, rule
Ausführungs- (Durchführungs-, Vollzugs-) carrying-out ordinance, executive order
Bundes- federal order
Gesetzes- decree, law, statutory order
Polizei- police ordinance
Regierungs- government decree
Verkehrs- traffic ordinance
— **erlassen** decree, issue (pass) a decree
Verordnungs
—**blatt** official gazette
—**gesetz** ordinance, statutory decree (order)
verordnungsgemäß (-mäßig) according to order, as enacted, by order, statutory
Verordnungs
—**gewalt** statutory power
—**recht** administrative law
—**weg, auf dem** by decree
verpachtbar leasable
verpachten farm out, lease, let (out), let on hire (lease), rent
Verpächter landlord, leaser, lessor
Verpachtung farming out, lease, leasing, letting on lease
verpfändbar mortgageable, pawnable, pledgeable
verpfänden mortgage, pawn, pledge, put in pawn (pledge)
Verpfänder mortgagor, pawner, pledger, pledgor
Verpfändung bailment, pawning, pledging
verpflichten bind (over), covenant, engage, lay under an obligation, obligate, oblige
—, **sich** commit oneself to, covenant, engage oneself for, make one's debtor, pledge oneself, put in one's debt, undertake
verpflichtet answerable, bound, engaged, in duty bound, indebted, liable, obliged
verpflichtet
— **sein zu** be bound (liable, obligated, obliged) to, be under an obligation to
gesetzlich — sein be bound by law
Verpflichteter debtor, obligee, obligor
Verpflichtung bond, commitment, covenant, duty, engagement, liability, obligation, responsibility
Beistands- assistance obligation
Garantie- guarantee obligation, indemnity (surety) bond
Gegen- counterobligation
Neben- collateral obligation
Unterhalts- maintenance obligation
Vertrags- contractual commitment (obligation)

Zahlungs- obligation to pay, payment obligation
—, **ohne** without obligation
— **eingehen** commit oneself, enter into a bond (an engagement, obligation), incur a liability, obligate oneself
— **einhalten (nachkommen)** fulfil (implement, meet) an engagement (obligation)
— **nicht nachkommen** default (an engagement)
Verrat betrayal, treachery, treason
Hoch- high treason
— **begehen** betray
verraten argue, betray, commit treason, disclose, divulge, indicate, prove, reveal, show, suggest
—, **sich** betray (commit) oneself
Verräter betrayer, traitor
Hoch- high treasoner, traitor
Landes- traitor
Verräterin traitress
verräterisch disloyal, faithless, perfidious, traitorous, treacherous, treasonable
verrichten accomplish, achieve, acquit, carry out, do, execute, fulfil, perform
Verrichtung act, business, discharge, doing, execution, performance, transaction
verringern curtail, cut down, decrease, diminish, drop, lower, reduce, retrench, slacken
—, **Tempo** slow down
Verringerung cut, decrease, diminution, reduction
Verruf discredit, disparagement, disrepute, ill repute
in — bringen bring in discredit (disrepute), decry, discredit, disparage, ruin one's reputation
verrufen disreputable, ill-famed, ill-reputed, in bad repute, of ill repute, notorious
Versagen failure
versagen decline, deny, fail, misfire, refuse, withhold
Versager failure, misfire
Versagung denial, refusal
—**sfall, im** in case of refusal

versammeln assemble, collect, convene, convoke, gather, rally
—, **sich** assemble, gather, meet, rally
Versammlung assembly, audience, conference, congregation, congress, convention, gathering, meeting, party, rally, rendezvous
Bundes- federal meeting
General- general assembly (meeting)
Haupt- general meeting
— —, **ordentliche** annual general meeting
— —, **außerordentliche** extraordinary general meeting
Jahres- annual meeting
Massen- mass meeting
Mitglieder- general meeting, meeting of members
National- national assembly
Plenar- plenary assembly (meeting)
Volks- popular assembly
Wahl- election meeting
Versammlung
—, **gesetzgebende** legislative assembly
—, **konstituierende (verfassunggebende)** constituent assembly
—, **öffentliche** public (open) meeting
—, **ordentliche** ordinary (statutory) meeting
—, **politische** political meeting
Versammlung
— **abhalten** hold a meeting
— **auflösen** dismiss (dissolve) a meeting
— **einberufen** convene (convoke) a meeting
Versammlungs
—**beschluß** resolution of a meeting
—**freiheit** freedom of assembly
—**leiter** conference leader
—**ort** meeting place, place of assembly (conference)
—**recht** right of assembly (meeting)
—**verbot** ban on public meetings, interdiction of a meeting

Versand delivery, dispatch, forwarding, mailing, shipment, shipping, transport(ation)
—anzeige consignment note, shipping advice (report)
—kosten forwarding expenses, shipping (delivery, transportation) costs
—unterlagen shipping documents
versäumen default, fail, forget, leave undone, miss, neglect, omit
Versäumnis contumacy, default, delinquency, dereliction, failure, loss of time, negligence, neglect, omission
—gebühr default fee
—urteil default judgement, judgement by (in) default
Versäumung noncompliance, omission
verschaffen bring, furnish, give, procure, provide, supply with
—, sich obtain, secure
verschärfen add to, aggravate, exacerbate, highten, intensify, raise, reinforce, sharpen, strengthen, tighten
Verschärfung aggravation, intensification, reinforcement, strengthening, tightening
verschenken give away, give as a gift (present), make a present of
verschieben adjourn, defer, delay, move, postpone, remove, sell underhand, sell on the black market, shift, smuggle abroad
Verschiebung adjournment, deferment, deferral, delay, dislocation, illicit sale, postponement, removal, shifting, smuggling
verschieden different, differing, discrepant, distinct (from), diverse, unlike, varied
verschiedenartig different, heterogeneous, miscellaneous, varied, various
Verschiedenartigkeit diversification, heterogeneousness
verschiedene different, divers, several, sundry, various
Verschiedenheit difference, divergence, diversity, disparity, heterogeneity, inequality, variety
Meinungs- controversy, difference (disparity, divergence) of opinion (views), disagreement, dissent
verschlechtern debase, degrade, depreciate, deteriorate, impair, lower, make worse, waste
—, sich change for the worse, deteriorate, sink, worsen
Verschlechterung change for the worse, debasement, degradation, depreciation, deterioration, worsening
verschleiern conceal, cook, disguise, dress up, obscure, screen, tamper, veil
Verschleierung camouflage, concealment, cooking, veiling, window-dressing
—smaßnahmen camouflage measures
verschleppen abduct, delay, deport, displace, kidnap, mislay, misplace, obstruct, pilfer, procrastinate, protract, purloin, spread
Verschleppter displaced (kidnapped) person
Verschleppung abduction, delay, deportation, kidnapping, misplacing, obstruction, procrastination, protraction, spread(ing)
Verschleppungs
—methoden obstructive measures
—politik obstructionism, policy of obstruction
—taktik obstructive tactics
Verschleuderer spendthrift, squanderer
verschleudern dissipate, dump, lavish, squander, waste, sell under price (at loss)
Verschleuderung dissipation, waste
verschließbar lock-up, lockable
verschließen blockade, bolt and bar, close, lock (up), padlock, seal, shut

verschlimmern aggravate, deprave, exacerbate, make worse, worsen
—, sich deteriorate, get (grow) worse
Verschlimmerung aggravation, change for the worse
Verschluß bond, lock, seal
—, unter in bond, bonded, under seal
unter — halten keep under lock and key
in — legen bond
verschlüsseln (en)code, cipher
verschmähen despise, disdain, refuse, reject, scorn, turn down
Verschmähung disdain, refusal, rejection, scorn
verschmelzen amalgamate, coalesce, consolidate, fuse, merge, unite
Verschmelzung amalgamation, coalescence, consolidation, fusion, merger
—svertrag amalgamation agreement, merger
verschollen disappeared, lost, missing
für — erklären declare dead
— sein be missing, be presumed dead
Verschollener missing person, absentee
Verschollenheit disappearance, presumption of death, want of appearance
verschonen excuse (exempt) from, spare
Verschonung exemption, forbearance, sparing
verschreiben assign, order, prescribe, transfer
—, sich miswrite, subscribe to
Verschreibung assignment, bond, deed, obligation, order, prescription, slip of the pen
Verschulden blame, cause, fault, guilt, negligence, wrong
verschulden be blamed for, be the cause of, be guilty of, encumber (with debts), involve in debts
—, sich involve oneself in debts, run into debts
verschuldet encumbered (with debts), in debt, indebted
verschuldetermaßen deservedly
Verschuldetsein indebtedness
Verschuldung fault, offence, indebtedness
verschwägert affiliated, related by marriage
nicht verwandt und nicht — related neither by blood nor by marriage
Verschwägerung affinity, relationship by marriage
Verschweigen concealment
verschweigen conceal, hide (from), hold back, keep secret, suppress, withhold
nichts — und nichts hinzufügen add and withhold nothing
Verschweigung concealment, silence
verschwenden be prodigal of, dissipate, lavish, squander, waste
Verschwender prodigal, dissipator, spendthrift, squanderer, waster
verschwenderisch extravagant, lavish, prodigal, profuse, sumptuous, thriftless, wasteful
Verschwendung dissipation, extravagance, squandering, waste (fulness)
—ssucht extravagance, lavishness, prodigality, squandermania, wastefulness
verschwiegen close, discreet, reserved, reticent, trustworthy
Verschwiegenheit discreetness, discretion, reserve, reticence, secrecy
—, unter dem Siegel der under the seal of secrecy
Verschwinden disappearance
verschwinden disappear, dissolve, face (pass, shade) away, vanish
verschwören abjure, curse, forswear, renounce
—, sich conspire, form a conspiracy, hatch (lay) a plot, plot
Verschwörer conspirator, plotter
Verschwörerin conspiratress

Verschwörerbande gang of conspirators (plotters)

Verschwörung abjuration, conspiracy, plot, renunciation

— **anzetteln** conspire (plot) against, hatch (lay) a plot against

— **aufdecken** discover a conspiracy (plot)

Versehen blunder, error, fault, inadvertence(cy), mistake, negligence, oversight, slip(-up)

—, **aus** by mistake, erroneously, inadvertently, through inadvertence (an error, an oversight)

versehen administer, attend to, blunder (in), do, err, hold, look after, miss, mistake, neglect, overlook, perform, run, take charge of, transact

— **mit** furnish (with), invest with, provide, supply (with)

—, **sich** commit an error, go wrong, make a mistake

versehentlich s. aus Versehen

Versehrter disabled (person), invalid

Kriegs- war disabled

versenden consign, convey, dispatch, forward, mail, post, send (off), ship, transport

versetzen deal, displace, give, move, pawn, pledge, promote, remove, shift, transfer, transplant, transpose

—, **in Angst** alarm, frighten, terrify

—, **in den Ruhestand** pension off, retire, superannuate

Versetzung bailment, displacement, pawning, pledging, removal, remove, superannuation, transfer, transplantation, transposition

— **in den Ruhestand** pensioning off, retirement

versicherbar assurable, insurable

Versicherer assurer, insurer, underwriter

versichern affirm, assert, assure, aver, avouch, certify, convince (of), declare, insure, protest, underwrite

—, **sich** insure oneself, make sure of, secure

—, **an Eidesstatt** affirm in lieu of oath

Versicherter assured, insured (person), insurant, policy holder

Versicherung affirmation, assertion, assurance, guarantee, insurance

—, **eidesstattliche** affidavit

—, **eidliche** sworn statement

—, **feierliche** solemn affirmation (declaration)

Alters- old age insurance

Angestellten- employees' social insurance

Arbeitslosen- unemployment insurance

Brand- fire insurance

Diebstahls- (Einbruchs-) burglary insurance, insurance against burglary and theft

Haftpflicht- liability insurance

Invaliden- (Invaliditäts-) invalidity insurance

Kraftfahrzeug- motor-car insurance

Kranken- health (sick, sickness) insurance

Lebens- life insurance

Leibrenten- annuity insurance

Pensions- (old-age) pension insurance

Personen- casualty (personal accident) insurance

Pflicht- compulsory insurance

Privat- private insurance

Renten- annuity insurance, pension insurance fund

Sozial- social insurance

Unfall- accident insurance

Zusatz- supplementary insurance

— **abschließen** effect an insurance, take out an insurance policy

Versicherungs

—**agent** insurance agent

—**anspruch** insurance claim

—**anstalt** insurance company

—anwalt insurance lawyer (solicitor)
—anzeige cover note, immediate notice
—beamter insurance officer (official)
—bedingungen insurance conditions, terms of insurance
—beitrag insurance premium
—bescheinigung insurance certificate
—bestimmungen insurance regulations, policy provisions
—betrag insured amount
—betrug insurance fraud
—betrüger insurance swindler
—büro insurance office
—dauer period (term) of insurance
—deckung insurance cover(age)
versicherungsfähig assurable, insurable
Versicherungs
—fähigkeit insurability
—fall insurance case
—fonds insurance fund
—geber insurer
—gebühr insurance fee (premium)
—gesellschaft insurance company
—gesetz insurance act (law), National Insurance Act (GB)
—grundlage insurance basis
—höhe amount of insurance, insured amount
—karte insurance card
—klausel insurance clause
—kosten (-lasten) insurance charges
—leistung (insurance) benefit
—makler insurance broker
—marke insurance (policy) stamp
—nehmer assured (insured) person, insurant, policy holder
—ordnung insurance regulations
—pflicht compulsory insurance
—police (-schein) insurance certificate, insurance policy
—prämie insurance premium
—recht insurance law
—risiko insurance risk
—sachverständiger insurance expert
—schutz insurance protection (cover, coverage)
—steuer insurance tax
—streitigkeiten insurance dispute
—summe insured amount
—system insurance system
—träger assurer, insurer, underwriter
—unterlagen insurance papers (documents)
—unternehmen insurance company
—vertrag insurance contract
—vertreter insurance agent
—vertretung insurance office
—wert insured value
—zwang compulsory insurance
versiegeln affix a seal (on), put under seal, seal (up)
versiegelt sealed, under seal
Versiegelung sealing
versiert experienced, skilled, versed
Versiertheit versedness
Version version
versöhnen appease, placate, reconcile (to, with)
sich — mit become reconciled with, resign oneself to
versöhnend conciliatory
Versöhner mediator, peacemaker, reconciler
versöhnlich conciliatory, forgiving, placable, reconcilable
Versöhnlichkeit forgivingness, placability, placableness
Versöhnung conciliation, reconciliation, reconcilement
versorgen furnish (with), look after, maintain, provide (for), provision, supply (with), take care of
Versorger bread-winner, maintainer, patron, provider, supplier, supporter
Versorgung care, furnishing, living, maintenance, providing, provision, subsistence, supply, support, sustenance
Alters— old age pension
Versorgungs
—amt pension office
—anspruch claim to maintenance, pension claim

versorgungsberechtigt entitled to maintenance (pension)
Versorgungs
—empfänger old age beneficiary, pensioner
—fonds provident fund
—gesetz law governing pensions and grants
—quelle source of supply
—lage supply situation
—leistung pension
verspäten delay, retard
—, sich be behind time, be late (overdue)
verspätet belated, delayed, late, overdue, tardy
Verspätung delay, lateness, retardation, tardiness
versperren bar, barricade, block up, obstruct
Versperrung barricade, blockade, blocking-up, obstruction
Versprechen (Versprechung) promise
Ehe— (Heirats—) promise of marriage
— abnehmen exact a promise from
— einlösen (erfüllen, halten) carry out (fulfil, keep) a promise
— geben make a promise
— nicht halten break a promise
versprechen promise
—, sich make a mistake in speaking
Versprecher slip of the tongue
Versprechender promisor
Versprechens
—empfänger promisee
—geber promisor
verstaatlichen nationalize, put under state (government) control, secularize, socialize, turn into state property
Verstaatlichung nationalization, socialization
Verstand comprehension, discernment, intellect, intelligence, judgement, mind, mental powers, reason, sense, understanding, wit
—, scharfer sagacity
Verstandes
—heirat marriage of convenience
verstandesmäßig intellectual, rational, reasonable
Verstandes
—mensch rationalist
—schärfe penetration, sagacity
—schwäche weak-mindedness
verständig intelligent, judicious, reasonable, sensible, understanding
verständigen advise, acquaint (with), inform (of), notify
sich — mit arrange with, come to an agreement (arrangement, understanding) with, come to terms
Verständigung advice, agreement, arrangement, information, understanding
Verständigungs
—friede negotiated peace
—politik policy of appeasement
verständlich clear, distinct, intelligible, perspicuous, popular, understandable
— machen explain
Verständlichkeit clearness, intelligibleness, lucidity
Verständnis agreement, appreciation, apprehension, comprehension, concord, discernment, insight (into), perception (of), sympathy, understanding
verständnislos irresponsive (to), unappreciative (of), uncomprehending
Verständnislosigkeit lack of comprehension
verständnisvoll intelligent, sympathetic, understanding
verstärken accentuate, add to, aggravate, augment, enlarge, fortify, increase, intensify, reinforce, strengthen, tighten
Verstärkung intensifying, intensification, reinforcement, strengthening
—struppen reinforcements
Versteck ambuscade, ambush, hide-out, hiding-place
verstecken conceal, hide
—, sich hide (out)

versteckt covert, hidden, indirect, latent, secret, veiled
— halten keep in concealment
verstehen catch, comprehend, get, grasp, know, realize, see, understand
sich — auf be a judge of, be skilled in, know
Versteigerer auctioneer
versteigern sell by (at) auction
— (lassen) bring to the hammer, put up for sale
Versteigerung (selling by) auction, public sale
Zwangs— compulsory auction
zur — bringen bring to the hammer, put up for sale
zur — kommen be sold at auction
Versteigerungs
—preis auction price
—bedingungen terms of auction
—gebühren auction fees
—termin auction day
verstellen, sich dissemble, feign, pretend, sham
Verstellung dissimulation, make-believe, sham(ming)
versterben decease, die, expire
versteuerbar dutiable, taxable
versteuern pay duty (taxes) on
versteuert duty (tax) paid
Versteuerung payment of duty (taxes)
—swert taxable value
verstorben dead, deceased, defunct, late
Verstoß breach, contravention, fault, infraction, infringement, mistake, offence (se), violation
— begehen gegen offend against, violate
verstoßen cast off, disown, expel, reject, repudiate
— gegen act contrary to, commit a breach (of), contravene, impinge (on), infringe, offend (against), not to be in keeping with, violate
Verstoßener outcast
Verstreichen expiration, lapse of time
verstreichen elapse, expire, lapse, pass (away), run, slip by
verstricken ensnare, entangle
sich — in be involved (mixed up) in, get entangled in, implicate in
Verstrickung entanglement
verstümmeln curtail, deform, disable, mutilate
Verstümmelung curtailment, mutilation
Versuch attempt, effort, experiment, tentative, test, trial, venture
Bestechungs— attempt at bribery, attempted bribery
Einschüchterungs- attempt at intimidation
Erpressungs— attempted blackmail (extortion)
Flucht— attempt to escape
Mord— attempt at (attempted) murder, murderous attempt
Selbstmord— attempted suicide
— machen make an attempt, try
versuchen allure, (make an) attempt, endeavour, entice, experiment (on), taste, test, try
Versucher seducer, tempter
Versuchs
—auftrag trial order
—fall test case
—stadium experimental stage
—station experimental station
versuchsweise as an experiment, by way of trial (experiment), experimentally, on approval (trial), tentatively
Versuchung temptation
in — führen lead into temptation
in — kommen be tempted (to)
vertagen adjourn, postpone, prorogue, (take a) recess
Vertagung adjournment, postponement, prorogation, recess
Vertagungs
—antrag motion for adjournment
—beschluß adjournment order
verteidigen advocate, defend, maintain, plead, protect, stand up for, support, uphold, vindicate

—, **sich** defend (justify) oneself, plead one's case, offer resistance
Verteidiger advocate, attorney for the defence, counsel (for the defence), counsellor, defender, defending counsel, supporter
Offizial— counsel assigned by the court
Wahl— appointed counsel
— **bestellen** appoint (assign, brief) a counsel (for the defence)
Verteidigung advocacy, defence (se), justification, maintenance, support, vindication
Landes— home (national) defence
Offizial— (**Pflicht—**) assigned counsel, official defence
Selbst— self-defence
Straf— defence in a criminal case
— **niederlegen** abandon the defence
— **übernehmen** assume the defence
Verteidigungs
—abkommen defence agreement (treaty)
—bündnis defensive alliance
—gemeinschaft defence community
—krieg defensive war
verteidigungslos defenceless
Verteidigungs
—maßnahme defensive measure
—rede (speech for the) defence
—schrift apology, (written) defence, statement of defence
—stellung defensive position
—waffe weapon of defence
—zustand state of defence
verteilbar available, distributable, divisible
verteilen allocate, allot, apportion, dispense, distribute, divide, pool, prorate, share (out)
—, **sich** spread
sich — auf be divided among
Verteilung allocation, allotment, apportionment, dispensation, disposition, distribution, division, repartition
Vertrag agreement, compact, contract, convention, covenant, deed, indenture, pact, settlement, treaty
Abfindungs— settlement (agreement)
Abtretungs— contract of assignment (conveyance, transfer)
Adoptions— contract (deed) of adoption
Anstellungs— employment contract
Arbeits— employment (labour, work) contract
Auslieferungs— delivery contract, extradition agreement (treaty)
Beistands— treaty (pact) of mutual assistance
Bündnis— treaty of alliance
Bündnis- und Freundschafts— treaty of alliance and friendship
Dienst— contract of employment, service (labour) contract
Ehe— marriage contract
Freundschafts— friendship pact, treaty of amity (friendship)
Friedens— peace treaty (pact), treaty of peace
Garantie— guarantee (warranty) contract
Geheim— secret treaty
Gesellschafts— articles of association, firm's contract, partnership agreement
Handels— commercial treaty, trade agreement
Kauf— purchase (sales) contract
Lehr— apprenticeship contract, articles of apprenticeship, indenture
Lizenz— licence contract
Miet— charterparty, hire contract, lease (contract), tenancy agreement
Options— option (agreement)
Pacht— lease (contract)
Schein— fictitious (sham, simulated) contract
Schieds— arbitration agreement

Tarif— collective agreement
Tausch— barter agreement (contract)
Verkaufs— sales agreement (contract)
Vor— preliminary agreement (contract)
Zusatz— supplementary agreement
Vertrag
— abschließen (schließen) conclude a treaty, conclude (enter into, make) an agreement (a contract)
— abfassen (aufsetzen) draft (draw up, make out, prepare) a contract
— beitreten accede to a treaty, become party to an agreement, join a contract
— brechen break (violate) a contract
— erfüllen carry out (execute, fulfil, perform) a contract
— erneuern renew a contract
— kündigen revoke (terminate) a contract
— verlängern prolong(ate) a contract
— verletzen violate a contract
vom — zurücktreten recede (withdraw) from a contract
—, durch (vertraglich) by agreement (contract), contractual, as stipulated, stipulated by agreement (contract)
vertraglich vereinbart contractual, conventional, provided in the contract, stipulated
Vertrags
—ablauf expiration of contract
—abschluß conclusion of agreement (contract)
vertragsähnlich quasi-contract (ual)
Vertrags
—artikel article of agreement, contract clause (stipulation)
—bedingungen contractual terms, terms (and conditions) of a contract (an agreement)
—bestimmung contract clause (provision)
—bestimmungen articles (terms) of an agreement, articles (conditions, provisions, regulations) of a contract
—bruch breach of contract
— —, Klage wegen assumpsit
vertragsbrüchig defaulting
— werden break an agreement (a contract)
Vertrags
—brecher breaker of a contract
vertragschließend contracting
Vertrags
—datum contract date
—dauer currency (life) of an agreement (a contract)
—entwurf draft agreement (contract)
—erbe contractual heir
—erfüllung fulfilment (performance) of contract
—erneuerung renewal of an agreement (a contract)
vertragsfähig having contractual capacity
Vertrags
—fähigkeit contractual capacity
—freiheit freedom of contract
—gegenstand subject of a contract
vertragsgemäß (—mäßig) according to contract, in accordance with the agreement, (as) stipulated, (as) agreed upon, contractual, conventional
Vertrags
—grundlage basis of contract (agreement)
—haftung contractual liability
—jahr contractual year
—klausel contract clause, stipulation, term
—kontrahent contracting partner (party), contractor, party to a contract
—land contracting state
—macht contracting (treaty) power
—partei (—partner) contracting party, contractor, party to a contract
—periode contractual period
—preis contract(ual) price
—punkte articles (terms) of an agreement (a contract)
—recht law of contract

—rechte contractual (treaty) rights
—schuld contractual debt
—staat contracting state
—strafe penalty
—termin contract date
—text wording of a contract
vertragstreu true to a contract
— sein abide by an agreement
Vertrags
—treue fidelity (loyalty, observance) of a contract
vertragsunfähig having no (without) contractual capacity
Vertrags
—unfähigkeit contractual incapacity
—verbindlichkeit contractual liability
—verhältnis contractual relation
—verhandlungen contract (treaty) negotiations (talks)
—verlängerung prolongation (renewal) of an agreement (a contract)
—verletzung breach (violation) of a contract
—verpflichtung contractual commitment (obligation)
—vorbehalt proviso, reservation
—vorschrift contractual clause (stipulation, provision)
vertragswidrig contrary to contract (agreement), contrary to the terms of an agreement (a contract), in violation of a contract
Vertragszeit contractual period
Vertrauen confidence, faith, trust
—, im confidentially, in confidence, privately
im — auf relying on, trusting to
— genießen be in the confidence of
— haben zu have confidence (faith) in, rely on, trust
kein — haben zu disbelieve in
sein — schenken (sein — setzen auf) place (put) one's confidence in
ins — ziehen admit (take) into one's confidence
vertrauen confide, entrust, place (put) confidence in, put faith (trust) in, rely (up)on, rest (up)on, trust (in)
Vertrauens
—amt (place of) trust
—arzt confidential medical adviser, public health commissioner
—bruch breach of confidence (faith, trust), betrayal of trust, indiscretion
—frage question (vote) of confidence
—mann authority, confidential agent (person), delegate, shop steward, trustee
—mißbrauch abuse of confidence (trust), breach of trust
—person confidential person
—posten position of trust, confidential (responsible) position
—rat shop steward, workers' council
—sache confidential matter, matter of confidence
—stellung confidential (responsible) position, position of trust
—verhältnis confidential relation(ship)
—votum vote of confidence
vertrauenswürdig creditable, reliable, responsible, sound, trustworthy
Vertrauens
—würdigkeit creditability, reliability, trustworthiness
vertraulich confidential, in confidence, familiar, intimate, private
—, streng strictly confidential
Vertraulichkeit confidence, confidentiality, familiarity, intimacy, privacy
vertraut acquainted (with), conversant (with), experienced (in), familiar (with), informed of, intimate, versed (in)
sich — machen mit acquaint (familiarize) oneself with, make oneself conversant with
— sein mit be conversant (familiar, intimate) with
Vertraute confidante
Vertrauter confidant, confidential (intimate, trusted) friend

Vertrautheit familiarity, intimacy, knowledge
vertreiben banish, dislodge, distribute, eject, exile, expel, extrude (from), market, oust, sell, turn out of
—, aus dem Besitz dispossess, evict
Vertreibung banishment, dislodgement, ejection, expulsion
—, aus dem Besitz dispossession, eviction
vertretbar defensible, fungible, justifiable, maintainable, pleadable, tenable, warrantable
vertreten act for (on behalf of), act as deputy (substitute) for, advocate, answer for, appear for, attend to, be an exponent of, champion, deputize for, expound, hold, intercede (with, for), plead (for), replace, represent, substitute (for), support, take, uphold
zu — haben be liable for
— sein be found, be represented be unrepresented
nicht — sein not to be found
Vertreter advocate, agent, assistant, attorney, champion, commercial traveller, delegate, deputy, holder, locum tenens, proxy, representative, salesman, substitute
—, gesetzlicher legal representative, legal (statutory) guardian, statutory agent
Vertreter
—provision agency (agent's) commission
—vertrag agency contract
Vertretung advocacy, agency, delegation, mission, replacement, representation, substitution
—, in acting for, acting as deputy (substitute) for, by attorney (proxy), in charge (commission)
Vertretungs
—befugnis (—macht) agent's authority, authority, power of agency (attorney), right of representation
vertretungsberechtigt representative
Vertretungs
—vertrag agency contract
—vollmacht power of attorney
vertretungsweise as representative, by proxy, vicariously
Vertrieb distribution, marketing, sale
Vertriebener expelled person, refugee
vertrösten put off (till, with)
vertuschen hush up, keep dark (secret), suppress
verüben commit, perpetrate, practise
Verüber perpetrator
Verübung commission, committing, perpetration
verunglimpfen abuse, backbite, calumniate, defame, denigrate, revile, slander
Verunglimpfer calumniator, defamer, detractor
Verunglimpfung calumniation, defamation, denigration, detraction, insult, revilement, reviling
verunglücken be killed, come to grief, fail, meet with an accident, miscarry, perish
verunglückt abortive
Verunglückter casualty, victim
verunreinigen contaminate, defile, pollute, soil
verunstalten deface, deform, disfigure, spoil
Verunstaltung blot, defacement, deformation, disfigurement
veruntreuen defraud, embezzle, misappropriate, peculate
Veruntreuer embezzler, peculator
Veruntreuung defalcation, defraudation, embezzlement, malversation, misappropriation, peculation
verursachen bring about (on, forth), call forth, cause, give rise to, involve, occasion, produce
Verursacher author, instigator, originator

verurteilen call down, condemn, convict, deprecate, pass judgement (sentence) on, sentence
—, zu Geldstrafe fine, impose a fine on
—, zu Gefängnis pass sentence of imprisonment on, send to prison
—, zum Tode condemn (sentence) to death, pass sentence of death on
Verurteilter condemned person, convict
Verurteilung condemnation, conviction, judgement, sentence
— aussprechen pass (pronounce) judgement (sentence)
vervollkommnen bring to perfection, improve, perfect
Vervollkommnung elaboration, improvement, perfection
vervollständigen complement, complete, improve, integrate, supplement
Vervollständigung completion, improvement, supplementation
verwahren guard, have charge of, have (hold) in custody, hold in trust, keep, preserve, take care of
sich — gegen protest against, raise protest against, secure oneself against
Verwahrer custodian, depositary (ory), guardian, keeper, preserver, safekeeper, trustee
Verwahrung care, charge, custody, deposit, guard, keeping, preservation, protest, prostestation, trust
Sicherheits— preventive detention
—, zur in trust
— einlegen gegen (enter a) protest against
in — geben commit to the charge (custody, trust) of, deposit, give into care (charge, custody), place in the hands of, put in trust
in — haben have care (charge, custody) of
in — nehmen put in jail, take charge of, take into custody, take in custody (trust)
in — sein be in the custody of
verwalten administer, be in charge of, conduct. control, direct, govern, hold, keep, manage, operate, rule, superintend, supervise
verwaltend administrative
Verwalter administrator, agent, assignee, custodian, manager, person in charge, receiver, steward, superintendent, trustee
Zwangs— sequestration
Verwaltung administration, agency, authority(ies), charge, conduct, control, direction, governing body, government, management, managing body, operation, trusteeship
Justiz— administration of justice
Selbst— autonomy, local government, self-administration (-government)
Staats— government, public (state) administration
Stadt- city (local, municipal, town) administration
Steuer— fiscal (tax) administration
Zentral— central administration
Zivil— civil administration
Zwangs— sequestration
Verwaltungs
—abteilung administrative branch (department)
—akt (—handlung, —maßnahme) act of administration, administrative act
—angelegenheit administrative matter
—anordnung administrative instruction
—apparat administrative apparatus (machinery)
—ausschuß administrative board, administrative (managing) committee
—beamter administrative officer (official), civil servant (officer), magistrate
—befugnisse administrative powers

—behörde administrative (administration) authority, board of management, governing (government) board
—bereich competence, jurisdiction
—bezirk administrative district
—dienst civil service
—gebühr administrative fee, management charge (fee)
—gericht administrative (administration) court
—gerichtsbarkeit administrative jurisdiction
—gerichtshof administration (administrative) court of appeal
—gremium (—körper) administrative body
—kosten administrative (administration) expenses (costs)
verwaltungsmäßig administrative
Verwaltungs
—maßnahme administrative means
—ordnung administrative regulations
—organ administrative organ
—rat board of directors, governing body, managing board
—recht administrative law
verwaltungsrechtlich administrative
Verwaltungs
—sache administrative matter
—schwierigkeiten administrative difficulties
—sitz headquarters
—tätigkeit administrative activity
verwaltungstechnisch administrative
Verwaltungs
—verfahren administrative procedure
—verfügung administrative order
—vorschriften administrative regulations
—weg, auf dem administratively, through administrative channels
—wesen administration
—zweig administrative department, branch of administration
verwandt allied (to), associated (with), cognate, congenial, kindred, related (to)
bluts— related by blood
nicht — und nicht verschwägert related neither by blood nor by marriage
Verwandter relation, relative
—, nächster next of kin
Verwandtschaft affinity, cogeniality, connexion, kindred, kinsfolk, kinship, relations, relationship, relatives
Bluts— consanguinity, kindred, kinship
Verwandtschaftsgrad degree of relationship
verwarnen admonish, caution, forewarn, give a warning, reprimand, warn
Verwarnung admonition, caution, reprimand, warning
—, gebührenpflichtige warning and fee
—, gerichtliche injunction
verwechseln change by mistake, confound (with), confuse (with), exchange, mistake (for), mix up
Verwechs(e)lung confusion, exchanging, mistake
verwehren debar (from), disallow, forbid, keep (from), prevent (from), refuse
verweigern decline, deny, refuse, withhold
—, Gehorsam disobey, refuse obedience
Verweigerung denial, refusal
Verweigerung
Annahme— non-acceptance, refusal to accept
Zahlungs— non-payment, refusal to pay
Verweigerungsfall, im in case of refusal
Verweis admonition, blame, censure, check, reference, reprehension, reprimand, reproach, reproof
— erteilen rebuke, reprimand
verweisen banish, exile, expel, rebuke, relegate (to), reprimand, reproach, refer to
— an commit to, defer to, direct to, remit to

Verweisung banishment, commitment, committal, exile, expulsion, reference, relegation, remittal
verweltlichen laicize, secularize
Verweltlichung laicization, secularization
verwendbar applicable (to), available, serviceable, suitable (for), useful
—, nicht unsuitable
Verwendbarkeit applicableness, serviceableness, usefulness
verwenden apply (to), appropriate, assign (to), dispose of, employ, expend, make use of, invest, spend (in, on), use (for), utilize
— auf bestow upon, devote to
verwenden
sich — für intercede (intervene) for (on behalf of), recommend
Verwendung application, appropriation, employment, expenditure, intercession, investment, use, utilization
—szweck intended purpose (use), purpose of application
verwerfen condemn, disallow, disapprove of, dismiss, ignore, overrule, quash, reject, repudiate, set aside, turn down
verwerflich abominable, condemnable, exceptionable, objectionable, reprehensible, wicked
Verwerfung condemnation, disapproval, dismissal, quashing, refusal, rejection, setting aside
verwertbar realizable, sal(e)able, utilizable
verwerten employ, make use of, realize, sell, use, utilize, turn to account
Verwertung employment, exploitation, realization, sale, use, utilization, turning to account
verwesen administer, manage
Verweser administrator
Verwesung administration, management
verwickeln complicate, embroil, entangle, implicate (in), involve (in), tangle
sich — in be embroiled in, become involved in, entangle oneself in, get entangled (involved) in, get mixed in (mixed up with)
verwickelt complex, complicated, implicated, intricate, involved
— sein in be entangled (involved, mixed up) in
Verwicklung complexity, complication, confusion, embroilment, entanglement, implication, intricacy, tangle
verwirkbar forfeitable
Verwirkbarkeit forfeitableness
verwirken forfeit, incur, lose
verwirklichen accomplish, achieve, carry out (into effect), effect, put into practice, realize
—, sich be realized, come true, materialize
Verwirklichung accomplishment, achievement, realization
Verwirkung forfeiture, loss
verwirren abash, bewilder, complicate, confound, confuse, disarrange, discompose, disconcert, embarrass, entangle, perplex, puzzle, throw into disorder, unsettle
verwirrt astray, complicated, disconcerted, distracted, entangled, intricate, puzzled
Verwirrung bewilderment, confusion, disorder, embarrassment, entanglement, perplexity
—, geistige aberration
in — bringen put to confusion
in — geraten become embarrassed
verwitwet widowed
verwundbar sensitive, vulnerable
verwunden hurt, injure, wound
Verwundeter wounded person
Verwundung hurt, injury, wound (ing)
—, tödliche fatal (mortal) wound
verzeichnen enrol, list, note down, record, register, specify, write down

Verzeichnis bill, catalog(ue), classification, docket, enrolment, file, index, invoice, inventory, list, record, register, roll, schedule, specification, statement, table, tariff
Bestands- inventory
Inhalts- (table of) contents, docket, index, register
Namens- index, list of names, roll
verzeihen condone, excuse, forgive, pardon, pass over
verzeihlich excusable, pardonable, venial
Verzeihung condonation, forgiveness, pardon
um — bitten beg one's pardon
Verzicht abandonment, abstention, cession, disclaimer, quitclaim, release, relinquishment, renouncement, renunciation, resignation, sacrifice, waiver
— leisten abandon, disclaim, renounce, waive one's claim to
verzichten abandon, cede, disclaim, dispense with, do without, forego, give up, refuse, release, relinquish, renounce, resign, waive
Verzichterklärung declaration of abandonment (renunciation), letter of renunciation, waiver
Verzichtleistung renunciation
verzinsen pay interest (for, on)
—, sich bear (pay, yield) interest
verzinslich bearing (paying, yielding) interest, interest-bearing, at interest
Verzinsung interest (rate), interest payment
verzögern defer, delay, procrastinate, protract, retard
Verzögerung delay, procrastination, protraction, retardation, (time) lag
—, ohne forthwith, immediately, without delay (loss of time)
Verzögerungs
—politik dilatory policy, policy of delay
—taktik delaying (dilatory) tactics
verzollbar dutiable, excisable, subject to duty
verzollen clear, declare, pay duty on
verzollt duty paid
un- duty unpaid
Verzollung clearance, payment of duty
Verzug default, delay
—, in defaulting, in default
—, ohne at once, without delay
im — sein default, be in default
Verzugs
—kosten demurrage
—tage days of grace
verzweifeln (be in) despair
verzweifelt despairing, desperate, in despair
Verzweiflung despair, desperation
Veto veto
— einlegen gegen put a veto upon, veto
Vetorecht (right of) veto
Vielehe polygamy
Viertel district, quarter, ward
Visitation inquiry, inspection, search
Leibes- bodily search
visitieren inspect, search
Visum visa, visé
—sgebühr visa fee
Volk nation, people
Völker
—bund League of Nations
— —statut Covenant of the League of Nations
—gemeinschaft commonwealth of nations
Völkerrecht international law, law of nations
völkerrechtlich under international law
Völkerrechtsbruch breach (violation) of international law
Volks
—abstimmung (-entscheid) plebiscite, popular vote, referendum
—angelegenheit national matter
—anwalt people's advocate
—aufruhr riot
—aufstand (-erhebung) insurrection, popular rising
—bank people's bank

—begehren initiative, demand for a plebiscite
—charakter national character
—eigentum national (public, state) property
—einkommen national income
—feind public enemy
—gericht (- -shof) people's court
—herrschaft democracy
—justiz lynch law
—partei people's party
—recht people's law
—regierung democracy, people's government
—staat people's state, republic
—stamm race, tribe
—vermögen national property (wealth)
—versammlung popular assembly
—vertreter deputy, representative of the people
—vertretung representation (representatives) of the people, parliamentary representation, representative government
—wirtschaft national (political) economy
—wohlfahrt national (public) welfare, national social service
—zählung census

vollberechtigt full, fully qualified
Vollberechtigung full qualification
vollbeschäftigt employed on full time, fully employed (occupied)
— sein be in full employment
Vollbeschäftigter full-time worker
Vollbeschäftigung full employment, full-time job
Vollbesitz full possession
im — seiner geistigen Kräfte of sound mind (and memory)
vollbringen accomplish, achieve, execute, perform, perpetrate
Vollbringung accomplishment, achievement, performance, perpetration
Vollbürger full citizen
vollenden accomplish, achieve, bring to a close, complete, finish, perfect, terminate
vollendet accomplished, complete, consummate, finished, perfect
—e Tatsache accomplished fact, definitive situation
Vollendung accomplishment, achievement, completion, finishing, perfection
vollgültig fully valid, of full value
Vollgültigkeit full validity
volljährig major, of (full) age
— sein be of (full) age
— werden attain majority, come of age
Volljähriger major, person of full age
Volljährigkeit full age, majority
— erlangen come of age
Volljährigkeitserklärung declaration of majority
vollkommen absolute, accomplished, complete, consummate, perfect, total
Vollkommenheit accomplishment, perfection
Vollmacht authorization, authority, commission, full (mandatory) power(s), mandate, power, power of attorney, procuration, proxy
General- general power of attorney, full power (authority)
Handlungs- power (of attorney), power to act
Verhandlungs- negotiating power, power of negotiation
—, ohne without authority
— erteilen (geben) authorize, confer (delegate, grant) power of attorney on, give authority (powers), grant authorization (full powers), empower
— haben be authorized (empowered), have authority (power), hold power of attorney
Vollmacht
—geber constituent, mandator, principal
—haber (-träger, -nehmer) mandatory, proxy
Vollmachts
—beschränkungen restraining powers

—**erteilung** authorization
—**inhaber** holder of a power
—**überschreitung** excess of authority (power)
—**übertragung** delegation of authority (power)
—**vertrag** agency contract
Vollmitglied full member
Vollmitgliedschaft full membership
Vollsitzung full (plenary) session
vollständig complete, entire, (in) full, integral, total, whole
Vollständigkeit complement, completeness, entirety, integrity, plenitude, totality
vollstreckbar enforceable, executable, executory
Vollstreckbarkeit enforceableness
—**serklärung** enforcement order, writ of execution
vollstrecken carry out, complete, enforce, distrain upon, execute
vollstreckend executory
Vollstrecker executioner, executor
Vollstreckerin executrix
Vollstreckung enforcement, execution
Zwangs- distraint, distress
Vollstreckungs
—**anordnung** writ of execution
—**aufschub** stay of execution, suspense
—**auftrag** distress warrant, enforcement order, warrant of distress, writ of execution
—**beamter** enforcement (execution) officer
—**befehl** s. -auftrag
—**gewalt** executive power
—**gläubiger** execution (judgement) creditor
Vollstreckungs
—**schuldner** distrainee, judgement debtor
—**schutz** exemption (protection) from execution
—**urteil** enforcement order, enforceable judgement, executory decree
—**verfahren** executory procedure
Vollversammlung plenary assembly (meeting)
Vollwaise parentless child
vollwertig full, of full value
vollzählig complete, full, in full number
Vollzähligkeit completeness
Vollzahlung full (complete) payment, payment in full
vollziehbar enforceable, executable
vollziehen accomplish, carry out, consummate, effect, execute, perform
—, **sich** happen, pass
vollziehend executive
Vollzieher executioner, executor
Gerichts- bailiff
Vollzieherin executrix
Vollziehung accomplishment, consummation, execution, fulfilment, performance
Vollziehungs
—**anordnung (-befehl)** warrant, writ of execution
—**gewalt** executive (power)
Vollzug accomplishment, execution, fulfilment
Straf- completion (execution) of sentence
Vollzugs
—**anordnung** executive order
—**anzeige** advice of execution (accomplishment)
—**ausschuß** executive committee
—**beamter** enforcement (executive) officer
—**bestimmungen** executive regulations
—**funktion** executive function
—**meldung** report of compliance
—**gewalt** executive (power)
—**verordnung** carrying-out ordinance, executive order
Volontär volunteer
vorab in advance
Voranfrage previous question
Voranmeldung (Voranzeige) advance notice, previous announcement (notice)
Vorankündigung advance (previous) notice
Voranschlag budget, estimate, rough calculation
Vorarbeit preliminary (preparatory) work

voraus, im beforehand, by anticipation, in advance
vorausbezahlen pay in advance prepay
Vorausbezahlung advance payment, payment in advance, prepayment
vorausdatieren antedate, foredate
vorausgehen precede
vorausgehend preceding, previous
vorausgesetzt (daß) on the condition (that), provided that, supposing that, subject to
Voraussage (Voraussagung) forecast, prediction, prophecy
voraussagen forecast, foretell, predict, prophesy
Vorausschau forecast
vorausschicken mention before, premise
voraussehbar foreseeable
voraussehen anticipate, foresee
voraussetzen assume, imply, presume, presuppose, require, suppose, take for granted, understand
Voraussetzung assumption, condition, precondition, prerequisite, presumption, presupposition, qualification, supposition
Voraussicht forecast, foresight, forethought, prescience, probability, providence, prudence
aller — nach in all likelihood **(probability)**
voraussichtlich expected, potential, presumable, presumptive, probable, prospective
vorauszahlen pay in advance, prepay
Vorauszahlung advance payment, payment in advance, prepayment
Vorbedacht aforethought, intention, premeditation
vorbedacht deliberate, intentional, on purpose, premeditated, prepense, with aforethought, with malice prepense
Vorbedingung condition, precedent, precondition, preliminary condition, prerequisite, qualification, requirement
Vorbehalt clause, proviso, reservation, reserve, restriction
—, mit (unter) with reservations
—, ohne unconditional(ly), without reservation (reserve, restriction)
unter — von reserving, subject to, under reservation (reserve) of
unter dem —, daß provided that, with the proviso (reservation) that
unter — aller Rechte all rights reserved
vorbehalten make a proviso, reserve, retain
—, sich reserve oneself
vorbehalten reserving, subject to
vorbehaltlich reserving, subject to, under reserve, with reservation as to, with the reservation that
vorbehaltslos unconditional, unqualified, unreserved, without reservation (reserve)
Vorbehalts
—klausel proviso, saving clause
—urteil provisional judgement
Vorbemerkung introduction, preamble, prefatory (preliminary) note
vorbenannt aforenamed, aforesaid, mentioned above (before)
vorbereiten arrange, fit for, make disposed for, prepare
—, sich get ready for, prepare (oneself) for
vorbereitend initiatory, preliminary, preparatory
Vorbereitung preparation, training
—en arrangements, dispositions
in — sein be in (under) preparation
—en treffen make preparations (arrangements) for, prepare
Vorbereitungs
—arbeiten preliminary (preparatory) work
—dienst preliminary training
—maßregel preliminary measure
—zeit preparatory period
Vorbericht introduction, preamble, preface, preliminary (preparatory) report

vorbesagt aforesaid
Vorbescheid advance notice, preliminary answer (decision, decree), interim action (order), interlocutory (provisional) decision
Vorbesitzer prepossessor, previous holder (owner, possessor), prior owner
Vorbesprechung preliminary discussion (talks), preparatory conference
vorbestimmen predetermine
Vorbestimmung predestination, predetermination
vorbestraft previously (formerly) convicted, having a criminal record
— sein have previous convictions
nicht — sein have a clean record, have no previous convictions
schwer — sein have a large (criminal, police) record
Vorbestrafung previous conviction
vorbeugen guard against, obviate, preclude, prevent
vorbeugend preventive, prohibitive, prophylactic
Vorbeugung prevention, prophylaxis
Vorbeugungs
—maßnahme (—maßregel) preservative, preventive measure
—mittel preservative, preventive, prophylactic
Vorbild example, model, pattern, standard
vorbildlich examplary, ideal, representative, typical
Vorbringen allegation, argument, assertion, pleadings, presentation, production, statement
vorbringen adduce, advance, allege, argue, assert, bring forward, furnish, give, interpose, maintain, make, offer, plead, prefer, present, produce, propose, propound, put forth (forward, in), quote, say, set forth, state, tender, urge, utter
Vordergrund foreground
vordringlich most important, urgent
Vordringlichkeit priority, urgency
—sliste priority list
Vordruck blank, form
vorehelich ante-nuptial, pre-marital, pre-nuptial
voreingenommen biassed, partial, prejudiced, prepossessed
un— free from bias, impartial, unbiassed, unprejudiced
Voreingenommenheit bias, prejudice, prepossession
vorenthalten conceal (from), deny, detain, keep back, retain from, withhold from
Vorenthaltung denial, detention, retention, withholding
Vorentscheidung interlocutory decree (decision), precedent, preliminary (provisional) decision
Vorentwurf (first, rough) draft, preliminary plan (scheme)
Vorerbe heir in tail, limited heir
Vorerbschaft estate in tail
vorerwähnt above-mentioned (-said), afore-mentioned (-named, -said), before-mentioned, mentioned (said) above
Vorexamen preliminary (previous) examination
Vorfahr ancestor
Vorfahren ancestors, ancestry, forefathers
Vorfahrt right of way
vorfahrtsberechtigt major
—, nicht inferior
Vorfahrts
—recht priority, right of way
—straße major road
—zeichen priority sign
Vorfall accident, case, event, happening, incident, occurrence
vorfallen come to pass, happen, occur
Vorfrage preliminary (previous) question
vorführen bring before (forward), demonstrate, display, exhibit, lead out, make appear in court, present, produce, put before, show
Vorführer demonstrator

Vorführung demonstration, display, exhibition, performance, presentation, production
—sbefehl (writ of) habeas corpus, warrant to appear
Vorgang antecedence, event, facts, goings-on, matter, occurrence, operation, practises, precedent, priority, proceedings, process, record, transaction
Vorgänger predecessor
  Amts— predecessor in office
  Rechts— assignor, predecessor in title
Vorgeben allegation, plea, pretence (se), pretext
vorgeben allege, assert, plead, pretend, purport, simulate
vorgeblich alleged, ostensible, pretended, sham, so-called, supposed
vorgefaßt preconceived
—e Meinung bias, preconception, prejudice
Vorgehen action, advance, antecedence, course (line) of action, precedence, proceeding(s), procedure
—, gemeinsames concerted action
—, gerichtliches court (legal) proceedings, lawsuit, proceedings at law
vorgehen advance, be more important than, go on, happen, have priority, have the preference, have (take) the precedence of, occur, operate, overrule, precede, prevail over, proceed (against), take action against
—, gemeinsam take concerted action
—, gerichtlich go to law, initiate legal proceedings, proceed by law, take legal steps (proceedings) against
vorgeladen summoned
— werden be summoned to appear
  als Zeuge — werden be called (summoned) as witness
Vorgeladener person summoned
vorgenannt s. vorerwähnt
Vorgeschichte antecedents, background, history
Vorgeschlagener nominee, presentee
vorgeschrieben compulsory, formulary, obligatory, prescribed, provided for, required, specified, statutory
—, gesetzlich prescribed (required) by law
vorgesehen intended, prescribed, proposed, provided for, stipulated
vorgesetzt superior, supervising
Vorgesetzter boss, chief, master, senior, superior
vorgreifen anticipate, encroach on, forestall, prejudge
Vorgriff anticipation
Vorhaben design, intent, intention, plan, project, purpose, scheme
vorhaben have in mind, intend, plan, project, purpose
vorhalten expostulate (with), remonstrate (with), reproach (with)
Vorhaltung remonstrance, representation, reproach
—en machen make representations, remonstrate (with)
vorhanden available, at (on) hand, effective, existing, present, ready
—, nicht non-existent
— sein be available (existing, in existence, present), be at (on) hand, be met with, exist
Vorhandensein availability, existence, presence
  Nicht— absence
Vorhängeschloß padlock
vorherbestimmen predestinate, predestine, predetermine, predict
Vorherbestimmung predestination
vorhergehen precede
vorhergehend antecedent, foregoing, preceding, previous
vorhergesehen foreseen
  un— unforeseen
vorherig (in) advance, former, last, preceding, previous

Vorherrschaft hegemony, predominance, superiority, supremacy
vorherrschen predominate, prevail
vorherrschend predominant, predominating, preponderant, prevailing, prevalent
Vorhersage (Vorhersagung) forecast, prediction, prophecy
vorhersagen forecast, foretell, predict, prophesy
vorhersehbar foreseeable
un— unforeseeable
vorhersehen forecast, foresee
vorig former, last, preceding, previous
im —en above
Vorinhaber previous holder (owner, possessor)
Vorinstanz lower (inferior) court, lower instance
Vorjahr previous year
vorkaufen forestall
Vorkaufs
—berechtigter preemptioner
—berechtigung preemptive right
—klausel clause of preemption
—preis preemption price
—recht option, (right of) preemption
Vorkehrungen arrangements, dispositions, precautions, (preventive) measures, provision, steps
— treffen make arrangements (preparations, provision) for, take measures (precautions, steps)
Vorkenntnis basic (preliminary, previous) knowledge
Vorkenntnisse elements, rudiments
Vorkommen deposit, incidence, occurrence, presence, resources
vorkommen appear, be found, be met with, happen, occur, seem, take place
Vorkommnis contingency, event, incident, occurrence
vorladen cite, invite, subpoena, summon
—, bei Strafe subpoena
—, als Zeugen call (summon) as witness
— lassen take out a summons against
Vorlader summoner
Vorladung citation, invitation, subpoena, summons, writ
—, auf on summons
—, gerichtliche court summons (invitation), notice of appearance, summons
— erlassen (ergehen lassen) indorse a writ, issue a summons
— erwirken take out a writ against
— Folge leisten (— nachkommen) answer (obey) a summons
Vorlage advance, bill, copy, exhibition, filing, model, motion, original, pattern, presentation, production, sample, specimen, source, submission, text
Vorläufer champion, forerunner, pioneer
vorläufig conditional, for the present, for the time being, interim, interlocutory, preliminary, provisional, provisory, so far available, temporary
Vorleben antecedents, background, past
vorlegen adduce, advance, display, exhibit, expose, file (with), present, produce, propound, put forward (on), submit
Vorlegung exhibition, presentation, production, submission
—sfrist limitation of presentation
Vorleistung advance payment, prepayment
vorliegen be in hand, be in the possession of, be under consideration, have come to hand
—, dem Gericht be before (in) the court
vorliegend at (in, to) hand, in question, present
vormachen impose upon, pretend
Vormacht hegemony, leading power
—stellung hegemony

vormerken book, make a note of, mark down, note (put) down, register, take note of

Vormerkung booking, entry, note, registration, reservation

Vormund curator, guardian, tutor, trustee
Mit— coguardian, joint guardian
Neben— ancillary guardian, coguardian, joint guardian
—, gesetzlicher guardian of court, statutory guardian
— bestellen appoint a guardian

Vormundschaft guardianship, tutelage
—, unter in ward, under guardianship
unter — stehen be in ward (under guardianship)
unter — stellen place under guardianship, place under the care of a guardian, put under tutelage

Vormundschafts
—behörde (-gericht) Court of Chancery (GB)
—gelder trust money
—gericht court of ward, guardianship court
—ordnung order in Chancery (GB)
—rat board of guardians
—richter judge of a guardianship court
—sachen guardianship matters, matters relating to guardian and ward

Vorname Christian (first, given) name

vornehmen carry out, deal with, effect, make, perform, take in hand, take up, undertake

vornehmen
—, sich design, intend, make up one's mind to, propose to oneself, purpose, resolve on

Vorprozeß preliminary proceedings, previous lawsuit

Vorprüfung preliminary examination (hearing), previous examination, pre-trial

Vorrang antecedence, precedence, preeminence, preference, priority, superiority
— einräumen give priority to
— haben go before, have preference (priority), precede
— haben vor have (take) precedence of, rank before
— lassen give precedence to

Vorrangstellung superiority

Vorrat inventory, provision, stock, storage, store, supply

vorrätig in (on) hand (stock)

Vorrecht benefit, preference, prerogative, priority, privilege, right of preference (priority), preferential (special) right
Alters- (right of) seniority
—, königliches (— der Krone) prerogative of the crown, royal prerogative
—saktie preference share, preferred stock

Vorrede preamble, preface, prefatory remark

Vorrichtung apparatus, appliance, contrivance, device, mechanism, preparation
Sicherheits- safety device

Vorrichtungen facilities

Vorsatz design, intent, intention, malice aforethought, plan, premeditation, purpose, resolution
—, mit deliberately, intentionally, on purpose, with deliberation (intent, malice aforethought)
— fassen form (take) a resolution
— haben design, intend

vorsätzlich deliberate, intended, intentional, on purpose, purposely, with deliberation (intent, malice aforethought, malice prepense)
un- undeliberate, undesigned, unintended, unintentional

Vorschau forecast, preview

vorschießen advance, lend, make an advance of

Vorschlag motion, nomination, offer, proposal, proposition, recommendation, suggestion

Gegen- counterproposal
Verbesserungs- proposal for (of) improvement
— zur Güte conciliatory (friendly) proposal, proposition for settlement
auf — von at the instance of, on the proposal of, upon suggestion by
— machen make a proposal, propose, suggest
vorschlagen make a proposal, nominate, offer, propose, put forth, recommend, suggest
Vorschlags
—liste list of nominations, slate
—recht right of nomination (to nominate)
vorschreiben direct, enact, enjoin, order, prescribe, provide, specify
Vorschrift command, copy, decree, direction, instruction, manual, order, precept, prescription, provision, regulation, rule, specification
Auslegungs- interpretation clause
Befreiungs- exemption provision
Betriebs—en operating instructions, shop (working) regulations
Dienst- service instruction (regulation)
Form- formal, requirements, formality
Polizei—en police regulations
Prozeß—en (Verfahrens— —en) rules of procedure, procedural rules
Sicherheits- precaution, precautionary (safety) provision
Straf- penal statute, penalty clause
Tarif—en tariff provisions
Verkehrs—en traffic regulations
Vertrags- contractual provision (clause)
Verwaltungs—en administrative regulations
Zoll—en customs regulations
—, gesetzliche legal regulations, rule (provision) of law, statutory provision
—, zwingende coercional (compulsory, peremptory) rule
—, nach according to regulations, as directed (prescribed)
Vorschrift
— erlassen pass a decree
—en erlassen make prescriptions, prescribe regulations
—en machen dictate, prescribe
vorschriftsgemäß (-mäßig) according to regulations (instruction, prescriptions, the rules), as directed (instructed, ordered, prescribed), by rule, correct, formulary, in accordance with instructions, in due form, proper, standard
vorschriftswidrig improper, irregular, against (contrary to) the regulations (the rules)
Vorschriftswidrigkeit irregularity
Vorschub aid, aiding and abetting, assistance, countenance, furtherance, support
— leisten aid and abet, abet, assist, connive, countenance, encourage, favour, further, help, pander
Vorschuß advance, advance(d) money, loan, payment in advance (on account), retainer, retaining fee
Gehalts- salary advance
Kosten- advance(d costs, expenses), retainer, retaining fee
— bewilligen grant an allowance
— leisten advance money, make an advance
vorschußweise as an (in) advance, by way of a loan
Vorschußzahlung advance payment
vorschützen malinger, make a pretext of, plead, pretend, pretext, allege (give, use) as a pretext
—, Krankheit allege ill health, malinger
—, Unerfahrenheit plead inexperience

—, Unkenntnis plead ignorance
Vorschützung plea, pleading, pretence, pretext
vorsehen assign for, consider, enact, foresee, plan, provide, make provisions for, schedule, stipulate
—, sich be careful, take care
sich — vor be on one's guard against, take precaution against
Vorsehung providence
Vorsicht care, caution, circumspection, foresight, precaution, prudence
—, mit cautiously, prudently, with caution
vorsichtig careful, cautious, circumspect, conservative, guarded, prudent, safe, wary, wise, with caution
vorsichtshalber by way of precaution
Vorsichtsmaßnahme (-maßregel) precaution, precautionary measure
—n ergreifen (-treffen) take precautions
Vorsitz chair, chairmanship, presidency
unter dem — von under the chairmanship (presidency) of, with ... in the chair (presiding)
— führen (haben, innehaben) be in the chair, preside
— übernehmen take the chair
vorsitzen be in the chair, preside
Vorsitzender chairman, president
Gerichts- presiding judge
—, stellvertretender deputy (vice) chairman, vice president
Vorsorge care, precaution, providence, provision
— treffen s. vorsorgen
vorsorgen arrange for, make arrangements for, make provision(s), provide, take care that, take precautions (against)
vorsorglich as a precaution, by way of precaution, precautionary, provident, thoughtful
vorspiegeln delude, make believe, make false appearances (pretences), pretend
Vorspiegelung delusion, illusion, pretence(se), sham
— falscher Tatsachen false pretences, misrepresentation (of facts)
unter — falscher Tatsachen by misrepresentation of facts, under false pretences
Vorspruch preamble
Vorstadium preliminary stage (state)
Vorstand board of administration (directors), board member, chairman, directing manager, director, executive board, executive (managing) committee, head, management, managers, managing board (director), president, principal
Vorstands
—bericht directors' report
—mitglied board member, director, member of the board of directors (of the managing committee)
—sitzung board meeting, meeting of the board of directors
—wahl board election, election of the (board of) directors
vorstehen administer, be at the head of, be in charge of, direct, govern, head, hold, keep, look after, manage, preside, represent, superintend
vorstehend above, aforesaid, foregoing, last, preceding
im —en above, hereinbefore
Vorsteher chairman, chief, director, governor, head, manager, principal, superintendent, superior, warden
Bezirks- district commissioner
Vorsteherin directress, manageress
vorstellbar conceivable, imaginable, presentable, thinkable
un- unconceivable, unimaginable, unthinkable
vorstellen introduce, mean, present, remonstrate (with), represent, signify, stand for
—, sich conceive of, envisage, imagine, introduce (oneself) to, present oneself to, think

vorstellig werden apply to, complain, make representations to, petition, present (send in) a petition to, protest against
Vorstellung conception, expostulation, idea, imagination, interview, introduction, notion, performance, presentation, remonstrance, representation
—, falsche misconception
—, persönliche presentation in person
Vorstellungs
—kraft imaginative power
—vermögen imagination, imaginative faculty
Vorstrafe former (previous) conviction
keine —n haben have a clean record, have no previous convictions
viele —n haben have a large (criminal, police) record
Vorstrafenregister (-verzeichnis) criminal (police) record, record of previous convictions
vorstrecken advance, lend
Vorstreckung advance
Vorstufe beginning, first step (stage), initial phase
Vorstudien preliminary studies
vortäuschen counterfeit, fake, feign, malinger, pretend, sham, simulate
Vortäuschung feint, pretension, simulation
Vorteil advantage, benefit, gain, interest, profit
—, von of advantage
zum — von in (on) behalf of, in favour (the interest) of, for the benefit of, to the advantage of
vorteilhaft advantageous, beneficial, favourable, lucrative, paying, profitable, remunerable, remunerative, with advantage
Vortrag address, delivery, elocution, lecture, paper, performance, pleadings, report, speech, talk
— halten make a report, deliver (make) a speech, read a paper
vortragen argue, deliver, express, lecture, plead, propose, report (on), set forth, state
Vortragender lecturer, speaker
Vortritt antecedence, precedence, prior rank, priority of rank
— haben vor take precedence of
— lassen give precedence to
vorübergehen pass (by)
vorübergehend passing, provisional, temporary, transitory, for a short time
Vorüberlegungen preliminary considerations
Voruntersuchung pre-trial, preliminary examination (hearing[s], inquiry, investigation, trial)
Vorurteil bias, preconceived notion, preconception, prejudice, prepossession
vorurteilsfrei (-los) free from bias, impartial, open-minded, unbiassed, unprejudiced
Vorurteilslosigkeit detachment, freedom from bias (prejudice), impartiality, liberality, open-mindedness
Vorverfahren preliminary proceedings
Vorverhandlung preliminary hearing (trial)
Vorverhandlungen pleadings, preliminaries
Vorverhör preliminary hearing (interrogation), pre-examination
vorverlegen antedate
Vorvertrag binder, preliminary agreement (contract), contract of agreement
Vorwahl nomination, pre-election, preliminary election, straw-vote
Vorwand excuse, plea, pretence (se), pretext
unter dem — von on (under the) pretext of, on (under) the pretence of, on the plea of (that)
Vorwarnung alert
vorweg before(hand), before the time, from before, in advance

Vorwegleistung advance payment, payment in advance, prepayment
Vorwegnahme anticipation
vorwegnehmen anticipate
vorweisen exhibit, present, produce, show
vorwerfen reproach with
vorwiegen predominate, prevail
vorwiegend chiefly, largely, mainly, mostly, predominant, preponderant, prevalent
Vorwissen foreknowledge, (previous) knowledge, prescience
Vorwort foreword, introduction, preface
Vorwurf blame, charge, remonstrance, representation, reproach
— **erheben** reproach with
Vorwürfe
— **machen** blame for, remonstrate (upon, with), reproach with
sich — machen reprove oneself (about)
vorwurfsfrei blameless, free from blame, irreproachable
Vorzeichen omen, prognostic, symptom, token
vorzeigen exhibit, present, produce, show
Vorzeigefrist limitation of presentation
Vorzeiger bearer, holder, presenter
Vorzeigung exhibition, presentation, production, showing, sight
—, **bei** on presentation, at sight
vorzeitig anticipated, before maturity (the time), early, in advance, premature, untimely
vorziehen give preference, prefer
Vorzug advantage, grace, preference, preferential treatment, prerogative, priority, privilege, virtue
— **geben** give preference to
— **genießen (haben)** be preferred (privileged) to, enjoy preference (preferential treatment), have the advantage over
Vorzugs
—**aktie** preference (preferential, priority) share, preferred share (stock)
—**aktionär** preference (preferential) shareholder (stockholder), preferred stockholder
—**angebot** exceptional (special) offer
—**anspruch** preference (preferential, preferred, priority) claim
—**bedingungen** preferential terms
—**behandlung** discrimination, preference, preferential treatment
—**gläubiger** preferential (prior) creditor
—**liste** priority list
—**preis** exceptional (preferential, special) price
—**recht** (right of) preference, preferential right, priority, privilege
—**satz** preferential (special) rate
—**tarif** preferential tariff
—**wechsel** preference bill
vorzugsweise by preference, for choice, especially, preferably, preferentially
—**zahlungen** preferential payments
—**zoll** preferential duty (tariff)
votieren vote
Votum suffrage, vote
Mißtrauens- vote of censure (no-confidence)
Vertrauens- vote of confidence
sein— abgeben cast one's vote

W

Wache guard, police station, watch
Polizei- police station
— halten be on duty (guard), keep guard
auf — sein watch
wachen care (for), guard, watch (over)
wachhabend on duty
Wachhund watch dog
Wachtposten guard
wachsam alert, vigilant, watchful
Wachsamkeit vigilance, watchfulness
Wächter custodian, guardian, guardsman, warder, watchman
Waffe arm, weapon
Dienst- service pistol
zu den —n greifen take up arms
—n tragen carry arms
—n wegwerfen abandon one's arms
Waffen
—ausfuhr export of arms
—ausfuhrverbot arms embargo
—beistand armed assistance
—besitz, unerlaubter illegal (unauthorized) possession of arms, unlawful possession of weapons
—depot (-lager) arsenal
—gewalt, mit by force of arms, with arms
—handel arms trade (traffic)
—ruhe armistice, cease-fire, suspension of hostilities, truce
—schein gun licence
—schmuggel gun running, arms smuggling
—stillstand armistice, cease-fire, truce
Waffenstillstands
—abkommen truce, armistice agreement
—bedingungen armistice terms
—verhandlungen truce (armistice) negotiations (parleys)
Waffenverbot ban on weapons
waffnen arm
sich — gegen guard against
wagen attempt, dare, hazard, (take the) risk, stake, venture
Wagnis danger, hazard, hazardous, enterprise, risk, risky undertaking, venture
Wahl alternative, ballot, choice, election, option, poll, polling, selection, voting
Nach- by-election, second ballot
Schluß- final vote
Stich- second ballot
Ur- preliminary (primary) election
Wieder- re-election
—, freie free choice
—, geheime secret ballot (vote)
—, nach at one's choice (option)
—, aus freier of one's own choice
— abhalten (durchführen) hold an election
— anfechten contest the validity of an election
— ausüben exercise an option
von der — ausschließen disfranchise
— gewinnen carry an election
— haben have the (one's) choice
keine — haben have no alternative (option)
in der — kandidieren run an election, stand as candidate, stand for an election
— treffen make a choice
zur — vorschlagen nominate as candidate
Wahl
—akt elective act, poll, polling act
—akten election returns
—alter voting age
—amt elective office
—ausschreibung election writ
—ausschuß election (electoral) committee, returning, board
wählbar eligible
—, nicht ineligible, non-eligible
wieder— reeligible

Wählbarkeit eligibility
Wahl
—beeinflussung electoral corruption
wahlberechtigt entitled to vote
Wahl
—berechtigter elector, (legal) voter
—berechtigung electoral qualification, franchise, right to vote, suffrage
—bericht electoral (election) return
—bestechung electoral corruption
—beteiligung percentage of voting, poll
—betrug electoral corruption, vote fraud
—bezirk constituency, (election, electoral) district, polling district (division), ward
—büro elective office, polling station
Wahlen elections
Kongreß— congressional elections
Neu— by-elections, new elections
Parlaments— general (parliamentary) elections
Präsidentschafts— presidential elections
Senats— senatorial elections
wählen choose, elect, go to the polls, make one's choice, pick out, poll, return, select, vote
Wähler constituent, elector, voter
Wählerin electress
Wahlergebnis election result, voting return, result of an election
Wähler
—liste ballot list, poll book, register of electors (voters)
—schaft body of voters, constituency, constituent body, electorate, voting population
—versammlung election meeting
wahlfähig eligible (for), entitled to vote, having a vote
—es Alter voting age
Wahl
—fähigkeit eligibility, franchise
—fälschung election fraud
—feldzug election (electoral) campaign
—gang ballot
—geheimnis secrecy of vote
—gesetz election (electoral) law
—gesetzgebung electoral legislation
—handlung poll, polling act
—kampagne s. -feldzug
—kampf electoral contest
—kandidat candidate
sich als — — aufstellen lassen run an election
—kreis s. bezirk
—leiter returning officer
—liste electoral list, poll book, register of electors (voters), slate
—lokal election room, polling station, polls, ward room
—mann constituent, delegate, elector
—mündigkeit voting age
—ordnung electoral regulations
—ort electoral place, polling station, polls
—periode electoral period
—pflicht voting obligation
—programm election programme, ticket
—propaganda election propaganda
—protest petition (against the return)
—prüfer scrutineer
—prüfung scrutiny
—recht electoral law, franchise, option, optional right, right of choice (option), right to vote, suffrage
Frauen- women's suffrage
— —, aktives franchise, right to vote
— —, passives eligibility
—(rechts)reform electoral reform
—rechtsverlust disfranchisement
—resultat s. -ergebnis
—schwindel s. -betrug
—spruch device, motto, slogan
—stimme choice, vote, suffrage
—system electoral system
—tag (-termin) day of election, election day

—umtriebe election disturbances, electioneering practices
wahlunfähig ineligible
Wahl
—urne ballot box, polls
—versammlung election meeting, electoral assembly
—versprechen election pledge, pre-election promise
wahlweise alternative, optional, selective
Wahl
—zeit election time
—zelle voting booth
—zensus voting census
—zettel (-schein) ballot (voting) paper
Wahn delusion, false (erroneous) opinion (idea), illusion, madness, mania
—begriff erroneous conception, false notion
—sinn insanity, lunacy, madness, mental alienation
wahnsinnig insane, mad
Wahnsinniger insane person, lunatic, madman, madwoman
wahr genuine, intrinsic, proper, real, right, sincere, true, truthful, veritable
un- (nicht-) false, truthless, untrue
als — erweisen substantiate
sich als — erweisen be verified
für — halten believe in
— machen fulfil, live up to
als — nachweisen verify
— werden be realized, come true, materialize
wahren attend to, comply with, defend, guard, keep up, look after, maintain, preserve, protect, reserve, safeguard, save, take care of, uphold, watch over
Wahrheit truth
—en verities
—, in in truth
die reine — the whole truth and nothing but the truth
— finden get to the truth
— sagen speak (tell) the truth
Wahrheits
—beweis proof of the truth
— — antreten embark upon the proof of truth, prove the truth of one's statement
wahrheitsgemäß (-getreu) in accordance with truth, faithful, true, truly, truthful
Wahrheitsliebe love of truth, truthfulness, veracity
wahrheitsliebend truthful, truth-loving, veracious
wahrheitswidrig against the truth, untrue, untruthful
wahrnehmen attend to, become aware of, look after, notice, observe, perceive, protect, safeguard, seize, take, take care of, make use of
Wahrnehmung attending, care (of), exercise, looking (after), maintenance, observation, perception, protection, safeguarding
—svermögen perceptive faculty, power of observation
wahrscheinlich likely, probable
un- improbable, unlikely
Wahrscheinlichkeit likelihood, probability
aller — nach in all probability
Wahrscheinlichkeitsbeweis presumptive evidence (proof)
Wahrspruch finding, verdict
Wahrung keeping, maintenance, protection, safeguarding
Währung currency, standard, monetary system (standard)
Währungs
—abkommen currency (monetary) agreement
—abwertung currency devaluation
—aufwertung currency revaluation
—bereich (-gebiet) currency area
—block currency block
—deckung coverage of a currency
—einheit monetary unit (standard)
—entwertung currency depreciation
—fonds currency (monetary) fund
— —, Internationaler International Monetary Fund

—gesetz currency (exchange) clause
—kontrolle controlled currency, currency control
—kredit foreign exchange loan
—krise monetary crisis
—kurs exchange rate
—manipulation currency manipulations
—ordnung currency regulations, monetary system
—parität exchange rate, parity, par of exchange
—politik currency policy
—reform (-umstellung) currency reform
—spekulant currency operator (speculator)
—stichtag currency reform day
—system monetary (currency) system
—umstellung currency reform
Wahrzeichen emblem, landmark, mark, omen, sign, symptom, token
Waise orphan
— werden be orphaned
Halb- fatherless (motherless) child
Voll- parentless child
Waisen
—haus orphanage, orphan, asylum, orphans' home
—kind orphan child, orphan boy (girl)
Wald
—aufseher (-hüter) forest keeper (guard), ranger
—brand forest fire
—frevel offence against the forest laws
—ordnung (-recht) forest laws
—schaden forest damage
walten govern, rule, sway
—, seines Amtes do one's duty, officiate
— lassen dispense, show
Wandel change, mutation
—, Handel und trade and traffic
Lebens- behaviour, conduct (course) of life, way of living
Wandel
—anleihe convertible loan
—schuldverschreibung (-obligation) convertible bond
wandelbar changeable, inconstant, variable
Wandelbarkeit changeableness, inconstancy
wandeln change
sich — (in) turn (into)
Wandlung change, redhibition, transformation
Wandlungs
—fehler redhibitory defect
—klage action for annulment (cancellation), redhibitory action
— — erheben sue for reversion
—verfahren redhibitory suit
Wappen (coat of) arms, crest
—bild (-figur) heraldic figure
—kunde heraldry
—spruch heraldic motto
—tier heraldic animal
wappnen arm
Ware article, commodity, goods, line, merchandise, product, ware
Waren goods, merchandise
—abkommen commodity agreement
—absatz sale of goods
—ausfuhr export(ation) of goods
—austausch exchange of goods, trade
—austauschabkommen trade agreement
—bestand stock (on hand) (of goods), stocks
—bezeichnung trademark
—einfuhr import(ation) of goods
—kontrolle merchandise control
—lager assortment, depot, stock (s), store, storehouse, warehouse
—lagerung storage, warehousing
—lieferung delivery (supply) of goods
—marke brand
—muster (-probe) pattern, sample, specimen
—prüfung quality control (inspection)
—rechnung invoice
—sendung consignment of goods
—tausch barter
—stempel trademark
—steuer duty, excise
—umsatz sales, turnover

—umsatzsteuer sales (turnover) tax
—verkauf sale of goods
—verzeichnis inventory, list of goods
—wechsel trade (commercial) bill
—zeichen trademark
—zeichengesetz trademark act
—zeichenrecht trademark law
—zeichenrechte trademark rights
—zeichenschutz trademark protection
—zeichenverletzung trademark infringement
—zoll (customs) duty
warnen admonish, caution (against), warn (of, against)
Warner admonisher, warner
Warn
—signal (-zeichen) warning signal
—tafel warning board
Warnung admonition, caution, warning
Warnungs
—anzeige public warning
—schuß summoning gun
—signal beacon, danger signal, warning siren
—streik warning strike
Warnvorrichtung warning device
Warte
—frist waiting period
—geld attendance fee, demurrage, half pay
—liste waiting list
warten attend to, look after, nurse, wait (upon)
— auf await, expect, wait for
Wärter attendant, custodian, guard, keeper, nurse, warden, warder, watchman
Wartezeit demurrage, grace, wait, waiting time
Wartung attendance, keeping, maintenance, nursing
Wasser
—polizei water (river) police
—schaden water damage
—schutz water protection
—weg water way
— —, auf dem by water
—zeichen watermark
—zoll water toll, waterage

Wechsel allowance, alternation, bill (of exchange), change, change-over, changing, draft, exchange, interchange, paper, shift, turn
Bank- bank bill
Besitz- change of title
Blanko- blank bill
Dato- dated bill
Finanz- financial bill
Gefälligkeits- accommodation bill
Gesinnungs- (Meinungs-) change of opinion
Handels- trade (commercial) bill
Prima- first of exchange, original (first) bill
Schatz- exchequer (treasury) bill (bond)
Sekunda- second of exchange
Sicht- sight bill
Termin dated bill
Vorzugs- preference bill
Wechsel
— akzeptieren accept a bill
— nicht akzeptieren dishono(u)r a bill
— ausstellen draw (issue) a bill
— begeben negotiate a bill
— einlösen hono(u)r (protect) a bill
— nicht einlösen dishono(u)r a bill
Wechsel
—agent bill broker
—akzept (-annahme) acceptance of a bill
—akzeptant acceptor of a bill
—aussteller drawer of a bill
—bestimmungen bill regulations
—beziehung correlation, interrelation, mutual relation
—bezogener drawee of a bill
—bürge bail (guarantor, surety) of a bill
—bürgschaft (-garantie) guarantee (surety) for a bill
—fälscher bill forger
—fälschung bill forgery
—forderungen bills receivable
—geber drawer of a bill
—geld change, small coin (money)

—gesetz Bill of Exchange Act (GB), Negotiable Instrument Act (Law) (USA)
Wechsel
—gläubiger bill creditor, holder of a bill
—inhaber holder of a bill
—klage action on account of a bill of exchange
—kommission bill brokerage
—kosten bill charges
—kurs exchange rate
—laufzeit currency of a bill
—makler bill broker
wechseln alternate, change, exchange, shift, vary
Wechsel
—nehmer payee, taker of a bill
—ordnung bill (exchange) regulations, Bill of Exchange Act (GB), Uniform Negotiable Instrument Act (USA)
—protest protest (of a bill)
—prozeß procedure on bills of exchange
—provision bill brokerage, exchange commission
—recht exchange law, law of exchange
—schuld bills payable
—schuldner bill debtor
wechselseitig mutual, reciprocal
Wechsel
—seitigkeit mutuality, reciprocity
—spekulant bill jobber
—spesen bill charges
—stube exchange bureau (office)
—verhältnis reciprocal relation
—verbindlichkeiten bills (notes) payable
wechselweise alternately, alternatively, by turn, mutually, reciprocally
Wechsel
—wirkung interaction, reciprocal action (effect)
Wechsler (money) changer, exchanger
Weg approach, course, line, manner, means, passage, path, road, route, way
Rechts- course (process) of law
— —, auf dem by legal proceedings, by suit, by process of law
Wege
—gebühr (-geld, -zoll) toll
—recht right of passage (way)
wegen on account of, for, because of, by reason of, on behalf of, due to, owing to, on the ground of, with regard to, regarding, as a result of, for the sake of
—, von Amts ex officio, officially
—, von Polizei by order of the police
—, von Rechts by law (right)
Wegfall abolishment, abolition, cessation, disappearance, drop, extinction, lapse, omission, suppression
wegfallen be abolished (discontinued, dropped, omitted, suppressed), become void, cease (to exist), disappear, fall away, not take place
weggeben give away, sell
weglassen dispense with, drop, leave out, omit
Weglassung omission
Wegnahme capture, confiscation, seizure, taking away
wegnehmen capture, confiscate, deprive of, occupy, remove, seize (upon), strip of, take away, withdraw
Wehr defence, resistance
—auftrag defence order
—dienst military service
—gesetz army act, national defence law
—macht armed (military) forces
—ordnung army statute
—pflicht conscription, compulsory service
wehrpflichtig liable to (subject to) military service
Wehr
—pflichtiger conscript, draftee
—wirtschaft defence economy
wehrlos defenceless, unarmed
Wehrlosigkeit defencelessness
weiblich female

weichen give (make) way, retreat, yield
weigern, sich decline, refuse
Weigerung refusal
Weigerungs
—fall, im in case of refusal
—grund reason for refusal
Weise custom, habit, manner, method, mode, style, way
weisen point out, show
— aus banish, exile, expel from
weismachen make believe
Weißbuch White Book (Paper)
Weisung direction, instruction, order
— ausführen (befolgen) comply with (follow) an instruction
—en einholen ask for instructions (directions)
—en erhalten receive instructions
—en geben give instructions
sich an die —en halten adhere to (comply with), instructions
weisungs
—gebunden subject to directions
—gemäß according to instructions, as directed (instructed)
weiteres, bis auf for the present, temporarily, until further notice
Weiterbestand continuance, continued (further) existence, survival
weiterbestehen continue (to exist), remain in existence, survive
weiterführen carry on, continue, maintain
Weiterführung continuation
Weitergabe handing over, passing on, transmission
weitergeben (-leiten) pass (on, to), hand over, transmit
weiterkommen advance, get on, progress
weiterveräußern (-verkaufen) resell
Weiterveräußerung (-verkauf) resale
weitervermieten sublet, underlet
weiterverpachten sublease
weiterverpfänden repledge
weitgehend extensive, far-reaching, large, sweeping, vast, wide
weitgreifend extensive
weitläufig ample, detailed, distant, extensive, large, spacious, vast, wide
weitreichend far-reaching
weitverbreitet common, prevalent, wide(ly) spread, widely circulated (held)
Welle wave
Streik- strike wave
Verhaftungs- wave of arrests
Welt world
Fach- experts
Halb- semi-monde (-world)
Juristen- lawyers
Welt
—all universe
—anschauung ideology, outlook on life, philosophy (view) of life, world concept
—bund international union
—frieden universal (world) peace
—gerichtshof Permanent Court of International Justice, world court
—gewerkschaftsbund World Federation of Trade Unions
—handel international trade, world('s) commerce (trade)
—herrschaft world domination
—konferenz international (world) conference
—kongreß world congress
—krieg world war
—krise world crisis
—lage international situation
weltlich mundane, profane, secular, temporal, worldly
Welt
—macht world power
—postverein Universal Postal Union
—sicherheit world security
—urheberrechtsabkommen Universal Copyright Convention
—verband international union
—verkehr international traffic
—währung world currency
—wirtschaft world economy
—wirtschaftskrise world's economic crisis
wenden turn
sich — an address oneself to, appeal to, apply to, contact, have recourse to, turn to

Wendepunkt crisis, juncture, turning point
Wendung turn, turning
werben apply for, canvass, make propaganda for, publicize, solicit, win over
Werber suitor, canvasser
Werbung advertising, canvass, propaganda, publicity
Werdegang career, development, evolution, history
Werk achievement, act, action, deed, enterprise, factory, gin, manufactory, mill, performance, plant(s), production, undertaking, work(s), workmanship
Werks
—angehöriger employee
—anlage plant
—spionage industrial espionage
—zugehörigkeit length of service
Werktag week-day, workday, working day
werktags on week-days (workdays)
werktätig active, on employment, labo(u)ring, operative, practical, working
Werk
—vertrag labo(u)r (work) contract
—zeug instrument, puppet, tool
Wert asset, merit, price, rate, standard, value, virtue, worth
Buch- book value
Gegen- countervalue, equivalent
Gesamt- total value
Nenn- (Nominal-) face (nominal) value, par (value)
Sach- real value
Vermögens—e assets, effects, property, resources
Versicherungs- insured value
dem — nach ad valorem
wert sein be valuable (worth), be worthy of, deserve
Wert
—abnahme decrease in (deterioration of) value
—angabe declaration of value, declared value
—ansatz estimate, valuation
—bestimmung appraisement, valuation
Werte assets, funds, securities, stock(s), valuables
Wert
—einbuße loss of value
—einheit unit of value
werten appraise, evaluate, rate, value
Wert
—erhöhung rise in value
—ermittlung (-festsetzung, -feststellung) appraisal, appraisement, assessment, valuation
—gegenstand article of value
—gegenstände valuables
—herabsetzung depreciation
wertlos futile, nugatory, of no (without) value, useless, valueless, worthless
Wert
—losigkeit uselessness, worthlessness
—messer standard
wertmindernd depreciating, depreciative
Wert
—minderung decline in (deterioration of) value, depreciation
—papiere bonds, negotiable instruments, securities, shares, stocks
—papiermakler sharebroker, stockbroker
—sachen valuables
wertschätzen appreciate, esteem, honour, value
Wert
—schätzung appreciation, esteem, estimation, regard (for)
—steigerung appreciation, increase in (rise in, improvement of) value
Wertung valuation
Wert
—verlust depreciation, loss of value
—verringerung depreciation, decrease in value
wertvoll precious, of (great) value, valuable
Wert
—zoll ad valorem duty

—zunahme (-zuwachs) appreciation, increment (value), increase in value
—zuwachssteuer increment value tax
Wesen being, character, condition, conduct, creature, entity, essence, existence, manners, nature, substance, virtue
—smerkmal characteristic feature
wesentlich essential, fundamental, intrinsic, material, principal, substantial, vital
Wett
—annahme (-büro) betting office
—bewerb competition, contest, rivalry
— —, ehrlicher fair competition
— —, freier free competition
— —, unlauterer unfair competition
—bewerber competitor, contestant, rival
Wettbewerbs
—basis competitive basis
—beschränkung restraint of trade
—bestimmungen competition regulations
—freiheit free competition, freedom of competition
—klausel competition clause
—lohn competitive wage
—system competitive system
—verbot restraint of trade
Wette bet, wager
— abschließen bet, make a bet, wager
— annehmen take (up) a bet
— eingehen make a bet, take up a wager
Wetteinsatz odds, stake
Wetten betting
wetten bet, wager, make a bet (wager)
Wetter better, weather
Un- row, storm, tempest
—schaden weather damage
Wett
—kampf (—streit) competition, contest
—kurs odds
—preis stake
—schwindler welsher
—vertrag wager contract
—zettel betting slip
wichtig essential, grave, important, material, of importance (moment), serious, weighty
— für relevant to
Wichtigkeit consequence, import, importance, moment, relevance (to)
wider against, contrary to, in the face of, in opposition to, versus
Für und Wider the pros and cons
widerfahren befall, happen (to), receive
— lassen, Gerechtigkeit give one's due, do justice
Widerklage counteraction, countercharge, counterclaim, counterplea, countersuit, cross action
— erheben cross-petition (-sue)
widerklagen file a counteraction (countersuit)
Widerkläger counterclaiming defendant
widerlegbar confutable, rebuttable, refutable
—, nicht irrebuttable, irrefutable
widerlegen confute, disprove, prove wrong, rebut, refute
Widerlegung confutation, disproof, rebuttal, refutation
widernatürlich unnatural
widerrechtlich against (contrary to) the law, illegal, unfair, unlawful, unjust, wrongful
— aneignen misappropriate, usurp
— betreten trespass (up) on
— verwenden misapply
—es Betreten trespass
Widerrechtlichkeit illegality, unlawfulness, wrongfulness
Widerrede contradiction, objection
Widerruf cancellation, countermand, disavowal, disclaimer, recall, recantation, repeal, retraction, revocation, withdrawal

—, **bis auf** unless countermanded, until recalled (cancelled)
widerrufen annul, cancel, countermand, quash, recall, recant, repeal, repudiate, retract, revoke, withdraw
widerruflich countermandable, removable, repealable, revocable
Widerruflichkeit revocability
Widerrufs
—klausel revocation (repealing) clause
—recht right of recantation
Widersacher adversary, antagonist, opponent
widersetzen, sich be opposed (recalcitrant) to, defy, disobey, fight (struggle) against, object to, oppose, resist
widersetzlich insubordinate, obstinate, obstructive, recalcitrant, refractory
Widersetzlichkeit insubordination, obstinacy, recalcitrance, refractoriness
Widersinn absurdity, nonsense, paradox
widersinnig absurd, inconsistent, nonsensical, paradoxical, preposterous
Widersinnigkeit absurdity, incongruity
widerspiegeln reflect
widersprechen argue, be opposed (repugnant) to, be in contradiction to, contest, contradict, gainsay, object to, oppose
widersprechen, sich be at variance (contradictory, inconsistent, repugnant to), contradict oneself, disagree
widersprechend conflicting, contradictory, inconsistent, repugnant
Widerspruch contradiction, discrepancy, inconsistency, objection, opposition, protest
—, **ohne** uncontradicted, unopposed, without opposition (contradiction)
— **einreichen** lodge an objection
— **erheben** interpose (make) an objection, oppose
— **hervorrufen** raise objection
— **stattgeben** sustain an objection
im — stehen be at variance (with), be in contradiction (to), be inconsistent (with), conflict with, disagree
sich in Widersprüche verwikkeln become entangled in contradictions
widerspruchslos uncontradicted, unopposed, without contradiction (opposition)
— **hinnehmen** leave uncontradicted (unopposed)
Widerspruchsrecht right to object (oppose)
widerspruchsvoll conflicting, (self-)contradictory, discrepant, incongruous, inconsistent
Widerstand opposition, resistance
— **gegen die Staatsgewalt** resistance to state authorities
—, **bewaffneter** armed resistance
—, **passiver** passive resistance
— **leisten** offer opposition (resistance), oppose, resist
keinen — leisten offer no resistance
auf — stoßen face (meet with) opposition
Widerstandsbewegung resistance movement
widerstandslos unresisting, without resistance
widerstehen be repugnant to, disagree, oppose, resist, withstand
—, **nicht** yield to
Widerstreben opposition, reluctance, resistance
widerstreben be opposed (repugnant) to, oppose, resist, strive (struggle) against
widerstrebend reluctantly, with reluctance
Widerstreit antagonism, clash (ing), collision, conflict, contradiction, opposition
widerstreiten be contrary to, clash with, conflict, mitigate against
widerstreitend antagonistic, clashing, conflicting, incompatible

widmen dedicate, devote, inscribe
—, sich abandon oneself (to), apply oneself (to), dedicate oneself, devote oneself (to), go in (for), follow
Widmung dedication, inscription
widrig adverse, contrary, inimical, untoward
—e Umstände adverse circumstances
widrigenfalls in default thereof (of this, of which), else, failing this (which), upon failure of which, otherwise
Widrigkeit adverseness, adversity, contrariety, untoward event
wiederabtreten retrocede
Wiederabtretung retrocession
wiederanschaffen replace
Wiederanschaffung replacement
—swert replacement value
Wiederaufbau reconstruction
wiederaufbauen rebuild, reconstruct
Wiederaufleben renascence, resurrection, revival
wiederaufleben revive
Wiederaufnahme reestablishment, renewal, resumption, revival
Wiederaufnahme
—antrag petition in error
—verfahren new hearing, rehearing, reopening of proceedings, retrial
wiederaufnehmen reestablish, renew, reopen, resume
wiederaufrüsten rearm
Wiederaufrüstung rearmament
wiederbekommen get back, recover
wiederbeschaffen replace
Wiederbeschaffung replacement
Wiederbeschaffungs
—kosten replacement costs
—preis replacement price
—wert replacement value
wiederbeschäftigen reemploy, reengage
Wiederbeschäftigung reemployment, reengagement
wiederbringen bring back, restore, return
wiederbringlich restorable, retrievable
wiedereinbürgern repatriate
Wiedereinbürgerung repatriation
wiedereinführen re-establish, reintroduce
wiedereingliedern rehabilitate, resettle
Wiedereingliederung rehabilitation, resettlement
wiedereinsetzen re-establish, rehabilitate, reinstall, reinstate, replace, restore
Wiedereinsetzung re-establishment, rehabilitation, reinstallation, reinstatement, restitution, restoration
wiedereinstellen s. -beschäftigen
Wiedereinstellung s. -beschäftigung
wiedereintreten recur, re-enter
Wiedereintritt recurrence, reentrance, re-entry
wiedereinverleiben reannex
Wiedereinverleibung reannexation
wiederergreifen recapture, reseize
Wiederergreifung recapture, reseizure
wiedererhalten get back, recover, retrieve
wiedererkennen recognize
Wiedererkennung recognition
wiedererlangbar recoverable
wiedererlangen be restored to, get back, recover, regain
Wiedererlangung recovery
wiederernennen reappoint
Wiederernennung reappointment
wiedererobern recapture, recover
wiedereröffnen reopen, resume
Wiedereröffnung reopening, resumption
wiedererstatten make up for, refund, reimburse, repay, restitute, restore
Wiedererstattung refund, refundment, reimbursement, restitution, restoration
Wiedererwerb reacquisition
wiedererwerben reacquire
wiederfinden recover

Wiedergabe rendering, representation, reproduction, restitution, return
wiedergeben give back, reflect, render, report, reproduce, restitute, restore, return
wiedergewinnen recover, regain, repossess, retrieve
Wiedergewinnung recovery, repossession, salvage
wiedergutmachen compensate, make amends for, make good (for), recompense, recoup, recover, redeem, redress, repair, restitute
Wiedergutmachung amends, compensation, reparation, restitution
Wiedergutmachungs
—abkommen reparations agreement
—anspruch claim for reparations, compensation (restitution) claim
Wiederheirat remarriage
wiederheiraten remarry
wiederherstellen re-establish, recondition, recover, redress, reinstate, renovate, restitute, restore, resume
Wiederherstellung readjustment, recovery, re-establishment, repair, restitution, restoration
Wiederherstellungs
—anspruch restitutory right
—klage action for restitution
—kosten cost of repair, repairs
—urteil restitution decree (judgement)
wiederholen bring back, recapitulate, reiterate, renew, repeat, resume, sum up
wiederholt repeated(ly)
Wiederholung recapitulation, recurrence, reiteration, repetition
—sfall, im in case of repetition (recurrence)
Wiederkauf redemption, repurchase
wiederkaufen buy back, rebuy, repurchase
wiederkäuflich redeemable
Wiederkaufsrecht right of redemption
Wiederkehr recurrence, return
wiederkehren come back, recur, return
wiederkehrend recurrent, recurring
—, nicht non-recurring
wiederkommen come back, return
Wiederkunft return
wiedervereinigen reunite
sich — mit rejoin
Wiedervereinigung reunification, reunion
Wiedervergeltung retortion
wiederverheiraten marry again, remarry
Wiederverheiratung remarriage
Wiederverkauf resale, retail
wiederverkaufen resell, retail, sell again
Wiederverkäufer reseller, retailer
wiederverkäuflich resaleable
Wiederverkaufs
—preis resale (retail) price
—recht right of resale (to resell)
—wert resale value
wiederverlangen redemand
wiedervermieten relet, sublet, underlet
Wiederversöhnung reconciliation
Wiederwahl re-election
wiederwählbar re-eligible
wiederwählen re-elect
wiederzulassen readmit
Wiederzulassung readmission
wild brutal, disorderly, dissolute, unlawful, wild, wildcat
—e Ehe cohabitation, concubinage
—er Streik illegal (outlaw, wildcat) strike
Wilderei poaching
Wilderer (Wilddieb) poacher
wildern poach
Wild
—dieberei poaching
—hüter gamekeeper
—schaden game damage
Wille(n) design, determination, inclination, intention, mind, purpose, volition, will, wish
—, böser ill will
—, freier free will
—, guter good will
—, letzter last will (and testament), last wishes, testament

Willen
aus freiem — of one's own accord, voluntarily, willingly
guten —s of good will, willing
guten — zeigen prove (give proof of) one's good will
willenlos irresolute, lacking will (will power), will-less
Willenlosigkeit indecision, lack of will power, want of will, weakness (of purpose)
willens sein be willing, have a mind, intend
Willens
—akt act of volition, voluntary action
—änderung change of intention (mind)
—anstregung effort of will
—äußerung expression of one's will (intention)
—bestimmung testamentary disposition, will
—erklärung declaratory act, declaration of one's will (intention)
—freiheit free will, freedom of will
—kraft power of volition, strength of mind, strong will, will power
willensschwach lacking will power, weak-minded (-willed)
Willensstärke strength of mind, strong will, will power
willentlich consciously, deliberately, designedly, intentionally, on purpose, purposely
willfahren accede to, comply with, grant, gratify, please, satisfy
willfährig complaisant, compliant, obliging, willing
Willfährigkeit complaisance, compliance, readiness
willig ready, willing
arbeits- ready to work
Willigkeit readiness, willingness
Willkür arbitrariness, arbitrary action (power), discretion
— ausgeliefert be at one's mercy
Willkür
—akt arbitrary act, discretionary action
—herrschaft arbitrary rule, despotism, tyranny
willkürlich absolute, arbitrary, despotic, discretionary
Willkür
—lichkeit arbitrariness, arbitrary act
—verfahren arbitrary proceeding
Windschaden wind damage
Wink hint, sign, tip
Winkel
—advokat hedge-lawyer, pettifogger
—zug trick
wirken be effective, cause, effect, have effect, operate, produce, work
— auf act (bear) on, affect, have influence on
wirklich actual, effective, genuine, positive, real, substantial, true, truthful, visible
Wirklichkeit actual fact, actuality, positive case, real life (existence), reality, truth
Wirklichkeit
—, in in fact (practice, reality)
in die — umsetzen materialize, realize
— werden be realized, come true, materialize
wirklichkeits
—fremd unrealistic
—nah objective, realistic
Wirklichkeitssinn common sense, realism
wirklichkeitstreu (-wahr) veracious
wirksam active, cogent, effective, effectual, efficacious, efficient, impressive, operative, valid
rechts- effective in law, final, legally effective (valid), of legal effect (force), operative, valid (in law)
un- inactive, ineffective, ineffectual, inefficacious, inefficient, inoperative, invalid, null, void, without effect
— werden become effective (operative), come into effect (force), take effect
Wirksamkeit activity, agency, effectiveness, efficacy, efficiency, impressiveness, opera-

tion, **strength**, validity, virtue
Rechts- force of law, legal effect (force, validity), operation, validity of law
Un- inactivity, inefficacy, inefficiency, inoperativeness, invalidity, nullity

Wirkung action, agency, consequence, effect, operation, reaction, result, virtue
Rechts- legal effect
mit — von coming into force on, effective, taking effect on, with effect from
—, mit sofortiger effective immediately, for immediate release
—, ohne ineffective, of no effect, without effect
— ausüben auf act upon, affect, impress
— haben have (take) effect, operate, work
— haben auf act upon, have bearing on
keine — haben produce no effect, prove ineffectual
in — treten come into force
— verlieren be deprived of effect, become inoperative

Wirkungs
—art mode of action
—bereich (-kreis) domain, field of action, province, scope, sphere of activity (influence)
—dauer duration of effect, persistency
—kraft efficacy, virtue

wirkungslos ineffective, ineffectual, inefficacious, inefficient, of no effect, without effect

Wirkungslosigkeit inefficacy, inefficiency, nullity

Wirren agitations, complications, confusions, connotions, disorders, riots, troubles

Wirtschaft economy
Kriegs- war economy
Land- agriculture
Markt— (— —, freie) free-enterprise (-market) economy
— —, soziale social market economy
Plan- planned economy
Privat- private economy
Volks- national (political) economy
Wehr- defence economy
Welt- world economy
Zwangs- controlled (planned) economy
—, freie free economy
—, gelenkte controlled (directed, planned) economy

wirtschaften administer, keep house, manage
—, schlecht mismanage
—, sparsam economize, operate economically, save

Wirtschafter housekeeper, manager

Wirtschaftler economist, economical expert

wirtschaftlich economic(al), commercial, financial, industrial, profitable, remunerative, trade

Wirtschaftlichkeit economy, profitability, profitableness, remunerativeness

Wirtschafts
—abkommen economic (trade) agreement, commercial treaty
—abordnung trade delegation
—ablauf economic process
—ausschuß economic committee
—berater economic adviser (expert)
—bericht economic report
—besprechungen trade talks (conference)
—bestimmungen commercial regulations
—bezeichnungen commercial (economic) relations
—bezirk industrial district (area)
—bilanz trade balance
—blockade economic blockade
—einheit economic entity
—entwicklung economic development
—form economic system
—frage economic problem
—freiheit economic freedom, freedom of trade
—frieden industrial peace
—gefüge economic structure
—geld housekeeping money
—gemeinschaft economic community
—gesetzgebung economic laws

—güter (economic) goods, assets
—hilfe economic aid
—interessen commercial (economic) interests
—jahr financial (business, fiscal) year
—konferenz economic (trade) conference
—kontrolle industrial control
—kredit commercial credit
—krise economic crisis
—lage economic situation
—lenkung controlled (directed, planned) economy, guidance of trade, governmental (state) control
—macht economic power
—ordnung economic system
—organisation economic (trade) organization
—plan budget, economic plan (programme)
—planung economic planning
—politik economic policy, economics
wirtschaftspolitisch political- (politico-) economical
Wirtschafts
—potential economic potential (capacity)
—problem economic problem
—prüfer (certified, chartered, incorporated) accountant, auditor
—prüfung accounting, audit
—prüfungsbericht audit(or's) report
—prüfungsgesellschaft auditing company
—rat economic council
—recht commercial (business) law
—sabotage industrial sabotage
—sachverständiger economic expert, economist
—schlichter trade arbitrator
—spionage economic espionage
—sprache economic terminology
—struktur economic structure
—system economic structure (system)
—union economic union
—unternehmen business (commercial) enterprise, business (trading) concern, commercial establishment, industrial firm
—verbindungen trade connections
—verband (—vereinigung) trade association (organization), marketing board
—verfassung economic constitution (structure, system)
—verhandlungen trade conference (negotiations)
—vertrag commercial treaty, economic (trade) agreement, trade contract
—wissenschaft economic science, economics
—zweig branch (line, sector) of economy, branch of trade
Wissen knowledge, learning
— um awareness of
Allgemein- general knowledge
Fach- expert (technical) knowledge
Halb- half-knowledge
—, juristisches knowledge of the law, legal knowledge
mit jemandens — with one's knowledge
ohne jemandens — without one's knowledge, unknown to
nach bestem — (und Gewissen) to the best of one's knowledge (and belief)
wieder besseres — against one's better judgement (knowledge)
wissen be aware (informed) of, be acquainted (familiar) with, have knowledge of, know, understand
—, genau be positive of
—, nicht be ignorant of
Wissenschaft intelligence, knowledge, learning, notice, science
Sozial- sociology
Staats- political science
Strafrechts- criminology
Wirtschafts- economic science, economics
Wissenschaftler man of science, scholar, scientist
wissenschaftlich scientific

wissentlich conscious, deliberate, knowingly, on purpose, scienter, wil(l)ful, willingly, with full knowledge
Witwe dowager, widow
Witwen
—geld widow's allowance
—pension (—rente) widow's pension
—stand widowhood
Witwer widower
—stand widowerhood
Woche week
Wochen
—ausgabe weekly edition
—ausweis weekly report (statement)
—bericht weekly report (return)
—blatt (—zeitung) weekly (paper)
—lohn weekly wages (pay)
—tag weekday
wochentags on weekdays
wöchentlich weekly
Wochen
—zahlung weekly payment
Wohl health, prosperity, weal, welfare, well-being
—, allgemeines general welfare
—, gemeines common (public) weal (welfare)
wohlbedacht deliberate, on purpose, well-considered
wohlbegründet well-established, well-founded, fully justified
wohlbekannt notorious, well-known
wohldurchdacht well-planned
wohlerworben duly acquired, well-acquired (-earned, -established), vested
—e Rechte vested rights
wohlbehalten safe (and sound)
Wohlfahrt prosperity, welfare
—, öffentliche public welfare activities, public relief (welfare assistance), social relief
Wohlfahrts
—amt relief (welfare) office
—ausschuß public welfare committee
—ausgaben welfare expenditure
—beamter welfare officer (inspector, worker), relief officer
—behörde relief (welfare) office
—einrichtung social (welfare) institution (organization)
—fonds benefit (relief) fund
—organisation charitable organization
—pflege charity work, social service, public (social) welfare, welfare work
—pfleger charity (welfare) worker, relief officer, social worker
—rente benefit (welfare) pension
—staat welfare state
—unterstützung poor (public) relief, welfare allowance
wohlgeordnet well-arranged (-disposed, -ordered)
wohlhabend moneyed, wealthy, well-off, well-to-do
Wohlhabenheit affluence, opulence, prosperity, wealth
wohlmeinend friendly, well-meaning
Wohlstand comfort, prosperity, wealth, welfare
Wohltat benefit, good action (deed), kindness, mercy
Wohltäter benefactor
Wohltäterin benefactress
wohltätig beneficent, charitable
Wohltätigkeit benefaction, beneficency, charitableness, charity
Wohltätigkeits
—anstalt charitable (beneficient) institution
—ausschuß charity commission
—einrichtung charitable establishment
—fond charity (benevolent) fund
—verein benevolent (charity, charitable, friendly) society
wohlüberlegt deliberate, well-considered
wohlunterrichtet well-informed
wohlverdient just, of great merit, well-deserved (-earned)
wohlverdientermaßen deservedly
Wohlverhalten good behaviour (conduct)
Wohlwollen benevolence, favour, goodwill, patronage
wohlwollend benevolent, kind, sympathetic, well-meaning
Wohn
—bezirk residential district

wohnen be domiciled, dwell, have one's residence (at, in), live, lodge (with), reside (at, in), room, stay (with)
Wohn
—gebäude (—haus) dwelling (apartment) house, residential premises
—grundstück residential estate (property)
wohnhaft in domiciled (dwelling, living, resident, residing) at (in)
— sein reside
Wohn
—heim residential home
—ort abode, domicile, dwelling place, home, place, (place of) residence
—partei tenant(s)
—raum housing (living, residential) space
—recht right of domicile (residence)
Wohnsitz abode, domicile, dwelling place, place, residence, seat
—, fester (ständiger) permanent residence
—, gesetzlicher legal domicile
— haben reside
seinen — nehmen settle down
Wohnung abode, accommodation, apartment, chambers, domicile, dwelling, flat, habitation, home, lodging(s), residence, rooms
Wohnungs
—amt housing office
—angabe address
—bedarf housing requirements
—bedingungen (—verhältnisse) housing (lodging) conditions
—frage housing problem
—geld lodging allowance
—gesetz housing act
—inhaber householder, lodger, tenant
—kosten housing costs
wohnungslos without fixed abode
Wohnungs
—mangel (—not) housing shortage
—miete rent
—nachweis accommodation (housing) registry, house agency
—problem housing problem
—suche house hunting
—wechsel change of address (domicile, residence), removal
Wohn
—verhältnisse housing conditions
—viertel residential quarter
Wollen aspiration, inclination, intention, purpose, volition, will, willingness
wollen be determined (resolved, willing), care, claim, demand, desire, intend, like, mean, request, want, will, wish
—, nicht refuse
Wort expression, saying, term, word
Ehren— parole, word of hono(u)r
Losungs— password
Stich— catchword, code (key) word, test word
Vor— foreword, introduction, preface
— abschneiden cut short
ums — bitten ask for leave to speak
sein — brechen break one's word
— einlösen (halten) keep (redeem) one's word
— entziehen rule out of order, stop (speaking), withdraw one's leave to speak
— ergreifen (begin to) speak, take the floor
— erteilen give leave to speak
— führen be spokesman
— haben have the floor, speak
sich zum — melden demand the floor
sein — zurücknehmen take back (withdraw) one's word
Wort
—bruch breach of one's word, treachery
wortbrüchig faithless, false to one's word, treacherous
— werden break one's word
Wortbrüchigkeit breach of promise, faithlessness
Wörterbuch dictionary
Fach— technical dictionary
Rechts— law dictionary

Wörterverzeichnis list of words, vocabulary
Wort
—führer foreman, speaker, spokesman
—gefecht debate, dispute, encounter, verbal duel
wortgetreu close, exact, faithful, literal, near, true, verbatim, word for word
wortgewandt eloquent
Wort
—klauber hairsplitter, quibbler, wordsplitter
—klauberei hairsplitting, quibbling, wordsplitting
—laut exact terms, reading, tenor, text, wording
wörtlich literal, verbal, verbatim, word for (by) word
Wort
—schatz vocabulary
—streit (—wechsel) altercation, discussion, dispute, quarrel, squabble, wrangle
Wort
—verdreher equivocator
—verdrehung distortion of words, equivocation
—verwechslung confusion of terms
—verzeichnis verbal index
—wechsel s. -streit
wortwörtlich word for word
Wrack derelict, wreck
Wrackgut flotsam, jetsam, wreckage, wrecked goods
Wucher profiteering, usury
— treiben practise usury, profiteer
Wucherer profiteer, profitmonger, usurer
Wucher
—geschäft usurious business (trade)
—gesetz law against usury (profiteering), usury law
—gewinn usurious (excess) profit
—handel usurious trade
wucherisch usurious
wuchern practise usury, profiteer
Wucher
—preis exorbitant (usurious) price
—zinsen excessive (illegal, usurious) interest
Wühlarbeit subversive (underground) activity, insidious agitation
Wunsch aspiration, desire, request, wish
—, auf at one's request, if desired, optional, on application (request)
wünschen desire, want, wish
Würde degree, dignity, hono(u)r, office, title
Würdenträger dignitary
würdig deserving (of), estimable, respectable, worthy (of)
glaub— authentic, credible, reliable, trustworthy, worthy of belief
kredit— creditable, good, reliable, sound, trustworthy, worthy of credit
— sein deserve
würdigen appraise, appreciate, consider worthy of, esteem, estimate, mention, respect, value
Würdigung appreciation, consideration, estimation, valuation
würgen choke, strangle, throttle
Würgegriff stranglehold
Würger cut-throat, slayer
Wut fury, mania, passion, rage
wüten foam, fume, rage, rave, storm
wütend enraged (at), fuming, furious, rabid, raving, with rage

Z

Zahl cipher, digit, figure, number, quantity, rate
zahlbar due, payable
— **werden** fall due
zählbar computable, countable, numerable
Zahlbarkeit maturity, payability, solvency
zahlen clear, discharge, make payment, pay, settle
zählen amount to, count, number, register, score, take the census of, tell
— **auf** count on
zahlend paying
Zahlender, nicht defaulter
zahlenmäßig by (in) number(s), numerical, in terms of figures
Zahlen
—**material** figures, data(s)
—**verhältnis** numerical proportion
—**wert** numerical value
Zahler payer
—, **säumiger** defaulter
Zähler counter, meter, scrutineer, teller
zahlfähig solvent
Zahlkarte paying-in slip, postal money order, money (postal) order
Zählkarte (—zettel) census paper
zahllos countless, innumerable, numberless
Zahl
—**losigkeit** numberlessness
—**meister** paymaster, purser, treasurer
—**meisterei** pay office
zahlreich numerous
Zahl
—**stelle** pay office
—**tag** day of payment, pay day
—**termin** date of payment
Zahlung clearance, discharge, disbursement, payment, settlement
Ausgleichs— discharge, equalization, payment, settlement, severance pay
Bar— cash payment
Gehalts— salary payment
Jahres— annual payment
Lohn— wage payment
Miet— rent(al) payment
Monats— monthly payment
Nach— additional (extra, subsequent, supplementary) payment
Nicht— default (of payment), nonpayment
Pauschal— lump-sum payment
Raten— instalment, part payment, payment by (in) instalments
Rück— amortization, redemption, reimbursement, repayment, return
Steuer— rate paying, tax payment
Teil— instalment, part payment
Voraus— advance payment, payment in advance, prepayment
Zins— interest payment
Zahlung
—, **sofortige** spot cash
an —s Statt in lieu of payment
zur — anweisen pass for payment
— **bescheinigen** receipt payment
— **bewirken** effect (make) a payment
— **einstellen** stop payment, suspend payments
— **empfangen** receive payment
in — geben give in payment, trade in
mit der — in Verzug kommen default (in payment)
— **leisten** effect (make) a payment, pay
in — nehmen accept as payment, receive in payment
— **stunden** allow (grant) a respite, extend the terms of payment
— **verweigern** refuse payment (to pay)
— **wiederaufnehmen** resume payment

zur — zwingen enforce payment
Zählung census, computation, counting, numeration, registration, scrutiny, telling
Zahlungs
—abkommen payments (clearing, monetary) agreement
—absicht intention to pay
—adresse domicile, payment address
—angebot bid, offer to pay, tender of payment
—anspruch payment (pecuniary) claim, demand for payment
—anweisung cheque, draft, money (postal) order, order to pay, post-office order
—anweisungen payment instructions
—anzeige advice of payment
—art mode (way) of payment
—aufforderung application (demand, request, summons) for payment, demand note, dun, order (notice) to pay, requisition of payment
—aufschub delay (respite) for payment, extension of payment
— — gewähren extend the term of payment, grant a respite
—auftrag order for payment (to pay), payment order
—bedingungen payment conditions, terms of payment
—befehl default (payment) summons, order for payment, order (summons) to pay, writ of execution
—beleg receipt (for payment), (pay) voucher
—berechtigter payee
—bereitschaft liquidity, solvency
—bescheinigung acquittance, receipt (for payment)
—bestätigung acknowledgement of payment, receipt (for payment)
—bilanz balance of payments
—einstellung default, failure, insolvency, stoppage (suspension) of payments
—empfänger payee
—erleichterungen easy terms, facilities for payment
—ermächtigung authorization to pay
zahlungsfähig able to pay, good, responsible, solvent, (financially) sound
Zahlungs
—fähigkeit ability (capacity) to pay, responsibility, solvency
—frist date (term, time) of payment, extension of time, grace period
zahlungskräftig responsible, solvent, sound, well-financed
— sein be financially strong
Zahlungs
—leistung payment
—methode method of payment
—mittel means of payment, currency, (current) money
— —, ausländische foreign money
— —, gesetzliches common tender, lawful currency (money), legal (currency, tender)
—nachweis receipt (for payment)
—ort domicile, place of payment
—periode pay(ment) period
—pflicht liability (obligation) to pay, financial responsibility
zahlungspflichtig answerable, liable, responsible
Zahlungs
—pflichtiger debtor
—plan payment (redemption) plan, hire purchase plan
—rückstand payment in arrear
—rückstände arrears, delinquent payments, outstanding debts
—schein acquittance, receipt (for payment)
—schwierigkeiten embarrassment, financial (pecuniary) difficulties
—sperre blocking, stoppage of payments
—tag day of payment, pay day
—termin date (time) of payment, date of maturity, due date
zahlungsunfähig bankrupt, defaulting, insolvent, unable to pay
Zahlungs
—unfähiger insolvent (debtor)

—**unfähigkeit** default, failure, inability to pay, insolvency
—**verbindlichkeit** financial obligation, liability to pay
—**verbot** stop order
—**vereinbarungen** financial arrangements, payment agreements (arrangements), stipulations of payment
—**verkehr** payment transactions, transfer
—**vermögen** ability to pay, solvency
zahlungsverpflichtet liable to pay
Zahlungs
—**verpflichteter** payer
—**verpflichtung** s. -pflicht
—**versprechen** promise to pay
—**verweigerung** nonpayment, refusal of payment (to pay)
—**verzug** default, delay of payment
—**vollmacht** authorization to pay
—**weise** manner (mode, way) of payment
—**wert** money value
—**zeit** expiration, grace period, maturity, term
—**ziel** date (term) of payment
Zedent assigner, ceder, endorser, transferor
zedierbar assignable, endorseable, transferable
Zedierbarkeit assignability, transferability
zedieren assign, cede, endorse, transfer
Zedierung assignment, cession, transfer
Zeichen brand, evidence, mark, proof, reference, sign, signal, signature, stamp, symbol, testimony, token, trademark
Ab- badge, decoration, distinguishing badge (mark), insignia, mark, sign
An- indication, mark, sign, signal, symptom
Erkennungs- distinctive (identification) mark
Grenz- boundary mark
Güte brand, quality mark (label)
Hand- hand signal
Kenn- brand, earmark, label, licence plate, (characteristic, distinguishing) mark
Schrift- character, letter
Unterscheidungs- distinctive mark
Verkehrs- traffic sign(al)
Waren- trademark
Warn- warning signal
Wasser- watermark
Zeichen geben give (make) a sign, give a signal, signal
Zeichensprache sign language
zeichnen brand, delineate, design, draw, label, mark, outline, sketch, subscribe, undersign
Zeichner designer, subscriber
Zeichnung delineation, design, diagram, draft, drawing, illustration, mark, signature, signing, sketch, subscription
Zeichnungs
—**bedingungen** terms of subscription, underwriting conditions
—**befugnis** authorization (power) to sign, signatory (signing) power
zeichnungsberechtigt authorized to sign, having signatory power, signing, entitled to subscribe
Zeichnungs
—**berechtigung (—recht)** authorization (power, right) to sign, subscription privilege (right)
—**frist** subscription period
—**gebühr** signing fee
—**list** subscription list
—**vollmacht** authorization (power) to sign, signatory power, subscription privilege (right)
zeigen demonstrate, display, exhibit, give evidence of, indicate, manifest, point at (out, to), present, prove, register, show
Zeile line
Zeit age, date, days, epoch, hours, period, phase, space of time, stage, term, time

Amts- tenure of office, term (of office)
Arbeits- working time (hours, period), hours of work
Ausbildungs- training period (time)
Bedenk- time for consideration (reflection)
Frei- free (leisure, spare) time, time off, vacancy
Friedens- peace time, time of peace
Geschäfts- business (office) hours
Karenz- waiting period (time)
Kriegs- war time(s)
Lauf- currency, due date, duration, life, maturity, period, term, validity
Lebens- lifetime, (term, time of) life
Lehr- (time of) apprenticeship
Liefer- time of delivery
Liege- lay days
Orts- local time
Probe- (period of) probation, probationary term, trial period
Ruhe- (time of) rest
Schon- close(d) time (season)
Schwebe- suspension period
Tages- daytime, time of day
Übergangs- transitional period, period of transition
Verfall- maturity, time of payment
Wahl- election time
Warte- demurrage, grace, wait, waiting period
Zwischen- interim, interval, meantime

—, **freie** free moment (time), leisure (spare) time
—, **verlorene** idle time
—, **auf** for a term of years, for time, on account (credit, term, trust)
auf — angestellt employed on the pleasure of
—, **mit der** in the course of time
—, **zur** at present, for the time being
—, **zu jeder** at any time
—, **zu keiner** at no time
—, **in absehbarer (angemessener)** within reasonable time
—, **auf bestimmte** for a fixed period
—, **zu einer bestimmten** at a given time
—, **zur festgelegten (vereinbarten)** at the appointed time, at the time fixed (agreed upon)
—, **zur geeigneten** in due time
—, **zur gleichen** at the same time, simultaneously
—, **im Laufe der** in the course of time
—, **zur rechten** in due time (course), at the right time, opportunely, timely
—, **auf unbestimmte** without date, sine die
—, **zur verabredeten** at the appointed time
—, **innerhalb der vorgeschriebenen** within the required (prescribed) time
— **festsetzen** appoint (fix) a time (for), time
— **gewinnen** gain time
versuchen — zu gewinnen play for time
— **sparen** save time

Zeit
—**ablauf** expiration of time, lapse of time
—**abschnitt** epoch, period (of time), time
—**abstand** interval
—**abständen, in regelmäßigen** periodically
—**alter** age, days, epoch, era, period
—**angabe** date, time signal
— —, **ohne** undated, without date
—**aufwand** loss of time
—**beschränkung** time limit (restriction)
—**bombe** time bomb
—**dauer** length (space) of time, period
—**einteilung** timing
—**ersparnis** saving of time
—**faktor** time factor
—**folge** chronological order

—frage matter (question) of time
—geld time loan
zeitgemäß opportune, seasonable, timely. up(-)to(-)date
Zeit
—genosse contemporary
—geschäft time bargain
—gewinn gained time
—grenze time limit
—kontrolle timekeeping
—kontrolleur timekeeper
—lage juncture
zeitlich chronological, temporal, temporary, time(ly)
zeitlebens for life
Zeit
—limit time limit
—lohn time wage
—lohnarbeit time work
zeitlos timeless
Zeit
—mangel lack of time
—ordnung chronological order
—plan schedule, time table
—planung time schedule, timing
—punkt date, time
—raum period, term, period (space) of time
—rente annuity
—schrift journal, magazine, periodical
—spanne lapse (period, space) of time, time span
zeitsparend time-saving
Zeit
—stempel time stamp
—umstände (-verhältnisse) circumstances, conjunctures, times
Zeitung journal, newspaper, paper
—, amtliche bulletin, gazette
Zeitungs
—annonce (-anzeige, -inserat) advertisement
—artikel newspaper article
—ausschnitt clipping, cutting
—bericht (-nachricht) newspaper (press) report
—ente canard, hoax
—meldung press report
—notiz (news, press) item
—wesen press
Zeit
—vergeudung (-verschwendung) waste of time
—verlust loss of time
— —, ohne immediately, without delay
zeitweilig provisional, temporary
zeitweise occasionally, for a time, from time to time
Zeit
—wert present (current) value
—zeichen time signal
Zelle cell
Gefängnis- prison cell
zensieren censor, censure, criticize, licence, review
Zensor censor, reviewer
Zensoramt censorship
Zensur censorship, censure, board of censors
Zensur
—behörde board of censors
—bestimmungen censorship regulations
Zensus census
zentral central
Zentral
—ablage central file
—ausschuß central committee
—bank central bank
—behörde central authority
—büro central (head) office, headquarters
Zentrale control station, central (head, main) office, headquarters
Zentral
—gewalt central power
Zentralisation centralization
zentralisieren centralize
Zentral
—kartei master (central) file
—mächte central powers
—regierung central government
—stelle central (head, main) office, headquarters
—verwaltung central administration
Zentrum centre
Zerfall decay, decadence, decomposition, disintegration, ruin

zerfallen collapse, decay, disintegrate, divide into, fail, fall apart, fall into ruin
zerlegen analyse, decompose, disintegrate, disjoin, dismantle, dissect, dissolve, divide, undo
Zerlegung analysis, decomposition, dissection, dismantling
zermürben wear down (out)
Zermürbung attrition
—skrieg war of attrition
Zerreißprobe endurance test
zerrütten derange, disarrange, disorder, disorganize, disrupt, ruin, shatter, unsettle, upset, wreck
zerrüttet broken, confused, in confusion, in disorder, disorganized, disrupted, distracted, ruined, shattered, unsettled, worn-out
Zerrüttung derangement, disorder, disorganization, disruption, distraction
zersetzen decompose, demoralize, disintegrate, dissolve, undermine
Zersetzung decomposition, demoralization, disintegration, dissolution, sedition, subversion
zerstörbar destructible
Zerstörbarkeit destructibility
zerstören demolish, devastate, disorganize, destroy, frustrate, overthrow, ravage, ruin, undo, wreck
zerstörend destructive, subversive
Zerstörer destroyer, subverter
zerstörerisch destructive, vandal (ic)
Zerstörung demolition, destruction, devastation, fall, frustration, overthrow, ravages, ruin
—skrieg war of destruction
Zertifikat certificate, warrant
zertrümmern break up, demolish, destroy, lay in ruins, shatter, smash, wreck
Zertrümmerung demolition, destruction, smashing, wreckage
Zerwürfnis difference, discord, dissention, disunion, quarrel
Zession abandonment, assignation, assignment, cession, conveyance, transfer
Zessionar assign, assignee, cessionary, transferee
Zessions
—akte deed of transfer
—anzeige notice of assignment
zessionsfähig assignable
Zessions
—fähigkeit assignability
—urkunde transfer deed, deed of assignment
Zettel bill, label, leaflet, list, note, paper, placard, poster, sheet, slip (of paper), tag, ticket
Zeuge attestor, deponent, testifier, voucher, witness
 Augen- eyewitness
 Belastungs- witness for the prosecution (crown)
 Entlastungs- witness for the defence
 Haupt- material (principal) witness
 Hauptbelastungs- principal witness for the prosecution, star prosecution witness
 Hauptentlastungs- principal witness for the defence
 Kron- approver, king's evidence, principal (chief, crown) witness, witness of the first class
 Ohren- ear witness
 Trau- marriage witness, witness to a marriage
Zeuge
—, falscher false witness
—, vereidigter sworn deposer, witness on oath
—, wichtiger material witness
Zeuge
 vor —n in the presence of witnesses
—n ablehnen challenge a witness
zu —n aufrufen call to witness (to)

als — aussagen bear witness, depose, (give) evidence, testify, bear testimony
als —n benennen call to witness
—n beeinflussen suborn a witness
als —n laden subpoena (summon) a witness
— sein evidence, testify, witness, be present at, be a witness (of)
—n verhören (-vernehmen) examine (hear) a witness
als —n vorladen call as witness, subpoena a witness
—n stellen produce evidence

zeugen bear evidence (witness) (of), generate, give evidence, produce, testify (for), witness
— von be evidence of, prove, show

Zeugen
—aussage evidence, statement of a witness, testimony
— —, schriftliche deposition
—bank witness box (chair, stand)
—beeinflussung corruption of witnesses
—bestechung corruption (subornation) of witnesses
—beweis evidence (proof) by witnesses, proof of evidence, testimonial proof
—eid oath of a witness
—stand witness box (stand)
—verhör (-vernehmung) (cross-) examination (hearing) of witnesses

Zeugnis attest, attestation, certificate, character, deposition, evidence
record, report, testimonial, testimony, voucher
Führungs- certificate of character (good behaviour, good conduct)
Herkunfts- (Ursprungs-) certificate of origin

Zeugnis
zum — dessen in witness thereof
— ablegen (geben) bear evidence (testimony, witness), give evidence (proof of), testify
falsches — ablegen bear (give) false evidence
gutes — ausstellen give a good character
— verweigern decline (refuse) to give evidence

Zeugnisabschrift copy of a testimonial
zeugnisfähig capable of giving evidence

Zeugnis
—fähigkeit capability of giving evidence
—pflicht obligation to give evidence
—verweigerung refusal to give evidence
—zwang obligation to give evidence

Ziel aim, butt, destination, end, goal, limit, mark, object, objective, prompt, purpose, target, term, time
—, auf on credit
—, ohne aimless
— erreichen attain an end, obtain an objective, reach a goal (an aim)

zielbewußt methodical, purposeful, stable, steady, systematic(ally)
ziellos aimless, purposeless, without aim

Ziffer cipher, digit, figure, number, rate
Kenn- code (index, key, reference) number

Zins interest, rent, rental, royalty, tribute

Zins
—abkommen agreement on interest rates
—abschnitt (-anteilschein) coupon, interest coupon (warrant)
—ausfall loss of interest

zinsbar tributary

Zins
—bedingungen terms of interest
—bogen coupon sheet

zinsbringend bearing interest, interest-bearing

Zins
—coupon interest coupon
—einkommen interest income
Zinsen interest(s)
— abwerfen (bringen, tragen) bear (yield) interest
Zinsenausfall loss of interest
Zinserträge interest returns (proceeds, yield)
Zinsforderungen interest claims (receivable)
zinsfrei (-los) free of interest, interest-free, rent-free
Zins
—freiheit exemption from paying rent
—fuß (-satz) interest rate, rate of interest
—klausel interest clause
zinslos non-interest bearing, free of interest, rent-free
zinspflichtig subject to rent (interest)
Zins
—schein interest compon (warrant), coupon
—tag rent day
zinstragend s. -bringend
Zins
—verbindlichkeiten interest payable
—verlust loss of interest
—verzug default of interest
—zahlung interest payment
Zirkular circular (letter)
Zirkulation circulation
zirkulieren circulate
Zitat citation, quotation, reference
—, falsches misquotation
Zitation citation, summons
zitieren cite, quote, summon
—, falsch misquote
Zivil, in in mufti, in plain clothes
zivil civil, civilian, moderate, reasonable
Zivil
—anzug mufti, plain clothes
—beamter civil servant
—behörde civil authority (office)
—bevölkerung civil(ian) population, civilians
—dienst civil service
—ehe civil marriage
—gericht civil court
—gerichtsbarkeit civil jurisdiction
—gesetz civil (common) law
—gesetzbuch civil code, code of civil law
—gesetzgebung civil legislation
Zivilisation civilization
zivilisieren civilize
Zivil
—klage civil action (suit)
—kleidung plain clothes, civilian dress
—person civilian
—prozeß civil action (lawsuit, procedure, proceedings, suit)
—prozeßordnung code of civil procedure
—recht civil law
zivilrechtlich civil, under civil law
Zivil
—rechtspflege civil jurisdiction
—sache civil case (matter)
—stand legal status
—trauung civil marriage
—urteil (civil) judgement
—verfahren civil proceedings
—verwaltung civil administration
Zoll customs, customs duty, dues, duty, tariff, toll, tribute,
Ausfuhr- export duty
Einfuhr- import duty
Vorzugs- preferential duty (tariff)
Zoll
—abfertigung customs clearance
—abgabe customs, (customs) duty
—abkommen tariff treaty
—amt customhouse, customs office
—angabe (-deklaration) customs declaration (entry)
—beamter customs (customhouse) officer (official)
—behörde board of customs, customs authority
—bescheinigung customs (clearance) certificate
—beschränkungen customs restrictions

—bestimmungen customs regulations
—bezirk customs district
—büro customs office
—buße customs fine
—dienst customs service
—dokumente customs documents, clearance papers
—erklärung customs declaration
—fahndung customs search
—fahndungsstelle customs search office
—formalitäten customs formalities
—fragen tariff matters
zollfrei custom-free, duty-free, exempt from duty
Zoll
—freiheit exemption from duty
—gebiet customs district
—gebühr duty
—gebühren customs duties, customhouse fees (charges)
—gesetz customs code (regulations), revenue law, tariff act (law)
—gesetzgebung tariff laws (legislation)
—grenzbezirk customs district
—grenze customs frontier
—haus customhouse
—hinterzieher defrauder of customs
—hinterziehung evasion of customs duties
—hoheit customs (tariff) jurisdiction
—inspektor customs officer (official)
—kontingent tariff quota
—kontrolle customs control (examination, inspection)
—krieg tariff war
—mauern tariff walls, wall of protections
—ordnung customs (customhouse) regulations
—papiere customs (clearance, customhouse) papers
—paß customs pass
zollpflichtig customable, dutiable, liable (subject) to duty
Zoll
—plombe customs (customhouse) seal
—politik customs policy
—quittung docket, customs (customhouse) receipt
—rechnung customhouse note, customs invoice
—revision customs examination
—rückforderung (—erstattung, —vergütung) drawback
—satz rate of customs (duty), tariff rate
—schein clearance bill, customs certificate, permit
—schranke customs barrier, tariff wall, toll gate (bar)
—schutz tariff protection
—siegel s. -plombe
—spesen customhouse charges
—station (—stelle) customs station, customhouse
—stempel s. -plombe
—strafe customs fine
—system customhouse system, tariff system
—tarif customs rate (tariff), tariff (of duty)
—umgehung s. -hinterziehung
—union (—verband, —verein) customs union
—untersuchung customs examination (inspection, search)
—vereinbarung tariff agreement
—vergehen customs (revenue) offence
—vergünstigung preferential tariff, sufferance
—vergütung drawback
—verhandlungen tariff negotiations
—vermerk tariff visa
—verordnung customs regulations
—verschluß bond, customs seal
— —, unter bonded, in bond
—vertrag customs (tariff) treaty
—verwaltung customs administration (authorities)
—verzeichnis customs tariff, tariff schedule
—visitation s. -untersuchung
—vorschriften customs regulations
—wert tariff value
—wesen customs, tariff system
Zone area, region, zone
Zonengrenze zone (zonal) border

Zubehör accessories, appurtenances, belongings, fittings, pertinents, requisites
zubilligen allow, award, concede, grant
Zubilligung awarding, concession, grant
Zuchthaus hard labo(u)r, house of correction, penal servitude, penitentiary
—, lebenslängliches penal servitude for life
Zuchthäusler convict
Zuchthausstrafe penal servitude
züchtigen chastise, correct, discipline, flog, inflict corporal punishment on, lash, punish, whip
Züchtigung chastisement, correction, flogging, (corporal) punishment, whipping
—srecht right of corporal punishment
zueignen ascribe, attribute, dedicate
—, sich appropriate, seize, take possession of
sich widerrechtlich — usurp
Zuneigung appropriation, dedication
—, widerrechtliche usurpation
zuerkennen acknowledge, adjudge, adjudicate, admit, allot, allocate, award, confer (on), condemn to, decree
Zuerkennung acknowledgement, adjudgement, adjudication, award, conferment
—surteil adjudicative sentence
zuerteilen allot, apportion to, assign, award, bestow (confer) on
Zufahrt approach
Zufall accident, chance, coincidence, fortune, hazard
—, durch accidentally, by accident (chance)
zufallen accrue (come, fall, go, result) to, devolve upon, fall to one's share, rest with
zufällig accidental, by accident (chance), casual, fortuitous, incidental
—es Ereignis contingency
Zufälligkeit accidentalness, casualness, casualty, contingency, eventuality, fortuitousness, unforeseen event
Zuflucht refuge, resource, resort, shelter
— gewähren afford refuge
— nehmen have recourse to, resort to, take refuge to (with), turn to
— suchen seek refuge
Zufluchtsort asylum, (place of) refuge, shelter
Zufluß afflux, inflow, influx, supply
zufrieden, content, contented, pleased, satisfied
—, nicht discontented, displeased, dissatisfied
Zufriedenheit content(ment), contentedness, satisfaction
zur — von to the satisfaction of
zufriedenstellen content, gratify, please, satisfy
zufriedenstellend satisfactory, satisfying
Zufriedenstellung satisfaction
zufügen add, cause, do, inflict (on)
Zufuhr importation, imports, provisions, supplies, supply
Zugabe addition, adjunct, bonus, extra, premium, surplus
Zugang access, accrual, accumulation, addition, admission, approach, avenue, entrance, entry, increase, increment, receipt, reinforcement
— haben have access (to)
zugänglich accessible, admissible, available, open
—, für die Öffentlichkeit open for the public
— machen make (render) available, render accessible
der Öffentlichkeit — machen make (throw) open to the public
Zugänglichkeit accessibility
Zugangsrecht easement, right of access
zugeben add, admit, agree, allow, concede, confess, grant, recognize, own to

zugegebenermaßen admittedly, avowedly
zugegen present (at)
— sein assist (at), attend, be present (at)
zugehören belong (to), appertain (to)
zugehörig accompanying, appertaining, appropriate, becoming, belonging (to), pertinent, proper, requisite
Zugehörigkeit adherence, affiliation, belonging (to), membership
zugelassen admitted, allowed, authorized, certified, chartered, lawful, licenced, listed, permitted, qualified, quoted, recognized
zugestandenermaßen admittedly
Zugeständnis admission, concession
—, gegenseitiges compromise
Zugeständnisse machen make concessions
zugestehen accord, admit, concede, grant, own, yield
zugrunde gehen perish, go to ruin
zugrunde legen take as (a) basis
zugrunde liegen form the basis of, underlie
zugrundeliegend underlying
zugrunde richten destroy, ruin, wreck
zugunsten von for the benefit of, in favo(u)r of
Zuhilfenahme
unter — von by (with) recourse to, with the aid (help) of
ohne — von without having recourse to
zuhören attend (to), listen (to)
Zuhörer auditor, audience, hearer, listener
Zuhörer
—raum auditorium, audience
—schaft attendance, audience, listeners
Zukunft future, prospects, time to come
—, in (für die —) for the future, from now on, henceforth, hereafter, in future
zukünftig future, intending, prospective
Zulage addition, advance, allowance, bonus, extra pay, increase, rise, surplus
zulassen accept, admit, allow, approve, authorize, enter, give admittance to, grant, grant leave for (to), let in, license, permit, receive, register, suffer, tolerate, yield
zulassen
—, als Anwalt admit (call) to the bar
zulässig admissible, allowable, allowed, approved, authorized, granted, lawful, permissible, permitted, receivable
—, nicht inadmissible, not permitted
Zulässigkeit admissibility, permissibility
Zulassung acceptance, admission, admittance, charter, concession, entrance, granting, licence, permission, permit
Nicht— nonadmission
Zulassungs
—anspruch right of admission
—antrag (—gesuch) application for admission, membership application
—ausschuß board of admission
—bedingungen terms of admission
zulassungsberechtigt admissible, eligible, qualified
Zulassungs
—berechtigung qualification
—bescheinigung car licence, licence, permit
—gebühr admission (entrance) fee
—nummer licence (permit) number
—marke voucher
—prüfung acceptance (admission) test, entrance examination
—schein entry permit, ticket of admission
—stelle board of admission
—verfahren admission procedure
—verweigerung nonadmission

zumessen admeasure, allocate, allot, apportion (to), determine, fix, measure out, mete out
Zumessung admeasurement, allotment, apportionment, meting out
zumutbar reasonable
Zumutung unreasonable demand
Zunahme advance, augmentation, growth, improvement, increase, increment, progress, rise
Zuname cognomen, family (last, proper) name, surname
zunehmen accelerate, advance (in), augment, gain (in), grow, improve, increase, progress, rise
Zunft association, company, corporation, guild, society
zunichte
— **machen** annihilate, blight, bring to nothing, condemn, destroy, frustrate, ruin, undo
— **werden** come to nothing
zunutze
— **machen** turn to account, utilize
sich — machen avail oneself of, make use of, play (practise) on, profit by, take advantage of, turn to one's profit
Zuraten
auf — von on the advise of
zuraten advise, persuade,
zurechnungsfähig accountable, competent, of sane (sound) mind, responsible, sane
un— insane
Zurechnungsfähigkeit accountability, capacity, competence, discernment, power, responsibility, sane state of mind, sanity, sound judgement, soundness of mind
Un— insanity
zurechtweisen advise, rebuke, reprimand, reprove, set right
Zurechtweisung instruction, rebuke, reprimand
Zurschaustellung display, exhibition, exposure
zurückabtreten reassign, retrocede
zurückbehalten detain, hold (keep) back, reserve, retain, withhold
Zurückbehaltung detention, recoupment, retention, withholding
—srecht lien, right of detention
zurückbekommen get back, recover, regain
zurückbezahlen clear, discharge, pay back, refund, reimburse, repay
Zurückbezahlung discharge, reimbursement, refunding, repayment
zurückbleiben be left over, fall (remain, stay) behind, remain, survive
zurückdatieren antedate, date back
—erhalten s. -bekommen
—erlangen get back, recover, regain, repossess, retrieve
Zurückerlangung recovery, retrieval
zurückerobern reconquer, recover
zurückerstatten pay back, refund, reimburse, render, repay, restitute, restore, return
Zurückerstattung refund(ing), reimbursement, repayment, restitution, restoration
zurückfallen an fall back to (into), revert to
— **auf** redound upon, reflect on
— **in** relapse into
zurückfordern ask (claim, demand, back), reclaim, redemand
Zurückforderung reclamation
zurückführen auf attribute to, trace back to
Zurückgabe giving back, restitution, return(ing)
zurückgeben give (hand) back, redeliver, render, restitute, restore, return, surrender
zurückgehen decline, deteriorate, diminish, recede, return, retreat
— **auf** date (go) back to
zurückgewinnen recover, recuperate, regain, win back

zurückgreifen auf go back to, revert to
zurückhalten conceal, delay, detain, hold back, keep, prevent, reserve, restrain, retain, retard, suppress, suspend, withhold
Zurückhaltung caution, cautiousness, detainment, detention, discretion, hesitation, reserve, reservedness, restraint, retention
—srecht lien, right of detention
zurückkaufen buy back (in), rebuy, redeem, repurchase
zurückkehren return, revert
zurückkommen come (get) back, return
— auf refer to, revert to
Zurücknahme reacceptance, recantation, retractation, retraction, revocation, taking back, withdrawal
zurücknehmen cancel, countermand, drop, recall, rescind, retract, revoke, take back, unsay, withdraw
zurückschicken (—senden) return, send back
zurücksetzen discriminate against, disregard, lower, neglect, reduce, set aside
Zurücksetzung discrimination, disregard, neglect, reduction
zurückstellen adjourn, defer, postpone, reserve, set aside, suspend from
Zurückstellung adjournment, postponement
zurücktreten cancel, recede, renounce, rescind, resign (from), retire, terminate, waive, withdraw
zurückübertragen reassign, reconvey, retrocede, transfer
zurückverfolgen retrace
zurückverlangen s. -fordern
zurückvergüten reimburse, repay, return
Zurückvergütung reimbursement, refund
zurückverkaufen sell back
zurückverweisen defer (refer, send) back to, recommit, remand, remit
Zurückverweisung exclusion, rejection, relegation, remand
zurückweisen decline, disho-no(u)r, dismiss, rebuff, rebut, refuse, reject, repel, repudiate, repulse, throw down, turn back
—, Klage nonsuit
Zurückweisung disallowance, dismissal, rebuff, rebuttal, refusal, rejection, repudiation, repulse
zurückwirken be retroactive, have a retroactive effect, react (upon), retroact
zurückzahlbar refundable, repayable
zurückzahlen discharge, pay back (off), redeem, refund, reimburse, repay, restitute, return
Zurückzahlung discharge, refund, reimbursement, repayment
zurückziehen abolish, call in, cancel, countermand, give up, quit, recall, recover, retire, retract, revoke, take back, withdraw
—, sich retire, retreat, withdraw
Zurückziehung retirement, retreat, revocation, withdrawal
Zusage acceptance, affirmation, answer in the affirmative, approval, assent, consent, pledge, promise, word
zusagen accept, agree with, answer in the affirmative, appeal to, consent, meet, please, pledge, promise, suit
zusagend acceptable, affirmative, pleasing
Zusammenarbeit co-operation, collaboration, teamwork
zusammenarbeiten co-operate, collaborate, work together
zusammenberufen call together, convene, convoke, summon
Zusammenberufung convening, convocation, summons

zusammenbrechen break down, collapse, fail, succumb
Zusammenbruch break-down, collapse, debacle, failure, ruin
zusammenfassen abridge, amalgamate, collect, combine, comprehend, compress, comprise, concentrate, concert, condense, consolidate, embrace, give a summary, include, integrate, recapitulate, resume, sum up, summarize, unite
zusammenfassend collective, comprehensive, recapitulatory
Zusammenfassung amalgamation, collection, compendium, concentration, condensation, digest, recapitulation, summary, summing up
Zusammenhang association, coherence, connection, connexion, context, contingency, continuity, relation
zusammenhängen cohere, (be) connect(ed)
zusammenhängend allied, coherent, connected, continuous, contiguous, interdependent, related
un- incoherent
zusammenhang(s)los disconnected, incoherent, loose
Zusammenhangslosigkeit incoherence(cy)
zusammenkommen assemble, come together, convene, meet
Zusammenkunft appointment, assembly, conference, convention, gathering, interview, meeting
Zusammenleben cohabitation, community, companionship, corporate (married, social) life, living together, mutual relationships
zusammenleben cohabit, live together
zusammenrufen call (together), convene, convoke, summon
Zusammenrufung convocation
zusammenschließen combine, consolidate, integrate into, join, link together, merge, pool, unite
—, sich amalgamate, bunch (up), enter into combination with, fuse, join hands, line up (against), merge, unite
Zusammenschluß alliance, amalgamation, association, bond, combination, consolidation, federation, fusion, integration, merger, union
zusammensetzen combine, compound, compose
sich — aus be composed of, consist of
Zusammensetzung combination, composition, compound, constitution, construction, make-up, structure
zusammenstellen arrange, assort, classify, combine, compare, compile, draw up, group, make (set) up, specify
Zusammenstellung arrangement, assortment, classification, combination, comparison, compilation, grouping, juxtaposition, schedule, statement, survey
Zusammenstoß clash(ing), collision, conflict, crash-up, encounter, smash-up
zusammenstoßen clash, collide (with), come into collision, encounter
Zusammentreffen assembly, coincidence, concurrence, conference, encounter, juncture, meeting
zusammentreffen coincide, concur, meet
zusammentreten assemble, combine, convene, ' join, meet, unite
Zusammentritt meeting
Zusammenwirken co-operation, concerted action, concurrence, united efforts
zusammen wirken coact, collaborate, concur, co-operate
zusammenzählen add (sum, total) up
Zusatz addendum, addition, admixture, alloy, amendment, annex, appended note, appendix, codicil, dash, postscript, rider, supplement

Zusatz
—abkommen supplementary agreement
—antrag amendment
—artikel extra clause, rider
—bedingung supplementary condition
—bestimmungen additional regulations
—gesetz supplementary act
—klausel additional (supplementary) clause
zusätzlich additional, auxiliary, extra, in addition, supplemental, supplementary
Zusatz
—protokoll supplementary protocol
—steuer additional tax
—versicherung additional (supplementary) insurance
—vertrag accessory contract, supplementary agreement
—wahl by-election
Zuschlag addition, additional (extra) charge, adjudication, bonus, premium, surcharge, surtax
zuschreiben ascribe to, assign to, attribute to, credit with, dedicate to, impute to, place to one's credit, write to
Zuschrift dedication, letter
—, amtliche official communication
zuschulden
sich — kommen lassen commit, do something wrong, make oneself guilty of, misconduct oneself, misbehave
Zuschuß additional payment, (extra) allowance, contribution, grant, subsidy, subvention
zusichern assure (of), guarantee, promise, warrant
Zusicherung assurance, guaranty (tee), promise, warranty
zusprechen adjudge, adjudicate, award, encourage
Zusprechung adjudgement, adjudication, award
Zuspruch encouragement
Zustand condition, frame of mind, order, position, repair, shape, situation, state (of affairs), status
zustande
— bringen accomplish, achieve, bring about, manage, reach
— kommen be effected, come about (to pass), materialize, realize, take place
— —, nicht fail
zuständig appertaining, appropriate, belonging, competent, having jurisdiction (cognizance of), proper, qualified, responsible
zuständig
—, nicht incompetent, not competent
sich für — erklären assume jurisdiction over
Zuständigkeit cognizance, competence(cy), jurisdiction, powers, province, responsibility, sphere
Zuständigkeits
—bereich competence(cy), jurisdiction, powers, province, scope, sphere of responsibility
—einwand jurisdiction plea
zuständigkeitshalber for reasons of competence
Zuständigkeits
—klausel jurisdiction clause
—streit clashing (conflict) of competence
—überschreitung excess of jurisdiction
—vereinbarung jurisdiction clause
zustehen accrue to, appertain (to), be due to, be entitled to, be vested in, belong to, have the right to, reside (in)
zustellen deliver, hand over, send, serve (on, with)
Zustellung consignment, delivery, service
—, öffentliche service by publication, summons
— bewirken effect service
Zustellungsurkunde writ of summons
zustimmen accede, agree to (with), approve (of), assent, consent (to), fall in with, fiat, ratify

—, **nicht** disagree (with)
Zustimmung agreement, approbation, approval, assent, consent, fiat, ratification
— **erteilen** approve (of), consent, give one's consent to
zuteilen adjudge, adjudicate, allocate, allot, allow, apportion, assign, attach, award, bestow (on), deal (measure, portion) out, distribute, grant, ration
Zuteilung adjudication, allocation, allotment, allowance, apportionment, assignment, attachment, distribution, granting, quota, ration(ing)
zutragen inform, report
—, **sich** come about (to pass), happen, occur, take place
Zuträger informer
zuträglich advantageous, useful
Zuträglichkeit advantageousness, usefulness
zutreffen be conclusive (correct, right, true, the case), come (hold) true, happen, prove right
— **auf** apply to, be true of
zutreffend applicable, apposite, correct, right, true, to the point
Zutritt access, admission, admittance
— **gewähren** admit, give admittance, grant access
— **haben** be admitted to, have access (admission, admittance) to
Zutrittsrecht easement, right of access
Zutun
ohne — von without one's aid (assistance, help, interference)
zuverlässig authentic, certain, creditable, dependable, exact, infallible, loyal, reliable, safe, sound, sta(u)nch, steady, sure, true, trusted, trustworthy, trusty
Zuverlässigkeit certainty, credit, loyalty, reliability, trustworthiness
Zuverlässigkeits
—**probe** endurance test
—**prüfung** reliability test (trial)
zuvorkommen anticipate, forestall, obviate, prevent
Zuwachs accession, accretion, appreciation, augmentation, expansion, growth, increase, increment
—**rate** growth rate, rate of growth
—**steuer** increment tax
zuweisen allocate, allot, apportion, appropriate, assign
Zuweisung allocation, allotment, apportionment, appropriation, assignation, assignment
zuwenden allocate, bequeath, bestow (upon), contribute, devise, present, procure
—, **sich** apply oneself to, enter, take up, turn to
Zuwendung allocation, allowance, benefit, bequest, contribution, devise, disposition, donation, gift, grant, gratification, gratuity
—, **letztwillige** gift by will
—, **testamentarische** legacy
zuwider adversely to, against, contrary to, opposed to, repugnant to
— **handeln** act contrary to (in contravention of), contravene, counteract, disregard, infringe, offend (against), trespass, violate
Zuwider
—**handelnder** infringer, offender, trespasser
—**handlung** contravention, infringement, noncompliance, nonobservation, offence, violation
zuwider laufen be against, be contrary to, contravene, infringe, run contrary (counter) to
zuziehen adjoin, call as (in), consult, immigrate, invite, join, move in, take one's advice
—, **sich** expose oneself to, get into, incur, involve oneself in
Zuziehung calling in, consultation
unter — von in the presence of, including, with the aid (assistance, help) of

zuzüglich add to this, adding, including, inclusive of, plus
Zwang coercion, compulsion, constraint, duress, force, pressure, violence
—, **moralischer** moral obligation
—, **aus** on compulsion
—, **unter** forced, under coercion (duress)
— **ausüben** bring pressure to bear on, exert (put) pressure on
unter — handeln act under coercion (duress, pressure)
zwanglos free (and easy), informal, unceremonious, unceremonial, unconstrained, unconventional
Zwanglosigkeit freedom, informality, unceremoniousness, unconstraint
Zwangs
—**abtretung** compulsory cession
—**anleihe** forced (compulsory) loan
—**arbeit** compulsory (forced, hard) labo(u)r, penal servitude
—**arbeiter** forced labo(u)rer
—**enteignung** expropriation
—**geld** fine
—**gesetz** coercive law
—**lage** coercion, constrained position, constraint, duress, embarrassing situation, exigency, position of constraint
zwangsläufig cogent, inevitable, mandatory, necessary, obligatory
Zwangs
—**läufigkeit** cogency
—**leistung** compulsory service
—**liquidation (-liquidierung)** compulsory liquidation
—**maßnahme (-maßregel)** coercive (compulsory) measure, reprisal, sanction
— —**n ergreifen** use force
—**mitgliedschaft** compulsory membership
—**mittel** coercive measures, compulsory means, force, means of coercion (constraint)
—**pensionierung** compulsory retirement
—**verfahren** compulsory procedure (proceedings)
—**vergleich** compulsory arbitration (settlement)
—**verkauf (versteigerung)** compulsory (forced) sale
—**verschickung** deportation
—**versicherung** compulsory insurance
—**versteigerung** s. -verkauf
zwangsverwalten sequester
Zwangs
—**verwalter** judicial trustee, (official) receiver, sequestrator
—**verwaltung** compulsory (forced) administration, sequestration, official receivership
in — — geben sequestrate
—**verwaltungsbeschluß** receiving order
zwangsvollstrecken foreclose, issue execution, levy (distraint)
Zwangs
—**vollstreckung** distraint, distress, execution, levy (of execution), seizure
— —**sbefehl** distress warrant, (writ of) elegit
—**beschluß** foreclosure decree
—**verfahren** execution proceedings
zwangsweise by coercion (compulsion, force), coercive, compulsorily, forced, forcible, mandatory, under coercion (duress)
Zwangswirtschaft controlled (planned) economy, government (state) control
Zweck aim, design, end, goal, intent, intention, object, point, purpose
End- final aim (purpose)
Haupt- main (principal) aim (purpose)
— **erfüllen** answer (serve, suit) the purpose
— **erreichen** accomplish (achieve, attain, gain, get) one's aim (purpose), carry one's point
— **verfehlen** miss one's aim
— **verfolgen** pursue an object
zweckdienlich appropriate, efficacious, efficient, expedient, pertinent, relevant, service-

able, suitable, to the purpose, useful
zwecklos aimless, purposeless, useless
Zwecklosigkeit aimlessness, purposelessness, uselessness
zweckmäßig advisable, appropriate, expedient, fit, practical, proper, rational, suitable, useful
Zweckmäßigkeit advisability, expedience(cy), fitness, practicability, usefulness
Zwecks by way of, for (the purpose of), with a view to
Zweckverband administrative union, county corporate, special association
zweckwidrig inexpedient, unsuitable
zweideutig ambiguous, equivocal
Zweideutigkeit ambiguity, ambiguousness, equivocality
Zweidrittelmehrheit two-thirds majority
—, mit by a two-thirds majority
Zweifel disbelief, doubt, hesitation, misgiving, scruple, suspicion
—, außer beyond doubt
—, ohne certainly, doubtless, without doubt
— hegen entertain doubts (have suspicions) about
zweifelhaft bad, doubtful, dubious, equivocal, precarious, questionable, shady, suspicious, uncertain, vague
Zweifelhaftigkeit doubtfulness
zweifellos doubtless, without doubt
zweifeln (an) doubt, have doubts (about)
Zweifelsfall, im in case of doubt
Zweig branch, department, division, line, section
Zweig
—abteilung branch, section
—anstalt branch (establishment)
—niederlassung branch (establishment, office)
—stelle branch (office)
Zweikampf duel, single combat
zweiseitig bilateral, bipartite, two-sided
Zweiseitigkeit bilateralism
Zweitschrift (-ausfertigung) copy, duplicate, second
Zwiespalt conflict, difference, discord, dissension, disunion
zwiespältig discordant, disunited, split, unbalanced
zwingen coerce, compel, constrain, force (on, upon), oblige, reduce, do violence to
zwingend absolute, binding, coercive, cogent, compulsory, conclusive, imperative, obligatory, peremptory, stringent, urgent
Zwischen
—bemerkung incidental remark, interruption
—bericht interim report, intermediate account
—bescheid intermediate (provisional) reply, interlocutory decree
—entscheid interlocutory decree
—fall incident, unforeseen event
—handel intermediary (intermediate) trade
—händler intermediary, commission (purchasing) agent, middleman
—lagerung intermediate storage, storage in transit
—prüfung (-examen) intermediate examination
—raum distance, interval, inter (mediate) space, space
—regelung provisional arrangement
—ruf interruption
—staat buffer state
zwischenstaatlich intergovernmental, international, interstate
Zwischen
—stadium intermediate (provisional) stage
—stellung intermediate position
—streit intervention
—summe subtotal
—urteil interlocutory decree (judgement, sentence), interim decree (judgement)

—verfahren interlocutory hearing

—verfügung interlocutory (intermediate) order

—zeit interim, interim (intermediate) period, interval, meantime, meanwhile

—, in der (zwischenzeitlich) in between, in the meantime (meanwhile), meantime, meanwhile, mesne

Zwist (-igkeit) difference, discord, dispute, dissension, feud, quarrel

Zyklus course, cycle

FSC
www.fsc.org
MIX
Papier | Fördert gute Waldnutzung
FSC® C083411

Kolibri 360 GmbH
Ferdinand-Jühlke-Straße 7
99095 Erfurt, Deutschland
produktsicherheit@kolibri360.de